Comparing Public Policies

Comparing Public Policies

Issues and Choices in Industrialized Countries

Second Edition

Jessica R. Adolino

Charles H. Blake

A Division of SAGE

Washington, D.C.

CQ Press
2300 N Street, NW, Suite 800
Washington, DC 20037

Phone: 202-729-1900; toll-free, 1-866-4CQ-PRESS (1-866-427-7737)

Web: www.cqpress.com

Cover design: Brian Barth
Composition: C&M Digitals (P) Ltd.

♾ The paper used in this publication exceeds the requirements of the American National Standard for Information Sciences—Permanence of Paper for Printed Library Materials, ANSI Z39.48-1992.

Printed and bound in the United States of America

14 13 12 11 2 3 4 5

Library of Congress Cataloging-in-Publication Data

Adolino, Jessica R. (Jessica Rose)
Comparing public policies : issues and choices in industrialized countries / Jessica R. Adolino, Charles H. Blake. — 2nd ed.
p. cm.
Includes bibliographical references and index.
ISBN 978-1-933116-78-5 (pbk. : alk. paper) 1. Industrial policy—Developed countries—Case studies. I. Blake, Charles H. II. Title.
HD3611.A34 2010
338.9—dc22

2009048893

Contents

Tables, Figures, and Boxes

Tables

Figure

Boxes

Preface

In the early twenty-first century, many news stories remind us of the growing interconnectedness of the world. Countries have never operated in complete isolation, but we increasingly define ourselves and our national priorities in a global context. Although learning about politics and governance by comparing different national experiences dates back to ancient civilizations, both Eastern and Western, we are perhaps more keenly aware than ever before of the relevance of other countries' actions.

This book is about comparative public policy in industrialized countries. It includes a conceptual discussion of policy making as well as treatment of specific areas from a cross-national perspective. The conceptual discussion provides a foundation for conducting political analysis of policy-making practices in the six largest industrialized economies with the six largest populations in the industrialized world—France, Germany, Italy, Japan, the United Kingdom, and the United States. In this second edition, we have added case studies of policy making in the European Union because decisions made in the EU have become increasingly important in many policy areas. We focus on large, industrialized countries so that the lessons drawn will have the greatest relevance for the United States—the largest industrialized country in terms of both economic output and population. The book is devoted to seven policy areas: immigration, fiscal policy, taxation, health care, social policy, education, and environmental policy. We chose these policy areas to expose readers to a variety of major issues on the policy agenda in the industrialized world. Although other policy concerns also form relevant elements of national agendas, each of these seven policy areas has maintained a visible profile for decades. Furthermore, by organizing this book across such diverse policy concerns, we encourage readers to ponder which policy-making dynamics are particular to a given issue and which travel across many issues.

We wrote this book as a primary text for courses on comparative public policy. We also hope that instructors and students in courses on European politics and on U.S. public policy find this book useful. Most books on comparative public policy tend to be written for professional analysts and graduate students and assume too much contextual and conceptual knowledge on the part of the reader. Conversely, books that provide such contextual and conceptual knowledge tend to provide minimal treatment of existing policy choices and even less analysis of the dynamics of those choices.

This book meets these dual challenges in a single text designed for undergraduates and general readers. Chapters 1 and 2 use real-world examples to summarize the field of comparative public policy and the literature on policy-making dynamics. Chapters 3 and 4 are intended for readers with little or no knowledge of political science or of the six countries studied in this book. Some readers, therefore, could skim this material or skip it entirely. The policy-oriented Chapters 5 through 11 form the core of the book. The first half of each chapter provides background material on policy issues, on the study of policy making regarding those issues, and on international factors framing domestic policy making. Then, in the case studies, readers are informed about contemporary policy efforts and about the dynamics of those policy decisions in the six largest industrialized economies and in the EU. In working through the case studies, readers are encouraged to apply the examined theories of policy making. These policy chapters are intended to be read in their entirety, but instructors and readers with an interest in the four European countries and the EU can focus on the case studies of interest to them without losing the thread of the book. Similarly, each policy chapter can be read on its own. Chapter 12 reexamines the internationalization of public policy in industrialized countries and returns to the opening theme: cross-national learning and the political constraints on learning, as observed in the case studies.

Throughout the book, terms defined in the glossary appear in bold print the first time they are used. We have included two types of feature boxes. "In Depth" boxes provide examples of issues examined in the book, whereas "At-a-Glance" boxes offer readers a quick review of the institutions of each political system examined. A series of tables summarize theoretical frameworks and provide data regarding national policy decisions and policy outcomes. The data focus on the 1990s and 2000s, thereby presenting readers with current information.

Acknowledgments

While writing and revising this book, we have benefited directly and indirectly from many exchanges about the politics of policy making with students and instructors here at James Madison University. In the years to come, we look forward to hearing from students and faculty using this book. We encourage you to send your comments to CQ Press.

We have also benefited from the counsel and hard work of many people beyond our campus. Don Reisman was generous in the early stages of this project with advice about how to organize a textbook on comparative public policy. At CQ Press, we have had the help of many talented individuals. Charisse Kiino provided a stimulating editorial climate in which to develop this project, and her counsel helped improve both the first and second editions. Both of the reviewers selected—Amy Mazur at Washington State University and Christopher Mobley at DePaul University—contributed helpful suggestions that have improved the content and the structure of this book. In this second edition, we have been ably guided through the production process by Dwain Smith and Sarah Fell and have benefited from the constructive copyediting of Amy Marks. Finally, we would like to thank our families for their ongoing love and support during this project and during all of life's many adventures.

An Introduction to Comparative Public Policy

In 1965 newly elected president Lyndon Johnson promised to extend health benefits to the elderly. Later that year the U.S. government created the Medicare program to provide senior citizens with hospitalization insurance paid for out of general government revenues. Many of the legislative leaders who voted in favor of the Medicare program had participated in failed efforts to create some form of national health insurance over the prior two decades. Medicare marked a change in legislative strategy from the original goal of comprehensive health insurance for all residents to a guarantee of hospitalization care for the elderly. This strategic change was a response to political obstacles facing prior initiatives. Advocates felt that it would be easier to build legislative and public support for public health insurance for retirees alone (and not discuss the merits of extending it to people still in the labor force). In part, this strategic change was also an effort to build on the experiences in neighboring Canada, where a national hospitalization insurance policy had just been created.

Three decades later, in 1993, newly elected president Bill Clinton renewed the call for some form of national health insurance program. It was the first time that sweeping health policy reform had reached a visible place on the presidential agenda since the Nixon administration in the early 1970s. President Clinton named a council on health reform that studied the current U.S. health care system as well as health policies in other industrialized countries. That council drafted a proposal based on the concept of managed competition and influenced by health policy reforms in the Netherlands and the United Kingdom. Meanwhile, legislative leaders proceeded to develop their own alternatives. Half of the subsequent major congressional bills proposed policies adapted from abroad. Sen. Paul Wellstone, D-Minn., sponsored a single-payer reform based on the Canadian system. Reps. Jim Cooper, D-Tenn., and Fred Grandy, R-Iowa, and Sen. John Chafee, R-R.I., sponsored bills advocating a form of employer-mandated health insurance—the most frequently observed health policy in the industrialized world.

These proposals sparked serious debate and controversy in the legislature, in the news media, and among a variety of interest groups during the 1993–1995 legislative session. By the end of that session, none of the various proposals had been passed by Congress. During the rest of Clinton's presidency, smaller reforms expanded the portability of health insurance for workers who change or lose their jobs and increased government funding to subsidize health insurance for children through the State Children's Health Insurance Program.

During George W. Bush's first term as president (2001–2005), the federal government made several important modifications to the Medicare program that had begun four decades earlier under Johnson. In addition, public debate continued over the issue of whether (and how) government might assist the over 46 million people in the U.S. population who lacked health insurance in 2005. During 2006 the debate over universal health care coverage shifted to the subnational level as many state governments debated bills that aimed to provide health insurance for many or all uninsured people. In 2009 the Obama administration chose to make health care reform the centerpiece of its domestic policy agenda. Central to the intensely partisan congressional debate on health care reform are questions about requiring all Americans to have health insurance and creating an insurance marketplace for those who are unable to obtain coverage at work and for those who are ineligible for public programs. The 2009 debate has involved a struggle to resolve profound partisan disagreement on these issues, despite some bipartisan consensus on the need for sweeping reform.

This brief discussion of health policy making in the United States illustrates three important features of public policy making. First, public policy making is an ongoing process. Over the years the United States has frequently discussed major modifications in its health policy. This is not unique to health care as an issue. Governments are always implementing and evaluating existing policies while they consider reform proposals for the creation of new programs, the modification of existing programs, and the termination of some current policies. Throughout this book we attempt to provide you with a richer understanding of policy making as an ongoing endeavor.

Second, you can see from the history of health policy making in the United States that countries try to learn from one another. Perhaps this is truer today than ever before. Marshall Raffel (1997) discussed this issue in an assessment of health reform in industrialized countries:

> The countries in this book are especially inclined to look at one another's efforts at reform because of the economic and social similarities and ties that exist among them. The Nordic countries are a case in point: They are in regular consultation and use the Nordic Council to facilitate the process. New Zealand has historically looked to the United Kingdom for leadership and many of its health care reforms were, and still are, adaptations of what the United Kingdom was doing. Government agencies in the United States have increased their study of the leading industrialized societies as witnessed by dedicated issues of the *Health Care Financing Review* (a journal published by the Health Care Financing Administration of the U.S. Department of Health and Human Services), and by reports from the General Accounting Office (an agency of the U.S. Congress) on Canada, Sweden, the United Kingdom, France, Germany, and Japan. Private professional journals such as

> the *New England Journal of Medicine*, the *Journal of the American Medical Association*, *Health Affairs*, the *Journal of Medical Practice Management*, and the *Journal of Health Politics, Policy and Law* have also printed accounts from time to time of the health systems in various industrialized countries (p. 293).

When countries study one another to draw lessons about which policies work best to reach particular goals, they are engaged in policy analysis. Policy analysts ask questions aimed at learning lessons about the strengths and weaknesses of different policy options. Policy analysis begins with a definition of the policy problem government wants to address. In turn, what are the policy objectives? How successful were the policies chosen in achieving those objectives? How should one account for these policy successes or failures? In this book we engage in policy analysis concerning seven major policy issues: immigration, fiscal (or budgetary) policy, taxation, health care, social (or welfare) policy, education, and the environment.

Third, in addition to viewing policy making as an ongoing process in which countries try to learn from one another about which options are desirable, you can also see in contemporary U.S. health policy that political dynamics can limit countries' willingness and ability to borrow from other countries. Although much of the health policy legislation proposed during Clinton's first term was inspired in good measure by foreign experiences, none of the proposed legislation was enacted at that time. In the most recent U.S. reform effort, cross-national comparisons have been used more frequently by the opponents of reform, who point to what they see as the failings of European health care systems (especially the British National Health Service) as evidence of why the United States should not adopt universal health coverage. Even if policy analysts can document that some form of universal health insurance is the norm across all other industrialized countries, that does not mean that U.S. policymakers are going to focus wholeheartedly on the foreign evidence in their public and private deliberations. Writing at the conclusion of another volume on health policy reform in the industrialized world, Theodore Marmor (1997) examined how political dynamics influence lesson learning:

> Policy-makers are busy with day-to-day pressures. Practical concerns incline them, if they take the time for comparative inquiry, to pay more attention to what appears to work, not academic reasons for what is and is not transferable and why. Policy debaters—whether politicians, policy analysts or interest group figures—are in struggles, not seminars. Like lawyers, they seek victory, not illumination. For that purpose, compelling stories, whether well-substantiated or not, are more useful than careful conclusions. Interest groups, as their label suggests, have material and symbolic stakes in policy outcomes, not reputations for intellectual precision to protect. None of these considerations are new—or surprising. But the increased flow of cross-national claims in health policy generates new reasons to reconsider the meaning of cross-national policy learning (p. 361).

Marmor's comments about the limits to learning make it clear that policy analysis should be complemented with political analysis. Public policies use government personnel and resources in response to challenges deemed worthy of government effort. Because the sum total of individual and collective complaints at any point in time is enormous, governments must choose which problems to address and how to address them. These choices are shaped by a variety of factors that are often common across countries. Political analysts study the dynamics of policy making in an effort to understand what sorts of policy choices are likely to be made in different scenarios. What policies have this country and other countries enacted in the past? What factors influenced their decision-making processes? Do the cultural, economic, political, or institutional conditions that exist in one country differ from those in other countries? If so, how will these differences affect policy decisions or the probability of long-term success for borrowing a given policy option?

In summary, research in comparative public policy tries to improve our understanding of these three major facets of policy making: its ongoing nature, the efforts in and out of government to build a better mousetrap via policy analysis, and the intensely political nature of policy choices made by government officials. Because we concur with Marmor's view that politics shape how the lessons of policy analysis will be applied, the primary emphasis in this book is on political analysis. By examining policy making in six industrialized countries and the European Union and in relation to seven major issues, we hope to enrich your understanding of other countries' policy making and increase your capacity to conduct political analysis. You will then be better positioned to consider strategies for adopting the policy option that seems preferable in light of a policy analysis of a given situation. Intervention in policy making—as a private citizen, as an interest group leader, or as a government official—also requires an understanding of the many stages of the policy-making process. If you do not get your way initially, you might later on in the process.

The Increasing Internationalization of Public Policy

When we hear the term *public policy*, we usually think of national issues dealt with by national governing institutions. In turn, when we hear the phrase *foreign policy*, our attention shifts to policies toward other countries' governments and societies. Since the 1970s, however, many issues formerly considered purely domestic concerns are becoming increasingly internationalized. Before we begin thinking about how governments make national policy decisions, let us consider how international obligations and pressures can frame public policy choices related to matters inside a country's own borders.

Perhaps the most overt examples of the internationalization of public policy stem from economic integration agreements adhered to by these countries. By ratifying the World Trade Organization agreement, all industrialized countries' governments commit themselves to a series of decisions that go beyond the scope of a narrow definition of trade policy. Within the European Union, the Maastricht Treaty and other directives and accords encroach on national governments' traditional sovereignty in areas such as environmental regulation, monetary policy, product safety, and (more slowly) health and social policy. Furthermore, other changes such as the elimination of border controls among members and the drive for monetary unification have tangible influences on immigration and fiscal policy, respectively. The North American Free Trade Agreement has not committed Canada, Mexico, and the United States to this degree of policy harmonization and supranational decision making. However, it does call for harmonization of certain areas (particularly investment laws and intellectual property rights) while focusing attention on differences in other areas such as education, the environment, fiscal and monetary policy, and social policy.

Beyond the realm of binding international agreements, market forces of various types motivate governments to internationalize their policy-making concerns and processes. If one conceives of human migration as a market choice, then the sustained high international demand to immigrate to wealthy countries places enormous pressure on the six countries examined in this book. These pressures go beyond calls for a more restrictive immigration policy. Increased ethnic diversity also can make equal opportunity and equal protection more visible policy issues. Demands for services from new arrivals affect decisions regarding basic government services, such as education, health, and social policy, that influence fiscal policy. Illegal immigration can place special demands on taxation policy because of the existence of underground economies.

The internationalizing forces need not be physically present in the country to have an impact. Over the past generation, foreign economic pressures and dynamics have had a growing effect on a variety of domestic policy areas. Foreign exchange market transactions in the 1990s had a significant impact on fiscal policy in Italy and the United Kingdom. The pressure to reduce deficits in order to stabilize one's currency influences just about every decision that governments make. Similarly, concerns about foreign economic competition affect a variety of policy realms that go beyond pressure for protectionist trade measures. Businesses in some countries lobby for educational reforms in the name of increasing economic competitiveness. In turn, business associations often complain that government environmental and social policies require too much taxation and impede economic growth and employment generation.

Given the growing sophistication and speed of communications and the importance of international trade in the global economy, this trend toward the internationalization of what were once considered domestic issues is unlikely to fade in the near future. Countries with poorer, less diversified economies than those in the industrialized world have long been seen as subject to international forces partially or wholly beyond their control. What is different in the twenty-first century is the increased visibility of interdependence in large, industrialized economies like those examined here.

The Organization of This Book

This book examines policy making in six major industrialized countries—the United States, Japan, Germany, France, the United Kingdom, and Italy—and the European Union. We chose to focus on industrialized countries so that the lessons learned will have the greatest relevance for the United States—the largest industrialized country in terms of both economic output and population. We selected the other countries to extend further the relevance of the comparisons involved by studying the six largest industrialized economies and the six largest populations in the industrialized world. In turn, we examine policy making in the European Union as the foremost example of the importance of a supranational organization that shapes public policy in the industrialized world.

The first four chapters of this book provide a foundation for conducting political analysis of policy-making practices in our six countries across the ongoing policy process. In Chapter 1 we discuss conceptual tools for the study of policy making in industrialized countries and introduce a five-stage model of the policy-making process. In Chapter 2 we examine cultural, economic, political, and institutional theories that attempt to explain policy-making choices. In Chapter 3 we extend our consideration of influences on policy making by reviewing concepts central to those cultural, economic, political, and institutional influences on policymakers. In Chapter 4 we summarize the political systems of the six countries at the heart of this book—France, Germany, Italy, Japan, the United Kingdom, and the United States—and we discuss the structure of the European Union as a key international influence on four of these six countries.

The main body of this book consists of Chapters 5–11. Considerable variation exists in the nature of policy making from country to country and across policy areas within a single country. For that reason, these chapters are organized by policy area rather than by country. In Chapters 5–7 we examine three broad sets of government decisions that frame individuals' prospects in their respective countries—immigration policy, fiscal policy, and taxation policy. In Chapters 8–11 we turn to four specific areas in which governments work to influence individuals' well-being more directly and often more overtly—health policy, social policy, education policy, and environmental policy. We chose these policy areas to expose readers to varied, major issues in public policy. Although other policy concerns form important portions of the national debate, each of these seven policy areas has maintained a visible profile for decades.

In each policy chapter we begin by discussing the policy area's principal problems and the major policy options available to address those challenges. This discussion provides us with information based on policy analyses. We then review research in political analysis that tries to explain the dynamics of policy making. We then move on to specific examples of policy making in our seven case studies—beginning with the United States and ending with the European Union.

In recognition of the increasing internationalization of national policy decisions, we frame the national case studies with a consideration of the international context for policy making in the issue area. Each case study starts with some background on the policy process and the history of policy making in the policy area. After that, we examine contemporary policy dynamics using the five-stage model of policy making presented in Chapter 1:

- Policy evaluation: How has the evaluation of past policy performance informed and shaped the current debate?
- Agenda setting: What policy problems are at the heart of the contemporary debate?
- Policy formulation: Who are the major participants in this policy area, and what are their preferred alternatives for addressing the problems?
- Decision making: What is the key arena to watch for a decision on this issue? What forces carried the day?
- Implementation: Are there any implementation concerns surrounding existing policies or the major alternatives under consideration?

Each case study concludes with an analysis of the choices made (or not made). This analysis is informed by the general political and policy dynamics discussed in Chapters 1–4 as well as by the nature of the specific policy issue(s) at hand.

At the end of each policy chapter we search for broader cross-national trends in policy choices, policy outcomes, and policy dynamics. The examination of policy choices and subsequent outcomes takes us to the task of policy analysis. Which governments have succeeded in reaching their major policy goals, and why? Finally, we reflect on the central question of political analysis: what influences contemporary policy decisions in these countries?

In Chapter 12 we conclude by returning to our opening themes. First, we reflect on how international factors shape contemporary policy making across the policy process and across policy issues. We then review some of the limitations on learning discussed over the course of this book. Finally, despite several obstacles to borrowing from other countries, we consider how cross-national perspectives can and do provide lessons for policymakers about which policy choices to make and about how to pursue those goals in the political process.

Chapter 1 The Policy Process

In this chapter we introduce some conceptual tools designed for the study of policy making in industrialized countries. Specifically, we use a five-stage model of the policy-making process. We start with the emergence of issues as policy problems on the political agenda and then move on to the formulation, adoption, implementation, and evaluation of public policies.

The Study of the Policy Process

The five-stage model is an analytical device used by researchers to study public policy; it is not a literal description of the policy-making process. Only on the rarest of occasions do governments march methodically from stage to stage in a given policy area. Most of the time, governments are working on all fronts simultaneously—continually shifting gears from the identification of problems to the creation of potential solutions and then back again. As an example, let's think this through in the area of health policy. At any given time, there are hundreds of health issues that different citizens want to see addressed (directly or indirectly) by public policy. Some people are concerned about the supply of certain health care options; others want government to help improve the quality of care for different health conditions; still others are concerned about the cost of health care; and so on. At the same time, many competing policy proposals are floating around that deal with each issue—several proposals are being actively considered by the bureaucracy and the legislature (in a federal system of government, such as the U.S. system, this is going on at multiple levels of government). While the government is making decisions about which (if any) policy proposals to adopt for each issue, the bureaucracy is overseeing thousands of aspects of existing health policies. While existing policies are being implemented, people inside and outside of government are evaluating the effectiveness of each existing government program using multiple sets of standards. The array of policy-making activity in any country on any given day in any given year would be just as dizzying in other policy areas.

It would be decidedly difficult to use a single set of tools to analyze everything that is happening simultaneously. It would be like trying to explain the outcome of a battle by applying the same principles to components as varied as supply lines, geography, weather conditions, weaponry, combat experience, morale, and tactics. To gain a greater appreciation of the entire policy process, analysts have worked over the years to conceptualize components of policy making that share common dynamics and common challenges. In this chapter we introduce these conceptual tools as lenses through which we can better understand public policy. We then apply these tools in analyzing public policy on seven different issues in industrialized countries and the European Union.

Because the study of public policy involves the analysis of what governments do, it is central to the work of political scientists. However, this was not always the case. When political science emerged as an academic discipline at the beginning of the twentieth century, it focused largely on the analysis of formal government institutions and made normative judgments about what institutions were preferable. This **traditionalism** remained the prevailing focus of professional political science until the end of World War II—even as critics from the 1920s and later years called for the systematic study of the dynamics of political events and decisions (rather than comparisons of constitutional provisions often divorced from the performance of those systems in practice). In the postwar era, Harold Lasswell (1951) sounded a clarion call for the creation of a **policy science** that would focus explicitly on what governments do rather than on how they are organized. In his view, this policy science should be multidisciplinary (combining legal studies with insights from economics, political science, and sociology); it should solve problems (focusing on relevant real-life policy problems rather than on obscure, sometimes semantic, legal distinctions); and it should be normative (admitting that the analysis of the policy process cannot be separated from the value judgments implicit in policy choices). Lasswell constructed a seven-stage model of the policy process: intelligence, promotion, prescription, invocation, application, termination, and appraisal. This model attempted to describe the steps taken by individual government decision makers: gathering information, promoting particular policy options, deciding on a particular policy, fleshing out that policy, carrying out the policy, deciding that the policy has outlived its usefulness, and evaluating the results of the entire enterprise.

This focus on people in government gave way during the 1960s and 1970s to efforts to conceptualize the policy process as one involving a variety of forces inside and outside of government itself. This broadening of Lasswell's initial formulation was driven largely by the other major development in political science during the 1950s: **behavioralism**. Whereas Lasswell reacted to traditionalist political science by focusing on government policies, other researchers such as Robert Dahl and David Truman led an effort to focus on the political behavior of individuals and groups throughout society. These two mid-century academic movements—policy science and behavioralism—combined to influence a new generation of public policy studies.

In the contemporary era, public policy analysts consider how and why governments enact and implement policies to address public needs and demands. **Public policies** are defined here as intentional courses of action designed by government bodies and officials to accomplish a specific goal or objective. These policies are usually enacted in response to a perceived need or demand and are thus problem oriented. In democracies, policy demands are made by a variety of actors, both within and outside government bodies, including private citizens, interest groups, bureaucrats, and legislators. Public policies may take the form of legislation (including budgets), government regulations, administrative and executive orders, or judicial decisions. They may also take the form of government actions that are not taken; in other words, the policy can be a decision *not* to use public authority to address a recognized problem. When we examine public policies, we are concerned not only with one specific decision to adopt a law or regulation but also with related subsequent decisions (such as amendments to the initial law or the regulations and procedures created to implement the law).

Studies of public policy and policy making examine not only government intentions but also specific government actions and the consequences of those actions. Thus such studies commonly examine **policy outputs**, or what governments do to implement and enforce their policies. Policy outputs can include the amount of money a government spends on education, the number of police officers it hires, the tax code provisions it passes to subsidize health care, and its penalties for violating environmental laws. Assessing the consequences of government activity involves the study of **policy outcomes**, or what the public policy has produced. This assessment entails evaluating a given policy's short-term effects and its long-term and unintended consequences. Analyses of policy outcomes examine whether public policies have, for example, improved literacy rates, reduced crime rates, made health care more accessible to the poor, or reduced air pollution.

Cross-national studies of the policy-making process in industrialized countries demonstrate that there is no single process through which public policies are made. Instead, different institutional frameworks, procedures, and traditions result in significant variation in the style and mechanisms of policy making. Despite such differences, however, it is possible to identify five stages of policy making that are common to all countries: **agenda setting**, **policy formulation**, **decision making**, **policy implementation**, and **policy evaluation**. The sections that follow are an introduction to what these commonly experienced stages entail in industrialized countries.

Agenda Setting

If we were to look at any given industrialized country today and attempt to catalog all of the needs and demands of its population, we would find the dimensions staggering. Most individual citizens and almost all organizations hold one or more pressing concerns that they believe merit government attention. These concerns, when combined with a country's domestic and international concerns more generally, create a seemingly endless list of potential items for the country's policy agenda. Many scholars refer to this potential list of policy issues as the country's **systemic agenda**. However, not all of these wants and demands occupy visible spots on the government's **institutional agenda**. In fact, only a relatively small number of these demands attain such institutional agenda status and become the focus of public policy making.

How then do problems attract the attention of government officials and become the objects of public policies? Comparative research in the 1960s and early 1970s focused on the level of economic development as a possible determinant of agenda setting and of decision making on a variety of policy issues. Some scholars working in this vein developed the **convergence thesis**, which posits that as countries industrialize, they develop similar policy concerns. For example, focusing on social security policy, Harold Wilensky (1975) asserted that the level of economic development in a country (as measured by gross domestic product per person) was the most important factor driving the level of social security spending in sixty-four countries. Wilensky argued that as countries industrialized, governments (whether democratic or not) would face increasing demands for policies to improve individuals' standards of living. Over time, Wilensky reasoned, governments would respond by spending increasing amounts of money to address those concerns via programs such as social security pensions, unemployment insurance, welfare benefits, and national health insurance.

During the rest of the 1970s and into the 1980s, the convergence thesis was attacked from a variety of angles. Some critics charged that spending levels were not the most appropriate measure for agenda status. If research focused on the variety of ways that governments construct public policy to influence people's standards of living, then we would find much more divergence among industrialized countries than Wilensky's study revealed. Others focused on redefining the role of political factors to understand better their importance in the process. Still others highlighted the role of ideas in shaping the issues to which policymakers attend in a given situation. The consensus in the field of comparative public policy today is that no single factor is the smoking gun that drives agenda setting in all policy areas or in all countries. To understand agenda setting, then, one must be open to exploring a variety of factors.

Instead of searching for universal determinants of agenda setting, many researchers have focused on understanding the process of agenda setting. Cobb, Ross, and Ross (1976) identified three different paths to agenda setting. In the **outside initiation** model, organized interest groups attempt to raise the profile of an issue on the systemic agenda. Interest groups form allegiances with other groups, raise citizen awareness, and lobby the government to get their concerns onto the institutional agenda. For example, during the 1960s a variety of grassroots organizations drew public attention to a series of environmental concerns in the United States. This dramatic change in public opinion and in the active expression of the public's concerns through petitions and protests paved the way for the formation of the Environmental Protection Agency at the start of the 1970s—all for a set of issues that was nowhere to be found on the systemic and institutional agendas just a decade earlier.

In the **inside initiation** model, influential interest groups seek to pressure the government to address particular concerns without expanding the visibility of the debate on the systemic agenda. In this model, interest groups do not engage in advertising campaigns and public rallies but instead attempt to influence government policymakers almost entirely in private meetings. Here the principal tools of the trade are information and analysis of the issue(s) at hand, along with, at times, the use of campaign donations. One of the most colorful examples of inside initiation in contemporary U.S. politics has been the quiet (and, to date, largely successful) effort of the honey industry to reinsert government subsidies into a series of budget proposals under successive presidencies that had initially removed the subsidies. The American Beekeeping Federation, the American Honey Producers Association, the National Honey Packers and Dealers Association, and other groups made campaign contributions to key legislators and provided a host of arguments about the importance of domestic honey—ranging from the jobs produced by the sector and its status as an environmentally friendly business to the purported need to maintain a substantial domestic bee population in the event of the arrival of so-called killer bees from abroad.

The **mobilization** model describes situations in which government constitutes the group interested in agenda setting. In these situations, government officials agree that an issue not currently visible in the systemic agenda needs to be addressed. The government works to get the issue onto the systemic agenda to increase public support for subsequent policy decisions and, often more crucially, for the implementation of those policies once created. The call for the privatization of several government enterprises during Prime Minister Margaret Thatcher's government in the United Kingdom provides one example of government officials expanding the visibility of an issue that had received much less attention prior to those efforts. The George W. Bush administration's attempt to increase support for sweeping social security reform in the United States during 2005 provides another example of mobilization led largely by the government.

Cobb, Ross, and Ross originally posited that these three models were each associated with a particular sort of political system: outside initiation with pluralist democracies; inside initiation with corporatist democracies; and mobilization with authoritarian (and, especially, totalitarian) governments. Over time, however, many researchers have concluded that all three models are potentially applicable in a variety of political systems. The more important determinant of which model will apply is not the political system but rather the policy issue in question. As we demonstrated earlier, contemporary democracies have engaged in all three forms of agenda setting.

Table 1-1 Four Models of Agenda Setting

		Public Support for Government Action	
		High	*Low*
Initiator of current debate	*Societal actors*	Outside initiation	Inside initiation
	Government	Consolidation	Mobilization

SOURCE: Modified from Howlett and Ramesh (1995): 116.

Peter May (1991) suggested a fourth model of agenda setting, **consolidation**, in which the government places an issue on the institutional agenda that already is visible on the systemic agenda. In this scenario the government does not need to mobilize support for maintaining the issue on the institutional agenda; it simply needs to work from the existing base of public interest in the issue. As an example of the consolidation model, one could point to the increased activity of Bill Clinton's administration in tobacco-related policy. Several of the proposed policy changes involving teenage smoking already had substantial support in public opinion polls.

The addition of the consolidation model leaves us with a basic typology of agenda setting that covers four different scenarios that vary from issue to issue in each country (Table 1-1). Low-profile issues tend to reach the institutional agenda via inside initiation or mobilization. More visible issues are more likely subject to the outside initiation or consolidation approach.

As we move on in subsequent chapters to the study of specific policies in particular countries, we will observe a considerable degree of cross-national divergence in problem definition. A pressing problem in one setting will sometimes be viewed as insignificant in another. In addition, the process through which problems are brought to policymakers' attention varies from country to country, particularly as a reflection of different participatory structures. More specifically, the structure and tactics of interest groups and the nature of political party systems (as well as the degree to which the political system is open to their influence) are key elements in defining the agenda-setting process in different countries. A new issue that is dominated by inside initiation in one country may be subject to the outside initiation model in another. In contrast, some long-standing policy issues (such as tax policy) may be so high on the systemic agenda that it would be difficult to take the inside initiation approach and unnecessary to conduct the mobilization gambit to place an item on the institutional agenda.

Policy Formulation

Once a problem has arrived on the institutional agenda, policymakers must create a course of action to solve, reduce, or dismiss the problem. The formulation stage entails developing and evaluating proposed solutions and programs. At this stage, many conceivable policy alternatives are rejected because they are viewed as technically not feasible or politically unacceptable by major participants in the policy-making process. Given the subjective nature of the technical and political judgments at issue here, understanding policy formulation requires an assessment of who the important participants are and where policymakers look for policy alternatives.

There is rarely a rational march from careful problem definition to the meticulous consideration of options. Often the agenda-setting process gets an issue on the institutional agenda without generating an accepted or a clear definition of the policy problem and its causes. As a result, the policy formulation process involves not only the evaluation of policy alternatives but also a vigorous debate about the nature of the problem itself. Consider for a moment the drug abuse problem in various countries. A variety of public and private organizations provide differing estimates of the percentage of the population that abuses narcotics and of the economic and human costs of that abuse. Opinions differ even more over the forces driving drug abuse that government efforts might try to tackle. People point their fingers at the personal background of drug abusers, the failure of law enforcement to prevent trafficking in illegal narcotics, the dire economic circumstances of many abusers, the failure of mass media to condemn drug use universally, and so on. This disagreement over what constitutes the drug problem creates a diverse range of potential policy proposals. Even when considerable agreement exists about the essential elements of the problem, multiple solutions are often proposed.

The government plays a crucial role in policy formulation. Government research can frame policy problems once they reach the institutional agenda. Our understanding of the dimensions of the problem is often shaped by government statistics. Different government agencies measure everything from the unemployment rate and the amount of air pollution to the infant mortality rate and the educational achievement of secondary school students—to name only a few examples. In addition, the bureaucracy provides formal and informal evaluations of different policy proposals that influence the debate over which options are more desirable. The historical stances of political parties in the legislature (as well as the partisan balance of forces) also tend to filter out some options while promoting others. For example, conservative legislators are likely to turn rather quickly to market-oriented policy instruments, but they can be slower to consider direct government intervention than are legislators from centrist or leftist parties.

In addition to the nature of relationships within government, the connection between society as a whole and government policymakers has an important effect on policy formulation. One of the oldest concepts in the analysis of U.S. policy making is the notion of an **iron triangle**. The iron triangle refers to a policy subsector controlled by the relevant bureaucratic agencies, the relevant legislative subcommittees, and the major interest groups dedicated to that policy area. For example, for many years national policy making on U.S. rivers and harbors was dominated by a small nucleus of actors: the Army Corps of Engineers (the key agency in charge of constructing and maintaining projects), the relevant congressional subcommittees with jurisdiction over public works in the House of Representatives and the Senate, and the National Rivers and Harbors Congress (the major interest group on the issue). Without fanfare, these groups spearheaded policy activity on water projects for decades—often working cooperatively in pursuit of shared goals.

Subsequent research in the United States and other countries demonstrated that few policy subsectors were governed by such a limited number of actors for long periods of time. Drawing on a series of comparative research projects on policy subsectors, Hugh Heclo developed a competing term, the **issue network**, to refer to situations in which a mix of government and nongovernment actors actively involved in policy formulation is much more flexible over time. For example, in health care policy making, a variety of public and private groups can be interested in one or more aspects of health policy. The precise number of groups and individuals actively participating in the process depends on the issues involved and the perceived urgency of those issues. As Heclo (1978) explained,

> Iron triangles and subgovernments suggest a stable set of participants coalesced to control fairly narrow public programs which are in the direct economic interest of each party to the alliance. Issue networks are almost the reverse image in each respect. Participants move in and out of the networks constantly. Rather than groups united in dominance over a program, no one, as far as one can tell, is in control of the policies and issues. Any direct material interest is often secondary to intellectual or emotional commitment (p. 102).

Over time, Heclo's notion of a continuum of policy formulation environments formed the foundation of subsequent research that tried to describe the **policy network** at play for different policy issues. A policy network can be thought of as a map detailing the different actors who typically participate actively in a given policy area and, in particular, the nature of the relationship between government and nongovernment participants. Heclo's initial typology focused largely on whether a given policy area was captured by a small number of actors. Frans van Waarden (1992) subsequently developed a broader typology consisting of eight distinct policy networks (Table 1-2).

Van Waarden's typology makes distinctions along two dimensions. First, is policy formulation dominated largely by government or by society? Second, how many major private groups are typically engaged in policy formulation in that issue area? In a bureaucratic network, government actors (especially in the executive bureaucracy) dominate with minimal effective participation from outside. The participatory statist network has the government bureaucracy playing the lead role in public but with key policy formulation conducted in

Table 1-2 Eight Types of Policy Networks

		Number and Nature of Network Participants			
		No Major Societal Groups	*One Major Societal Group*	*Two Major Societal Groups*	*Three or More Major Societal Groups*
Government-society relations within the network	*Government dominated*	Bureaucratic network	Clientelistic network	Triadic network	Pluralistic network
	Society dominated	Participatory statist network	Captured network	Corporatist network	Issue network

SOURCE: Modified from Howlett and Ramesh (1995): 130.

private by major nongovernment actors (often in the business community). In a clientelistic network, the government uses its resources to ensure the loyalty of a major interest group active in the policy area. In a captured network, that power relationship is reversed: a major interest group forces the government to formulate policies to its liking. In a triadic network, the government leads a policy network in which two major interest groups are key players. In a corporatist network, that power relationship is (again) turned on its head, and the two major interest groups tend to play the lead role in tripartite bargaining. In a pluralistic network, many interest groups are active, but more often than not government tends to retain the policy formulation initiative. In an issue network, as Heclo originally suggested, a large number of actors drop in and out of the policy formulation process, and government does not play a leading role over time (nor does any other single group).

This typology of policy networks will be a guide to thinking about policy formulation in the chapters that follow. In industrialized countries, most policy networks include one or more major interest group participants, and policy networks on major issues are often subject to multiple influences. In the policy-oriented chapters, we discuss who participates in several specific policy networks, and how they do so.

Decision Making

Once the political process inside and outside of government has weeded out many potential policy options, the moment arrives to make a decision to create a new policy, revise an existing policy, or, alternatively, take no new action. The decision-making stage is the component of the policy-making process that involves the smallest number of direct participants. With the infrequent exception of policy questions put to a vote via a referendum or an initiative, only the appropriate elected or appointed government officials can make decisions about the use of public authority. A variety of formal and informal rules determine the precise procedures by which the government can make decisions, and these rules vary considerably from country to country.

For instance, meaningful cross-national variation exists at the decision-making stage and hinges on the nature of executive-legislative relations. In presidential systems, decision making occurs in both the executive and the legislative branches of government—especially in the United States. In parliamentary systems, policy decisions are largely the responsibility of the executive branch with legislatures playing more limited, often symbolic, roles—particularly when a single political party has majority control of the government, as has tended to be the case in the United Kingdom. When legislatures are important, one must pay attention to specific rules that govern how committees screen bills, how legislative proposals come to a full vote, what constitutes a quorum, and how new spending (if needed) gets authorized.

The distinction between a unitary and a federal system also plays a key role in the decision-making stage. In a unitary system, formal decisions that shape policy must usually be made at the national level (although sometimes governments in unitary systems delegate authority to lower levels of government). In federal systems, many policy decisions can be made at the national, provincial, or local level. This flexibility naturally expands the number of potential formal participants in the decision-making process. For example, educational standards in a federal system could conceivably be set by the national, provincial, or local legislature or by the relevant executive branch agency at the national, provincial, or local level. Funding decisions also could be made by government at all three levels. Federalism also allows decisions at one level of government to be formed in reaction to decisions made at other levels. For instance, a national government might choose to modify its own educational standards to emulate a standards model first implemented at the provincial level. Alternatively, a provincial government might choose to alter its own policy in response to an unwanted change in national policy.

Despite the formal exclusion of nongovernment actors from the policy process at this stage, government decision makers work in a context shaped by the policy preferences found in society as a whole. Individual citizens and organized interest groups voice their approval of some options (and, perhaps more crucially, their objections to other alternatives). The more important and visible the issue is to the public at large, the more decisions are constrained by public opinion. Not surprisingly, the less salient the issue is to the public, the more decisions are influenced primarily by the interest groups most directly affected by the policy under discussion.

Amid this variety of formal and informal constraints, how do decisions get made? In the early years of formal policy research in the postwar era, the **rational decision-making** model emerged as the primary conceptualization of decision making. The rational model arose out of an effort to prescribe an ideal path to sound decisions rather than from an attempt to describe reality. After defining a policy problem, firm goals should be established; all possible paths to reaching those goals should be identified; each option's ability to achieve the stated goals should be evaluated, as should its cost; and, finally, decision makers should approve the option that has the greatest likelihood of reaching the goals at an acceptable cost. At its most formalized, the rational model calls for all items to be evaluated in monetary terms. The results of this **cost-benefit analysis** can be evaluated against different criteria. One such standard is **Pareto optimality**, according to which policy decisions must make at least one person better off while making no one worse off. However, because most public decisions involve transferring resources (directly or indirectly), few policy decisions can hope to be Pareto optimal. Instead, formal cost-benefit analyses tend to adopt the utilitarian principle of the **Kaldor criterion**, according to which a policy must provide more benefits than costs to society as a whole (even if some people suffer net losses) in order to be adopted. The preferred policy option, then, is the one that provides the greatest net benefits.

During the 1950s, future Nobel Prize winner Herbert Simon conducted studies that detailed serious limitations to the application of the rational decision-making model under real-life conditions. First, all human beings have cognitive limitations that Simon termed bounded rationality—we cannot and do not consider all possible alternative courses of action. Instead, we consider a much more limited number of options. In the policy realm, these options are selected using the ideological or political filters that are part and parcel of the policy formulation process. Second, it is simply impossible for anyone to predict the positive and negative consequences of each examined alternative. To use the phrase favored by economists, people do not have perfect information—especially about the future. Finally, most policy decisions affect so many people in so many different ways that it is difficult to conduct formal cost-benefit analysis for society as a whole. Faced with these constraints, Simon argued that real-life decision makers could not hope to make Pareto-optimal or Kaldor-efficient decisions on most matters. Instead, they would engage in **satisficing decision making**, setting some basic guidelines for a decision and then trying to meet them. For further discussion of how formal cost-benefit analysis contrasts with Simon's satisficing model, see Box 1-1.

Over the next decade, the **incremental decision-making** model emerged out of further criticism of the limited usefulness of the rational model. Political scientists embraced Simon's critique of cost-benefit analysis, and they went further in detailing the real-life dynamics of public decisions. Charles Lindblom (1959, 1968) and others argued that in most circumstances the principal elements of bounded rationality are the existing policy and the institutions created to implement the policy. New policy problems emerge not from consideration of all conceivable alternatives but rather from specific problems associated with the existing state of affairs. In turn, the policy options under consideration need not be an exhaustive list but rather a short list varying only incrementally from the status quo. This incrementalism is driven by the cognitive limitations of human beings as well as a desire to

Box 1-1 **Decision-making Processes: Cost-benefit Analysis versus Satisficing**

Richard Layard and Stephen Glaister (1994) outline a specific framework for conducting cost-benefit analysis. This approach calls for the relative valuation of all costs and benefits at various points in time across the life of the project and an assessment of the costs and benefits accruing to residents at different income levels and with different relationships to the policy. From these valuations, analysts calculate the sum total of costs and benefits for each year of the proposed project. At that point, they try to estimate the present value of the total project by discounting the costs and benefits in the future. This discount rate, like the cost and benefit totals, varies by category of resident and is an effort to make projections about the future more conservative; inflation and many other unpredictable factors can reduce people's enjoyment of the policy in the future. Finally, these individual calculations are compiled into the present value estimate, and policymakers can then determine whether benefits exceed the proposed costs of the project.

Herbert Simon (1957) argued that this detailed accounting of costs and benefits did not match up with reality. He wrote:

> While economic man maximizes—selects the best alternative from among all those available to him; his cousin, whom we shall call administrative man, satisfices—looks for a course of action that is satisfactory or "good enough." Examples of satisficing criteria that are familiar enough to businessmen, if unfamiliar to most economists, are "share of market," "adequate profit," "fair price."
>
> Economic man deals with the "real world" in all its complexity. Administrative man recognizes that the world he perceives is a drastically simplified model of the buzzing, blooming confusion that constitutes the real world. He is content with this gross simplification because he believes that the real world is mostly empty—that most of the facts of the real world have no great relevance to any particular situation he is facing, and that most significant chains of causes and consequences are short and simple. Hence, he is content to leave out of account those aspects of reality—and that means most aspects—that are substantially irrelevant at a given time. He makes his choices using a simple picture of the situation that takes into account just a few of the factors that he regards as most relevant and crucial (p. xxv).

Simon's criticisms of the rational decision-making model have proven fairly persuasive. Few, if any, contemporary political analysts consider cost-benefit analysis as a model of how most decisions are conducted. Instead, cost-benefit analysis is seen as one of many ways that policy analysts attempt to inform (and to influence) the decision-making process. In the political process, if satisficing decision makers find a cost-benefit study that supports their position, it can be a useful tool in the debate. If they want to support a conclusion not supported by cost-benefit analysis, they will try to find some reason to dismiss its importance.

minimize the political costs of the new decision. This model assumes that—under most circumstances—it is much easier politically to gain approval of minor changes in existing policies than to negotiate a decidedly different approach. Consider briefly the income tax code in any country. The tax code contains several exemptions and deductions for various categories of personal and business expenses. Most proposed reforms in the tax code are generated by opposition to particular components of the existing tax structure. Even calls for sweeping reform, however, are still potentially subject to the incrementalist tug highlighted by Lindblom: it is easier for politicians (and involved citizens) to hammer out minor deviations in the existing system than to embrace a wholesale change that might create new opponents of reform who see their favored elements of the current system under challenge.

The conservatism implied by the cognitive and political dynamics of incrementalism is bolstered by additional dynamics. First, people usually have greater confidence in their ability to predict the costs and benefits of minor changes than major ones; as a result, major reform proposals are vulnerable to the criticism that the proposed costs and benefits are miscalculated. Second, the existing policy already has a government bureaucracy conducting analyses of the current state of affairs and it tends to call for minor changes for a variety of reasons: an ideological commitment to the success of the existing policy, self-interest in the policy's continuation, and the bounded rationality constraints identified by Simon. Critiques of this incremental decision-making model run the gamut from those who believe it encourages people to give up on systematic, rational decision-making to those who believe the incremental model still describes a more orderly consideration of alternatives than exists in real life.

James March and Johan Olsen (1976) developed the **garbage can decision-making** model, which rejected even the limited rationality of the incremental model. March and Olsen argued that policymakers do not engage in any systematic consideration of alternatives. Instead, a variety of circumstances thrust decision opportunities on the government. Unforeseen economic developments, political dynamics at home and abroad, the sum total of a variety of actions taken by elected and nonelected government officials, and the mood of decision makers can all shape the decision. March and Olsen called each decision opportunity a garbage can in an effort to dramatize the ad hoc, even chaotic nature of many policy decisions. A key notion in this garbage can metaphor is that spare policy problems and spare solutions are always sitting around in the can. This means that when the government is called into action, officials will sometimes choose a solution they find handy—for ideological or political reasons—rather than search for solutions specific to the problem at hand. For example, faced with public criticism of existing child care facilities, a governing party that favors government intervention on a variety of issues may be more prone to consider direct government provision of child care or greater public regulation.

Table 1-3 Four Scenarios of Subsystem Decision Making

		Complexity of the Policy Network	
		High	*Low*
Policy issue constraints	*High*	Incremental decision making	Satisficing decision making
	Low	Optimizing adjustment	Rational decision making

SOURCE: Modified from Howlett and Ramesh (1995): 148.

Conversely, a more market-oriented party might consider issuing a call for personal responsibility or a public call for dedicated individuals to take advantage of market opportunities in child care. In the garbage can model, decision makers are often depicted as being addicted to a particular problem-solving approach—not unlike a child who enjoys drumming and looks at every household object as another opportunity to play the drums.

Although some decisions undeniably have a "garbage can" feel to them, many decisions are made more systematically. During the 1980s and 1990s, policy researchers moved from efforts to generate a one-size-fits-all characterization of decision making to the study of decisions as made in different policy areas. This contemporary approach departs from the premise that all the models described earlier occur in real life—depending on the context and on the will of the participants. To attempt to understand the likelihood of different decision-making styles, one must try to understand the specific policy area and the formal and informal rules governing decisions in that area. This subsystem decision-making model analyzes the context of decision making along two dimensions. First, how complex is the policy network for that issue? In other words, are the political constraints on decision makers high or low? Are there many groups and individuals actively lobbying with differing goals, or are there relatively few groups with goals that overlap in several respects? Second, how compelling are the logistical constraints? These constraints include the complexity of the policy problem, the pressure of time, and the availability of sound information. In short, are the logistical constraints high or low? The income tax reform dynamics we discussed earlier are an example of an area with high political and logistical constraints with many divided participants dealing with a laundry list of complex alternatives. Working from these two sets of constraints, Martin Smith (1994) generated a four-model typology of decision making at the subsystem level (Table 1-3).

In Smith's typology the model of rational decision making is most applicable to situations in which the policy network is not complex and the logistical constraints are low. In turn, incrementalism is most likely at the other extreme—when the policy subsystem is highly complex and the logistical constraints are also high. Simon's satisficing behavior is most likely when logistical constraints are high but the policy network is not very large. Finally, Smith carved out a new model of decision making, **optimizing adjustment**, to refer to situations in which decision makers do not consider widely divergent options but are willing to consider fairly significant changes from the status quo. Such a model of decision making is deemed most likely when the political constraints are high and the logistical constraints are low.

If we pause briefly to reflect on the preceding discussion of decision making, we might assume that sweeping policy change is close to impossible in major policy areas. Only the rational decision-making model holds out the possibility of tremendous change, and that model is not likely to occur in major policy areas. However, both common sense and the consideration of major reforms of the past in various countries tell us that change is possible—even in policy areas with major political and logistical constraints. What breaks the logjam in such situations? Since the late 1980s a variety of analysts have argued that a perception of crisis is the driving characteristic common to most major policy changes. Studies of both industrialized countries (Hall 1990; Jenson 1989) and late-industrializing countries (Grindle and Thomas 1991) concur that an economic, political, or social crisis can drive sweeping policy change from the agenda-setting stage through to policy formulation—culminating in the adoption of decidedly different public policies. For example, the perception of an emerging ecological crisis in many industrialized countries in the 1970s helped to create a policy climate in which major departures from previous policies were considered and, in many cases, adopted by governments.

Be forewarned, however, that what constitutes a crisis is in the eye of the beholder. There is no ironclad, objective definition of crisis; it is entirely subjective. For that reason, in many policy settings we should anticipate that the advocates of sweeping change will be calling the current state of affairs a crisis. Conversely, the advocates of lesser (or no) change will attempt to convince the general public and decision makers that there is no crisis that warrants major reform.

Policy Implementation

When speaking of the implementation stage, we are concerned with what is done to put a public policy into effect. In the early years of policy research, most analysts focused on the first three stages of policy making because they assumed that the real action centered on policy decision making (and the events leading up to the decision). However, by the early 1970s a variety of studies had demonstrated that the implementation stage is crucial to the success or failure of a policy (Pressman and Wildavsky 1973).

Implementation is important because prior to this stage a great many public policy decisions are loosely defined. Individuals and agencies responsible for policy implementation are often given a great deal of latitude in determining the specific terms and requirements of a new law or regulation. Because of this delegation of authority, in most countries the bureaucracy is the major location for policy implementation and enforcement and thus plays a large role in interpreting and elaborating the government's broad policy guidelines. How the bureaucracy approaches this task can vary widely from country to country and across policy areas within the same country. We consider both sides of the implementation coin: the specific provisions made to enforce the core elements of the policy and the behavior of the persons responsible for policy implementation as they interpret and elaborate policies.

Many policy implementation studies examine issues such as the amount of money spent on a program, the types of fines or penalties to be imposed on those who violate the law, or the number of new employees hired to implement a program. In short, these studies consider the specific **policy instruments** used to put the policy into effect. Policy instruments can be grouped into four basic types. When most people think of public policies, they tend to think of the use of **direct government instruments**—whether through regulation, the direct provision of services, or the operation of state-owned enterprises. However, direct action is just one of several possible approaches to achieving policy goals. Sometimes governments attempt to reach policy goals by the operation of **market instruments**—ranging from deregulation to incentives intended to motivate certain behaviors within a largely free market. In other situations, governments mobilize their powers of persuasion to convince the public to address policy concerns via **voluntary instruments** at home or in their local communities. A fourth course of action remains: the combination of some or all of these options into a **mixed instruments** approach.

In the early years of scholarly research on implementation, theories focused on the nature of instrument choice at the upper levels of the bureaucracy via a focus on **top-down implementation**. In a top-down approach, the resources dedicated to an agency, its organizational structure, and the goals adopted by the agency are crucial to successful implementation. For instance, the analysis of implementation problems in secondary education focused on identifying the missing resources or organizational patterns that could improve schools' performance. As case studies of various programs in several countries showed, however, important decisions are often made at the lower levels of the executive branch. Civil servants can shape policies at the ground level not only by using the discretion left to them by the implementation decisions at higher levels but also by the speed and dedication with which they use their resources.

Critics of the top-down approach, such as James Wilson (1989), countered with a conceptualization of **bottom-up implementation**. The debate between top-down and bottom-up theories of implementation is not just about who shapes implementation but also about the core nature of implementation problems. In a top-down approach, the crucial issue in implementation is policy design: good implementation is driven largely by sound, detailed decisions made at the highest levels of government. In a bottom-up

Table 1-4 Four Scenarios of Subsystem Instrument Choice

		Complexity of the Policy Network	
		High	*Low*
Government capacity	*High*	Market instruments	Direct government instruments
	Low	Voluntary instruments	Mixed instruments

SOURCE: Modified from Howlett and Ramesh (1995): 163.

world, the central concern is building a motivated, trained civil service that makes good instrument-choice decisions when reacting to situations that the policy designers did not anticipate. For example, can school principals motivate teachers and students while providing sanctions for those who do not meet certain expectations?

Since the early 1980s researchers shifted from trying to characterize entire countries to studying what drives instrument choice at the policy subsystem level within countries. Stephen Linder and B. Guy Peters (1989) argued that the two crucial factors determining decisions at this stage are the complexity of the policy network and the nature of government capacity in the policy area (Table 1-4). When the policy network is complicated (again, meaning that there are many participants in and out of government) and government capacity is low, government is most likely to resort to voluntary instruments—exhorting citizens to change their behavior to address the policy problem. Conversely, when government capacity is high and the policy network is less complicated, government is most likely to use direct instruments. It may be surprising to see research indicate that the use of market instruments is associated with high government capacity. Linder and Peters (and others) argued that although the flexibility of market instruments lends itself to situations in which the policy networks are complex, only governments with high capacity are likely to use them. This is because governments need substantial administrative capacity to monitor market activity and to enforce market outcomes. They also need substantial political capacity to defend the use of markets in the face of opposition in complex, mobilized policy networks. For example, a responsive judicial system is needed to enforce contracts and an effective regulatory system is needed to monitor the provision of services such as education and utilities via the private sector. In both examples the government that adopts market-oriented approaches to an issue must have sufficient support for tackling these concerns through the up-and-down world of the free market. Finally, Linder and Peters asserted that when the number of participants in the policy network is low and government capacity is low, an eclectic, mixed instruments approach is most likely.

In addition to analyzing instrument choice, many studies of implementation focus on the bureaucrats themselves. As noted in Table 1-4, the capacity of the bureaucracy plays a crucial role in public policy. Just as some instruments are not chosen because of a lack of capacity, other instruments can fail in practice because the bureaucracy lacks the motivation to carry out the program. Studies of implementation failure often focus on the human factor. For example, Wilson (1989) discussed how situational imperatives and the internal norms of police forces frame daily work activity in ways that differ from the stated goals and policies of the overall law enforcement policy.

When the focus turns to bureaucrats' motivations, many scholars turn to insights from the **principal-agent model** of delegation. The principal (here the supervisory government authority) may have one vision of policy implementation but cannot carry it out without the cooperation of many individual agents to whom specific responsibilities are delegated. The principal has certain potential sources of leverage over the agents' behavior, including the power to hire and fire and the possibility of rewarding faithful implementation with raises and promotions. That said, there are constraints on the use of each of these strategies by elected officials because they usually have the power to hire and fire only the top-level appointed officials who, in turn, face legal and political constraints both in firing employees and in rewarding some employees disproportionately over others.

An even greater limitation on the power of the principal may be the problem of imperfect information. If the principal were all-knowing, perfect information could be used to identify implementation failure everywhere it happened and to propose specific remedies for each situation. However, legislators (and even executive agency heads) will never have anything approaching perfect information on the implementation process. Accordingly, it can be difficult to identify which bureaucrats are not carrying out the policy as designed. Clearly the larger the population to be served by a policy, the bigger this potential problem becomes. This information constraint on the principal is magnified further when you consider that the source of much of that information on implementation is the bureaucracy itself. As a result, managers and politicians have to try to motivate bureaucrats to carry out the work independently.

The implementation process can be critical in explaining cross-national differences in policy outcomes and effectiveness. In some instances, countries that have adopted similar policy goals and frameworks in response to a given problem have observed different policy outcomes. Often the resources for policy implementation and the specific instrument choices made by governments play major roles in determining policy effectiveness. In other situations the willingness and ability of government officials to implement the specified program in a coherent manner can be the deciding factors in policy success.

Policy Evaluation

The evaluation of policy effectiveness constitutes the fifth and final stage in the policy-making process. People in and out of government are often conducting formal and informal evaluations of government performance in different policy areas. The potential criteria for evaluation are diverse. Sometimes evaluations focus primarily on the nature of policy outputs—that is, the resources government uses to address a problem. An output-oriented study might focus on the amount of money spent on a policy area or on the number of government employees dedicated to work in that policy area. Other evaluations focus on policy outcomes, examining whether government action has produced desired objectives. For example, did education policies increase access to schooling or improve students' test scores? Still more ambitious evaluations might focus on policy efficiency, asking whether current policies constitute money well spent. In other words, are existing policy outputs the best path to the current outcomes, or would some alternative produce better outcomes using similar resources?

There are three major arenas for policy evaluation. **Administrative evaluation** is conducted by government itself. Most government programs are required to provide regular self-assessments that are reviewed by the upper levels of the executive branch or by the appropriate legislative committee(s). In addition, many programs periodically undergo external evaluations—by another government agency, by private consultants, or by some mixture of the two. Even external evaluations are shaped by information provided by the program itself.

Judicial evaluation is conducted by the courts in response to a particular legal complaint against the program. In most industrialized countries the central issue of judicial evaluation is the legal authority of the government to make policy in that area. Many countries employ administrative courts to determine whether a particular government employee or agency had legal authority to take action in a certain sphere. Sometimes, however, especially in the United States, the courts examine not just the statutory authority to take action but also whether that action was in compliance with the policy intent of the law in question. In such a scenario, judicial evaluations may move from the determination of the scope of government authority to the determination of whether such authority was used appropriately in a given situation. For example, courts in the United States may determine that a local school board's plan for rezoning to generate a more racially integrated student body is insufficient. In most other countries, the courts would simply be ruling on whether the school board had the authority to engage in rezoning.

A third major arena is the realm of **political evaluation**. Sometimes governments attempt to gauge the public's evaluation of government policies via the interpretation of election results and by tracking public opinion polls on certain issues. However, it is difficult to interpret election results as turning on a single policy's evaluation, and public opinion polls are often better indicators of where governments should focus attention (rather than on how to approach a problem). Instead, most political evaluation takes place within the active policy network for each issue. Perhaps the major role of interest groups lies in their efforts to shape government (and, at times, public) opinion via formal and informal policy evaluation. For example, think briefly about the debate over immigration reform in the United States in the early twenty-first century. Interest groups calling for major changes, such as lower limits on legal immigration flows and stricter policies toward illegal immigrants, distributed studies asserting that immigrants were costing U.S. taxpayers and the U.S. economy more money than they were producing. In contrast, groups opposed to those changes presented analyses arguing that immigrants tend to pay more money in taxes than they receive in government benefits and emphasizing immigrants' role in the increased dynamism of the contemporary U.S. economy in contrast to most other industrialized countries. A similarly diverse range of studies sponsored by interest groups dots the policy landscape of every major issue area.

Consultation within policy networks about the current state of affairs provides the feedback that closes the circle of the policy cycle by shaping the institutional agenda for the next round of policy formulation, decision making, and implementation. Such consultation among those dedicated to a policy area is shaped broadly by perceived trends in public opinion and voting. That said, decisions within the boundaries set by general public opinion at all five stages are in turn crucially influenced by the policy network for the specific issue.

Since the late 1980s policy researchers have moved from the study of how to conduct different types of policy evaluation to a focus on how administrative, judicial, and political evaluations merge to influence subsequent choices in the earlier stages of the policy process. Again, contemporary research has focused on the policy subsystem level because of the wide variation within and across countries from one policy area to the next. Wesley Cohen and Daniel Levinthal (1990) argued that the crucial determinants of the effect of policy evaluation on future behavior are the level of government capacity and the nature of links between those in and out of government in the policy network (Table 1-5).

For Cohen and Levinthal, major changes in behavior are most likely when government capacity is high. When governments have expertise and good information, they are most able to learn from past experience. In turn, when policy networks have clear lines of communication between the public and private sectors, learning is likely to take place both in government and in society as a whole. When government has high capacity but has minimal links to those outside of government, past experience will have the largest impact on those within government itself. Conversely, when government has little expertise or minimal good information, policy evaluation continues but far less learning takes place. When nongovernment actors have multiple links to government in a policy network, the government is more likely to engage in formal policy evaluation than when the policy network is less vibrant. In both scenarios, however, the impact of those formal and informal evaluations will be smaller on future decisions in subsequent rounds of the policy cycle.

Table 1-5 Four Scenarios of Policy Evaluation and Policy Learning

		Government-Society Links in the Policy Network	
		High	*Low*
Government capacity	*High*	Maximum learning in government and society	Substantial government learning with minimal societal learning
	Low	Formal evaluation with minimal learning	Informal evaluation with minimal learning

SOURCE: Modified from Howlett and Ramesh (1995): 177.

The Policy Process Revisited

The study of the five stages of the policy process indicates that it is difficult to make sound generalizations about any stage that apply to policy making throughout an entire country—much less to all countries. Perhaps the lone exception is in the number of participants in the policy-making process across the five stages. In most countries and in most policy areas, the number of active participants has an hourglass shape across the five-stage policy-making process (Figure 1-1).

The agenda-setting stage is filled with participants in and out of government at many levels. Once a policy problem reaches the active political agenda, the number of meaningful participants begins to decrease as the debate shifts from what is important to the analysis and promotion of competing policy solutions to the problem at hand. At the decision-making stage, given the rule-based nature of most public authority, we find the smallest number of active participants as government decision makers outline the new policy (or ratify the existing one). This decision, however, is not the end of the process. Instead, it leads to a wider struggle to implement the policy. The implementation process involves more participants as many more individuals in government (and often outside of government) have a direct role in bringing the policy to life. Implementation is complex not just because government policy decisions leave room for interpretation by the executive branch but also because the broader number of participants leaves multiple points for opponents of the prior decision to attempt to change the course of the policy. Finally, at the policy evaluation stage, the number of participants gets broader still as the executive, judicial, and legislative branches review policy performance—as do a variety of forces from outside of government. These evaluations form the context in which subsequent agenda setting takes place as the policy process continues.

Beyond this pattern of participation across the policy process, one finds substantial differences in the precise nature of policy making from country to country and across policy areas within a single country. For that reason, our examination of policy making focuses on the dynamics in different policy

Figure 1-1 The "Hourglass" Nature of Participation in the Policy Process

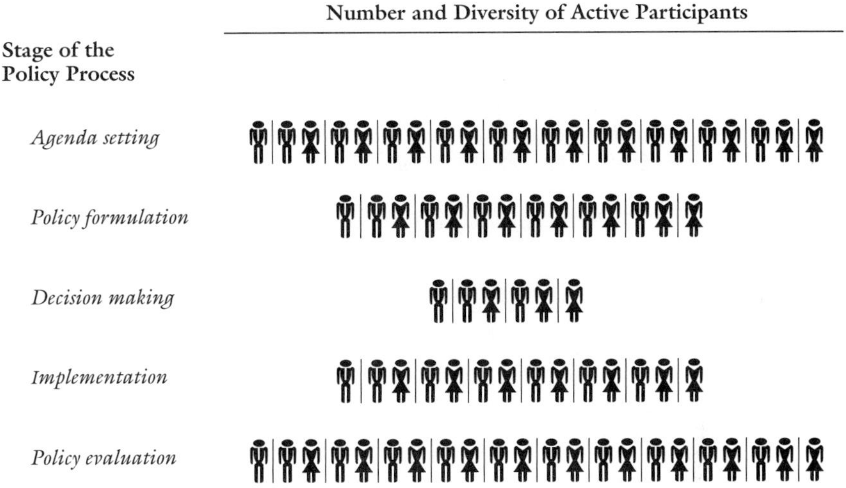

Number and Diversity of Active Participants

Stage of the Policy Process

Agenda setting

Policy formulation

Decision making

Implementation

Policy evaluation

areas. In analyzing those policy areas, we consider what motivates government to create, reform, and terminate specific policies. Those decisions constitute choices made in an intensely political process shaped by many factors.

SUGGESTED READINGS

Castles, Francis G. 1998. *Comparative Public Policy: Patterns of Post-war Transformation*. Northampton, Mass.: Edward Elgar.

Gowda, Rajeev, and Jeffrey Fox, eds. 2002. *Judgments, Decisions, and Public Policy.* Cambridge: Cambridge University Press.

Harris, Phil, and Craig Fleisher, eds. 2005. *The Handbook of Public Affairs.* London: Sage.

Hill, Michael, and Peter Hupe. 2002. *Implementing Public Policy: Governance in Theory and Practice.* London: Sage.

Howlett, Michael, and M. Ramesh. 2003. *Studying Public Policy: Policy Cycles and Policy Subsystems,* 2nd ed. Toronto: Oxford University Press.

Kingdon, John W. 2003. *Agendas, Alternatives, and Public Policies,* 2nd ed. New York: HarperCollins.

Levin, Martin, and Martin Shapiro, eds. 2004. *Transatlantic Policymaking in an Age of Austerity: Diversity and Drift.* Washington, D.C.: Georgetown University Press.

Marsh, David. 1998. *Comparing Policy Networks.* Buckingham, England: Open University Press.

McCombs, Maxwell. 2004. *Setting the Agenda: The Mass Media and Public Opinion.* Malden, Mass.: Polity.

Miyakawa, Tadao, ed. 1999, 2001. *The Science of Public Policy,* vols. 1–7. New York: Routledge.

Nagel, Stuart, ed. 2002. *Handbook of Public Policy Evaluation.* Thousand Oaks, Calif.: Sage.

Parsons, Wayne. 1995. *Public Policy: An Introduction to the Theory and Practice of Policy Analysis.* Northampton, Mass.: Edward Elgar.

Peters, B. Guy. 2001. *The Politics of Bureaucracy,* 5th ed. New York: Routledge.

Sabatier, Paul, ed. 2007. *Theories of the Policy Process,* 2nd ed. Boulder: Westview Press.

Stone, Deborah. 2002. *Policy Paradox: The Art of Political Decision Making,* rev. ed. New York: Norton.

Chapter 2 Theories of Policy Making

Across the policy process, what are the major factors that shape the policies adopted by governments? The attempt to explain why governments create, modify, or terminate policies has produced theories that focus on various potential influences. Cultural, economic, political, and institutional factors have received significant attention from scholars.

The Cultural School

The cultural school maintains that some societies are more skeptical about government than others. This skepticism reduces the probability of government policy creation and expansion. In other settings, cultural traditions, attitudes, and values are more supportive of government intervention and tend to support the expansion of government activity. In the sections that follow, we examine two major approaches to the study of cultural influences on policy making.

The Family of Nations Approach

Industrialized countries often differ in how they approach a given policy area; however, groups of countries may traditionally handle a given issue in a similar way. What explains those differences across groups of countries? Some researchers focus on deeply rooted cultural and historical traditions that lend themselves to different attitudes about society and distinct ways of organizing policy making. Francis Castles (1993) led a team of researchers to examine whether there are **families of nations**, that is, groups of countries whose cultural similarities help to produce similar policy-making dynamics and, in some cases, similar policy decisions. They identified four distinct cultural families in the postwar industrialized world: the Anglo-American family (Australia, Canada, Ireland, New Zealand, the United Kingdom, and the United States), the German family (Austria, Germany, and Switzerland), the Latin family (France, Greece, Italy, Portugal, and Spain), and the Scandinavian family (Denmark, Finland, the Netherlands, Norway, and Sweden).

What characterizes each family of nations is a particular set of historical and cultural traditions that have continued to shape policy making in the postwar era. For instance, the Anglo-American countries have had a greater tendency to emphasize the role of the individual than have societies from different cultural traditions. As a result, some scholars assert that Anglo-American traditions serve as a brake on government expansion (or as a force for contraction). Conversely, the Scandinavian family of nations is seen as more collectivist in its cultural norms, which helped to fuel more support for government expansion in range and degree. The German and Latin families' traditions stand between those contrasting Anglo-American and Scandinavian traditions. The German family of nations has a deeply rooted federalist approach to political organization that serves as a check on government expansion. At the same time, societal groups have tended to organize nationwide in a more corporatist fashion that makes collectivist public policies more possible when those national groups work closely with government. The Latin family of nations, in turn, has a long historical tradition of support for a powerful central government, which many scholars attribute to its historical desire to catch up economically and militarily to northern European countries. This big government tradition, however, has been counterbalanced by a variety of cultural norms that center on the family and breed distrust of the national government.

The Public Opinion Approach

Some scholars prefer to focus not on broad, long-standing cultural and historical traditions but rather on the impact of contemporary, specific attitudes as reflected in public opinion polls. Working in this vein, scholars use responses to questionnaires to measure support for government intervention or, conversely, belief in the role of individual responsibility. Cross-national studies of public attitudes toward policy making began to flourish in the 1970s and expanded to include more countries by the 1990s.

Regarding the range of government activity, opinion surveys from the 1970s and later have found that considerable majorities in industrialized countries have supported government intervention in a broad range of policy areas. Table 2-1 shows that virtually all citizens in these six countries support government activity to provide health care, to protect the environment, and to care for the elderly. Large majorities support government responsibility for other issues as well. This pattern of broad support for some form of government intervention on a variety of issues characterizes the situation in the industrialized world since the 1970s: government is expected to play a role. Support for some form of government action or responsibility places a broad array of policy concerns on every country's systemic agenda. This does not mean, however, that large majorities of citizens will consistently agree on the specific form of government activity in each policy area, nor do polls on attitudes about the range of government activity tell us very much about citizens' attitudes about spending priorities.

Indeed, public attitudes regarding the degree of government intervention (as measured by support for increased spending) have been less stable. In the

Table 2-1 Attitudes toward the Range of Government Responsibility, 2006 (in percent)

Issue	France	Germany	Italy[a]	Japan	United Kingdom[b]	United States	Average
Provide health care	92%	96%	99%	87%	99%	90%	*94%*
Protect the environment	96	94	97	90	91	94	*94*
Provide for the elderly	94	94	98	89	98	90	*94*
Control prices	78	78	93	92	85	77	*84*
Assist industry	83	59	80	67	88	74	*75*
Reduce income differences	78	72	75	66	69	52	*69*
Provide for the unemployed	70	71	75	57	57	52	*64*
Provide jobs	62	68	77	52	56	40	*59*
Average	*82%*	*79%*	*87%*	*75%*	*80%*	*71%*	

SOURCE: Data for all countries but Italy are from International Social Science Programme (ISSP 2006). Italian data are from ISSP (1996).

NOTE: Percentages of respondents who think the issue "definitely should be" or "probably should be" the government's responsibility.

[a]The data for Italy are for 1996.

[b]The respondents for the United Kingdom were all located in Great Britain.

1960s and 1970s, there was overall support for the expansion of government spending in most countries—though with greater differences across countries than we observed on the range-of-activity dimension. From the 1980s through the 2000s, this situation changed. On many specific policy issues, majorities (albeit smaller ones) still favored higher spending. Regarding total government spending, however, societies were more divided, as large minorities favored more spending and large minorities supported a contraction of overall spending by the 1980s (Huseby 1995). By the early twenty-first century, majorities in many industrialized countries supported cuts in the overall level of government spending. Table 2-2 illustrates the challenges faced by policymakers when citizens call for a reduction in total spending while supporting spending increases in most specific policy areas. In this 2006 poll, we observe two-thirds or more of respondents calling for lower government spending everywhere except for the United Kingdom. Large majorities among these same respondents, however, want government to increase or maintain spending on every listed policy issue except for national defense.

Policymakers must face public opinion that is united over its desire for government action yet divided over the issue of spending. Elected officials attempt to satisfy calls for government program spending increases on certain issues (and from certain quarters) while avoiding visible increases in overall spending that are likely to alienate another sizable segment of voters. To avoid seriously angering one side or the other, governments try to strike a balance. Continued overall government growth risks mobilizing much of the public; however, so, too, does a refusal to expand government activity on at least some fronts. To deal with this complicated situation, policymakers would be well advised to examine the flow of opinion in each specific policy area.

Table 2-2 Attitudes toward Government Spending, 2006 (in percent)

Issue	France	Germany	Italy[a]	Japan	United Kingdom[b]	United States	Average
ATTITUDES regarding CUTS in OVERALL GOVERNMENT SPENDING							
Strongly support cuts	68%	45%	33%	57%	12%	28%	*41%*
Support cuts	21	31	37	23	26	36	*29*
Neither	6	15	17	14	29	23	*17*
Oppose cuts	3	7	11	4	24	10	*10*
Strongly oppose cuts	3	3	3	3	8	4	*4*
SPENDING on HEALTH							
Increase spending	30	66	77	65	82	80	*71*
Spend same	33	28	18	26	16	14	*23*
Decrease spending	8	6	5	9	1	6	*6*
SPENDING on the ENVIRONMENT							
Increase spending	54	38	60	58	57	54	*57*
Spend same	36	52	30	35	40	33	*35*
Decrease spending	10	11	10	7	3	13	*8*
SPENDING on RETIREMENT/PENSIONS							
Increase spending	46	52	68	56	75	65	*60*
Spend same	47	42	25	37	24	28	*34*
Decrease spending	7	6	7	7	2	7	*6*
SPENDING on EDUCATION							
Increase spending	59	82	71	53	73	83	*66*
Spend same	33	16	24	41	27	13	*30*
Decrease spending	8	2	5	7	1	4	*5*
SPENDING on UNEMPLOYMENT BENEFITS							
Increase spending	14	33	49	28	16	37	*31*
Spend same	46	49	30	52	46	49	*45*
Decrease spending	41	18	21	20	39	14	*25*
SPENDING on DEFENSE							
Increase spending	9	12	7	21	31	36	*19*
Spend same	42	33	20	42	45	36	*35*
Decrease spending	49	56	73	37	24	27	*47*
TAXES per GDP	*44*	*35*	*41*	*27*	*37*	*27*	

SOURCE: Data on taxation as a share of gross domestic product (GDP) for 2006 are from Organisation for Economic Co-operation and Development (2008d). Polling data for all countries but Italy are from International Social Science Programme (ISSP 2006). Italian data are from ISSP (1996).

[a]The data for Italy are for 1996.

[b]The respondents for the United Kingdom were all located in Great Britain.

The Economic School

The economic resources available to a country shape the expectations of citizens and policymakers alike. Efforts to study the influence of economic conditions on policy making have taken into account both short-term and long-term effects of economic change.

The Role of Short-term Economic Conditions

Economic perceptions can be based on short-term trends in the economy, such as the gross domestic product (GDP) growth rate of the economy as a whole. If the economy is growing, policymakers might be more prone to expand government activity for a couple of reasons. First, economic growth can also spawn policy reform by generating optimism about a society's ability to solve its problems through public action. Second, rising economic growth rates generate additional government revenues even if all tax rates remain the same. In short, more money is available to create new programs and to expand existing efforts. For a hypothetical example of how economic windfalls and crises can affect the public purse, see Box 2-1.

Some scholars have challenged the notion that economic growth will be associated with growth in the government's size relative to the economy as a whole. Among others, Aaron Wildavsky (1975) argued that governments blessed with growth rates that exceed the rate of inflation could expand government spending in real terms without taking a larger slice of the growing economic pie. For example, Wildavsky noted that Japanese public spending rose during the 1960s by 16 percent annually while inflation rose at an annual rate of 5.5 percent. As a result, spending rose in real terms (controlling for inflation) by over 10 percent annually. By the end of the decade, however, public spending comprised a slightly smaller share of the economy. How did this happen? Annual economic growth in Japan averaged nearly 12 percent during that time period (232–235).

Bad economic conditions can also influence fiscal policy making. A recession breeds a decline in government revenues that forces governments to borrow money if they want to maintain or increase spending. Amid a recession, the fiscal incentives to reexamine and curtail government activity can be substantial. Also, just as growth can breed optimism among decision makers and the general public, an economic downturn can generate pessimism about the prospects for successful government action.

A potential product of economic downturns—rising unemployment rates—deserves special attention in many policy areas. Unemployment presents complex challenges for policymakers. As just noted, economic problems can breed a pessimism that makes policy activity more difficult. At the same time, rising unemployment places new demands directly on existing policies such as unemployment insurance, poverty relief, and, at times, health insurance. These demands for increased government benefits raise issues for fiscal and taxation policy as governments must find ways to fund the increased services. These funding decisions are made more difficult than usual because rising unemployment is often associated with falling government revenues—due to a reduction in the workforce paying payroll taxes and to a fall in economic activity more generally. If that weren't enough, spikes in unemployment can spawn calls for immigration restrictions as a potential path toward alleviating unemployment problems among voting citizens.

Box 2-1 The Relationship between Economic Growth and Deficits

Assume that last year your national government ran a balanced budget. In an economy that produced 100 dollars, the government collected 30 dollars in taxes and spent 30 dollars. For the current year, the government announces that it plans to increase spending to 31 dollars (an increase of 3.33 percent) but will leave the overall tax rate stable at 30 percent. Does this mean the government will be engaging in deficit spending this year?

Whether the government runs a deficit or surplus in this scenario is entirely contingent on economic growth. If the economy grows by exactly 3.33 percent, the budget will remain balanced. If it grows by more than 3.33 percent, the government will run a surplus. Conversely, the farther the economy falls short of that target, the larger the deficit will become, as the table indicates:

Economic Growth Rate (%)	Gross Domestic Product (dollars)	Rate of Taxation (%)	Public Revenues (dollars)	Public Spending (dollars)	Budget Outcome (dollars)	Budget Outcome as a Percentage of GDP
–5%	$95	30%	$28.50	$31	–$2.50	–2.6%
–2	98	30	29.40	31	–1.60	–1.6
0	100	30	30.00	31	–1.00	–1.0
2	102	30	30.60	31	–0.40	–0.4
3.33	103.33	30	31.00	31	0.00	balanced
5	105	30	31.50	31	0.50	0.5
10	110	30	33.00	31	2.00	1.8

The Role of Longer-term Economic Trends

Policy making can also be influenced by longer-term economic conditions such as the wealth of the country as a whole. For example, one could say that the greater a country's GDP per person, the wealthier the country is. This national wealth, along the lines of the convergence thesis of agenda setting we discussed in Chapter 1, can serve as a force pushing for the expansion of government. Overall national affluence helps to make the remaining pockets of poverty more noticeable while it also can generate confidence that poverty can and should be eliminated, that everyone can be provided a sound education, that health care can and should be made available to all, and that environmental preservation can be achieved—all without major sacrifices in the national standard of living. Harold Wilensky (1975) and others (Lindert 2004) demonstrated in comparisons of countries from around the world that the affluence of industrialized countries was associated with greater welfare spending than was typically found in less wealthy countries. This is the essence of the convergence thesis: wealth helps make national policy agendas, and public spending levels in the industrialized world look different from those elsewhere.

Table 2-3 Size of the Labor Force per Elderly Person, 2000–2020

Country	2000	2005	2010	2015	2020
France	2.8	2.7	2.6	2.2	1.9
Germany	3.0	2.7	2.4	2.4	2.2
Italy	2.4	2.3	2.1	2.0	1.8
Japan	3.7	3.1	2.6	2.2	2.0
United Kingdom	3.5	3.4	3.2	2.8	2.6
United States	4.8	4.8	4.5	4.0	3.4
EU-15 Average*	*3.0*	*2.8*	*2.6*	*2.4*	*2.2*

SOURCE: Organisation for Economic Co-operation and Development (2006: 19).

*The average for the EU-15 refers to the initial 15 member countries of the European Union.

The convergence thesis is not necessarily as useful in comparisons of policy dynamics within the industrialized world itself. Once we focus on the industrialized countries alone, we begin to see enduring differences in spending levels between countries. In the 1980s and 1990s, some countries tended to spend around one-fourth of the GDP, whereas others tended to spend as much as half. In contrast to the logic of the convergence thesis, two of the wealthiest industrialized countries, Japan and the United States, have been among the lowest spenders. Another limitation of the convergence thesis is that spending is not the only way to characterize a country's policy outputs. Two countries might spend similar amounts of money to implement decidedly distinct policies. This is true even in policy areas that demonstrate the convergence detailed in Wilensky's worldwide study. Take health care, for example. Every industrialized country in the world except the United States has adopted some form of national health insurance. Even so, the precise nature of national health insurance provision varies considerably from country to country. Some countries have government-managed national health services. Others mandate that employers provide insurance. Still others use a mix of these strategies along with government-provided health insurance. Spending priorities are important policy decisions, but they are not the only concern facing policymakers in each issue area.

Another longer-term economic trend consists of demographic changes common to industrialized countries. In particular, these countries are experiencing a so-called graying factor: an increasing percentage of their residents are senior citizens. This shift, especially if it is not accompanied by an increase in the average age at which people retire, has implications for a variety of policy areas. Just as with unemployment, a rise in the percentage of retirees in a society tends to generate an increase in demands for certain government services—especially public pensions and health care. At the same time, the aging dynamic reduces the number of active workers per retiree. As Table 2-3 indicates, this trend will accelerate over the coming years as the bulk of the postwar baby-boom generation reaches retirement age during the 2010s. The potential influence of these demographic pressures will probably increase as this trend deepens in the future.

Another long-term economic trend that became increasingly visible during the 1990s is the increasing interconnectedness of the world economy. As trade increases, as production processes are less frequently national (but instead truly global), as communication speed increases, and as international economic agreements grow more complex, what were once considered domestic policy issues must now be decided with an eye toward a variety of international contextual influences. Sometimes those influences are ongoing phenomena with heightened visibility—such as a concern for the impact of government policies on the country's economic competitiveness. In other situations an increase in the number of intergovernmental organizations and international agreements can have direct implications for domestic policy-makers. Sometimes international agreements redefine the existing problem in a policy area. On other occasions the agreements can place explicit and implicit limitations on national sovereignty in the exercise of government authority within national boundaries. The most ambitious example of this latter influence on industrialized countries is the European Union.

The Political School

In the 1970s a variety of policy analysts began to criticize what they saw as an overemphasis on the role of cultural and economic influences on policy making. Their chief contention was that policy dynamics were not necessarily driven primarily by those conditions. The political strategies and actions of political parties and interest groups could often play a central role as well.

The Role of Labor-oriented Political Parties

Many explanations of government activity (and, in particular, of the creation of the modern welfare state) have focused on the rise to popularity of political parties with ties to the organized labor movement. The contention that parties matter is the core of the **partisanship thesis** of policy making. Labor parties are likely to support an expansion in the scope of government in support of policy issues generally supported by labor unions, including education, the expansion of economic activity, health care programs, job creation and protection, old-age pensions, and unemployment insurance. Labor parties are considered likely to be faithful to this agenda for two main reasons. First, labor parties often have organizational or financial ties to organized labor that make the parties more likely to adopt policy positions in harmony with labor unions' priorities. Second, labor parties tend to focus their campaign efforts on citizens living at the lower end of the economic scale. To mobilize votes to gain and retain power, labor parties have an additional incentive to follow through on a welfare state agenda that has tended to be popular with working class voters in most industrialized countries during the postwar era. Scholarly research in the 1970s and 1980s provided empirical support for the contention that the range and degree of government activity was more likely to expand when labor parties had total or partial control of the executive and legislative branches (Castles 1982a).

Events in Europe during the 1990s caused modifications in the consideration of labor party influence on government spending. In the drive to reduce deficit spending, most European governments reduced spending levels. Some of those cuts were undertaken by labor party governments. Accordingly, it would be a misinterpretation of earlier research to conclude that labor parties will not engage in spending cuts. Instead, one might hypothesize that labor parties are likely to make lower cuts than conservative parties (particularly in welfare spending) when spending reductions are adopted—just as they were likely to raise spending at a higher rate than conservative parties in past decades when spending was on the rise throughout the industrialized world.

The Influence of One-party Government

In addition to the ideologies and constituencies associated with major political parties, the partisan balance of forces in the legislative and executive branches also can play a role. When one party controls the executive branch and holds a majority in the legislative branch, the **party government model** argues that such one-party governments will find it easier to engage in quick reforms (Castles and Wildenmann 1986). In the industrialized world the party government model has referred mainly to three Anglo-American countries (the United Kingdom, Australia, and Canada) that follow the **Westminster model** of government, in which a parliamentary system is combined with a plurality electoral system. Other scholars (Pempel 1990) have also included Japan as an example of a parliamentary system in which a single party has controlled both branches of government for long periods of time. We explore the Westminster model and the party government model in greater detail in Chapter 3.

The party government dynamic has an influence on the ease of policy change and is not necessarily a force for government expansion or contraction. These majority governments could use this power in either direction—to expand or to contract the scope of government activity. Conversely, divided governments in presidential systems (that is, when the presidency is in the hands of a party that does not have a majority in the legislature) and multiparty coalition governments in parliamentary systems tend to be less likely to engage in sweeping reform because multiple parties must be consulted to generate a working majority.

The "Overloaded Government" Thesis

Other scholars working in the 1970s and 1980s focused on the implications of party competition itself on policy making (King 1975). In a democracy, political parties strive to win elections. The party or parties in control of the government often believe that spending increases can be useful to mobilize people to vote. Conversely, tax increases are dangerous because they mobilize votes against the governing party or coalition. As a result of these dynamics, the size of government will grow in good economic times but may also grow in bad economic times. However, because governments are reluctant to increase tax rates to pay for higher spending, they are prone to run budget deficit spending. Furthermore, over time, this pattern of government growth may generate demands for even more growth as voters and interest groups refine their strategies for increasing spending on behalf of their own policy priorities. In the end, this process generates an **overloaded government**, in which the sum total of demands grows faster than both public spending and public revenues.

The notion of overloaded government certainly captures an important portion of democratic policy making: elected officials can and do attempt to retain office through the use of public authority. In fact, the gloomy implications of the thesis were lived out in many countries during the stagflationary economic crisis of the 1970s and early 1980s. Many democracies experienced increasing levels of deficit spending and a list of public demands that exceeded government efforts by increasingly larger margins. However, the last decade of the twentieth century did not witness an extension of the crisis of overloaded government. Many industrialized countries slowed the growth of spending and reduced their annual budget deficits. The overload dynamic can certainly have an impact on policymakers, but it is not always and everywhere going to be the dominant influence that it seemed to be in the late 1970s.

The Interest Group Politics Approach

Interest group activity is central to many discussions of agenda setting and policy formulation (Cigler and Loomis 2007; Norton 1999). The strategies of interest groups and their direct appeals to government officials also form part of the context of decision making and implementation. Indeed, interest groups are often directly involved in the implementation of public policies—especially regarding health care, education, and the environment. At the evaluation stage, many interest groups engage in political evaluation directly while others focus their activity on publicizing evaluations conducted by others in an effort to influence the agenda-setting process.

When are interest groups most likely to be influential? Generally speaking, increases in the size of a group's membership and in its financial resources improve its chances to be effective. However, organizational size and strength are only part of the story. As we noted in Chapter 1, the number of interest groups that are usually active in a policy network also affects the roles of those interest groups. In policy networks in which the issue is narrow and has a relatively low profile, the notion of an iron triangle emphasizes a particular interest group that has a predominant role above all others. Usually, however, the policy network is more complicated, and a variety of major interest groups have visible roles. This is perhaps especially true for the major policy areas covered in this book.

In policy networks in which many interest groups participate, the interactions among groups and between those groups and the government become important influences on policy making. Two major conceptualizations of interest group activity exist for such complex policy networks: **pluralism** and **corporatism**. Under a pluralist scenario, many interest groups compete openly for the government's attention, and the government does not often make a clear effort to bring the different groups to the negotiating table to seek a consensus. In a corporatist scenario, fewer, larger groups participate actively, and the government tries more often to include the major groups in systematic discussions of policy-making issues relevant to the policy network. We discuss the pluralist and corporatist models of interest group activity in more depth in Chapter 3.

The Institutional School

Some scholarly analyses focus on how institutions frame policy-making decisions. Rules shape how decisions get made at many stages of the policy process. Within government, some rules make it easier to take action, thereby making the expansion of government more feasible. A new institutionalist school of scholars has emerged that examines not only the impact of formal government rules but also the impact of informal norms in government and nongovernment institutions.

The Role of Formal Government Institutions

The study of the effects of government institutions on policy making has tended to focus on two sets of rules: those structuring the relations between the national and subnational governments (**federal political systems** versus **unitary political systems**) and those framing the interaction between the executive and legislative branches (**presidential systems** versus **parliamentary systems**). For many years, scholars have recognized that federal governments tend to have a harder time engaging in national policy reform. This notion begins from the premise that subnational governments are autonomous on some issues and share authority with the national government on other issues. The multi-tiered decision making of federal systems makes them prone to slower change because more people in and out of government have a chance to challenge policy proposals (Tsebelis 2002). This common-sense dynamic has been associated with long-term trends in the extension of the scope of government in the postwar era (Cameron 1978). Industrialized countries with federal governments tended to have smaller governments in both range and degree. In a unitary system, government claims ultimate authority throughout the national territory, which makes the national government the supreme policymaker unless it chooses to delegate authority to subnational government units. When unitary governments remain fairly centralized, decisions have to be ratified or carried out in fewer arenas. This makes expansion of the government's range and degree easier to achieve because fewer decisions have to be made to ratify the expansion.

As in the party government model, the unitary system's relation to the expansion issue is ultimately indeterminate. The centralization of authority lends itself to faster change, but that change could occur in either direction. An expansionist central government could expand its activities more quickly, and a contraction-oriented central government could shrink government more quickly. The Conservative government led by British prime minister Margaret Thatcher provides a clear example of how centralized authority in a unitary state can be used to reverse the expansion of government.

Executive-legislative relations also can influence the government's ability to engage in policy reform. Some scholars have argued that a presidential system provides more decision points because the chief executive and the legislature need not be from the same party or governing coalition of parties. The presidential system, similar to the federal system, generates additional decision points that tend to slow potential changes in government activity. In contrast, a parliamentary system has rules that require the executive branch to retain the support of a majority of legislators. These rules may do a better job of ensuring that the executive and legislative branchs will act together—thereby increasing the possibility of speedy reform. As with the centralization of power, this institutional factor has more of a potential role in shaping the pace of reform than its direction. When the executive and legislative branches work together, they can do so to expand government or to slow the growth of government. Prime Minister Thatcher's government was not simply working within a unitary system; it was working in the context of a parliamentary system in which Thatcher had a solid working majority in the legislature.

The effects of formal institutions on policy making can perhaps best be described as contingent on other policy-making influences. First, both federal systems and presidential systems can affect the speed of reform—provided that the political party or parties in power desire reform at all. Other factors may create a climate so unfavorable to reform that the effects of institutional arrangements on those decisions are negligible. Second, if major actors in and out of government desire change, reform can come despite the obstacles posed by these institutional rules. In other words, federal systems and presidential systems often serve as obstacles to change, but

Box 2-2 **The Contingent Influence of National Government Institutions**

In *Do Institutions Matter? Government Capabilities in the United States and Abroad*, Kent Weaver and Bert Rockman reviewed comparative case studies of issues such as energy policy, environmental policy, the management of ethnic and social cleavages, fiscal policy, industrial policy, pensions policy, national security policy, and trade policy. Their summary analysis captures the complexity of policy making and reiterates the simple truth that national-level government institutions are part of the larger whole (1993b: 446–453):

- Although institutions affect governmental capabilities, their effects are contingent.
- Specific institutional arrangements often create both opportunities and risks for individual governmental capabilities.
- Policy-making capabilities may also differ substantially across policy areas within a political system.
- Institutional effects on governmental capabilities are channeled through governmental decision-making characteristics.
- Differences in electoral rules and the norms that guide the formation of governments may have as much impact as institutions themselves.
- Parliamentary systems are not better than presidential systems, and vice versa.
- Divided party control of the executive or legislative branch exacerbates the problems of governance—especially that of setting policy priorities.
- Institutional arrangements involve a trade-off in capabilities.
- Governments may work around institutional constraints by generating countervailing mechanisms.

they do not pose insurmountable obstacles. If they were insurmountable, change would never occur in such systems, and that clearly has not been the case. Reviewing comparative research on the role of institutions in policy making, Kent Weaver and Bert Rockman (1993b) asserted that an institution's role is contingent on other policy influences and that each set of governing institutions has its own strengths and weaknesses (Box 2-2).

The Bureaucratic Politics Approach

The prior two sets of institutional influences focus on the nature of interaction among elected officials across levels and branches of government. A third set of institutional influences stems from the actions of nonelected officials—especially in the executive branch. Bureaucrats are particularly relevant in policy formulation and implementation. Peters (1995: 211–35) argued that a variety of characteristics shape a given agency's influence over policy making:

- The degree of consensus within the agency about its mission (and the path to achieving that mission)
- The degree to which the agency is seen as the prevailing expert authority regarding the feasible implementation of policies
- The personnel stability of the agency
- The managerial skill demonstrated by the agency over time
- The agency's ability to mobilize political support for its view
- The agency's ability to claim an apolitical distance from partisan and electoral disputes
- The degree of monopoly an agency holds over a policy sector (versus a situation in which two or more agencies compete for a role)

Generally speaking, the more each of these factors is present, the more effective the bureaucracy will tend to be in influencing policy making.

This list of characteristics makes clear the many reasons why the bureaucracy forms an important part of the politics of policy making. That said, it is important to remember two things. First, in many situations individual agencies lack several of these features in significant ways. Second, there are many more situations in which subunits within a single agency compete for leadership in a policy area. As a result, we should not think of the bureaucracy as a faceless, monolithic group working in unison toward a single vision of public policy. Instead, just as we are accustomed to hearing about disagreements within and among political parties and interest groups, we should be open to the possibility of divisions within and among bureaucratic agencies.

The New Institutionalism

Researchers from the 1980s forward have placed renewed interest in institutional influences on policy making (Congleton and Swedenborg 2006). This **new institutionalism** has expanded the examination of institutions in a couple of senses (March and Olsen 1984). First, the concern for institutions has broadened from a focus primarily on formal rules to include consideration of how informal norms and patterns can frame policy making. For example, the seniority rule dominant in the U.S. House of Representatives in the middle half of the twentieth century was not a formal rule of the House. It was an informal tradition passed on from session to session within each political party. For decades, congressional committees elected as chair the senior member of the majority party within the committee. Only in the 1970s did both political parties explicitly embrace the possibility that nonsenior members could be nominated (and thereby elected) as committee chairs; however, the informal practice of seniority as a decision rule has continued to dominate committee chair elections to this day. During the age in which House committee chairs were not bound to many formal rules, this informal seniority system had a crucial impact on policy making. The policy impact of the seniority system was not lost on legislators often frustrated by the dominance of committee chairs. Indeed, that frustration led to a call for new formal and informal institutions that would constrain House committee chairs over the last quarter of the twentieth century.

Second, although government rules remain an important potential influence, scholars have begun to consider the role of institutional considerations that frame the participation of nongovernmental organizations in policy making (Hall 1986; Scharpf 1997). For example, in the debate over health care reform in the United States during the early 1990s, the directors of the U.S. Chamber of Commerce initially voted to endorse the drive for some form of national health insurance. Most of the directors were representatives of large firms who generally felt that health reform would work to reduce their costs. In the membership rolls of the Chamber, however, small and medium-sized firms greatly outnumber the large firms. Since voting within the Chamber is based on the principle of one vote per firm, the members voted not to endorse national health insurance because the smaller firms feared that reform would raise their costs. If the Chamber had voting rules based on the size of the firm, the vote might have affirmed the directors' inclination to support health care reform. This reversal of course had a visible impact on the push for reform because it deflated the Clinton administration's claim that the Chamber's initial decision demonstrated that the business world supported the president's plan. This is but one of many examples of how institutional rules in nongovernmental organizations influence policy making.

An Eclectic Approach to Examining Policy Theories

Past efforts to explain public policy dynamics demonstrate the need to examine policy making from several theoretical perspectives. No single set of factors emerged as the dominant influence on policy making in the second half of the twentieth century. Cultural, economic, political, and institutional influences all played roles.

As we saw in Chapter 1, many studies of the creation, reform, and termination of policies remind us that the context of policy making varies not just from country to country but also across policy areas within each country. Similarly, the specific nature of factors that influence policy decisions will vary from one policy area to another. Accordingly, our effort to explore the influence of cultural, economic, political, and institutional factors on policy choices and outcomes also focuses on the individual policies.

Although each policy area has its own particular context and dynamics, the national context for policy making forms an essential element of the backdrop that shapes policy making on each issue. Before we move on to specific policy issues, we consider national conditions more thoroughly. In Chapter 3 we review a variety of societal dynamics that frame policy making. Then in Chapter 4 we explore the context for policy making in the European Union and the six countries featured in the policy chapters that follow.

SUGGESTED READINGS

Borre, Ole, and Elinor Scarborough, eds. 1995. *The Scope of Government.* Oxford: Oxford University Press.

Castles, Francis G., ed. 1982. *The Impact of Parties: Politics and Policies in Democratic Capitalist States.* London: Sage.

Castles, Francis G., ed. 1993. *Families of Nations: Patterns of Public Policy in Western Democracies.* Aldershot, England: Dartmouth Publishing.

Colebatch, H. K., ed. 2006. *The Work of Policy: An International Survey.* Lanham, Md.: Rowman and Littlefield.

Congleton, Roger, and Birgitta Swedenborg, eds. 2006. *Democratic Constitutional Design and Public Policy: Analysis and Evidence.* Cambridge: MIT University Press.

Flora, Peter, and Arnold J. Heidenheimer, eds. 1981. *The Development of Welfare States in Europe and America.* New Brunswick, N.J.: Transaction.

Gelissen, John. 2002. *Worlds of Welfare, Worlds of Consent?: Public Opinion on the Welfare State.* Boston: Brill.

Lindert, Peter. 2004. *Growing Public: Social Spending and Economic Growth Since the Eighteenth Century,* vols. 1–2. Cambridge: Cambridge University Press.

Maloney, William, et al. 2007. *Interest Group Politics: Internal and External Dynamics.* Basingstoke, United Kingdom: Palgrave Macmillan.

Pierre, Jon, and B. Guy Peters. 2005. *Governing Complex Societies: Trajectories and Scenarios.* Basingstoke, United Kingdom: Palgrave Macmillan.

Poguntke, Thomas, and Paul Webb, eds. 2005. *The Presidentialization of Politics: A Comparative Study of Modern Democracies.* Oxford: Oxford University Press.

Scharpf, Fritz W. 1997. *Games Real Actors Play: Actor-centered Institutionalism in Policy Research.* Boulder: Westview.

Tsebelis, George. 2002. *Veto Players: How Political Institutions Work.* Princeton: Princeton University Press.

Weaver, R. Kent, and Bert A. Rockman, eds. 1993. *Do Institutions Matter? Government Capabilities in the United States and Abroad.* Washington, D.C.: Brookings Institution Press.

Wilensky, Harold. 2002. *Rich Democracies: Political Economy, Public Policy, and Performance.* Berkeley: University of California Press.

Chapter 3 Political and Economic Dynamics in Industrialized Countries

We do not have to stretch our imaginations far to recognize that a country's policy-making process is affected by its political and economic institutions and traditions. For example, the policy-making process in an authoritarian political system looks different from the policy-making process in a democratic system. We also expect policies to look different in market economies and centrally planned economies. Among democracies, meaningful variations in policy-making processes are based on a country's institutions and its society. In this chapter we examine the basic distinctions in industrialized countries' political and economic dynamics and the relevance of these dynamics to the policy-making process. In so doing we lay the foundation for the specific policy analyses offered in the remainder of the book.

Social Cleavages

The pattern of **social cleavages**, or social divisions, is an important contextual factor for understanding any country's political system. Social cleavages are those social criteria by which people are grouped in a society. The politically relevant social cleavages found in industrialized countries have traditionally included socioeconomic status (or class), religion, ethnicity, region, and language. These cleavages find expression in various interest groups and political parties and are important for understanding a country's patterns of conflict, its distribution of political authority, its choice of an electoral system, and the formation of individuals' political attitudes and their political behavior.

The manner in which social cleavages are expressed through a country's interest group and political party systems is of particular significance for our understanding of the policy-making process. A country's social cleavages can be linked directly to certain patterns in this regard. For example, in industrialized countries from 1945 to the late 1980s, upper-middle-class voters were more likely to vote for right-wing parties, whereas working-class voters were more likely to vote for leftist parties. Thus class was a strong predictor of partisan identification and the vote. Similarly, until at least the late 1960s, religious cleavages were strong predictors of party choice and voting behavior. Social changes (for example, a growing middle class and increasing secularization) in industrialized countries since the 1970s, however, have reduced the degree to which these two cleavages are related to political behavior. Both class and religion have decreasing influence on party identification and voting choice in many industrialized countries.

Having observed this change, researchers have begun to look at new sources of social cleavage in industrialized countries, including divisive issues among the growing middle class (such as environmental protection and women's rights) that appear to influence individuals' political behavior. As we discuss later in this chapter, changes in social cleavage patterns have had an impact on contemporary patterns of partisan competition in industrialized countries, particularly through the emergence of new social movements and political parties. These changed patterns often have resulted in less predictable voting practices in these countries. For example, as noted earlier, through the 1980s in most industrialized countries the working class voted for left-wing social democratic or labor parties; these parties tended to favor increasing social welfare spending, bigger government, and higher taxation rates. Consequently, when these parties were elected to office, public policies largely reflected these preferences. Today we no longer observe such a clear connection between working-class status and support of such parties. Thus our ability to establish a clear relationship between social cleavages and party identification or voting choice, as well as the policy choices of a political party once elected, is no longer as strong. As a result, understanding the policy-making process in these countries is less straightforward than it once was.

Interest Groups

Political parties and **interest groups** serve as democratic linkage mechanisms, connecting citizens to their political systems by communicating citizens' interests and demands. However, interest groups define for themselves goals clearly different from those associated with political parties. Interest groups do not seek the election of their representatives to political office. Instead, they set out to influence public policy in specific areas of concern to their members. Interest groups do not aggregate interests; instead, they directly communicate the specific and particularized interests of their members, and, typically, most of their members share similar interests and concerns. Interest group systems tend to reflect a country's social cleavage patterns: the more socially and economically diverse a society is, the more interest groups we expect to find. Today interest groups proliferate in industrialized countries, with multiple, independent groups pressuring governments externally in most countries (although these groups have varying degrees of influence on the content of public policies).

Interest groups' prevalence, behavior, and effect are partly a reflection of the characteristics of a country's wider political system. Countries with more centralized political systems are likely to have few key interest groups that have privileged access to policymakers and a greater likelihood of meaningfully influencing the policy-making process. For example, interest groups in the United Kingdom typically have had less influence on the policy process because policy making is highly centralized and party discipline is strong (making members of Parliament less subject to the influence of lobbyists). British interest groups tend to be relatively weak, their access to the policy-making process is limited (with the exception of a few large and powerful interests that are given special access to policymakers), and they have been less able to regularly influence policy decisions.

In more decentralized political systems, where there are multiple points of access to key policymakers, interest groups are often more numerous, active, and effective. In such systems, the greater the size, internal coherence, and financial resources of an interest group, the more influential it is likely to be. In addition, in systems where political parties and party discipline are weak, interest groups may be more active for at least two reasons. First, weak political parties tend to rely on interest groups for fundraising and for sparking the public's interest. Second, if party discipline is weak, interest groups will have a much better chance of influencing the votes of members of the legislature because those members are less likely to be subject to reprisals from their party for voting against the party line in favor of an interest group's position.

The best example of interest group activity in a decentralized political system is found in the United States, where strong interest groups (such as AARP and the National Rifle Association) have large membership numbers and substantial financial resources with which to exert influence. Complementing this strength is the fact that the political system offers to these powerful groups multiple points of access to the policy-making process via members of Congress as well as the executive branch. When this ease of access is combined with the weak party discipline found in congressional parties and the legislature's decentralized and powerful committee system, we find all the ingredients for a pervasive pattern of interest group influence on the policy-making process.

The pattern of interest group activity in a country, particularly the relationship between interest groups and the government, is crucial to understanding the impact of these groups on the policy-making process. All industrialized countries have interest groups, but we find important differences from country to country when we examine the nature of the relationship between interest groups and government. Political scientists usually describe this relationship as either **pluralism** or **corporatism**. In pluralist systems, such as those found in the United Kingdom, France, and the United States, power is dispersed throughout society rather than concentrated in a few actors within and around the government. Interests organize independently, compete freely, and have no formal connections to government. In such systems, competition between interest groups is viewed as making a vital contribution to the political process, and public policies frequently reflect interest groups' demands. In a pluralist setting the government responds to outside pressures but does not

Box 3-1 **The Swedish Corporatist Model**

One of the best examples of a corporatist interest group system among the industrialized countries is found in Sweden. Sweden has a highly centralized, unitary parliamentary political system. Policy making takes place in an environment that emphasizes cooperation and compromise and in which government and interest groups act to develop a high degree of policy consensus. Sweden has many powerful interest groups that are formally incorporated into the policy-making process, enabling them to exert a considerable degree of influence over policy making.

Swedish interest groups work together in powerful associations empowered to represent all their members. For example, trade unions in all economic sectors operate under the umbrella of the National Federation of Trade Unions, while employers throw their lot together in the Swedish Association of Employers. These and other interest organizations are consulted regularly in the policy-making process, primarily through their work on state commissions. These commissions serve in a number of specific issue areas and play an important advisory role in the policy-making process. They are appointed by the Swedish cabinet and include members of relevant interest associations as well as bureaucrats and politicians. These commissions' recommendations are incorporated into government policy proposals and also may be an important source of policy initiation.

In addition to forming these commissions, the government is constitutionally required to submit all legislative proposals to those interests involved with any given policy. In this process, known as *remiss*, groups and the bureaucracy are given the opportunity to comment on pending policy proposals. Their comments are included with the legislation submitted to the parliament. When combined, the state commissions and the remiss procedure make for a strong corporatist arrangement between government and organized interests, and as a result of these arrangements, organized interests in Sweden have a direct influence on policy making.

intervene in interest groups' activities in any systematic fashion. The extent of an interest group's influence on the policy-making process in a pluralist system often depends on an interest group's individual characteristics such as expertise, financial resources, and organizational unity.

In corporatist systems, fewer interest groups participate in the political process and the ties between interest groups and the government are often institutionalized and quite explicit. Among the countries we examine in this book, Germany is the most strongly corporatist, although Italy and Japan also demonstrate corporatist tendencies (see Box 3-1 for an example of a corporatist model elsewhere in Europe). Where corporatism occurs, we typically find one large interest group in each of the major interest sectors in a country (for example, labor, farmers, government workers). This one group will coordinate the demands of active organizations in that sector and speak authoritatively for them. Such groups usually are incorporated directly into the official policy-making process as members of a council or committee that is consulted systematically when policy is made and implemented. In corporatist systems, governments do not simply respond to interest group pressures at their own discretion; rather, they create an institutionalized pattern of active consultation and cooperation between groups and the policymakers. Policy decisions therefore are viewed as negotiated outcomes between the government and those most affected by the policy. Corporatist arrangements are intended to reduce conflict in the policy-making process, to develop policy consensus, and to increase the likelihood of policies being implemented effectively.

Some evidence indicates that corporatist relationships are of declining influence in those industrialized countries where they once flourished (such as in northern Europe). This decline appears to be a flexibility issue: corporatist arrangements tend to reduce the ability of both governments and organized interest groups to respond to a more complicated policy environment because of the complex relationship between the two. As a result, it can be difficult for actors in corporatist arrangements to adjust to changing conditions. Further, corporatist arrangements require unanimity in group interests; in the contemporary era, it has become increasingly difficult for interest associations to organize diverse interests around one clear policy position. Finally, societies that emphasize corporatist relationships make it more difficult for new interests to be heard, which results in demands for weakening corporatist linkages. Nevertheless, these arrangements remain important in some countries in key policy sectors, particularly in agriculture and in more technical policy areas.

Political Parties and Party Systems

Political parties are viewed widely as the most significant political institutions in a representative democracy because they play a key role in linking citizens to their political systems and the policy-making process. Parties are fundamental to the policy-making process because of their role in **interest aggregation**. Political parties are responsible for taking a wide range of citizen viewpoints and demands (for example, on education, health care, and the environment) and translating them into a more manageable and more specific number of policy alternatives. Parties then enter elections and voters choose between the various parties' competing partisan programs. Once elected to office, parties form the basis for the executive branch and the legislature (usually, but not necessarily, as a reflection of partisan majorities) and then exercise control over the policy-making process, thus translating these policy alternatives into actual public policies. Because these political parties try to fulfill many of their campaign promises once in office, they play a key role in the policy-making process in any country.

We must evaluate the role of political parties and party systems in the policy-making process along several dimensions. The first dimension involves those partisan characteristics that affect the way parties aggregate citizens' interests, namely, the nature of their membership bases and their internal cohesion. Traditionally, the primary form of partisan organization in industrialized countries was known as a **mass party**. This term describes parties that (1) have a large number of active members drawn from a specific social cleavage (for example, the working class or a religious group), (2) are well organized, and (3) are committed to pursuing a particular political ideology or a distinctive set of policy goals (that clearly reflect their members' interests). In the past, European Socialist and Communist parties, especially those found in Italy and France, were considered to be model mass parties, in that their memberships tended to be drawn from one particular group (the working class) and they pursued a clear ideological vision—namely, some version of Marxist philosophy. Mass parties have become less common in modern political systems as political, social, and economic changes (such as the growth of the middle class and the declining strength of labor unions) have eroded their traditional bases of support.

Today, mass parties have for the most part given way to far looser coalitions of voters with weaker organizational structures, memberships drawn from disparate backgrounds, and programs based on less clearly defined goals or visions. These forms of partisan organization are often described as **catch-all parties**, and they are commonly seen more as electoral organizations (focused on achieving elected office) than as membership parties (focused on pursuing a set of policy goals that directly reflect their members' concerns and ideology). The German Christian Democratic Union and the Japanese Liberal Democratic Party are both catch-all parties. These partisan organizations have broadly based memberships drawn from across socioeconomic and occupational groups, they are programmatically vague, and they are concerned with issues rather than ideologies. Historically, these parties have been highly effective electoral machines, with most of their activities directed toward ensuring that their parties secured and maintained positions of political power.

Mass parties are generally seen as a far more effective mechanism for performing the interest aggregation function, particularly because their members, based on a set of shared characteristics, can be more easily focused and mobilized around a set of common goals. Catch-all parties tend to have diverse membership bases and are much less focused and unified around a common policy vision. Thus we might expect governing catch-all parties to provide less policy coherence than more traditional mass parties. Further, when catch-all parties are in power, we might expect the policy-making process to be less focused on large-scale reform, particularly reform driven by some wider vision or plan for society. Catch-all parties are the predominant form of partisan organization operating in the six countries we examine.

The internal cohesion of each party's behavior in the legislature is another key element of the policy-making process. The term **party discipline** refers to the likelihood of legislators voting with their own party in the legislature.

The more often party members vote the party line, the more disciplined the party. A higher degree of party discipline implies a greater degree of partisan control over the policy-making process. More specifically, disciplined parties are considered to be more likely to fulfill their campaign promises because they can be confident that their members will support their party's policy proposals. British political parties are among the most disciplined of those found in the six countries we examine, whereas parties in the United States provide a clear example of undisciplined partisan organizations. In Britain, parties are structured, centralized, and cohesive, and their members vote as a bloc in the legislature. In the United States, none of this is true of political parties. Parties in the other four countries vary with respect to discipline, but all lean toward greater discipline than is found in U.S. parties.

Another important feature of a country's political system is the nature of its **party system**, meaning the number of parties viewed as having a serious chance of winning elections in that country as well as the extent of competition among these parties. The number of parties operating in a country affects the way in which parties aggregate interests. Two principal types of party systems are found in industrialized countries: **two-party** and **multiparty systems**. In the two-party systems of the United States and the United Kingdom, the two major political parties (both of which are increasingly "catch-all") present broad and relatively undefined policy alternatives to the electorate. This approach reflects the parties' desire to appeal to the broadest segment of the electorate possible and to avoid alienating potential supporters. As such, these parties do a great deal of interest aggregation. In contrast, in France the multiparty system is characterized by multiple parties that represent a much more narrow range of interests and thereby do very little interest aggregation. These characteristics are key factors in understanding the role that these countries' legislatures play in the policy-making process.

The emergence of two major parties may have roots in a country's political culture, its social cleavage patterns, or its political institutions (see the discussion of electoral systems later in this chapter). In two-party systems, two major parties receive the vast majority of votes cast at any given election. These two parties are not necessarily the only parties that run in an election. Rather, they are the only two parties that have a serious chance of winning. In two-party systems, the victorious party usually wins with a large enough majority to govern independently—the Labour Party in Britain currently finds itself in this position, where it enjoys a 62-seat majority in the House of Commons. As a result, this type of party system usually is associated with more stable patterns of governance, and public policies generally reflect the preferences of the majority party in the legislature (assuming that the majority party is disciplined). In such instances, **party government** is said to prevail. Two-party systems also encourage parties to moderate their policy positions to attract a wider base of support; this tendency toward centrist parties and policies further contributes to government stability in these systems.

Multiparty systems are more common than two-party systems in industrialized countries. This is true for two main reasons: First, many of these countries traditionally were characterized by social cleavages that created the basis for several different parties. Second, the use of proportional representation electoral laws in most industrialized countries makes it easier for multiple parties, and especially smaller parties, to take seats in the legislature.

A fairly clear association exists between multipartism and coalition governments. Coalition governments in multiparty systems are currently found in four of the six countries we examine: France, Germany, Italy, and Japan. In coalition governments, the executive branch must negotiate with coalition members to obtain support for policies and get them passed, or sometimes even to remain in office. The executive branch's success in acquiring and maintaining support for its policies will be affected by the degree to which the parties in the coalition are disciplined—if party leaders cannot ensure their party members support the coalition's policy proposals, the policy-making process is further complicated. Thus policy making in multiparty systems is often less straightforward than in two-party systems because no single party in the legislature controls enough seats to govern alone. In multiparty systems, political parties often continue the interest aggregation process well after being elected to office, as their policy positions are refined in negotiations between the parties in the coalition. As a result, the link between voters and policy choice can be less direct in a multiparty system than in a two-party system.

Countries with multiparty systems have a greater tendency toward government instability because of the difficulties associated with either forming or maintaining a governing coalition. The assumed culprit is the existence of too many parties in the coalition; however, evidence suggests that this instability is related to the degree of **polarization** between the parties in the system, or the amount of emotional or political distance between parties. It is argued that the more ideologically distant the parties are (referring to the distance between them on the political spectrum), or the greater the degree of antagonism and conflict between parties drawn together in a governing coalition (in other words, where there is **polarized pluralism**), the more likely political instability is to occur. Polarized systems are more likely to have extremist or antisystem parties in their midst. Conversely, in political systems where the "pulls" are toward a moderate center (in other words, where a centripetal tendency or **moderate pluralism** exists), multiparty systems are not associated with unstable government. In short, the greater the ideological distance between the parties involved in a governing coalition, the more likely we are to observe government instability.

The situation in France during its Fourth and Fifth Republics illustrates the effects of polarized and more moderate pluralism. Prior to 1958, the French party system consisted of multiple parties clustered around the extreme right and left, with a wide distance between these extremes, leaving a political vacuum at the more moderate center. The result was a debilitating tendency toward parliamentary and governmental instability and resulting governmental ineffectiveness. Since the beginning of the Fifth Republic in 1958, we observe a pattern of much more moderate pluralism and consequently a much more stable government structure. Today, France still has a multiparty system that continues to lack a truly moderate centrist party (or parties), although the number of politically significant parties has shrunk, so that we now observe two broad political blocs on the left and right. However, the ideological distance between the ends of the political spectrum has narrowed considerably, and the possibility of workable coalitions between parties of the left and right has risen. As a result, persistent government and parliamentary instability has not been a problem during the Fifth Republic. Instead, frequent transitions between right- and left-wing governments have proceeded easily, and coalitional arrangements have remained fairly secure.

France is not the only example of changes in degrees of partisan polarization. As social cleavages have declined in significance since the mid-1970s, we have observed in most industrialized countries a tendency for political parties to move toward the moderate political center because voters tend to look so much more like one another. As a result, we have also seen a general pattern of more stable party and political systems. Although increased government stability has some positive effects for policy making, this movement toward the center (or **depolarization**) can make it more difficult to identify significant policy differences between parties, so that at election time voters' partisan choices seem to be less about policy and more about perceptions of competence. This often complicates the policy-making process once parties come to office because they lack a clearly defined program and must quickly develop coherent policy proposals.

Voting Behavior

Voting is the most common form of political participation in industrialized countries. Citizens enter the voting booth with the expectation that their actions affect not only who governs but the policies that governments adopt. Voting citizens select candidates who have adopted certain policy positions that they will then try to enact in the legislature, thereby communicating their policy preferences. Thus some knowledge of why citizens decide to vote for a particular party or candidate is important for understanding the policy-making process.

In some industrialized countries, such as France and Italy, voters are given the opportunity to make policy choices directly through the use of a **referendum**—elections in which voters choose among specific policy options, typically involving a yes-no vote on one issue. For example, should we ratify the treaty establishing a constitution for Europe? Should we increase education spending? In some countries such elections are used fairly regularly; in others they are used only for decisions considered to be of such importance that the people should be involved directly. In policy-making terms, when referenda are used, they can have a direct and significant effect on the policy-making process.

Because the use of referenda is not widespread, typically we are less concerned with citizens' voting patterns in referenda and more with their behavior concerning the selection of elected representatives. As mentioned earlier, in industrialized countries electoral choice traditionally was most directly related to group membership and social cleavage patterns and not to specific policy positions. Through the late 1970s, an individual's association with a particular societal cleavage (for example, class, religion, or region) or his or her attachment to a particular ideology gave that individual a certain set of characteristics that clearly made him or her part of the natural constituency of one political party over another. Thus voters were seen as making voting choices based on partisan ties that almost exclusively reflected their class background, ethnic identification, religious affiliation, or a shared ideological perspective. For example, belonging to the British working class until very recently was directly related to voting for the Labour Party. Although we observe today some lessening of working-class support for Labour in Britain (for example, with the emergence of "working class Tories"—members of the working class who vote for the other major British party, the Conservatives or Tories), the Labour Party continues to receive the greatest proportion of the working-class vote. In this situation, we talk about a form of party loyalty that reflects an individual's social characteristics more than his or her assessment of parties' and candidates' policy positions.

In most industrialized countries, voting based primarily on social cleavages has yielded ground to more **issue voting**. Rather than voting for the same party at every election because of their strong sense of party identification, voters are increasingly likely to compare policies advocated by competing parties on issues that matter to them and to make their choice on the basis of which party's program seems to best suit their own interests and beliefs. This is a much more pragmatic style of voting than traditional partisan voting and can result in a great deal of **volatility** in election results—patterns of partisan support may shift dramatically from election to election as both the issues of the day and parties and the electorate's positions change. Increasingly volatile voting patterns across industrialized countries demonstrate voters' growing willingness to punish governments that fail to deliver, as well as more widespread feelings of disillusionment among electorates.

A consequence of this volatility has been a marked rise in support for marginal parties as support for mainstream parties declines. For example, in both France and Germany left-wing green parties have enjoyed greater success since the 1980s; the same is true for far-right extremist parties. In Italy, we observe increased support for regional leagues and movement away from mainstream traditional parties. Such movement has raised some concern that volatility will destabilize party systems in the long run. This possibility does exist when voters move to the margins; however, in systems where vote swapping is between mainstream parties, this prospect seems less likely. More worrying in the latter instance is increasing evidence that volatility is accompanied by decreasing electoral participation overall.

Elections in France since the 1980s clearly reveal such electoral volatility. Since 1978 French electoral majorities have moved back and forth from left to right in nearly every national election. Voting data indicate that parties' traditional bases of support have eroded. For example, Catholics who in the past were strong right-wing voters increasingly vote for parties of the left, and working-class voters have moved from the left wing to the right wing. Such results support the view that a substantial number of **swing voters** demonstrate no strong loyalty to any political party but rather cast their vote on the basis of considerations such as candidates' personalities, perceptions of their competence and leadership abilities, or more specific policy promises of one party or another. These patterns hold true in France and in other industrialized countries.

Economic conditions also appear to have a powerful effect on electoral choice. Where we observe what is known as **pocketbook voting**, election results reflect the state of the national economy and, at times, individual economic fortunes. If the economy is seen as reasonably strong, the incumbent party tends to do well with many voters—regardless of their traditional party ties or ideology. Many analysts argue that such voting patterns were observed in the United Kingdom in the 1980s and early 1990s, when voters who seemed otherwise dissatisfied with the ruling Conservative Party (because of their policy positions or their views of the party's leader) continued to vote for the party because of their belief that the Conservatives were responsible for improving economic conditions and that they were the party of economic competence. (This pattern applied to both Tory voters and traditional Labour voters who switched to the Conservatives in this period because of their belief in their own party's economic incompetence.) With the emergence of issue voting and pocketbook voting, predicting the vote is much less straightforward today than it was when being a member of the working class meant that you would almost invariably vote for a party of the left, irrespective of the issues or the economic climate of the day.

Political scientists describe this general pattern of weakening ties to existing political parties and shifting voting behavior as **dealignment**. This pattern emerged as old cleavage patterns in industrialized countries have become less significant, particularly as class lines blur and shift (especially as a result of the increasing size of the middle class in most of these countries). As a result, parties become less meaningful agents for channeling political conflict. In addition, the process of building effective electoral coalitions has become more challenging.

There is some speculation that these changes may be part of a trend toward eventual **realignment**, in which individuals form attachments to new political parties resting on new bases of social identification. This trend is suggested by the appearance of several new partisan movements in industrialized countries, such as green parties in Germany and France, that have sought to attract voters concerned about issues that tend to cut across class lines, such as environmental problems, human rights, regional nationalism, or xenophobia. Such a process of realignment is blocked in some countries by institutional barriers, namely, electoral laws that impede the success of smaller, emerging parties. The absence of a meaningful green party movement in the United Kingdom or the United States, for example, can be attributed at least in part to electoral laws that discourage small parties from running for office.

The extent to which such issue-based politics may be forming the basis for enduring, institutionalized partisan alignments remains unclear. These new movements may turn out to be the major parties of the future, or a more fluid and volatile pattern may be the continuing trend, as more stable bases of partisan identification continue to erode. Following on this, political leaders are faced with a more uncertain policy-making environment. In particular, in policy terms increased volatility and partisan dealignment make it more difficult for governments to engage in widespread reform, especially when reform involves actual costs to the citizens. For example, in France in the early 1990s, the right-wing government of Jacques Chirac and Alain Juppe attempted to reduce significantly levels of public spending by cutting public sector employment and reducing public sector benefits. These reforms were rejected by French citizens (as indicated by massive public demonstrations), and in subsequent parliamentary elections there was a clear swing away from a large right-wing majority to left-wing control. Needless to say, the new left-controlled government has been much more cautious in its approach to reform, presumably in recognition of the electoral risks associated with both large-scale change and the enactment of policies that reduce benefits for large numbers of French citizens—no matter how necessary the policies may be.

Changing patterns of voter choice affect the way parties develop their policy positions and have changed the very nature of parties themselves. As parties' traditional bases of support have eroded, they have struggled to redefine themselves. As part of this effort, parties seek to tailor their policy positions to capture as many votes as possible; this results in an overall moderation of parties in industrialized countries. Increasingly, we observe political parties trying to develop policies that will appeal to the widest range of voters (following what is known as the **median voter model**), regardless of whether those policy positions contradict the party's traditional perspective on the issue at hand. The result is a clear trend toward the aforementioned catch-all parties with elections becoming nothing more than contests for the median voter.

Electoral Systems

Electoral laws determine the manner in which the votes cast in an election are translated into seats in the legislature. The nature of a country's electoral system can have an important impact on election outcomes—the same percentage of votes can yield very different shares of seats in the legislature. Electoral laws are important for understanding the policy-making process because they affect not only the distribution of seats in the legislature and its subsequent operation but also citizens' access to politics and the nature of political party systems. For example, electoral laws influence whether smaller parties form in a political system, what sort of say they will have in the policy-making process, and whether such parties continue to exist at all. In most industrialized countries, two main types of laws are used to allocate legislature seats. Countries may adopt either **single-member district plurality** or **proportional representation** electoral systems, although some choose a combination of the two. Table 3-1 summarizes the electoral systems used in the six industrialized countries we examine in this book.

Single-member district plurality (SMDP) electoral systems (also known variously as plurality, winner-take-all, or first-past-the-post systems) divide a given country into a relatively large number of legislative districts and assign one seat in the legislature to each district. Once an election is held in a given district and the results are tallied, the candidate who receives the most votes (a **plurality**) is the elected representative from that district. A candidate may win a seat under such a system without capturing a majority of the votes cast (particularly when more than two candidates are running for a seat), and no seats are awarded to any other candidate receiving votes in that district. Some countries, such as France, require a candidate to win a majority of votes to be elected. This usually entails a second runoff election between a group of top vote-getters in the first round of balloting. This **ballotage system** variation of SMDP encourages the participation of smaller parties in the first round—when they are more likely to receive enough votes to make it to the second ballot—while ensuring that the eventual winner of the election enjoys strong support among the electorate. Of the six countries we examine, only the United States and the United Kingdom employ SMDP systems.

SMDP systems are often valued for the strong legislative majorities they produce, resulting in a politically stable legislature, and for the clear and direct ties they create between elected representatives and their constituents (because there is only one representative from a district, everyone living in that district knows who is representing him or her). These systems often are criticized, however, for favoring larger parties, particularly if support for smaller parties is not geographically concentrated in certain electoral districts, so that the smaller parties have some chance of achieving a plurality in at least a few districts. If a small party's support is spread across a country, the party is unlikely to win a plurality of the vote in a district. Because the prospects for such parties are so poor, support for small parties generally declines over time

Table 3-1 Electoral Systems in Six Industrialized Countries

Country	Type	Institution	System
France	Mixed	President	Two-ballot plurality
		National Assembly	Two-ballot SMDP (second ballot only if no absolute majority in first round)
Germany	Mixed	Bundestag	Half SMDP Half PR with party lists
Italy	PR	Chamber of Deputies	PR with party lists
		Senate	PR with party lists
Japan	Mixed	House of Representatives	300 seats SMDP 180 seats PR with party lists
		House of Councillors	146 multiseat constituencies 96 PR with party lists
United Kingdom	SMDP	House of Commons	Plurality of popular vote
United States	SMDP	President	Plurality of popular vote Electoral College majority
		House of Representatives	Plurality of popular vote
		Senate	Plurality of popular vote

SMDP = single-member district plurality; PR = proportional representation.

or never emerges in countries using SMDP systems. Two-party systems are more likely to evolve and endure under SMDP systems, and those parties are more likely to be moderate in the interest of attracting the widest possible range of voters. As a result, it is often argued that SMDP systems sacrifice the wider representation of political interests (by creating two-party systems) for the sake of greater political stability (resulting from single-party control of the legislature rather than coalition governments), which in turn produces greater policy coherency and follow-through but may exclude important interests from having a say in the policy-making process.

Proportional representation (PR) electoral systems involve a smaller number of large electoral districts, with multiple seats in the legislature allocated to each district. Instead of voting for individual candidates at election time, voters under PR systems usually cast one vote for a single party or choose several candidates from a party list. When the votes are tallied after an election, the seats available in the district are allocated roughly according to the proportion of the vote that the party's slate received. For example, if ten seats are available in a district and party A received 40 percent of the vote, and parties B, C, and D received 20 percent each, then party A would win four seats in the legislature and parties B, C, and D would win two seats each. This is in contrast to a SMDP system in which only party A would win the only available seat. The precise formula used to translate the vote into seats varies from country to country. Strict proportionality often is qualified somewhat in PR systems through the introduction of a threshold of votes: a minimum percentage of the votes cast nationally (usually between 4 and 9 percent) that a party must receive to win any legislative seats. This threshold is intended to consolidate the representation of parties in the legislature by reducing the participation of electorally smaller parties, thereby increasing the likelihood of government stability.

This emphasis on proportionality in PR systems results in their being rated as more equitable and representative than SMDP systems. Box 3-2 illustrates how the SMDP system compares to the PR system. Because PR systems increase the electoral chances of smaller parties, countries that adopt these laws tend to have multiparty systems with both small and large parties and a wider array of ideological positions represented in the legislature—thus the belief that they are more representative and fair. Rather than excluding smaller interests from political institutions, PR systems are designed to ensure their inclusion. For example, under a PR system, sixteen different parties took seats in Italy's Chamber of Deputies after the 1992 national elections (over fifty parties sought office). In 1994 a nationwide referendum resulted in the adoption a mixed electoral system, based primarily on SMDP principles, with the intention of reducing the significance of smaller parties and encouraging the formation of two party blocs (although loopholes in the new system meant that the absolute number of parties operating in Italy remained large, as did the number of parties gaining representation in the parliament). The system was reformed again in 2005, when the ruling party adopted a complicated and unusual version of a PR system that involved a system of thresholds designed to encourage party coalitions. Reflecting the highly proportional emphasis of the newer system, following the 2006 election no fewer than 36 parties were seated in the parliament.

Critics often argue that PR systems produce a weaker linkage between representatives and their districts because citizens are less clear about who is really charged with representing them. Further, although they expand inclusiveness, PR systems also increase the likelihood of multiparty coalition governments by making it more difficult for a single party to achieve majority control of the legislature. In addition, depending on the degree to which a country's population is divided and prone to conflict, and the extent to which the electoral system has allowed the representation of more radical and extreme groups, a pattern of parliamentary instability can emerge. This consideration is important for the policy-making process because stable government means more straightforward and effective policy making. If a coalition has numerous, hostile parties, it is often impossible for that coalition to work together cooperatively and govern effectively. Italy again serves as the best example of such a pattern—here multiparty governing coalitions have been the norm because of proportional representation. These coalitions often were formed by parties that had little in common and were unable to form effective working groups. This resulted in fifty-five different governments from 1946 to 1997 (each averaging less than one year in office)—more than in any other industrialized

Box 3-2 **The Effects of Electoral System Choice**

2005 General Election Results in the United Kingdom

	Voter Support (percentage)	Seats in House of Commons	
		Percentage	*Number*
Labour	35.2%	54.6%	355
Conservative	32.3	30.7	198
Liberal Democrat	22.1	9.6	62
Other	10.4	4.8	31

The results of the 2005 British general election illustrate the effects of a single-member district plurality (SMDP) electoral system on the distribution of the seats in a legislature. The Labour Party commands an overwhelming majority of seats in the House of Commons, despite having received less than a majority of the votes cast (only 35.2 percent). The Liberal Democratic Party, which garnered 22 percent of the vote, received only 62 seats in the House, which is less than 10 percent of Parliament. As these results demonstrate, the SMDP system overrepresents the strength of the larger parties and underrepresents the smaller ones—in so doing, the distribution of seats in Parliament becomes a distortion of the electorate's political preferences.

2005 General Election Results in the Federal Republic of Germany

	Voter Support (percentage)	Seats in Bundestag	
		Percentage	*Number*
CDU/CSU[a]	35.2%	36.8%	226
Social Democrat	34.2	36.2	222
Free Democrat	9.8	9.9	61
Left Party	8.7	8.8	54
Alliance 90/Greens	8.1	8.3	51

[a]CDU/CSU = Christian Democratic Union/Christian Social Union.

In the German system, where a variant of a proportional representation electoral system is used, the relationship between the votes cast in the election and the actual distribution of seats in the legislature is much less distorted. In comparison to the British system, German electoral laws deliver a far more equitable distribution of legislative power among political parties. The use of a form of proportional representation after the 2005 general election resulted in a far closer alignment between partisan strength in the legislature and the distribution of votes in the election, thereby creating a far more accurate expression of the public's preferences. The only parties who fail to gain representation are those who do not reach a 5 percent threshold, which ultimately creates a more stable pattern of governance because fringe parties do not gain representation.

democracy. Some of this instability was clearly related to the presence of too many parties in the parliament, although this was not necessarily the sole cause; parties in Italy also lack internal cohesion, have ideological differences, and have leaders who are prone to personality-based conflicts with one another. Taken together, these factors account for the observed patterns of Italian governmental instability. The results of this instability for policy making were important: citizens lost confidence in the political process, and policy making was defined by the lack of a consistent vision or coherence.

Executive-Legislative Relations

Industrialized countries have two general models of executive institutions: presidential and parliamentary governments. Despite the heightened awareness of the presidential model in the United States, the presidency is clearly in the minority as a framework for executive-legislative relations. The vast majority of the world's enduring democracies have parliamentary arrangements. Of the six countries we examine in this book, only the United States has a presidential system of government; France has a mix of presidential and parliamentary institutions; and Italy, Japan, Germany, and the United Kingdom operate under parliamentary arrangements (Table 3-2).

Presidential democracies have one chief political executive—the president—who is directly elected for a fixed term of office. Perhaps the most distinctive feature of presidential democracies is their formal **separation of powers** between the executive and legislative branches of government. In presidential systems, central-level policy-making authority is constitutionally divided among the executive, legislative, and judicial branches of government. This formal separation of powers involves a system of checks and balances in which each branch is given certain constitutionally defined mechanisms through which it controls the actions of the other branches (through the use of vetoes, overrides, filibusters, and the like). This division of authority was intended primarily to prevent the abuse of power by any one government branch. In practice, it has three direct effects on the policy-making process: (1) it decentralizes power, (2) it requires negotiation and compromise among government branches, and (3) it creates inefficiency in the decision-making process.

In addition to recognizing the importance of a separation of powers, we must also consider the effects of a **separation of mandate** on presidential systems. The chief executive derives his or her strength from the fact that the president is elected independently from the legislature and therefore has a personal mandate to govern. At the same time, the legislature has its own independent electoral mandate. A president's personal mandate means that, in theory, he or she should be able to take charge of the policy-making process and provide clear policy leadership. In reality, however, the legislature often goes against a president's wishes, claiming that it is rightfully pursuing its own electoral mandate.

The emphasis of presidential systems on the structural independence of the government branches is argued to have several negative consequences for

Table 3-2 Governmental Forms in Six Industrialized Countries

Country	State Form	Government Form	Executive		Bicameral Legislature	
			Symbolic	*Political*	*Upper*	*Lower*
France	Republic	Presidential and Parliamentary	None	President Prime minister	Senate	National Assembly
Germany	Federal	Parliamentary republic	President	Chancellor	Bundesrat	Bundestag
Italy	Republic	Parliamentary	President	Prime minister	Senate	Chamber of Deputies
Japan	Constitutional monarchy	Parliamentary	Emperor	Prime minister	House of Councillors	House of Representatives
United Kingdom	Constitutional monarchy	Parliamentary	Monarch	Prime minister	House of Lords	House of Commons
United States	Republic	Presidential	None	President	Senate	House of Representatives

policy making. Because the legislature is independent of the president, it is not bound by law or tradition to support the president's policies. One of the central premises of the system, then, is the legislature's freedom to deny the president's wishes. In other words, its members must be convinced to offer their support. As such, presidents cannot ensure that they will be able to fulfill their campaign promises unless they secure the legislature's support. In the United States, the president cannot even introduce legislation independently to Congress; he or she needs the support of a legislative sponsor who will introduce the bill. To receive such sponsorship, the president usually compromises over policy content or offers the sponsor incentives. Reflecting this relationship, the legislative agenda and calendar are not under the president's control but are set by the legislative leadership. Given these dynamics, most adopted policies reflect a series of compromises between the legislature and the executive branch rather than the clear intentions of the executive branch alone. The policy-making division of labor in presidential systems usually is described as one in which the legislature is responsible for decision making, and the executive branch is responsible for policy implementation, that is, making sure that policies are carried out.

In presidential systems, the smooth flow of the policy-making process may be interrupted by a clear tendency toward government immobilization. This often occurs in times of **divided government**, when the legislature and the president are from different parties, as was the case in the United States in the late 1990s. In such a situation, the president often finds it difficult to achieve much of anything. Instead, we often observe a process in which the executive branch and the legislature set out to frustrate each other rather than cooperate, mostly for political and electoral gain. This condition is often described as **gridlock**—when political, ideological, or other differences between the executive branch and the legislature make it more difficult for the government to develop policies to address important problems. Even when gridlock does not occur, the weak position of the president relative to the legislature also may reflect a tendency of presidential systems toward weak party discipline. Parties tend to be less disciplined because of the separation of mandate; legislators do not directly owe their election success to the president and vice versa. Often, a lack of party discipline in the legislature makes it difficult for presidents to secure support for their policies, even if their party controls a legislative majority.

Such obstacles make comprehensive policy making, in particular, large-scale reform, difficult to pursue in presidential systems. Instead, policies require extensive bargaining and negotiation and usually represent a compromise between the two branches. Voters find it difficult to assign responsibility for policies—because it is not immediately apparent which branch or institution created a particular policy (despite a clear focus on the president for policy leadership). As a result, voting in elections is not typically seen as an opportunity to pass judgment on a party's or an individual's ability to fulfill policy promises.

A presidential system does have some positive policy-making features. Because presidents serve a fixed term of office and are not subject to immediate removal by the legislature if their opinion poll ratings drop precipitously once a policy is implemented, they are freer to make politically less popular policy choices (particularly when they have the support of the legislature). Further, policy making in presidential systems tends to be a slow, deliberative legislative process in which many actors have the opportunity to weigh in on the decision—thus increasing the possibility for citizen participation and input and avoiding the problem of snap decision making by politicians for immediate political gain. Finally, separation of powers results in a fragmented decision-making process (which may reduce efficiency), but citizens have many more opportunities to influence the policy-making process.

Parliamentary systems usually have a dual executive that consists of a ceremonial head of state and a chief political executive known most often as the prime minister. Citizens vote for parties, not individual candidates, and members of the parliament are selected from the winning parties. The majority party in the parliament (or a coalition of parties that forms a majority of the legislature) then selects a prime minister. Typically this individual serves as the leader of the majority (or largest) party in the parliament and continues to act in this capacity while serving as prime minister. Thus the prime minister is not directly elected, and we observe a **fusion of powers**—meaning the executive derives from and is responsible to the legislature.

The prime minister and the cabinet (collectively known as the government) play both a policy-making and a policy implementation role in parliamentary systems. They control the overall process by formulating policies, overseeing their passage in the legislature, and controlling implementation. Whereas in presidential systems, chief executives must find sympathetic members of the legislature to sponsor their bills, in parliamentary systems the government introduces its legislation directly and independently into the parliament. (Few individual members' bills are introduced, and even fewer are passed.) The government controls the legislative calendar and agenda as well. Generally speaking, parliaments play a secondary role in the policy-making process in these systems—their role is essentially advisory, particularly when one party controls a strong majority.

In parliamentary systems the executive's policies are almost guaranteed to be adopted and implemented, provided that party discipline is intact. When the governing party (or coalition) controls a strong and disciplined majority in the parliament, the executive is virtually assured of obtaining its policy wish list. Only a small percentage of bills introduced by the government will not be successful (unless party discipline has broken down, in which case the government will resign or be removed by the legislature). Under these conditions, legislative policy making tends to proceed quickly because there are no meaningful barriers to policy adoption in the legislature—an opposition party or parties will be present and participate in debate in the parliamentary chamber, but they typically will not be able to influence the policy-making process. Further, and unlike presidential systems, the lines of policy responsibility are clear in parliamentary systems—the electorate expects the government to fulfill its campaign promises, and at election time voters know who to blame or reward for policy decisions: the party or parties in power.

Several characteristics of parliamentary systems can have a negative effect on the policy-making process. First, prime ministers do not enjoy the same job security that presidents have: they may be removed from office at any time by a legislative majority. If the executive loses the support of the parliamentary majority, the prime minister will typically be forced to leave office. This may be accomplished by way of pressure to resign, a negative vote on a major piece of legislation, or a vote of no confidence. As a result, parliamentary executives are not likely to adopt policy positions that the legislature clearly does not support, for fear of being removed from office (although prime ministers are not typically so out of step with their parliaments that this occurs frequently). Second, prime ministers and their cabinets have the ability to dissolve the legislature at any time and call for new elections, or to call for a vote of confidence to confirm the executive's power. Thus the legislature is also unlikely to ignore consistently the executive's preferences, because if legislative-executive interactions become too contentious, the legislature will be dissolved, risking the careers of its members. Third, although parliamentary systems are able to deliver policies quickly, some danger is associated with the pace of this policy-making process. More specifically, there is a risk of adopting inappropriate or poorly designed policies in the absence of a more deliberative process. Further, the faster pace at which policies are introduced, debated, and passed in parliamentary systems also decreases the opportunities for citizen input into the policy-making process.

Intergovernmental Relations

Any discussion of the policy-making process in industrialized countries must consider the degree to which a country's governmental authority is centralized. Where are government policy decisions made? At the central level, or by lower levels of government? Such discussions about the distribution of political authority usually focus on a single constitutional feature: does a country have a unitary or federal political system? Among the six countries we examine in this book, only the United States and Germany have federal political systems (Table 3-3).

A **unitary political system** has only one meaningful level of government above the local level. In such systems, only the central government has constitutionally derived policy-making authority (for all stages of the policy-making process). For the most part, local governments in unitary systems are charged with simply administering decisions made at the central level. Under most unitary arrangements, central governments assign some decision-making authority in a few specific policy areas to local level governments as they see fit, with local governments having only limited independent policy-making discretion. In the United Kingdom, for example, acts of Parliament make local governments responsible for delivering many important government services (such as primary schooling, refuse collection, and policing); however, the central government strictly controls the ability of local authorities to raise revenue to pay for these services. In unitary systems, government finances often are controlled by the center, thus limiting the scope of local efforts. Reflecting this distribution of authority, political power is centralized.

Unitary political arrangements are often praised for their simplicity, uniformity, and clear lines of accountability. Power is exercised at the central level, and the electorate will hold this level of government responsible for public policies. Policy implementation in most unitary systems is expected to be more uniform within the country because of the limited discretion given to local governments in administering policies. As such, we expect to observe a more equal pattern of government service delivery within a unitary system—that is, living in one locality or another should not affect substantially the type, quality, or quantity of service citizens receive, particularly because local governments operate with similar financial resources. A noted disadvantage of unitary arrangements, however, is their tendency to reduce citizen involvement in policy making because of the remote nature of the policy process. Policies are made in some distant, impersonal central government structure, rather than in citizens' own backyard by individuals with whom they have a more personal connection.

A **federal political system** involves one or two meaningful levels of government above the local level, and each level has its own institutionally defined policy-making responsibilities. Usually, lower government levels (including state, regional, or local governments) are assigned powers in specific policy

Table 3-3 State Structures in Six Industrialized Countries

Country	Structure	Composition
France	Unitary	22 administrative regions with 96 metropolitan departments
Germany	Federal	16 *Länder* (states)
Italy	Unitary	20 regions and 94 provinces (several regions have some autonomy)
Japan	Unitary	47 prefectures
United Kingdom	Unitary	Municipalities and counties
United States	Federal	50 states

areas (for example, education, policing, or transport), and these powers go beyond administration. Constitutionally, lower levels of government are given the power to determine policy in these areas at their own discretion. Typically they have their own revenue-raising capacity, thereby ensuring that their independent policy jurisdictions translate into a meaningful role in a country's policy-making process. Reflecting such distributions of authority, political power is fragmented.

Federal systems are most often adopted by larger countries (especially in terms of population size) because they provide for more flexibility in addressing the demands of their typically more diverse populations. This flexibility is viewed as federalism's strength: it enables governments to develop policies that are more responsive to the needs of smaller groups or more particularized interests. For example, in the United States a federal system of government is argued to make it easier to hold together such a large and culturally diverse political entity. The needs of different groups can be met at the state and local levels—wherever their populations may be more concentrated. For example, policies may be required in California to address the needs of migrant farm workers from Latin America, whereas such policies have no widespread application in Minnesota, where such farm workers are not a significant presence. Federal political arrangements allow California to develop such policies, while Minnesota is free to address other concerns. If these problems could be solved only by a national government at the center, the likelihood of their being addressed would be far smaller. In this way, federalism is argued to make the political system more responsive to the needs of a diverse population. Federalism also encourages policy experimentation and innovation (whereby new solutions are tested at lower levels of government before being introduced nationwide). Because there are multiple points of policy decision making in federal systems, they also provide greater opportunities for citizen involvement.

Some disadvantages are associated with federal systems, however. Because significant variation exists in the type, quality, or quantity of government services delivered across a federal system, citizens may receive different treatment depending on where they live. This occurs for several reasons: differences in resources across levels of government (since lower levels of government typically have their own revenue-raising powers), with some localities or states more affluent than others; the effects of alternative policy choices across and within levels of government; and, more generally, variations in government performance. Difficulties can also arise owing to a lack of control by the central level over the pace and effectiveness of central-level policy implementation by lower levels of government. In addition, some duplication of government services is common in federal systems, when the central and the lower levels of government enact policies in similar policy areas. Such duplication often results in unnecessary government spending or government programs that pursue conflicting goals.

The Bureaucracy

Public bureaucracies play a powerful role in policy making in all industrialized countries. As the size of the welfare state and the role of government more generally (especially its economic activities) have expanded over the past several decades, public bureaucracies have increased in size as agents for both the formulation and the implementation of government programs. Even as governments seek to reduce their size, bureaucracies continue to flourish and to occupy a powerful role in the policy-making process.

Industrialized countries have well-established bureaucratic traditions. At one time, public bureaucracies were based on the distribution of the political spoils: people were appointed to the bureaucracy for their political loyalty and were expected to demonstrate this loyalty in their work. In European bureaucracies, these so-called spoils systems often involved wealthy citizens buying positions in the bureaucracy for their children. Such bureaucratic systems often were inefficient and of poor quality because of this lack of control over hiring—appointees were often unqualified and lacked any specific policy expertise. In addition, these systems generally lacked mechanisms for control over performance; employees would perform to get their jobs and then fail to perform once the position was secured, with no effective provisions for compelling them to do their jobs (their removal was unlikely given that they were protected by powerful political leaders). Today, however, industrialized countries pride themselves on having bureaucracies characterized by a modern civil service. By this we mean that bureaucratic institutions have become increasingly professionalized. They are viewed as impartial, permanent, and meritocratic; and bureaucrats are highly valued in the policy-making process for their knowledge, skills, and experience.

The question of political control of the bureaucracy, that is, the ability of the central government to control bureaucratic behavior and influence, has been raised now that the modern civil service has become the norm in industrialized countries. When bureaucracies consisted primarily of political appointees, political leaders exercised a significant amount of control over their actions. Leaders could simply remove the bureaucrats from office if they went against the leaders' wishes or political preferences. As a result, political appointees were not likely to contradict or challenge these leaders. Today, with professionalized and expert bureaucracies, there is some concern about bureaucracies' seeming immunity to the influence or control of politicians. Often this concern is expressed as a worry about a so-called democratic deficit, reflecting the fact that bureaucrats are not elected officials. When bureaucrats are seen as exercising too much influence on the policy-making process, citizens may question whether policy decision making is truly democratic.

Beyond the common denominator of a modern civil service, we observe a considerable degree of variation from country to country in the policy-making functions of bureaucracies. This variation reflects organizational factors, cultural traditions, and norms as well as the structure of party systems. Civil servants influence public policy in all political systems in some fashion, but the degree and manner of this influence vary. In particular, bureaucrats' ability to pursue and realize their own policy preferences, especially in the face of opposition from elected officials or the public, varies significantly both from country to country and across policy areas within countries. In some situations, the bureaucracy is seen as dominating the policy-making process, often going so far as to render parliaments and elected officials almost irrelevant. In other cases, the bureaucracy is seen as playing only a limited role beyond the implementation of policies made elsewhere. Bureaucratic policy making has traditionally been an important feature of the Japanese political system. In Japan, the majority of bills passed in the parliament are drafted by the bureaucracy. During the period of Liberal Democratic Party dominance in Japan (until 1993), bureaucrats worked closely with party politicians and representatives of special interests (especially big business) to develop and implement policies in what were known as iron triangles. Even after 1993, such patterns of policy making persisted. The bureaucracy's policy-making role was further enhanced in Japan because most adopted legislation is broad and vague, and the bureaucracy uses its power to draft rules and regulations to further control the nature of public policy.

The Judiciary

Industrialized countries also vary in the degree to which they have allowed judicial institutions to play a role in the policy-making process. In most of these countries, the judiciary traditionally was considered a branch of government that had no role to play in lawmaking. This area was seen instead as the exclusive domain of the elected representatives of the people in the legislature and the executive. Despite this tradition, we now find constitutional courts in some industrialized countries, such as Germany, that have the power of **legislative judicial review**, meaning that they have the power to declare legislation unconstitutional and thereby nullify laws. From country to country, we observe significant differences in these courts with respect to their constitutionally derived powers, their interpretation of these powers, the kinds of decisions they make, and their levels of judicial activism (Table 3-4).

Table 3-4 Constitutional Courts in Six Industrialized Countries

Country	Court
France	Constitutional Council
Germany	Federal Constitutional Court
Italy	Constitutional Court
Japan	Supreme Court
United Kingdom	No court with powers of judicial review
United States	Supreme Court

Generally speaking, constitutional courts do not seek out cases independently but instead consider issues that others (for example, a parliamentary party or the central government) send them. Because the policy-making process is not subject to the courts' independent influence or control, we do not consider the judiciary to play a consistent role in this process; however, they do have an important role to play. The courts' decisions cannot be overturned by any other institution; thus their ability to modify or nullify laws represents an important power in the policy-making process. In all countries we observe an increased willingness on the part of constitutional courts to engage in judicial interpretation and to make decisions about the substance of laws when cases are referred to them. A second and perhaps more apparent influence is that the courts' rulings set a standard or precedent by which future policies will be measured, not only by the courts but also by the legislatures and executives. Future policies must comply with the guidelines established by earlier court rulings; thus the courts become a participant in the policy-making process, albeit indirectly. Third, policy making begins to reflect some effort on the part of the legislature to anticipate the reaction of the court in developing policies—in this sense the legislature is not necessarily reacting to precedents but is attempting to avoid making policy decisions that might trigger the process of judicial review. Although the judiciary may not actively initiate policy-making activities, the fact that it may be asked to act, in conjunction with knowledge about how it acted in the past, can significantly influence policy decisions.

Economic Dynamics

Many of the policy decisions we examine later in this book undoubtedly affect countries' economies. At the same time, economic conditions and institutions clearly influence policymakers' decisions. An understanding of politics and policy making today requires some consideration of the role of economic factors in these processes for two reasons. First, many of the problems facing countries today are a byproduct of the economic choices they have made—for example, the commitment to the welfare state or a social market economy today presents real policy problems for many industrialized countries' governments as they are faced with skyrocketing costs and falling revenues. Second, a country's economic system often determines the manner in which the government responds to certain problems on its policy agendas. For example, an economic choice for trade liberalization may result in a loss of price protections for farmers, thus creating new policy demands in the agricultural sector.

Industrialized countries have in common one key characteristic: they are all capitalist **market economies**. They all adhere, with varying degrees of commitment, to certain core economic principles, although their economies do not all operate in the same fashion. Industrialized countries are considered to be capitalist because business remains predominantly in the hands of the private sector. In addition, the central coordinating mechanism for economic activities in these countries is the market, not the state. In a market economy, producers and consumers are key actors who enter the marketplace as individuals and behave in a rational manner. Their preferences and behaviors, through competition in the marketplace, set prices, control supply, and allocate resources, with producers responding to consumers' demands because of the profit motive. In this way the balancing effects of supply and demand are expected to provide maximum societal wealth and efficiency at minimum cost. A pure free-market economic system demands no strong role for government in the marketplace; the market is intended to regulate itself and requires minimal government interference. As such, market economies should be based on private sector rather than government decision making. In a pure market economy, therefore, the government's role is limited to maintaining order at home, enforcing laws to allow the market to function properly, and protecting the country from external threats.

Today, however, no industrialized country has reduced government to such an exclusively external role. Instead, the governments of industrialized countries play, to varying degrees, important economic roles—and these roles have expanded since the end of World War II. For example, all governments in industrialized countries provide for **public goods**—those services generally deemed necessary for a basic quality of life but that are unlikely to be provided by the marketplace because it is not in any individual's self-interest to produce them. Public goods include roads, schools, a clean environment, mass transportation, and public parks.

The governments of industrialized countries also determine to some extent how their economies operate overall: they regulate markets and industries to varying degrees, control inflation, oversee money supplies, and more generally enact policies designed to control or promote economic growth. In Japan, for example, where we clearly observe a capitalist market economy, government in the postwar era has played a major role in shaping the economy, especially through planning and assistance to specific industries. In some countries, the increase in the government's role since the end of World War II has been dramatic. This is particularly true in countries with **mixed economies**, such as France, Germany, Italy, and the United Kingdom. Mixed economies combine capitalist free-market principles, including private ownership, with some level of state ownership (usually of key industries and utilities), some central economic planning, and a higher level of regulation. As such, they mix public ownership with private control. Countries with mixed economies vary in the degree to which the state intervenes in the marketplace. In the United Kingdom, for example, the government does not engage in economic planning, it intervenes in the marketplace less directly, and it tends to regulate economic activities to a lesser degree than is observed in France or Germany. By the 1980s, some of these countries, especially the United Kingdom and France, began to reduce the economic role played by their governments in order to pursue policies of privatization, deregulation, and liberalization. These efforts were aimed at decreasing public spending and increasing government revenues (especially by selling off government assets). Despite these efforts, the economies of many industrialized countries are still characterized by a rather high level of government economic intervention.

In all of these mixed economic systems, **social insurance programs** provide for health care, old age and unemployment benefits, and the like and typically cover individuals from cradle to grave. Countries that provide such benefits are often referred to as **welfare states**. These programs generally involve a high level of public expenditure and high taxation rates, which, taken together, create some of the most vexing political policy issues faced by leaders in industrialized countries. Although the six countries we examine in this book provide some level of social welfare benefits to their populations (and all increased their levels of expenditure on these benefits after World War II), the French, German, and Italian governments do so far more comprehensively than do the governments of Japan, the United Kingdom, or the United States.

In Germany, we find a more specific type of mixed economy: the **social market economy**. Here the government combines support for the private sector and the free market (with nearly all enterprises under private control), with a high level of government intervention designed to create a framework for economic growth. The German government's economic activities are intended to achieve a clearly defined and widely accepted social goal—the well-being of all German citizens. Government thus is charged with providing a more extensive and generous array of social welfare benefits to its citizens than is found in most other industrialized countries. These generous social programs are viewed as essential to the workings of the marketplace. These economic arrangements are often described as "capitalism with a human face." The market is free and private, but government remains vigilant to ensure that citizens are protected from economic insecurity or other wants. Although public ownership is not an important dimension of the social market economy, close cooperation between public and private sector institutions is central to the development and implementation of economic policies. Both sectors work together in a consensual environment to create policies designed to provide maximum social gain.

Economic life in industrialized countries today also clearly reflects the effects of **globalization**. This term has many meanings but may be captured by the idea that national economic, social, and political life, in both industrialized and late-industrializing economies, is increasingly affected by what occurs beyond a country's borders. Those who consider the effects of globalization believe that the world has become more and more one market for goods and capital through technological innovations and improved global communications. As a result, policy agendas and policy making in industrialized countries increasingly are influenced by events and conditions outside their territorial borders. Thus economic policies that once could be decided on in isolation are more subject to international constraints. Global financial and currency markets, multinational corporations, and the European Union are external forces that bring their influence to bear on national economic life in all industrialized countries, and their effects continue to grow. Further, events in the global environment, such as increasing industrial capacity in Southeast Asia, increases in interest rates in the United States, and increasing civil war in Africa, may create policy problems for countries to address in an ever-more globalized context.

Economic systems in industrialized countries today are often referred to as **postindustrial**. If we look at where jobs are concentrated in most industrialized countries, we find that more people work in service industries (such as insurance, banking, and computing) than in manufacturing industries or agriculture. This represents a change in employment structures that began in the early 1980s and accelerated throughout the 1990s. This move to postindustrial status is argued to have several political implications. First, changing employment patterns can be associated with changes in the class structure of industrialized countries: the growing middle class discussed earlier is at least in part the result of the growing service sector and a higher standard of living associated with higher-paying jobs. Second, and following on the first implication, the relative decline in manufacturing jobs has produced a decrease in union membership that has reduced the political influence of these organizations in most countries. Today only public sector unions have seen their membership numbers increase. Third, the shift in employment away from traditional manufacturing occupations, which were often low-skill jobs, to high-skill service sector jobs has left many citizens in industrialized countries in a state of long-term unemployment, which has translated into higher levels of dissatisfaction with the performance of democratic institutions and political leaders in these countries and has created new political pressures and policy demands. It is often argued that this postindustrial development, when combined with rapid, unprecedented economic growth since World War II that vastly improved standards of living, also has produced attitudinal change in industrialized countries. Some political scientists believe that the new economic structure of these societies has produced long-term value change known as **postmaterialism**. This term was introduced by the political scientist Ronald Inglehart, who argued that by the early 1980s citizens in industrialized countries, who were increasingly members of the middle class, were less concerned about physical and economic security, or material well-being, than they were about less tangible concerns such as freedom of expression, quality of life, greater political participation, the environment, or gender and sexual equality. Inglehart claimed that because these new values were the result of generational, not short-term, changes, they would be of continuing political relevance.

The emergence of green parties in several industrialized countries, especially in Germany, as well as the strength of various new social movements, such as the women's and disarmament movements, support such arguments. Such groups often have a significant effect on public policies, even in countries where they do not have a share of governing power. Often they have been able to force the major parties in a country to adopt positions that reflect postmaterial concerns (as the parties attempt to reduce the effects of these movements on their own electoral support), and some of the partisan dealignment we discussed earlier is a result of the activities of new parties that espouse these postmaterial values. Supporters of the idea of postmaterial value change in industrialized countries argue that its effects on public policy are likely to increase in the future as greater proportions of their populations consist of people born in the postindustrial era.

SUGGESTED READINGS

Aberbach, Joel, Robert Putnam, and Bert Rockman. 1981. *Bureaucrats and Politicians in Western Democracies.* Cambridge: Harvard University Press.

Bartolini, Stefano, Richard Gunther, Juan J. Linz, and J. R. Montero, eds. 2003. *Political Parties: Old Concepts and New Challenges.* Oxford: Oxford University Press.

Baumgartner, Frank, and Beth Leech. 2001. *Basic Interests: The Importance of Groups in Politics and Political Science.* Princeton: Princeton University Press.

Benoit, Kenneth and Michael Laver. 2007. *Party Policy in Modern Democracies.* New York: Routledge.

Berry, Jeffrey M., and Clyde Wilcox. 2009. *The Interest Group Society,* 5th ed. New York: Pearson/Longman.

Beyers, Jan, Rainer Eising, and William A. Maloney, eds. 2008. *Interest Group Politics in Europe.* London: Routledge.

Bond, Jon, and Richard Fleisher. 1990. *The President in the Legislative Arena.* Chicago: University of Chicago Press.

Dalton, Russell, et al., eds. 1985. *Electoral Change in Advanced Industrial Democracies: Realignment or Dealignment?* Princeton: Princeton University Press.

Dalton, Russell, and Martin Wattenberg, eds. 2002. *Parties Without Partisans: Political Change in Advanced Industrial Democracies.* Oxford: Oxford University Press.

David, Rene, and John Brierly. 2000. *Major Legal Systems in the World Today,* 3rd ed. Delran, N.J.: Legal Classics Library.

Diamond, Larry, and Richard Gunther, eds. 2001. *Political Parties and Democracy.* Baltimore: Johns Hopkins University Press.

Diamond, Larry, and Marc F. Plattner. 2006. *Electoral Systems and Democracy.* Baltimore: Johns Hopkins University Press.

Farrell, David. 2001. *Electoral Systems: A Comparative Introduction.* Basingstoke, United Kingdom: Palgrave.

Harrop, Martin, ed. 1994. *Power and Policy in Liberal Democracies.* Cambridge: Cambridge University Press.

Hayward, Jack, and Edward Page. 1995. *Governing the New Europe.* Durham: Duke University Press.

Hershey, Marjorie Randon, and Paul Allen Beck. 2003. *Party Politics in America,* 10th ed. New York: Longman.

Hix, Simon. 2005. *The Political System of the European Union.* New York: Palgrave Macmillan.

Inglehart, Ronald, and Christian Welzer. 2005. *Modernization, Cultural Change and Democracy: The Human Development Sequence.* Cambridge: Cambridge University Press.

Jackson, Donald, and C. Neal Tate. 1992. *Comparative Judicial Review and Public Policy.* Westport, Conn.: Greenwood Press.

Jacob, Herbert, et al., eds. 1996. *Courts, Law and Politics in Comparative Perspective.* London: M. E. Sharpe.

Laver, Michael, and Norman Schofield. 2001. *Multiparty Government: The Politics of Coalition in Europe.* Ann Arbor: University of Michigan Press.

Leduc, Lawrence, Richard Niemi, and Pippa Norris, eds. 2002. *Comparing Democracies 2: New Challenges in the Study of Elections and Voting.* Thousand Oaks: Sage Publications.

Lehmbruch, Gerhard, and Philippe Schmitter, eds. 1982. *Patterns of Corporatist Policy-making.* Beverly Hills, Calif.: Sage Publications.

Luther, Kurt, and Ferdinand Muller-Rommel. 2005. *Political Parties in the New Europe: Political and Analytical Challenges.* New York: Oxford University Press.

Moe, Terry. 1980. *The Organization of Interests.* Chicago: University of Chicago Press.

Müller, Wolfgang, and Kaare Strøm, eds. 1999. *Policy, Office or Votes? How Political Parties in Western Europe Make Hard Decisions.* Cambridge: Cambridge University Press.

Müller, Wolfgang, and Kaare Strøm, eds. 2000. *Coalition Governments in Western Europe.* Oxford: Oxford University Press.

Poguntke, Thomas, and Paul Webb, eds. 2007. *The Presidentialization of Politics: A Comparative Study of Modern Democracies.* Oxford: Oxford University Press.

Rose, Richard. 1974. *The Problem of Party Government.* New York: Free Press.

Rose, Richard, and Ezra Suleiman, eds. 1980. *Presidents and Prime Ministers.* Washington, D.C.: American Enterprise Institute.

Sartori, Giovanni. 1976. *Parties and Party Systems.* Cambridge: Cambridge University Press.

Strom, Kaare. 2008. *Minority Government and Majority Rule.* New York: Cambridge University Press.

Ware, Alan. 1999. *Political Parties and Party Systems.* Oxford: Oxford University Press.

Webb, Paul, et al., eds. 2002. *Political Parties in Advanced Industrial Societies.* Oxford: Oxford University Press.

Chapter 4 The Policy-making Context

The policy-making process in industrialized countries is often more dissimilar from country to country than we might expect in a set of countries that appear to have a great deal in common as democracies and comparatively wealthy societies. As we touched on in Chapter 3, much of this variation is related to institutional arrangements that allocate power and resources in distinctly different patterns in each country. The choice, for example, between presidential and parliamentary systems of executive-legislative relations, or between federal and unitary patterns of organization, has a definite impact on the style and often the effectiveness of government policy making. In light of these and other important differences, we offer here a capsule discussion of the formal and informal political institutions in the United States, Japan, Germany, France, the United Kingdom, Italy, and the European Union (EU). Basic knowledge of these political systems provides useful background for the case studies offered in Chapters 5–11.

The United States

The United States has a presidential, federal system of government. This system is based on a separation of powers among the executive, legislative, and judicial branches of government, accompanied by a system of checks and balances that prevents each branch from overstepping its constitutional authority. The policy process in the United States is often viewed as being less orderly and efficient than in parliamentary systems. In particular, the executive does not have the ability to control the legislative agenda in the United States. Instead, each house of Congress controls its own agenda, and the president has a more limited capacity to generate legislative cooperation or compliance with the government's policy proposals or objectives.

The president may not introduce legislation directly to the legislature but must work with members of Congress to persuade them to adopt and propose the government's policy program. Presidential success in this regard usually depends on the pattern of party support in the legislature, the president's bargaining skills, and the state of public opinion. Thus policies are generally made by assembling issue-specific coalitions through a process of bargaining and deal making, typically involving all sorts of public officials, from bureaucrats to cabinet members to members of Congress, as well as interest group representatives. This approach results in less clear lines of policy accountability than are found in parliamentary systems. Unlike many of their prime ministerial counterparts, presidents must also constantly

Box 4-1 **United States at a Glance**

Political System
Federal republic
Presidential democracy

Administrative Structure: Federal state with fifty states and one district

Executive:

- Head of state and head of government: President
  Directly elected, four-year term
  Barack H. Obama, Democratic Party (since January 2009)
  Presidential election results (2008): Barack H. Obama, 52.4 percent; John McCain, 46.3 percent; other, 1.3 percent

Legislature: Bicameral congress

- Lower house: House of Representatives (directly elected, two-year term), 435 seats
  Majority party: Democratic Party, 257 seats (since January 2009)
  Other parties: Republican Party, 178 seats
- Upper house: Senate (directly elected, six-year term), 100 seats
  Majority party: Democratic Party, 58 seats
  Other parties: Republican Party, 40 seats; Independent Democrat, 1 seat; Independent, 1 seat

Party System: Two party

- Principal parties: Republican Party, Democratic Party
- Other parties: Democratic Socialists of America, Green Parties of North America, Libertarian Party

Judiciary: Supreme Court with powers of legislative review

Economic Indicators
Gross domestic product (GDP), purchasing power parity, 2007: $13,811.2 billion
GDP per capita, purchasing power parity, 2007: $45,790
Exports as a percentage of GDP, 2007: 11.7 percent
Economic growth, 2007: 2.0 percent
Average economic growth, 1997–2006: 3.10 percent
Unemployment, 2007: 4.6 percent
Average unemployment, 1997–2006: 4.94 percent
Inflation rate, 2007: 2.9 percent
Average inflation rate, 1997–2006: 2.54 percent
Budget deficit as a percentage of GDP, 2007: 2.9 percent
Average budget deficit as a percentage of GDP, 1997–2006: –1.68 percent

maneuver to avoid deadlock with the legislature, especially when Congress is controlled by a party different from their own. This situation makes it especially difficult for the president to realize any broad policy goals.

The U.S. legislature exercises far more control over policy making than is the case in other industrialized (and in particular parliamentary) countries. This is partly a reflection of a strong congressional committee system that involves a large number of specialized, permanently staffed, and powerful committees. U.S. committees are independent and activist, and most of their decisions are supported by their relevant legislative branches.

The federal structure in the United States grants considerable powers of self-government to individual states. In addition, state and local governments in the United States have more independent sources of revenue than is the case in most industrialized countries. This structure has restricted the U.S. government's policy reach far more than is found in industrialized countries with unitary structures. In many policy areas, however, the division of policy making and administrative responsibilities between federal and state levels creates implementation and coordination difficulties.

Interest groups in the United States play a larger role in the policy process than in most other industrialized countries. This is partly a reflection of a much weaker party system. Parties in the United States generally lack the discipline, programs, and organization that characterize many European party systems. Party leaders in the United States do not have as much disciplinary authority as they do in other countries; as a result, party members often demonstrate low levels of party loyalty, especially when voting in Congress. Although party membership can be an important predictor of how members of Congress will vote, it is by no means the sole or even primary influence on their voting decisions. Hence, political parties in the United States are viewed widely as ineffective agents of interest articulation and aggregation—these functions are performed instead by interest groups.

With multiple points of access to the policy-making process in the United States, interest group activity is substantial and influential. Interest groups lobby bureaucrats and politicians at all levels of government—federal, state, and local. The large number and important role of congressional committees, when combined with weak party discipline, encourage widespread interest group activity because of the strong possibility of influencing legislators' decisions. These interest groups usually fall into one of two categories: political action committees that attempt to influence campaigns and elections at all levels of government, and groups that focus on lobbying members of Congress. Interest groups often make specific proposals for legislation to the bureaucracy and the legislature, and then work with executive and legislative officials in developing, enacting, and implementing policies.

Judicial review is an important aspect of the policy-making process in the United States. The U.S. Supreme Court is a very activist institution, compared with the constitutional courts found in other industrialized countries. This is true not only with respect to its position as the final arbiter of policies but also because of its tendency to initiate policy through its decisions. The Supreme Court is more powerful than the other constitutional courts because of its role as the highest court in the land for all matters—civil, criminal, and constitutional. This role gives the Court more opportunities to make policy indirectly and also more status when it exercises the explicit power of judicial review.

The U.S. government has allowed the economy to operate according to the dictates of the market. Although there is government regulation of the marketplace in the United States, this takes place to a lesser degree than is observed in other industrialized countries. The U.S. economy is not based on a tradition of public ownership, and the public sector overall is smaller than in other countries. In general, the government does not engage in either long- or short-term economic planning nor does it coordinate economic policy. The government also does not provide guidance to various sectors of the economy (with the exception of agriculture and some defense-related industries). The United States is not a social welfare state, although the government maintains a variety of social insurance programs. The scale of this coverage is more limited than in most other industrialized countries.

Japan

The Japanese government is organized along parliamentary and unitary lines. Policy making in Japan is highly centralized, although it does not follow the traditional parliamentary policy-making pattern. Most notably, the Japanese prime minister does not have absolute control over the policy process, although the prime minister is still considered to be the country's most important policymaker. In contrast to the British or German executive, the Japanese prime minister lacks a disciplined majority party in the legislature and as such cannot enact major policy initiatives as easily. From 1945 to 1993 the majority party in Japan, the Liberal Democratic Party (LDP), was composed of a number of competing factions that resisted strong discipline. LDP members of the House of Representatives (the lower and more powerful branch of the Japanese Diet, or parliament), senior civil servants, and interest group leaders worked together in small groups referred to as subgovernments. These powerful groups exercised a large degree of influence over policy making in their areas of expertise, making it difficult for the prime minister and cabinet to intervene effectively in the policy-making process.

A related effect of this pattern of influence was the marked absence of comprehensive national policies. The strong influence of particularized interests allowed prime ministers to manage the policy process but made it difficult for them to control the policy agenda or institute overarching policy reform. Since 1993 and the end of continuous LDP control, the policy position of the executive has not changed dramatically in Japan. The first non-LDP prime ministers after 1993 were hampered by unstable multiparty coalitions.

Box 4-2 **Japan at a Glance**

Political System
Constitutional monarchy
Parliamentary democracy

Administrative Structure: Unitary state with forty-seven prefectures

Executive: Dual executive
- Head of state: Emperor
  Ceremonial, hereditary
  Akihito (since January 1989)
- Head of government: Prime minister
  Elected by National Assembly, leader of largest parliamentary party
  Yukio Hatoyama, Democratic Party of Japan (since August 2009)

Legislature: Bicameral parliament (Diet or Kokkai)
- Lower house: House of Representatives (directly elected, four-year term), 480 seats
  Coalition government, since August 2009: Democratic Party of Japan, Social Democratic Party, People's New Party
  Largest party: Democratic Party of Japan, 308 seats
  Other parties: Liberal Democratic Party, 119 seats; New Komeito, 21 seats; Japan Communist Party, 9 seats; Your Party, 5 seats; Social Democratic Party, 7 seats; People's New Party, 34 seats; New Party Nippon, 1 seat; New Party Daichi, l seat; others, 68 seats
- Upper house: House of Councillors (directly elected, six-year term), 242 seats

Party System: Multiparty
- Principal parties: Liberal Democratic Party, New Komeito, Democratic Party of Japan, Japan Communist Party, Social Democratic Party

Judiciary: Supreme Court with powers of legislative review

Economic Indicators
Gross domestic product (GDP), purchasing power parity, 2007: $4,283.5 billion
GDP per capita, purchasing power parity, 2007: $33,525
Exports as a percentage of GDP, 2007: 19.2 percent
Economic growth, 2007: 2.1 percent
Average economic growth, 1997–2006: 1.12 percent
Unemployment, 2007: 3.9 percent
Average unemployment, 1997–2006: 4.58 percent
Inflation rate, 2007: –0.1 percent
Average inflation rate, 1997–2006: –0.08 percent
Budget deficit as a percentage of GDP, 2007: 2.4 percent
Average budget deficit as a percentage of GDP, 1997–2006: –6.67 percent

The majority of bills proposed to the legislature by the Japanese prime minister and cabinet are formulated by Japan's powerful, highly professionalized bureaucracy after consultation with relevant interest groups (especially business interests) and advisory councils (*shingikai*) comprised of experts in a given policy area. The bureaucracy's recommendations then go to parliamentary committees. The Japanese parliament has little influence over policy content but can be somewhat effective in blocking the passage of bills through the use of established parliamentary procedures. Because of bargaining between LDP factions, however, the Japanese parliament tends to play more of a policy-making role than other parliaments—although party discipline remains an important operating principle.

Through the national bureaucracy, the Japanese government also retains control over policy implementation. Laws passed in the Japanese parliament tend to be loose framework policies that leave ample room for interpretation at the implementation stage. Although local governments follow the lead of the national government under a system known as administrative guidance (reinforced by the local governments' high degree of dependence on the national government for funding), local adaptation of centrally defined policies is still possible. A notable feature of Japan's policy implementation process is the relative absence of policy coordination across bureaucratic jurisdictions. This lack of coordination can result in conflict, policy overlap, and inefficiency.

Japanese political parties as organizations play an insignificant role in the policy process. Unlike their counterparts in the European parliamentary democracies, Japanese political parties are elitist, with limited membership and weakly structured organizations. These parties do not seek to serve as agents of interest aggregation by representing local and grassroots-level interests, and they do not concern themselves with developing policy proposals to reflect those interests. Instead, these parties (particularly the LDP) have close ties to interest groups and bureaucratic leaders who are concerned primarily with representing elite interests.

Japan's wide range of interest groups fall into two categories: those that are clients of government agencies and ministries, and those that are not. Groups in the first category have a close relationship with bureaucratic and relevant party officials and have a great deal of influence on public policy making through these personal contacts, and through their role on advisory councils and their influence on bureaucrats at the policy implementation stage. In this sense the Japanese interest group system is corporatist. Interest groups that participate in the system in a pluralist manner (that is, those in the other category) are not officially shut out of the policy-making process, but they do not have the privileged access that groups tied to the LDP traditionally have enjoyed. As a result, they have far less influence on policy making.

Japan has an elected Supreme Court that has powers of judicial review. Unlike most of its counterparts in industrialized democracies, the Japanese court has not been activist. Reflecting a belief in parliamentary supremacy, the court has only rarely nullified parliamentary laws and does not appear likely to do so in the future.

The Japanese government plays a key role in the country's economy, while operating a free-market capitalist system. The government's immediate postwar industrial policies were central to Japan's rapid and remarkable economic growth. These policies provided financial assistance, tax breaks, foreign exchange, and imported technologies to targeted industries that were integral to economic development. The government intervenes in the market to guide investment decisions, and restrictive trade policies are implemented to protect key or developing industries. Most of the country's important domestic industries operate under the guidance and protection of bureaucratic agencies, especially the small but powerful Ministry of International Trade and Industry—this ministry and other economic ministries have a strong role in economic decision making. In the early postwar years these bureaucratic agencies, through administrative guidance, encouraged business mergers and cartelization to prevent counterproductive domestic competition. The government thus played a key role in directing the country's economic recovery through close collaboration with industry. Despite this strong guiding role for the government, the Japanese economy is not based on public ownership (the public sector is small relative to other industrialized countries). Free enterprise is the rule, although the government does not leave the market completely free to its own devices. The Japanese government continues to intervene in the market and restrict trade to protect its own industries and as such continues to play a major role in economic decisions.

Germany

The German government is a parliamentary system organized on a federal basis. Most legislation arrives in the German parliament through the executive—the chancellor's office is constitutionally responsible for setting the policy agenda, formulating policy, and overseeing policy implementation. As is typical of parliamentary systems, the legislature plays a more limited role in the policy process in Germany. Because policy initiation takes place at the executive level, the legislature is left with the task of evaluating and amending policies but only in a reactive manner. The German parliament typically plays a larger role in revising legislation than other parliamentary legislatures, through the efforts of both its committees and its legislative party groups. German parliamentary committees tend to be stronger than most of their counterparts, because they are more specialized, active, and powerful (although not to the degree observed in the United States). Nonetheless, the principle of party discipline reduces the likelihood of these committees making major changes to proposed legislation without government approval.

Box 4-3 **Germany at a Glance**

Political System
Federal republic
Parliamentary democracy

Administrative Structure: Federal with sixteen states (*Länder*)

Executive: Dual executive
- Head of state: President
  Ceremonial, five-year term
  Elected by an electoral college consisting of federal and state parliament members
  Horst Koehler, Christian Democratic Union (since July 2004)
- Head of government: Chancellor
  Elected by Bundestag, leader of largest party in the Bundestag
  Angela Merkel, Christian Democratic Union (since November 2005)

Legislature: Bicameral parliament
- Lower house: Bundestag (directly elected, four-year term), 622 seats
  Coalition government (since September 2009), Christian Democratic Union/Christian Social Union and Free Democratic Party
  Largest party: Christian Democratic Union/Christian Social Union, 239 seats
  Other parties: Social Democratic Party, 146 seats; Free Democratic Party, 93 seats; Left Party, 76 seats; Alliance 90/Greens, 68 seats
- Upper house: Bundesrat (elected and appointed from sixteen states, four-year term), 69 seats

Party System: Multiparty
- Principal parties: Social Democratic Party, Christian Democratic Union, Christian Social Union
- Other parties: Alliance 90/Greens, Free Democratic Party, Left Party

Judiciary: Constitutional court with powers of legislative review

Economic Indicators
Gross domestic product (GDP), purchasing power parity, 2007: $2,727.5 billion
GDP per capita, purchasing power parity, 2007: $33,154
Exports as a percentage of GDP, 2007: 46.5 percent
Economic growth, 2007: 2.6 percent
Average economic growth, 1997–2006: 1.50 percent
Unemployment, 2007: 8.4 percent
Average unemployment, 1997–2006: 8.97 percent
Inflation rate, 2007: 2.3 percent
Average inflation rate, 1997–2006: 1.40 percent
Budget deficit as a percentage of GDP, 2007: 0.0 percent
Average budget deficit as a percentage of GDP, 1997–2006: –2.41 percent

In most policy areas, responsibility for policy formulation is found at the federal level of government. The sixteen German states (*Länder*) are directly responsible for educational, cultural, policing, and regional planning policies. Jurisdiction over some policy areas is shared between the federal and state levels (federal policy takes precedence over state policy in the event of conflicts). The states influence federal policy making and administration through the Bundesrat (the upper house of the German parliament), which is designed to represent state interests. A number of informal channels are used for policy consultation and coordination between the federal and state governments.

German states are integral to federal policy implementation. The states have primary responsibility for policy implementation and administration. In contrast to the situation in most other industrialized countries, German federal legislation and regulations tend to be very detailed to ensure that the government's objectives are met at the policy implementation stage. Because of wide-ranging responsibilities, state bureaucracies are larger than federal and local administrative agencies, and few federal ministries have sufficient resources to implement federal policies. The federal bureaucracy has the right to oversee state bureaucracies, but the German states typically have a good deal of autonomy and exercise some discretion in applying federal law. States typically are allowed to alter laws to fit local needs and circumstances when necessary, although this power is exercised within limits. In particular, states have limited policy latitude because their finances are centrally controlled—they have no independent revenue-raising powers. These characteristics of the federal-state relationship in Germany have created an environment conducive to effective policy implementation.

Germany has a competitive multiparty system, and parties play an important role in the policy process. German political parties are highly disciplined and have considerable influence on the government's policy agenda. In particular, parliamentary party groups in the Bundestag (the lower house) play an important policy-making role. They meet frequently to debate policy issues and are often successful in persuading the government to change the content of legislation, either before it is proposed or while the parliament is considering it.

The German interest group structure is considered to be corporatist because a clear pattern of cooperation exists between the government and interest groups—interest groups are systematically involved in making and implementing public policy. German law requires that the relevant interest groups be contacted when new policies are being formulated to ensure that the government benefits from the expertise of the groups and that the groups agree with and will cooperate with the new policies. The relationship between German administrative agencies and interest groups is strong. The leaders of major German interest groups are important actors in the policy process, and interest groups are seen as performing an important and necessary role at all stages of the policy-making process. A good deal of interest group lobbying occurs in the German legislature, particularly at the committee level, because German committees have some influence over the content of parliamentary legislation. Although this influence is not as extensive as is observed in the United States, it exceeds the legislative roles of interest groups in many other industrialized countries.

The principle of judicial review is an important aspect of the German policy-making process. The German constitutional court has independent powers that enable it to nullify any law on constitutional grounds. The court hears appeals from private citizens; through referrals from lower courts; at the request of federal, state, or local governments; or in response to members of the parliament. In recent years this court has played an increasingly activist role in the policy-making process, especially in the areas of human rights and federal-state relations.

Germany, like Japan, also experienced a remarkable postwar economic recovery, though in response to a different model of government intervention. In Germany, the government plays a leading but not directing economic role. The German economy is based on a social market model that emphasizes private ownership (although a small state sector exists), accompanied by an active role for the government in guiding the economy. In practice, the German government uses regulations to establish a broad framework for economic activity and within this framework encourages business organizations to coordinate their activities to achieve the government's objectives. The German government does not play a directing role like the Japanese government does; rather, it allows market forces to operate within a framework of government supervision. The German economic system places a strong emphasis on social responsibility, and the government provides a generous social insurance system.

France

The French political system is commonly described as a hybrid because it mixes elements of presidential and parliamentary systems. The existence of both a directly elected president and a prime minister who represents the dominant party (or coalition) in the parliament creates a distinctive semi-presidential policy process. With the exception of periods of so-called cohabitation, when the president and prime minister represent different parties (as is the case as of this writing), nearly all government policy making since 1958 has been the responsibility of the French president and a small circle of advisers. The president, with bureaucratic assistance, dominates the policy process through the development of detailed legislative proposals and through control over policy implementation. During periods of cohabitation, control of domestic policy tends to move to the prime minister and the cabinet, whereas foreign policy remains in the president's domain. The few policies formulated by the prime minister and the cabinet outside periods of cohabitation generally require presidential approval.

Box 4-4 **France at a Glance**

Political System
Republic
Semi-presidential democracy

Administrative Structure: Unitary state with twenty-two administrative regions containing ninety-six departments

Executive: Dual executive

- Chief of state: President
  - Directly elected, five-year term
  - Nicolas Sarkozy, Union for a Popular Movement (since May 2007)
  - Presidential election results (2007, second round): Nicolas Sarkozy, 53.1 percent; Segolene Royal, 46.9 percent
- Head of government: Prime minister
  - Appointed by president, leader of largest parliamentary party
  - François Fillon, Union for a Popular Movement (since May 2007)

Legislature: Bicameral parliament

- Lower house: National Assembly (directly elected, five-year term), 577 seats
  - Majority government since May 2007, Union for a Popular Movement control
  - Largest party: Union for a Popular Movement, 313 seats
  - Miscellaneous right-wing parties, 9 seats
  - New Center Party, 22 seats
  - Left parties: Socialist Party, 186 seats; French Communist Party, 15 seats; Left Radical Party, 7 seats; Greens, 4 seats; miscellaneous left-wing parties, 15 seats
- Upper house: Senate (indirectly elected, six-year term), 321 seats

Party System: Multiparty

- Principal parties: Union for a Popular Movement, Democratic Movement, Socialist Party, French Communist Party
- Other parties: National Front, New Center, Left Radical Party, Rally for France, Greens, multiple smaller parties on right and left

Judiciary: Constitutional Council with powers of administrative review

Economic Indicators

Gross domestic product (GDP), purchasing power parity, 2007: $2,061.9 billion

GDP per capita, purchasing power parity, 2007: $33,014

Exports as a percentage of GDP, 2007: 26.9 percent

Economic growth, 2007: 2.1 percent

Average economic growth, 1997–2006: 2.34 percent

Unemployment, 2007: 8.3 percent

Average unemployment, 1997–2006: 9.55 percent

Inflation rate, 2007: 1.6 percent

Average inflation rate, 1997–2006: 1.64 percent

Budget deficit as a percentage of GDP, 2007: –2.7 percent

Average budget deficit as a percentage of GDP, 1997–2006: –2.70 percent

The French parliament during the Fifth Republic has played a minor role in policy making, especially on important issues. This situation reflects in part an explicit constitutional decision to limit the parliament's policy-making role, especially its lawmaking powers. Nearly all legislation considered by the parliament is proposed by the executive, which has a wide range of specific powers to encourage (or even coerce) the parliament to adopt its policies. As tends to be the norm in parliamentary systems, the French legislature for the most part reviews and approves legislation formulated elsewhere. The parliament has begun to play a somewhat larger policy-making role in recent years as its committees have increased their influence (through their powers of amendment), but overall the policy-making activities of this institution remain limited.

France is a unitary state and has been one of the most centralized of the industrialized countries. The country is divided into 96 departments under the administrative control of a prefect. In addition, there are 22 French regions (consisting of the 96 departments and 36,551 communes or local governments). Each lower level of government is controlled by an elected body of some sort. Since the 1980s some movement has been made toward decentralizing policy responsibilities and power to these lower levels of government. However, compared to most countries, the French government remains highly centralized, with the bulk of policy development and implementation occurring at the central government level. The policy implementation process in France has been among the most effective of the industrialized countries because of strong linkages between the executive and the bureaucracy and the general public's tendency to support a strong government apparatus.

France has a weak multiparty system troubled by fragmentation and polarization. This, in combination with the strong role assumed by the executive, means that political parties do not have as much influence on agenda setting and policy formulation as is observed in parliamentary systems that have stronger partisan organizations. To some degree, parties exert greater influence on policy making in periods of cohabitation, especially when a partisan majority has strong control in the parliament.

The interest group system in France is generally considered to be pluralist, with multiple groups and actors vying for influence over policy making. French interest groups tend to be smaller, less organized, and less cohesive than are those found in other countries. In particular, ideological divisions, both between and within groups (especially labor unions), have led to a marked pattern of interest group fragmentation that reduces their effectiveness. French interest groups generally do not have privileged access to policymakers. The possible exceptions to this pattern are agricultural and big business groups, which have some stronger connections to the government. Interest groups have a limited role in bureaucratic advisory committees in France, although not to the degree observed in some other industrialized countries. Further, because of a generally strong pattern of party discipline in the French parliament and its committees, members of the parliament are not important channels of influence for lobbyists.

The French system does not subscribe fully to the principle of judicial review. Laws passed by the parliament are not subject to further scrutiny by a constitutional court; however, the Constitutional Council has the power to assess the constitutionality of a bill before it is adopted by the parliament. This council does not hear appeals from individual citizens but will examine legislation at the request of the president, the presiding officers of the parliament, or through a joint appeal from members of the parliament. Increasingly it has been used by opposition party members seeking to block a law's adoption. Since the 1980s the council has been very partisan and controversial as it has increased both its scope and its willingness to reject bills.

The government plays an important role in directing and managing the French economy. Since the 1960s France has had one of the world's strongest economies, based on a high level of public ownership, regulated market competition, and government economic planning. This strong government role typically was advocated by both conservative and leftist governments in France, reflecting the country's strong statist tradition. Government economic intervention and state ownership increased markedly in the early years of Socialist rule in the 1980s but were then reduced because this approach was viewed as economically counterproductive. Despite recent widespread privatization and an emphasis on market forces, France still has a relatively high level of public ownership and a higher level of economic intervention than is found in the United Kingdom or the United States. Thus the general economic context is one of a free-market economy, with the government playing an important guiding role. France has a well-developed social welfare system that provides the most extensive cradle-to-grave coverage among the six countries examined in this book.

The United Kingdom

The United Kingdom is a parliamentary democracy organized around a unitary structure. Although parliamentary sovereignty is an important foundational principle for the United Kingdom, policy making is in reality the responsibility of the prime minister and the cabinet. Policy formulation takes place within both the cabinet and the bureaucracy: the cabinet is solely responsible for determining the parliamentary agenda, and civil servants play an important role in drafting the legislation sent to Parliament.

As noted in Chapter 2, the United Kingdom's Westminster model of party government combines parliamentary democracy with a plurality electoral system. This model is characterized by an executive that, as a rule, is highly successful in seeing its policy agenda adopted in its entirety. The plurality electoral system in the United Kingdom produces a two-party system that

Box 4-5 **United Kingdom at a Glance**

Political System
Constitutional monarchy
Parliamentary democracy

Administrative Structure: Unitary state with forty-seven counties and seven metropolitan counties

Executive: Dual executive

- Head of state: Monarch
  - Ceremonial, hereditary
  - Queen Elizabeth II (since 1952)
- Head of government: Prime minister
  - Elected by House of Commons, leader of largest parliamentary party
  - Gordon Brown, Labour Party (since June 2007)

Legislature: Bicameral parliament

- Lower house: House of Commons (directly elected, five-year term), 646 seats
  - Majority party government since May 1997, Labour Party control
  - Majority party: Labour Party, 355 seats (since May 2005)
  - Other parties: Conservative Party, 198 seats; Liberal Democratic Party, 62 seats; others, 30 seats
- Upper house: House of Lords, 739 (as of July 2009)
  - 621 life peers (title ceases upon death)
  - 92 elected hereditary peers (replaced through indirect election upon their death)
  - 26 clergy (will not be replaced upon their death)
- Other legislative bodies: Scottish Parliament (since July 1999), Welsh Assembly (since May 1999), Northern Ireland Assembly (established 1998, currently suspended)

Party System: Two party

- Principal parties: Labour Party, Conservative Party
- Other parties: Liberal Democratic Party, Democratic Unionist Party, Scottish Nationalist Party, Sinn Fein, Plaid Cymru, Social Democratic and Labour Party, Ulster Unionist Party, Respect Party

Judiciary: No constitutional court with powers of legislative review

Economic Indicators

Gross domestic product (GDP), purchasing power parity, 2007: $2,046.8 billion
GDP per capita, purchasing power parity, 2007: $33,535
Exports as a percentage of GDP, 2007: 26.1 percent
Economic growth, 2007: 3.0 percent
Average economic growth, 1997–2006: 2.93 percent
Unemployment, 2007: 5.3 percent
Average unemployment, 1997–2006: 5.42 percent
Inflation rate, 2007: 2.3 percent
Average inflation rate, 1997–2006: 1.51 percent
Budget deficit as a percentage of GDP, 2007: 2.8 percent
Average budget deficit as a percentage of GDP, 1997–2006: –1.25 percent

grants significant power to a prime minister who controls a strong majority in the House of Commons—and majority control by a single disciplined party is the norm. Parliament and its individual members play only a small role in the policy-making process. Opposition party members have no real ability to influence policy making, and even the ability of majority party members to amend the government's policies is highly restricted. It is often argued that this pattern produces clearer lines of policy accountability between government and citizens than is the case in most other industrialized countries.

The unitary structure of the United Kingdom means that policy implementation is largely the responsibility of central government ministries. Adopted policies tend to be broad, with the bureaucracy left to work out the details. The British civil service has a strong reputation for efficient, professional, and effective policy implementation and administration. Policies that are made at the central government level are legally binding on local governments. Local government institutions serve as the mechanism for the delivery of services, but they exercise little discretion in the policy implementation process, largely because funding is controlled at the center.

The British interest group structure can best be described as pluralist, with many kinds of active interest groups attempting to influence politicians and bureaucrats. The bureaucracy maintains an important consultative relationship with interest groups, particularly in the development of administrative regulations included within the broad framework of parliamentary acts. Bureaucrats regularly submit draft regulations to interest groups for comment, in an effort to draw on the groups' expertise and improve the chances of successful policy implementation.

In recent years, interest group lobbying of both the government and members of Parliament (particularly the latter) has increased, reflecting in part the growth in the size and powers of parliamentary select committees. Generally speaking, however, parliamentary lobbying has not significantly reduced the importance of party discipline in predicting the vote in the House of Commons. Nonetheless, lobbying is argued to have made Parliament a more informed and critical participant in the policy-making process, as well as having given interest groups at least some voice in parliamentary debates. A notable feature of the interest group system in the United Kingdom has been the formal organizational linkage between labor unions and the Labour Party, which traditionally gave unions tremendous influence over Labour policies. Under the leadership of Prime Minister Tony Blair, the Labour Party endeavored to restructure and reduce this pattern of influence, with the result being that labor unions play a less significant, although still influential, role in defining Labour Party policy than was the case in the past.

Courts do not have a policy-making role in the United Kingdom. The founding principle of parliamentary sovereignty denies the possibility of judicial review—only Parliament can overturn an act of Parliament. British courts may question the application of laws and the authority of government's actions, but their impact is on policy administration, not formulation.

The British government's economic approach traditionally involved a more limited role for the state than is found in France, Germany, or Japan, in that there has been no role for industrial guidance or economic planning. However, the British government in the postwar period played an active role in governing the economy through state ownership of key industries, the provision of a wide range of economic management policies, and the maintenance of a generous social welfare system. By the early 1980s, however, the country's economic decline persuaded the government to reduce its strong economic presence through privatization, deregulation, the downsizing of public sector employment, and reduction of social welfare benefits. The government's current approach to the economy does not involve any overall planning or guidance but attempts to support market mechanisms and advocates pro-business and growth policies. The British government continues to support a wide array of social insurance programs, though not to the extent found in France and Germany.

Italy

Italy has a parliamentary, unitary system of government. The country has a strong tradition of parliamentary predominance. In comparison to other European parliaments, the Italian legislature is far more responsible for policy formulation and adoption, with party leaders developing and controlling the legislative agenda. Although most policy development takes place within government ministries, political parties and interest groups are also influential. Legislation is introduced by party leaders into parliamentary committees, and the president of each committee has a high degree of influence over the country's policy agenda. Unlike most other parliamentary committees, Italian committees are capable of completely rewriting legislative proposals. These standing committees have the right to pass bills on behalf of the Chamber of Deputies without sending them to the chamber for consideration. About three-fourths of Italy's bills are passed in this manner.

The cabinet and prime minister have relatively limited control over the content of Italy's public policies. This unusual pattern is not only a reflection of a tradition of parliamentary dominance but also the result of a marked tendency toward cabinet instability that has resulted in a weak executive and the empowerment of the legislature and the political parties. Because of the multiparty nature of Italian cabinets, the cabinet and prime minister as a group are too weak to address divisive issues. They also have difficulty defining a clear government agenda and perspective—resulting in governmental immobility—a consistent characteristic of Italian government.

Although the Italian parliament plays a dominant role in policy making, much of its legislation takes the form of loose framework policies that are vaguely designed and difficult to implement effectively. The quality of these policies is yet another reflection of recurring and fragile multiparty coalition governments. It is also a reflection of the nature of Italy's political parties

Box 4-6 **Italy at a Glance**

Political System
Republic
Parliamentary democracy

Administrative Structure: Unitary state with ninety-four provinces, twenty regions

Executive: Dual executive
- Head of state: President
  - Ceremonial, seven-year term
  - Elected by parliament and regional delegates
  - Giorgio Napolitano (since May 2006)
- Head of government: Prime minister
  - Appointed by president, confirmed by parliament
  - Silvio Berlusconi, People of Freedom Party (since May 2008)

Legislature: Bicameral parliament
- Lower house: Chamber of Deputies (directly elected, five-year term), 630 seats
  - Silvio Berlusconi coalition government, since May 2006, 344 seats
    - Largest party in coalition: People of Freedom Party, 276 seats
    - Other coalition parties: Lega Nord, 60 seats; Movement for Autonomy, 8 seats
  - Walter Veltroni coalition, 246 seats
    - Largest party in Veltroni coalition: Democratic Party, 217 seats
    - Other coalition parties: Italy of Values, 29 seats
  - Other parties: 40 seats
- Upper house: Senate (directly elected, five-year term), 315 seats

Party System: Multiparty
- Principal parties: People of Freedom, Lega Nord, Movement for Autonomy, Democratic Party, Italy of Values
- Other parties: Union of the Centre, numerous other small parties on right and left

Judiciary: Constitutional court with powers of legislative review

Economic Indicators
Gross domestic product (GDP), purchasing power parity, 2007: $1,777.4 billion
GDP per capita, purchasing power parity, 2007: $29,934
Exports as a percentage of GDP, 2007: 28.6 percent
Economic growth, 2007: 1.4 percent
Average economic growth, 1997–2006: 1.47 percent
Unemployment, 2007: 6.2 percent
Average unemployment, 1997–2006: 9.25 percent
Inflation rate, 2007: 2.0 percent
Average inflation rate, 1997–2006: 2.25 percent
Budget deficit as a percentage of GDP, 2007: –1.5 percent
Average budget deficit as a percentage of GDP, 1997–2006: –2.94 percent

themselves. These parties lack clear and coherent policy visions and historically have been fragmented and polarized. The major political reforms of the early 1990s (including the adoption of a hybrid single-member district plurality/proportional representation electoral system) did not reduce markedly the fragmentation of the political party system. Although members of the Italian parliament vote along party lines, their leaders find it difficult to adopt focused policy instruments. Most major policies tend to represent the least common denominator position on which the representatives of the many parties forming a majority coalition can agree.

Policy implementation is the responsibility of the Italian bureaucracy. Compared to most of its European counterparts, Italy lacks a strong bureaucratic tradition and its administrators have low status and command little respect. Overall, Italian citizens view the bureaucracy as corrupt, inefficient, and overly centralized—an institution renowned for its red tape. Such perceptions create significant problems for the implementation stage of the policy-making process.

Theoretically the Italian government has engaged in a process of decentralization. The country is divided into twenty regions whose powers have increased since the 1970s—today more than 30 percent of the national budget is formally under regional control. Even so, key policy areas, such as education, policing, and taxation, remain in the central government's hands, and financial control also remains at the center. Many policies that require regional implementation are ineffective, as a result of both poor policy design and a lack of sufficient central coordination or oversight of the implementation process.

Italian interest groups traditionally reflected divisions within the party system because they were linked directly to the political parties (in groups known as *parentela*, which resemble party factions, especially within the parliament). Today Italian interest groups increasingly act autonomously in both the parliament (especially in its committees) and the bureaucracy. Most bureaucratic agencies and departments have established sets of client groups (*clientela*) with which they regularly work to develop and implement policies. In this role, interest groups are an important source of political support for government agencies, and these agencies work to accommodate the demands of these groups.

Italy has a constitutional court that has powers of judicial review. The court may overturn any national law and has played a significant policy-making role, particularly with respect to civil liberties. It is far more activist than other such courts in industrialized countries. The court hears cases in response to appeals from private citizens, groups, or regional governments.

The Italian government has played a major economic role in the postwar period. In the early 1990s Italy had one of the largest state-owned sectors among the industrialized countries. The vast array of publicly owned enterprises in the country were controlled by public sector holding companies (such as the Institute for Industrial Reconstruction) that dominated all economic decisions and created close ties between government and industry. A large economic bureaucracy resulted that was prone to inefficiency and corruption. This close and corrupt relationship led to the scandals of the early 1990s that ultimately resulted in the collapse of the government system. The economy has traditionally been heavily regulated. Following the government crisis, a process of privatization and deregulation began, although the government still plays a significant role in economic decision making. The Italian government continues to provide a wide array of social benefits to its citizens, although these benefits are not as generous as those afforded to citizens in the other European countries examined in this book.

European Union

The EU traces its roots to the European Economic Community that was created by the Treaty of Rome in 1957. The treaty was intended to create a common economic marketplace through the elimination of trade barriers between its member states (which then numbered six). It also included common policies in areas such as agriculture and transport. The common market the treaty envisioned was established gradually through the 1960s. The 1987 Single European Act broadened the community's areas of responsibility, made changes to its decision-making processes, and established 1992 as the target year for the official completion of the single market—this latter provision was legally binding on member states. The 1992 Maastricht Treaty on European Union extensively revised the community's vision for the future. The treaty formally created the EU and introduced three pillars, or foundations, upon which this union would be built. The first pillar calls for cooperation on trade and economic affairs (including economic and monetary union), the second for the creation of a common foreign and security policy, and the third for cooperation on justice and domestic affairs. These three pillars create a substantial agenda for reform for the EU's member states. The 1997 Treaty of Amsterdam clarified, and in some cases extended, the union's vision under these three pillars and called for a strengthening of its governing institutions.

The EU currently consists of twenty-seven member states that are governed at both the supranational and intergovernmental levels.[1] The union's supranational elements have the authority to make decisions that are binding on all member states. The European Parliament, the European Court of Justice, and the European Commission are all supranational bodies—the members of these bodies act as representatives of the EU and its population rather

[1] The twenty-seven member states are Austria, Belgium, Bulgaria, the Czech Republic, Cyprus, Denmark, Estonia, Finland, France, Germany, Greece, Hungary, Ireland, Italy, Latvia, Lithuania, Luxembourg, Malta, the Netherlands, Poland, Portugal, Romania, Slovakia, Slovenia, Spain, Sweden, and the United Kingdom.

Box 4-7 **European Union at a Glance**

Political System

Intergovernmental organization with plans for full economic and political union
Intergovernmental and supranational institutions

Administrative Structure

European Commission

- Twenty-seven commissioners appointed by member states (one from each member state) and confirmed by European Parliament
- President José Manuel Barroso (since 2005), chosen by European Council
- Staff of 28,000
- Thirty-six directorates-general charged with policy initiation and management
- Supranational

Executive

Council of the European Union (also known as Council of Ministers)

- Various ministers of twenty-seven member states (depending on issue being discussed)
- European Council: twenty-seven heads of state and president of commission
- Rotating six-month presidency
- Intergovernmental and supranational

Legislature

European Parliament (directly elected, five-year terms), 736 seats as of June 2009

- Close to 100 political parties represented, organized into seven political groups
- Twenty standing committees
- Supranational

Party System

Seven political groups in 2004 European Parliament:

- Dominant groups:
  - Group of the Progressive Alliance of Socialists and Democrats in the European Parliament
  - Group of the European People's Party (Christian Democrats)
- Smaller groups:
  - Group of the Alliance of Liberals and Democrats for Europe
  - Group of the Greens/European Free Alliance
  - Europe of Freedom and Democracy Group
  - European Conservatives and Reformists Groups
  - Confederal Group of the European United Left–Nordic Green Left

Judiciary

Court of Justice of the European Communities

- Twenty-seven judges appointed by member states for six-year renewable terms than their own countries. The Council of Ministers and the European Council are both intergovernmental arrangements—representatives to these bodies act in the interest of their own countries. Decisions made by the EU's intergovernmental bodies do not require the approval of the supranational bodies before they become binding—as a result, individual member states remain powerful actors in the EU's policy-making process. The EU is more than an international organization (primarily because it has legally binding authority over its sovereign member states), but at the same time its institutions do not replicate the legislative and executive bodies characteristic of political systems in industrialized countries. Policy making in the EU essentially takes place within three bodies, beginning with the European Commission.

As is the case in domestic political systems, responsibility for policy formulation in the EU is a bureaucratic function. The European Commission has twenty-seven members (one from each member state) selected by member state governments. These European commissioners are sworn to represent and act in the interest of the EU, and their activities are important in the push toward further integration. The commissioners oversee the EU's bureaucracy and civil service. The European Commission also consists of twenty directorates general (DGs), each of which is responsible for drafting and implementing policy in specific policy areas. Each DG reports to a commissioner. The EU's bureaucracy resembles national bureaucratic institutions, although it is smaller.

The European Commission has the sole right to initiate legislation for the EU. In the policy formulation process, the Commission interacts, as in other bureaucracies, with all those who have a stake in a given policy area. These actors include interest groups, individual national governments, national governments acting collectively in the Council of Ministers, and the European Parliament. The Commission attempts to ensure that its proposals will be mutually acceptable to all relevant actors while at the same time developing policies that represent the interests of the EU overall. It is responsible for monitoring policy implementation in member states and for serving as the EU's administrative apparatus (although it depends on national bureaucracies to implement EU laws). It also issues technical and administrative laws and is the European Union's sole representative in international trade negotiations.

The European Commission sends two types of legislation forward for adoption. Regulations tend to be general policies that upon adoption by the Council of Ministers automatically become national laws. Directives, in contrast, require member states to create policy instruments within a certain time period to put these directives into effect in the countries. Both types of proposals are sent to the Council of Ministers for approval. The Commission has been an important institution for coordinating and promoting the process of European integration by developing policies that consistently focus on further integration as a primary policy goal. For example, the Commission is widely seen as having maintained the EU's focus on specific objectives, such as economic and monetary union or the creation of the single market, even in the face of setbacks or waning enthusiasm.

The European Parliament is the EU's only directly elected body, and its members organize on a partisan rather than national basis. The 736 European members of the Parliament adopt a European outlook, with their views varying as a reflection of the members' partisan preferences. Like the Commission, the Parliament tends to support policies designed to encourage further integration and is more supranational in outlook. Traditionally, the Parliament has played the least important policy-making role of all the EU institutions. The Parliament itself cannot initiate or adopt legislation; it was intended to be a reactive institution. Policy proposals developed by the Commission are sent to one of the Parliament's twenty policy-specific committees for review. These committees then make their recommendations to the full Parliament; any amendments they call for will usually be adopted by the Parliament and then referred back to the Commission. The Commission is free to accept or reject these amendments as it sees fit. Beginning with the 1987 Single European Act, with further changes in the Maastricht, Amsterdam, and Nice treaties, the European Parliament's role in amending and approving legislation has been strengthened. Over time, the Parliament's powers have been extended such that it now has equal say with the Council of Ministers in most areas of EU law.

Policy proposals enter their third round of consideration with their submission to the Council of Ministers. The Council is simultaneously an executive and a legislative body and has been the EU's main decision-making institution. The Council most often directly represents the interests of EU member states individually; national political concerns are a prime influence, despite its commitment to European goals (although the Council sometimes acts on the basis of a unified European outlook, this is not the norm). The Council is comprised of elected politicians, one from each member state, who are empowered to speak authoritatively for their countries. The Council also has one nonvoting member from the European Commission. The exact membership of the Council is not fixed; it changes depending on the issue being discussed. For instance, if environmental policy is being discussed, then the environment ministers attend. If agricultural policy is the topic, then each country's agriculture minister attends. If a more general topic is on the agenda, then the foreign ministers or the prime ministers attend. The Council must approve all policies initiated by the Commission before they can be implemented. The Council is free to make policy decisions based on its own counsel alone; it may reject policies that have the support of the Parliament, the Commission, or both, and it may accept policies that both bodies oppose. Since 1993 the Council has shared legislative powers with the European Parliament. However, the Council remains more powerful than the Parliament because it grants final approval on legislation through other procedures that allow it to overrule the Parliament when it sees fit to do so. Although the

Council cannot initiate policy proposals independently, it usually commands sufficient influence to pressure the Commission to develop policies it considers necessary.

The Court of Justice of the European Communities has binding jurisdiction over all EU member states, and its decisions overrule the decisions of national courts. The Court does not have powers of judicial review—it does not overturn the policy decisions of the Council of Ministers. The Court may, however, overturn national laws in member states that are judged to be in violation of EU laws. The decisions of the Court pertain mostly to member states' application or interpretation of EU laws, not the content of the laws themselves.

SUGGESTED READINGS

Bull, Martin J., and James Newell. 2005. *Italian Politics: Adjustment Under Duress.* Cambridge: Polity.

Conradt, David. 2008. *The German Polity,* 9th ed. New York: Longman.

Edwards, George, Martin P. Wattenberg, and Robert L. Lineberry. 2008. *Government in America: People, Politics and Policy,* 13th ed. New York: Longman.

Hayes, Louis D. 2009. *Introduction to Japanese Politics,* 5th ed. Armonk, N.Y.: M. E. Sharpe.

Kavanaugh, Dennis. 2006. *British Politics,* 5th ed. New York: Oxford University Press.

Nugent, Neill. 2007. *The Government and Politics of the European Union,* 6th ed. Durham: Duke University Press.

Safran, William. 2007. *The French Polity,* 7th ed. New York: Longman.

Shafer, Byron. 1996. *Postwar Politics in the G-7: Orders and Eras in Comparative Perspective.* Madison: University of Wisconsin Press.

Chapter 5 Immigration Policy

The question of what to do about immigration and immigrants is on the systemic agendas of most industrialized countries today, as a reflection of changing patterns of population movement and settlement, continuing labor shortages, demographic change and national security concerns. In addition to addressing how much immigration to allow, governments construct policies about asylum seekers and refugees, about residents without papers, and about foreign temporary workers—many of whom have resided in these countries for years. New political organizations and initiatives among immigrants have emerged that call for government responses to their concerns. At the same time, electorally relevant anti-immigration political parties have been formed that call for more restrictive policies. Since 2001, terrorist attacks in the United States, the United Kingdom, and Spain have highlighted the nexus between immigration and national security, while demographic change and labor needs further complicate the reform picture. In response to these developments, reformation of immigration control systems is a political priority. Most notably, governments are modifying policy instruments, or inventing new ones, to address the questions of who, how many, and why?

Common Policy Problems

Immigration in most industrialized countries takes one of three forms: **legal immigration** (usually as a result of family reunification or labor importation schemes), **humanitarian immigration** (involving asylum seekers or refugees), and **illegal immigration** (typically through clandestine entry or visa overstaying). Despite the introduction of substantial control mechanisms since the 1970s, legal immigration continues to constitute the bulk of immigration into most industrialized countries. The vast majority of legal immigrants arrive as a result of **family reunification** that is usually limited to the spouses and children of legal residents and citizens. A second major source of legal immigration is employment based, in which individuals are admitted on the basis of their specialized skills. Entry to a country through such legal means is often referred to as **front door immigration**.

Legal, employment-based immigration has been especially important in European countries. Following World War II, many of these countries instituted **guest-worker programs**, in which foreign workers were given temporary work and residence permits. These workers were expected to return to their home countries when their services were no longer needed; however, most of them remained in the countries to which they emigrated, and often their families were subsequently permitted to join them. The result is the presence of significant immigrant populations that lack a clearly defined status. Most European countries banned foreign workers in the mid-1970s but continue to allow limited employment-based immigration in sectors of the economy where labor is scarce. Today, this immigration focuses on the recruitment of highly skilled migrants and temporary, often seasonal, low-skilled immigration. Entry to a country through a temporary labor program is often referred to as **side door immigration**, because these immigrants are not intended as permanent settlers.

The problem of humanitarian immigration encompasses the issue of what to do about asylum seekers and refugees. **Asylum seekers** are typically individuals who are already present in the country where refuge is sought or are at the border requesting entry. **Refugees** are usually found outside their home country (typically in refugee camps), where they are usually interviewed by a country's immigration officials before being given entry permits (see Box 5-1). Humanitarian immigration is often considered side door immigration.

Preventing illegal immigration is perhaps the most difficult problem for policymakers to address effectively. In this case, the term **back door immigration** is frequently used. An increasing problem for most industrialized countries, illegal immigration is often the result of a variety of mechanisms. Some illegal immigrants enter a country legally and then remain after their visas expire; others cross clandestinely over relatively open borders. Illegal immigration has increasingly been a problem for European governments, as a result of their effective end to legal immigration by the mid-1970s and the more recent tightening of asylum policies, both of which forced would-be immigrants to find other means of entry. Until recently the bulk of European illegal immigrants were rejected asylum seekers who did not leave the country after their claims were refused.

A final area of concern is a government's ability to control so-called push and pull factors. In the immigration context, **pull factors** refer to a country's characteristics that make it attractive to immigrants. These factors include existing family ties, job opportunities, and the availability of public services and social welfare benefits. The nature of industrialized countries' labor markets—with abundant low-wage, low-skill jobs that these countries' populations are either unwilling or unavailable to fill—is another strong pull. National immigration policies usually attempt to modify or eliminate such pull factors, in the hope of reducing the incentive to immigrate. At the same time, **push factors** affect individuals' decisions to emigrate from their home countries. These factors include overpopulation, poverty, unemployment, natural disaster, and war. The ability of immigrant-receiving countries to control push factors is far more limited than is the case with pull factors. Industrialized countries attempt to control these push factors primarily through development assistance to the countries that provide them with substantial immigrant flows.

Box 5-1 **In Depth: The International Refugee Problem**

The United Nations High Commissioner for Refugees (UNHCR) defines a refugee as a person who has fled his or her country because of a well-founded fear of persecution for reasons of race, religion, nationality, political opinion, or membership in a particular social group and who cannot or does not want to return. Some refugees flee from acts of terror perpetrated by their governments; others may be seeking refuge from violence resulting from ethnic conflict that does not involve the government or from other forms of oppression that the government can no longer control. Under existing international agreements, refugees have a right to safe asylum—defined as the right to seek and receive refuge from persecution or war. In this sense, refugees differ from other migrants in that they need protection because their own government has failed to protect their rights or physical security. Migrants applying for refugee status, or asylum, in a country are required to establish that their fear of persecution is well founded. Having done so, receiving countries are bound to afford refugees the same rights and assistance as any other foreigner who is a legal resident, including the extension of civil, social, and economic rights. Under these same agreements, receiving states may not forcibly return refugees to a country where they may face danger.

The problem of refugees increased significantly in the 1970s. At that time, a worldwide refugee crisis emerged as hundreds of thousands fled from such far-flung places as Vietnam, Cambodia, Laos, Lebanon, and Afghanistan—all of whom were seeking to escape repression, persecution, or civil war. By the 1990s refugees were moving across the globe, fleeing ethnic conflict in particular. The global refugee population peaked at nearly 18 million in 1993. In 1997–2001 the number of refugees worldwide fell by 24 percent compared to the previous five years. The global refugee population fell to its lowest level since 1980 in 2005, to 8.4 million. This significant drop was accounted for in part by the voluntary return home of more than 6 million refugees since 2001, as well a significant drop in the mass movement of new refugees, with the arrival of only 136,000 new refugees to neighboring states in 2005—the smallest number in twenty-nine years. However, in 2006, for the first time in five years, the global refugee population increased, to 9.9 million, in large part because of the growth of the Iraqi refugee population to an estimated 1.2 million (by September 2007, this number had grown to well over 2 million). In addition to Iraq, there were large new outflows from the Central African Republic, Chad, Sri Lanka, Sudan, and Somalia. Outflows from Afghanistan were the most significant, with 2.1 million refugees (20 percent of the entire global refugee population) distributed across seventy asylum countries.

Worldwide, the number of asylum applications has been dropping steadily since the early 1990s. Across fifty industrialized countries, asylum claims dropped for the fifth year in a row in 2005 to their lowest level in nearly twenty years. In Western Europe the number of asylum applications rose from under 170,000 in 1985 to more than 690,000 in 1992. Owing to stricter policies, the number of applications has declined steadily since 1992, to about 299,000 (or half the worldwide total) in 2006. France now receives more asylum applications than any other European country, with nearly 30,750 applications in 2006. Asylum applications in the United States increased from about 20,000 in 1985 to almost 148,000 in 1995 and dropped to just over 41,100 in 2006. Of all the major industrialized countries, Japan receives the fewest asylum applications, only about 950 in 2006.

SOURCE: Data are from UNHCR (2006, 2007).

Major Policy Options

The most basic policy choice in the area of legal immigration involves the task of establishing who may legally enter a country for long-term or permanent residence. Beyond this, countries must also plan and manage the inflow of migrants to best serve national goals, whether economic, social, or demographic. The most common policy instrument is the **preference system**, which allocates a certain number of visas for categories of immigrants per year. Such systems may employ strict quotas, targets, or ceilings to regulate the flow of immigrants. Restrictions on the type of family reunification permitted have also been a common policy tool to control the flow of legal migrants. Family reunification policies have proven to be a rather ineffective control mechanism, largely because there is no accurate way to predict how many claims for entry on the basis of family ties will be made in any given year. Countries that permit employment-based immigration usually identify particular skills or economic sectors experiencing labor shortages for which immigration will be allowed. Some countries officially ban foreign workers entirely but continue to allow employment-based immigration on a smaller scale based on workers' skills and employment needs in particular economic sectors. These countries often have an immigrant labor quota, and governments reserve the right to deny work permits as they see fit, usually based on changing labor conditions.

In addressing asylum and refugee problems, governments generally are not completely free to develop policy unilaterally due to international treaties and agreements that reduce their range of options. Most countries' asylum and refugee policies reflect the provisions of the United Nations Convention Relating to the Status of Refugees, which calls for the admission of refugees and asylum seekers "owing to well-founded fear of being persecuted for reasons of race, religion, nationality, membership of a particular social group or political opinion." The treatment of asylum seekers is a particularly difficult problem for democratic states to resolve because denying asylum is viewed by many citizens as compromising democratic values and a concern for human rights.

Despite these constraints, since the 1990s industrialized countries have responded to unprecedented flows of migrants with increasingly restrictive asylum policies. Most countries sought to regulate flows through policies making it more difficult for asylum seekers to enter countries and obtain resident status. These policies involve what are known as preentry (or external) and postentry (or internal) controls. Designed to prevent asylum seekers from making it across a country's borders, **preentry controls** may include sanctions against airlines for transporting individuals who lack legal documents, stricter visa requirements for citizens of countries known to be sources of asylum applicants, the invention of so-called international zones in airports to detain undocumented foreigners, or the streamlining of asylum procedures. Many countries signed bilateral agreements with other countries that permit the return of asylum seekers at the border to the first so-called safe country they passed through before they arrived at the nation where they are seeking asylum. (Safe countries have asylum processes of their own, meet international standards, and are not themselves a source of asylum seekers.) Finally, many countries increasingly used the standard of **manifestly unfounded claims** to assess requests for asylum. Claims may be rejected as such because of insufficient evidence of persecution or false evidence presented by the applicant.

Postentry controls attempt to control the rights and activities of asylum applicants who are already within a country's borders, including limiting access to social welfare benefits, denying work permits, and using computerized registration systems to prevent asylum seekers from disappearing into society before a decision is reached or after an application is rejected. Many European countries have also created government-run reception centers in which asylum applicants must reside until a decision is reached on their status. These policies are intended to reduce asylum claims by making life more difficult for applicants once they are in the country.

The task of managing illegal immigration is clearly the most difficult problem in this policy area, because it involves controlling individuals who are deliberately attempting to avoid detection. Policy responses to illegal immigration generally take one of three forms: internal controls, external controls, and regularization programs. **Internal controls** allow for the legal supervision of immigrants to be sure they leave when their visas expire and that they do not work without authorization. Such policies include deportation programs for those with expired visas and sanctions against employers who hire illegal immigrants. **External controls** usually involve measures designed to prevent foreigners from entering the country without permission, such as more effective policing of borders and airports or installation of elaborate fences and surveillance devices. **Regularization programs** provide legal amnesty (and usually naturalized citizenship) for illegal immigrants who satisfy certain conditions such as entry into the country before a certain date, good health, regular employment, or a valid passport. Regularization measures are usually adopted jointly with increased enforcement efforts to prevent additional inflows of illegal immigrants.

Explaining Policy Dynamics

The politics of the immigration policy-making process is an area of research that lacks any broadly comprehensive theorizing. In surveying the literature, we find relatively few attempts to clarify this process across the industrialized countries. The vast majority of empirical explanations are based on studies of a single country (or occasionally two or three countries). Based on this existing work, we can offer a set of potential explanations—cultural, economic, political, and institutional—for immigration policy reform.

Cultural Explanations

Cultural factors influence immigration policy reform. One cultural thesis focuses on a country's historical experiences with immigration. According to this view, immigration policy in countries that have longer histories of population inflows from abroad and larger immigrant populations overall (the so-called countries of immigration) differs from policy in countries that have experienced immigration for shorter periods of time and have smaller immigrant populations. In these latter countries, immigration is often unwelcome, particularly as immigrants become a permanent part of the population. More specifically, if immigration is incorporated into the country's "founding myth," that country is less inclined to favor more restrictive or exclusive immigration policies (Freeman 1998; Joppke 1998, 1999). Joppke (1999) argues that where immigration coincides with the nation-building process (in that immigration occurs as the nation is developing its self-identity), one finds a belief that immigration is a good thing and stronger support for continued immigration. National myths and self-images can be particularly important for understanding policy reform because they allow political leaders to portray their preferred policy outcomes as consonant with a nation's self-identity. In countries where immigration is not a crucial aspect of national identity, more exclusive immigration policy reforms are more easily adopted and implemented.

Other historical explanations for immigration policy reform consider the nature of the relationship between immigrant-receiving and immigrant-sending states. Immigrant-receiving states have less control over immigration policy relative to immigrant-sending states with whom they have strong historical ties. Often this argument points to the importance of past colonial relationships between countries that create special immigration obligations, although it may point to other aspects of a country's experiences as well, such as its record during World War II (Layton-Henry 1992; Rich 1990).

Pressures for immigration policy reform also may be explained by trends in public opinion. Today most governments face pressure to pass laws to slow or end immigration. Public opinion is often far more restrictionist than that held by political parties or government officials. Baldwin-Edwards and Schain (1994), for example, observe that most Europeans feel that there are too many immigrants in their countries. They note that the effects of these opinions on public policy are largely contingent on other factors. In particular, where political parties that specifically represent these negative views exist, reform tends to be more reflective of public opinion. In other contexts, these negative public sentiments do not dictate public policy. For example, Gimpel and Edwards (1998) argue that in the United States immigration is not usually an issue that motivates people to vote (unless the economy is weak), which they say explains an observed gap between public opinion and policy.

A final cultural explanation found in the literature on immigration policy reform concerns the effects of liberal political values on reform. These values are embedded in the fabric of industrialized countries, as well as in the international system in which they operate, and include nondiscrimination, political equality, and civil rights. Where rights-based liberalism figures prominently in policy making, it is difficult for states to treat immigrants in ways that violate these fundamental tenets (Gurowitz 1999; Heisler 1986; Hollifield 1992, 2004; Jacobson 1996; Joppke 1999, Soysal 1994). Because stricter immigration policies often require a rollback of civil and human rights for noncitizens, the prevalence of these norms can impede more restrictive reform.

Economic Explanations

Changes in a country's employment patterns also influence immigration policy reform. Schnapper (1994) notes that industrial restructuring has meant that there are fewer such jobs for both native populations and immigrants in industrialized countries. In response, immigrants (who until the early 1970s had been accepted in most industrialized countries because of their economic contribution) are argued to cost more (in social welfare benefits) than they contribute to national economies. Support for more restrictive immigration policies is then mustered more easily among the general public, notably among the unemployed. Feelings of economic deprivation are frequently used to explain support for extreme right-wing parties and the more restrictive reforms they advocate (Money 1999). Economic depression, long-lasting unemployment, and budget deficits may all have an impact on the demand for immigration policy reform, especially where foreign workers are seen as unwanted competitors who take away jobs from native workers or who live on social benefits for which others have paid.

Short-term trends in economic growth can stimulate fluctuations in the focus of immigration policy, or its tendency to oscillate between restrictionism and liberalization. Some researchers claim that a close connection exists between business cycles and so-called admissionist or restrictionist reforms. Immigration is tolerated or even encouraged during periods of economic growth and prosperity. During bad times, immigrants are targeted as scapegoats for conditions they may have no part in causing, and immigration policies may become more restrictive (Brochman and Hammar 1999; Freeman 1998; Hollifield 1992, 2004; Kindleberger 1967).

A final economic explanation for policy reform concerns the effects of economic globalization and interdependence. Here, reform is viewed as a function of the connections between economic internationalization and labor market demands. In a world in which economic change is in the direction of deregulation and liberalization, countries are pressured to keep their borders open. Sassen (1999) argues that it simply is not possible for countries to have an open policy for circulating capital and a very different regime for circulating people. The free movement of people is an integral part of the movement of trade and investment across borders. Transnational economic processes become key factors influencing immigration policy. Policy reform reflects the wishes of governments and private economic actors in immigrant-receiving countries that are concerned with creating economic linkages with immigrant-sending countries—such linkages naturally serve as bridges for immigrants.

Political Explanations

Research points to several important political explanations for immigration policy reform. The first explanation emerges from studies of the growth and success of anti-immigration, extreme right-wing parties in European countries. These parties, which base their appeals to the electorate on anti-immigration, racist, and xenophobic views, have disrupted traditional party systems by creating opportunities for the political expression of such sentiments. They increasingly influence public debates on immigration and immigrants. Perhaps more important for immigration policy reform, these right-wing movements also have forced the more moderate established political parties, on both the right and left, to place these issues high on their own agendas and to favor tougher reforms. Often these xenophobic, anti-immigration parties can force traditional parties to rearrange their policy platforms, their priorities for government, and ultimately the very nature of immigration policy reform (Brochman and Hammar 1999; Hollifield 1992; Messina 1995). The ideology of parties beyond the extreme right is also an important influence on immigration policy preferences. Lahav (2004) finds that ideology is a better indicator of immigration preferences than national or cultural values: parties of the left are more likely to amend social inequalities and to extend immigrant rights and to be open to increased immigration than are parties of the right.

A second explanation, the role of public opinion more generally in immigration policy today, is the subject of scholarly debate. Some argue that liberal immigration policies have emerged because negative public opinion is not factored into elite decision making (Apap 2004; Beck and Camarota 2002; Hansen 2000; McLaren 2001). Still others contend that public opinion influences policy far more than previously thought; the public's opinions are much closer to elite views than most would believe, and the public is much more rational and informed than typically assumed (Fetzer 2000; Freeman 1995; Guiraudon 2000; Hansen 2000).

A third political explanation is based on research into the role of interest groups in immigration policy reform. Freeman (1995, 2001, 2006) advanced what he calls a client politics thesis in his examination of ethnic and economic interest group pressure on the immigration policy process. In his view, client politics involves a number of small and well-organized groups that have a strong influence on the policy-making process. He argues that such client politics is oriented heavily toward expansive immigration policies because of the more organized and effective efforts of interest groups (employers, ethnic advocacy groups, or human rights organizations) that favor more liberal policies. In Freeman's view, governments may pay more attention to these interests than to public opinion because of the fear of promoting right-wing extremism if these issues are debated publicly. Thus governments seek to reach an early and private consensus to avoid the emergence of these issues on the national systemic agenda, where they may quickly spiral out of control. This tendency for the major parties to try to defuse the immigration issue while responding to interest group pressure offers one explanation for situations in which policies do not reflect public opinion.

Institutional Explanations

Freeman's client politics perspective generated considerable debate among scholars in this area. Perlmutter (1996) responded that Freeman's model applies only when a strong political party controls the institutional agenda in a relatively unitary political system. In many other situations, the declining strength of mass parties creates the opportunity for other actors—dissident regional politicians, dissatisfied small parties in governing coalitions, or radical parties—to pose real challenges to immigration policy reform. Perlmutter argues that in multiparty or federalist polities, there are more chances to politicize immigration and only limited ability to keep these issues off the institutional agenda. In his view, the nature of immigration policy reform will be influenced strongly by the location of power in a political system. Perlmutter contends that because federalism allows for the regional expression of demands (which then often reach the national political agenda) and because immigrants tend to be concentrated in specific regions, the ability of advocates for change to influence policy reform could be increased in a federal system. More recently, Statham and Geddes (2006) and Schain (2006) also challenge Freeman's arguments, with research that suggests that pro-immigrant groups may capture policymakers' attention less, and anti-immigration groups more, than previously thought.

Many scholars make similar arguments about the effects of the long-term erosion of political parties and other traditional political institutions as policymaking bodies and as vehicles for political representation in industrialized countries. They note that as traditional actors lose influence, immigration policy falls increasingly within the jurisdiction of national courts or becomes the preoccupation of pro-immigrant welfare groups and activists or of anti-immigration extremists on the right. Hence, an area of public policy that was once controlled by executives and bureaucracies (and took place outside the domain of legislatures and electoral politics) becomes increasingly politicized and more difficult for governments and political parties to develop and implement (Betz 1991, 1994; Messina 1989, 1990; Schain 1987, 1988).

Other research describes an important role for the judiciary in immigration policy reform. In countries where the judiciary is inclined to (and empowered to) hold legislation to constitutional norms via judicial review, more restrictive immigration policy reforms are less likely to survive (Shapiro and Stone 1994). In many countries, courts also have limited the ability of governments to restrict or stop asylum seekers from crossing national borders (Cornelius, Martin, and Hollifield 1994; Guiraudon 1997, 2001; Hollifield 1992; Joppke 1998, 1999; Sassen 1998). In some states, however, governments may attempt to circumvent judicial constraints by delegating authority over immigration policy to subnational or supranational authorities (Guiraudon 2001; Guiraudon and Lahav 2000; Messina 1989).

International Policy Making

Immigration policy is one of the least developed areas of international policy making because decision making in this area is most likely to take place at the national government level. Countries have demonstrated a marked reluctance to surrender their sovereignty and policy-making flexibility to a higher-level authority on this matter. This is true with respect not only to the European Union (EU) but also to broader international policies intended to govern population flows.

The most important international agreement affecting many countries' asylum and refugee policies is the 1951 Geneva Convention. Article One of the agreement calls on signatory nations to grant refugee status to any person who, owing to a well-founded fear of persecution on racial, religious, political, or other grounds, is unwilling or unable to return to his or her home country. This article, along with the 1951 United Nations Convention Relating to the Status of Refugees and the 1967 Protocol (which made the Convention more comprehensive), imposes both legal and moral obligations on countries not to reject foreign asylum applicants if such rejection entails their being returned to a place where they are in danger of being persecuted. This is known as the **non-refoulement principle**. Countries that have signed these agreements are to establish procedures for evaluating asylum and refugee claims and are obligated to admit those who qualify as refugees and have nowhere else to go. In practice, we observe considerable variation in how countries interpret their individual obligations under these commitments. Most industrialized countries have adopted more restrictive asylum and refugee policies than in the past; however, in keeping with their international commitments, they maintain that real refugees will not be turned away.

EU member countries have made progress on immigration and asylum policy coordination in only two areas: movement of EU nationals within the union and visa requirements. The elimination of borders between EU member countries was first proposed in a European Commission consultation in

1988, and by 1995 the removal of border controls had been largely implemented. Progress has been made on the adoption of EU-wide visa policies through the development of a common list of non-EU countries whose citizens require visas to enter any EU country. The 1992 Maastricht Treaty officially acknowledged for the first time an EU vision of immigration as an area of "common interest" for member states. Until 1997 immigration policy fell primarily under the third pillar of the treaty, justice and home affairs, although these matters were also addressed in the first pillar on economic integration (in particular concerning visa policies). In the 1990s the most limited policy activity in the EU occurred in areas that fell under the third pillar. The 1997 Treaty of Amsterdam moved the area of justice and home affairs to the first pillar and fully committed the EU to creating a common "area of freedom, security and justice." Under this treaty, EU member states agreed in principle to develop common immigration and asylum policies. The treaty introduced community decision-making procedures to immigration policy and increased the role of the European Commission in this policy area.

The 1999 Tampere Program involved the first binding EU-level agreements on asylum policies. These included a policy about temporary protections for persons displaced by conflicts, a common understanding of refugee status and "subsidiary" protection, minimal procedural guarantees, minimum conditions for the reception of asylum seekers, and a regulation on deciding which member state is responsible for assessing which asylum claim. Tampere was based on four themes: partnerships with countries of origin, a common European asylum system, fair treatment of third-country nationals, and the management of migration flows. The Hague Program, introduced in 2004, aimed to improve the EU's ability to guarantee fundamental rights, procedural safeguards, and access to justice; fight organized crime; repress the threat of terrorism; provide protection to refugees; and regulate migration flows and control external borders of the union. The program is divided into five parts: a common European asylum system, legal migration and the fight against illegal employment, integration of third-country nationals, the external dimension of asylum and migration policy, and the management of migration flows. The Hague Program was not intended to lead to an EU-wide immigration system but was nonetheless wide ranging in perspective and set out an ambitious agenda. Whether its long-term goals are achievable is a matter of some debate.

In recent years European countries have been shaping their national immigration policies to reflect international agreements developed beyond EU institutions. The most important of these is the Schengen Agreement, which was implemented in 1995 among the Benelux countries, France, and Germany. The 1997 Treaty of Amsterdam fully incorporated the Schengen Agreement into the existing EU structure (with a five-year phase-in period) as the Schengen *acquis*. The Schengen Agreement abolished internal EU border controls and instituted common policies on visas and asylum applications. More specifically, the agreement was intended to allow for the freedom of movement of EU nationals within the EU. The agreement also introduced a single computer system for maintaining immigration information that encourages customs policy cooperation (known as the Schengen Information System). At the end of 2008, twenty-five countries had signed on to the Schengen Agreement. This included all the EU countries with the exception of the United Kingdom and Ireland, which reserved their rights to maintain border controls with other Schengen countries. Although the agreement is technically open only to EU member states, three non-EU members, Iceland, Norway, and Switzerland, are parties to the agreement. These countries were part of an older passport-free agreement among the Nordic countries and were thus allowed to join the Schengen area.

The 1993 North American Free Trade Agreement (NAFTA) signed by the United States, Canada, and Mexico does not directly mention immigration issues (beyond minor attention to the temporary movement of business persons). Unlike EU policies, NAFTA neither guarantees the right to free movement for workers between its signatory countries, nor does it impose strict requirements on member states' immigration policies or behaviors. In fact, NAFTA supporters argued before its signing that the agreement was likely to decrease immigration flows as increased trade flows would reduce immigration push factors. However, Mexican-U.S. migration in fact increased in the 1990s and early 2000s, in particular as demand for labor increased in the United States in the face of falling unemployment rates and strong economic growth. In North America, immigration policy is solely the province of national governments.

The Security and Prosperity Partnership of North America (SPP) is a trilateral alliance adopted in 2005 by Canada, Mexico and the United States. The SPP covers two major areas—development and security. With reference to immigration, the SPP includes provisions for shared technology, access to databases, special clearances for border residents, coordinated visa policies, the exchange of intelligence information on persons of "special interest," and fast-track lanes for travelers.

United States

Background: Policy Process and Policy History

Immigration policy making in the United States is controlled at the federal level of government. This control is relatively comprehensive, particularly because the Supreme Court has prohibited states from passing any laws that contradict federal policies in this area. At the federal level, policy making is led more by Congress than by the executive branch. There are two important congressional committees for immigration policy making: the House and Senate Judiciary Committees. Since 2002 immigration policy development, implementation, and enforcement has been the responsibility of the cabinet-level Department of Homeland Security (DHS). The threat to U.S. national security posed by terrorism prompted the creation of the DHS through the merger of twenty-two federal agencies. This merger abolished the Immigration and Naturalization Service, which had been the Department of Justice's agency responsible for immigration matters. The DHS division of the U.S. Citizenship and Immigration Services now handles immigrant visa petitions, naturalization applications, and asylum and refugee applications, whereas the Customs and Border Protection division oversees admission of all people and goods at all ports of entry. Other federal agencies may be involved in specialized areas of immigration. For example, the Departments of Labor and Commerce may determine appropriate levels of foreign worker inflows. The judiciary also plays an important role in determining the constitutionality of many policy decisions in this area.

Because Congress plays a greater role in immigration policy making than do the executive or judicial branches, interest groups also figure prominently in the immigration policy-making process. Congress is very sensitive to immigration interests, and interest groups sometimes determine the political agenda or propose legislation that members of Congress will introduce and advocate. Prominent interest groups in this policy arena include ethnic, business, human rights, and community groups as well as trade unions.

Historically, the United States has been considered by many to be a country of immigration, so much so that it is often referred to as a melting pot. Until 1875 the United States had no national restrictions on immigration. In the nineteenth and early twentieth centuries, policymakers viewed immigration as important to national economic growth and constructed policies to maximize the flow of immigrants. As a result, the vast majority of the U.S. population today are descendants of immigrants from the 1800s or early 1900s who came to the United States in search of economic opportunities. The total foreign-born population in the United States in 2000 was nearly 36.5 million, or 12.4 percent of the population overall.

The United States' legal immigration policy has been largely independent of the dictates of the labor market. The Immigration and Nationality Act of 1990 and its amendments are the basis for most of the immigration policies in place today. U.S. law provides for legal immigration (or legal permanent resident status) for family reunification, employment preferences, and diversity immigration (for foreign nationals of countries with low levels of immigration to the United States), and for refugees and asylum seekers. Permanent immigration rose sharply in 2006, with a 13 percent increase over 2005 levels, to the highest level since 1991. Consistent with past trends, legal immigration in 2006 was primarily for family reunification (70.3 percent); only about 5.6 percent of population inflows consisted of skilled labor. Currently, all immigrants are admitted under a preference system that allocates a certain number of visas for each category of immigrant. Since the late 1990s the number of temporary worker visas authorized has fallen far short of the demand—the annual cap for these visas is filled soon after the beginning of each fiscal year. The American Competitiveness in the Twenty-First Century Act of 2000 and the Real ID Act of 2005 increased the number of temporary work visas available per year.

The last significant new restrictions on legal immigration were introduced in 1924. In marked contrast to the other countries examined in this book, in the United States almost all organized pressure related to immigration policy in the 1990s was on raising immigration levels. In this period, a rapidly growing economy generated, for example, an increasing need for skilled and unskilled workers. Historically, support for continued legal immigration clearly reflected a belief that restrictions on legal immigration were antithetical to the U.S. immigration tradition. Early in the twentieth-first century, however, pressure for increased immigration to meet labor shortages has been counterbalanced by demands that immigration be restricted because of the presumed connection between immigration and terrorism and rising illegal immigration.

The Refugee Act of 1980 sets targets for humanitarian immigration to the United States. Refugees and asylum seekers accounted for 17 percent of all persons granted legal permanent residence status in 2006. Under the 1980 law, the number of applicants admitted per year is determined jointly by Congress and the president, with an annual recommended inflow of 70,000 refugees (although actual inflows are far below this level—48,300 in 2006). Refugees living in the United States are authorized to work and may apply for legal permanent resident status after one year of residence in the country. The number of refugees granted immigrant status has increased in recent years but remains well below pre–September 11 levels (28,000 in 2003, compared to 72,143 in 2000 and 68,925 in 2001). The United States' asylum program was reformed in 1995 to reduce application backlogs, to recognize legitimate claims within 180 days, and to improve the process of identifying fraudulent claims. In 2006, 41,101 persons were granted asylum. Asylees must wait one year after they are granted asylum status to apply for legal permanent residence. Until 2005 the number of persons authorized to adjust their asylum status was capped at 10,000. The Real ID Act 2005 removed this limit.

Among the industrialized countries examined in this book, the United States faces the largest illegal immigration problem, mostly because of the country's vast geographic area. The country's long borders—over 2,000 miles with Mexico and 3,000 miles with Canada—as well as innumerable points of entry at airports and along an extensive coastline present a logistical nightmare for immigration officials. Estimates of the illegal immigrant population in the United States vary. The DHS Office of Immigration Statistics estimates that nearly 11 million illegal immigrants were in the United States in January 2006, whereas in March 2006 the Pew Hispanic Center estimated this population at between 11.5 and 12 million, or 30 percent of the foreign-born population in 2005. The DHS estimates that an additional 408,000 illegal immigrants entered the country each year during 2000–2004—amounting to nearly 1,400 people a day, whereas the Pew Center estimates that the illegal population has averaged more than 500,000 a year since 2000. The Pew Center further estimates that in 2005 nearly two-thirds of the unauthorized population had been in the country ten years or less and that 40 percent had been in the country five years or less. Mexicans make up the largest proportion (roughly 57 percent) of illegal immigrants.

In the early twenty-first century, illegal immigrants have spread to nontraditional settlement regions in the United States, such as the Midwest and the South. Whereas 88 percent of the illegal immigrant population was concentrated in six states (California, Florida, New York, Texas, Illinois, and New Jersey) in 1990, today these six states hold only 61 percent of that population. The rising presence of immigrants in nontraditional settlement areas has generated a political backlash among some citizens. The 1996 Illegal Immigration Reform and Immigrant Responsibility Act provides the framework for the country's approach to the problem of illegal immigration. Externally the act was designed to assist the then-Immigration and Naturalization Service by increasing the number of border patrols, strengthening enforcement abilities, improving detection technology and improving barriers along the Mexican border. Internally the act restricted the rights of illegal immigrants already in the country and strengthened the ability of immigration officials to deny entry to the country or deport those who had already entered. Since the terrorist attacks of September 11, 2001, many people in the United States have come to view illegal immigration as a national security matter. The terrorist acts catalyzed the passage of a series of laws that affect not only suspected terrorists, but all immigrants. Included among these are the USA PATRIOT Act of 2001, which strengthened border enforcement; the Enhanced Border Security and Visa Entry Reform Act of 2002, which tightened visa screening, border inspections, and the tracking of foreigners; and the Real ID Act of 2005, which blocks states from issuing driver's licenses to illegal immigrants. More recently, the Secure Fence Act of 2006 endorsed plans to build a 700-mile fence along the U.S.-Mexican border and to further strengthen border patrols.

Contemporary Dynamics

U.S. policymakers face a continual challenge: to balance effectively the economic necessity of continued labor immigration expansion with rising anti-immigration pressures and popular calls for an end to immigration entirely. The conflict between expansionists (usually business leaders and immigrants' rights groups) and restrictionists (such as governors and citizens in states with large immigrant populations) flares up repeatedly. Since 2001 the approach to immigration policy has been more restrictionist, as many members of Congress, and particularly many Republicans, view as a threat to national security the presence of a large illegal immigrant population, whose size, composition, and movements cannot be monitored effectively. As such, they are intent on reducing illegal immigration and opposed to further opening the country to immigrants. At the same time, because immigrants continue to play an important role in the U.S. economy, especially in the agricultural, construction, and information technology sectors, the pressure from some quarters to maintain an open immigration stance continues to be significant. Hence, immigration politics in this period has been characterized by an increasingly contentious debate over the effects of immigration on the U.S. economy, society, and security.

Agenda setting for the most recent immigration policy reform effort began with President George W. Bush's 2004 declaration that the current immigration system was "broken" and that repairing it was one of his top priorities. To fix the system, he proposed a temporary worker program for both undocumented workers already in the country as well as new foreign workers, but not a path to full legal status or citizenship. The introduction of specific legislative proposals to achieve these ends was left to members of Congress. Anti-immigration forces viewed the president's proposal as an amnesty program that would do nothing to stem the flow of illegal immigrants. Conservative Republicans believed a temporary worker program would reward those who entered the country illegally and encourage more illegal immigration. They further argued that existing border control and interior enforcement policies were inadequate and unable to deter future illegal immigration. Many Democrats, immigrant advocacy groups, and human rights organizations also voiced concerns about the president's proposal, saying that it did not go far enough to protect temporary workers and provided too few incentives for undocumented workers to come forward. Trade union leaders also argued that illegal immigrant flows could not be reduced without a clear path to citizenship.

Few, if any, issues divided Republicans in the 109th Congress (2005–2007) more than immigration, especially the question of what to do about illegal immigration. Consequently the decision-making phase of the immigration reform was highly contentious. In late 2005 and early 2006, vastly different immigration reform bills were introduced and passed in the Senate and the House of Representatives, with subsequent efforts to reconcile the two measures failing. HR 4437, sponsored by House Judiciary Committee chair James Sensenbrenner, R-Wisc., focused on border security and tougher workplace enforcement of immigration laws. The centerpiece of the bill was a mandatory employee verification program and tamperproof identification cards for all workers. The bill also included provisions that would have made illegal immigration a felony punishable by jail, eliminated the possibility of legalization, funded a fence along much of the U.S.-Mexican border, and punished those who assisted illegal immigrants (including clergy and humanitarian workers). The Sensenbrenner bill in no way conformed to the agenda set by the president in 2004; it passed in the House in December 2005 by a vote of 239 to 182.

The approval of the House bill prompted a swift and strong reaction among those who wanted to stop illegal immigration, employers who wanted to legalize the employment of unauthorized workers, and church and immigrant groups that wanted to legalize unauthorized foreigners. The legislation was praised by most opponents of illegal immigration because it would send resources to the border and would require employers to screen employee documents against federal databases, without rewarding illegal immigrants with a path to U.S. citizenship. A coalition of business groups, religious leaders, and immigrants' rights advocates complained that the bill would make felons out of illegal immigrants caught working in the United States and those who assist them for humanitarian reasons and did not address the fact that illegal immigrants provide a vital labor pool for some industries. Dissatisfaction with the bill became the catalyst for mass protests across the country. In March and April 2006, hundreds of thousands of immigrants in more than 100 U.S. cities marched against the proposed House reforms. Trade unions and the Catholic Church provided much of the organizational support for the marches. May 1, 2006, was designated as "A Day Without Immigrants" or the Great American Boycott of 2006. This protest was intended to demonstrate immigrants' economic importance to the country; nearly a million immigrants and their supporters boycotted workplaces, schools, and stores. To counter these demonstrations, members of Minuteman border watchdog groups launched a month-long campaign on the Arizona border to call attention to continuing illegal immigration.

Senate debate on its immigration reform legislation took place in the midst of the April and May protests against the House bill. The Senate took a different approach to immigration reform, with an unusually large number of Republicans joining Democrats in supporting a bill closer to that proposed by the president in 2004. The Comprehensive Immigration Reform Act, introduced by the chair of the Judiciary Committee, Arlen Specter, then–R-Penn., combined border security and worksite enforcement with a temporary worker program and a path to citizenship for most illegal immigrants already in the country. After two weeks of contentious floor debate on the bill and six Judiciary Committee markups, the bill passed in May 2006 on a 62–36 vote (with 22 members of the 55-member Republican majority voting for it). House Republicans immediately dismissed the Senate measure as too lenient on illegal immigrants, labeling it "amnesty" and the work of Democrats.

In June 2006 the House and Senate bills should have moved to a conference committee to be reconciled (the normal step when both chambers pass nonidentical measures). In an election year, however, it was soon clear that a compromise was unlikely. House Republicans refused to convene a conference, choosing instead to hold field hearings around the country in a systematic effort to undermine the Senate legislation—at the hearings the Senate legislation was attacked on grounds ranging from its being too costly to its likely detrimental effects on U.S. national security. The Senate held its own hearings. When Congress reconvened in the fall, House Republicans held to their original position that the Senate measure was unacceptable, and both immigration bills died at the end of the session. In an attempt to salvage something from this contentious reform process in the lead-up to the 2006 midterm elections, House Republicans passed a series of narrowly cast bills based on their failed legislation. In September 2006 only one of these measures was approved in the Senate: Congress passed the Secure Fence Act. However, Congress appropriated only a small proportion ($1.2 billion) of the funds required for implementation of the law. Subsequent attempts to pass similar, although pared down, immigration reform failed in the 110th Congress (2007–2009), and immigration is not expected to be among the first issues tackled by Barack Obama's administration.

Throughout the 2006–2007 debates, the American public was clearly divided in its views on immigration in general and the two policy proposals more specifically. Bolstering supporters of the more moderate Senate legislation, public opinion polls indicated that a majority of Americans supported a path for legalization of illegal immigrants if they had a job, were made to pay back taxes, and had been living in the United States for a number of years. However, Republicans tended to take a somewhat tougher approach to the question of illegal immigration: in 2006, 49 percent of Republicans thought illegal immigrants living in the country for at least two years should be given a chance to keep their jobs and eventually apply for citizenship (compared to 59 percent of the general electorate), and 45 percent said they should be deported immediately (compared to 36 percent of the general electorate). At the same time, a small majority of both Republicans and the general population believe that all forms of immigration should be decreased. Complicating matters further, in an election year both parties were concerned with appealing to the growing Hispanic electorate, for whom a more open and tolerant immigration policy obviously was a key issue.

The policy process just described reveals the importance of cultural, economic, and political explanations for immigration policy reform. First, the intensity of the congressional and national debate over immigration reflects the power of immigration as a national symbol. Even in an environment in which national security concerns entered into the debate, for many citizens the founding myth of the United States as a country that values immigration played an important role in preventing the adoption of a noticeably more restrictive policy. Second, the business community's strong opposition to reducing immigration flows revealed the influence of economic considerations. This policy decision occurred at a time when the demand for highly skilled and unskilled workers was rising; hence, employers were motivated to block any additional restrictions on immigration. Third, the ability of interest groups to mobilize their supporters for mass action and to involve themselves directly in the decision-making process resulted in a highly politicized policy debate and stalemate. Finally, Congress's failure to approve the 2006 and 2007 reforms reflected a high degree of partisanship on the issue and the difficulty of reconciling major differences of opinion between the parties in an election year.

Japan

Background: Policy Process and Policy History

Immigration policy making in Japan involves a number of cabinet-level ministries. There is no ministry specifically organized around immigration issues. Instead, the following ministries play specific roles: Justice (through its Immigration Bureau, which is responsible for border controls), Labor, and Construction. All immigration policy decisions are discussed and debated among these ministries, with input from relevant governing officials and no meaningful opportunity for public input. Policy making in this area is often characterized as a tug-of-war, with the various departments and ministries involved struggling to represent the distinct interests of their constituencies. The prime minister and cabinet perform a coordinating rather than initiating role.

Historically, Japan was not a country of immigration. It still has the smallest foreign population of any industrialized country, but immigration into Japan increased substantially during the 1990s. Between 1950 and 1988, foreigners made up only 0.6 percent of the total population, and by the end of the 1990s the foreign-born population had grown to just over 1.0 percent, rising further to 1.7 percent by 2007. The largest immigrant group in Japan is from Korea, and many others are from China, Brazil, or Southeast Asia. The number of immigrants in Japan has grown by half since the late 1980s, but their proportion of the population remains well below that of any other industrialized country.

Japan is known for its preference for cultural, racial, and ethnic stability that reflects a traditionally homogenous population. Japan in the postwar period was the only major industrialized country that was not forced to import foreign workers to fill low-level employment gaps. Guest workers were not needed because of a large rural labor supply and the massive use of labor-saving technologies by large industries. The situation had changed markedly, however, by the mid-1980s. Japan faced its first labor shortage as a result of a low fertility rate, a declining labor supply from rural areas, and government policies that encouraged employers and workers to reduce their working hours. A growing reluctance among younger Japanese to take so-called 3K jobs—*kitsui, kitanai, kiken* (dirty, dangerous, and demanding)—as well as the greater availability of higher skilled jobs, also spurred the labor shortage. This shortage, in a time of economic boom in the late 1980s to early 1990s, created a strong pull for immigrants from other Asian countries. Today, some social and economic factors are pushing Japan toward a more open immigration policy. In particular, faced with labor shortages resulting from an aging and shrinking population, many in the business community have stepped up their call for reducing labor-based immigration controls. However, despite these pressures, increasing public concerns about rising crime rates and international terrorism have prompted the country to adopt even stricter immigration controls and Japan remains a low legal entry country. As yet, there are few, if any, signs of an increasing recourse to immigration to satisfy labor needs.

Currently, Japanese immigration policy is based on the 1990 Immigration Control and Refugee Recognition Act and its amendments. This policy is organized around three defining principles. First, the entry of foreign workers should be allowed only as a last resort in response to severe labor shortages. Second, under no circumstances will unskilled labor be admitted. Third, all foreigners will be admitted as temporary, not permanent, settlers, regardless of their reasons for entry. The 1990 law limited legal foreign labor immigration to a supplementary role only when absolutely necessary and created a number of new categories, mostly professionals and those with specific expertise, who could enter and remain in the country legally. Japan discourages family reunification as a general policy. Today, government policy is centered on the acceptance of a limited number of foreign workers in highly skilled occupations, control of illegal immigration, and caution with respect to the admission of low-skilled workers. There were approximately 590,000 legal foreign workers in Japan in 2004. Most immigrants enter only as short-term residents; permanent residency is typically granted only after ten years of problem-free residence in the country.

Despite these restrictionist principles, side mechanisms exist through which unskilled foreign labor is imported, often on a permanent basis. One such mechanism permits descendants of Japanese emigrants to Latin America (known as *Nikkeijin*) to immigrate and settle permanently in Japan. Since 1990 these individuals have had essentially unrestricted access to the Japanese labor market. In 1990, 56,000 foreigners entered under this status, by 2004 their numbers had risen to 286,000. This policy is widely accepted on the grounds that these individuals, being of Japanese descent, are not viewed as upsetting Japan's ethnic and cultural homogeneity.

The government also allows the entry of foreign workers through two other side door immigration policies: corporate trainee programs and student visas. These programs are basically legal labor importation programs the government has not formally recognized (and that it does not attempt to end) and through which a substantial number of foreigners flow into the country. Small and medium-sized enterprises use this mechanism to import cheap, unskilled foreign labor in the name of training. Foreign workers who enter the country as trainees are not protected under Japanese labor laws, resulting in their poor treatment. In 2004 the number of trainees entering the country reached a new high, at 75,000. The government introduced stricter review procedures in 2005 in response to a sense that these flows were now too high. The decision to use these side and back door mechanisms allows the Japanese government to import labor to meet an economic need without stirring up Japanese public opinion in opposition to the immigrant presence. These practices undermine the government's overall policy of restricting immigration.

Despite its participation in the major international agreements concerning humanitarian immigration, there are essentially no asylum seeker or refugee problems in Japan because the government is generally hostile to applicants. From 1982 to 2004, Japan accepted 3,544 asylum applications and granted asylum to only 313 (9 percent) of them. The prime exception was the acceptance of about 8,000 Southeast Asian refugees who were accepted as political refugees from the Vietnam War in the 1970s and early 1980s. This situation clearly reflects a lack of support for accepting refugees, particularly economic refugees, as well as the principle that no foreigners should be admitted for permanent settlement. Any limited movement toward the acceptance of refugees has been in the interest of maintaining an image of international cooperation and humanitarianism rather than a wholehearted commitment to fulfilling Japan's international obligations. Although Japan's asylum rules were somewhat liberalized in 2006, only 34 of 954 applicants for asylum were recognized as refugees in that year.

A large part of the illegal immigration problem in Japan currently consists of foreigners who were allowed into the country on short-term visas (such as tourists, students, or those employed in the entertainment industry) but who did not leave when their visas expired. The estimated number of foreigners who overstayed their visas increased threefold to nearly 299,000 between 1990 and 1993. By 2006, however, this figure declined to 171,000 (a 43 percent drop since 1993) through better enforcement of border controls and the use of more sophisticated detection systems. It is further estimated that over 90 percent of these illegal immigrants are participating in the workforce. This increase in illegal resident foreigners followed the implementation in 1990 of a more restrictive immigration law that involved severe employer and immigration broker sanctions and the extension of visa requirements to immigrants (primarily from Southeast Asia) known to be likely to remain in the country illegally. The government introduced in 2003 an "Action Plan for the Realization of a Society Resistant to Crime" intended to reduce the number of illegal foreign residents through increased cooperation between the government and the police to halve the number of illegal immigrants by 2008. This plan was greeted with skepticism, however, because the government is seen as having little political will for a strict immigration crackdown, given Japan's economic dependence on its illegal workforce. According to official estimates, illegal immigrants made up about 0.2 percent of the total population in 2006, one of the lowest rates among industrialized countries.

Contemporary Dynamics

Immigration policies in Japan have not been reformed significantly in recent years. Japan has continued to pursue a closed-door immigration policy despite persistently strong demand for foreign workers in several key areas of the economy. To the limited extent that Japan has opened to additional foreigners, it has done so grudgingly. The last notable immigration reform in Japan was a revision of the Immigration Control and Refugee Recognition Law in 1990, which simplified immigration procedures and strengthened existing restrictions on employment of foreign labor. Japan's struggle to develop a comprehensive immigration control policy continues.

Since implementation of the 1990 law, only incremental changes have been made. The lack of comprehensive reform reflects in part a lack of governmental consensus about basic policy directions. The prime minister's office exercises little control over the immigration policy process, leaving agenda setting largely to the competing bureaucratic agencies. The bureaucracy continues to dominate the immigration policy-making regime and is relatively insensitive to lobbying by the small and medium-sized employers that have the most pressing labor needs, or by pro-immigration groups. Similarly, although political parties have study groups or ad hoc committees to develop policy positions on immigration, they generally do not affect the immigration policy agenda. The Diet has little active participation in immigration policy-making; it generally rubberstamps legislation handed down by bureaucrats after pro forma debates. Instead, the immigration debate is dominated by unelected bureaucrats in the Ministries of Justice and Labor. The Ministry of Labor supports legal immigration in economic sectors facing labor shortages, but only at very restricted entry levels. Such positions tend to be supported by ministries involved with globalization (Foreign Affairs and International Trade and Industry) and by those involved with labor-scarce industries (Construction, Fisheries, and Transportation). In contrast, the Ministry of Justice regularly argues against expanding legal immigration on the grounds that it is harmful to Japanese workers and that immigrants are more likely to engage in criminal activities than are native Japanese. The ministry continues to push for additional employer sanctions against those who hire illegal immigrants. To date, the bureaucracy has been relatively unresponsive to pressure from employers and business owners, and because bureaucrats are not publicly accountable or elected, they have no incentive to respond. Further, the separate ministries compete for power rather than coordinating or cooperating, often resulting in policy incoherence.

As unemployment rates rose through the early 1990s, the demand for foreign workers diminished. Declining population growth, an increasingly aged population, rising economic growth, and mounting demand for skilled and unskilled labor suggest that, from early in the twenty-first century, Japan will need at least a half million new workers each year, clearly indicating a need for an expansion of legal immigration. Despite such expectations, significant public pressure for reform is lacking and a coherent or comprehensive national immigration policy framework has not been developed. However, recognition of the challenges presented by a declining workforce appears to be changing once-fixed views about immigration in the country. In 2008, for the first time, an eighty-strong group of economically liberal politicians in the Liberal Democratic Party (LDP), led by Hidenao Nakagawa, a former LDP secretary general, began promoting a dramatically different approach to immigration policy. This group called for the number of foreigners in Japan to rise to 10 million through 2050 and for many of these immigrants to become nationalized Japanese citizens. In addition, they supported entry for entire families, not just individual foreign workers. Small and medium-sized companies are increasingly calling for more immigrant workers, and *Keidanren*, a large manufacturers' association, has indicated its support for immigration policy reform designed to attract highly skilled workers. However, in the current political environment, the government seems unlikely to heed such calls and pursue comprehensive immigration reform.

Public opinion in Japan weighs heavily on immigration policy and pushes against substantial reform in the direction of greater openness, despite the pressures described above. There is a growing feeling in the country that foreigners, particularly those in the country illegally, are responsible for increasing crime rates and an overall decline in public security. In 2003, 92 percent of Japanese did not want more foreigners allowed into the country, fearing rising crime rates. Such feelings have been exacerbated by the media, which tend to be conservative and nationalistic in outlook and, as such, opposed to more open immigration policies. Both politicians and the media regularly assert the certainty of social instability should the number of foreigners rise. Most policymakers view the public's strong anti-immigration sentiments as a significant impediment to major reform. To the limited extent that we find human rights or immigrant advocacy groups in Japan, they exercise little influence. In the absence of public pressure for change or effective interest group activity, immigration issues are unlikely to be propelled on to the country's systemic agenda.

The absence of significant reforms to Japanese immigration policies in the early twenty-first century reflects the country's rejection of immigration as an aspect of Japanese social or economic life. This is not a country with a historical pattern of immigration. Reflecting this legacy, a strong commitment to excluding foreigners continues today, despite evidence that such foreign labor is already in high demand and will be even more necessary in the future. Further, there appears to be little interest in policies that allow immigrants to settle in Japan and become citizens. Finally, the absence of effective immigrant interest groups or political parties concerned with these issues also eliminates other sources of pressures for reform. Generally speaking, then, reform has failed to occur in Japan because no one with any capacity to influence the policy agenda is particularly interested in pursuing policy change.

Germany

Background: Policy Process and Policy History

German immigration policy is developed at the central level but is implemented and enforced at the state level. Multiple institutions at the federal, state, and local levels are responsible for immigration policy making and implementation. The federal Ministry of the Interior is most involved with immigration policy making, although the Ministry of Foreign Affairs has several subdepartments that also address immigration issues. Each of the sixteen German states (*Länder*) has an aliens authority charged with carrying out national immigration policies. Federal offices are responsible only for the initial reception of ethnic Germans (foreigners who share blood lines with Germans) and for deciding whether asylum seekers should be accepted as refugees. States decide, under federal guidelines, about family reunification, naturalization, and deportation. Little policy coordination occurs between individual states and the federal government, even though a working group that includes the federal interior minister and the interior ministers of each of the states has been created to coordinate policy enforcement. This distribution of authority means that immigration is governed by a variety of ad hoc rules and policies rather than a single overarching policy.

In the 1990s Germany received more immigrants than any other European country. Immigration, however, has not been part of Germany's national self-definition, and preventing further immigration continues to be the country's first principle of immigration policy making. Immigration policy reform trends echo the increased calls for immigration restrictions observed elsewhere. As a result, since the mid- to late 1990s, immigration has declined steadily. By 2006 the foreign-born population was 6.7 million, or 8 percent of the total population. This population consists primarily of immigrants from Turkey, Yugoslavia, Italy, and other European countries from which Germany used to recruit workers, as well as central and eastern Europe.

Germany was traditionally a country of emigration, although it had a small foreign worker population prior to World War II. Immediately after the war, until the early 1960s, the majority of immigrants to Germany were ethnic German refugees. However, reflecting postwar labor shortages, Germany's guest-worker population rose from 1 million to 2.6 million, or from 5 percent to 12 percent of the German workforce, by 1972. In the early years of guest-worker importation, immigrants were largely of European origin, but by 1972 Turkish workers formed the majority of the immigrant worker group.

Amid the economic downturn of the early 1970s, the German government in 1973 put a stop to the recruitment of foreign workers. Policies tripled the employer-paid recruitment fee and banned all further foreign recruitment.

This ban was highly ineffective in controlling immigration flows because of continued and increasing rates of family reunification. The 1990 Aliens Law had three objectives: to promote the return of foreigners to their home countries, to restrict further immigration, and to facilitate the integration of those who remained. The law made it more difficult for foreigners to obtain permanent residence rights and made a clear distinction between EU nationals and non-European citizens (the former did not need work permits to enter the country and had complete freedom of movement within the country). The 1990 law did not, however, establish standards or categories, or numerical targets, to control population inflows. After labor recruitment came to a stop, the primary form of legal immigration was family reunification and refugees. By early in the twenty-first century, Germany had yet to adopt comprehensive policies that attempted to restrict the number of persons eligible to enter (except for ethnic Germans) or that disallowed family reunification. Nor had it attempted to stem the tide of immigration by reducing push factors through development assistance. Until recently, the situation in Germany was unusual: the government announced that the country was closed to immigrants, but few official policies ensured that this was the case.

Among the industrialized countries, Germany has one area of population inflow that is unique: the return of ethnic Germans. In the 1980s and early 1990s these individuals claimed full rights to German citizenship. German citizens tend to view these returning Germans as foreigners who speak different languages, who observe different customs and traditions, and who have no real right to German residence. In reaction, a 1993 law was implemented that restricts the number of entering ethnic Germans, limits the cash payments they can receive on arrival, restricts their access to language training programs, and provides funds for development and cultural assistance to discourage their emigration to Germany. By 2006 the migration of persons of German origin from the successor countries of the former Soviet Union had dropped dramatically (to less than 8,000, compared to more than 35,000 in 2005 and between 100,000 and 230,000 in the 1990s).

Germany's 2005 Immigration Act reduced the number of legal residence permits from five to two (one with limited duration and one with unlimited; the duration varies according to the permit's purpose). Under the new law, entry depends on the immigrant's skill level: highly qualified persons are given the full right to work upon arrival, whereas unskilled and low-skilled workers are still banned. Admission to work is based on a priority check to ensure that positions cannot be filled by a German or EU national. Family reunification is still permitted, and those admitted in this way now have the same labor market access as the relative they are joining (they previously had to wait one year to work). Family migration reached its lowest point in more than a decade in 2006. Most analysts view the new law as falling short of what is needed to meet Germany's current and future labor and demographic challenges.

Asylum seekers and refugees are admitted to Germany under Article 16 of the Basic Law, which, in an explicit commitment to human rights, states that "persons persecuted on political grounds shall enjoy the right of asylum." Before 1993 the number of asylum applications was not restricted, and applicants were entitled to social welfare benefits and housing until decisions were made about their applications. Such liberal policies made Germany the primary destination for asylum seekers among all the industrialized countries. Between 1945 and 1993, Germany attracted half of all applications for asylum in Europe. The number of asylum seekers entering Germany began to increase significantly in the mid-1980s and peaked at 440,000 in 1992. In response, and after lengthy political debate, Germany reformed its asylum process in 1993, through an amendment to the Basic Law. The constitutional right to asylum was protected in the reform process. However, asylum applicants who arrive in Germany through safe countries are required to return to these countries and make their asylum claims there. Since 1992 the number of asylum seekers has fallen consistently: in 2006 asylum seeking continued to decline, to about 21,000, its lowest level since early 1980s.

Traditionally, illegal immigration was not as significant a problem in Germany as in other industrialized countries (reflecting the effective policing of its borders), but today it presents a growing policy challenge. The size of the country's illegal immigrant population has increased since 1993, particularly as rejected asylum applicants manage to remain in the country. The number of illegal immigrants has also risen because of criminal trafficking operations that smuggle people in and because some foreign workers remain in the country after their work permits expire. Germany has traditionally resisted regularization programs for illegal immigrants on the grounds that such programs would encourage further illegal immigration. However, a new policy was introduced in 2007, making it easier for some unauthorized immigrants to remain in the country. Foreigners whose deportations had been suspended and who had resided in Germany for many years were granted a right to stay "on a trial basis" for a period of two and a half years with the possibility of extension. These individuals have to be self-supporting; under the new policy, after four years they are given unlimited access to the labor market. Germany has yet to develop comprehensive policies in response to the illegal immigration problem, and the country has devoted insufficient resources to border control and internal enforcement. German political leaders have been unwilling to act more strongly to control illegal immigration due to opposition from employers and business leaders who are concerned that stringent controls will hurt the economy, as well as from pro-immigrant groups.

Contemporary Dynamics

Immigration policy has been one of the most politically significant areas of policy reform in Germany since the late 1990s. Although through the early years of the twenty-first century many German political leaders (especially conservative leaders) have continued to state that Germany was not, nor would it become, a country of immigration, in reality the country had a substantial permanent immigrant population, and immigration inflows continued to grow. A key challenge, therefore, was how to develop an immigration policy for the country that accurately reflected the problem at hand—namely, that further reduction in immigration inflows appeared unlikely because the country's large resident immigrant population makes family unification growth inevitable, economic and demographic changes make foreign labor a necessity, and Germany remains an attractive destination for immigrants.

By the end of the twentieth century, German political leaders were confronted with a public that believed widely that the government had lost control over immigration and that was clamoring for a more realistic and effective policy regime. At the same time, the country was faced with vast demographic and market challenges that could not be denied. The Social Democratic Party (SPD)–Green Party coalition elected in 1998 promised a new approach to immigration by first acknowledging that Germany was an immigration country. However, the new government held only a slim majority in the lower house of parliament and was initially fearful of pushing comprehensive immigration reform in the chamber. To build an immigration consensus, the Social Democratic minister of the interior, Otto Schily, created an independent commission chaired by a prominent leader of the opposition Christian Democratic Union (CDU) and including representatives of trade unions, employers' associations, churches, local governments, and all political parties. In its 2001 report the commission drew attention to the rapidly aging German population, the country's low birth rate, and the future labor market gap that would emerge as a result. To address these problems, it recommended the active recruitment of qualified immigrants based on a skills-based point system, the promotion of integration, and an overhaul of the country's asylum rules.

With its agenda thus set by the commission's report, the government in 2002 introduced Germany's first comprehensive immigration policy. In introducing the bill, SPD chancellor Gerhard Schröder said that Germany needed immigrants and a new law to regulate their entry and integration. Interior Minister Otto Schily said that the proposed new law would give Germany "the most modern immigration legislation in Europe. With this law, Germany shows itself to be an open country." The CDU-CSU (Christian Social Union) stridently opposed the legislation in both the Bundestag and Bundesrat, even though many of the party's members served on the 2001 commission. The opposition parties argued that Germany should not increase immigration at a time of high unemployment; that accepting more foreigners, a large proportion of whom could be expected to be unemployed, would add to the country's welfare costs; and that the law would entice more immigrants to enter Germany. The CDU also questioned German society's capacity to integrate more foreigners. However, most business, trade union, humanitarian, and church groups supported the law. A 2002 poll showed that 51 percent of Germans were in favor of the law, 30 percent against. Many of these key stakeholders were dissatisfied with some aspects of the legislation, but they viewed it as an important step toward a modern immigration policy. These groups supported the bill in hopes that it would pave the way for future reform more in line with their own preferences. After heated debates, the law passed in July 2002 by a vote of 320–225 in the Bundestag and 35–34 in the Bundesrat. The opposition parties immediately shot back, however, challenging the law in the German Constitutional Court on accusations of procedural voting errors in the Bundesrat. The court subsequently overturned the law, finding that the vote had been conducted improperly.

Immigration was a major issue in the 2002 parliamentary election campaign. The opposition CDU-CSU parties argued against liberalizing immigration and persistently held to the position that Germany was not a country of immigration. CDU leader Edmund Stoiber asserted that "Germany cannot handle any more immigrants . . . where there are more than four million jobless, then it is irresponsible to open up the job market to everyone." A CSU minister accused the SPD government of compromising Germany's economic future with its immigration policy, as well as threatening Germany's national identity by engineering a multicultural society. The Social Democrats and Greens responded that their opponents were desperate and would use any issue to "find a topic with which one can arouse emotions."

In fall 2002 the narrowly reelected SPD-Green government reintroduced its 2002 immigration legislation unchanged in the parliament. The CDU characterized this as a "provocation"—saying that the new bill would never get a majority in the upper house, where, following the elections, partisan control had shifted to the CDU-CSU. CDU leader Edmund Stoiber stated flatly that the CDU wanted a law that would restrict immigration, not increase it. As fears of terrorism increased citizens' concerns and as the country's unemployment rates continued to rise, the CDU's strong opposition to any proactive migration policy began to garner widespread public support. The bill passed in the lower house in May 2003 but was voted down in the upper chamber, where the opposition parties controlled the majority. The legislation thus entered into a protracted period of legislative gridlock, as a parliamentary conciliation committee tried to reach a difficult compromise behind closed doors. It took direct talks between the chancellor, the minister of the interior, and opposition leaders to engineer a compromise. The resulting law, passed in June 2004, was diminished significantly relative to the law passed in 2002. Its central measure, the skills-based point system for labor migrants, was lost during the bargaining process, and, as such, the recruitment ban on labor immigration by and large remained intact. Ultimately, a drawn-out, highly politicized and polarized decision-making process resulted in a law that did not introduce a dramatically new framework for immigration policy.

Implementation of the country's new immigration policy proceeded smoothly regarding the legislation's primary goals. Although many German political leaders (especially conservative leaders) continue to state that Germany is not, nor will it become, a country of immigration, the country has a substantial permanent immigrant population, and immigration inflows continue. A remaining key challenge, therefore, is how to develop an immigration policy for the country that accurately reflects the problem at hand. Further reduction in immigration inflows appears unlikely, primarily because the country's large resident immigrant population makes family unification growth inevitable, the demand for skilled and unskilled labor is rising, and Germany remains an attractive destination for immigrants. In 2009, the CDU-led governing coalition had no plans for a new immigration law and continued to support a zero-immigration policy, whereas its then-coalition partner, the SPD, wanted a new immigration law along the lines of the legislation originally introduced in 2002.

The most recent reform to Germany's long-standing restrictive immigration policies can be explained in large part by cultural factors. The German population's response to a continuing inflow of foreigners continues to be conditioned by a widespread and deep-seated belief that Germany is not (and never should be) a country of immigration. As the country experienced ever-increasing population inflows and in particular as national security concerns increased, public opinion strongly opposed changes in the direction of liberalizing the country's immigration policy regime. Although the bill enjoyed the support of business and immigrant rights' groups, their ability to influence the decision-making process was ultimately overridden by changing public opinion on the issue. Political and institutional factors also played a role in the decision-making process: in particular, the nature of Germany's federal political system was instrumental in assisting the opposition parties in blocking the second version of the government's policy. When the opposition CDU took control of the upper house of the parliament in 2002, it gained significant influence over the policy-making process. During the 2002 election campaign, the CDU had successfully politicized immigration at the state level. With public opinion shifting in its favor by 2004, the opposition was able to gain the upper hand in negotiations with the government over policy content, producing a very different immigration law than the government intended. The CDU did not have this sort of political leverage in 2002 when the law first passed. At that time the SPD government controlled both houses of parliament and public opinion was disposed toward a more open policy. As national security and immigration became connected more closely in the public's minds, a more restrictive immigration policy regime was able to gain ground.

France

Background: Policy Process and Policy History

As in Germany, immigration policies in France are developed at the central level of government. At the cabinet level, the Ministry of the Interior traditionally was charged with immigration control and overseeing policing and border control. The Ministry of Foreign Affairs was responsible for refugee and asylum policy. Illegal immigration issues were previously monitored by the Central Agency for the Control of Immigration and the Struggle Against the Employment of Illegal Immigrants. In 2007 newly elected president Nicolas Sarkozy created a new central agency, the Ministry of Immigration, Integration, National Identity and Co-Development. The new ministry is charged with better managing immigration, combating irregular immigration, fostering integration, maintaining national identity and citizenship, and promoting development in immigrant-sending countries. Both the French Council of State and the Constitutional Council play important roles in immigration policy making, with the latter demonstrating a willingness to reject strict immigration and asylum policies on constitutional grounds. The Office of International Migration deals with the problems of immigrants who are already residing in the country. Immigration policies in France are implemented at lower levels within the government.

Among European countries, France has the longest history as a country of immigration; however, immigration is not part of the country's nation-building experience as it was in the United States. Rather, immigrants have entered France in large numbers since the mid-1800s in response to industrialization, lower French population growth, and a republican tradition that involves a respect for human rights and civil liberties and that prescribes a more open and inclusive idea of citizenship. By the early 1930s, 6.6 percent of the French population was foreign. Although this figure dropped during World War II and the early postwar years, by the 1950s immigration was again on the rise in response to labor shortages.

Despite its immigration legacy, the French population generally is reluctant to recognize immigration as either an economic or a demographic necessity or benefit, with the result being an increasing emphasis on immigration control. As the twenty-first century began, worsening economic conditions, high unemployment, public anxiety about the rapidly increasing number of Muslim immigrants to the country (around 5 million by 2003, for the largest concentration in Western Europe), and the threat of terrorism compelled the French government to take an increasingly negative policy stance. Although immigration into France slowed in the 1990s, the country's borders have remained relatively open, particularly when compared with its European neighbors. The 1999 census reported the foreign population at 4.3 million (only a 3.5 percent increase from 1990), and by 2005 foreigners constituted 4.9 percent of the country's total population. Over 40 percent of the foreign population in France is from Algeria, Morocco, or Tunisia, and a large Turkish population is present.

The French government maintained an open immigration policy from the early 1900s through the early 1970s. Labor shortages, as well as a falling birthrate, created continuing support for liberal immigration policies. Beginning in the 1950s and continuing to the early 1980s, the French set specific targets and imported foreign labor as guest workers who arrived in France on a temporary basis. These immigrants supplied France with the labor needed to keep its economy growing. In the early years of these programs, immigrants were mostly European in origin. By the 1960s immigration from North Africa (especially Algeria) became more widespread. The changing nature of the immigrant population, in combination with the economic recession that followed the 1973 oil crisis, made the open immigration policy more controversial. Immigrants quickly became scapegoats for rising unemployment. In response, the government declared an official end to worker recruitment abroad and announced a goal of zero immigration in 1974. However, France's agreements with its former colonies remained in place, and its borders remained porous to these immigrants.

The government's attempts to restrict immigration further in the 1980s and 1990s were largely unsuccessful. French law continues to allow legal immigration on a small scale for family reunification or based on labor needs for temporary, seasonal, or permanent skilled workers. Few permanent work permits are issued to foreigners who do not already have temporary residence or refugee status. Family reunification presently accounts for nearly two-thirds of the total permanent immigration into the country, and labor immigration accounted for 12 percent of all entries in 2005. The French government overhauled the country's immigration system in 2006. The new immigration law, which took effect in early 2007, and follow-on legislation implemented later that year, emphasizes labor-based immigration over family reunification. The laws give the government new powers to encourage highly skilled labor migration in areas of recruitment difficulty. New restrictions on family reunification are designed to ensure that immigrants respect French values, to promote integration, and to fight forced and polygamous marriages.

After World War II, and through the 1970s, France had a liberal asylum and refugee policy, reflecting traditional support for civil and human rights and a desire to compensate for the discriminatory policies of the Vichy regime during the German occupation. Until 1960 an average of 15,000 asylum applications were received each year, and virtually all applications were accepted. The number of asylum seekers rose steadily from the mid-1970s to 1990, and their ethnic composition changed, with Europeans replaced by immigrants from developing countries. The government began to restrict significantly asylum claims in the late 1980s, resulting in reduced asylum seeker inflows in the 1990s. Asylum claims numbered 17,408 in 1996, but rose to 50,050 in 2005 as other countries significantly increased their restrictions on asylum seekers and as the French relaxed some of their controls. Although French asylum policy now relies heavily on the principle of manifestly unfounded claims, asylum applicants are denied entry unless they provide absolute proof of political persecution. Policy reforms in 2004 extended the scope of conventional asylum and added a new category of subsidiary protection. The 2007 immigration law placed new restrictions on the rights of asylum seekers already in the country. The net result of these changes has been a decrease in the number of foreigners granted asylum in France since 2005.

Illegal immigration in France emerged in 1974 with the government's efforts to stop legal immigration. In addition, a considerable number of foreigners in temporary worker programs chose to remain in the country illegally when their work permits expired. Current estimates of the illegal immigrant population in France are around 200,000 to 400,000 in 2006. In response to rising numbers of illegal immigrants in the 1970s, France enacted a generous amnesty policy for illegal immigrants in the early 1980s. Those who entered France prior to 1981 were eligible for temporary residence permits that allowed them to enter the application process for legal status. In 1995 the government introduced another regularization program that allowed some illegal foreigners to obtain temporary residence permits. This program was pursued again in 1997 and 1998, during which time over 200,000 immigrants were legalized. Legalizations, however, have not eliminated the problem of illegal immigration. Recent immigration laws put in place strong measures against illegal immigration and set annual targets of 25,000 deportations of unauthorized foreigners per year.

Contemporary Dynamics

French immigration policy since the 1990s has alternated between increasingly restrictive measures and public pressure to weaken those restrictions once their impact was recognized. Persistent unemployment problems, weak economic growth, rising global immigration pressures, and strident right-wing opposition have compelled political leaders to enact stronger controls. At the same time, many on the left remain committed to France's republican values, which makes stricter policies difficult to implement. While immigration issues in France have been highly politicized for a long time, today the political debate has intensified as the public has become increasingly focused on questions of national identity and integration and as public anxiety has risen in the face of growing numbers of Muslim immigrants and national security concerns.

Agenda setting on immigration issues in France also is influenced by the success of the anti-immigration, extreme right-wing party Front National (FN) in French electoral politics. The electoral breakthrough of the FN in the 1980s and 1990s changed the face of French immigration politics. The party's leader, Jean-Marie Le Pen, is strongly opposed to further immigration and a permanent foreign population, which compels competing parties across the political spectrum to exploit France's underlying xenophobia. The FN's success has created a sense that immigration is one of the country's most pressing issues, with public opinion polls indicating that most French citizens blame immigrants for France's economic and cultural decline and think immigration should stop. An April 2006 poll found 53 percent of the population agreeing with the statement that France has too many immigrants. As the FN has gained power and acceptance among the electorate, French political leaders, particularly on the right, have sought to redefine and reassert themselves on immigration issues out of fear of losing their traditional bases of support to the FN. In 2002 Le Pen placed second in voting for president, furthering this tendency. This mobilization by forces on the extreme right has fed the political debate on immigration, pushing the mainstream center-right parties to address the immigration issue or risk losing votes to the FN.

Reflecting this increased politicization of immigration issues, policy formulation debates played themselves out in recent years both in the National Assembly and on the streets of France. Riots between black and Arab youth and the police in the Paris suburbs in fall 2005 were interpreted widely as evidence of the lack of integration of immigrants and their children, many of whom are French by birth, and renewed an intense debate about what to do about integration, as well as immigration. The unsettled environment created by the riots, coupled with the approach of the 2007 presidential elections and increasingly negative public opinion on immigration issues, set the stage for the most recent rounds of immigration policy reform.

In early 2006 then–interior minister and presidential hopeful Nicolas Sarkozy introduced a new immigration bill in the French parliament. In presenting the legislation, Sarkozy said: "the violence which exploded in our suburbs is not unconnected with the shocking failure of our policies of integration and immigration." He asserted that the proposed immigration law finally would allow the government to control immigration. In Sarkozy's words, the bill would allow France to have "chosen immigration"—with the country choosing, rather than having to "undergo," the process of immigration for the first time. The bill included a selective system for labor immigration, placed limits on family reunification, and eliminated the ability of unauthorized foreigners living in the country for at least ten years to gain legal residence. To justify its more restrictive approach, the government argued that more controlled migration would lead to better integration of migrants.

Although most policymakers agreed that France's immigration system was failing, the legislation elicited a strong, hostile reaction from left-wing opposition parties, human rights groups, the Catholic Church, and even some African countries. The opposition center-left parties strongly criticized the proposed law in the National Assembly debate. One Socialist Party member of parliament described the selection system in the bill as "organized pillaging of brains" from developing countries, intended to attract the most talented people from countries where their talents were badly needed. Human rights groups called the law racist and said it would be a "black stain" on the country: "The proposed bill is a blatant violation of immigrants' rights and is based on a selective racist approach," said eight groups led by the French League for Human Rights. The antiracism organization SOS Racisme was completely opposed to the bill, saying, "We think that it tries to kill every liberty and every right of the French immigrants . . . it is very dangerous for the country." Reflecting the intense opposition to the bill, large-scale demonstrations were carried out in spring 2006 in defense of immigrant rights. The marches were organized by over 600 immigrants' rights groups and many left-wing parties, including the Socialists, Greens, and Communists.

Despite such popular outcry, the legislation passed in the National Assembly 367–164 in May 2006, reflecting the strong legislative majority commanded by Sarkozy's party; the bill similarly passed in the Senate in July 2006. After the bill's final passage, Sarkozy argued that "selective immigration . . . is the expression of France's sovereignty. It is the right of our country, like all of the great democracies of the world, to choose which foreigners it allows to reside in our territory." The law's critics continued to insist that it was unacceptably damaging to French immigrants, would potentially split up families, and was sure to damage France's reputation of accepting foreigners, especially asylum seekers and refugees.

While the law did not come into force until early 2007, its effects were felt immediately upon its passage: deportations of those without legal papers reached nearly 13,000 by end of July 2006; this was over halfway to the government's goal for that year of 25,000. This stepped-up rate of deportation even before implementation of the law incited further protests by thousands of French citizens. Such unrest suggested that the country's transition to a more selective immigration system will not be an easy one. By July 2006 thousands of citizens also had signed petitions supporting the sheltering of children to prevent their deportation, and the government was forced to pull back on its timeframe for implementing its plans.

Immigration issues promise to remain prominent on the French political agenda in the coming years, particularly as high unemployment rates and worldwide immigration pressures persist, as the public continues to associate unemployment and national security with immigrants, and as the extreme right continues to agitate popular opinion. Although France will continue to admit immigrants, inflows are likely to fall, leaving the question of what to do about illegal immigration as the most likely reform issue for the future.

The reform pattern just described resulted from the interaction of various factors. Culturally, the introduction of stricter controls reflected strong sentiment in some quarters favoring further limits on immigrants' ability to enter the country. When these sentiments were echoed and reinforced by the influential extreme right-wing party FN, and when violent unrest broke out in areas of immigrant settlement, the French government responded by placing stricter controls on the institutional agenda. Despite strident opposition from left-wing parties, employers, and immigrant advocacy groups about the nature of the reform, majority control of the parliament by the center-right allowed relatively easy passage of a fairly extreme law. Typically at the implementation stage, the tendency of French citizens is to voice their policy outrage in the streets, with the government then reversing its policy course. President Sarkozy, however, has demonstrated a distinct willingness to go against this traditional pattern of backing-down by the government; and while immigrant advocacy groups continue to reject key aspects of the 2006 and 2007 laws, they have not been successful in forcing reform in the direction of greater openness. Their discontent, however, suggests the continuing influence of rights-based liberalism on many citizens' attitudes about immigration policy. Many of those who protested the 2006 and 2007 reforms view them as violating fundamental human and civil rights principles. Although they were unsuccessful in blocking the introduction of stricter control policies, public outcry for a more open, less restrictive approach may continue as the effects of these policies are fully realized.

United Kingdom

Background: Policy Process and Policy History

The immigration policy-making process in the United Kingdom is centralized to a greater degree than in the other five countries examined in this book. Traditionally, decisions in this policy area are made at the cabinet level, primarily through the prime minister's office, with little opportunity for influence from other interested parties. Although the House of Commons is often the site of heated debates over changes to immigration policies, it has not played an appreciable role in either policy formulation or amendment. The government dramatically changed its approach to immigration in 2008 with the creation of a Borders and Immigration Agency (BIA). The government's objective in creating BIA was to clarify lines of accountability regarding immigration policy implementation and to establish clear lines of responsibility. The agency will play a central role in immigration policy development and implementation. Local governments are charged with implementing some aspects of immigration law, but they have no ability to interpret policies. To date, the judiciary has not played a role in immigration policy.

Among the six countries we examine, the United Kingdom historically has been considered to be a model of successful immigration control. This reputation reflects a marked ability on the part of the British government to prevent unwanted immigration through effective policy instruments. Until the end of World War II, the British government dealt with emigration rather than immigration. Employment-based immigration in the postwar period, primarily from former British colonies, reversed this pattern, and questions of immigration control became politically significant. By 2005 the foreign-born population in the United Kingdom was nearly 4.8 million, or 8.6 percent of the total population.

Immediately after World War II, citizenship policy for residents of former British colonies was extremely liberal, reflecting a continuing sense among the British that they had a special relationship with their former satellites. Citizens of former colonies retained full British citizenship, including the right to enter the United Kingdom without restriction. Postwar economic conditions both in the colonies and in the United Kingdom served as powerful push and pull factors for these so-called New Commonwealth citizens. The flow of these citizens was substantial in the 1950s and 1960s (peaking at over 90,000 in 1962) and declined steadily during the 1970s and 1980s (to a low of 46,000 in 1987).

The British public did not, however, welcome the racially and ethnically distinct migrants from the New Commonwealth, believing they would not be easily assimilated. Thus strict controls have always been justified by political leaders as being essential for good race relations in the country. Traditionally, British policymakers of all political stripes championed policies of strict control and reaped political benefits in terms of the vote. Beginning in the 1960s a succession of increasingly stricter immigration control policies was adopted, resulting in the effective end to new immigration from former colonies in 1981 and to family reunification in 1988. Family reunification is now permitted only for persons who can prove that they have guaranteed housing and financial support in the country.

Continuing to reflect public opinion, Prime Minister Margaret Thatcher's government (in power from 1979 to 1990) emphasized strict controls on entry, employing visa requirements for New Commonwealth countries, genetic fingerprinting to establish family ties, and carrier sanctions for transporting undocumented foreigners. In the 1990s immigrants entering the United Kingdom (around 50,000 annually from the late 1980s to the mid-1990s) generally were spouses or dependents of legal residents. In this period, a small percentage of immigrants entered as highly skilled workers, professionals and managers, or refugees. Immigration to the United Kingdom rose dramatically beginning in the mid-1990s (exceeding 100,000 annually): sustained economic growth, historically low unemployment rates, and increasing asylum applications and family reunification combined to produce historically high immigration levels.

When the Labour government came to power in 1997, its initial approach to immigration policy was to relax the previous government's labor-based immigration controls, in recognition of the robust economy's rising labor demands, a rapidly aging population, and increasing global competition for skilled workers. An increase in the number of employment-related permits reversed the pattern of increasingly restrictive immigration policies since

1962. These policy changes have resulted in a 62 percent rise in labor migrants since 1999. In 2002 around 130,000 work permits were issued—more than 87 percent of these were for highly skilled occupations via quotas set by the Highly Skilled Workers Scheme. In 2003 the Seasonal Agricultural Workers Scheme and the Sector Based Scheme allowed into the country temporary low-skilled workers in agricultural services, hospitality, and food services. Britain remains a labor migration country today, with some 30–40 percent of permanent immigrants arriving for work-related reasons.

The Labour government's rhetoric and policy inclinations toward greater openness were reversed with the July 2005 terrorist attacks in London, which were perpetrated by British citizens of immigrant stock. Once this became apparent, the political climate surrounding immigration changed markedly as popular calls for reversing immigration trends became more strident. In response, a five-year immigration plan was announced by the government in late 2005 that proposed revising and consolidating the country's newly more expansive labor migration schemes. The plan was billed by the government as the most significant change in immigration policy in fifty years. The centerpiece of this reform is a points-based immigration system under which potential non-EU immigrants will be channeled through one of five "tiers." The new system is intended to simplify the country's immigration regime by replacing more than eighty different ways to enter Britain for work with five tiers, as well as to ensure that the country receives only the workers it needs. The top tier allows for independent highly skilled professionals; the second for employer-sponsored skilled workers; the third for temporary low-skilled workers; the fourth for students; and the fifth for trainees and short-term specialist workers. A phased-in implementation of the plan began in 2008.

Unlike the other EU member states discussed in this book, the United Kingdom did not restrict immigration from the ten new EU member states after 2004. The government saw labor migration from these countries as a way to respond to its own pressing labor shortages. Workers from these countries were required to register soon after obtaining employment in the United Kingdom. Between May and December 2004 alone, the country received some 133,000 applications under the Worker Registration Scheme for workers from new EU member states. A majority of these immigrants were low-skilled workers. These flows remained substantial in subsequent years, with 218,000 registered entrants between June 2006 and June 2007. Strong and steady inflows of these so-called A8 citizens led the United Kingdom to impose a transitional period on Romanian and Bulgarian citizens following their entry to the EU on January 1, 2007.

The United Kingdom did not face the same sort of crisis in the 1990s as its European counterparts did with respect to asylum seekers and refugees. Although the United Kingdom also experienced a rise in asylum applications in this period, the rise was tempered by the country's island geography, close scrutiny of asylum applications, and specific policies aimed at keeping the number of asylum seekers and refugees in check. In the 1980s the United Kingdom received fewer than 5,000 asylum applications per year. These numbers increased significantly beginning in 1989 to peak at around 45,000 in 1991 and ranged from 22,000 to 44,000 between 1992 and 1995. However, in the period 2000–2002 the country had the highest number of asylum seekers of any EU country, with a dramatic rise in applications between 1996 (29,640) and 2002 (84,130).

The British government responded to these increases with a strategy of preentry and postentry controls. Because most asylum seekers enter the United Kingdom through another country (given the country's island status), the British government makes full use of the safe country concept, returning asylum seekers to the countries where they first landed. Further, the government levies stiff fines against airlines for carrying passengers who lack proper documentation and has also instituted a strict set of visa requirements as an important instrument of control. The 1999 Immigration and Asylum Act further streamlined the government's approach to immigration and asylum with the intention of preventing abuse of the system and eliminating a massive backlog in applications. The act established the National Asylum Support Service (NASS), which provides assistance to asylum seekers and settles them in accommodation centers dispersed across the country. Under this dispersal system, asylum seekers have no choice as to where they are accommodated unless they are able to support themselves (through family or friends). NASS also was intended to provide better monitoring of asylum seekers while they awaited decisions and to limit the amount of government support they received while waiting. Subsequent laws in 2002 (the Nationality, Immigration and Asylum Act) and 2004 (the Asylum and Immigration Act) were further intended to curb the number of asylum applications, speed up their processing, and achieve more effective removals of failed asylum seekers. The 2002 law also limited the right of asylum applicants to work or receive vocational training until they received a positive decision. The 2004 law created a new criminal offense for asylum seekers and illegal immigrants arriving in the United Kingdom without documents and no reasonable excuse for failing to have their papers; this resulted in a 50 percent decline in the number of undocumented asylum seekers in 2004. The 2004 law also simplified the asylum appeals system to reduce delays. Additional nonlegislative reforms included the introduction of a target to decide at least 80 percent of claims within two months and restrictions on access to free legal aid for asylum seekers. The cumulative result of these new policies has been that applications have fallen since 2003, to 33,930 in 2004. Acceptance rates also have declined: in 1999, 19 percent were decided positively, with 6 percent granted full refugee status. By 2004 these rates had dropped to 11 percent receiving a positive decision and only 3 percent being granted refugee status. Asylum applications continued to drop in 2005 and 2006.

Because of a very effective and well-established policy of border control and strict monitoring of foreigners in the country, the United Kingdom historically has not had a significant problem with illegal immigration. By 1995, however, concern about the weakening of internal border controls in the EU prompted the government to introduce new proposals to ward off the problem of illegal immigration. Such measures included the government's requiring employers to check the immigration status of prospective employees and denying social welfare benefits to suspected illegal immigrants. Nevertheless, illegal immigration in the United Kingdom is increasing steadily, especially as asylum restrictions increase. Like other EU countries, the United Kingdom is increasingly a destination for people trafficking, people smuggling, and forced labor. Unofficial government estimates in 2005 counted the number of undocumented migrants at around 500,000. The public and the media have become increasingly hostile to what is widely perceived as an illegal immigration crisis. Largely as a result of focused media attention on the arrival of illegal immigrants via the Eurotunnel, the popular impression is that the United Kingdom's borders are insecure. In response, the government has imposed stiff fines for carrying undocumented migrants, similar to carrier sanctions, especially on freight carriers across the English Channel. At the same time, continued poor enforcement of employers' sanctions allows a high number of undocumented workers to remain in the country. Post-2005 security concerns about illegal immigrants led the government to announce its intention to introduce a compulsory identity card system for all U.K. residents.

Contemporary Dynamics

Since 1997 Britain has gone from being a nation of low immigration to one with rising numbers of foreign workers and asylum seekers. From early in its tenure in office, the Blair government pursued a rapid pace of immigration policy reform in the direction of a more liberal policy regime. In response to a shortage of skilled and unskilled workers, the government dismantled many long-standing barriers to labor migration, adopting in particular a more liberal approach to the admission of skilled immigrants. Until recently, the Labour government's policy was, on the one hand, to encourage legal migration to the United Kingdom and the integration of resident foreigners while, on the other, cutting the numbers of illegal immigrants and asylum seekers.

The political debate on immigration in the United Kingdom in recent years has been driven by mounting public skepticism about a rising number of immigrants and, since 2005 in particular, the security of the country's borders. Although the heightened tenor of the immigration debate predated the July 2005 London bombings, public concern continued to intensify in their aftermath. This was evident in the central role immigration played in the 2005 general election: over a quarter of likely voters identified immigration as a major issue, whereas in 2001 only 14 percent listed immigration as their top priority. Opinion polls in early 2005 found that 78 percent of Britons thought the government's policies on immigration were "not tough enough." Seeking to capitalize on such feelings, Conservative Party leader Michael Howard argued that Britain had lost control over immigration; the party's campaign motto was "it's not racist to impose limits on immigration." Then–prime minister Tony Blair agreed, saying that "concern over asylum and immigration is not about racism. It is about fairness," and he promised to introduce after the election "strict controls that work." Howard declared that at the election voters would be faced with a choice between "unlimited immigration under Mr. Blair or limited, controlled immigration under the Conservatives." Although the Labour Party was returned to power, the government could not disregard the public's fears about possible connections among national security, international terrorism, and immigration. As a result, the government has pursued a notably stricter immigration policy agenda since 2005.

The most recent phase of immigration policy reform in the United Kingdom began in early 2005 as part of Labour's preelection campaign with the introduction of the government's five-year strategy for asylum and immigration. After the Labour government was returned to power, many of the strategy's proposals were put forward in a new Immigration, Asylum and Nationality Bill, which was signed into law in 2006. The bill returned the country to the more restrictive approach to immigration that had been the country's trademark prior to 1997. A subsequent immigration bill, put before Parliament in January 2007 (the UK Borders Bill), was the third piece of primary legislation in as many years and was introduced even before parts of previous acts had been brought into force. This bill also adopts a more restrictive approach to all forms of immigration. The single-party majority parliamentary system in the United Kingdom made the decision-making phase of these reforms straightforward: the government introduced its bills, and they were agreed to by the members of the majority party.

Unlike in several other countries considered in this book, increasing levels of public concern about immigration policy in the United Kingdom have not stimulated mass political participation. In the main, the country's immigration debate is confined to the media and the main parties in Parliament. Although there are two specifically anti-immigrant parties in the country—the UK Independence Party (which opposes immigration and European integration) and the British National Party (which opposes immigration and the idea of a multiethnic population)—neither party enjoys nationwide support, which, combined with the country's plurality electoral system, has rendered them electorally insignificant. Further, although a wide range of civil and human rights groups strongly opposed the government's post-2005 immigration strategies, they have been relatively ineffective in influencing the policy reform process.

The current state of immigration policy reform in the United Kingdom can be explained by the fact that the British population and its political parties have returned to a strong commitment to restrictionist policies. Today, immigration policy in the United Kingdom is not driven by those who benefit from continued immigration, such as employers or ethnic groups—rather, it reflects the wishes of an overwhelmingly hostile public, with both political parties representing these views. The ability of the majority party to enact its policies as formulated—because of strong party government—means that this coincidence between public opinion and partisan views is fully represented in the country's immigration policies. The Labour Party that came to power in 1997 originally embarked on a policy course designed to encourage needed labor immigration. However, rapidly rising immigration rates, as well as genuine fears about national security in the aftermath of the 2005 London bombings, resulted in a dramatic shift in the country's immigration policies, recalling earlier British governments' limitations on all forms of population inflows.

Italy

Background: Policy Process and Policy History

Italian immigration policy is developed primarily by the central government through the Ministry of the Interior (which oversees the local police, who issue residence permits, and the prefectures, who oversee regularization of immigration flows). The Ministry of Labor and Social Policy also plays a role in regulating issues concerning the labor market. Within the Labor Ministry, the Non-EU Immigrants' Service is responsible for determining annual immigration quotas and monitoring regularization programs and bilateral agreements. The successful implementation of immigration control policies in Italy is impeded by a fragmentation of authority on immigration matters and a lack of coordination between government agencies. Policies made at the central level tend to be constructed loosely, and when implemented at lower levels of government these policies are often misinterpreted. A pressing need exists for stronger monitoring from the center as well as for increases in resources allocated to authorities charged with maintaining border controls. The overarching political crisis of the early 1990s reduced the likelihood that a systematic and comprehensive immigration policy would be implemented.

Italy has traditionally been a country of emigration, not immigration. Between 1946 and 1975, over seven million Italians departed from their homeland, primarily in search of economic opportunities. Thus Italians constituted a large proportion of many of the guest-worker populations of other European countries. By the late 1970s immigrants began to outnumber emigrants in Italy for the first time, and by the early 1980s the emigration trend had been reversed and Italy had become an immigrant destination. The delay in immigration to Italy partly reflected the belief that greater opportunities existed elsewhere. Also, the existence of a relatively large supply of low-skilled labor prevented the pull factor of labor shortages experienced elsewhere. Not surprisingly, the increase in immigration to Italy occurred at the same time that Italy's European neighbors were closing their doors to economic immigration. These new population inflows included returning guest workers who had sought opportunities in other European countries as well as new immigrants from Africa, Latin America, and Asia.

The precise number of immigrants in Italy today is difficult to estimate because of poor accounting procedures. The 2001 reported estimate of the foreign-born population was 1.4 million legal foreigners (2.7 percent of the total population). The majority of legal immigration to Italy is in the form of family reunification, accounting for more than 60 percent of long-term visas in 2004, representing a 23 percent increase over 2003. Permanent immigration to Italy continues to be significant and largely employment based.

Before 1986 Italian immigration policy was neither well defined nor adequately implemented. Immigration was controlled primarily through a series of ministerial directives that lacked a unifying vision of Italy's immigration future. In 1986 the Italian government introduced the country's first comprehensive immigration legislation, the Foreign Workers and the Control of Illegal Immigration Law, which attempted to regulate labor inflows (by tying immigration controls to the country's labor needs) and launched the country's first major regularization program. The law, however, was criticized as being too vague and excessively bureaucratic and for being so restrictive that it created an incentive for illegal immigration.

In response, the 1990 Martelli law established categories of foreign workers to be admitted on an annual basis and identified which countries' citizens would need visas to enter. This law was designed to bring Italy's immigration policies into line with those of other EU member states, particularly by focusing on more restrictive external controls. Legal immigration to Italy is currently restricted to those who have arranged employment or who are joining their families.

In response to criticism from other EU member states about Italy's lax immigration control approach, as well as to a more general sense that the 1986 and 1990 laws were ineffective and weak, a new comprehensive immigration control act regulating the entry and residence of foreigners was adopted in early 1998. Law 40/1998 (the so-called Turco-Napolitano law or Testo Unico act) focuses on immigration control and labor market regulation. Bureaucratically the law was designed for more effective implementation at both the national and regional levels of government, as well as for cooperation with employers and employees' organizations in regulating labor inflows. The law established, for the first time, the use of quotas for foreign workers, family reunification (while guaranteeing a right to such unification), and temporary asylum for humanitarian reasons. Entry to Italy was allowed within the national quotas and with an employment offer, or with sponsorship by a legal Italian resident.

The law was revised in 2002. Law 189/2002 (known as the Bossi-Fini law) imposed further restrictions on entry and tightened the conditions for stay. The new law continued the use of a quota system for employment-based residence permits. It also introduced needs tests for foreign workers, requiring employers to publish job openings for twenty days before the employment office would authorize the entry of a non-EU worker. Immigration quotas are in theory set annually, but the process is beset by delays and backlogs, and quota numbers have always fallen short of demand. The legal entry quota for work was set at 58,000 in 1998 and 1999, increasing to 83,000 in 2000, and 79,500 annually in 2002–2004 (with 50,000 of these for seasonal workers only). These quotas were raised in 2006 to 171,000, twice the 2005 limit. There are no quotas for family reunification. Italy completely opened its labor market to citizens of the EU countries that joined in 2004. During 2007 the legally resident Romanian population was estimated to have risen by about 50 percent, to more than 500,000, replacing Albania as the most important origin country. Following several publicized crimes, a decree was issued in late 2007 facilitating deportation of EU citizens who break laws.

The 1948 Italian constitution recognizes the right of asylum and the need for Italy to conduct itself within the requirements of international law. More specifically, the constitution provides that "any foreigner who in his own country is denied democratic rights guaranteed by the Italian constitution has the right of asylum in Italy." In addition, Italy had ratified the Geneva Convention. The 1990 Martelli law eliminated geographic limits on asylum seekers and extended these rights to all nationalities. Despite this relatively open policy, Italy has received few asylum claims historically (fewer than 2,000 asylum requests were received in 1993, and only 675 were received in 1996). The number of asylum requests rose to over 33,000 in 1999, but then dropped to 16,000 by 2002 and to 10,348 by 2006 (although this number represents an increase over 2004 and 2005). Italy does not have a framework asylum law—asylum is regulated by Article 1 of Law 39/1990 and a few articles of the 2002 law. In 2005 Italy engaged in the most significant reform of its asylum system to date: the asylum seeker review process was accelerated, and the country implemented the EU directive on minimum standards for asylum seekers. The country's new decentralized asylum application system significantly increased processing efficiency.

The Italian economic system is distinguished from many other industrialized countries through the existence of a large and flourishing underground (informal or black market) economy. This underground economy accounts for 25–30 percent of Italian economic activity. For immigrants, this has meant disproportionate illegal employment opportunities in small- and medium-scale manufacturing and the service sector. For the government, this has meant that policies dealing with illegal immigrants differ from those of other countries not so much in their content (in that they involve attempts at regularization and the use of employer sanctions) but rather in their effectiveness.

Italy's location in the center of the Mediterranean, with its extensive coastline and importance as a tourist destination, makes it a relatively accessible country for Europe-bound immigrants. The existence of a considerable informal economy, the rapid growth of the domestic and personal services sector, and the predominance of small businesses all provide ample work for illegal immigrants. As a result, Italy has experienced continued robust growth in the number of illegal immigrants. Further, because the setting of labor immigration quotas has been so out of step with demand, many workers arrive undocumented and work unregistered in the hopes that they will be able to convert their status during a regularization.

Italy's first attempts at addressing illegal immigration, in 1986, involved employer sanctions and the introduction of a regularization program, both of which were largely unsuccessful. A second and more effective version of these programs was introduced with the 1990 Martelli law. This law was followed in 1992 by the Boniver Decree, which outlined new rules for the expulsion of undocumented immigrants, including asylum seekers and refugees. It permitted the police to transport foreigners who lacked visas or stay permits to the border for immediate expulsion without a court hearing. Finally, a decree issued in 1995 instituted a four-month regularization program for as many as 300,000 illegal immigrants who had been employed for at least four of the preceding twelve months, with a special provision for seasonal agricultural workers. The 1998 immigration law confronted illegal immigration via bilateral agreements and new criminal penalties. The Italian government returned to the regularization approach again in 1998 and 1999 in a continuing effort to draw illegal immigrants out of the underground economy. In 1999 some 300,000 unauthorized foreigners applied for legalization, and 150,000 received legal immigrant status. The 2002 law included a regularization program for domestic workers, home helpers, and other low-skilled workers. The program closed in early 2004 with the granting of nearly 690,000 permits. In total, the five regularizations between 1986 and 2002 converted the status of more than 2 million immigrants (although many of these may have been repeat regularizations of those who failed to maintain their permits).

Contemporary Dynamics

As is the case for the other countries considered here, Italy in the first decade of the twenty-first century has attempted to balance a strong labor demand with the appearance of restrictions in its immigration policy in response to the increasing politicization of immigration issues. Demographic concerns are more pressing in Italy than in any of the countries considered in this book. For example, Italy has the lowest birthrate and the most rapidly aging population. These characteristics, when combined with an indigenous labor force disinterested in taking difficult, low-wage jobs, create the possibility of pressing labor shortages and a resulting strong demand for foreign labor. Italy's generous welfare state also effectively encourages unemployment and early retirement among workers, while strong labor unions demanding high wages and benefits for their employees increase the attractiveness to employers of cheap foreign labor. The idea that foreign labor is inevitable thus has permeated the public discourse. Despite this seeming awareness of legitimate and growing demand for immigrants, public concern about immigration issues has been running high since the late 1990s.

The 2001 election of a center-right government led by Silvio Berlusconi (leader of the far-right party, the Northern League) set the stage for significant immigration reform. Berlusconi's cabinet included other members of the Northern League (which made opposition to immigration its central electoral plank), representatives from the National Alliance (a party with fascist roots), and members of center-right parties. The far-right parties have garnered considerable support in some parts of the country using anti-immigrant appeals, and, during the election campaign, the parties that came together to form Berlusconi's government signaled their intention to quickly introduce legislation to reverse many of the more liberal aspects of previous governments' immigration policies. Within the governing coalition, the Northern League and the National Alliance were partners in drafting a restrictive piece of immigration legislation that was introduced in the Italian parliament in 2001.

Ultimately the government's plans for a dramatically more restrictive approach to immigration were reined in during the decision-making phase of the reform process by strong employer lobbying and massive public protests organized by immigrant advocacy groups. The early stages of the decision-making phase on the legislation was marked by intense debate with the governing coalition, reflecting its partisan composition, with the center-right parties much less inclined toward more restrictive policies. In particular, the center-right came under intense pressure from a powerful coalition of pro-immigrant groups including employers' associations, labor unions, and religious groups that opposed key elements of the proposed law. Significant differences between members of the coalition resulted in repeated delays in the bill's passage and major modifications of its content in the direction of greater openness. In particular, the more moderate members of the coalition succeeded in getting their coalition partners to agree to a wide-scale regularization to accompany this bill—this was a major concession on the far-right's part. In this phase, the government's intention to more comprehensively and strictly control immigration was eventually overwhelmed by the combination of public mobilization on the issue, powerful market forces, and divisions within the governing coalition. The bill passed in 2002 tightened immigration rules somewhat but was less restrictive than the prime minister and the far-right parties had promised to their supporters in the 2001 campaign. In the end, the far-right parties had made promises to the public about controlling immigration that they were unable to keep as popular pressures for control in some quarters were counterbalanced by powerful market demands and humanitarian appeals.

During the 2008 presidential campaign, former prime minister Berlusconi pledged to fine-tune the 2002 immigration law to expedite the removal of illegal foreigners, and he won the election partly by promising to crack down on crime and immigration. In May 2008 the newly elected Berlusconi government approved a tough "security package" to stem illegal immigration and remove unwanted foreigners from the country. The package was based on Berlusconi's guarantee to protect "the right of Italians not to be afraid." The implementation of this package has been fraught with difficulty, however, in particular because many of its main provisions have run up against EU directives. Of the four main provisions of the package, only one has been introduced: the deployment of troops in support of the policy. Other elements have run into trouble because they contradict EU freedom-of-movement principles. For example, a plan for the automatic expulsion of EU citizens who cannot show that they have adequate means of support has been abandoned because it clashes with EU laws.

Public opinion on immigration in Italy is highly polarized. On the one hand, public opinion polls indicate that the Italian public is one of the most tolerant in Europe. On the other hand, public opinion reflects media prone to focus on criminality and poverty when they discuss immigration, resulting in growing public antagonism toward immigrants based on beliefs that they threaten public safety and take jobs from native-born workers. The dominant media image is one of boatloads of "clandestines" or long lines of visibly foreign people waiting outside police stations or post offices to receive their documents, an image that both creates and reinforces a sense that the country is being overrun by immigrants. This polarization is captured in the most recent immigration policy reform process. Although some Italians supported greater restriction, compelling the government to introduce stricter legislation, others favored continued openness and tolerance, resulting in a weaker law than was intended.

Immigration laws in Italy have traditionally proved difficult to implement effectively. The laws are often weak, overly bureaucratic, and contradictory. The process often is marked by confusion within the government over who has implementation responsibility in a highly bureaucratic system. Laws passed by parliament are poorly articulated, leaving them open to interpretation by legislative staff and administrative bureaucrats. For example, the regulations for implementing the 2002 law were debated and contested for years, creating significant delays in application of the law. Policy implementation is complicated further by the fact that the main stakeholders in immigration policy—employers' associations, trade unions, and immigrant associations—lobby extensively while the regulations to apply the legislation are written. This results in a marked diversion between the law as adopted and as implemented, as well as policy that is often contradictory in its interpretation and effects.

In Italy, as in the other countries examined in this book, public opinion and the mobilization of a wide variety of interest groups played a critical role in the policy reform process. Changes in public attitudes about immigration were critical in placing these issues on the country's institutional agenda and continued to influence the reforms as they moved through the policy process. The ability of a wide range of interest groups to intervene at key points in the policy-making process, especially to effectively pressure the center-right parties in the governing coalition, had a significant impact on the compromise policy, and resulted in the introduction of additional legislation to effect a generous amnesty program (a proposal that originally was flatly rejected by the prime minister and all the far-right parties). The 2002 immigration policy reforms also reflect the difficulty of policy making by multiparty coalition governments. Differences within the governing coalition meant that the debate during the decision-making stage was heated and divisive, with the policy's supporters within the government ultimately having to settle for a less restrictive bill because of intense pressure from their center-right coalition partners who faced strong pressure from a variety of interest groups and whose support was vital for the government to survive.

European Union

Background: Policy Process and Policy History

The EU has for some time endeavored to develop a common approach to immigration policies. This policy-making process began in the 1980s when internal borders were eliminated as part of the process of creating the internal market. In the 1990s the EU's immigration policy focus shifted to humanitarian immigration, as EU countries began to experience unprecedented inflows of asylum seekers and refugees. At this time, the EU put in place policies that, when taken together, were viewed as having created a "Fortress Europe," because of their emphasis on ensuring the "non-arrival" of such migrants. Cumulatively, the policies adopted by the EU were intended to deny foreigners without documents access to Europe. Since the adoption of these policies, little more has been accomplished with respect to the creation of a fully articulated immigration and asylum policy regime, while the flow of immigrants into EU member states has continued at a steady and increasing pace.

In 2005 all the countries of western Europe (the EU-15, Norway, and Switzerland) and six of the ten new EU member states had a positive migration balance. Each year, about one and a half million legal immigrants arrive in the EU, proportionally twice as many as arrive in the United States. Europe's population increases of more than 2 million people between January 2005 and January 2006 were driven mainly by immigration. About 13 million non-EU nationals resided legally in the EU before enlargement in 2004, making up about 4 percent of the total population. Of the 474 million citizens and legal foreign residents of the EU and Switzerland, some 42 million were born outside their European country of residence. In the majority of these countries, the foreign-born population accounts for between 7 and

15 percent of the total population. As we have seen in the European case studies in this book, national situations with respect to numbers of immigrants vary significantly across the EU. Under the Hague Program, all types of immigration remain under the control of individual member states. The only action recommended in this area was that, by 2005, the European Commission should have a policy plan for legal migration, including admission procedures capable of responding promptly to fluctuating demands for migrant labor. Although aspects of this plan have been developed, meaningful EU policy development in this area has yet to occur.

The number of asylum seekers coming to Europe declined from 479,762 in 1998 to 403,465 in 2000. Reflecting the global decline in asylum seeking, asylum levels across the EU have dropped significantly since then, to 226,245 in 2005. The Hague Program does not introduce the notion that there will someday be an EU-wide valid refugee status, but it does request the exploration of the legal and practical implications of jointly processing asylum applications within the union. It also asks that the European Commission, along with the United Nations High Commissioner for Refugees, investigate the practicality of joint processing of asylum applications outside EU territory. The major task of the Commission in the asylum section of the Hague Program is to monitor and evaluate how member states have implemented the Tampere Program–era legislation. This should be completed in 2007; by 2010 the Commission is to produce proposals for the next phase of a common asylum system based on this review.

Illegal immigrants are of rising significance across all EU countries. Although their exact numbers are impossible to determine, estimates were at about 3 million in 1998, with anywhere between 120,000 and 500,000 arriving annually across the EU. The Hague Program focuses on three areas designed to address the flow of undocumented migrants: borders, biometrics, and visas. The primary objective is to fully abolish internal borders while providing the maximum security and orderly passage at external borders. Policies are to be developed for biometric identifiers for EU citizens and EU residents' travel documents, visas, and residence permits. The union will also develop minimum standards for national identity cards and the development of policies for common visa offices and mechanisms to fight trafficking and smuggling. Although a series of proposals have been developed in this regard, no common policies have been adopted.

Contemporary Dynamics

As was true in the four European countries examined in this book, by the early twenty-first century, immigration and asylum had become issues of high politics across the whole of the EU and as such had moved to the top of the EU's systemic agenda. Nonetheless, creating common immigration and asylum policies has been a slow and arduous process. By the late 1990s the growth of illegal immigration in particular created a call for a new series of cooperative initiatives among EU countries. Member governments made a determined effort to cooperate more closely on border management, immigration, and asylum—by the late 1990s these were the most commonly discussed issues at meetings of the Council of Ministers.

Despite the lofty goals set out at Tampere in 1999 (and at the Hague in 2004), by 2005 no common immigration policy was in place. The increased visibility and politicization of immigration issues across the member states have compelled many European leaders to embrace the view that managing immigration is the greatest challenge facing all European governments; however, agreement on the future direction of policy in this area has been elusive. In fact, few actual policy documents have been agreed upon since 1992, and those that have been approved have been minimalist in approach. The elaborate rhetorical commitments to a common approach agreed to at Tampere and the Hague notwithstanding, at present, policies pertaining to legal migration channels are left almost entirely to the member states, and the political will to have a truly European immigration policy remains in short supply.

In this context, the 2004 Hague Program, decided upon at the first Interministerial Conference on Integration, was viewed as a major achievement of the Dutch EU presidency. Here, the European Council set out ten priorities for the EU with a view to strengthening the area of freedom, security, and justice. With the acceptance of the Hague Program, the EU set its policy agenda for immigration and asylum-related policies. Agreement on the Hague Program did not involve any binding commitments on the part of member states. Instead, member states agreed on a set of proposals and deadlines for the areas in which the Council wanted to see decisions in the future.

Turning the Hague Program into meaningful policies to be implemented by the member states is the responsibility of the European Commission, the Justice and Home Affairs (JHA) Council (the 27 ministers responsible for immigration policy in each member state), and the European Parliament. The Commission is responsible for drafting and issuing proposals, which are then considered by the JHA Council and the European Parliament, who have the sole decision-making powers in this policy area. At the decision-making phase of the EU-level policy process, tensions between all of these players have slowed down the process. This has always been a policy area in which there have been continued disagreements between the Commission and the Council over the distribution of competences. The decision-making process in the European Council is intergovernmental, and in this policy area member states are reluctant to surrender too much power to the Commission or the European Parliament. In the view of the member states, the Commission does not recognize the political pressures surrounding immigration issues. The Commission views this as avoidance by the Council, seeing it as afraid to act in an area that is politicized. As a result, considerable tension exists between the two bodies; such differences in perspective generally have produced immobility.

Further, national governments have been reluctant to pool their sovereignty or hand over decision making to "Europe" in this particular policy area. They also have been concerned that the Commission will force politically unpopular measures on them, jeopardizing their political situations at home.

Policy cooperation on immigration also is negatively affected by the way in which public opinion and media coverage influence national government priorities. Across the member states, increasingly anti-immigration and anti-European attitudes are visible in both the public and the media. A key driver in the push for common policies in this area has been public pressure for EU governments to find a solution to what is viewed as at least in part a European immigration crisis, especially regarding asylum and illegal immigration. However, persistently negative media coverage of a lack of progress at the EU level also drives public frustration with this EU policy process. Further, national governments are under intense pressure to satisfy public demands to control migration while at the same time protecting their country's economic interests. Because their publics tend to be hostile to too much EU involvement in their domestic affairs, national leaders have been reluctant to commit to substantial policies at the EU level. Such contradictory messages from the public are an obstacle to developing a meaningful common policy. An ongoing dilemma, then, has been striking a balance between the motivations of member states in seeking EU action and their perceptions of their own interests at home. To date, most member states have preferred as little interference in their own approaches as possible, while they acknowledge the utility of common policies to solve problems against which they have made little progress on their own.

To add to these decision-making difficulties, whatever is agreed to under the Hague Program's ambitious agenda also will be difficult to achieve fully because implementation is in the hands of the member states. The EU's framework treaties require national governments to agree to a text at the EU level and also to include that text in their national laws. As such, the European Council's member states usually can be expected to continue to seek legislation that is similar to their existing national laws. In the area of immigration and asylum policies, many existing national laws are much weaker than the EU-level plans envisioned by the Hague Program. Thus member states lack any real incentive to strive for EU-wide policy in this area, and they cling to their sovereignty on this issue in spite of common problems and interests. As a result, at best, incremental change is likely. Further, in the area of immigration, sanctions for nonimplementation of EU directives are weak. Although the Court of Justice of the European Communities may issue rulings on the interpretation of justice and home affairs measures, its role is circumscribed. In particular, the Court has no jurisdiction over national border-crossing policies intended to safeguard internal security.

From the outset, and despite these reforms, it remains unclear how far European-wide policy integration will go in this policy area. To a greater degree than is observed in other policy areas, countries resist having more decision-making authority transferred to Brussels when it comes to immigration. This resistance arises from two concerns: first, that accepting supranational decision making on immigration policy involves the loss of yet another fundamental aspect of national sovereignty—border control; and second, that some member states cannot yet be trusted to effectively police their own borders, causing problems for other countries as inter-EU border controls are lessened. Most analysts agree that a truly common European policy on immigration and asylum that addresses individual member states' interests and needs as well as the reality of global migration flows is unlikely to be achieved by the time the Hague Program concludes in 2010. Its agenda is ambitious, and although some progress is likely to be made toward a common approach, the development of a genuine EU-wide immigration and asylum policy regime will require a more deliberate commitment by member states than has been observed to date.

Cross-national Trends

When considering the broader cross-national trends in the six countries discussed in this book, one must note the choices these countries make with respect to immigration policy and how effective they are in achieving their immigration objectives. Two clear patterns emerge. First, immigration and asylum have moved to the center of the political debate in these countries, and all moved in the direction of increasingly stricter controls over immigration in the recent past. Second, despite their best efforts, they have not succeeded in reducing population inflows to their desired levels.

Policy Outputs

In comparing the immigration policies of these six industrialized countries, we see a marked convergence in their policies over the past several decades. The long-term trend is toward asserting greater control over all types of population inflows. These countries have adopted restrictive attitudes toward foreigners' right to enter and remain within their borders. In most of these countries, governments have tightened restrictions that apply to the flow of both legal immigrants for purposes of employment or family reunification and asylum seekers and refugees. Accompanying these stricter definitions of who has a right to enter legally, most industrialized governments also have fortified their border management systems to forestall further illegal immigration. The bottom line is that the industrialized countries have become less welcoming to foreigners. These six countries have restricted legal access so that entry is allowed for family reunification or to meet labor needs, although entry even on these bases has become more limited. The United States uses preference or quota systems to define the extent of legal immigration. The traditional use of such preference systems is generally considered to be evidence of a strong planning instinct in the United States, in that an explicit effort is made to link immigration to labor or demographic needs. In the past in most other countries, legal immigration was defined by categories (such as temporary workers, families, or seasonal migrants) but was not based on strict numerical targets or quotas for these categories. This remains true in Japan and Germany, but since the late 1990s both Italy and the United Kingdom have adopted quota systems for employment-based residence permits. In countries without numerical targets, the goal is generally to admit as few new entrants as possible by eliminating whole categories of possible entrants.

Humanitarian immigration policies have also become more restrictive in these six countries. As popular opinion crystallized and mobilized against continued population inflows, governments in most industrialized countries responded with new policies that generally involved a stricter interpretation of the major international agreements protecting individuals' human rights and rights to asylum. Many countries introduced measures to control the entry of refugees, such as restrictions for those judged to have manifestly unfounded claims, the extension of visa requirements to include more countries, and the return of asylum seekers to safe third countries. These countries also increased the rates at which they process asylum applications and at which they dismiss applicants who make invalid or fraudulent requests. Most countries now attempt to evaluate asylum applications before individuals have the time to become settled in the country. Such moves are the norm in all but Italy and Japan, neither of which accepts a large number of asylum seekers or refugees.

In countries with large illegal immigrant populations, such as France and the United States, citizens place substantial pressure on government to stop all unauthorized entry and to reduce the size of the illegal foreign population. As a result, policymakers in these countries adopt much more stringent controls. Policies are designed that focus on the removal of undocumented foreigners (through deportation schemes and workplace inspections), increase barriers to illegal entry (such as visa requirements or stricter border controls), or penalize employers that hire illegal entrants (generally through employer sanctions and fines). Other countries with large illegal immigrant populations, such as Italy, have introduced policies intended to assist illegal immigrants already in the country (through regularization programs or the extension of legal and political rights). France has adopted similar programs (despite its stringent efforts to prevent illegal immigration), reflecting the country's republican tradition of protecting individuals' human rights.

Policy Outcomes

In the previous section we observed a marked convergence among the types of immigration policy instruments used in these six countries. The effects of

Table 5-1 Inflows of Foreign Population

	Foreign Population Inflow, by Year (in thousands)		
Country	*1997*	*2001*	*2006*
France	74.5	106.9	135.1
Germany[a]	615.3	685.3	558.5
Italy	n.a.	232.8	181.5
Japan[a]	274.8	351.2	325.6
United Kingdom	237.2	373.3	509.8
United States	797.8[b]	1058.9[b]	1266.3[b]
	999.62	1375.1[c]	1457.9[c]

SOURCE: Organisation for Economic Co-operation and Development (2008b).

[a]Data for Germany and Japan are from population registers. Data from the other countries are based on residence permits or other sources. Data from population registers are not fully comparable across countries because the criteria governing who gets registered differs from country to country.

[b]Figures are for permanent population inflows. These figures include persons already present in the United States who changed status.

[c]Figures are for temporary population inflows. Data refer to nonimmigration visas issued, excluding visitors, transit passengers and crewmembers, and including family members.

n.a. = not available.

these policies have been nearly as uniform across these countries. The adoption of increasingly restrictive immigration policies has resulted in these countries more effectively controlling their borders with respect to some forms of immigration since the mid-1990s. However, the overall trend among the industrialized countries is rising immigration since the mid-1990s, after experiencing significant decreases between 1990 and 1995 (Table 5-1). The only exception to this pattern among these countries is found in Germany. The persistence of a wide range of push and pull factors that encourage immigration worldwide has presented these countries with an uphill battle as they introduce increasingly strict policies designed to reduce or even end population inflows. Gaining control of immigration requires a challenging balancing act between encouraging immigration to meet rising demands for labor in the face of demographic and workforce change and maintaining sufficient controls to respond to growing public anxiety about the connections between terrorism and immigration, high levels of illegal immigration, and a perceived failure to effectively integrate immigrants already resident in their countries.

Reflecting the intent of most immigration policies, family reunification was the principal form of legal immigration in industrialized countries in 2006. The exception to this pattern among these six countries is Japan, where family-based immigration is actively discouraged as a policy goal—here too, though, policy outcomes match policy intentions. Ancestry-based legal immigration was prominent only in Germany and Japan. The second major form of legal immigration in the industrialized countries is employment-based immigration. In all countries, family-based immigration far exceeds employment-based inflows, although the balance between the two has shifted since the late 1990s, with family reunification falling in most countries and labor-based migration rising. In most places, though, family migration still outweighs labor migration; work-related immigration was the minority form of entry in all industrialized countries in 2006. Although there has been an opening up to skilled migration in many countries, movement in this direction remains limited. In general, most countries remain even more reluctant to accept low-skilled migration, except for temporary stays (often through bilateral agreements, as in Italy). Thus, to the limited extent that labor migration is encouraged in industrialized countries today, most policies are designed to recruit skilled workers and discourage unskilled migrants, despite rising demand for all forms of labor in these countries.

Humanitarian immigration is another area in which policy reforms were reflected in policy outcomes in these six countries. As they tightened their asylum rules, those countries that had been most attractive to asylum seekers and refugees witnessed a notable decline in the number of asylum claims they received. Policy measures designed to stem the flow of new arrivals, combined with efforts to lower rates of acceptance, led to a dramatic drop in the number of asylum applications in Germany after 1992, and these numbers have continued to fall. Inflows of asylum seekers dropped dramatically in the United States after September 11, 2001, as stricter controls were imposed, and their numbers have yet to approximate the levels experienced previously. Contrary to the trend observed elsewhere, asylum applications increased dramatically from the mid-1990s until 2000 in the United Kingdom. This increase may reflect the imposition of stricter policies in the other industrialized countries, especially Germany, as well as the later timeframe in which the British themselves moved to a more restrictive asylum policy. Subsequent reforms to the British asylum system in 2002 and 2004 dropped the level of asylum seekers from nearly 100,000 in 2000 to just over 30,000 in 2005. Since 2000 France has received more asylum requests than any other industrialized country, including the United States and the United Kingdom. The reason for this shift is most likely the movement of asylum seekers to France following the implementation of more stringent controls at entry and during processing in the United Kingdom. Inflows of asylum seekers remained relatively low in Italy and Japan over this period. Across countries, asylum acceptance rates remain well below 20 percent and continue to decline (Table 5-2).

Success in controlling immigration through the front door (that is, legal immigration) and side doors (mainly asylum seekers and refugees) in the 1990s resulted in increased back door, or illegal, immigration to meet continuing labor demands in these six countries early in the twenty-first century. A significant and growing number of employers rely on foreign workers to fill labor gaps, which serves as a powerful pull factor for illegal immigrants. In this context, it is more difficult to control population inflows, especially because employers are willing to risk penalties. Further, as employment-based illegal immigration rises, so too does the likelihood of increased illegal

Table 5-2 Inflows of Asylum Seekers

Country	Asylum Seeker Inflow, by Year (in thousands)		
	1996	*2001*	*2006*
France	17,405	54,291	30,748
Germany	116,367	88,287	21,029
Italy	675	9,620	10,348
Japan	147	353	954
United Kingdom	37,000	91,600	28,320
United States	107,130	59,432	41,101

SOURCE: Organisation for Economic Co-operation and Development (2008b).

family-based immigration. As the industrialized countries, particularly in Europe, adopted more restrictive controls on legal and humanitarian immigration, back door points of entry became increasingly significant, as witnessed by the rising numbers of illegal immigrants in most countries. Thus, although most countries have had some success in controlling important aspects of their foreign population inflows, they generally have not been effective in ending immigration, especially when illegal population inflows are considered.

Understanding Policy Reform

The case studies in this chapter indicate that the interaction of cultural, economic, political, and institutional variables is key to understanding immigration policy reform. If we begin with cultural variables, we see that countries that have not traditionally been countries of immigration (such as Germany) are more likely to impose restrictive immigration control policies than are countries that have always valued immigration (such as the United States). If there is no tradition of immigration to uphold or respect, policymakers face fewer constraints in imposing harsh restrictions. In such countries (most notably Germany and Japan), the imposition of restrictive immigration measures is seen as a laudable effort to protect the country from the damaging social and economic effects of population inflows. In countries with traditions of immigration, especially the United States, supporters of continued population inflows have the upper hand in immigration policy making, and policies remain open and less restrictive. Even in these countries, however, the government is under increasing pressure to restrict flows, especially in areas where immigrants are concentrated, in times of economic contraction, where persistent unemployment is endemic, and in the face of growing public fears about terrorism and national security. Nonetheless, the government's responses to such pressures are not as extreme as those observed in countries that do not traditionally value immigration as part of their national heritage.

A county's approach to immigration policy reform is also related to the degree that its population demands stricter controls—the greater the popular outcry, the stricter the controls. Since the late 1990s citizens in industrialized countries, especially in Europe, have been more highly mobilized around immigration control issues, in response to economic downturns, increasing numbers of immigrants in their countries, and national security concerns. With the exception of the United States, the case studies show that citizens' demands for greater controls resulted in these countries' developing new, more restrictive policy instruments (or, in the case of Japan, choosing not to respond to employers' demands for more foreign labor by relaxing strict controls). The United States is the only country in which we observe a gap between increasingly hostile public opinion in some quarters and policymakers' actions, reflecting the ability of interest groups to influence the policy-making process.

We also see the effects of another cultural factor in our examination of these countries' reform efforts. In both France and the United States, liberal political values clearly influenced the policy-making process. In the United States, advocates of continued legal immigration into the country appealed to lawmakers on the grounds that denying immigrants access to the country would violate the United States' fundamental belief in protecting individuals' human rights and would violate the constitutional principle of nondiscrimination. In France, citizens protested the government's adoption of its newly enacted immigration policies on the grounds that they were too harsh and went against the country's republican values. When such political values remain a strong element of the national psyche, they may have a significant impact on the nature of immigration policies.

As seen in the case studies, short-term economic conditions can play an important role in explaining immigration policy reform. Immigration policies tend to become stricter in times of economic difficulty. If a visible proportion of the citizenry blames immigrants for increased unemployment, job loss, and other economic ills, calls for stricter policies or opposition to relaxing policies may arise. For example, in Japan, concerns about declining economic growth and rising unemployment through the middle 1990s made the Japanese population unreceptive to any increases in legal immigration to meet employers' demands for low-skilled workers. Restrictions on immigration also may follow significant increases in the number of new entrants, particularly when economic conditions are poor. This explains the German response to a surge in the number of asylum seekers in the early 1990s. Strict immigration control policies seem to be cyclical: they are more likely to be implemented when economic conditions are uncertain; when citizens feel less threatened (economically, culturally, or socially) by the foreign presence in their countries, pressure for stricter policies is less apparent.

In times of economic difficulty (especially when unemployment is high), immigrants tend to be treated poorly by the receiving population and are blamed for an array of social and economic problems, even when foreign workers are needed to maintain global economic competitiveness. This was clearly the case in Germany in 2004. In the European countries, a desire to reduce the size of the social welfare state, especially in the face of rising costs due to demographic change, also resulted in increased pressure to deny immigrants access to benefits. The tendency to treat immigrants as scapegoats for all of a society's ills creates a strong incentive for policymakers to adopt stricter controls, because a tougher stand on immigration has tended to pay off in electoral terms, particularly in regions where immigrants are concentrated. A final economic consideration in understanding immigration policy reform involves the role of employers' and business associations: when demand for highly skilled and unskilled workers is rising, employers are highly motivated to block additional restrictions on immigration.

Finally, political factors can have an important effect on immigration policy reforms. The existence of far-right parties in industrialized countries has a significant effect on the immigration policy-making process. Such parties may force reforms onto the institutional agenda, change the policy positions of more moderate mainstream parties (as in Italy and France), or both. An institutional factor also is influential here: the ability of right-wing parties to play a role in the policy process is affected by the country's type of electoral system. For example, such parties noticeably affected the policy process only in countries with proportional representation electoral systems, such as Italy. Such systems significantly increase the possibility of electoral success for these parties, which affects their overall credibility in the political system. The multiparty governments that proportional representation electoral systems often produce also create conditions in which right-wing parties may disrupt the policy-making process, even when they are not included in governing coalitions. In Italy, these parties were able to control the governing coalition, allowing them to establish the institutional agenda on immigration and actively participate in decision making on immigration reforms. However, the presence of the more moderate center-right parties in the governing coalition compelled the far-right parties to agree to less strict policies than they had promised their supporters. In France, where far-right parties are electorally significant but have not played a role in the governing coalition, their impact is still felt. Here, other parties based their positions in part on the appeals of more right-wing parties in the country. In this instance, where right-wing parties play a role, the entire political climate becomes more anti-immigration, as parties of all political persuasions begin to favor tougher reforms.

The ability of interest groups to influence the political process was a key dimension of the policy decision-making stage only in the United States. Here, the central role of the legislature in U.S. policy decision making was critical. Because congressional decision making provides multiple points of access to policymakers, a well-organized and highly mobilized pro-immigration movement was able to prevent the adoption of legislation to which they were fundamentally opposed. Interest groups may also be able to influence the policy process at the implementation stage, as has happened in France and Italy. In the other countries, interest groups, though they exist, were not integral to the policy reform process, beyond playing a role in agenda setting as part of a general public outcry for reform.

At the same time that the populations of most industrialized countries push for even stricter immigration controls, and political leaders cater to these demands, these countries are faced with many compelling reasons to continue and even increase immigration levels. First, many industrialized countries need immigrant labor to fill jobs their own populations are unwilling to take. In European countries and Japan, foreign workers are also needed to respond to workforce declines and to sustain the welfare state, as these countries' populations age and their young people have fewer children. Second, the increasing mobility of labor internationally, especially as a result of technological advances in travel and communication, makes it difficult to cut off immigrant flows entirely. International agreements and norms also increasingly compel countries to protect individual human rights, even when state sovereignty may be limited as a result. Finally, most countries also have made explicit commitments, often in their constitutions, to protect individual human rights. Strict immigration controls are argued to interfere with this commitment and often generate significant criticism and public outcry from those who defend human rights and democratic values.

SUGGESTED READINGS

Bernstein, Ann, and Myron Weiner. 1999. *Migration and Refugee Policies: An Overview.* London: Pinter.

Boswell, Christina. 2003. *European Migration Policies in Flux: Changing Patterns of Inclusion and Exclusion.* Oxford: Blackwell Publishing.

Brochman, Grete, and Tomas Hammar, eds. 1999. *Mechanisms of Immigration Control: A Comparative Analysis of European Regulation Policies.* Oxford: Berg Publishers.

Chebel d'Appollonia, Ariane, and Simon Reich. 2006. *Immigration, Integration, and Security: America and Europe in Comparative Perspective.* Pittsburgh: University of Pittsburgh Press.

Cornelius, Wayne. 2004. *Controlling Immigration: A Global Perspective.* Stanford: Stanford University Press.

Daniels, Roger. 2004. *Guarding the Golden Door : American Immigration Policy and Immigrants Since 1882.* New York: Hill and Wang.

Faist, Thomas, and Andreas Ette. 2007. *The Europeanization of National Policies and Politics of Immigration: Between Autonomy and the European Union.* New York: Palgrave Macmillan.

Douglass, Mike, and Glenda Roberts, eds. 2003. *Japan and Global Migration.* Honolulu: University of Hawaii Press.

Geddes, Andrew. 2003. *The Politics of Migration and Immigration in Europe.* London: Sage Publications.

Gimpel, James, and James Edwards. 1998. *The Congressional Politics of Immigration Control.* Boston: Allyn and Bacon.

Lahav, Gallya. 2004. *Immigration and Politics in the New Europe: Reinventing Borders.* New York: Cambridge University Press.

Lynch, James, and Rita Simon. 2003. *Immigration the World Over: Statutes, Policies and Practices.* Lanham, Md.: Rowman and Littlefield.

Messina, Anthony. 2007. *The Logic and Politics of Post-World War II Migration to Western Europe.* New York: Cambridge University Press.

Odmalm, Pontus. 2005. *Migration Policies and Political Participation: Inclusion or Intrusion in Western Europe.* New York: Palgrave Macmillan.

Rudolph, Christopher. 2006. *National Security and Immigration: Policy Development in the United States and Western Europe Since 1945.* Stanford: Stanford University Press.

Schain, Martin. 2008. *The Politics of Immigration in France, Britain, and the United States: A Comparative Study.* New York: Palgrave Macmillan.

Chapter 6 Fiscal Policy

Fiscal policy is perhaps the most fundamental macroeconomic policy pursued by governments. Fiscal decisions help to frame the national economic environment in which all residents operate. At the same time, decisions about the budget are also driven by policy considerations regarding all other issues considered by governments. Policymakers must make difficult decisions about which policies to pursue, how much to spend in each area, and how to pay for those policies. The sum total of that multitude of decisions is reflected in the government budget. Over the years, elected officials, budget analysts, and ordinary citizens have debated the consequences of running budget deficits. During the middle portion of the twentieth century, budget deficits became increasingly common in industrialized countries. During the 1980s and especially during the 1990s, a variety of public officials, interest groups, and private citizens placed deficit reduction in a highly visible place on the systemic and institutional agendas of industrialized countries. In the early twenty-first century, budget deficits rose slightly but remained below the levels observed from the 1970s through the mid-1990s.

Common Policy Problems

Governments (democratic and nondemocratic alike) face a core problem that has implications for all their decisions: ideally the citizenry as a whole would like to receive more services from the government than they are willing to pay for in taxes. If this assumption about public desires is correct, governments will feel some pressure to run a budget **deficit**. When governments spend more money than they take in, they must borrow money to cover the deficit. In most countries—including the six examined in this book—some degree of deficit spending has been common for decades.

The idea of deficit spending would have seemed ridiculous in the nineteenth century. Government leaders and economic experts of the day preached the importance of running a budget **surplus**. This approach was politically more feasible back then given limited political participation. In most democracies only a minority of the total adult population could vote, and many other countries did not have democratic political systems. In the era before radio and television, print news media dominated the coverage of public policy and only a minority of the population was literate. In this context, governments typically intervened in fewer policy areas and in a more limited way. A fiscal surplus was seen as virtually synonymous with sound government. Budget deficits often were incurred during wartime, but surpluses were the order of the day during peacetime.

In the first half of the twentieth century, particularly during the Great Depression, governments ventured into the world of prolonged deficit spending in peacetime. John Maynard Keynes and other economists began to argue that deficit spending was a policy tool that governments could use to help the economy grow out of tough times. **Keynesianism** as a school of economic thought became a watchword for governments for the rest of the century. A core element of Keynesian thought is that no fiscal policy is universally desirable under all circumstances. Instead, fiscal policy decisions should be made to react to the state of the economy as a whole. In general, if the economy is contracting, governments should consider deficit spending as a fiscal stimulus designed to shorten the recession. If the economy is growing so quickly that inflationary pressures may result, governments should consider running surpluses (or at least smaller deficits) to deflate the economy. As a result of the influence of Keynesianism, such **countercyclical fiscal policies** are used to smooth out the performance of the economy.

The rise of Keynesianism also met the pressure of the postwar political environment, in which citizens placed increasing demands on government. Deficit spending could be used to escape hard economic times as well as to resolve the imbalance between demands for government services and people's willingness to pay taxes. Fiscal conservatives tied to the nineteenth-century push for budget surpluses had argued that deficit spending would bring national economic ruin. However, when industrialized economies did not collapse in the face of prolonged deficits during the Depression and afterward, opponents of deficit spending seemed less persuasive. The gloom they associated with prolonged deficits of any size did not appear to materialize.

The use of deficit spending to solve these two problems (escaping a recession and handling the political pressure toward deficits) generates a third problem in fiscal policy: how big of a deficit is too big? The whole concept of deficit spending is based on borrowing money to cover the deficit. This need to borrow implies that government deficits cannot get so big that government creditworthiness is lost. If that were to happen, the health of the entire economy—and, hence, the political health of the government—would be seriously challenged.

Another potential problem is raised by the **supply-side school** of economics that emerged to challenge the Keynesian perspective in fiscal policy. Supply-siders argue that prolonged deficits have insidious effects even before a country's creditworthiness collapses. They believe that prolonged budget deficits (and the expansion of government more generally) serve as a drag on the private sector because government borrowing and wasteful government spending soak up financial resources. Supply-siders assert that this money could be used more productively if it remained in private hands.

Major Policy Options

When governments run budget deficits, they must borrow money to cover the excess of expenses over revenues. Like a private citizen, a government can simply go to the bank and ask for a loan. The government can negotiate over the amount of money lent, the length of time over which the loan will be paid back, the interest rate, and other loan provisions.

In addition to contracting loans from banks, governments can also sell **government bonds**. The government offers bonds for sale to cover a certain amount (perhaps all) of its fiscal shortfall. The bond is still basically a loan. Investors pay the government today, and the government agrees to pay back the value of the bond plus interest over a period of time. Bonds have some advantages over loans, however. First, the government can place a similar set of conditions on its borrowing from multiple sources without engaging in negotiations with each lender. This holds true provided that enough investors purchase bonds under the terms offered by the government. Second, by selling bonds, the government borrows funds from a variety of sources—large and small—rather than simply from the banking community. Banks, investment firms, foreign governments, businesses, and private citizens are all potential purchasers of bonds. Finally, bonds—in contrast to loans—often postpone all interest payments until the end of the bond term.

The **national debt** is the sum total of future financial obligations incurred by a government (by both loans and bond payments owed). Interest and principal payments on the debt become an additional stream of expenses that the budget must cover every year. In other words, current deficits can lead to future deficits because this year's shortfall becomes next year's **debt service**. Debt service refers to the interest and principal payments made on the debt.

A desire to avoid collecting revenues today to cover yesterday's expenses is a major motivation cited by proponents of a balanced budget. Opponents of deficit spending also claim that government borrowing is a drag on the economy because the government attracts capital that might otherwise go to more productive use. The truth of this assertion rests on two assumptions that may or may not hold true: (1) that this money would indeed have been lent to others and (2) that money lent to the government will be used less productively than money lent elsewhere.

Conversely, others claim that governments can run budget deficits indefinitely with no substantial negative effects on the economy provided that they retain sufficient creditworthiness. In this view, the deficit and the debt are problems only when people believe that the government will not make good on its obligations. When this happens, the government will either be forced to borrow money at exorbitant interest rates in excess of current market levels or, in a worst-case scenario, find it hard to borrow money under any terms whatsoever. To avoid this scenario, governments need to pay their debts on time. See Box 6-1 for a look at how the negative impact of budget deficits is tied to perceptions of the government's creditworthiness.

Box 6-1 **In Depth: A Tale of Two Deficits**

In 2002 the U.S. government ran a budget deficit of $396 billion—equal to 3.8 percent of its gross domestic product (GDP). In that same year, the public debt of $6.2 trillion represented 60 percent of the GDP. In response to these and other financial developments, the U.S. Federal Reserve Bank did not face a major run on the dollar. The economic growth rate rose from 0.8 percent in 2001 to 1.6 percent in 2002.

That same year, the Argentine government ran a budget deficit equal to 0.8 percent of its GDP. It did so, however, in an economy that had not grown since late 1998. At the beginning of 2002, a beleaguered Argentine government announced that it would delay payments on many of its debts. Over the course of 2002, the Argentine peso lost two-thirds of its value against the dollar. The GDP shrank by 11 percent as domestic and foreign investors shied away from Argentina. Due to the economic collapse and a currency devaluation that made it harder to repay debts denominated in U.S. dollars, Argentine public debt skyrocketed from 65 percent of GDP in 2001 to 184 percent in 2002.

Why did a smaller budget deficit in Argentina lead to a crisis of confidence, whereas a larger deficit in the United States caused no noticeable problems? Part of the difference stems from the trends underlying the two deficits. The U.S. government deficit in 2002 was its first substantial deficit since 1995. Conversely, Argentine deficits during 1999–2001 had averaged nearly 5 percent of GDP, and the economy showed no signs of pulling out of its doldrums. In addition, the Argentine government faced many debt obligations that came due in 2002. When it postponed most debt repayments, investors took notice of the defaults and of the bleak economic picture more broadly. During 2002 the Argentine government found it literally impossible to borrow money by issuing new bonds.

The moral of the story is that the perception of a deficit is the true driving force that distinguishes a deficit from a deficit crisis. If, for various reasons, many people and firms active in financial markets lose confidence in the government's ability to defend its currency or to meet its financial obligations, even a small deficit can be considered an indicator of an unresolved crisis. Larger deficits elsewhere, viewed in light of past credit history and other factors, may not be perceived as cause for concern. A crisis is in the eye of the beholder.

Proponents of fiscal restraint are not as optimistic about the effects of chronic budget deficits and rising national debts. They believe large debts or deficits may lead to higher interest rates—thereby slowing economic growth. A large debt—relative to the size of the economy and the government's creditworthiness—may also generate greater speculation against the national currency. As a remedy to this scenario, supply-side economists recommend dramatic cuts in both government spending and taxes. Supply-siders argue that this course of action should increase economic activity, thereby increasing economic growth (and partially compensating for government revenues lost in the tax-rate cuts).

Although experts differ over the nature of the negative consequences of chronic budget deficits and disagree about the precise threshold at which deficits or debts become highly problematic, few would recommend that governments run chronic deficits in excess of 10 percent of the gross domestic product (GDP). Indeed, many analysts assert that a deficit nearing 3–5 percent of GDP should serve as a clarion call for greater fiscal restraint. When such fiscal restraint is called for, how can governments reduce the deficit?

Simply put, governments can reduce the deficit by raising revenues, by reducing spending, or by a combination of the two. In the rest of this chapter we examine the dynamics of choices made about spending. In Chapter 7 we take a look at how countries raise revenues.

Explaining Policy Dynamics

In this chapter we focus on the issue of budget deficits. Under what conditions are governments more likely to run budget deficits? The study of budget deficits has relied on a mixture of cross-national statistical analyses (often conducted by economists) and comparative case studies of particular budgetary decisions. Here we review four major sets of potential explanations: cultural, economic, political, and institutional. Along the way you will see the complex web of factors that can influence the final balance sheet of public finances.

Cultural Explanations

Cultural factors have been offered as one explanation for deficit spending choices in the postwar era. One school of thought has been characterized as the something for nothing phenomenon (Sears and Citrin 1985). This notion emerges from public opinion research posing separate questions about government spending and taxation. If we look at polling data on spending, a majority of citizens in most industrialized countries support increased spending for a variety of specific purposes. At the same time, responding to questions on the general level of taxation, majorities oppose tax increases and many assert further that taxes should be cut (Hadenius 1985). The polling data on these sorts of questions have been so stable over the years that they have helped to fuel in the media the notion that policymakers face a nearly impossible task: they must always provide more government services without increasing government revenues.

Another body of research has responded to the something for nothing thesis by arguing that citizens' individual opinions are not as selfishly inconsistent as the general polling trends indicate (Confalonieri and Newton 1995; Peters 1991; Weissberg 2002; Welch 1985). When citizens are asked more detailed questions—for example, asking them to respond to trade-offs among spending, taxation, and deficits—their answers are not as contradictory as their responses to isolated questions might imply. Peters (1991) concludes that "citizens have demonstrated that they are not really as naïve about public finance as is sometimes assumed. Most citizens appear to recognize that if they want more services they will have to pay for them through taxes" (p. 160). Perhaps the most detailed examination of these issues to date analyzed U.S. opinions on twelve budgetary trade-offs among deficit levels, domestic spending, defense spending, and taxation (Hansen 1998). Hansen found that 40 percent of citizens had entirely uncontradictory opinions across the twelve fiscal questions, and another 40 percent had only one opinion inconsistent with some of their other answers. Although this finding would need to be supported by similarly detailed research in other industrialized countries, it suggests that the something for nothing paradox emerges because citizens are asked the questions about spending and taxation in isolation from one another. Yes, citizens ideally prefer more services to fewer, and lower taxes to higher taxes. Nevertheless, people can and do recognize the trade-offs involved when asked to do so in public opinion research.

Economic Explanations

Short-term economic conditions have been central influences on annual budget deficits. Generally speaking, the healthier the economy, the lower the deficit will be. Grilli, Masciandaro, and Tabellini (1991), Freitag and Sciarini (2001), and others demonstrated that changes in economic growth rates, interest rates, and unemployment rates all have a significant effect on budget deficits. First, if the economic growth rate increases from one year to the next, this tends to reduce deficits—provided that policymakers did not already anticipate all of the economic expansion in making expenditure decisions and revenue predictions for that fiscal year.

As noted in Chapter 2, that same dynamic can cut the other way in an economic recession. First, decreases in economic growth tend to increase deficits because the drop in economic activity reduces tax revenues coming into public coffers. Second, if interest rates increase, the cost of financing the existing public debt within the annual budget goes up. This pushes deficits upward unless policymakers account for the increased costs of debt service. The higher the public debt, the more vulnerable annual budgets are to spikes in interest rates. This relationship demonstrates one of the future costs of past deficit spending: policymakers in future governments find it more difficult to steer a sound fiscal course. Third, increases in unemployment rates tend to generate higher deficits. Rising unemployment tends to increase demand for government services—unemployment insurance, poverty relief programs, and the like. This increased demand for government spending usually occurs with no compensating rise in economic growth that would generate more revenues to pay for those higher expenditures.

This discussion of short-term economic influences on fiscal policy demonstrates the climate of uncertainty in which fiscal policy decisions are made. Government budget proposals total the expenditures and revenues and project a deficit or surplus; however, it is a projection. Although many of the line items in the public budget are fixed levels of expenditures, the majority are projections of expenditures for varied government activities: debt service, so-called entitlement programs (health care, pensions, poverty relief programs, unemployment insurance), and other areas of public policy where expenditures may exceed projections due to unforeseen circumstances (such as defense policy, environmental clean-up, and relief for natural disasters). As we discuss in Chapter 7, tax revenues are almost entirely projections tied to the level of economic activity in the coming year. If economic growth exceeds projections, deficits will tend to be smaller than projected and vice versa. Accordingly, when we analyze fiscal policy decisions, we must recognize that fiscal policymakers are piloting a sailboat. They can chart a course to certain fiscal outcomes, but unfavorable economic winds sometimes force them to reach their final goal more slowly than anticipated. Conversely, an unusually favorable economic climate can do wonders for fiscal policy fortunes.

International financial markets form another economic influence on fiscal policies. Financial markets have long had a possible influence on fiscal policies because high deficits can create a crisis of confidence in the financial community at home and abroad. Technological changes and rising globalization, however, have caused some analysts to give this factor a higher profile today (Yergin and Stanislaw 1998). The 1980s and 1990s brought quantum leaps in the size of the currency market, in the speed with which it operates, and in the information flows provided by the Internet. In 1986 the normal daily volume of foreign currency transactions was less than \$200 billion; that figure increased to well over \$1.5 trillion by 1998. Trading is a nonstop enterprise because financial transactions can now be made instantaneously in major trading venues around the clock—beginning with Japan, moving on through European markets, and ending the day in the United States. Worldwide television news and the Internet provide a constant stream of information for financial analysts. Professional traders abroad can track national economic and governmental developments just as quickly as their counterparts in other countries. Even if the prospect of a devastating run on currencies is more remote in industrialized countries than in smaller, poorer economies (such as occurred in the Asian financial crisis of 1997), the governments of industrialized countries strive to maintain the confidence of investors around the globe as part of their overall economic strategy.

Political Explanations

Political factors also influence budgetary dynamics. As noted in Chapter 2, King's (1975) overloaded government thesis asserts that democracies are prone to deficits because voters like spending increases and tax cuts more than they value tax increases, spending cuts, and balanced budgets. In a study of fifteen European countries during the years 1960–2000, Mulas-Granados (2004) found that incumbent governments that pursued fiscal adjustments were less likely to be reelected—especially if they tried to balance the budget largely through spending decreases. However, he also notes that this relationship between fiscal policy and incumbents' chances for reelection weakened during the years following the 1991 Maastricht Treaty's call for greater fiscal discipline. The ability of European politicians to "blame Brussels" for spending cuts provides a clear example of the internationalization of domestic policy making.

The unity of the governing party or coalition is another political factor that could influence fiscal deficits. Roubini and Sachs (1989) are most associated with what they call the strength of government thesis (a variant on the party government model discussed in Chapters 2 and 3). Single-party governments and coalition governments dominated by a single major party find it easier to say no to deficit spending because of their greater cohesiveness. Conversely, Roubini and Sachs argue that multiparty coalition governments (those with more than two parties represented in the cabinet) tend to run higher deficits because they paper over their policy differences with deficit spending. Franzese (2000) later modified this finding when his study showed that multiparty governments tended to have an inertial effect on fiscal policy: countries with large deficits ran slightly larger deficits under larger coalitions, whereas countries with historically smaller deficits tended to run slightly smaller deficits as the size of the coalition increased.

Some observers hold that the political ideology of the governing party (or coalition of parties) influences the likelihood of budget deficits. Because numerous studies demonstrated that leftist parties in industrialized countries supported the expansion of public spending, scholars have examined the hypothesis that rightist governments are more likely to run lower deficits than are center-left governments. Although Hicks and Swank (1992) and Clingermayer and Wood (1995) determined that leftist parties were slightly more deficit prone, many more studies have found no significant relationship between political party ideology and budget deficits. Cowart's analysis (1978) of the 1960s and early 1970s found that center-left and leftist governments tended to fund government expansion by riding the tide of steady economic growth, by raising tax rates, or both. Similarly, De Haan and Sturm (1994), Borelli and Royed (1995), Hahm, Kamlet, and Mowery (1996), and Alesina, Roubini, and Cohen (1997) found no support for the partisanship argument in their study of deficits in the late twentieth century.

Institutional Explanations

Perhaps in an effort to provide shelter from political demands, some countries have chosen to create institutions that place greater authority for fiscal policy in the hands of the finance ministry. Hahm, Kamlet, and Mowery (1996) focus on three dimensions of bureaucratic strength in fiscal matters: centralization, dominance, and quasi-independence. Centralization refers to the unification of most or all responsibility for fiscal policy formulation in a single ministry. A second, related issue is the power that the finance ministry has after the initial budget proposal is formulated and circulated within the executive branch. A dominant finance ministry can have a veto over additional spending requests from other ministries. Weaker finance ministries might be forced to arbitrate in conjunction with the office of the chief executive. The least dominant finance ministries might simply be viewed as first among equals in the final stages of the budget formulation process. The third dimension of bureaucratic strength lies in the independence of the employees of the finance ministry. The finance ministry's power is enhanced when most of its analysts have permanent civil service protection, which makes firing them difficult. Conversely, the higher the percentage of political appointees in the ministry and the weaker the civil service laws, the weaker the bureaucracy becomes. A subsequent study by Hallerberg and von Hagen (1999) also found that countries where budgetary decision-making authority is centralized are less likely to incur budget deficits.

The logic of this explanation focuses on two aspects of stronger finance ministries that would tend to reduce deficits. First, centralization and dominance limit access to fiscal decisions. These limits reduce the demands to approve spending above the level of revenues. Second, the more independent the finance ministry is, the more likely that its core employees can distance themselves from the world of political demands faced in other ministries. Although other ministries' prestige is enhanced by a growth in the size of their programs, the prestige of the finance ministry (in the eyes of bureaucrats and the international financial community) is more likely to be enhanced by riding herd over deficit spending demands coming from other sectors of the government (Pempel 1992).

International Policy Making

Historically, countries around the world have been reluctant to make international commitments regarding their respective fiscal policies. Fiscal autonomy has traditionally been seen as a key element of national sovereignty. However, the shift toward monetary unification in the European Union visibly expanded the sphere of international influence for countries interested in participating in the new common currency, the euro. The 1991 Maastricht Treaty set a series of five major conditions that countries must meet in order to participate in the euro. Advocates of these convergence criteria argued that if countries were to share a currency, then they needed to engage in greater coordination in other macroeconomic policies. Many of the countries that pledged to join

Box 6-2 **In Depth: The Race to the Euro**

The Maastricht agreement to create a common European currency tied countries' participation to a series of macroeconomic criteria. The following formal targets were set for admission to the euro zone:

- An annual budget deficit below 3 percent of the GDP
- An inflation rate within 1.5 percentage points of the average rate in the three member states with the lowest inflation
- Long-term interest rates within 2 percentage points of the average rate in the three member states with the lowest inflation
- An exchange rate with a fairly stable relationship to the euro
- A public debt of less than 60 percent of the GDP

At the beginning of 1996, just two years prior to the selection of participants for the launch of the euro planned for 1999, only one of the thirteen European countries pledged to participate met all five of the economic criteria for inclusion—Luxembourg. Italy had not met any of the targets. Most countries were in compliance with the goals for inflation, exchange rate stability, and interest rates. However, all countries except for Luxembourg and France had public debts in excess of 60 percent of the GDP, and all but Luxembourg and Ireland had failed to meet the budget deficit guideline of 3 percent of the GDP.

To make matters even worse, only Germany's budget deficit was fairly close to the target (at 3.3 percent). All other countries' deficits were at or above 4 percent. Finland, Greece, Italy, the Netherlands, Portugal, Spain, and Sweden all ran deficits above 5 percent. All eyes turned to fiscal policy in 1996 and 1997 as countries worked to meet the target in 1997.

The race to the euro fueled a visible reduction in budget deficits throughout Europe, including the two EU countries not pledged to participate (Denmark and the United Kingdom). Through a variety of fiscal measures, all countries but Greece managed to meet the target in 1997 (Greece subsequently met the criteria in 2000 and entered the euro zone in 2001). Once the euro was launched, attention in the early twenty-first century within the euro zone then shifted to the fiscal constraints imposed by the Stability and Growth Pact.

the euro zone had to make tremendous strides to meet these criteria during the 1990s (Box 6-2).[1]

This pursuit of greater fiscal policy harmonization did not end upon the creation of the euro zone. Instead, in 1997 a series of European Council resolutions bound countries participating in the euro to the Stability and

[1]Deficit statistics and macroeconomic statistics on growth, unemployment, and inflation are from the Organisation for Economic Co-operation and Development (OECD, 2008c). Government finance statistics on debt and debt financing are from OECD (2008d).

Growth Pact (SGP). The SGP required these countries to maintain relatively harmonious fiscal policies and suggested that countries aim to have balanced budgets. In particular, the pact retains the Maastricht deficit ceiling of no more than 3 percent of GDP unless the deficit is a product of a recession or an exceptional, unforeseeable event beyond the member state's control. Violation of this policy (or of targets for the public debt-to-GDP ratio) can lead to sanctions. We examine the SGP and its evolution later in this chapter when we look at the EU's fiscal policies.

With the SGP in place, three of the six countries examined in this book (France, Germany, and Italy) have made an international pledge to limit budget deficits as a percentage of their GDPs. They are not alone: as of January 2008, sixteen of the twenty-seven member states of the EU have committed themselves to considerable fiscal restraint as part of their participation in the EU's common currency. The United Kingdom (along with Denmark) retains the option to participate in monetary unification should it eventually decide to do so. The United States and Japan have not made any international commitments regarding their budget deficits (although, like all industrialized countries, their participation in some international organizations and treaties does bind them to engage in related spending that typically constitutes a tiny fraction of overall government spending).

United States

Background: Policy Process and Policy History

More than any of the six countries examined in this book, the United States has a decidedly pluralist fiscal policy process. These procedural differences have their roots in differences in core governing institutions as defined by the Constitution; however, the major distinction is not the constitutional provision requiring fiscal policy to be controlled by the legislature. Instead, what makes the ultimate enactment of budget legislation potentially more difficult (and usually more time consuming) in the United States than in the other countries is the presidential system of executive-legislative relations. As we will see in the other national case studies, in parliamentary systems the governing party (or coalition) controls both the executive and legislative branches. This arrangement streamlines the fiscal policy formulation and decision-making processes by giving the executive branch the lead role in formulation and a stronger set of tools with which to negotiate legislative approval of many elements of the draft budget. In the Italian and Japanese systems, the existence of more fractionalized political parties that support the executive branch often leads to a process that involves more negotiation and more revisions than in France, Germany, and the United Kingdom. In the United States, however, the process is even more decentralized than in Italy and Japan.

As in other countries, the budget formation process in the United States originates in the executive branch, centered in the Office of Management and Budget (OMB). The OMB prepares the budget proposal, after receiving direction from the president and consulting with presidential senior advisers and officials from cabinet departments and other government agencies. After formulating a budget, the president presents it to the legislature. At this point the U.S. process begins to diverge markedly from that found in other countries.

After the legislature receives the budget proposal, the locus of activity shifts markedly to Congress. Members of both houses of the legislature first pass a budget resolution that guides legislative committees as they make their decisions about spending and taxes. This resolution includes targets for expenditures and revenues, and allocations within the spending targets for discretionary and mandatory expenditures. Mandatory expenditures required by existing legislation currently make up over three-fifths of all spending. The rest of the budget's discretionary spending is determined by eleven (or more) separate annual appropriations processes that fund most ongoing government programs that are not formula-driven entitlements. The 1990 Budget Enforcement Act put a firm cap on total discretionary spending through 2002. In addition the law required legislation that would raise mandatory spending or lower revenues (relative to existing law) to be offset by revenue increases or spending cuts. This requirement (often called pay-as-you-go or paygo) was intended to prevent new legislation from increasing the deficit.

Congress begins to decide on discretionary appropriations bills by examining the president's budget in detail. Committees and subcommittees hold hearings on appropriations proposals under their jurisdiction. These hearings and informal meetings provide opportunities for interest groups and agencies to debate budgetary priorities in different sectors. If the president's budget calls for changes in taxes, the House Ways and Means Committee and the Senate Finance Committee would need to hold hearings on the matter. The budget director, cabinet officers, and other executive branch officials work with Congress to try to maintain what the executive branch views as key elements of the president's initial proposal. In the end, these complex negotiations must produce a budget agreement in both houses of the legislature that will not be vetoed by the president. A presidential veto can be overridden only by a two-thirds majority. Congress has ample opportunity to inject many of its own priorities into the budget, but serious departure from presidential priorities runs the risk of a veto. As a result, although the U.S. legislature plays a much larger role in fiscal policy than in other countries, the presidential veto enables the chief executive to generate a meaningful role in the process even when Congress is controlled by a different party.

The dollar's position as the world's major reference currency during the second half of the twentieth century gave the United States a comparatively privileged position in the realm of deficit financing. It was easy for the United States to attract domestic and foreign investors willing to purchase long-term government bonds. During the early twenty-first century, the rise of the euro as an alternative reference currency reduced the primacy of the dollar. In turn, a rising public debt during 2002–2007 also posed a potential challenge to confidence in dollar-denominated bonds. Roughly half of U.S. federal debt obligations were held by nonresidents in 2007, and a majority of outstanding bonds were medium-term instruments.

The United States entered the twenty-first century on an economic upswing. Nine years of steady growth, from 1992 to 2000, combined with more restrained spending (especially in social security and welfare), reduced a budget deficit that had constituted over 5 percent of GDP in 1992. In 1998 the government ran its first budget surplus since 1969. Larger budget surpluses in 1999 and 2000 shifted the political debate away from deficit reduction and toward the issue of what to do with the budget surplus.

Contemporary Dynamics

In the 2000 elections, held amid a rising budget surplus, the two major presidential candidates presented contrasting proposals regarding the fiscal surplus. Democratic Party candidate Al Gore pledged to maintain a surplus and to use some of the excess funds to bolster the finances of the Social Security pension system and to improve the Medicare health care program for senior citizens. Republican candidate George W. Bush emphasized his desire to cut taxes, and he also proposed a few new spending initiatives in defense and education policy. The inauguration of George W. Bush in January 2001 placed tax cuts firmly on the institutional agenda while fiscal conservatism took a back seat; Chapter 7 discusses the tax cuts passed during 2001 in more detail. Initial forecasts following the 2001 tax reforms predicted a continuation of small surpluses, but a series of events changed budgetary dynamics early in Bush's presidency. A stagnant economy in 2001 and 2002 depressed government revenues. In turn, higher commitments to homeland security programs and the U.S. military invasion of Afghanistan in late 2001 increased spending. Within two short years the agenda had shifted from what to do with the budget surplus to how to deal with a budget deficit that reached 3.8 percent of GDP in 2002.

Some fiscally conservative Republicans called for deeper cuts in nonmilitary spending to achieve a balanced budget or, at least, a smaller deficit. They also called for an extension of the spending constraints tied to the 1990 Budget Enforcement Act. President Bush countered with a proposal to extend the paygo provisions for spending, but not for additional tax cuts. The Republican leadership in the legislature refused to pursue an extension of the paygo rules and of the cap on discretionary spending on the grounds that the country was at war. Furthermore, they and President Bush argued that additional tax cuts were needed to stimulate a faster economic growth rate. The Democratic Party's legislative caucus was in disarray following an unexpected defeat in the 2002 midterm elections. Many Democratic legislators criticized the president's spending priorities and the tax cut: when they briefly gained a one-seat majority in the Senate, they used it to block the president's budget proposal during 2002. Critics of the proposal claimed that additional tax cuts were irresponsible in the face of rising budget deficits and potential military operations in Iraq. Business interest groups tended to line up with Republicans calling for tax cuts, whereas labor tended to side with the Democrats.

In this difficult climate, the fiscal year 2004 budget barely made it through a Republican-controlled legislature in 2003. With a thin majority restored in the Senate, the Republican leadership negotiated a compromise to mollify senators who criticized the tax cuts: they agreed to shrink the tax cuts by $200 billion. Even after this change, the budget resolution passed the Senate only via a tie-breaking vote cast by Vice President Dick Cheney. Subsequent budgetary decision making grew even more conflictual. In 2004 a coalition of fiscally conservative Republican and Democratic senators tried to restore the paygo rules that had expired in 2002. When the Republican leadership thwarted this attempt, they blocked the president's budget for the rest of the year. When Bush won reelection in November 2004, the president pledged to make permanent the tax cuts that were scheduled to expire in 2010. Fiscal conservatives argued that the tax cuts could not be extended without cuts in spending. During 2005 Congress worked to cut mandatory spending programs in health, education, and welfare by nearly $40 billion. Democrats remained united in opposition on the grounds that the spending cuts were tied to over $70 billion in additional tax cuts. To pass the budget bill in the Senate via a 51–50 vote, Vice President Cheney again broke a deadlock. During the rest of Bush's second term, the close balance of forces tilted over time in the direction of the president's critics. A coalition of fiscally conservative Republicans and Democrats worked over the years 2006 and 2007 to bring deficits back below 3 percent of GDP. As the Democratic Party regained small majorities in both chambers of Congress in the November 2006 elections, its leaders spoke of a need for greater fiscal responsibility; the now-Democratic-led House restored paygo principles via a rules change. Meanwhile President Bush continued to emphasize the desirability of extending the tax cuts that were scheduled to expire over the next decade. A banking crisis and a sharp economic downturn in 2008 altered the fiscal policy stalemate as many leaders of both parties began to speak of the need for a fiscal stimulus to rescue the financial sector and to rebuild consumer credit. The House circumvented the paygo principle to back an economic stimulus package in early 2008 and a financial sector rescue plan in fall 2008.

Because of the divided nature of government in the United States, fiscal policy implementation faces more potential problems there than it does in other countries. The executive branch can use its control over the implementation of programs to create a set of priorities more to its liking and less like what an opposition-controlled legislature might have intended. By the same token, legislative appropriations committees have the power to block funds to projects favored by the president or the president's party. These sorts of actions could be carried out in any political system, but they are far more common in presidential systems where the executive and legislative branches may be dominated by different parties. In addition, varying patterns of representation in the bicameral legislature often create divisions between the lower and upper houses even when the same political party holds a majority in both chambers. This phenomenon could be observed repeatedly during the George W. Bush presidency.

What is on the fiscal horizon for the United States? Preliminary estimates for 2008 said that the deficit would exceed 5 percent of GDP as the country entered a recession. Dealing with financial uncertainty and economic recession became major issues in the November 2008 presidential and legislative elections. As the recession deepened in late 2008, Barack Obama's transition team discussed proposals for an additional spending package designed to reactivate the economy and avoid further financial panic. Republican leaders criticized the call for public spending and countered with proposals for tax cuts.

The visible conflict in the U.S. budgetary process demonstrates the impact that a presidential system can have on fiscal policy making. The president tries to set the fiscal agenda but faces a lot of competition: conflicting voices from fellow party members in the legislature and the distinct possibility of a legislature controlled by the opposition. We can see the president's relative weakness in the extreme difficulty the Bush administration had in shepherding the majority of its first budget through the legislature, which was controlled by Bush's own party. The U.S. position regarding the party government model does not clear the path for quick responsiveness in fiscal policy. That difficulty is perhaps an even more telling comment on fiscal policy making in presidential systems than were the highly charged, partisan budget battles of the mid-1990s between a Democratic-controlled White House and a Republican-led Congress.

The rapid return of the deficit in the early twenty-first century is also a testimony to the role of political considerations and the potential fragility of economic circumstances. For the years 1998–2000, nearly a decade of steady economic expansion, stable inflation rates, declining interest rates, and declining unemployment rates played a considerable role in paving the way for budget surpluses. Within one year, a political willingness to reduce the surplus via new tax cuts and spending increases combined with minimal economic growth led to deficits that rivaled the levels observed in the early 1990s during the George H. W. Bush presidency. Citizens and government officials will now have to decide how much of a deficit can and should be tolerated during the economic crisis that began in 2008.

Japan

Background: Policy Process and Policy History

As in the United States, the budget process in Japan has tended to be more pluralist than in most major European economies in that a wider variety of forces participate actively in the process. While top Ministry of Finance officials generate the framework estimates for the new budget, the Budget Bureau of the ministry examines requests compiled by all ministries and agencies. As the Ministry of Finance puts the finishing touches on the draft budget, representatives from the different ministries and individual legislators from the governing coalition in the Diet begin to lobby the drafters for additional resources. Ultimately disputes are arbitrated in meetings between the Ministry of Finance and the leaders of major coalition partners (and party factions within those partners) to generate support for passage of the budget in the Diet.

Deficit financing was not a major policy issue in Japan in the late 1980s and early 1990s. Japan's comparatively limited needs for deficit financing, combined with a strong economic reputation forged by high economic growth from the 1960s forward, made it fairly easy to market long-term bonds. The economic stagnation of the 1990s generated a shift toward a mix of medium- and long-term debt obligations. The country has relied largely on domestic financing.

In 1992, however, things began to change. An overheated domestic investment market (in both real estate and stocks and bonds) lost a significant amount of its value. In turn, a stronger national currency began to reduce the competitive advantage of many Japanese exporters. Growth slowed to 1.0 percent in 1992. From 1993 to 1995 the economy remained stagnant—growing at around 1 percent per year. In 1994 a weak coalition government narrowly passed a stimulus package of temporary tax cuts and spending increases; the budget bill included a compromise for fiscal conservatives tied to Ministry of Finance officials: sales taxes would rise in 1997. The economic growth rate rose to 2.0 percent in 1995 and 2.7 percent in 1996. However, the tax hike in 1997 knocked back the fragile Japanese economy—provoking a recession in 1998 and 1999. Japan's economy had entered a period of stagnation that it had not known for over a generation.

In the early twenty-first century, fiscal policy involved a vigorous debate between fiscal conservatives bred from the boom decades of the past and other politicians and interest groups arguing that prolonged deficit spending would be essential to restructuring the financial sector and reinvigorating the Japanese economy. Deficit hawks argued that Japan should control spending and perhaps raise tax rates to bring down a deficit that had ballooned to an average of 9.3 percent of GDP during the recession of the late 1990s. Advocates of a fiscal stimulus argued that the spending increase and tax cuts of the 1994 budget bill stimulated the economy until they were snuffed out by the 1997 sales tax increase.

Contemporary Dynamics

From 1993 through 1996, a series of unstable coalition governments—the first governments not led by the Liberal Democratic Party (LDP) in nearly forty years—had debated how to revive an economy in which many banks held nonperforming loans that were unlikely to be repaid. As the recession emerged in mid-1998, veteran LDP leader Keizo Obuchi became prime minister of a smaller, three-party coalition government in which the LDP was the largest partner. The Obuchi government pledged to launch an increase in public works spending and to stimulate consumer spending. In 1999 the LDP captured a majority in the lower house (yet honored its pledge to continue its coalition with two smaller parties), and the economy began to expand toward the end of the year. In April 2000, however, Obuchi suffered a massive stroke. The LDP selected Yoshiro Mori as his successor, and the new prime minister made a series of public relations and political gaffes that dragged his public approval ratings down below 10 percent. Mori's poor performance created a political opening for one of the most reform-minded leaders of the LDP—Junichiro Koizumi—to become prime minister in April 2001. Koizumi's views were controversial in the minds of many in the Ministry of Finance and in the LDP, but the photogenic, outspoken leader had the highest approval rating of any Japanese politician at the time.

Koizumi had spent the 1990s arguing in the legislature and in the media for a serious financial restructuring that would revive the economy by expanding private credit markets. In addition to assisting private banks, Koizumi called for the privatization of the largest financial entity in the world, the government-owned Japan Post. The postal service operated a network of banks and insurance companies through the country. At the same time that the Koizumi government argued for deficit reduction in the medium run, it also pledged not to raise tax rates for the foreseeable future. These plans were initially opposed by the senior bureaucrats in the Ministry of Finance and by Koizumi's own finance minister, Hakuo Yanagisawa. In 2002 Koizumi shuffled his cabinet and inserted his former economic minister, Keizo Takenaka, as the new finance minister. Takenaka energized the restructuring of the banking system by using public money to retire bad loans. These actions pushed deficit spending up from 6.3 percent of GDP in 2001 to an average of 8.0 percent during 2002 and 2003.

The battle of fiscal policy and financial sector reform was now fully joined in a complex political and economic environment. Economic growth had resumed in 2004 and 2005, yet domestic and foreign analysts continued to call for further financial restructuring. Koizumi pressed ahead with his call to privatize the Japan Post; he claimed that taxpayers were subsidizing a financial network that made loans based on political networks. Koizumi claimed that privatizing Japan Post would reduce the likelihood of future government deficits. Many traditional factions within the LDP stridently opposed its privatization precisely because they saw its actions as supportive of their electoral bases and political supporters. In turn, the major opposition party, the Democratic

Party, opposed the reform on the grounds that the public network provided benefits for ordinary citizens.

Koizumi narrowly pushed the privatization bill through the lower house by a five-vote margin. Then a coalition of opposition parties and rebel LDP legislators blocked the reform in the upper house. Koizumi resolved to overcome the obstacle by calling new elections. To the surprise of many observers, Koizumi's call for snap elections culminated in a major victory for the LDP in September 2005. It won sixty seats from the Democratic Party—primarily in urban districts that had traditionally been a stronghold for the LDP's opponents. With a massive majority in the lower house and a public approval rating at historically high levels, Koizumi then passed a privatization bill through both chambers of the legislature in October 2005.

In building support for the implementation of its initiatives, the Koizumi government performed a delicate balancing act. Although Ministry of Finance officials initially moved slowly on his plans for injecting public money into the banking system, Koizumi passed on an opportunity to shake up its bureaucracy when the most senior bureaucrat retired at the start of the Koizumi government; Koizumi adhered to Japanese custom by appointing a senior civil servant seen as loyal to the traditional ministry viewpoints. Instead of risking alienating the bureaucracy via personnel changes, Koizumi tried to mobilize public opinion and used his most loyal cabinet appointees, especially Takenaka, to interact with the bureaucracy and the business sector. Eventually the injection of government funds reenergized the banking system and culminated in a reduction of the budget deficit from 8.0 percent of GDP in 2002 down to 1.4 percent in 2006 (Koizumi's last year in office).

The fiscal policy-making dynamics in contemporary Japan illustrate the difficulties of steering a clear policy path in troubled political waters. The major fiscal policy reform of 1994 produced a mixed bag of contradictory initiatives designed to please different elements of the weak governing coalition. Although a weak coalition government was in place, the government's lack of strength did not produce as large a deficit as one might think because of the role of bureaucratic politics in the Japanese system. Cabinet instability and factionalism from the mid-1990s through the short-lived Obuchi government increased the latitude given to an already powerful Ministry of Finance. In turn, the successes of the Koizumi government testify to the agenda-setting power of a politician able to mobilize public opinion—even in a political party as prone to faction-driven rivalries as the LDP.

The impact of Koizumi's skill in mobilizing public opinion as a tool to deal with intraparty rivals and opposition parties became even more evident following his resignation as prime minister in September 2006. His successor, Shinzo Abe, lasted less than a year in office—as did Abe's successor, Yasuo Fukuda. When Taro Aso took office as prime minister in September 2008, it remained to be seen how his government would forge a fiscal policy amid the burgeoning global economic downturn under way.

Germany

Background: Policy Process and Policy History

The budget formulation process is more centralized in Germany than in the United States or Japan. This greater centralization stems partly from more disciplined political parties and partly from more centralized formal government procedures. The chancellor sets a general fiscal target in consultation with a variety of actors. At that point, the chancellor delegates much of the remainder of the formulation process to the finance minister. The finance minister can veto any calls for expenditures that exceed the targets outlined by the chief executive but does not typically act alone in ratifying additional increases. Ultimately any troubling disputes are arbitrated by the chancellor, the finance minister, and senior figures in the governing coalition to ensure passage of the budget in the legislature. The Budget Committee in the Bundestag usually works closely with Finance Ministry officials in reviewing the budget proposal. Legislative activism in the budget-making process is constrained further by two additional procedures. First, any additional spending proposals made in the Bundestag must contain a proposal for a revenue source. Second, the executive branch retains a legislatively mandated veto over any spending increases authorized by the legislature that were not in the government's draft budget. The total effect of these procedures is to limit the role of the legislature to that of a brainstorming second opinion on spending decisions.

As Germany's financing needs grew in the 1990s, the country increased its use of foreign financing somewhat, but domestic sources remain central. In the early twenty-first century, Germany continued to finance its shortfalls primarily through long-term bonds. Low inflation rates and a central bank system with a long tradition of political independence helped to maintain investor confidence in long-term bonds. A key element of German support for monetary unification resided in the pledge to create an independent European Central Bank similarly dedicated to fight inflation.

German economic policy in the 1990s was colored by the obligations assumed with reunification. Historically, postwar German economic policy had emphasized fiscal restraint and tight monetary policies in a sustained effort to avoid a return to the hyperinflation of the 1920s. In the 1980s the deficit averaged markedly less than 2 percent of GDP. Reunification generated enormous fiscal pressures—particularly in light of the Kohl government's pledge to raise living standards in the east to those of the west as quickly as possible. The decisions to convert East German marks on an even footing and to extend government social programs immediately upon reunification implied a rapid rise in expenditures. Deficits averaged around 3 percent of GDP in the 1990s.

Contemporary Dynamics

The 1998 elections proved to be a watershed. Helmut Kohl had served as chancellor since 1982—presiding over the upswing in European integration and the reunification of Germany. In 1998 the Christian Democratic leader told voters that his experienced leadership would prove central to pulling Germany out of its economic stagnation. Annual average economic growth was a paltry 1.7 percent during 1995–1997, and the unemployment rate climbed to 9.4 percent. The costs associated with reunification had driven public debt up such that interest payments on the debt comprised one-fourth of government spending.

Historically, both major parties had emphasized price stability (and fiscal responsibility) in an effort not to lose voters who might fear the specter of the runaway inflation of the 1920s. German business associations were vocally supportive of fiscal austerity and lower taxes—in part because many major German firms are owned by holding companies controlled by banks. Banks, as lenders of money over time, are particularly sensitive to inflation. The major labor confederation, the *Deutscher Gewerkschaftsbund*, called for the protection of social programs but expressed willingness to compromise on some issues in an effort to keep inflation in check. As the costs of reunification became visible, several small right-wing parties attempted to mobilize voters in the west who complained of the costs of subsidizing the east. Although the Christian Democrats at times talked tough about stern measures to deal with so-called eastern freeloaders, an additional impetus for returning to Germany's fiscally conservative roots was the need to stay within the bounds of the Stability and Growth Pact. The new Social Democratic leader in the 1998 elections, Gerhard Schröder, promised a heterodox mix of tax cuts and well-managed social programs as a path toward invigorating the German economy. Although many preelection polls indicated a dead heat with no clear majority emerging in the legislature, a coalition of Social Democrats and Greens won 345 seats in the 669-seat Bundestag.

The time had come for Schröder to push through his "Third Way" agenda of tax cuts, controlled spending, and effective administration of social programs. His first finance minister, Oskar Lafontaine, hailed from the left wing of the Social Democratic Party and pushed vigorously for increased public spending. Within five months, Lafontaine resigned citing differences with Schröder; the chancellor replaced him with a more fiscally conservative party member, Hans Eichel. Eichel brokered a tax-cut program and froze most government spending in real terms. The deficit fell to below 2 percent of GDP in 1999 and 2000. Schröder and Eichel became the visible leaders of a reshaped Social Democratic Party (although many in the party's left wing criticized these measures publicly or privately). Despite an economic downturn in 2001, Schröder's coalition held on for a narrow victory in the 2002 elections in which he pledged to continue his agenda of tax reduction, spending restraint, and effective governance. In its second term, however, the center-left coalition confronted a major economic slowdown: the average annual growth rate was a mere 0.4 percent during 2002–2005. The deficit averaged 3.7 percent of GDP during that same time period.

Few implementation problems clouded the fiscal policy horizon in Germany on an administrative level. Capability concerns were virtually nonexistent as demonstrated by the ability of the Schröder government to track and enforce spending caps under difficult political and economic circumstances. The major implementation challenge faced by German fiscal policy under Schröder was an uncooperative economy. Economic stagnation flattened revenue growth while creating demands for social spending on several fronts—thus preventing the attainment of the balanced budget promised by Schröder. When the deficit exceeded 3 percent for the second consecutive year in 2003, the SGP rules called on Germany to enact deficit control measures. Germany argued successfully that it needed more time; however, the effort to bring down the deficit during 2004–2005 likely extended the economic downturn.

Schröder's move toward the center of German politics caused a realignment of the party system. In 2005 Oskar Lafontaine led a group of more left-leaning legislators out of the Social Democratic Party to form a new party, The Left (in association with the former communist party, the PDS). The Left entered the 2005 election campaign criticizing the failure of the two main parties to help ordinary Germans via their similar recipes of fiscal responsibility and tax cuts. Meanwhile, the programmatic differences between the Social Democrats and the Christian Democrats had become narrower than ever before. In the end, the 2005 election results produced an indeterminate outcome as the newly formed Left won nearly 9 percent of the seats—thus preventing the most recent center-left and center-right coalitions from winning enough seats to control the Bundestag. Rather than risk building broader coalitions with parties less supportive of their respective platforms, the Christian Democrats and the Social Democrats ultimately resolved to form a government jointly based on a common program that would balance the budget via spending restraint combined with tax reform (see Chapter 7 on this point). Spending austerity mixed with economic growth averaging 2.9 percent during 2006–2007 to produce a balanced budget by 2007. Critics of this approach argued that fiscal conservatism had become too extreme in the early twenty-first century; Germany was the one major country that did not engage promptly in deficit spending in response to the global economic downturn in 2008.

In contemporary German fiscal policy, we see three sets of policy influences in succession. First, the experience of hyperinflation in the 1920s created a cultural norm against inflation that powerfully frames choices about fiscal policy toward an aversion of budget deficits. German citizens and leaders still fear inflation more than do people in most industrialized countries. Second, an international commitment to European monetary integration played a role in reinforcing the Schröder government's call for spending austerity in the early twenty-first century—especially during the stagnation of 2002–2005. Finally, the events of the early twenty-first century testify to the power of partisan influences. When Schröder faced potential opposition to more stringent spending reforms from the Greens and from within his own party, he was not able to adopt the fullest vision of those reforms. In turn, after the leftist rebels vacated the Social Democratic Party and the center-right Christian Democrats became the Social Democrats' coalition partner, it became easier for the Merkel grand coalition government to adopt the fiscal measures pursued during 2006–2007.

France

Background: Policy Process and Policy History

The French budget process historically involved executive branch negotiations on spending levels. The prime minister and the finance minister consulted to set budget targets for every ministry with the power to spend. Then the finance minister negotiated one-on-one with each spending minister about adjustments to those targets. This process of negotiation gave spending ministers (and the interest groups who lobbied them) an opportunity to influence budget formulation. However, the power to arbitrate disputes, which is held by the finance minister and ultimately the prime minister, constrained adjustments during formulation. Once the budget was completed, approval in the legislature was sealed by an agreement brokered among the senior figures in the governing coalition. Interest groups attempted to influence this process in various ways ranging from quiet lobbying to mass demonstrations.

The 2001 Organic Law Related to Finance Laws overhauled this process via a new set of rules that entered into effect in 2006. Rather than incrementally adjusting spending over hundreds of budget lines in each ministry, the new system organizes spending by over one hundred programs grouped into over thirty policy areas (called "missions"). The finance minister still works out the overall spending targets in consultation with ministers, but managers of programs and subprograms are given greater discretion over how to spend the funds allocated and accrual-based accounting replaces more traditional public finance bookkeeping. The most sweeping aspect of the reform is its attempt to link budgeting to management, program evaluation, and legislative oversight. Each annual budget bill must attach an annual program evaluation for each of the policies and programs funded. In turn, these program evaluations must be considered by the parliament before it votes on the budget. In addition, the legislature's ability to amend the budget has been extended by its ability to propose changes among the various programs within each functional mission. As of this writing, it remains too early to say whether this process will transform public management in France, but it has clearly expanded the amount of time that the legislature dedicates to the budgetary process.

Historically, most French debt was financed domestically. However, with the advent of the euro, French debt internationalized further with each passing year from 1998 forward. By 2007 roughly three-fifths of outstanding debt obligations were held by nonresidents. The government relied primarily on a mix of medium- and long-term instruments. In 2007 the average maturity of debt was longer in France than in any of the other countries covered in this book.

Since the 1990s the major economic issue in France has been stubbornly high unemployment. In the 1990s the unemployment rate averaged slightly more than 11 percent. Slow economic growth made reducing unemployment more difficult; the annual average GDP increase was just 1.6 percent in that decade. These developments, in turn, flattened revenue growth while increasing demands for public programs. The budget deficit reached an average of 5.8 percent during 1993–1995. In light of France's Maastricht commitments, this change moved the deficit to near the top of the policy agenda. Massive strikes against Alain Juppe's center-right government blocked many of its major spending cut proposals; with the election of a new center-left government in 1997, it seemed that France's policy course had been set firmly toward the preservation of social spending. To meet the target without drastically alienating either center-left voters (by cutting spending) or center-right voters (by raising taxes), Lionel Jospin's government pushed through a series of temporary tax increases and slowed the growth of spending. The deficit fell from 3.3 percent in 1997 to 1.6 percent in 2002.

Contemporary Dynamics

Policy problems at the heart of contemporary French spending policy result from a clash between two conflicting imperatives setting the fiscal agenda. On the one hand, the French government has been a consistent supporter of monetary unification—thereby placing fiscal responsibility high on the country's agenda. On the other hand, prolonged unemployment has stirred calls to preserve (or even extend) the social programs that make up the majority of national expenditures.

This turbulent clash of imperatives has made for some high-voltage policy formulation in France. As is the case in most political systems around the world, the center-right bloc of parties (led by the Gaullists) has emphasized fiscal austerity, whereas the center-left bloc of parties (led by the Socialists) call for the protection of social spending. Both coalitions have found it difficult to set a durable policy course while in office. Center-right governments find it difficult to cut spending as much as they promised, and center-left governments find it hard to improve programs as vigorously as they pledged—as illustrated by the Jospin government formed following the 1997 elections. French businesses have advocated tax reductions while French unions and social movements have fought doggedly to resist reductions in public services and social spending.

The reemergence of the center-right as a large governing majority in 2002 seemed to signal a move toward even greater fiscal austerity. When Jospin surprisingly failed to reach the decisive runoff in the presidential elections,

Gaullist leader Jacques Chirac handily defeated far-right candidate Jean-Marie Le Pen in May 2002. This outcome put the center-left bloc on the defensive in the June 2002 legislative campaign as Gaullists campaigned for an end to the "cohabitation" between a Chirac-led presidency and a parliament controlled by his opponents. In the end, voters gave the center-right bloc a massive majority of 399 seats in the 577-seat National Assembly. The Gaullist UMP had a sturdy majority even without its allied parties. Although Jean-Pierre Raffarin's government still encountered strident political opposition to spending cuts, it had greater legislative success than the prior center-right government led by Juppe. In 2003 the government reformed the pension system for public employees despite a series of strikes that tried to emulate the successful efforts to protest the Juppe-era proposals in the 1990s. Several publicly owned enterprises were privatized. The government also froze public spending in real terms in most spending categories. These policies were generally extended when Dominique de Villepin replaced Raffarin as prime minister in 2005 following the defeat of the referendum regarding a new EU constitution. Public finances were also improved by steady (albeit unspectacular) economic growth averaging 2.2 percent annually from 2004 to 2007. As a result of policy change and improved economic conditions, the deficit fell from 4.1 percent in 2003 to 2.7 percent in 2007.

Few technical considerations blocked the implementation of most spending increases or decreases in France. The bigger implementation challenge was decidedly political. As the Balladur and Juppe governments saw when they reversed course on spending cuts in 1990s, opponents of those cuts were able to place visible public pressure on the government to reconsider its policies. Several cuts that had been announced were pulled back before full implementation proceeded. These potential implementation obstacles also have served as constraints framing policy formulation and decision making in the early twenty-first century.

What will the future of French spending policy hold? The new Gaullist leader, Nicolas Sarkozy, won the May 2007 presidential elections with 53 percent of the vote. Although his center-right coalition lost seats in the 2007 legislative elections, it still controlled three-fifths of the National Assembly. Sarkozy promised to reduce taxes and to reduce public spending gradually. Perhaps his boldest proposal called for the government to leave vacant the jobs of one out of every three retiring civil service employees.

French spending reflects the role of cultural and institutional influences on policy making. First, the polarization of the party system reflects deeply felt divisions in French society about the role of government. As a result, national spending priorities are politically explosive. Second, the unitary nature of the French state creates an expectation that governments can implement new priorities quickly—adding to the all-or-nothing flavor of debate over social spending. Nevertheless, the two major parties agree that France will remain in the euro zone. Until the EU fiscal guidelines for monetary union are revised markedly (or one of several small anti-EU parties in France becomes a major coalition partner), the SGP will continue to shape policy debates in the major parties. Globalization is a visible force in contemporary fiscal policy making—especially inside the euro zone.

United Kingdom

Background: Policy Process and Policy History

As in France, budget formulation in the United Kingdom is centered on the prime minister and the finance minister (known as the chancellor of the exchequer). They work out a general set of targets, and then the finance minister negotiates with each spending minister. Disputes are arbitrated by a committee of senior ministers who have no power to spend and therefore are not in a position to trade votes for spending increases in each other's ministries. Instead, these ministers have tended to reflect the position of the prime minister and, often, the finance minister. The budget then goes to the legislature, where its passage with minimal revision is generally a foregone conclusion—although sometimes the flow of debate in Parliament can spark a change in the government's plans. In formal terms, the legislature can only block spending proposals; it has no power to authorize new programs or to increase appropriations for existing programs beyond the budget bill. To provide for more debate of major issues before public presentation of the government's draft budget, in late 1997 the newly elected Blair government introduced the practice of having the finance minister present a so-called Green Budget speech in which preliminary economic projections and major policy considerations that guide budget formation could be aired publicly. In 1998, under then-chancellor Gordon Brown, the United Kingdom began a process of biennial budgeting for spending decisions that subsequently became a triennial process in 2004. Rather than negotiating spending allocations each year, the contemporary British budget locks in spending for three-year cycles during which public agencies can carry over unspent money from one year to the next inside each triennial budget.

The United Kingdom has traditionally relied on a mix of foreign and domestic sources to finance its deficit. However, when the pound's position deteriorated on international markets in the early 1990s, the government was forced to turn more heavily to domestic investors. A long tradition of meeting its obligations—combined with what many observers depict as the risk-averse stance of British investors—helped the government to finance its debt in the domestic capital market without hiking up interest rates. In the early twenty-first century, the improved fiscal situation under the Blair government and a lowered debt-to-GDP ratio increased foreign investor confidence once more. The share of debt held by nonresidents nearly doubled to over 30 percent by 2007.

Like Japan, the United Kingdom also began the 1990s with a certain amount of economic optimism. Economic growth, combined with spending cuts in 1988 and 1989, converted the budget deficit of 2.9 percent of GDP in 1985 into surpluses of around 1 percent in 1988 and 1989. The British surplus proved precarious. Flat growth in 1990 and a recession in 1991 and 1992 pushed the deficit back up to 6.5 percent of GDP in 1992. The newly formed Major government carried out real expenditure increases throughout the recession in preparation for an ultimately successful, come-from-behind general election campaign in 1992. With the election won, the Major government faced the challenge of bringing down the deficit without jeopardizing its slim majority in the legislature. The 1997 elections brought an end to nearly two decades of Conservative governments and ushered in an overwhelmingly large Labour majority. Tony Blair campaigned on a New Labour platform that stressed fiscal responsibility, but with a large, disciplined majority party behind him he did not confront the same political constraints faced by his predecessor. Furthermore, the United Kingdom's option on European monetary unification meant that the British government was under no firm pressure to meet the precise target of a deficit no larger than 3 percent of GDP. In Blair's first term as prime minister, he pursued modest increases in social spending teamed with the occasional accompanying tax provision to ensure fiscal stability. This approach converted a 1997 deficit of 2.0 percent of GDP into a balanced budget in 1998 and then a small surplus in 1999.

Contemporary Dynamics

As noted earlier, the Blair government began by honoring its pledge to reduce the budget deficit. Chancellor Brown enforced caps that kept expenditures from rising faster than GDP growth. A large, disciplined Labour majority enabled the Blair government to pursue this policy despite complaints from Labour backbenchers that their party needed to do more to improve core social services. Spending restraint combined with steady economic growth—averaging 3.4 percent a year during 1997–2001—to produce three consecutive budget surpluses in 1999–2001. These surpluses changed the political agenda.

The Labour Party had demonstrated fiscal responsibility, and calls for addressing other policy areas grew louder at the start of the twenty-first century. Labour legislators to the left of Tony Blair pressed harder for increased social spending, which they deemed critical to improving capacity and outcomes in education and health care. Conservative critics bolstered the hand of those advocates of social spending by arguing that the Blair government had not achieved its ambitious goal of significantly lowering waiting times for a variety of health care treatments. Labor unions and social movements increased their mobilization in support of increased social spending. When Labour triumphed handily again in the 2001 elections, the pressure increased further.

The 2002 budget responded to these calls from within Labour and several of its key supporters. The Blair government proposed a visible increase in health care spending and launched some new initiatives in education. In this instance, there was little disagreement within the Labour majority; indeed, many legislators rejoiced. The difficult issue in Blair's second term stemmed from his decision to send troops to Iraq in support of the U.S. invasion in 2003. The war effort was opposed by a majority of the British public in opinion polls, and many Labour legislators were also against it. Nevertheless, as has been the case historically, the presence of a large, disciplined majority in the Westminster model (in which a plurality electoral system is combined with a parliamentary executive) put decision-making power firmly in the hands of the cabinet. The Labour majority backed the first increase in military spending in excess of GDP growth since 1991.

The fiscal responsibility mantra of the Blair campaign was an electorally successful effort to deflect the traditional Tory argument that Labour could not be trusted to govern. From Margaret Thatcher forward, two decades of Conservative politicians had campaigned on the charge that they were more fiscally responsible than Labour. This charge was bolstered by anecdotal evidence that Labour's ties to the trade union movement might lead to a host of expensive social spending should Labour return to power. Many business leaders echoed the call for Conservative leadership in fiscal matters. Given the tendency toward majority party government in the United Kingdom, the challenge for Blair was not to build a unified coalition but rather to win over a disciplined majority within his own party. This process, begun under earlier party leaders, reached a fever pitch under Blair's leadership as he worked hard to use his authority and his public visibility to reshape fiscal policy formulation within the party itself.

No technical implementation problems blocked the execution of these budgetary decisions. Instead, the principal potential obstacle was political—public opposition to the war effort. Blair's approval ratings plummeted; he announced prior to the 2005 elections that he would retire as party leader prior to the next election cycle. In the end, Labour held on to a parliamentary majority but its share of the vote fell from 40.7 percent in 2001 to 35.3 percent in 2005. The main reason that Labour did not lose power is that antiwar Labour voters threw their support to smaller parties (and not to the Conservative Party as it had backed involvement in the Iraq war). The sobering electoral result may have sped up Blair's resignation as he left office in June 2007. He was replaced by Gordon Brown, the chancellor of the exchequer throughout the Blair era.

Given Brown's long involvement in fiscal policy, the Labour Party will likely continue its course of modest increases in social spending teamed with the occasional accompanying new tax provision to ensure fiscal stability. The major potential obstacle to the continuation of that approach is the overall economic climate. The Brown government responded to the global economic downturn and financial crisis in 2008 with a countercyclical upswing in public spending to recapitalize banks and increase the availability of credit for firms and consumers.

This case study demonstrates in practice some of the principles of the Westminster model of parliamentary government: one-party majority governments, two major parties dominating the political scene, and a unitary state capable of making great changes fairly rapidly. With no coalition partners to satisfy, most British governments have faced less political pressure to run large deficits. At the same time, the relative unity of British governments is no panacea from a policy outcome perspective. Just because the British government is often capable of making faster decisions and implementing them more quickly does not mean that the United Kingdom is immune to disappointing economic conditions or unpopular governmental policy commitments (such as the Iraq war). In fact, the responsiveness of the political system may paradoxically raise some people's expectations about government's capacity to work miracles.

Italy

Background: Policy Process and Policy History

The Italian fiscal process during the 1980s and most of the 1990s tended to be somewhat more intricate than the French and German processes—both in theory and in practice. Although a specific Budget Ministry existed, it was not the central arena for annual fiscal policy; the Budget Ministry's principal task was to design medium- and long-term economic plans. The annual budget process centered on the Treasury. The General Accountancy Office within the Treasury drafted the budget within rough guidelines established by an inter-ministerial committee on economic planning chaired by the budget minister. Since 1978, legislators in both chambers had been able to make amendments to the budget bill. Although some of these changes were last-minute adjustments worked out between leaders of the governing coalitions or their respective major factions, many amendments were members' initiatives from legislators without leadership positions. The inability or unwillingness of the governing coalition to restrain decentralized additions to spending was often cited as a major factor in rising budget deficits in the 1980s and early 1990s. The statutory procedures prevented legislators from spending beyond the revenues and from writing new revenue provisions into the budget bill. Members often skirted these obstacles by basing the funding on changed economic projections or on projections of authorized funds not spent. These less centralized practices at the decision-making stage delayed the timely passage of the annual budget and opened the budget approval process to the participation of a wider variety of actors.

In reaction to these various problems—and with considerable pressure and political commitment to meet the Maastricht deficit target for monetary unification—the Prodi government passed a major reform of the budget procedures in April 1997 (Law Number 94). This procedural reform reduced the number of budgetary categories greatly (to improve control over the administration of spending), streamlined the procedures for parliamentary approval, and expanded the authority of the bureaucracy in monitoring expenditures (as opposed to planned spending). Perhaps the most striking change was a move from the past incrementalist approach to budget formation to a zero-based budgeting approach that requires all spending proposals to be justified on their individual merits. A further administrative reform merged the Budget, Treasury, and Finance Ministries—thus unifying the implementation of spending and taxation measures. With these tools in place, the Italian governments prepared to meet the challenge of trying to maintain consistently low deficits in accord with the EU's Stability and Growth Pact.

Some of the consequences of perennially high deficits were visible in the Italian experience in the 1980s and 1990s. Italy found it very difficult to market long-term bonds. High deficits decreased investors' confidence in the government's ability to make good on a long-term obligation. More important, comparatively higher inflation rates in Italy (associated in part with higher deficits) decreased the value of Italian bonds relative to other countries' debt instruments—forcing the Italian government to pay higher interest rates in its debt financing. Deficit reduction in the late 1990s and the creation of the euro helped to improve Italian bonds' creditworthiness. During the years 1998–2007, the average maturity increased and the percentage of debt held by nonresidents increased from one-third to over half of all Italian public debt.

Throughout the 1980s Italy ran the highest deficits in the G-7 as the average deficit exceeded 10 percent of GDP. By 1989 interest payments on the debt constituted nearly one-fifth of all government spending. Among G-7 countries, only Canada faced a similar debt service burden. Many observers cited the political dynamics of perennially vulnerable coalition governments as a major contributor to Italy's seeming inability to cut its deficit. Political reform in Italy in the 1990s—manifested by continued anticorruption efforts and a substantial change in its electoral system—renewed optimism in some circles that the deficit could be reduced. The Maastricht commitment provided another new tool that Italian governments could wield to build political support for (or at least acceptance of) deficit reduction measures. This scenario helped to create the new budgetary process highlighted above.

Contemporary Dynamics

Despite these changes over the course of the 1990s, coherent policy formulation on fiscal policy remained difficult amid the fractious coalition politics that characterized Italian politics following the collapse of the old party system and the emergence of a new, hybrid electoral system. The first center-right government to emerge in the new era lasted less than one year before internal divisions brought down Silvio Berlusconi's first prime ministership. In turn, the center-left coalition that followed pushed for a series of budgetary reforms between 1996 and 1997 before Romano Prodi lost a confidence vote framed around budgetary priorities in 1998. His successor, Massimo D'Alema, also found it difficult to forge a stable coalition—resigning prior to the 2001 general elections. During the 1990s, both coalitions headed governments careful to call simultaneously for the preservation of social spending and for fiscal responsibility. Major business associations and labor union confederations have echoed this dualistic call for having one's cake and eating it, too. The end to the secret legislative ballot and the 1997 budget reforms helped to centralize authority in government; however, the tenuous nature of coalition governments continued to enable many actors to influence policy.

Partisan wrangling notwithstanding, the deficit was reduced substantially in Italy from the mid-1990s through 2000. The caretaker government led by banker Lamberto Dini reduced government spending in 1994 and 1995 by a series of across-the-board cuts. By 1995 the deficit was down to just below 8 percent of GDP. The newly elected center-left Prodi government had a long way to go to push the deficit down to 2.7 percent in 1997 to meet the Maastricht target. D'Alema continued this commitment to monetary unification, pushing the deficit down to 0.9 percent of GDP by 2000. As in France, the desire to join the euro zone was a powerful force helping the government to reduce the deficit.

These sea changes in Italian public finance—along with nearly 4 percent annual GDP growth in 2000—framed the 2001 election campaign. Silvio Berlusconi boldly promised to halve the unemployment rate via a combination of a massive, ten-year public works program and a tax reform that would simplify and reduce the income tax rate structure (discussed further in Chapter 7). Francesco Rutelli, the new standard bearer on the center-left, talked of an expansion of public spending in the service of ordinary Italians. A multitude of interest groups put forward specific proposals for varied initiatives. In the end, Berlusconi's coalition won a more convincing victory that seemed to promise a new era of more party discipline in fiscal policy and other matters. His party's share of coalition seats rose markedly—and he no longer depended on the votes of the Northern League allies that had brought down his first government back in 1995.

However, despite the rosy outlook during the campaign for the May 2001 elections, fiscal decisions during Berlusconi's second government were constrained by a worsening economic context and the continued ability of individual politicians to retain some autonomy in fiscal matters. The first bad news came early in Berlusconi's term: the economy cooled off. The GDP grew by 1.7 percent in 2001 and then stagnated for the rest of Berlusconi's term. During 2002–2005, annual GDP growth averaged a paltry 0.7 percent. Demands for social spending increased while tax revenues could not keep pace. The deficit increased immediately to 3.1 percent in 2001. Over the years 2002 to 2005 it stayed at or above 3 percent of GDP. Rather than presiding over a new era of high growth, public works, and lower taxes, the Berlusconi coalition found itself immediately in the crosshairs of the Stability and Growth Pact's mandate to keep the deficit from rising above 3 percent of GDP. Economic Minister Giulio Tremonti called for deeper spending cuts than coalition members would accept and was removed briefly in 2004. When his successor proved even less able to mobilize a coalition for reform, Berlusconi reappointed Tremonti and gave him a mandate to cut taxes in 2005—in advance of the pending 2006 elections. Tremonti followed through on some of these ideas, but the tax cuts initially pushed the deficit up to 4.4 percent in 2005.

Although these events testify to the difficulties of building political support for fiscal austerity amid economic stagnation, the same period also bore witness to the improved implementation capacity of the reformed Italian Economic Ministry. The reforms of the 1990s created a more streamlined system in which the Economic Ministry was better poised to monitor the spending of each ministry as well as changes in tax revenues. This improved capability helped the second Berlusconi government to walk a tightrope near the SGP target from 2001 to 2004—before abandoning the target in the build-up to the 2006 elections.

The dynamics of fiscal policy in Italy reinforce the points raised by the strength of government thesis about divided electorates and unstable coalition governments. Although parliamentary governments may prove more responsive when a stable majority or majority coalition emerges in control of the government, the absence of a durable majority can make governing difficult. In short, institutions help to frame policy making, but they do not determine the final outcome. Parliamentary and cabinet institutions may make fiscal policy easier to conduct, but only if the political influences on policy making are not too polarizing.

Controlling a budget deficit amid economic stagnation presents serious challenges. Given the turmoil in the Italian political system in the 1990s, it is striking that Berlusconi's second government avoided increasing the deficit for nearly four years before pursuing a portion of its tax cut agenda. That improved fiscal discipline is a testament to the power of shared political will by major government and nongovernment leaders to remain in the euro zone. In this instance, the globalization thesis appears to have triumphed in the face of potentially fragile coalition governments and divided electorates.

European Union

Background: Policy Process and Policy History

Prior to the Single European Act, the creation of the EU's budget was an annual process characterized by considerable conflict between the major decision-making bodies—the European Parliament and the Council of Ministers. Beginning in 1988, the EU moved toward multiyear budgeting; from 1993 forward the EU has enacted seven-year budgets (which permit minor annual changes in response to unforeseen events). In stark contrast to the national governments examined in this book, the EU is forced to produce a balanced budget each year and is not permitted to shift funds from one spending category to another within the overall budget. Budgets are drafted by the European Commission and then voted on by both the Council of Ministers and the European Parliament; the Parliament takes the final vote on the multiyear budget and must approve each successive year's budget before it can be implemented.

The EU's budget process does not fit well into common discussions of the role of fiscal policy as a potential countercyclical instrument capable of affecting macroeconomic conditions more broadly. The requirement for balanced budgets eliminates its ability to engage in deficit spending to stimulate recoveries amid economic downturns. In turn, the small size of the budget limits its economic impact still further. The budget's total expenditures comprise just 1 percent of the EU's overall GDP. The impact of EU expenditures is limited further by their narrow focus. Over the years 2003–2007, the EU spent over two-fifths of its budget on agricultural policy and another third on structural cohesion policies intended to reduce regional disparities within and across member states. In turn, the EU spent no money on health, education, or social welfare programs. Instead, as we will observe in subsequent chapters, the EU influences national policy decisions in health, education, and welfare via rulemaking and the negotiation of treaties.

In the area of fiscal policy as well, the EU's primary influence is via its creation of rules and commitments that frame the decisions made by the national governments of its member states. As noted earlier, the EU's ability to shape fiscal policy is a relatively recent development. The push for monetary unification produced the 1997 SGP, which constituted the EU's first major effort to shape national fiscal policies. Created at the urging of the German government, the SGP called for governments to pursue budgets in surplus (or, at least, nearly balanced) over the medium term. Furthermore, under the SGP's excessive deficit procedure, member states could face sanctions for annual deficits exceeding 3 percent of GDP, except in the special circumstances mentioned earlier. Finally, the SGP also called for governments to contain overall public debt at below 60 percent of GDP.

Contemporary Dynamics

At its initiation, the SGP's deficit target was not that hard for most countries to meet amid the largely favorable global economic conditions of the late 1990s. In the euro zone as a whole, the average deficit fell steadily during 1998–2000 from 2.3 percent of GDP to 0.0; the medium-term objective of a balanced budget seemed to have been met in the aggregate. In the three largest countries inside the euro zone—Germany, France, and Italy—average deficits fell steadily during this period but remained around 1 percent of GDP in 2000. The European Commission suggested even greater efforts to constrain spending during periods of economic growth. Many business groups in member states echoed this recommendation. Labor union leaders and some external economic analysts countered that the SGP's threat of sanctions for failure to meet fiscal targets during economic declines could culminate in longer recessions.

A widespread economic downturn in 2001 tested the fragility of the deficit reduction achieved during 1996–2000. In 2001 Portugal's deficit of 4.3 percent of GDP exceeded the SGP target; under the excessive deficit procedure, EU authorities gave Portugal one year to comply with the 3 percent target. They judged that the deficit's size exceeded the depth of the economic slowdown in Portugal given that its GDP had grown by 2.0 percent in 2001. To avoid possible sanctions, Portugal reined in spending and raised the national sales tax rate by two percentage points. These fiscal policies brought the deficit within the 3 percent SGP limit. However, they also slowed the Portuguese economy, which grew by just 0.8 percent in 2002 and shrank by 0.8 percent in 2003. During that same period, the growth rate slowed in the euro zone as a whole.

In 2002 Germany, France, and Italy ran deficits slightly over 3 percent; in 2003 each country was informed that it should reduce its deficit. However, all three countries continued to run deficits in excess of 3 percent during 2003–2004. In theory the SGP should have sanctioned these countries after they violated the excessive deficit procedure's rectification process, but sanctions were not implemented. Technical considerations did not cause implementation failure in this instance; the European Commission received timely updates regarding the fiscal situation in each country. Instead, political and policy considerations blocked implementation: it proved difficult in practice for the EU authorities to punish three of its four largest economies. Politically, some decision makers did not want to risk angering powerful countries. The United Kingdom joined France and Germany in arguing that the SGP was insufficiently flexible. Policy concerns also entered into play: if sanctions succeeded in producing a rapid drop in these deficits, the abrupt change might negatively affect growth throughout the EU.

Indeed, German, French, and Italian authorities made just these sorts of policy evaluation arguments both privately and publicly. They said that the SGP's inflexibility harmed the interests of member states and of the EU as a whole. In this debate, the Portuguese case was often cited as an example of the SGP's excessive harshness. Such policy evaluations framed a new round of decision making regarding the SGP's future. In 2005 a series of resolutions from the Council of Ministers revised the SGP in pursuit of additional flexibility. The deficit and public debt targets remained the same, but the new regulations called for an adjustment period of sixteen months (rather than the prior twelve-month period for compliance). The new system also mandates further consideration of low growth as a factor that could produce admissible deficits above the 3 percent threshold. The budgetary impact of policy reforms that could imply higher spending in the short term but lead to lower spending over time also became a recognized exception.

The dynamics of the SGP illustrate the role of institutional and economic factors in EU policy making. First and foremost, the formal and informal impact of weighted voting favors the perspectives of the largest members in major policy decisions. Tellingly, Germany and France succeeded in helping to push for the creation of the SGP in 1997 and then—after their national interests were potentially threatened by the excessive deficit procedure—the same two countries led the charge to reform the policy. In addition, economic factors play a key role in policy change here as the growth outlook framed the evolution of this policy considerably. After the SGP's initial launch, steady economic growth made compliance relatively easy for most participating countries. Conversely, once economic conditions soured, staying within the prescribed 3 percent target became difficult.

The events of 2002–2005 also contributed to the global debate regarding the relative priority of fiscal discipline and countercyclical measures. Fiscal hawks argue that without a threat of sanctions, some members of the euro zone will be tempted to run considerable deficits in the hopes that their borrowing can be subsidized by other euro partners more committed to balanced budgets. Neokeynesians, on the other hand, assert that excessive obsession with fiscal discipline will reduce economic growth in good times and prolong recessions in bad times. The advent of a sharp economic downturn in 2008 signaled that this particular policy debate will likely continue both within the EU and beyond.

Cross-national Trends

Five of the six countries discussed here demonstrated a visible trend toward deficit reduction. Although deficit reduction has reduced inflation, in the late 1990s it was rarely associated with a decline in unemployment and faster economic growth. The lone exception to this trend was in the United States. Given that deficit reduction tended to take place amid slow economic growth, it presented these countries with a series of political challenges. As the case studies demonstrated, global economic factors proved crucial in the move toward deficit reduction.

Policy Outputs

Among the six countries, Japan sat at one extreme of the fiscal policy continuum while the United Kingdom and the United States found themselves

Table 6-1 Deficit Spending Trends, 1985–2007

	Government Deficit, as a Percentage of GDP							
	France	*Germany*	*Italy*	*Japan*	*United Kingdom*	*United States*	*Average*	*Euro Zone*
Annual average, 1985–1989	–2.44%	–1.24%	–11.02%	0.56%	–1.18%	–4.28%	–3.27%	—
Annual average, 1990–1999	–3.73	–2.51	–7.11	–1.97	–3.65	–2.86	–3.64	—
Annual average, 2000–2004	–2.79	–2.59	–2.82	–7.20	–1.01	–2.35	–3.13	–2.09
Annual average, 1998–2007	–2.64	–2.13	–2.83	–6.51	–1.31	–1.88	–2.88	–1.86
1998	–2.6	–2.2	–3.1	–11.2	–0.1	0.4	–3.1	–2.3
1999	–1.8	–1.5	–1.8	–7.4	0.9	0.9	–1.8	–1.4
2000	–1.5	–1.3	–0.9	–7.6	3.7	1.6	–0.6	–0.0
2001	–1.6	–2.8	–3.1	–6.3	0.6	–0.4	–2.3	–1.8
2002	–3.2	–3.6	–3.0	–8.0	–2.0	–3.8	–3.9	–2.6
2003	–4.1	–4.0	–3.5	–7.9	–3.7	–4.8	–4.7	–3.1
2004	–3.6	–3.8	–3.6	–6.2	–3.7	–4.4	–4.2	–3.0
2005	–3.0	–3.3	–4.4	–6.7	–3.3	–3.3	–4.0	–2.5
2006	–2.4	–1.5	–3.4	–1.4	–2.7	–2.2	–2.3	–1.3
2007	–2.7	0.1	–1.5	–2.4	–2.8	–2.9	–2.0	–0.6

SOURCE: For years 1985–1997, Organisation for Economic Co-operation and Development (OECD 2000); for years 1998–2007, OECD (2008c).

NOTE: Positive numbers indicate a budget surplus.

GDP = gross domestic product; — = not applicable.

at the other extreme at the turn of the twenty-first century. Table 6-1 shows that Japan had, on average, considerable budget deficits from 1998 to 2001. In contrast, both the United Kingdom and the United States ran a net budget surplus over the same period. Germany, France, and Italy held an intermediate stance as all three countries ran relatively small deficits that declined over the course of that four-year period.

An economic downturn beginning in 2001 and lasting until 2003 across much of the industrialized world placed renewed pressure on public finances in these six countries. In addition, the decision to wage war in Iraq had human, political, and fiscal costs for the United States and its British ally. Deficits exceeded 3 percent of GDP in all six countries by 2003 and remained at or above that level through 2005. Thus, if a deficit of over 3 percent of GDP is deemed by some to be the litmus test of fiscal problems, then during 2003–2005 none of these countries proved able to meet that overall fiscal target.

Higher economic growth rates during 2006 and 2007 relieved some fiscal pressures and enabled all of these countries to reduce their deficits during that time. By 2007 all six countries had deficits below 3 percent of GDP. Can these countries continue to meet this deficit target over time? If governments are capable, is it desirable that they pursue fiscal responsibility as a central priority? Part of the answer to the capability question certainly lies in the political ingenuity of the governments. An assessment of the relative desirability of fiscal discipline may in turn be tied to the economic outcomes associated with efforts to keep the deficit in check.

Policy Outcomes

The need for spending austerity to meet the deficit target set for monetary unification in Europe during the 1990s was magnified by markedly slow GDP growth. As Table 6-2 shows, the average annual growth for the six countries examined in this book was 3.46 percent during 1985–1989. During the race to the euro, however, growth averaged a paltry 1.89 percent for the period 1990–1999. Only the U.S. and British economies managed to grow at rates in excess of 2 percent per year in the 1990s. During 2000–2004, the average growth rate remained limited at 1.89 percent annually. While average growth rates picked up slightly to 2.2 percent in 2005–2007, preliminary forecasts for 2008 and 2009 indicate a considerable economic decline, which will probably pull the average annual growth rate for the entire second half of the decade well below 2 percent.

Although growth fell significantly between the periods 1985–1989 and 1990–1994, inflation increased slightly from an average of 3.51 percent to 3.66 percent. During 1995–1999, however, inflation in all six countries fell markedly, to an average of 1.85 percent. Fairly tight monetary policies were used by most of these governments in the mid-1990s to keep inflation in check in the face of persistent budget deficits. During the first decade of the twenty-first century, average annual inflation remained below 2 percent as central banks maintained fairly restrictive monetary policies through 2006.

Tight monetary policies helped to check inflation, but at the cost of slower growth. Slow growth dampens government revenues—thereby increasing pressures on the expenditure side of the fiscal equation. Slow growth also makes it difficult to escape high unemployment. Although inflation was the major economic problem in many industrialized countries during the 1970s, unemployment has been the bugbear of the industrialized world from the 1980s forward. By the mid-1990s only Japan and the United States had low levels of unemployment. Those two countries were joined in the late 1990s by the United Kingdom.

In contrast, unemployment rose in France, Germany, and Italy during the period 1995–1998. Part of the rise in unemployment stems from efforts to reduce the budget deficit rapidly in 1997. Slow economic growth and fiscal austerity do not entirely explain these countries' disappointing unemployment outcomes. Other explanations focus on the relative lack of pro-labor legislation in Japan and the United States, in comparison with the European countries. The average annual unemployment in all three countries continued to exceed 8 percent during the years 2000–2007.

Table 6-2 Major Economic Indicators, 1985–2007 (in percent)

Country	Indicator	Annual average 1985–1989 (%)	Annual average 1990–1999 (%)	Annual average 2000–2004 (%)	2003 (%)	2004 (%)	2005 (%)	2006 (%)	2007 (%)
France	Growth	*2.98*	*1.64*	*2.05*	1.1	2.2	1.9	2.4	2.1
	Unemployment	*10.04*	*11.24*	*8.84*	9.0	9.3	9.3	9.2	8.3
	Inflation	*3.56*	*1.94*	*2.01*	2.2	2.3	1.9	1.9	1.6
	Deficit/GDP	*–2.44*	*–3.73*	*–2.79*	–4.1	–3.6	–3.0	–2.4	–2.7
Germany	Growth	*2.62*	*2.18*	*1.07*	–0.2	0.7	0.9	3.2	2.6
	Unemployment	*6.36*	*7.49*	*8.52*	9.3	9.8	10.6	9.8	8.4
	Inflation	*1.26*	*2.51*	*1.50*	1.0	1.8	1.9	1.8	2.3
	Deficit/GDP	*–1.24*	*–2.51*	*–2.59*	–4.0	–3.8	–3.3	–1.5	0.1
Italy	Growth	*3.06*	*1.42*	*1.50*	0.0	1.4	0.7	1.9	1.4
	Unemployment	*9.32*	*10.61*	*8.88*	8.5	8.1	7.7	6.8	6.2
	Inflation	*6.22*	*4.17*	*2.52*	2.8	2.3	2.2	2.2	2.0
	Deficit/GDP	*–11.02*	*–7.11*	*–2.82*	–3.5	–3.6	–4.4	–3.4	–1.5
Japan	Growth	*4.50*	*1.83*	*1.49*	1.4	2.7	1.9	2.4	2.1
	Unemployment	*2.60*	*3.05*	*5.02*	5.3	4.7	4.4	4.1	3.9
	Inflation	*1.14*	*1.20*	*–0.50*	–0.2	0.0	–0.6	0.2	0.1
	Deficit/GDP	*0.56*	*–1.97*	*–7.20*	–7.9	–6.2	–6.7	–1.4	–2.4
United Kingdom	Growth	*3.94*	*2.00*	*2.81*	2.8	2.8	2.1	2.8	3.0
	Unemployment	*9.94*	*8.24*	*5.04*	5.0	4.7	4.8	5.4	5.3
	Inflation	*5.26*	*3.71*	*1.20*	1.4	1.3	2.0	2.3	2.3
	Deficit/GDP	*–1.18*	*–3.65*	*–1.01*	–3.7	–3.7	–3.7	–2.7	–2.8
United States	Growth	*3.66*	*2.33*	*2.43*	2.5	3.6	2.9	2.8	2.0
	Unemployment	*6.24*	*5.75*	*5.20*	6.0	5.5	5.1	4.6	4.6
	Inflation	*3.60*	*3.00*	*2.55*	2.3	2.7	3.4	3.2	2.9
	Deficit/GDP	*–4.28*	*–2.86*	*–2.35*	–4.8	–4.4	–3.3	–2.2	–2.9
Average	*Growth*	3.46	1.89	1.89	*1.3*	2.2	*1.8*	2.6	2.2
	Unemployment	7.42	7.73	6.62	*7.0*	*7.0*	*7.0*	6.6	6.0
	Inflation	3.51	2.76	1.54	*1.6*	*1.7*	*1.8*	2.0	*1.9*
	Deficit/GDP	–3.27	–3.64	–3.13	*–4.7*	*–4.2*	*–4.0*	–2.3	–2.0

SOURCE: For years 1985–1997, Organisation for Economic Co-operation and Development (OECD 2000); for years 1998–2007, OECD (2008c).

NOTE: Positive numbers regarding the deficit indicate a budget surplus.

GDP = gross domestic product.

Although no crystal-clear link exists between falling deficits and rising, persistent unemployment in the industrialized countries, the two issues are connected in the policy debate within the systemic agenda for two main reasons. First, many deficit-cutting politicians raise expectations that a more fiscally sound government could help reduce the unemployment rate. Across all industrialized countries, that sequence has occurred in only four countries to any visible degree—Denmark, Ireland, the United Kingdom, and the United States. Second, as noted earlier, persistent unemployment in many countries (even where it has declined slightly) puts increasing pressure on governments to provide social expenditures. The effort to control the deficit amid slow growth and rising demands for some services increases the conflict involved in fiscal policy making.

Understanding Policy Reform

Partisanship may still matter in determining spending priorities within budgets, but the contours of fiscal policy decisions regarding deficits do not line up well with the historical notion that center-left parties are more prone than center-right parties to produce deficits. Not only did parties of all stripes pledge lowered deficits in the late 1990s, they also delivered deficit reduction. New center-left governments were formed in 1997 and 1998 in France, Germany, Italy, and the United Kingdom. Although these governments included movements historically associated with an expansion of government programs (particularly in health and social policy), all pledged to combine fiscal responsibility with the maintenance of most existing government programs in some form. The Clinton administration in the United States set a policy course along roughly the same lines. In turn, governments led by conservative parties presided over rising budget deficits in Japan during the 1990s and in France and the United States during the first decade of the twenty-first century.

The situation in Japan is a reminder of the role of short-term economic conditions in shaping budget deficits. The weak economy in Japan—including a strong recession in 1997 and very slow growth during 2000–2004—produced strong pressure toward deficit spending in two senses. First, the contraction in the economy forced government revenues down. Second, that recession and the stagnation that preceded it provided a strong political rationale for engaging in deficit spending to promote economic growth. A less severe version of the same scenario can be observed in France, Germany, and Italy amid limited growth during 2001–2005.

Further, although some analysts argued for more vigorous use of deficit spending (and more permissive monetary policy) to accelerate economic growth and to reduce unemployment in continental Europe, governments of varied political parties in France, Germany, and Italy all pointed to the monetary union as a rationale for limiting the application of countercyclical policies to a level only minimally out of line with the SGP guidelines. In addition to that international agreement, governments in all six countries pointed to a need to control deficits in order to lower domestic interest rates (to attract foreign capital) and to decrease pressure on the national currency (especially from abroad). In short, global economic factors—both formal integration and de facto interdependence—were the most visible influences at the agenda-setting and decision-making stages of fiscal policy from the 1990s through the early twenty-first century in these countries.

SUGGESTED READINGS

Dyson, Kenneth H. F. 2002. *European States and the Euro: Europeanization, Variation, and Convergence.* Oxford: Oxford University Press.

Farrier, Jasmine. 2004. *Passing the Buck: Congress, the Budget and Deficits.* Lexington: University of Kentucky Press.

Garrett, Elizabeth, Elizabeth Graddy, and Howell E. Jackson, eds. 2008. *Fiscal Challenges: An Interdisciplinary Approach to Budget Policy.* Cambridge: Cambridge University Press.

Hallerberg, Mark. 2004. *Domestic Budgets in a United Europe: Fiscal Governance from the End of Bretton Woods to EMU.* Ithaca: Cornell University Press.

Kaarlejärvi, Jani. 2007. *Fiscal Policy Without a State in EMU?: Germany, the Stability and Growth Pact and Policy Coordination.* New York: Palgrave Macmillan.

Kaul, Inge, and Pedro Conceição, eds. 2006. *The New Public Finance: Responding to Global Challenges.* Oxford: Oxford University Press.

Mulas-Granados, Carlos. 2006. *Economics, Politics and Budgets: The Political Economy of Fiscal Consolidations in Europe.* New York: Palgrave Macmillan.

Roy, Ravi K., and Arthur Denzau. 2004. *Fiscal Policy Convergence from Reagan to Blair: The Left Veers Right.* London: Routledge.

Schick, Allen. 2007. *The Federal Budget: Politics, Policy, Process,* 3rd ed. Washington, D.C.: Brookings Institution Press.

Sturm, Roland. 1999. *Public Deficits: A Comparative Study of Their Economic and Political Consequences in Britain, Canada, Germany and the United States.* Harlow, England: Longman.

Talani, Leila Simona, and Bernard Casey, eds. 2008. *Between Growth and Stability: The Demise and Reform of the European Union's Stability and Growth Pact.* Northampton, Mass.: Edward Elgar.

Wanna, John, Lotte Jensen, and Jouke de Vries, eds. 2003. *Controlling Public Expenditure: The Changing Roles of Central Budget Agencies—Better Guardians?* Northampton, Mass.: Edward Elgar.

Wright, Maurice. 2002. *Japan's Fiscal Crisis: The Ministry of Finance and the Politics of Public Spending, 1975–2000.* Oxford: Oxford University Press.

Yergin, Daniel, and Joseph Stanislaw. 2002. *The Commanding Heights: The Battle for the World Economy,* 2nd ed. New York: Simon & Schuster.

Chapter 7 Taxation Policy

Contemporary governments need money to carry out the wide variety of activities they pursue. Some of that money is raised by the sale of government-provided goods and services. However, in the six countries examined in this book (and in most countries around the world today), the vast majority of government revenues are generated by taxation.

More is at stake here than the generation of revenue. Governments make countless decisions about whom to tax and at what rate to tax them. These decisions can have important implications for other policy areas. Often governments encourage certain activities (and discourage others) through tax incentives. In this way the tax code—in addition to funding government activity—is itself a policy instrument, used in pursuit of goals on a multitude of issues.

Common Policy Problems

In the nineteenth century, government was much smaller than it is today. Because it provided far fewer services to its citizenry, it needed less money. Many countries managed to meet their revenue needs largely by taxing foreigners—in particular by taxing imports and by selling import licenses. In this way, governments minimized the visible tax burden on their citizens (a less visible tax remained in the form of higher prices for consumers of those imported goods).

During the twentieth century, governments began to provide a growing number of services to many people and organizations. All things being equal, most people and most businesses would still prefer to pay little or no money in taxes. Expressed in the language of rational choice theory, actors prefer to free ride on the cooperation of others. People want to receive as many government services and subsidies as possible, but they would prefer that those services be paid for by other people's taxes.

This simple truth provides the backdrop against which governments try to achieve the three fundamental goals of tax policy. First, how can the tax code be constructed to ensure that needed revenues are generated? Second, how can the government generate those revenues while generating the smallest degree of discontent possible? Third, how can the government use the tax code to provide tax incentives to encourage desired behaviors and tax disincentives to discourage other behaviors?

People's distaste for taxes gives individuals and firms an incentive to reduce the total taxes paid regardless of the tax system employed. Tax reduction efforts can take the form of **tax avoidance** (managing one's money in a way that minimizes tax liability) or outright **tax evasion** (the illegal refusal to pay taxes owed under the law).

In general, people would prefer to pay few or no taxes; however, they can be persuaded to pay taxes for a variety of reasons. For instance, they may pay taxes because they support the services the government provides with the tax revenue. This concept implies that governments have an incentive to fund popular programs out of funds raised explicitly for that purpose. As an example, old-age pensions are normally funded via payroll taxes earmarked for the pension fund. In an effort to increase tax compliance with many disparate programs, governments will sometimes bundle a popular program with several other initiatives paid for out of a given revenue stream.

People also are sometimes willing to pay taxes out of a sense of burden-sharing. If they believe that most (if not all) people are shouldering a fair share of the load, they may be more likely to pay (and less likely to criticize the government for its tax policies). Thus a major policy challenge for governments is to create a tax code that is viewed as equitable.

A second policy challenge results because people are more likely to pay taxes owed when they face a credible possibility of apprehension and punishment for tax evasion. When apprehension of evaders is likely, taxes are easier to collect. Some taxes are easier (or harder) to collect than others. Unfortunately for governments, many of the taxes that are relatively easy to collect are viewed by many as inequitable—thereby conflicting with the goal of equity.

We earlier alluded to a third problem in contemporary tax policy. The tax code is a major avenue of interaction between a government and its citizenry. As a result, the tax code presents an opportunity to pursue goals in other policy areas by providing preferential (or penalizing) tax treatment to encourage (or discourage) certain types of behavior. These provisions are generally referred to as **tax expenditures**—a term that captures how tax incentives spend revenues that otherwise would have been collected. For example, the tax code can be used to promote savings investment, discourage pollution, subsidize health care and education, provide extra tax relief to the impoverished, and so on.

The potential for using the tax code to promote different policy goals is seemingly endless. Nevertheless, the use of tax policy to meet various ends often runs counter to the challenges of tax equity and ease of collection. Too many tax expenditures may create the impression that some people are not paying their fair share—generating calls for a simpler tax code. Additionally, widespread use of tax expenditures may provide an incentive for tax fraud—the evasion of taxes by understating one's tax burden.

How governments manage this complex and conflicting triad of tax challenges (equity, ease of collection, and tax expenditures)—while still meeting the fundamental goals of generating needed revenues without substantial discontent—is central to government success in many areas. Governments that achieve a working equilibrium in this area can provide a stable economic and political environment. Governments that fail are headed for economic and political trouble.

Major Policy Options

When dealing with the equity issue, policymakers face a difficult series of choices. Sometimes equity is in conflict with other priorities. Moreover, the definition of equity depends on one's perspective. For some, equitable burden-sharing entails the rich paying a larger share of total taxes collected; this is deemed fair because the well-off presumably can pay more in taxes and still live comfortably. When a tax system calls on the wealthy to pay a higher percentage of their income in taxes than the poor, the tax system is said to be **progressive** because it is redistributing money from the rich to the poor. For others, equity implies that all persons and firms pay an equal percentage of their earnings in taxes—regardless of wealth and regardless of the source(s) of income. Such a tax system would be **income-neutral**; it would have no impact on the distribution of income. Finally, if a tax system forces the poor to pay a higher percentage in taxes than the rich, it is said to be **regressive** because it redistributes income from the poor to the wealthy. The progressive and income-neutral notions of equity face difficult technical challenges owing to the multitude of taxes collected. Different sorts of taxes lend themselves better to meeting the dueling concepts of progressivity and income neutrality, respectively.

Tax instruments are usually divided into two major groups. **Direct taxes** are levied as a percentage of income earned by a person or a firm. Personal income tax, corporate income tax, and employee payroll contributions to social security or other government programs (such as health insurance) are examples of direct taxes. Because direct taxes are calculated based on income data, they are a major potential instrument for redistribution. The government can choose to apply increasingly higher tax rates at higher income levels (via the use of **tax brackets**). Alternatively, the government can choose to have income-neutral direct taxes and charge all citizens the same uniform rate; this option is often referred to as the **flat tax**.

Although direct taxes provide the government with a ready means for redistribution via progressive tax brackets, they can be harder to collect than indirect taxes. Because direct taxes are based on income levels, the potential exists for the taxpayer's income to be underestimated by the tax collector, the taxpayer (at times intentionally), or both. During the twentieth century, governments worked hard to improve their information about income levels in order to reduce this problem.

Indirect taxes are not based on the taxpayer's income. Employer payroll taxes (based on earnings of employees) represent a major form of indirect taxation found in virtually every country around the world. Another common form of indirect tax is the sales tax—a tax charged on the sale of a good or service. In the United States, sales taxes have tended to be charged and collected at the final point of retail sale. In postwar Europe and in many developing countries, governments have increasingly turned to a value-added tax (VAT) charged on every transaction in the production of a good. A special form of sales tax is the **excise tax**—a tax charged on a particular good (for example, tobacco, liquor, or luxury yachts). Property taxes are also deemed to be indirect taxes because they do not take into account income earned but rather are a percentage of the assessed value of a given piece of property, for example, a house, a vacant lot, or an automobile.

Indirect taxes provided the bulk of government revenues in the nineteenth century because they were easier to collect than direct taxes. During the twentieth century, the sales tax was criticized as regressive because the wealthy spend a smaller portion of their income on consumer purchases than the poor. Efforts to address this problem by charging higher tax rates on luxury items have been problematic in industrialized countries because few products are purchased exclusively by the rich. Instead, the wealthy buy pricier, luxury-brand versions of the same products bought by others: cars, alcohol, food, and the like. Furthermore, the excise and property tax rates needed to address the inequities in the basic sales tax are so high that they are difficult to defend politically.

In industrialized countries during the twentieth century, proponents of both the progressive and the income-neutral notions of equity used the generally regressive nature of indirect taxes to argue for the implementation of progressive income taxes. Late-industrializing countries, however, rely heavily on indirect taxes because of the relative ease of collection. To the extent that indirect taxes in a given country's tax system are regressive, impoverished citizens in many poor nations are caught in a vicious cycle. Government programs to aid the poor are often insufficient, and the means used to fund the programs often place a disproportionate burden on the poor.

One might think that a tax system's effect on income distribution in the industrialized world could be readily evaluated. The information on the progressivity of direct taxes is inherent in the tax structure, and one could estimate the amount of money that people spend in sales taxes each year. Nevertheless, gauging the redistributive nature of a tax system is in practice extremely difficult because of the widespread use of tax expenditures. The estimate of sales taxes paid can be hard to calculate because many goods are subject to different sales tax rates (or, occasionally, no tax at all). Governments charge lower sales taxes on products they want to subsidize—sometimes making the good or service tax-exempt. Things can get even more complicated in the realm of direct taxes because governments can provide income tax expenditures to promote or subsidize a variety of activities. Sometimes governments provide **tax credits**, through which the cost of the activity is counted as a credit toward the taxes owed. For example, charitable donations could conceivably generate

Box 7-1 **In Depth: Income Tax Expenditures in the United States**

Tax credits and deductions are used more frequently in the United States than in any other industrialized country. For 2007 the Joint Committee on Taxation of the U.S. Congress tracked a total 136 specific tax expenditures in the individual income tax code and another 102 provisions in the corporate income tax code. These provisions apply to 171 different specific uses of money or categories of beneficiaries. The estimated revenue loss tied to these tax expenditures totaled $1.103 trillion in 2007. By way of perspective, the budget deficit in that fiscal year was $160.7 billion. Total government revenues were $2.729 trillion.

Governments engage in tax expenditures to promote specific activities. The ten largest tax expenditures in 2007 (accounting for nearly two-thirds of all tax expenditures) are as follows (the value in parentheses is the amount of revenue loss estimated for each provision):

- Capital gains exemptions in the individual income tax ($127.1 billion)
- Net exclusion of employee contributions to employer pension plans ($108.6 billion)
- Exclusion of employer contributions to employee medical insurance ($105.7 billion)
- Deductibility of mortgage interest on owner-occupied homes ($73.7 billion)
- Step-up basis of capital gains exemptions at death ($51.9 billion)
- Child tax credit ($45.0 billion)
- Earned income tax credit ($44.7 billion)
- Deductibility of nonbusiness state and local taxes other than those paid on owner-occupied homes ($33.9 billion)
- Deductibility of charitable contributions by individuals ($32.0 billion)
- Exclusion of employee job benefits ($30.0 billion)

a tax credit in an effort to promote giving. Much more often, governments provide **tax deductions**—a reduction in the amount of taxable income. Pursuing further the example of charitable donations, assume that a taxpayer making $50,000 a year donates $1,000 to a charity. If the donation were treated as a tax deduction, the individual's taxable income would be $49,000. If the tax rate were 10 percent, the taxpayer would owe $4,900 in income tax. If the same individual had received a $1,000 tax credit, the income tax bill would be only $4,000. For a look at the major tax expenditures written into the U.S. corporate and individual income tax codes, see Box 7-1.

Once you consider the multitude of tax expenditures written into the tax code, you can begin to appreciate the complexity of evaluating the equity of a tax system based on the concepts of either progressivity or income-neutrality. Why should governments complicate matters by pursuing policy goals via tax expenditures? Tax expenditures are attractive for a couple of reasons. First, governments can subsidize certain activities without collecting money in taxes and then paying out the subsidies to the relevant individuals. This approach can be an effective means of promoting the activity in question as long as the tax assessment process is not subject to fraud. Second, once the use of tax expenditures becomes widespread, they can have political advantages as well. When tax expenditures clutter the tax code, many citizens and firms have a stake in their retention such that the tax expenditures can be used to build political support for tax policy as a whole. Although all countries have a mix of direct and indirect taxes spiced with tax expenditures, various taxation models have proven to be politically viable in the six countries examined in this book.

Explaining Policy Dynamics

The complexity of the tax code presents a series of issues that can promote demands for change in one or more of its major provisions. Some citizens, interest groups, and public officials are concerned about the overall level of taxation. Others mobilize around particular components of the tax code itself. Under what conditions are governments more likely to reform the tax structure? Although the overall level of taxation is amenable to cross-national statistical analysis, the intricacy of the tax structure has made it difficult to study via quantitative analysis. Instead, research has centered on national and comparative case studies of tax policy. In different situations, cultural, economic, political, and institutional factors can shape the emergence of tax reform on the agenda, the particular reform decisions made, and the nature of implementation concerns.

Cultural Explanations

Some research indicates that deep cultural traditions help to shape the tax structures that governments choose. In particular, significant distrust of government can result in a trend toward tax evasion that prods governments to favor indirect taxes over direct taxes because the former are easier to collect. If tax evasion becomes enshrined in the culture, even if its pervasiveness is exaggerated in national folklore, governments may remain reliant on indirect taxation. When new revenues are needed in this context, governments would be more likely to raise rates on existing indirect taxes (or create new ones) than to expand direct taxation. Italy and France have demonstrated this dynamic more frequently than the other countries examined in this book (Haycraft 1987; Peters 1991).

Other research focuses more directly on public opinion regarding the nature of taxation. As we noted in Chapter 6, a stable majority in most

Table 7-1 A Model of Citizens' Attitudes toward Taxation

		Perceived Fairness of Tax System	
		Fair	*Unfair*
Perceived Justice of Tax System	*Just*	Tax compliance	Tax formalism
	Unjust	Tax protest	Tax revolt

SOURCE: Modified from Confalonieri and Newton (1995: 126).

industrialized societies would prefer to see taxes decrease or, at a minimum, stay at current levels. If and when that desire changes from an idle wish into a firmly stated demand, public opinion can tilt toward strident calls for reform that shape the policymakers' environment. Confalonieri and Newton (1995) present a four-scenario typology of public attitudes toward taxation (Table 7-1).

In this model, public attitudes about a tax system are measured along two dimensions—fairness and justice. Fairness concerns people's willingness to accept as fair the tax structure's general, fundamental principles. Justice involves judgments about whether the tax structure in practice calls on all citizens to pay their share in accordance with the tax system's founding principles. Confalonieri and Newton assert that most of the public opinion data do not support a situation of open revolt against taxation but rather a frequently held perception that wealthy citizens are not paying their just share of taxes. If too many citizens' sense of justice has been violated by their perceptions of the tax system's operation, then the prospects for public mobilization in protest of the existing tax structure increase. Confalonieri and Newton steadfastly hold to a distinction between a **tax protest** generated by perceived injustice and an open **tax revolt** in which many citizens find taxation unjust in its execution and unfair in principle. The latter scenario would involve a much more fundamental challenge to governments' very existence. Grant and Mockabee (2002), in turn, argue that the electoral salience of public attitudes toward taxation increases when voters believe that much of the country is collectively harmed by certain tax policies and decreases when voters find themselves harmed yet do not believe the country as a whole is harmed.

Economic Explanations

Given the impact of economic growth on government revenues, it should come as no surprise that the health of the economy shapes the climate of tax policy making. A growing economy expands revenues, thereby decreasing pressure for reform. In contrast, a recessionary economy contracts revenues while frequently expanding demand for government services. Governments can consider responding by altering the tax code to meet the fiscal challenges of a recession (Swank and Steinmo 2002).

Another economic factor that can build support for reform is sales and investment competition within and across countries. The more open the environment regarding international trade and domestic economic regulation, the more visible tax distinctions that favor some firms or sectors of the economy will become (Hagemann, Jones, and Montador 1988; Winner 2005). Tax rates on investment capital may drop as a result of economic competition in what some observers have termed "a race to the bottom," in which governments make increasingly large concessions to businesses. In turn, taxes designed to fund pensions and unemployment insurance may well rise in an effort to cushion workers from the higher level of economic competition (Adam and Kammas 2007; Katzenstein 1985; Rodrik 1998). These dual logics of reform exemplify the policy pressures posed by globalization. Economic integration in the European Union (EU) has created a variety of reasons to reconsider tax provisions as movement toward a level economic playing field continues within the EU.

Yet, across all industrialized countries, there are limits to the impact of investment competition on tax policy decisions. Basinger and Hallerberg (2004) examined tax reform trends across twenty industrialized countries during the 1980s and 1990s. They found that domestic political dynamics can limit the possibility that tax cuts in one country breed tax reform elsewhere. Where ideological commitments or institutional dynamics make reform more difficult, it is less likely to occur.

Political Explanations

Political parties will almost always play some role in studies of policy making, and tax policy is no exception. Generally speaking, left-leaning parties tend to speak out for a more progressive tax code as an agent of income redistribution, whereas right-leaning parties tend to call for income-neutral taxation and often favor regressive sales taxes over potentially progressive forms of direct taxation. Research has found that changes in partisan control of government can affect the course of tax policy (Basinger and Hallerberg 2004; Castles 1982b; Morrissey and Steinmo 1987; Steinmo 1993).

That said, the role that partisanship can play is contingent on other factors. The effect of partisanship will be greatest when a single party controls the executive and legislative branches of government along the lines of the party government model. Substantial tax reform is more likely when a single party is in control than in a divided government or in a multiparty coalition government. Steinmo (1993) argues that the United Kingdom has seen greater swings in its tax system over the years as the two major parties have alternated in power and have had greater opportunity to realize their visions for reform. Conversely, coalition governments provide the impetus for a more incrementalist approach to tax reform as the coalition partners find it more difficult to work out a shared vision of sweeping tax reform (Rose and Karran 1986).

Interest group politics can also shape the tax system. In more pluralist settings, one should expect to see a greater fight for tax reforms that benefit a particular segment of the population. Conversely, in more corporatist settings, the encompassing nature of the major interest groups should tend to limit calls for tax provisions that benefit a single firm or group of firms. At the same time, existing corporatist commitments to social spending tied to indirect taxation can make reform of those taxes more difficult (Beramendi and Rueda 2007).

Institutional Explanations

Steinmo's work (1993) on the party government model's effects on taxation finds the roots of party government in the electoral and executive-legislative institutions of the three countries whose tax politics he examined—Sweden, the United Kingdom, and the United States. In short, Steinmo believes that party government occurs more frequently in the United Kingdom because of the Westminster model of government, in which a plurality electoral system is combined with a parliamentary executive.

The institutional setting specific to tax policy making can also influence tax decisions. Peters (1991) notes that tax policy making settings can differ in a couple of significant ways. First, the technical nature of tax policy can leave a role for at least three different cultures of expertise: lawyers, economists, and bureaucrats. This approach holds that lawyers are more likely to stress the need for detailed codes, economists are more worried about the incentives associated with taxation changes, and tax bureaucrats are frequently focused on the implementation issues associated with different forms of taxation. This diversity of expert cultures can be a force for incrementalism as the different mindsets make sweeping reform more difficult to deliver in a consensual form.

Second, the division of spending and taxing policy into various executive agencies and legislative committees shapes the context of tax reform. Spending decisions made elsewhere in the government can force the people actively involved in formulating tax policy to create new plans to respond to changed levels of expenditures. The role of government units not charged with forming the tax code is potentially much greater still because legislators, bureaucrats, and lobbyists active in other policy areas may try to place on the institutional agenda specific tax expenditures or particular tax rate changes. Crepaz (2001) finds that the total number of veto points in the political system matters less than their nature: veto points generated by judicial review and by federalism present greater obstacles to tax reform than do veto points presented by interest group dynamics or by executive-legislative relations.

International Policy Making

Few binding international agreements influence the specific tax policy choices individual countries make in an effort to meet the challenges discussed earlier in this chapter. Countries negotiate a variety of bilateral tax treaties with other countries to determine the tax status of persons and firms spending portions of the year in both countries. These bilateral negotiations have their own challenges that go beyond the scope of this chapter.

The EU's push for a single market has generated an incentive for national governments to harmonize their tax policies with other member countries' tax codes. These pressures, for the most part, have been more informal than formal. In other words, the context of economic integration has had more impact on national tax policies than has EU regulation itself. We examine the pursuit of VAT tax harmonization in greater detail in the EU case study later in this chapter.

A word of caution is in order regarding our treatment of national tax structures. Governments set tax rates, but tax revenues are largely dependent on economic activity. When we discuss tax structure in these six countries and in the European Union, remember that the figures presented can and do change from year to year. When these figures are noticeably out of line with other years, we discuss the difference. In an effort to maintain a similar context across all cases under examination, the discussion of tax structures below is based on national experiences in 2006. Unless otherwise noted, information on tax rates refers to 2008.[1]

United States

Background: Policy Process and Policy History

The tax policy process in the United States is more centralized than is the country's spending policy process, but these formal and informal procedures remain much more pluralist and open-ended than in other countries. Although tax changes can be written into the annual budget, they can also be proposed separately. As a result, policy formulation does not necessarily originate formally in the executive branch (unlike the budget process). As with most other legislation, the president must find legislative members willing to sponsor proposals that could have originated in executive branch discussions among the Office of Management and Budget, the Treasury, the Internal Revenue Service, the President's Council of Economic Advisers, or from many other sources. Alternatively, the tax proposal could originate directly from a legislator.

Although the initiation of formal policy discussions is more decentralized for tax decisions than for spending decisions, the formal review of those ideas in Congress is more centralized. Spending decisions are reviewed by the relevant committees in both chambers, but taxation proposals must be reviewed

---

[1]Data on the tax structure in 2006 are taken from Organisation for Economic Co-operation and Development (OECD 2008c). Data on tax rates in 2008 are from OECD (2009d).

in the House of Representatives by the Ways and Means Committee and in the Senate by the Finance Committee. Despite this degree of centralization, interest groups have multiple legislative targets to lobby for particular changes in the tax code because ultimate approval depends on passage in both chambers. The open-ended nature of the tax policy process, and a political philosophy in many sectors that favors tax expenditures over direct transfers, have worked together to produce a lengthy list of tax expenditures for both corporate and individual income taxes (review Box 7-1). The presidential veto is not a useful institutional threat in most cases because tax changes can be attached to legislation that on balance the president supports.

The U.S. tax structure stands out for its reliance on personal income taxes. The United States is the only country among the six examined in this book in which individual income taxes make up well over one-quarter of tax receipts (35.1 percent in 2006). Other direct taxes are also slightly more important in the United States than in other major industrialized countries. The sum of shares represented by employee social security taxes and corporate income taxes in the United States (22.2 percent) exceeded the average for the EU (17.9 percent) by over 20 percent in 2006. The United States relies on sales taxes less than do all of these other countries. In 2006 sales taxes accounted for 17.4 percent of total government tax receipts in the United States. Sales taxes account for less than 4 percent of tax receipts at the federal level, with excise taxes levied on only a few products and no universal sales tax.

The highest marginal rate for corporate income tax is 35 percent. A series of surtaxes force most medium-sized and large firms to pay taxes at close to one-third of taxable income. States and localities are free to establish corporate income taxes. A multitude of systems exist; rates average under 7 percent, and taxable income can be calculated in many different ways. There is no capital gains exemption at the federal level, but capital losses can be used to offset capital gains. The individual income tax code has five tax brackets with marginal rates ranging from 10 to 35 percent. The top rate on individual dividend income is capped at 17 percent. As with corporations, a variety of state and local personal income tax systems exist. Employees pay a basic social security tax of 7.65 percent of the first $102,000 in earnings and 1.45 percent thereafter. Employers pay an equal percentage of payroll taxes plus an additional assessment for unemployment insurance, which varies from state to state.

As noted earlier, the United States has no national sales tax. The federal government levies excise taxes on alcohol, gasoline, luxury automobiles, telephone services, and tobacco. Most state governments and many localities levy a sales tax at the point of sale. These combined state and local tax rates vary across the country from 3 to 11 percent. Similarly, the United States has no national property tax, but states and, especially, localities often rely heavily on property taxes. The sort of property taxed, how the property value is assessed, and the rate of tax charged vary across the country.

The 1986 federal tax reform marked the realization of a central piece of the Reagan administration's agenda: the reduction of tax rates and a simplification of the tax code. A major element of that reform was a change in individual income taxes. The number of tax brackets was reduced from eleven to two, and the top marginal rate was cut from 50 to 28 percent. The top corporate tax rate fell from 48 to 34 percent. Part of the revenue lost was replaced by raising excise tax rates, and another portion was replaced by an increase in the applicability of corporate income taxes. In addition, changes in tax deduction regulations increased many individuals' taxable income.

Upon taking office in 1993, the Clinton administration argued that the 1986 tax cuts had produced higher budget deficits that were hurting the economy by diverting credit markets to finance the deficit. In 1992 the deficit had reached 5 percent of GDP. By a single tie-breaking vote cast by Vice President Al Gore in the Senate, the top tax bracket (with a marginal rate of 28 percent) was raised to a maximum of 39.6 percent. The top corporate rate rose from 34 to 35 percent, and the income cap on Medicare payroll taxes was eliminated: wealthy taxpayers now had to contribute payroll taxes on all income earned. At the same time, personal income tax brackets were indexed for inflation—avoiding the phenomenon of bracket creep, in which inflation pushes people into higher tax brackets without raising their purchasing power. This loss of revenue was justified by the administration on redistributive grounds because it would limit the share of income taxes paid by low- and middle-income taxpayers. These tax changes—combined with sustained economic growth—worked to eliminate deficits as the government produced its first budget surpluses in a generation during the years 1998–2000. During Clinton's second term, tax reform changes centered on incremental changes to the tax code—primarily the expansion of tax expenditures.

Contemporary Dynamics

Amid the new federal budget surplus, the 2000 presidential campaign featured contrasting visions of what improved government finances implied for tax policy. The Democratic Party's candidate, Al Gore, pledged to use the surplus to bolster the financial health of the federal government's two major programs, Social Security pensions and the Medicare program of health insurance for senior citizens. The Republican candidate, George W. Bush, campaigned on a platform of across-the-board cuts in the personal income tax. Business interest groups tended to line up with Republicans calling for tax cuts, whereas labor tended to side with the Democrats.

At the start of George W. Bush's first term as president, the Republican Party held a slim majority in the House of Representatives and faced a 50–50 split in the Senate. When Sen. James Jeffords left the Republican Party in mid-2001, the Republicans faced an uphill battle in the Senate until special elections and the midterm election of November 2002 gave them a small majority in the Senate that lasted until 2006. To push through the tax cut bill, Bush compromised by agreeing to phase in the cuts over time, by providing new tax expenditures supporting social policy, and, most important, by agreeing to a sunset provision: all major tax reforms enacted would revert to prior law on January 1, 2011. These 2001 tax reforms were the most sweeping since 1986. Tax rates for all personal income tax brackets were lowered by roughly 10 percent. Taxes on dividends and some capital gains were lowered, and the estate tax was phased out over a ten-year period, thus eliminating estate taxes in 2010. On the social policy side, the so-called marriage penalty (in which couples often paid higher taxes filing jointly than they would as single individuals) was eliminated, and the child tax credit was doubled.

Upon passage of the bill, government estimates stated that the 2001 tax changes would initially reduce the size of the budget surplus, but that surpluses would continue throughout Bush's first term. A series of factors made the implementation of these tax cuts more troubling than had been forecast. A weak economy in 2001 and 2002 depressed government revenues. In turn, higher spending commitments to homeland security programs and the U.S. military invasion of Afghanistan in late 2001 pushed the budget into a deficit comprising 3.8 percent of GDP in 2002. President Bush and the congressional leadership in the Republican Party argued that these economic struggles provided a rationale for new tax cuts to try to fuel an economic recovery. Rather than focusing on stimulating consumer spending (which a team of Nobel laureate economists advocated in a public letter in 2003), the 2002 and 2003 tax reforms provided tax subsidies for businesses and a substantial reduction in tax rates on dividends and capital gains. Upon winning reelection in November 2004, President Bush pledged to make the tax cuts of his first term permanent. However, rising budget deficits (growing larger amid the spending associated with the 2003 invasion of Iraq) made it harder for the Bush administration to rally the nearly universal support that his tax bills had received from Republican legislators during his first term. Some fiscal conservatives in the Republican caucus joined Democratic legislators in a refusal to pass new legislation to eliminate the 2011 sunset clause. In addition, in the 2006 midterm elections, voters replaced the slim Republican legislative majorities with Democratic majorities in both houses of Congress. These partisan changes doomed efforts to extend the tax cuts during the last two years of the Bush presidency.

The severe economic downturn of late 2008 in the United States and beyond generated a new discussion of the role of tax policy in the 2008 presidential campaign. Republican candidate John McCain resumed a call for extending all of the temporary tax cuts enacted under the Bush administration. In contrast, Democratic candidate Barack Obama's economic team argued that a stimulus should focus on targeted tax relief for consumers and businesses and on spending programs designed to stimulate job creation. Obama's electoral victory in November 2008—accompanied by the expansion of Democratic majorities in Congress—made it more likely that his vision would be pursued in 2009.

The battle over tax policy during the Bush administration illustrates the crucial importance of taxation for many politically active citizens and interest groups. In a country in which citizens are generally more skeptical of government expansion than are residents of most industrialized countries, tax cuts can have a visceral political appeal with voters. At the same time, when the enactment of tax cuts threatens government programs that many people support, political parties, interest groups, and individual citizens often rally to protect government revenues needed to pay for those programs. In addition, the dynamics of tax policy also illustrate the extent to which politicians and voters make decisions in a shifting national and global context. In 2001 many people were optimistic that the economic boom of the 1990s could be sustained indefinitely. Rising budget deficits and then a financial crisis have reshaped markedly people's expectations with an eye toward the 2010s.

Japan

Background: Policy Process and Policy History

As with spending policy, tax policy formulation in Japan has centered around the Ministry of Finance. Proposed changes (which can originate from forces outside the ministry as well) are then reviewed by major coalition leaders and the leadership of affected interest groups. Often the relative power of the prime minister in this process is determined by his or her prior experience (or lack thereof) in the Ministry of Finance.

Historically, the Diet's role in tax policy has been limited because agreements were typically arrived at among major Liberal Democratic Party (LDP) factions before bills were presented in the legislature. In the contemporary period, however, multiparty coalitions formed by unstable parties have been the rule of the day. As a result, the process of securing passage of tax reforms announced by the government is no longer a foregone conclusion.

Japan's tax structure is different from most other industrialized countries' systems in two notable respects. First, Japan relies less on sales taxes, which account for only 19.4 percent of tax receipts. Second, corporate income taxes are much more important. In 2006 corporate income taxes accounted for 15.5 percent of all taxes—more than 72 percent larger than the average share found in the other five countries examined in this book. The portions of the tax structure represented by personal income tax (18.3 percent) and by social security (32.6 percent) are more in line with other countries' tax systems.

The basic corporate income tax rate is 30 percent; smaller businesses pay a lower rate (22 percent) on the first eight million yen of taxable income. A local corporate income tax code also exists, with an average rate of 11.56 percent. Localities also levy a corporate inhabitant tax of roughly 5 to 6 percent on the income of businesses headquartered in their jurisdictions.

The personal income tax code has six brackets ranging from 5 to 40 percent. Local income taxes vary and provide a variety of deductions and exemptions. With the exception of accident compensation insurance, social security taxes are borne equally by employers and employees. Rates vary somewhat depending mainly on occupation. Most employees pay roughly 12.2 percent of earnings. Most employers pay a little under 13 percent of payroll.

As we noted earlier, sales taxes are much less important in Japan than in the other industrialized countries. Traditionally, Japan had no general sales tax but rather a series of excise taxes. In the late 1980s, after several failed attempts by prior governments, the Takeshita government finally managed to gets its LDP legislative majority to replace the excise taxes with a 3 percent consumption tax (in large part because opposition parties had expressed uniform disapproval of the measure). After considerable debate, the VAT was ultimately raised to 5 percent in a 1996 reform, effective April 1, 1997; it has remained there ever since. Property taxes on buildings and on land are levied at several different rates.

Japan was the one major economy that did not encounter rising budget deficits in the late 1980s or early 1990s. In fact, Japan ran surpluses from 1987 through 1992. When economic growth slowed to 1.0 percent in 1992 and then to 0.3 percent the next year, pressure mounted on the Japanese government to consider a fiscal stimulus. From 1993 through 1996, several unstable coalition governments—the first governments not led by the LDP in nearly forty years—were divided regarding how to place Japan's economy on a stronger footing. The coalition governments pursued temporary tax relief and spending programs in 1994 and 1995. However, the Ministry of Finance (dominated by officials with long-standing ties to the LDP and with a historical commitment to deficit control) worried that an excessive stimulus would lead to a growing budget deficit. In 1996, partly to please the Ministry of Finance, the Murayama government passed a permanent increase in the consumption tax from 3 to 5 percent, effective April 1997. The consumption tax hike, along with continuing domestic financial crises and a burgeoning regional economic crisis, led to renewed economic stagnation that culminated in a recession in 1998, during which the GDP shrank by 2.5 percent.

Contemporary Dynamics

Japan's deepening economic problems produced varied tax cut proposals from all major political parties and interest groups in the late 1990s. As the recession emerged in mid-1998, veteran LDP leader Keizo Obuchi became prime minister of a smaller, three-party coalition government in which the LDP was the largest partner. He promised a major stimulus package along with structural reforms designed to modernize the Japanese economy. In turn, the bad outcomes associated with the 1997 sales tax hike muted opposition from more fiscally conservative members of the LDP as well as from officials the Ministry of Finance. The Obuchi government also cultivated the support of business groups supportive of his call for sweeping tax reform.

Obuchi's predecessor, Ryutaro Hashimoto, had been roundly criticized for backing away from his initial commitment to sweeping tax reform. Obuchi, in contrast, vigorously pursued new tax legislation upon taking office in June 1998 following Hashimoto's resignation. In his opening address to the 1999 legislative session, Obuchi made a commitment to permanent reductions in personal and corporate income tax central to the political agenda. He worked with other cabinet members to try to convince LDP legislators that the LDP risked electoral defeat if it failed to heed the call for tax reform. In turn, Obuchi's smaller coalition partners had already committed themselves to tax cuts. By February the government had already gained lower house approval, and a series of tax cuts were enacted for implementation in 1999. The top marginal rate for personal income tax was slashed from 50 to 37 percent; the lower tax brackets retained their existing rates in an effort to avoid further alienation of fiscal conservatives. The overall corporate income tax rate was cut from 46 percent down to 41 percent. These and other policy reforms proved popular with voters initially as the LDP regained a majority in the 1999 legislative elections.

The implementation of the 1999 tax reform produced uneven results. The economy did not immediately pull out of its decade-long slump. When Obuchi suffered a stroke, his successor Yoshiro Mori proved unpopular, which led to the selection of Junichiro Koizumi as prime minister in 2001. Koizumi presented himself as an outspoken advocate of bold economic reforms. As we saw in Chapter 6, his central initiative focused on the privatization of the financial network controlled by the Japanese postal system. His dedication to that privatization project limited his willingness and his ability to pursue his pledge to decrease further corporate tax rates and inheritance taxes. Instead, slightly improved economic conditions during 2003–2006 increased pressure on Koizumi to reduce Japan's large budget deficit. In the end, the major tax reforms of the Koizumi government were revenue-seeking in nature. He reduced tax expenditures; raised the top marginal rate for personal income tax in 2006 (from 37 to 40 percent); and raised social security payroll taxes on employers and, especially, on employees.

Koizumi's personal popularity bolstered his ability to pursue tax increases that other politicians might have avoided. By late 2008, however, the political agenda for tax policy in Japan had shifted yet again. His two immediate successors—Shinzo Abe and Yasuo Fukuda—each lasted less than one year in office prior to resigning in the face of a discordant legislature and declining public approval ratings. This political turbulence, combined with an economic downturn in 2008, put tax reform back on the systemic agenda when Taro Aso became prime minister in September 2008.

The Japanese experience demonstrates a couple of the principles discussed in Chapters 2 and 3. First, large governing coalitions make it harder to craft a coherent policy. Whereas Obuchi and Koizumi enjoyed several legislative successes as prime ministers, most chief executives in Japan have struggled to remain popular with voters and with legislators from the mid-1990s forward. In the eyes of many observers, the weakness of the Japanese government has negatively influenced tax policy making by producing "stop-go" policy changes in which tax cuts alternate too abruptly with tax hikes and vice versa. Second, visible failures of the governing party or coalition are often grist for the policy formulation mill of the opposition parties. As soon as the LDP became identified with the failings blamed on the consumption tax increase, other political parties swept in with different plans to reduce the tax burden on individuals. The Obuchi government was sly enough to adapt to these shifting political winds and make tax cuts part of the LDP's agenda.

Germany

Background: Policy Process and Policy History

As with spending policy, tax policy in Germany involves the chancellor consulting with all relevant members of the cabinet in forming a proposal before presenting it to the entire cabinet for approval. Historically, coalition governments in Germany have often split the Economic and Finance Ministries among the coalition partners. As a result, both coalition partners have tended to play a major role in tax policy decisions by heading the two major ministries involved. Ultimately any coalition disagreements are arbitrated by the chancellor, the economic and finance ministers, and senior figures in the governing coalition. Leaders of the major business and labor confederations are usually included in the policy formulation process—although formal, mandatory consultation has not taken place for three decades.

In the German tax structure, the largest share of tax revenues comes from social security taxes (36.3 percent). Sales tax accounted for another 29 percent of tax revenues, and personal income taxes comprised 23 percent of revenues in 2006. Corporate income taxes made up a little less than 5 percent of total tax revenues.

The basic federal corporate income tax rate is 15 percent, but subnational governments levy additional corporate taxes averaging nearly 15 percent nationwide. Individual income tax rates range from 15 to 45 percent; the precise rate for each individual is calculated using a sliding-scale formula (rather than via the fixed income brackets used in most countries' tax codes). Both corporate and personal income taxes have been subject to a so-called solidarity surcharge of 5.5 percent of taxes owed (beginning January 1, 1998) to help pay for the costs associated with national reunification. This surcharge raises the highest corporate rate to 30.2 percent and the top individual rate to 47.5 percent. Employee social security taxes are levied at 20.4 percent on the first 43.200 euros earned and then at 11.6 percent on the next 19,800 euros earned. Employers pay social security taxes at the slightly lower rate of 19.5 percent on the first 43,200 euros paid in salaries and then at the same 11.6 percent rate paid by employees on wages up to a maximum of 62,000 euros. As elsewhere in Europe, the main sales tax is a VAT. The standard VAT rate from 1998 through 2006 was 16 percent; a major tax reform raised that rate to 19 percent from 2007 forward. Food, plants, books, and a few other items are taxed at 7 percent. Several transactions are exempt from the VAT including banking, insurance, and financial services; property transactions; education; health care services; cultural activities; and some nonprofit activities.

In the late 1980s tax reform under the center-right Helmut Kohl government focused on rate reduction and simplification. The basic corporate rate was cut from 56 to 50 percent. The number of personal income tax brackets was reduced slightly from eleven to ten; the top marginal rate fell by 3 percentage points, and the lowest rate was raised from 21.4 to 22.1 percent. Amid the steady growth of 1983 to 1989, a small reduction in some tax rates presented no revenue problems.

As we noted in Chapter 6, reunification generated substantial fiscal pressures in Germany. Its budget deficit grew precisely when the course of monetary unification called for small budget deficits. A difficult challenge resulted in the early 1990s as two potentially conflicting imperatives reached the institutional agenda: a need to generate more revenues emerged simultaneously with a desire to avoid a significant tax increase (because it might further deepen the recession). The watchwords for the late 1980s had been tax simplification and tax reduction. Now, very quickly, revenue enhancement was added to the agenda. The Kohl government responded with a series of revenue-seeking measures—an increase in the VAT rate, the reduction of some tax expenditures, and the creation of a "solidarity surcharge" designed to produce revenues targeted for economic recovery in eastern Germany. In response to criticism from business groups and from their coalition partners in the Free Democratic Party, the Christian Democrats also backed a reduction in corporate income taxes.

Contemporary Dynamics

The 1998 election campaign was a battle of contrasting styles and proposals despite the presence of two major candidates who each labeled himself as a pragmatist. Helmut Kohl, who had served as chancellor since 1982, presented himself as a steady hand amid the challenges of national reunification and European integration. Gerhard Schröder, the new Social Democratic leader, called for an eclectic mixture of tax cuts and well-managed social programs. The center-left coalition of Social Democrats and Greens pledged to protect ordinary Germans' living standards better than the Kohl government. Business groups generally backed Kohl's coalition, whereas labor groups supported Schröder's coalition. In the end, the center-left gained a majority and the Schröder cabinet took power in October 1998.

Vigorous debate ensued within Schröder's governing coalition of the Social Democrats and Greens. Many members of both parties called for tax increases on the wealthy to fund a swift increase in social spending. The first tax reform initiative created a new "ecological tax" on fuel consumption that was designed to pursue two objectives simultaneously. It would encourage energy conservation while also generating a new source of government revenues for social programs. Schröder ultimately backed a modest increase in social spending and a major tax cut package. The 1999 tax reform phased in a series of across-the-board personal income and corporate tax reductions that would take full effect in 2002. The top marginal rate for personal income tax declined from 53 to 48.5 percent while the bottom marginal rate fell from 25.9 to 19.9 percent. The top marginal rate for the federal corporate income tax was slashed from 40 to 25 percent. In addition the government reduced both employer and employee payroll tax rates by 0.4 percentage points; this payroll tax relief was funded via the revenue generated by the new energy tax.

Upon passage and implementation of these heterodox measures, Schröder emphasized that they were emblematic of his "third way" approach to economic policy. The leader of the more progressive wing of the Social Democrats, Oskar Lafontaine, resigned from his cabinet post; Lafontaine had argued that wealthy citizens and businesses did not need substantial tax relief. Most of these policy changes were decidedly easy to implement because they involved no new tax instruments. However, the brand-new energy tax required the creation of a new set of administrative practices and also faced a series of legal challenges as opponents tried to block its implementation in the courts. Debate over the new measure filtered back into the legislative cycle as Greens pushed for higher energy taxes, especially on coal, whereas the initial law had focused primarily on motor fuels. Faced with stagnant economic growth and high deficits following reelection in 2002, the Schröder government turned its attention to revenue-seeking via the reduction and elimination of several tax expenditures.

Persistent economic stagnation culminated in a divided 2005 general election. The creation of the Left Party pulled some voters away from the Social Democrats, yet the Christian Democrats also lost ground. As a result, neither the SDP-Green coalition nor the CDU-CSU coalition with the Free Democrats had enough seats to form a legislative majority. Complicated negotiations ensued regarding the formation a new government. Ultimately, the Social Democrats decided that they would rather form a "grand coalition" with the other major party, the Christian Democrats, than risk a volatile coalition with the new Left Party. This heterogeneous marriage of convenience between the major center-left and center-right parties produced a multitude of often contradictory tax reform proposals. In its first three years in office, the Angela Merkel government introduced several changes favored by Christian Democrats. A visible cut in the federal corporate tax rate from 25 to 15 percent was financed by raising the VAT rate from 16 to 19 percent. At the same time, Social Democrats supported other tax measures such as an increase in the top income tax rate from 42 to 45 percent, the reduction of some tax expenditures for large businesses, a small reduction in payroll taxes, and the creation of some new tax expenditures for working families.

In addition to demonstrating the clear role of international factors in framing contemporary tax policy, the German experience illustrates the power of a perceived emergency as a political tool that can overcome opposition to tax increases. The dual challenges of reunification and European monetary integration enabled the Kohl and Schröder governments to implement tax increases of much greater size than those pursued in other European countries. Once those emergencies faded, however, tax reduction bubbled back up onto the systemic and institutional agendas. More recent events in Germany under the Merkel government demonstrate the challenges of designing tax policies to suit the preferences of an ideologically diverse governing coalition. It will be interesting to see how German voters evaluate the performance of these two major parties in tax policy when Germany returns to the polls in September 2009.

France

Background: Policy Process and Policy History

As with spending policy, the Finance Ministry is central to tax policy in France. Once budget parameters are set using estimates from the Finance Ministry, the finance minister formulates recommendations for tax changes associated with the coming budget. If changes affect sectors of the economy that correspond to other ministries, those ministries are brought into consultations before the prime minister makes a decision to present the changes as part of the budget bill or as a separate measure. The decision to move ahead with the proposal can also be shaped by consultations with relevant interest groups or senior parliamentary leaders, particularly if the government believes the reforms could be controversial. After the public announcement, the Finance Ministry leads the effort to secure passage in the legislature.

In the French tax structure, roughly one-third of tax receipts are generated by social security contributions (34.2 percent in 2006). Income taxes are less important in France than in other industrialized countries. Individual income taxes accounted for 17.3 percent of revenues, and corporate income taxes represented 6.2 percent. Direct taxes constituted only one-third of tax receipts, compared to over 43 percent in the average industrialized country. Sales taxes accounted for an additional 25.3 percent of revenues.

The individual income tax code has four brackets with progressive rates ranging from 5.5 to 40.0 percent. Because of a relatively high income threshold, roughly half of French households pay little or no income taxes. Residents are assessed an additional generalized social contribution of 7.5 percent of earnings (raised in 1997 from 3.4 percent). The corporate income tax rate is 34.43 percent. Social security rates vary slightly by occupation.

Most employees pay around 20 percent, whereas employers pay approximately 40 percent of payroll. The basic sales tax is a VAT with a standard rate of 19.6 percent. A lower rate of 5.5 percent is levied on most food products, books, water, and a few other items. On entities with over 90 percent of their production exempt from the VAT, France levies a special payroll tax of between 4.25 and 13 percent.

Like many industrialized countries, France simplified its income tax structure and lowered income tax rates during the 1980s and 1990s. Many of these changes came under the so-called cohabitation center-right governments serving alongside center-left French president François Mitterrand. The corporate tax rate fell from 45 to 42 percent under the first cohabitation government led by Jacques Chirac in the late 1980s. To replace some of the revenues lost in these measures, the government began to levy an income tax surcharge of 1.2 percent of earnings—the generalized social contribution (GSC). After a large center-right electoral victory in 1993, Edouard Balladur's government lowered the corporate rate to 33.33 percent and slashed the number of brackets in the individual income tax from thirteen to seven. It doubled the GSC rate to recoup some of the lost revenues. After Chirac won the presidency in 1995, many analysts predicted a prolonged period of center-right dominance. However, the deficit-cutting economic program of the new cabinet led by Alain Juppe faced a firestorm of criticism from all sides. Conservatives opposed the tax increase proposals, whereas progressives launched strikes and street protests against proposed spending cuts. The Juppe government raised the VAT rate from 18.6 to 20.6 percent and increased the corporate tax rate to 36 percent.

In the wake of the turmoil, in the 1997 legislative elections the center-left bloc led by Lionel Jospin won control and a new cohabitation government emerged. The Jospin government used the need to meet the Maastricht deficit target by the end of 1997 as a justification for quick action on the fiscal front. To maintain the support of organized labor, the government reduced the sales tax rate by one percentage point to 19.6 percent; the top personal income tax rate rose to 54 percent; and the corporate tax rate paid by large companies increased from 36 to 41.6 percent. In the name of burden-sharing and in pursuit of the Maastricht target, the GSC rate was increased from 3.4 to 7.5 percent.

Contemporary Dynamics

In 2002 the political winds in France shifted yet again. Jospin's failure to qualify for the presidential runoff in the April elections set into motion a rising tide of support for the center-right forces led by Chirac, who won overwhelmingly in May. His center-right coalition campaigned successfully for an end to divided government in the June legislative elections. Jean-Pierre Raffarin's government enjoyed a large legislative majority.

The new center-right government proposed a series of decreases in personal and corporate income tax rates. These measures were backed by business groups. However, the tax cuts were linked by opponents to the Raffarin government's call for major public-sector reforms in retirement pensions and health care. These proposals, as had been the case during the Juppe government, produced a new wave of protests and strikes from center-left political parties and labor unions.

Amid the opposition protests, the center-right coalition limited the scope of the tax cuts that it pursued in practice. The top personal income tax rate fell from 49.6 to 48.1 percent. Similarly, corporate tax rates fell from 35.4 to 34.4 percent. To deal with chronic financing difficulties in pension policies, payroll rates roses slightly (by roughly 0.3 percentage points) for both employees and employers.

The reforms pursued by the Raffarin government faced few technical implementation obstacles. Instead, their implementation generated a new cycle of policy evaluation. Conservatives argued that France had not done enough to reduce taxes on wealthy individuals and firms. Progressives countered that the Raffarin government had deepened the process of shifting the tax burden from the wealthy to the poor. In the 2007 elections, the new leader of the Gaullist movement, Nicolas Sarkozy, campaigned vigorously for deeper tax cuts. When he won the presidency and his coalition retained control of the legislature, Sarkozy worked quickly in the first weeks of his presidency to back Prime Minister François Fillon's proposals for tax reductions. The top rate for personal income taxes fell from 48.1 to 40 percent, and a sweeping reform of the inheritance tax reduced its impact to less than 5 percent of the population.

France's experience demonstrates the potential power of international constraints (and commitments) on domestic policymakers. Although tax increases tend to be divisive, the push to join the euro zone eventually built support for various tax measures to lower the deficit in order to meet the target, once the deadline loomed larger. In the decade following the 1997 Maastricht deadline, the dynamics of domestic politics played a greater role. The emergence of a large center-right legislative majority paved the way for major tax cuts once that majority was reaffirmed in the 2007 presidential and legislative elections. A question now looms on the horizon for policymakers and political analysts: what will be the impact in the 2012 electoral cycle of over 18 billion dollars in annual tax cuts focused largely on affluent citizens?

United Kingdom

Background: Policy Process and Policy History

The tax policy formulation process is much more centralized in the United Kingdom than in most other countries. The prime minister and the finance minister (known as the chancellor of the exchequer) work together to discuss potential reforms proposed from within the Finance Ministry. Those reforms are then discussed with relevant ministers and senior officials at other ministries. The prime minister is the arbiter of any disputes. Tax reforms are usually worked into the draft budget. Once the budget is announced, the government is typically confident that it will pass in Parliament. As discussed in Chapter 6, the Blair government introduced in late 1997 the practice of an annual Green Budget speech in which the Finance Ministry provides a broad outline of possible tax reform initiatives and the economic concerns that motivate them. Some observers have noted that this procedural innovation is a response to Margaret Thatcher's problems with the poll tax initiative (discussed later in this section).

The British tax structure relies more heavily on sales taxes than do the tax structures of the other industrialized countries we examine here. Throughout the early twenty-first century sales taxes have accounted for over 30 percent of tax receipts. In 2006 social security taxes were just 18.2 percent of taxes received, largely because health care is funded out of other revenues and not via an earmarked payroll tax. Shares from individual income taxes (28.6 percent) and corporate income taxes (9.3 percent) are similar to those found in the other countries.

The basic corporate income tax rate is 28 percent. Small firms with incomes below $2.6 million receive tax relief. There are no subnational or local income taxes. The two individual income tax brackets are set at 20 and 40 percent. Employee social security taxes are set at 11 percent on roughly the first $1,500 earned each week and at a 1 percent rate for all earnings above that threshold. Employer payroll taxes are set at 12.8 percent of all earnings; employer social security contributions have no upper limit.

The central sales tax is a basic VAT of 17.5 percent on most goods and services. An economic stimulus package enacted in late 2008 lowered the VAT rate to 15 percent until January 1, 2010. A lower tax rate of 5 percent is levied on fuel and power for domestic use. Food, books and publications, and passenger transportation are exempt from the VAT, as are many services commonly exempted elsewhere (banking, insurance, and finance; education; health care; and some nonprofit activities). Insurance premiums are subject to a special tax of 2.5 percent. Taxes on residential and business real property are the main source of local government revenues.

The Thatcher government came to power in 1979 on a Conservative platform of smaller government and, in turn, lower taxes. Although some tax reduction took place during the government's first two terms, a persistent budget deficit and pressure on the national currency in foreign exchange markets made it difficult to pursue major tax reform. In the late 1980s, fresh after leading her party to an unprecedented third consecutive electoral victory in 1987, Thatcher set into motion a series of substantial tax changes placed at the top of the institutional agenda. The House of Commons ratified substantial reforms at both levels of government. At the national level, a simplification of the individual income tax code reduced the number of brackets from six to three, and the top rate was lowered dramatically from 60 to 40 percent. The basic corporate income tax rate decreased slightly from 35 to 33 percent. In turn, the government looked to recoup lost revenue in these direct taxes by raising the basic VAT rate from 15 to 17.5 percent.

At the local level, however, the shift from property taxes to a single poll tax charged to all residents produced a firestorm of opposition once it was fully implemented in 1990. A wave of public demonstrations ensued that included the worst riot in London in recent history. Some citizens openly refused to pay the poll tax in protest. When public opinion polls showed that Conservatives were in danger of being trounced in the next national elections, Thatcher faced a leadership challenge within her own party. After failing to win a clear majority of support within her own party's bloc in the legislature, Thatcher resigned as prime minister. Her successor, John Major, quickly replaced the controversial poll tax with a modified property tax system and used this reform as a central element of his subsequently successful 1992 election campaign.

Contemporary Dynamics

In 1997 the Labour Party pursued its first parliamentary majority in nearly two decades. Tony Blair had spent the 1990s arguing that the Labour Party would find a "third way" in economic policy. With regard to tax policy, his electoral campaign promised not to return to the level of income tax rates observed in the 1970s. Instead, he promised to reforms the priorities and the implementation of government programs. Conservatives countered that Blair would ignore his campaign promises by raising income taxes on all Britons. In the end, the Labour Party won a massive majority in the House of Commons.

Amid the euphoria of a sizable electoral triumph, policy formulation proceeded confidently within the executive branch. The minimalist tax reform agenda called for tax cuts for lower-income taxpayers and for small businesses. In addition, the government proposed to eliminate some tax expenditures that reduced taxes owed by businesses and individual taxpayers. Finally, the government proposed to simplify employer payroll taxes by moving from a five-bracket system to a single rate that would raise the level of employer contributions by an average of 3 percentage points. Although some of the more progressive members of the Labour Party called for tax rate increases on wealthy Britons, the Blair leadership team held firm to its campaign promises. The absence of tax hike proposals helped to block potential protests from business confederations and opposition parties.

The House of Commons approved a dramatic reduction in the tax rate for the lowest tax bracket; the rate fell from 20 to 10 percent. In turn, the corporate tax rate for small businesses was reduced from 24 to 19 percent and the top corporate rate decreased from 33 to 31 percent. Although the corporate tax rates fell and the top marginal rate on individuals remained the same, the simplification of the corporate and personal tax code actually increased the taxes owed by some businesses and by many wealthy individuals. The employer payroll tax reform created a single rate of 12.2 percent.

Implementation of the initial Blair tax reforms went smoothly amid a growing economy. The Blair government's unity surprised its opponents who had expected the Labour Party to fail to live up to its pledge not to increase income tax rates. The political and economic results of the initial tax reforms strengthened Blair's pledge not to raise income taxes in his successful reelection campaigns in 2002 and 2005.

Although tax policy decisions did not pose the problems for Tony Blair that the poll tax reform did for Margaret Thatcher, the Blair government's decision to participate in the U.S. invasion and occupation of Iraq proved increasingly unpopular over time. The troop commitment also placed new fiscal pressures on the government. When the 2005 election produced a visibly smaller Labour majority, Blair resigned as prime minister in 2007 and his chancellor of the exchequer, Gordon Brown, became the new leader of the British government. Faced with rising fiscal pressures and a stagnating economy, the Brown government reversed the signature income tax reform of the first Blair government: it raised the tax rate for the lowest income bracket from 10 percent back to the 20 percent rate levied by the Major government. In an effort to produce a stimulus for consumer spending, the Brown government also authorized a temporary reduction in the VAT from 17.5 to 15 percent; the tax reduction is scheduled to expire at the start of 2010.

The perceived successes of the Blair government in tax policy speak to the manner in which party discipline is aided by the Westminster model of executive-legislative relations. Blair used his authority and popularity as prime minister to resist requests from his own core base of legislators and supporters to increase income tax rates on wealthy individuals and large businesses. In turn, the government's early political successes reinforced Blair's leadership in the years that followed.

At the same time, the poll tax affair and its subsequent ramifications for the Thatcher government serve as a cautionary tale about the double-edged sword of executive power in the Westminster model. On the one hand, with a sizable majority and the varied resources of the prime minister's post, Thatcher was correct in assuming that she could drive through the poll tax despite criticisms of the plan both within and outside the governing party. On the other hand, the executive's ability to enact with relative ease the poll tax reform left it blindsided by a level of public opposition that was difficult to forecast given the limited public debate over the initiative prior to implementation.

Italy

Background: Policy Process and Policy History

The Italian fiscal process has differed from most industrialized countries' by formally separating tax legislation from spending legislation. Any changes to the tax code have to be written outside of the budget bill. As with spending policy, the Treasury has taken the lead role in formulating tax reforms.

Nevertheless, the greater size of governing coalitions and the weaker party discipline of the participants have made it difficult to negotiate major tax reforms through the legislature. As a result, tax policy has tended to follow the same incrementalist dynamic present in spending policy.

In the Italian tax structure, social security payroll taxes, personal income taxes, and sales taxes each account for just over 25 percent of tax receipts. Employers pay the lion's share of social security taxes—nearly 80 percent. Corporate income tax rates were lowered significantly in 1998 and now constitute 6.8 percent of total revenues.

Since 2008 the corporate income tax rate in Italy has been 27.5 percent. In addition, businesses pay a regional tax of 4.5 percent (which can be raised to a maximum of 5.5 percent at the discretion of the regional government). The individual income tax code has five brackets with rates ranging from 23 to 43 percent. Like corporations, individuals also pay an additional regional tax that ranges from 0.9 to 1.4 percent of income; some local governments levy an additional surcharge up to a maximum rate of 0.5 percent. Social security payroll tax rates are among the highest in the world. Most of the responsibility for social security taxes falls on employers, who pay at a rate of 32.1 percent on the first 88,669 euros earned. Most employees pay around 10 percent of earnings up to the same income threshold of 88,669 euros. The self-employed pay, on average, around 5 percent of earnings.

The basic VAT rate is 20 percent. Several goods and services are charged lower rates ranging from 4 to 10 percent. Property taxes of less than 1 percent are levied by local governments. Excise taxes are charged on several items including furs and luxury automobiles. Effective in 1998 a new regional VAT of 4.5 to 5.5 percent replaced the local income tax and the social security payroll tax. This major change increased Italy's reliance on indirect taxes in its quest to reduce tax evasion.

Throughout the 1980s and 1990s Italy had the highest budget deficit among the six countries examined in this book. During the 1980s the deficit was consistently greater than 10 percent of GDP. Following the lead of many other countries, Italy simplified the individual income tax code in the late 1980s by reducing the number of brackets from nine to seven, dropping the top rate from 62 to 51 percent. Although Romano Prodi's government committed itself to the Maastricht guidelines related to European monetary unification upon taking office in 1995, the center-left coalition government was under tremendous stress. In addition to the problems associated with getting multiple coalition partners to agree on a reform proposal, the situation was complicated by the large fluctuations in the Italian party system during that decade. Reductions in the top rates for individual and corporate income taxes were compensated for by a broadening of the tax base achieved by the elimination and reduction of several tax exemptions. As in Germany and France, a temporary surtax, the Eurotax, was enacted in 1997 with an eye toward the Maastricht target. The government also created a regional VAT (varying from

4.5 to 5.5 percent) that would pay for health care and some other social services previously funded by payroll taxes; this particular reform combined efforts to reduce tax rates on employers with efforts to reduce tax evasion associated with social security contributions. As noted in Chapter 6, this program enabled Italy to meet the deficit target at the last minute. However, the fight over continued budgetary austerity in 1998 culminated in the ouster of the Prodi government via a failed vote of confidence in which the government's budget bill failed to pass by a single vote. The subsequent government led by Massimo D'Alema reduced the top marginal rate for personal income taxes from 51 to 46.5 percent and increased the rate for the lowest tax bracket from 10 to 18 percent.

Contemporary Dynamics

The 2001 elections in Italy were a hard-fought affair. Communications magnate Silvio Berlusconi boldly promised voters that a center-right triumph would lead simultaneously to a major public works program and a series of tax cuts. The center-left coalition countered that it would do a better job of protecting the interests of all Italians. Berlusconi won the election with a tighter-knit coalition and a larger legislative majority than he had enjoyed during his short-lived government following the 1994 elections. In particular, his Forza Italia party controlled a greater share of the seats and he no longer needed the support of the Northern League to preserve his legislative majority.

The 2001 electoral triumph, however, had unclear implications for tax policy. Berlusconi had committed to tax cuts, but he had also promised to cut the unemployment rate in half via an ambitious public works campaign. Furthermore, the Stability and Growth Pact (SGP) committed his government to hold deficits to 3 percent of GDP, which placed his two signature economic agenda items in conflict. With a budget deficit right at the maximum level in 2001 and 2002, his government's latitude was limited. Business groups pressured for tax cuts, but many businesses also welcomed government expansion during the recession in place. Labor groups and center-left parties strongly criticized any discussion of funding tax cuts for the affluent by raising taxes on lower-income families.

At the decision-making phase, the government relied on its legislative majority and reminded all skeptical legislators that party discipline was needed to avoid another short-lived government. Tax reforms took place in the direction indicated by Berlusconi, but (to try to hold budget deficits near the SGP limit) the government postponed the major tax cuts until the latter part of his term. This strategy tried to maximize the visibility of the tax cuts for the 2006 election campaign while attempting to delay any expansion of the deficit until after the campaign was over. The top corporate tax rate declined gradually from 36 percent in 2002 to 34 percent in 2004.

To compensate for lost revenues, the lowest income tax bracket's marginal rate was increased from 18 to 23 percent in 2003. The top marginal rate for personal income tax declined from 45 to 43 percent in 2005, and employer payroll taxes decreased by one percentage point in the election year of 2006.

Implementation of Berlusconi's tax reforms pleased some of his most ardent supporters but also met with stiff opposition from center-left political parties and their labor union allies. Rather than reducing taxation on all Italians, the Berlusconi tax reforms raised taxes on lower-income Italians and lowered them only for businesses and affluent taxpayers. The center-left opposition, led once again by Romano Prodi in the 2006 elections, attempted to rally voters around a pledge to protect the interests of ordinary Italians. Berlusconi countered by trying to cultivate voters' skepticism regarding the ability and willingness of the center-left coalition to use government resources effectively.

Winning by a razor-thin electoral margin, the center-left's nine-party coalition formed a new government in the wake of the 2006 elections. However, with almost no margin for error in the Senate, the Prodi government found it difficult to formulate and pursue policies. It narrowly gained approval of its fiscal year 2008 budget proposal in October 2007 by retaining centrist coalition members' support via a provision that lowered the corporate tax rate from 33 to 27.5 percent. In January 2008 the Prodi government won a vote-of-confidence measure in the lower house but lost in the Senate when one of its Christian Democratic allies removed its support from the government. In the subsequent April 2008 general election, Berlusconi's coalition regained control of the legislature. As of this writing, it remains unclear what that will mean for tax policy, but the trend toward lowering taxes on the wealthy seems likely to continue.

The dynamics of Italian politics in the early twenty-first century provide a tale of two different coalition blocs. The center-left coalition involved more political parties and a considerable ideological diversity that made policy making more difficult. By contrast, the Berlusconi coalition during the same period relied on fewer parties, enjoyed greater ideological agreement about the priorities of tax policy, and had the benefit of a larger legislative majority. The center-left bloc's vulnerability made it face several difficult votes of confidence, whereas the Berlusconi coalition, perhaps chastened by the rapid collapse of his first government in 1996, demonstrated the political and policy-making advantages of a more disciplined governing coalition.

European Union

Background: Policy Process and Policy History

The European Union conducts two forms of tax policy. First, it pursues tax policies designed to finance its own activities. The EU itself has no power to create and levy taxes; instead, it must work through the member states. As noted in Chapter 6, the EU budget's total expenditures comprise just

1 percent of the union's overall GDP. Accordingly, revenue pressures are smaller on the EU system than they are in the member governments themselves. Second, the EU designs tax policies in an attempt to guide and frame the nature of taxation in the member states. In both policy areas, proposals are drafted by the Commission and then voted on by the European Parliament and the Council of Ministers.

Observers of the United Nations can always find news stories about the many member states that are behind on their scheduled national contributions to that international organization's shared budget. From its founding in 1957 until 1970, the European Community (EC) faced the same problem: the EC depended on the collection of pledged revenues from each member state rather than on a particular set of tax instruments. In April 1970 the Luxembourg Agreement profoundly changed the tax profile of the EC. It called for three sets of tax revenues to be earmarked directly into the EC budget: customs duties on imports coming from outside the EC, special levies on agricultural imports, and a percentage of the VAT collected in each member state (not to exceed 1 percent). Fiscal pressures amid the stagflation of the late 1970s and early 1980s led to reform in this formula at the Fontainebleau summit, where the maximum rate for the EC portion of the VAT was raised to 1.4 percent. In 1992, in response to a changed fiscal picture for both member states and the EU, the maximum VAT rate was returned to 1 percent in 1999.

The decision to dedicate so-called own resources to the EU achieved its stated purpose. We do not open the newspaper to read a listing of the back contributions owed the EU from its member states every fiscal year. The dedication of certain resources also has a small but visible influence on the taxation options available to EU member states. First, no member state can use import tariffs as part of its domestic revenue mix; all such revenues go straight into the EU budget. Second, the decision to earmark a percentage of the VAT collected by member states quietly deepened the trend in these countries toward the adoption of this form of taxation—as opposed to a sales tax at the point of sale or other options. The use of the VAT instrument avoids the possibility that sales taxes across the member states could visibly inflate the price of a good via a cascading, multiplier effect. When sales taxes are charged at the point of sale, there is a possibility that sales taxes could be charged on the full value of a manufacturer's materiel inputs at the start of the production process, and then taxes could be charged on the full value of the good again at the end of the production process. The VAT mechanism avoids this cascade effect by levying taxes only on the value added at each step of the production and distribution process.

Contemporary Dynamics

With the finances of the EU on a reasonably solid footing, contemporary EU tax policy in the era of heightened integration has focused on the coordination of member states' tax policies. Although the goal of a single European market implies the pursuit of comparable tax policies among the member states, policymakers have always faced the challenge of national sovereignty. The governments in the member states view tax policy as a crucial policy area over which they are unwilling to cede much of their authority.

The mandate for tax harmonization forms part of the EC Treaty. Article 90 prohibits any tax discrimination that would create an unfair national advantage at the expense of other member states. In turn, Article 93 expressly calls for the harmonization of indirect taxes. Not surprisingly, policy formulation within the EC has focused largely on harmonizing indirect taxes because there is no explicit mandate to regulate other taxes unless they constitute a form of illegal tax discrimination.

With the VAT earmarked as a community-wide endeavor since 1970, political momentum made it easiest to focus the EC's special claim as a VAT stakeholder. The European Commission and many large businesses favored the vigorous pursuit of VAT harmonization. By reducing the variation in taxation across member states, paperwork associated with the VAT's implementation could be reduced and the costs of doing business would vary less across national boundaries. In contrast, member state governments of all political stripes were extremely reluctant to embrace a universalization of VAT procedures. They wanted to retain some meaningful control over which goods and services could be taxed, over the rate of taxation, and over where and when items would be taxed.

After seven long years of debate, in 1977 the Council of Ministers endorsed a common policy that established minimum and maximum levels of all member states' VAT rates. The new policy also defined the precise mix of goods and services over which the VAT could be levied in any and all member states. However, a desire for policy autonomy limited the impact of the community-wide directive in two important senses. First, most countries (as illustrated in the national case studies in this book) permit some important goods and services to be taxed at a lower rate. As a result, the 1977 VAT harmonization directive expressly acknowledged the right of member countries to charge a lower VAT rate (as low as 5 percent) as long as it did not pose a form of illegal discrimination against other member states' economies. Further, the harmonization process permits member states to apply for exceptions via which they can charge even lower VAT rates than the community-wide norm would otherwise permit. In short, the official band of permissible VAT rates was born full of exceptions. Second, despite the recommendations of the European Commission, the member states proved unwilling to permit tax collection to be shifted to the member state of origin (where the finished good or service was produced). Instead, the member governments chose to retain the existing system of collecting the final stage of the VAT in the member state where the item is destined to be purchased. The member state governments did not want to sort out the political trade-offs implicit in shifting where taxes would be collected because the majority of the VAT revenues go directly to the member state that ultimately collects the tax.

The implementation of the VAT harmonization directive and the pursuit of the 1987 Single Market Act each bred pressures to place the harmonization of indirect taxation back on the EU's institutional agenda. The procedures permitting exceptions to the official VAT rate band permitted a diverse landscape of taxation rules to exist in the face of the harmonization initiative. This forced the EU to process a number of requests for exceptions—beyond the considerable variation permitted by the ability of countries to levy rates as low as 5 percent on goods and services without special permission. In addition, as intra-community trade expanded, businesses complained about the logistics of needing to request VAT refunds from the country of origin so that they could avoid double taxation when VAT rates were levied in the destination country.

In response to these issues, bureaucrats at the European Commission again served as official advocates for a deepening of tax harmonization. By 1993 their efforts produced an agreement to harmonize indirect excise taxes on tobacco products, alcohol, and mineral spirits as well as a tweaking of the VAT harmonization. The new 1993 directive permitted EU residents to carry VAT-dutiable goods across member-state borders without facing customs and taxation procedures; only businesses were left subject to the need to process VAT refund requests. However, the member states (via the Council of Ministers) again left considerable discretionary "wiggle room" within the VAT harmonization policy. A lower rate band and the possibility of requesting exceptions were retained as features. VAT taxes also continued to be levied in the destination country, necessitating the use of various refund mechanisms for goods and services crossing national borders. Business pressure persisted and, in 2006, the EU approved the levying of the VAT only in the country of origin for certain services that travel across national boundaries upon delivery. Although the European Commission continues to call for greater harmonization of VAT rates, no real progress has been made on that front.

The dynamics of the four-decade-long pursuit of harmonized VAT rates—and of tax policy more broadly—illustrate the role of institutional and economic factors in EU policy making. First and foremost, the willingness and ability of member-state governments to protect their sovereignty on matters of importance remain considerable. Although the staff of the European Commission is charged with viewing the EU as a single entity, the national governments see the EU as just one of several arenas in which they pursue their interests. Second, in spite of political opposition in the Council of Ministers, the economic pressures associated with European integration (and with economic globalization more broadly) helped to create tax harmonization well beyond the level dictated by the EU. For example, there is no EU directive regulating the band of permissible corporate and personal income tax rates, but all six of these economies have moved toward more similar rates on corporate and personal income taxes during the 1990s and 2000s.

Cross-national Trends

A cross-national summary of tax structures in these six countries highlights the greater reliance on indirect taxes in the continental European countries. This distinction was deepened by tax reforms pursued in the push toward monetary unification in the 1990s—most notably by the creation of a new regional VAT in Italy that replaced local income taxes and national payroll taxes for social security. All six countries pursued a simplification of their income tax structures and a reduction in rates for the highest bracket in line with the supply-sider argument, yet the desired policy outcome of higher economic growth rates did not materialize in most countries. Consideration of the dynamics of tax reform in the 1990s and 2000s leads us to focus on the role of economic and political factors as central to contemporary tax policy making.

Policy Outputs

The tax challenge is lowest in Japan and the United States, where taxes represent less than 28 percent of GDP. Conversely, France and Italy gather about 43 percent of GDP in taxes. How do these countries collect taxes?

Several trends and exceptions are visible in Table 7-2. Three of the six countries generate around one-quarter of tax revenues via personal income taxes. The United States generates over one-third of its revenues in this way, whereas in France and Japan personal income taxes account for less than one-fifth of each country's revenues.

Corporate income taxes are a more important source of revenue in Japan than in the other five countries. Corporate income taxes account for over 15 percent of revenues—double the average share for the other five countries. Corporate income taxes are least important in France, Germany, and Italy.

Dependence on payroll taxes (including employee and employer social security contributions) varies even more widely. In the United Kingdom, payroll taxes account for less than one-fifth of revenues. In the United States and Italy, they make up roughly one-quarter of tax receipts. Japan (32.6 percent), France (34.2 percent), and Germany (36.6 percent) are noticeably more reliant on payroll taxes. Table 7-2 also details how payroll tax obligations are divided between employers and employees. In all six countries, employers pay over half of payroll taxes. On average, employers pay 61 percent of the total. At the low end of the spectrum, Japanese employers pay around 51 percent of payroll taxes; at the high end, Italian employers carry a comparatively heavier load (80 percent).

Sales taxes in France, Germany, and Italy account for roughly one-quarter of tax receipts. Sales taxes are most important in the United Kingdom, where they make up over 30 percent of tax revenues. They are noticeably less important components of the tax structure in Japan (19.4 percent) and the United States (17.4 percent). Remember from the case studies that the United States

Table 7-2 Tax Structures as a Percentage of Tax Receipts, 1996 and 2006

Country	Personal Income Tax	Corporate Income Tax	Employee Social Security	Employer Social Security	Sales Taxes	Other Taxes	Total Taxes per GDP
France 1996	14.1%	3.8%	13.0%	26.6%	27.3%	15.2%	*45.7%*
France 2006	17.3	6.2	9.2	25.0	25.3	16.9	*44.1*
Germany 1996	24.7	3.8	17.6	20.5	27.9	5.5	*38.1*
Germany 2006	23.3	4.9	17.4	19.2	29.0	6.1	*34.8*
Italy 1996	25.1	9.2	6.8	23.7	25.9	9.3	*43.2*
Italy 2006	25.5	6.8	5.5	21.4	26.4	14.4	*41.0*
Japan 1996	20.2	16.4	14.2	18.6	15.4	15.2	*28.4*
Japan 2006	18.3	15.5	15.9	16.7	19.4	14.1	*27.4*
United Kingdom 1996	25.9	10.5	7.2	9.6	35.2	11.6	*36.0*
United Kingdom 2006	28.6	9.3	7.8	10.4	30.3	13.1	*36.5*
United States 1996	37.6	9.6	10.6	12.9	17.2	12.2	*28.5*
United States 2006	35.1	11.4	10.8	12.6	17.4	12.7	*27.3*
Average 1966	*24.6*	*8.9*	*11.6*	*18.7*	*24.8*	*11.5*	*36.7*
Average 2006	*24.7*	*9.0*	*11.1*	*17.6*	*24.6*	*12.9*	*35.2*
EU Average 1996	*26.0*	*7.5*	*10.1*	*16.3*	*31.2*	*8.8*	*42.4*
EU Average 2006	*24.7*	*8.6*	*9.3*	*16.3*	*30.3*	*10.7*	*39.7*
OECD Average 1996	*26.8*	*8.2*	*7.8*	*14.5*	*32.5*	*10.2*	*37.7*
OECD Average 2006	*24.6*	*10.3*	*8.4*	*14.5*	*31.9*	*9.0*	*36.2*

SOURCE: For 1996, Organisation for Economic Co-operation and Development (OECD 1999); for 2006, OECD (2008d).

is the only one of these countries with no comprehensive national sales tax; most sales taxes are collected at the state and local levels.

What drives some of these differences in tax structure? A major force behind smaller payroll taxes in the United Kingdom is the decision to fund government health care programs out of general revenues. This decision is somewhat of a double-edged sword. On the one hand, by funding out of general revenues a basic government program that is popular with many citizens, the government can try to increase popular support for the tax system as a whole. On the other hand, such an approach makes these programs potentially more vulnerable to a generalized tax protest. If health care were funded in the United Kingdom out of an earmarked tax, it might be easier to maintain support for that particular tax instrument, even in the face of major pressures to cut (or maintain) tax rates.

Income taxes have been least important in France because of the government's suspicion that tax avoidance and evasion are relatively common. In response, French governments have responded over the decades by relying much more heavily on payroll and sales taxes, which are easier to implement. Property taxes have also been an important substitute.

Policy Outcomes

A crucial outcome for tax policymakers is public acceptance of the tax structure. Since the early 1980s, protests calling for tax simplification emerged in all of these countries. These pressures have helped to increase commonalities

Table 7-3 Personal Income Tax at the National Level, 1985, 1994, and 2008

	Top Rate			Lowest Positive Rate			Number of Brackets			
Country	*1985*	*1994*	*2008*	*1985*	*1994*	*2008*	*1985*	*1994*	*2008*	Tax Unit in 2008
France	65%	56.8%	40%	5%	12%	5.5%	13	6	4	Family
Germany[a]	56	53	45	22	19	15	—	—	—	Optional
Italy	62	51	43	18	10	23	15	7	5	Individual
Japan	70	50	40	10	10	5	9	3	6	Individual
United Kingdom	60	40	40	30	20	20	6	3	2	Individual
United States	50	39.6	35	11	15	10	14	5	5	Optional
Average	*60.5%*	*48.4%*	*40.5%*	*16%*	*14.3%*	*13.1%*	*11.4*	*5*	*4.4*	

SOURCE: Organisation for Economic Co-operation and Development (2009d).

[a]The German system includes a sliding-scale formula and not formal brackets. — = not applicable.

across the countries' tax systems. For instance, the major trend in tax reform during the 1990s was the simplification of the personal income tax code and a decrease in the top marginal rate (Table 7-3). During the early twenty-first century, this trend continued and these six countries' top marginal rates converged considerably. In the mid-1990s, the three countries with a tradition of smaller government (Japan, the United Kingdom, and the United States) were the only countries with a top rate of 50 percent or less. By 2008, as this trend of falling income tax rates deepened and spread, the average top marginal rate fell to 40.5 percent. Thus between 1985 and 2008 the top marginal rate across these countries fell by one-fifth or more; the average rate reduction was a cut of one-third.

Lowering of upper marginal rates was expected to increase revenues by stimulating additional economic activity. The added growth would generate new revenue streams to compensate for the tax rate cuts. In most of these countries, however, economic growth slowed during the 1990s and the early twenty-first century in comparison with prior decades. Slower growth stymied the hopes of providing politically popular rate cuts without increasing budgetary pressures. The supply-sider argument reviewed in Chapter 6 has yet to realize its promised goal in practice.

In response, governments often resorted to increases in payroll taxes and sales taxes earmarked for popular government programs (combined with restrained spending) in an effort to reduce the deficit. Italy and the United Kingdom took the further step of increasing income taxes for the lowest tax bracket during the early twenty-first century. Tax cuts tended to exceed tax increases such that real revenue growth trailed economic growth during the same time period in these six countries. Given the commitment to deficit reduction, this situation motivates governments to try to promote economic growth without raising tax rates or spending significantly. The global economic downturn in 2008 will pose a serious challenge to the continuation of this trend in fiscal policy.

Understanding Policy Reform

If the 1980s were characterized as the decade of tax protest, tax simplification, and tax reduction, the 1990s and the 2000s might be considered a period of quiet revenue-seeking. Center-left and center-right governments alike tried to lower their highest personal and corporate income tax rates while also increasing revenues in other ways. These hunts for revenue expansion were motivated largely by the desire to reduce (or, in Japan's case, to control) the budget deficit. As we saw in Chapter 6, most of the motivation for deficit reduction stemmed from international financial markets and from the monetary unification agreement in continental Europe. To understand the nuances of how governments went about revenue enhancement, we need to consider additional factors.

Prevailing short-term economic conditions clearly played a role in most of these countries. Slow economic growth in all but the United States forced taxation rate increases onto the institutional agenda as a path toward deficit reduction because political considerations made wholesale spending cuts undesirable. Stronger economic growth enabled the United States to zero out its deficit briefly in the 1990s with only one specific tax increase—the jump in the top rate enacted in 1993 at the beginning of the Clinton administration. By the end of the decade, continued economic growth and the budget surplus put tax rate reduction back on the U.S. agenda.

In the other countries, slow growth created pressure for tax rate increases, but the public remained unsurprisingly skeptical. In the case studies, we saw three major strategies used to pursue revenue enhancement in the absence of strong economic growth—increases in indirect taxes, increases in the bottom rate of taxation for individuals and corporations, and the creation of a surcharge income tax. In the three countries pushing to meet the Maastricht fiscal target by 1997, governments tried to blunt opposition by using the proposed benefits of monetary unification as a rationale for tax increases. To reduce further the vibrancy of opposition, governments often placed sunset clauses on tax increases. This sunset clause approach was used differently by the Bush administration to cement legislative support for his tax cut measures in the United States during the early twenty-first century.

We also observed how political unity within the government provides a force for policy stability, whereas divisions within governing coalitions and visible swings in election outcomes make it difficult for governments to steer a coherent course. In particular, multiparty coalitions and major voting swings made policymakers' jobs more difficult in the 1990s in France, Italy, and Japan. Although these three governments used approaches seen in all six countries, we observed situations in which French, Italian, and Japanese governments had to reverse recent decisions in tax policy. The creation of larger, more sustained center-right majorities in France and Italy in the early twenty-first century buoyed the leaders of those governments, whereas the fragmented Japanese political system continued to struggle to find a successful electoral and policy formula. After the 2005 elections in Germany, the "grand coalition" government headed by Angela Merkel also found it difficult to formulate and pursue coherent tax policies in the face of the ideological diversity within the cabinet. Ideological unity, however, is no panacea for sustained electoral success. Both the Thatcher government in the United Kingdom and the Bush administration in the United States implemented bold policy reforms that bred vibrant opposition and a subsequent change in their political fortunes. Unity makes policy making easier, but it does not necessarily ensure the decisions taken will please a majority of the citizenry.

SUGGESTED READINGS

Ault, Hugh J., and Brian J. Arnold. 2004. *Comparative Income Taxation: A Structural Analysis,* 2nd ed. The Hague: Kluwer Law International.

Cnossen, Sijbren, and Hans-Werner Sinn, eds. 2003. *Public Finance and Public Policy in the New Century.* Cambridge: MIT Press.

Cordes, Joseph J., Robert D. Ebel, and Jane Gravelle, eds. 2005. *The Encyclopedia of Tax and Tax Policy.* Washington, D.C.: Urban Institute Press.

Eccleston, Richard. 2007. *Taxing Reforms: The Politics of the Consumption Tax in Japan, the United States, Canada, and Australia.* Cheltenham, U.K.: Edward Elgar.

Haufler, Andreas. 2002. *Taxation in a Global Economy.* Cambridge: Cambridge University Press.

Howard, Christopher. 1997. *The Hidden Welfare State: Tax Expenditures and Social Policy in the United States.* Princeton: Princeton University Press.

Ishi, Hiromitsu. 2001. *The Japanese Tax System,* 3rd ed. Oxford: Oxford University Press.

James, Malcolm. 2005. *The U.K. Tax System: An Introduction.* London: Spiramus.

Lamb, Margaret, Andrew Lymer, Judith Freeman, and Simon James, eds. 2005. *Tax: An Interdisciplinary Approach to Research.* Oxford: Oxford University Press.

Messere, Ken, ed. 1998. *The Tax System in Industrialized Countries.* Oxford: Oxford University Press.

Reed, Colin, and Greg N. Gregorio, eds. 2007. *International Taxation Handbook: Policy, Practice, Standards, and Regulations.* Oxford: CIMA Publishing.

Slemrod, Joel, and Jon Bakija. 2008. *Taxing Ourselves: A Citizen's Guide to the Debate over Taxes,* 4th ed. Cambridge: MIT Press.

Steuerle, C. Eugene. 2004. *Contemporary U.S. Tax Policy,* 2nd ed. Washington, D.C.: Urban Institute Press.

Thorndike, Joseph J., and Dennis J. Ventry, Jr., eds. 2002. *Tax Justice: The Ongoing Debate.* Washington, D.C.: Urban Institute Press.

Tömmel, Ingeborg, and Amy Verdun, eds. 2009. *Innovative Governance in the European Union: The Politics of Multilevel Policymaking.* Boulder: Lynne Rienner Publishers.

Chapter 8 **Health Care Policy**

The most basic element of human welfare is good health. For centuries, governments were largely "off the hook" in this area because most people did not hold government directly responsible for individuals' poor health. Governments tried to slow the spread of infectious diseases but did little else. Since the twentieth century, as preventive public health initiatives expanded, governments have also played a growing role in the curative care sector via regulation, funding, and, at times, the provision of care itself.

Common Policy Problems

Health outcomes are the fundamental test of government success in the area of health policy. If many citizens are ill and dying, people will likely say that government efforts are insufficient to deal with the problem—even if government inaction is not the sole (or even principal) cause of these undesired outcomes. The complexity of health outcomes is what makes health policy such a difficult challenge for governments. Should policy focus largely on preventive measures such as vaccinations, clean air and water, and the like? Or is the problem the absence of medical intervention at the right time? Here, too, government can make a difference by sponsoring research to discover new treatments and by providing access to curative care.

Access to curative care is understandably important to most people. People want to protect their most important asset: their lives and those of their families and friends. Perhaps the most fundamental aspect of modern health care policy stems from the widespread belief in the possibility of curing any and all illnesses: citizens' demands in the health sector are almost unlimited. Once people became confident that even devastating illnesses could be overcome, demands for curative care expanded and many of those demands involved the government as the provider of last resort. As a result, access to curative care is a major public policy issue.

Curative care is often expensive. Specialized health care professionals demand high wages, and new medical technologies and medicines fuel our hope that virtually any illness can be conquered. In many industrialized and late-industrializing countries, the cost of curative care has risen faster than the general rate of inflation. Whether most curative care is provided publicly or privately, governments frequently face pressure to control health care costs.

Major Policy Options

In virtually every country the government manages and provides an array of public health projects, including health education through schools and the broadcast media, vaccination programs, sanitation projects, and the regulation of food and drug quality. In most industrialized countries these projects have covered such a high percentage of the population for so long that they tend to be taken for granted despite their crucial importance for health outcomes. In late-industrializing countries, public health programs vary more substantially from one country to the next in several key respects, including money spent per person; the organizational structure of public health; the number of public health professionals per person; and crucially, the percentage of the population reached by public health initiatives. Despite the undeniable importance of these differences in public health around the world, in this chapter we focus on the organization of curative care and cost-control issues because they represent more visible public policy issues in industrialized countries (and in many late-industrializing countries).

National policy models for curative care range from direct provision of care by the government to minimal government activity in providing care or even access to that care. The polar extremes here are not absolutes: private activity still occurs in government-run systems, and government has a considerable role in market-oriented systems. All countries are searching for what they believe is an optimal mix of public and private activity.

In the **national health service** model, citizens are guaranteed access to most curative care services through a system paid for and administered directly by the government. This approach has been prevalent in many communist economies, but it has also been used in some market economies, most notably the United Kingdom. In this model the government pays hospitals, physicians, and nurses directly to provide comprehensive care to all citizens. Access is guaranteed, but all or almost all costs are absorbed by the government, which has a direct interest in cost-control measures and the authority to carry them out. This can mean, however, that demand for certain services may exceed supply—sometimes significantly. For example, waiting lists for elective procedures can be lengthy. As a result, the national health service approach is sometimes called rationed care.

In many late-industrializing countries, a much more limited national health service is constructed via a system of government-run hospitals that frequently lack the resources needed to meet the demands on their services. Although citizens are legally guaranteed a right to care at these facilities, the quality and availability of care are more often insufficient. A much higher percentage of citizens in these countries seek out private care or forego care than has been the case in the United Kingdom, Italy, or most command economies.

The **single-payer** model guarantees all citizens access to health care via a single program in which almost all funds come from the government, but care is provided privately. This approach tries to control costs and guarantee access by pooling all citizens into a single insurance program run directly by the government. The single insurer then negotiates the best rates from hospitals and physicians. Although conceivably all citizens could pay the government a premium earmarked for health insurance, in Canada the single-payer system is funded out of general government revenues. For further discussion of the development of the single-payer system in Canada, see Box 8-1.

Through **mandatory national health insurance,** government guarantees all citizens access to care but with multiple payers and multiple providers. Germany pioneered such efforts in the late nineteenth century, and many other countries followed this model during the twentieth century. In this approach, many citizens receive health coverage through private insurance (often tied into their jobs), but government regulations guarantee certain benefits or control costs and fees. The government provides health insurance to the unemployed, the self-employed, and retired citizens through various programs.

In the **market-maximized** model, the government provides no guarantee of access through either public hospitals or mandatory health insurance. In this approach the government might provide access for some categories of people but not all. This approach assumes that access to health care is not a right of citizens but rather a choice each citizen makes. Government regulation of private health insurers, while still significant, is not at the level found in the mandatory national health insurance model. The United States has been a proponent of the market-maximized model. Health care in the market-maximized model is also rationed—not by the availability of services relative to the urgency of their need but rather by one's ability to pay.

In addition to policy options dealing with access, policymakers have an array of alternatives for dealing with cost-control concerns. Some cost-control measures try to limit costs by altering the behavior of certain individuals in the health care system. For example, one way to reduce health care costs is to make patients pay at the time care is delivered. Even if private or public insurance will pay the lion's share of the bill, forcing patients to make a **copayment** may make them monitor their use of medical services more carefully. Conversely, if care is free at the point of service, patients may be more likely to pursue care even if, in the long run, it will result in higher health insurance costs for them. Critics of this cost-control approach argue that patients' decisions to pursue treatment should not be constrained by economic considerations.

Other cost-control measures try to influence the behavior of physicians. Many countries employ a **fee-for-service** system, in which doctors are paid a fee for each service performed. If the number of services that can be provided is not constrained, physicians can provide additional services to rule out certain diagnostic possibilities or to enhance their incomes. In contrast, doctors are sometimes paid on a **capitation** basis; they receive a fee based on how many patients they treat, not on how many services they provide. In the

Box 8-1 **In Depth: Canada's Single-payer Model**

For the first half of the twentieth century, Canadian health policy generally resembled the situation in the United States. The desirability of publicly mandated or financed health insurance was debated several times, but no such policies were adopted. In the middle of the century, a series of five provincial governments created universal hospitalization programs—beginning with Saskatchewan in 1947. The popularity of these programs put national health insurance back on the institutional agenda, and in 1957 the government passed the Hospital Insurance and Diagnostic Services Act. The law required all provincial governments to provide hospitalization insurance for their residents under financing shared jointly by the federal and provincial governments.

As this policy was being implemented in the 1960s, its popularity raised the issue of providing a comprehensive insurance plan that would also cover outpatient services. Despite opposition from private insurers and the Canadian Medical Association, the 1968 Medical Care Act expanded the system to its present scope. The Canadian Medicare system—in which each provincial government serves as a single payer for covered services in its jurisdiction—was in place in all provinces by 1971.

Under this single-payer system, each provincial government provides universal health coverage to its residents. The federal legislation dictates the basic coverage of the Medicare system; provinces are allowed to provide additional coverage should they choose to do so. Coverage is portable from province to province, although citizens generally must reside three months in a new province prior to joining its plan. The Medicare system features fee-for-service billing in accordance with a fee schedule worked out between provincial governments and physicians' associations. Physicians who choose not to obey the fee schedule cannot provide treatment to Medicare patients; this aspect of the Canadian system expands greatly the number of physicians in the system. As a result, citizens are able to choose their physicians from virtually the entire medical community. Covered physician services include general medical and maternity care, surgical and laboratory services, and other specializations. Medicare covers all basic hospitalization services. Hospitals in Canada are nonprofit organizations, and most are privately run. However, the government controls the annual public budget associated with the Medicare program as well as the technology acquisition decisions made by hospitals.

Under the terms of the single-payer system, private insurance companies are not permitted to write policies for benefits provided under Medicare. However, private insurers are allowed to provide supplemental medical insurance to cover benefits not provided by the government. Over 65 percent of all Canadians have some form of private supplemental health insurance, often paid in whole or in part by employers. Since 1984, when the 1984 Canada Health Act virtually outlawed patient copayments, the system has been free to the user at the point of service. The vast majority of program funding comes from general government revenues at the federal and provincial levels (although nine provinces also levy earmarked taxes or patient premiums).

United States, **health maintenance organizations** (HMOs) provide most services based on capitation reimbursement. In the capitation system, physicians presumably will restrain themselves in providing services to strictly necessary care in order to remain within the bounds of their per-patient budget. Again, critics of this approach do not want economic considerations front and center when treatment options are being decided.

Another cost-control measure that focuses on the behavior of the medical community involves **limits on technology acquisition**. Studies have shown that making expensive technologies more available increases the likelihood that they will be used. Although this seems logical enough, cost-control advocates charge that much of this technology is overused—especially in countries that operate on a fee-for-service reimbursement system. They also argue that placing limits on the acquisition of medical technology by hospitals and private physicians can help keep costs under control. Limits on technology acquisition are associated with lower costs but also imply waiting lists to use certain technologies for which demand exceeds supply.

An organizational measure that tries to change cost dynamics in the health sector involves the use of a gatekeeper. Some health plans give patients the freedom to go to not just the general practitioner (GP) of their choice but to any physician of any specialty. In contrast, in a **gatekeeper system**, patients must see a GP and get a referral before going to see a specialist. In this way, the GP serves to control costs by trying to make the appropriate referral or no referral when the diagnosis or treatment does not require the participation of a specialist. This is the cost-control measure most widely used across countries—whether the health insurance plan is public or private. In the United States, **preferred provider organizations** (PPOs) use gatekeepers. PPOs also limit patients to the selection of doctors who agree to the insurer's fee schedule. The notion at work here is that the physician is a better judge of where the patient should go than is the patient. GPs are often preferred as gatekeepers because in most countries they make significantly less money than more specialized physicians. The gatekeeper approach is not without its controversies. In some countries, gatekeeper physicians at times complain that they are under pressure to keep costs low by keeping referrals under a certain budgetary limit.

The most frequent criticism of these cost-control alternatives stems from a desire to make health care decisions without reference to economic considerations. We cannot present ironclad evidence about the optimal amount that a country (or an individual) should spend on health care; it is a choice that must be made. Choices in health policy, as in other policy areas, are made by government officials who are responding to a variety of constituent groups. In turn, individual citizens also make choices with regard to their own health spending habits.

What is the average citizen concerned about in the health sector? Everyone needs medical attention from time to time, and people know that they could incur serious medical problems (and expenses) due to illness or injury. That said, not everyone is equally risk-averse in his or her approach to health care. Some people want to spend as little as possible on health care, and others want complete coverage almost regardless of cost.

These different individual perspectives on health insurance are related to different approaches to medical insurance: the principle of **actuarial fairness** and the principle of **risk-pooling**. Actuarial fairness calls for people to be grouped by risk factors—enabling healthy individuals in low-risk occupations to join health insurance plans with other similar individuals. Thus high-risk patients (including those already diagnosed with chronic health problems) would be forced to pay higher health insurance premiums in recognition of the greater likelihood that they will require care. The principle of risk-pooling calls for solidarity of citizens based on a recognition that everyone is at risk of needing care because of chronic illness or accidents. That risk is then pooled across a large body of currently healthy and unhealthy individuals to provide maximal coverage at a lower cost. Advocates of actuarial fairness criticize risk-pooling because they claim that it asks the healthy to subsidize the unhealthy when they have no responsibility for the illnesses involved. Advocates of risk-pooling counter that even narrowly self-interested individuals should pool risks together to lower the costs of illness to the sick because today's healthy could become tomorrow's ill.

Explaining Policy Dynamics

Health policy has become an increasingly visible issue on the systemic agenda during the late twentieth and early twenty-first centuries. That visibility has motivated a new wave of research on the dynamics of health policy making. Most research has consisted of national case studies, but several analysts have conducted cross-national comparisons. Although in past decades primary attention was paid to cultural, economic, and political factors, a series of studies at the turn of the century brought new attention to the role of institutions.

Cultural Explanations

Cultural factors have been used most frequently in analyses of U.S. health policy making. A series of studies have emphasized the role of an individualistic and antigovernment culture in blocking the emergence of legislation that ensures universal access to medical care in the United States (Anderson 1972; Blank and Burau 2004; Jacobs 1993; Patel and Rushefsky 1998; Starr 1982). As we noted in other chapters, cultural differences are frequently used to explain countries' use of government authority in responding to various policy challenges.

This approach, however, has proven more problematic in building an explanation of health policy making that holds up to cross-national examination.

When we look at the rest of the Anglo-American family of nations, we see a delay in the adoption of some form of universal access policy (especially in Australia and Canada). That said, we also see that two of those countries developed health policy models that are among the most government-intensive in some respects: the first national health service (in the United Kingdom) and the first single-payer system (in Canada). In fact, during the twentieth century, health care was one of the policy areas in which most countries actively debated fairly similar policy options (Immergut 1992: 11–12). Perhaps a more nuanced version of the cultural argument merits consideration. Citizens in the Anglo-American family of nations tend to prefer a limited government role and private responsibility. These attitudes can conceivably be exploited by organized groups and political parties seeking a smaller role for government (Morone 1995).

Economic Explanations

The convergence thesis (Wilensky 1975) introduced in Chapter 2 has played a role in comparative studies of health politics. Recall that Wilensky argued that as countries become industrialized—usually measured by gross domestic product (GDP) per capita—they are likely to experience similar social and political pressures. These pressures culminate in the adoption of a wide range of similar welfare policies—in part because those greater economic resources provide more breathing room for the expansion of government spending and activity. Roemer (1977) applied this logic to explain the expansion of government activity and spending in health care across the industrialized world during the postwar era. In addition to Wilensky's emphasis on affluence, Roemer noted that advances in medical technology developed in industrialized countries provide an additional force driving toward convergence of spending levels. This logic has been less useful, however, for explaining differences among industrialized countries regarding the specific choice of policy models and the ongoing reform of those models since the 1980s.

A central feature of contemporary reform debates, as we noted at the beginning of this chapter, is a desire to control costs. These pressures continue to intensify as the populations of industrialized countries age, owing to the observed connection between age and demands for health care services (Abel-Smith 1994; Giaimo 2002). These demographic changes are particularly relevant in the area of health policy. Senior citizens are more likely than younger citizens to want and need medical attention. Accordingly, as the elderly constitute a rising percentage of the population, health care utilization tends to rise while the amount paid into the overall system tends to decrease (especially in countries with the **employer-mandate** model in which premiums are tied to wages). This graying factor, as we noted in Chapter 2, is projected to intensify further through the 2010s as the postwar baby-boom generation reaches retirement age (Raffel 1997).

Political Explanations

Interest group politics approaches have also been used to explain health policy making. In fact, health care constitutes the one policy area discussed in this book in which a single interest group—the medical profession—has been argued to hold a defining role all by itself. As we note throughout this book, many interest groups work to influence policy making, and their effectiveness is tied to a variety of factors such as financial and organizational resources, personal connections to policymakers, and strategies for mobilizing public opinion in favor of their positions. Several analysts of health policy making have asserted that physicians' associations have a special form of political power not found in other spheres: they are the only group licensed to provide most forms of curative care (Anderson 1972; Quadagno 2004; Starr 1982). This power is deemed greatest when health policy concerns touch directly on physicians' professional domain, for example, regarding the form of payment: "As producers of a crucial service in industrial countries, and a service for which governments can seldom provide short-run substitutes, physicians have the overwhelming political resources to influence decisions regarding payment methods quite apart from the form of bargaining that their organizations employ" (Marmor and Thomas 1972: 436–437). Stated in its most extreme view, this assertion implies that physicians' associations hold a veto power over varied policy proposals not to their liking.

Over the years, however, a series of studies has demonstrated that doctors do not always have the ability to block reforms they oppose (Eckstein 1960; Glaser 1978; Immergut 1992; Klein 2006; Stone 1980). Instead, medical associations' policy-making influence varies in accordance with their own unity (Wilsford 1991) and with the constellation of other influences on policy making. For example, a study of health policy reform in ten industrialized countries concluded that a variety of factors—including internal divisions in the profession, the political cost of being labeled as obstructionist in prior reform debates, and the increasing importance of cost-control concerns—diminished medical associations' political influence during the 1990s (Raffel 1997). As more people perceive health care activities as affecting their own sectors of the government budget or the economy as a whole, other stakeholders (for example, government officials, business leaders, and diverse interest groups) become more reluctant to defer to physicians' associations in disagreements over health policy.

Other political explanations focus on the positions of the major political parties (Maioni 1997; Navarro 1995). When one steps back to consider the role played by political parties from a broader cross-national perspective in the welfare state literature, leftist political parties played an important role in stimulating the emergence and evolution of the welfare state in most industrialized countries, whereas rightist parties worked to slow its development (Castles 1982a; Esping-Andersen 1990). Health care proved no exception to this trend as the countries with the least important leftist parties—Canada and the United States—were the slowest to devote active consideration to some form of national health insurance. In the contemporary period, center-right and rightist parties have played a visible role in promoting reforms deemed to reduce government's role in health policy by encouraging more discretionary behavior by health care providers and patients alike (Marmor 1997), whereas left-leaning parties have tended to be more critical of many of those measures. The ability of reform-minded political parties is contingent not only on the size and unity of its governing majority but also on a variety of factors beyond the parties' direct control (Tuohy 1999).

Institutional Explanations

Cultural, economic, and political factors traditionally received the most attention in studies of health politics. Since the 1980s, however, scholars (Blake and Adolino 2001; Giaimo 2002; Hacker 2004; March and Olsen 1984; Morone 1995; Steinmo and Watts 1995) have attempted to highlight the role of institutional influences that past studies understated or, in some cases, ignored entirely. Perhaps the most widely read comparative institutionalist study is Immergut's (1992) analysis of the evolution of health policy in France, Sweden, and Switzerland. Immergut focused on how distinctions in government organization (federal versus unitary), the nature of executive-legislative relations (parliamentary versus presidential systems), and the ability to call a binding referendum shape health policy making by determining the number of veto points available across the policy-making process. In this analysis, the Swiss system characterized by federalism, a multimember chief executive, and frequent use of referenda in politics makes large reforms more difficult. Conversely, the unitary Swedish government, in which the prime minister frequently enjoyed a firm legislative majority with no threat of a referendum, provided a path toward party government. The number of veto points in France during the twentieth-century evolution of health policy lay between those two extremes. Although Immergut emphasized the role of institutional factors in preventing a straight line from groups' stated positions to policy making, she concluded her study with a call to remain open to a variety of influences (1992: 242–244).

International Policy Making

No binding set of international agreements guides the curative care policies of the six countries examined in this book. All six countries are members of the World Health Organization (WHO) through their participation in the United Nations. The WHO serves as a clearinghouse for disseminating data on health outcomes, public health initiatives, and medical practices. It has reached consensus behind some binding commitments regarding the prevention of infectious diseases and, more recently in this century, regarding a set of public health initiatives related to tobacco use. However, the WHO does not set firm parameters for the curative care measures at the center of contemporary health policy.

As discussed in Chapter 9, the Maastricht Treaty includes a series of social policy goals (the so-called social chapter). The language of the social chapter itself contains no specific references to curative care initiatives in the health sector. The language emphasizes public health policy instruments and outcomes—as was the case subsequently in the health component (Article 152) of the Treaty of Amsterdam that entered into effect in 1999. Despite the EU's focus on public health, one of the social chapter's major themes—a call for harmonized social policies among member states—coincides with the pressures associated with the single-market initiative in the EU. As we will see in our examination of EU health policy activity later in this chapter, the evolution of the single market has inserted EU governing bodies into some health policy questions despite the absence of any treaty-based agreement to have EU-wide standards for medical care. Beyond the activities of the EU authorities, the move toward more open competition among the member states also makes businesses more sensitive to varying costs associated with health care expenses. The cost pressure implied by economic globalization affects countries in and outside of the EU and its Social Community.[1]

United States

Background: Policy Process and Policy History

Throughout this book we turn repeatedly to different policy sectors to discover a shared truth: the policy process in the United States is usually the most decentralized among the six countries. With the possible exception of budgetary appropriations decisions, this is most true of contemporary health policy making. In part, the diffuse nature of health policy making stems from the absence of a unified national health policy. The United States has multiple segments to its health care policy:

- A government-mandated and -managed health insurance Medicare program for the elderly
- A Medicaid program for the poor with basic guidelines set by the federal government but with most specific standards and benefits determined by the state governments
- A majority of the population covered by private insurance providers regulated by both federal and state legislation

---

[1]The statistics presented in the case studies on benefit levels and funding are taken from U.S. Social Security Administration (2009). Data for the United States are from July 2007, data for Japan are from July 2008, and data for the other four countries are from January 2008. The data on overall health care expenditures are from Organisation for Economic Co-operation and Development (2009b).

As a result, health care reform initiatives can emerge from a variety of public arenas. The decentralization of Medicaid and insurance regulation means that any of the state governments can make health policy. The field is even broader in terms of federal policy. A variety of executive agencies are engaged in health policy formulation, including the Centers for Medicare and Medicaid Services (in charge of Medicare implementation), the Department of Health and Human Services, and the Surgeon General's office. In addition, presidents can convene working groups to formulate policy recommendations. Many congressional committees hold hearings on one or more aspects of health policy; the percentage of congressional hearings held by the presumably dominant health committees in the House and the Senate comprises less than half of all hearings held on health care.

The United States is the only industrialized country that has no form of national health insurance. During the twentieth century, a series of (mainly Democratic) legislative efforts to generate some form of national health insurance failed as government focused instead on providing tax incentives for the provision of private insurance as a job benefit. This approach left many elderly and low-income citizens without health insurance. Criticism of this large block of uninsured people eventually resulted in the 1965 establishment of the Medicare and Medicaid programs as part of Lyndon Johnson's Great Society initiatives. Medicare is a federally managed insurance program that covers people aged sixty-five and over (later extended in 1972 to cover the disabled). About 14 percent of the population is served by the Medicare program. The Medicaid program provides care to different categories of low-income citizens, covering about 11 percent of the population.

The basic Medicare program (Part A) provides up to 90 days of hospitalization coverage (and up to 100 days of nursing home care) to pensioners over age sixty-four, to those who have been disabled for over two years, and to patients suffering from chronic kidney disease. A supplemental program (Part B) covers general and specialist physician services, laboratory services, and physical therapy. Medicaid covers many inpatient and outpatient services for uninsured pregnant women and children whose family incomes are below a specified minimum. In the early twenty-first century, roughly 15 percent of the U.S. population at any point in time had no health insurance and did not qualify for Medicaid coverage. Uninsured individuals who do not qualify for Medicaid benefits must either pay for services out of pocket or seek care from a limited number of nonprofit clinics.

Roughly 60 percent of U.S. residents have some form of private insurance (often, but not always, linked to employment). These plans had traditionally featured fee-for-service billing; however, from 1988 through 2005 the portion of the insured population covered by unmanaged fee-for-service billing fell from 73 percent to 3 percent. One-eighth of the population is covered by HMOs. These comprehensive health care providers try to limit the utilization incentives associated with fee-for-service billing by hiring an array of GPs and specialists on a salary or capitation basis. Most private insurance is provided by managed fee-for-service plans. More than one-third of the population is enrolled in standard PPO networks, and another one-tenth in **point-of-service** (POS) plans that are a hybrid of managed care and unrestricted fee-for-service insurance. In POS health plans, patients can participate in a managed care system in an HMO or in a preferred provider network headed by a gatekeeper. However, they retain the option to see physicians outside of the network at a lower rate of reimbursement from the insurer.

Most hospitals are privately owned. Since the 1980s a noticeable shift has occurred from nonprofit to for-profit private hospitals. In recognition of the substantial number of uninsured citizens, the law requires all hospitals to provide emergency treatment to all citizens; in practice, violations of this principle occur. Under both Medicare and Medicaid, inpatient and outpatient services are paid for on a fee-for-service basis.

Medicare Part A is funded by payroll taxes. Employees pay 1.45 percent of earnings; employers pay an identical percentage of payroll. The self-employed pay the full 2.9 percent themselves; pensioners pay a flat-rate monthly premium (almost $94). Medicare participants can pay a monthly premium to gain access to Part B, which covers outpatient care. The vast majority of participants choose to do so. The federal government covers the balance of expenses for the supplemental plan out of general revenues. Wealthy seniors can choose to replace these traditional Medicare programs with an optional Part C, through which they contract with a private insurer or invest in a health savings account. The 2003 Medicare Modernization Act created a new Part D, through which patients receive prescription drug benefits by paying an additional premium that is supplemented with government funds to cover catastrophic care; the average monthly premium is about $30. About 90 percent of eligible seniors are enrolled in Medicare Part D. The Medicaid program is administered at the state level; funding is shared between the federal and state governments out of general revenues. Federal contributions now take the form of block grants, in which states have greater freedom to determine how to spend the federal funding.

Medicare rules include a variety of deductibles and copayments. Similarly, Medicaid patients can be held responsible for billing above the relevant Medicaid reimbursement schedule; however, they are not responsible for copayments. In the private sector, deductibles and copayments are also a substantial component of the system for most people. Out-of-pocket payments account for around one-eighth of the country's health expenses.

During 1980s and 1990s the U.S. health reform debate was dominated by two issues. The first, cost control, is quite familiar to other industrialized countries. The second issue is unique to the United States: the large number of uninsured residents. Some political forces approached coverage for the uninsured as a moral imperative. Others, especially many business groups, focused on how the cost of covering the uninsured is passed on to the insured by overbilling by private providers to compensate for losses stemming from services for which uninsured patients failed to pay. Despite the notion that market competition among insurers and providers would lead to quality care at low cost, the United States was spending more money per capita and as a percentage of GDP than any other industrialized country. In addition to overbilling, predominant reliance on fee-for-service reimbursement, administrative costs associated with the multitude of payers and providers, and so-called defensive medicine (that is, tests conducted to rule out unlikely scenarios in an effort to avoid malpractice lawsuits) all increased U.S. health care spending. The willingness and ability of many providers to purchase the latest technology also led to greater utilization of expensive services.

In the 1980s the government attempted to control rising costs through fee schedules. A uniform fee schedule based on diagnosis-related groups (DRGs) was introduced unilaterally in 1983 to try to limit the government's rising obligations under the Medicare supplemental program. Over the rest of the decade, the government kept a keen eye on fee structures in the Medicare and Medicaid programs in an effort to cut costs. However, higher utilization rates per insured in Medicare and an extension of the covered population in Medicaid kept expenses on the rise. Beyond the halls of government itself, the implementation of cost-control efforts in the private sector placed new issues higher on the systemic and institutional agendas. The expansion of HMO activity and the extension of PPOs and other utilization-controlling efforts by traditional insurers generated debate over the pros and cons of managed care. In 1988 only 30 percent of the insured population was covered by some form of managed care plan; by 1998 that figure had risen to 86 percent. These cost-control measures drew complaints from both physicians and patients, who argued that necessary tests and treatments were sometimes not provided in the effort to control costs. These public discussions of perceived decreases in the quality and freedom of care, implied by curtailed utilization, placed insurer regulation on the agenda.

Against this agenda-setting backdrop, in 1993 the newly elected Clinton administration pledged to create a national health insurance system to deal with the twin problems of high costs and unequal access. Given the high-profile commitment of the president and the many business leaders who had spoken in favor of reform, many observers felt that some major reform would take place. However, once policy formulation began in earnest, the Democratic majority in Congress was divided on which model to adopt, and most Republican legislators bitterly opposed the managed competition plan favored by the president. In addition, the Health Insurance Association of America launched a biting media campaign aimed at reducing popular support for the president's plan by asserting that the proposal would reduce patients' choice, increase their costs, and decrease the quality of services provided. In the end, none of the handful of major health care bills proposed during the 1993–1995 session received a floor vote. For the remainder of the decade, health reform efforts focused on incremental changes rather than on a government-led reform of the entire health care system.

Contemporary Dynamics

The 2000 presidential campaign took place in a novel context of government budget surpluses obtained during the years 1998–2000. The Democratic Party candidate, Al Gore, pledged to use much of the surplus to shore up the finances of the Medicare program and of the Social Security retirement pension program. In addition, he proposed adding a prescription drug benefit to the Medicare program. The Clinton administration had pursued this idea during its second term, but it was blocked by Republican legislative opposition. On the campaign trail, Gore criticized Republicans in general (and presidential candidate George W. Bush in particular) for not protecting the elderly. The Bush campaign stressed a desire to eliminate most of the budget surplus via tax cuts. However, in a response to the Gore campaign, Bush also promised to generate a new prescription drug benefit for senior citizens. While interest group advocates of more sweeping health policy reform had pinned their hopes on a potential Gore-led presidency, the inauguration of George W. Bush in January 2001 turned most health reformers' attention squarely to the issue of prescription drug benefits for senior citizens.

Despite bipartisan support for some sort of Medicare prescription drug coverage, the policy formulation process revealed significant differences across and within party lines. President Bush and most Republicans in the House initially backed a proposal that would provide drug benefits only to seniors who opted to shift to the privatized Part C component of the Medicare program. In turn, moderate Republicans, especially in the Senate, preferred a bill that would provide some sort of benefit to all seniors but also wanted to increase private insurance providers' participation in Medicare. Democratic legislators sponsored alternative proposals that would provide the same drug benefits to all seniors from within the traditional, publicly managed Medicare program. Senior citizens' groups lobbied for benefits for all seniors, insurance companies pressured for a role in Medicare, and drug companies mobilized to head off any effort to control drug prices as a result of Medicare reform. The division of opinions fueled a series of nonevents during the 107th Congress (2001–2003). The Bush administration did not insist on a floor vote for its proposal because it believed (probably correctly) that it could not gain passage in the Senate. In turn, Democratic proposals for more sweeping reform failed to make it out of committee in the Republican-controlled House.

Once the Republican Party regained a small majority in the Senate via the November 2002 legislative elections, the Bush administration and the Republican congressional leadership agreed to make Medicare reform the major domestic policy initiative for 2003. When this ran into opposition from moderates in both parties in the House and (especially) the Senate, the Republican bill was modified to grant drug benefits to all seniors but required that the drug insurance plans be offered by private insurance companies. Both the House and the Senate pursued a "donut-holed" drug benefit: in the final version of the legislation, seniors would receive coverage up to a $2,400 spending threshold; then they would pay 100 percent of prescription costs until they reached a catastrophic threshold of $3,850 in out-of-pocket spending—after which point the government would pay 90 percent of any additional prescription costs. The catastrophic component is an unfunded commitment to be paid from general government revenues. This particular program feature caused a rebellion on the House floor as several fiscally conservative Republicans initially voted against the bill. The House leadership took the unusual step of leaving the vote count open for several hours while furiously lobbying a handful of legislators to change their votes. The measure passed by a one-vote margin with a small number of Democratic votes.

The implementation of the 2003 Medicare Modernization Act did not proceed smoothly. Many senior citizens struggled to come to grips with a dizzying array of new prescription drug benefit plans. The law gave them only a few months to make a decision in order to access Part D without paying a penalty. In addition, the law and its implementing legislation permitted the private insurance companies participating in Part D to change their benefit packages and premiums frequently. Skeptics claimed that the Republican leadership had used the bill to bankrupt the Medicare system while filling the coffers of insurance companies and the pharmaceutical industry.

Complaints about the new system motivated the Democratic Party to make reform of Part D its first legislative initiative upon gaining a legislative majority in 2007. On a party-line basis, the Democratic bill to empower the Medicare program to negotiate drug prices (a power already enjoyed by the Veterans Health Administration, by Medicaid, and by large private insurers) passed the House. However, 41 Republicans in the Senate supported a filibuster that prevented consideration of the bill in the upper house during the 2007–2009 legislative session. Meanwhile, continuing concerns over both health costs and the plight of the uninsured reinserted those issues into the 2008 presidential campaign. The victory of Democratic candidate Barack Obama provided the potential to reinsert discussion of some form of universal health care proposal into the institutional agenda of the U.S. Congress during the 2009–2011 session.

The health care reform experience under the Clinton and George W. Bush administrations demonstrates a series of obstacles that make major expansion of government activity difficult in this sector. Many citizens are skeptical of government intervention. Interest groups are able to mount private and public lobbying campaigns on behalf of their preferred policy positions so that reformers find it difficult to see their vision rise to the top of the systemic agenda unchallenged. The federal system dictates that policy can be made (and blocked) at multiple levels of government. The presidential system of executive-legislative relations permits not only the possibility of divided government but also the daily reality of a decentralized legislative process in which multiple poles of power exist in both houses of Congress. Remember, the Clinton health care proposal did not fail in a Republican-controlled legislature. It failed to get a floor vote in a session in which the Democratic Party held majorities in both houses. In a similar vein, the Bush Medicare reform initiative nearly failed because of opposition from Bush's own party in the Republican-controlled House of Representatives. This is a telling reminder about the limitations on the president's ability to generate major legislation in the U.S. political system. Advocates of sweeping health reform during the Obama presidency will need to devise strategies to mobilize public opinion and interest groups to pressure legislators to back an expansion of health insurance coverage in the United States.

Japan

Background: Policy Process and Policy History

National policy making in Japan has a corporatist element. The government interacts with sickness funds established by individual businesses and sectors of the economy. These sickness funds are in constant contact with the relevant health care provider organizations. The fee schedule is set in formal negotiations between the Central Social Insurance Medical Council and the Ministry of Health and Welfare. The central council represents various groups, including health care payers (sickness funds, management, and labor), the general public (represented by lawyers and economists), and health care providers (who have eight seats). Surprisingly, hospitals have historically been excluded from the council. It should not be surprising, then, that hospital physicians have tended not to fare as well as outpatient physicians and clinic heads in fee negotiations. Major reforms have been brokered historically not just in negotiations between the council and the Ministry of Health and Welfare but also in negotiations between various factions in the Liberal Democratic Party (LDP).

In contrast to the U.S. experience but in line with developments in Europe, Japanese health policy was built on a foundation of occupationally grounded government-mandated insurance plans, which began in the industrial sector in 1922 and expanded gradually to cover most employee groups. A separate, government-run National Health Insurance (NHI) program was established in 1958 by the LDP government to provide care for those not covered by employee health plans; every locality was required to have an insurance plan for such residents by 1961. Approximately two-fifths of the population is currently covered by the NHI program while 60 percent of Japanese residents have employment-based health insurance.

The sickness funds and the NHI program often have health care providers under contract. The system calls for outpatient physician services to be paid on a fee-for-service basis; fee schedules are negotiated by physicians and insurers. In many cases the NHI fees are lower than the employer-mandate fee schedules. Both the employee plans and the NHI program cover physician services, hospitalization, prescription drugs, and dental care. The employee plans often provide additional benefits or require smaller copayments.

Most hospitals are privately owned. Hospital physicians are salaried employees; however, reimbursements for hospital procedures are made on a fee-for-service basis. Many physicians own small clinics that provide inpatient treatment and, often, long-term care. Furthermore, many physicians are also pharmacists—enabling them to profit from the medicines they prescribe. Japan has tended to have the highest per-capita pharmaceutical consumption in the world.

Funding varies considerably across different employee plans. Most employees in such plans pay between 3.7 and 4.1 percent of their total income. Most employers also contribute at rates ranging from 3.7 to 4.1 percent. Government subsidies from general revenues cover 13 percent of most benefit costs and 16.4 percent of costs for elderly employees and covered retirees. In the main NHI system the insured pay a flat-fee premium that varies somewhat by locality; the average annual NHI premium was roughly $750 in 2006. The government bears the brunt of the costs out of general revenues because it pays for half of all medical care provided and all administrative costs and provides additional subsidies to certain localities. In 1982 the government introduced a separate NHI program for the elderly that was intended to limit government obligations to less than half of total costs with the remainder paid by contributions from the sickness funds. In practice the system did not limit government obligations as much as anticipated. In 2008 the government created a new system for so-called old-old residents, aged seventy-five and older. In this system, older senior citizens will now pay a premium designed to cover 10 percent of costs (and the law mandates that this cost-sharing will increase as the aged's share of the population increases over time). In turn, the government and the sickness funds will share responsibility for the remaining costs.

Copayments are a major feature of the Japanese system. In the employee plans and in the NHI program, patients aged 3 to 69 pay a 30 percent copayment on all care up to a monthly out-of-pocket maximum, which varies by family income, up to a ceiling of about $450. Patients aged seventy and over pay a 10 percent copayment unless they are classified as high-income, in which case they are billed the standard 30 percent. Hospitalized patients also pay a small per diem of roughly $3, earmarked for food services, that is reduced for low-income patients.

The demographic transition has framed the evolution of the Japanese health care system. Japan had the oldest population in the world by the 1980s, which helped to drive up health care spending. Copayment provisions were initially adopted in 1984. In 1994 a multipartisan consensus (shared by business leaders) led to a monthly copayment increase that was followed by another hike in 2002 up to the current 30 percent rate. Apart from that debate, in the late 1980s and 1990s reform discussions centered primarily on the elderly and, in particular, on the issue of long-term care. Historically, Japan has had high hospital occupancy rates (above 80 percent) and a long average length of stay (often over 50 days), largely because hospitalization has been used to provide long-term care.

These trends generated serious debate within and between the major factions of the LDP regarding how to address the need for long-term care. Rising costs in the 1980s were viewed as the first wave of a much larger problem, given the demographic trend toward an aging society. As was often the case during the LDP's heyday, policy formulation involved extensive consultation among party faction leaders, civil servants, business leaders, health professional associations, and (to a lesser extent) labor unions. Nearly a decade of debate culminated in the presentation of the LDP's Gold Plan for long-term care. A 1997 law created a new long-term care insurance system launched in 2000. The goal was to curtail costs by sharing financial burdens and by trying to stimulate the use of home care as an alternative to hospitalization.

Contemporary Dynamics

The end to Japan's long period of sustained economic growth reshaped the health policy debate. In the 1970s and the 1980s, concerns for cost control were leavened by growing government revenues and by private sector commitments to employees. As the economic downturn of the 1990s extended into the new century, a broadening coalition of government officials began to look for ways to limit health spending. Despite the expansion of copayments discussed above, health spending as a share of GDP grew from 6 percent in 1990 to nearly 8 percent in 2002. When reform-minded Junichiro Koizumi became prime minister in 2001, his newly formed Council on Economic and Fiscal Policy took up the costs of caring for the elderly as a major arena for policy reform.

The most aggressive reformers in the Koizumi government wanted to combine new limits on health spending with decentralization and injection of new business activity via an expansion of competition in the hospital sector. Sickness funds vigorously backed the idea of changing the provision of insurance for the elderly because they viewed the existing NHI system for the elderly as an open-ended requirement in which they transferred money from their sickness funds to subsidize the NHI program. Many subnational governments also welcomed any reform that might reduce their financial obligations. In contrast, opposition political parties accused the LDP of abandoning its responsibilities and commitments to care for senior citizens; interest groups for the elderly were similarly opposed. Japanese physicians' groups lobbied strenuously against proposed efforts to transform health care delivery. The diversity of opinions and the public visibility of the health system made the pursuit of reform difficult. Over time the Koizumi government abandoned some of its deregulation proposals in a successful effort to reduce physicians' opposition to the overall reform package.

Koizumi's electoral victory in 2005 broke the logjam regarding health reform. His successful effort to campaign against members of his own LDP party opposed to the privatization of the Japanese post financial network gave him a more disciplined legislative majority. The 2006 Health Reform Law focused on five areas. The major reform was the 2008 establishment of the old-old insurance system. This system placed explicit caps on the financial subsidies provided by the national government, subnational government, and private insurance companies while creating a system of patient premiums that would increase over time as the number of participants grew. This change is significant given that the share of the Japanese population aged seventy-five and older doubled from 5 to 10 percent during the years 1990–2007. The 2006 reform also decentralized oversight and management of the NHI system to forty-seven prefecture-level governments charged with determining financing schemes in accordance with local actuarial trends and tax bases. To reduce costs, the 2006 reform mandated efforts to promote healthy lifestyles via annual checkups and (like the previous Gold Plan) calls for reduced use of hospitalization for patients in long-term care situations. Finally, the law required a dramatic expansion of the use of electronic billing and electronic medical records. The heightened use of information technology aims at providing a more comprehensive database from which to review utilization patterns and to guide physicians in following evidence-based standards of care.

The implementation of the Koizumi-led health reform required a substantial shift in administrative staffing and practices. Prefectural agencies had to be established to manage the entire health insurance system. In addition, the lofty goals of instilling healthy lifestyles and promoting more cost-effective patterns of long-term care depend not just on administrative reforms but also on convincing patients to change their own behavior. The government's official cost-saving target in 2006 was an annual savings of $20 billion nationwide by 2011. By 2008 the government had already reduced its forecast to a potential annual cost savings of perhaps as much as $7 billion by 2011. As of this writing, it remains to be seen whether even this more modest goal will be attained.

The difficulties in shifting bed-usage rates faced by the Gold Plan and then by the subsequent 2006 Health Reform Law demonstrate another facet of the complexity of policy implementation. During the policy formulation and decision-making stages, the interaction of government officials and interest groups dominates our attention. In many policy areas, including health care, the activities of these players are crucial to effective policy implementation as well. However, when the realization of policy goals also depends on the behavior of individual citizens, substantial cooperation between organized interests and government may not eliminate all implementation problems. In this case, generalized cultural norms form a barrier to full implementation. Culture—as discussed in Chapters 2 and 3—is a factor that can be slow to change.

Germany

Background: Policy Process and Policy History

In contrast to other countries, in Germany the health policy process has historically been more inclusive and more decentralized. An 1883 statute called for the establishment of labor-management boards to administer the sickness funds. Government played the role of the honest broker in disputes—but it was a broker with the power to alter the rules and provide subsidies. Over time, physicians began to form associations specific to each sickness fund through which to bargain over budgets and fees.

Since 1977 health policy making in Germany has been even more formally corporatist in its approach to interest group participation. Legislation established the federal Concerted Action process to oversee the government-mandated health insurance program. Twice a year representatives from over seventy groups meet to review the state of the health care system and to negotiate budgetary, fee, and utilization guidelines for the next six months in a variety of health subsectors including hospitals, outpatient services, pharmaceuticals, and dental care. These measures were taken to provide an inclusive setting from which to deal with the inflationary problems of the late 1970s. The Concerted Action group sets guidelines—often based on recommendations formed by its permanent professional staff—intended to shape subsequent formal negotiations between the regional sickness fund associations and the corresponding regional physicians' associations.

Germany adopted the first government-mandated health insurance program in 1883. A series of German governments gradually extended the mix of sickness funds tied to job categories until arriving at truly nationwide coverage during the postwar era. After reunification into a single Federal Republic of Germany, residents of the former German Democratic Republic (who retained their original pension and disability benefits in many instances) became participants in the German health insurance system.

As in Japan, Germany has a patchwork of government-mandated sickness funds with special systems existing for miners, seamen, public employees, and self-employed farmers. Almost all other employees, the unemployed, pensioners, and the self-employed are required to join the government sickness fund system if their annual income does not exceed a threshold determined by the government. In 2008 the threshold was over $70,000; about one-quarter of the population has been above the threshold since reunification.

Those earning more than the threshold can choose to join the sickness fund system voluntarily; around two-thirds of such Germans do so. Most of the other third (less than 10 percent of the total population) have private insurance; however, citizens who choose private insurance cannot return to the sickness fund system. Through the year 2008, roughly 1 percent of the total population consisted of people above the income threshold who chose not to have health insurance. Beginning in 2009, however, all residents are now required to join the sickness fund system or to purchase private insurance. All sickness funds are required to cover physician services, maternity, hospitalization, and prescription drugs. A 1994 reform added a series of long-term care provisions (along with a boost in the payroll tax earmarked for that purpose). Semiprivate rooms and eyeglasses are not covered, but many Germans have supplemental private policies for these services.

Outpatient physician services are provided on a fee-for-service basis in accordance with fee schedules negotiated at the national and regional levels. Hospital physicians, however, work on salary. Hospitals are paid an all-inclusive per diem by the insured's sickness fund. The per diem varies by region and, since 1996, by illness. The government controls the acquisition of capital equipment by hospitals.

A majority of sickness fund revenues is generated by payroll taxes charged up to the annual income ceiling used to determine mandatory participation. Historically, as in Japan, funding varied across different sickness funds in Germany. A 2007 health finance reform, however, set a new uniform contribution rate effective in 2009. All employees now pay 8.2 percent of income on the first $65,000 earned. Employers usually pay 7.3 percent up to the same income threshold. However, employers pay the full employee share for low-income workers (those earning less than $600 monthly in 2008). The government contributes subsidies for maternity benefits, to pay for children's health care, and to help cover pensioners, the unemployed, students, and apprentices; these subsidies constitute around one-quarter of sickness fund revenues. Patients make 10 percent copayments for prescription medicines, and they must cover the difference in price between a brand-name drug and a generic. In addition, they pay a supplemental per diem for the first four weeks of hospitalization and roughly $15 per outpatient visit.

Most contemporary health policy reform efforts in Germany have focused on cost control, beginning with the aptly named 1977 Health Care Cost Containment Act, which established annual spending targets for physician services and the current mechanism for fee negotiations. When the government squeezed the fee schedules, physicians often provided more services. In 1986 the government replaced the targets with annual caps; once the cap is breached in a region, the sickness fund pays out less than 100 percent of the normal fee. Because physicians submit fee vouchers to physicians' associations that are reimbursed by the sickness funds, the move to a cap gave physicians an incentive to police themselves. If a doctor bills for too many services, he or she is eating into the fee schedule of all other physicians in the regional association. In 1988 the government responded to rising expenditures on prescription drugs by requiring the use of generic drugs. It also implemented several of the copayments applied in today's system. A 1993 reform introduced a host of new cost control measures: additional copayments, reference prices for prescription drugs, a cap on the supply of physicians, and a new formula to keep physicians' incomes in line with other workers' incomes. In 1997 most patients were given the ability to choose among all of the sickness fund options. In 2003 the Schröder government pursued a substantial increase in copayments and created a new "smart" identification card as a platform for holding prescription information and other forms of electronic medical records.

Contemporary Dynamics

Reform measures were largely successful in controlling costs in the 1980s, during which time health spending stayed at just over 8 percent of the GDP. However, in the 1990s reunification placed additional fiscal pressure on the government (as described in Chapter 6). Health spending rose to over 9 percent upon reunification in 1991 and then reached 10 percent by 1995. Sickness fund managers complained of rising cost pressures, and patients disliked the increases in copayments. The network of mandatory sickness funds faced grim actuarial trends. Cost containment had gained a nearly permanent place on the systemic and institutional agendas.

A variety of possible solutions were brought forward from different elements of the policy network in the early twenty-first century. The two major political parties favored contrasting reforms in the 2005 election campaign. The Social Democratic Party backed a call for truly universal health care in which all citizens would be required to pay a uniform payroll tax in support of the health care system. The existing ability of affluent citizens to opt out of sickness fund system would be eliminated; private insurance plans could exist but only to provide supplemental benefits (similar to the system in place in Japan and in most of Europe). Labor unions backed this initiative and were particularly insistent on moving toward a universal system. The Christian Democrats countered with a call to transform the system into a flat-rate annual premium that would be identical for all residents regardless of income. The government would contribute subsidies to assist low-income residents, and all people would be encouraged to pay additional contributions to create a rainy-day fund. Major business confederations supported the Christian Democratic proposal along with some alternative ideas that would also place a firm cap on employer health insurance costs. Physicians' associations criticized the possibility that either reform might jeopardize the quality of care and leave some sickness funds unable to meet their obligations.

The stalemate in the 2005 legislative elections framed the decision-making phase. The two major parties in the subsequent "grand coalition" government led by Angela Merkel had both committed to major health reform, but they disagreed on specifics. In the end the Merkel government negotiated a brokered set of reforms over two years that embraced elements of both major proposals while leaving open to future governments some key decisions. The 2007 Act to Strengthen Competition in Statutory Health Insurance introduced several changes that entered into effect on January 1, 2009. In line with the prior Social Democratic proposal, the reform set a uniform, total percentage contribution rate of 15.5 percent of income; there was no shift to a flat-fee payment system. However, all contributors into this unified national health fund can select the sickness fund of their choice—a market-oriented component favored by Christian Democrats. Sickness funds can determine if they want to offer additional benefits and can also provide refunds if they run a profit; this is intended to inspire greater cost-effectiveness in the sickness funds. To avoid having some sickness funds harmed by adverse selection (that is, by having too many sick insurees), a third major element of the reform created a morbidity-based adjustment system in which sickness funds would receive funds in accordance with the risk factors associated with their members. A fourth component of the law provided an additional safeguard for sickness funds by permitting them to levy a surcharge contribution of up to 1 percent of their total revenues if they are running a deficit; however, use of the surcharge clause permits all insured contributors to change sickness funds should they choose to do so. A fifth feature of the reform, favored especially by Social Democrats, increased government subsidies into the new health fund. Finally, the Christian Democrats were most insistent on the new cap on employer contributions. While the contribution rate for most employees increased, the contribution rate for most employers declined in the new system.

As of this writing, only very preliminary information is available regarding implementation of the reform measures that began in January 2009. Many analysts criticized the decision to permit sickness funds to continue to collect contributions during 2009 (as they had done in the prior system); the sickness funds then distribute funds to the government, which redistributes them to the sickness funds based on patient enrollment and morbidity trends. The principal criticism is that this incremental change in how payments are collected is needlessly inefficient. Critics are mobilizing for the creation of a single government agency into which health fund contributions will be paid because that will stop employers from having to earmark payments toward a variety of sickness funds. However, with the September 2009 elections on the horizon, few people expect any tinkering with this or other aspects of the new health care system until a new government is in place.

The intentionally mixed nature of the 2007 reform law leaves the future of the system tied to the results of the next elections. Business groups tend to place their hopes on the notion that a Christian Democratic victory will provide the best chance of retaining the cap on employer contributions obtained in the last reform. Conversely, labor unions and center-left political parties assert that the recent reforms placed the costs of adjustment on working families.

The response to cost pressures in contemporary health policy demonstrates the consensus-seeking nature of German political dynamics. The pursuit of consensus was amplified by the emergence of Merkel's "grand coalition" following the 2005 elections. Neither of the two major political parties wanted to abandon its respective commitments to health reform, but they now each lacked the legislative might needed to ensure that their vision would take clear precedence. Seeking consensus by producing a multifaceted compromise avoids more vibrant conflict, but it does not ensure that all (or even most) major constituencies are fully satisfied. In this situation, most participants consoled themselves (and their constituents) with the knowledge that the 2009 elections might provide a new constellation of forces more in line with their preferred policy options.

France

Background: Policy Process and Policy History

Health policy making in France takes place largely at the national level. The action centers around two agencies—social security and finance. Historically, major proposals for reform have emerged out of the social security agency and are then reviewed by the Finance Ministry staff. At times, however, the initiative for reform has stemmed from the Finance Ministry in response to pressure to cut costs.

The ongoing debate over budgets and fee schedules also takes place at the national level. The association of sickness funds negotiates with the three major physicians' associations over fee schedules. These agreements must then be approved by both the finance minister and the social security minister. The sickness funds can use the central government's veto power in disagreements over fee schedules in two ways. First, the funds can try to reduce demands from physicians by claiming that the government will simply reject them later. Second, if the funds want to appear conciliatory, they can go along with physicians' demands when they are confident the government will reject that portion of the agreement. In both cases the strength of the sickness funds' negotiating position is determined in part by having open communication with the relevant ministries. The funds' position is enhanced further because they need consent from only one of the three physicians' associations in order to form an agreement. The physicians' bargaining strength lies in their predominant role in establishing the relative values among different service groups such as the ratio of the cost of open heart surgery to the cost of a heart stress test.

Government intervention in the curative care sector in France began in earnest with the 1930 Social Insurance Act, which provided health insurance to low-income workers. After World War II, a series of laws expanded the system until it covered virtually all citizens by 1978. The resulting patchwork of programs, comprising a variety of plans directed toward different occupational groups, is a government-mandated insurance system. The system is dominated by the general health insurance plan, which covers over 84 percent of the population. Special systems exist for occupations including the agricultural and mining sectors, public employees, and the self-employed. Because the majority of French citizens are covered in the general system, our discussion focuses on that plan.

The general system covers all eligible employees with 60 hours of paid employment in the previous 30 days (or 120 hours in the previous 90 days) with contributions duly paid into the system. Because it is a national health insurance system, coverage is portable across the country. Physician services are provided on a fee-for-service basis. The insured usually pays for services first and is then reimbursed by the local sickness fund for a percentage of the cost (usually around 70 percent, but reimbursements vary from 30 to 100 percent). Reimbursements are calculated in accordance with negotiated fee schedules for the fund; the patient is responsible for excess fees. Covered services include general medical and maternity care, surgical and laboratory services, other specializations, dental care, and medicines.

Hospitals are a mix of public and private institutions. Although fewer than one-third of all hospitals are public, they account for over two-thirds of the available beds in the system. In response to cost-control concerns, in the mid-1980s French public hospitals were placed on fixed global budgets while private hospital care was financed by reimbursements via the sickness fund system. A 2003 reform under the center-right Raffarin government will merge financing for both public and private hospitals into a unified system by 2012. Rather than global budgeting or fee-for-service, all hospitals will be financed primarily on a per-patient basis via the use of DRGs—supplemented by a fixed yearly grant to cover emergency room expenses and by additional, optional grants to fund research initiatives and other special projects. The insured pays a flat per diem (almost $24 in 2008) for hospital room and board. Disabled children, soldiers injured in war, and employees injured in job-related accidents are exempt from the per diem. All inpatient medical services are handled as part of the insurance program and reimbursed as described earlier. The system as a whole provides comprehensive coverage for everything but semiprivate rooms and, in some instances, eye care and chiropractors. Patients enjoy unrestricted access to specialists; the system has no gatekeeper provisions. Approximately 85 percent of the population has supplemental private insurance to cover copayments and additional services not covered in the general plan.

The bulk of sickness fund revenues comes from payroll taxes. Employers pay 12.8 percent of total payroll into the general system. Employees pay just 0.75 percent of total earnings; however, most of the funds collected by the 7.5 percent income tax surcharge (the general social contribution) go toward the sickness fund system. The government contributes subsidies into the system taken from a 12 percent surtax on automobile premiums and from excise taxes on pharmaceutical advertising, tobacco, and alcohol. The government also provides funds for hospital construction.

The French system is not free to the user at the point of service. As we noted earlier, patients generally pay for services and are then reimbursed by the insurance program. In addition, most services call for a 30 percent copayment on the part of the patient. In fact, copayments for many users tend to exceed 30 percent annually because more services are reimbursed at less than 70 percent (either by regulation or in practice because of fee differences) than the few reimbursed at over 70 percent. Treatment for serious prolonged illnesses (including cancer and diabetes) is exempt from copayments. These twin funding measures—initial payment in full by the patient and a substantial copayment—are cost-control aspects of the system that try to limit utilization by influencing patient behavior. The effectiveness of copayments as utilization control is limited because over 85 percent of the population has supplemental insurance to cover the copayments.

Health reform efforts in the 1980s and early 1990s tried to control costs by focusing on providers. In 1983 public hospitals were placed on fixed annual budgets to control average lengths of stay. In subsequent years the government took a stronger stance in negotiations with physicians over the national fee schedule. As in Germany, many physicians responded by billing for additional services. An increasing percentage of physicians were permitted to bill for certain services in excess of the established fee schedule; by the late 1980s nearly 30 percent of all physicians could do so. That extra billing had to be paid out of pocket by the patient (or, in turn, by private supplemental insurance). The center-right Juppe government proposed a firm cap on physician services only to see the proposal fail amid fierce opposition from physicians' associations.

Upon taking office in 1997, the center-left Jospin government shifted the reform debate to persistent inequalities faced by users. In 1998 all insured adults received an electronic card to maximize the portability of their insurance information for billing purposes. The government then turned toward the unequal availability of supplemental insurance, which historically represented a stark division in coverage and utilization between low-income citizens and the rest of the population. The 1999 Universal Health Coverage Act created a truly universal health care system by creating government funding for the small minority of poor citizens (less than 1 percent of the population) who did not qualify for coverage under the previous rules. More important, the law created a subsidy by which French residents under the poverty line could qualify for government financing of a supplemental insurance policy to cover the large copayments in the French system—thereby leveling the playing field for utilization decisions made by low-income citizens.

Contemporary Dynamics

The 2002 elections provoked a sea-change in the balance of forces in French politics. Jospin's defeat in the first-round presidential elections in April was followed by a massive victory by Jacques Chirac in the May presidential run-off and then by a major victory by his center-right bloc in the June legislative elections. The Raffarin government was formed with a large parliamentary majority that it took as a mandate for reform in several policy areas.

The Raffarin government, emboldened by its large electoral victory, took up the banner of sweeping health reform that had been one of the downfalls of the previous center-right governments led by Alain Juppe and Dominique de Villepin in the mid-1990s. The government proposed a "Hospital 2007" reform package to modernize French hospital care via a shift to DRG-based billing—which would move public hospitals away from global budgets while moving private hospitals away from fee-for-service billing. In addition, public hospitals and their medical staff would receive new operating autonomy. The Raffarin government also proposed to reopen the controversial issue of physician reimbursement for outpatient care. The Juppe reforms of the mid-1990s had created a legal mechanism for reaching formal contracts with physicians' associations, but in the ensuing years only the general practitioners had ever reached an agreement with the government. Medical specialists welcomed the end of a Jospin government that they felt had suppressed official fees, but they also viewed these new negotiations in an atmosphere of conflict and mistrust dating back to the strikes against the Juppe government. Labor unions and center-left political parties opposed many elements of the Raffarin package as focusing more on the use of market mechanisms and less on the issues of access and quality of care. The Raffarin government, in response, labeled its hospital proposals a pursuit of equality for public and private hospitals (rather than as an attempt to inject competition into the hospital sector).

At the decision-making stage, the government moved most quickly in the areas where public opinion most sided with its reform ideas: controlling drug costs and hospital reform. A reform of the social security law authorized the pilot creation of a series of reference prices and the shift toward generic drugs for a small minority of pharmaceuticals. The 2003 hospital reform law will merge financing for both public and private hospitals into a unified system by 2012. Private hospitals moved immediately in 2003 to billing on a per-patient basis via the use of DRGs, whereas public hospitals will gradually increase the use of that financing mechanism over a ten-year period culminating in 2012. For both public and private hospitals, these funds can be supplemented by a fixed yearly grant to cover emergency room expenses and by optional grants to fund research initiatives and other special projects. Regional health authorities also received new funds to renovate several aging hospital facilities. In 2005 a second reform law gave hospital boards and clinical staffs more managerial autonomy in terms of how facilities would be used and in how to subcontract services from other providers. The goal of the overall reform is to encourage hospitals to work efficiently within each DRG to provide care as needed. The 2004 Health Insurance Reform Law focused on the dynamics of outpatient care. All insured adults would receive an enhanced electronic identification card suitable for containing their medical records; they also gained legal control over those records. The 2004 law also introduced a gatekeeper mechanism into the French system of outpatient care. Patients could refuse to contract a primary gatekeeper physician; however, if they did not use the gatekeeper system, all reimbursements would decrease by 10 percentage points.

The initial implementation of these reforms went more smoothly than many analysts had predicted. Firm consensus on the need for modernization galvanized support from the hospital community. In turn, patients opted for the gatekeeper system option in larger numbers than had been anticipated; by 2008 roughly three-fourths of insured residents had contracted a gatekeeper physician. Some analysts argued that the reimbursement penalty was driving patient behavior, whereas others claimed that a considerable number of citizens mistakenly thought that the gatekeeper system was mandatory rather than optional. To reduce the ongoing conflict with the major physicians' associations, the Raffarin government reached collective contracts in 2005 with several major associations for the first time this decade. To get specialists to agree to the new gatekeeper system, the new contracts authorized a wider variety of specialists to engage in extra-billing in any situation in which patients are consulting specialists outside of the gatekeeper system.

The reelection of the center-right bloc in the 2007 presidential and legislative elections produced an extension of the call for decentralization that began in earnest under the Raffarin government. In 2008 the Fillon government was preparing a series of proposals to create a network of regional health authorities to govern the hospital system. Some observers called this a first step toward decentralizing all medical care. As of this writing, it is premature to predict the outcome of this particular reform effort.

The ability of physicians to block the Juppe reform proposals demonstrates a situation in which the policy network privileged the physicians' position. The formal inclusion of physicians' unions in bargaining over fee schedules enabled physicians to play the labor card despite their historical emphasis on free-market principles in the health sector. The physicians' associations depicted themselves as unionized workers attempting to protect the other unionized workers jeopardized by the threat of inferior care that doctors claimed would result from the cap. Divisions among doctors had weakened their bargaining position in fee negotiations in the past, but the threat of a firm cap enabled the three major physicians' groups to speak with one voice on this particular issue, further enhancing the doctors' ability to mobilize opposition to the cap from elements of organized labor and from the public at large. Conversely, the emergence of a large center-right majority in 2002 showed that the relative power of physicians' groups is contingent not just on its unity but also on that of the government. The Raffarin government's legislative power and internal discipline enabled it to pursue successfully several of the reforms that the Juppe government felt forced to abandon.

United Kingdom

Background: Policy Process and Policy History

The National Health Service (NHS) plays a major role in policy formulation in the health care sector in the United Kingdom. The senior administrators are charged with setting fee schedules and global budgets in consultation with the health minister, the Treasury, and relevant health providers' associations. Because services are provided directly under NHS supervision, the agency also provides the vast majority of data suitable for program evaluation. For three decades after its inception in 1948 the NHS was largely autonomous—at least once it demonstrated an ability to meet most of its core functions with limited annual funding increases from the national government. Prime ministers and their health ministers tended to view the NHS as a popular government program that had proven itself relatively free of the cost pressures evident in other countries in the 1970s. This set of assumptions gave the NHS more freedom to determine how to allocate limited resources, but it also made it difficult for the NHS to generate political support for increasing its funding. Nevertheless, this historical autonomy was neither unlimited nor formally guaranteed. The executive always retained the capacity to consider reshaping not just the flow of NHS funding but also its basic mode of operation. The potentially activist role for the prime minister in health care policy was realized by the Thatcher government in the 1980s, and subsequent governments retained an activist stance in the 1990s and the early twenty-first century.

The United Kingdom's first national health insurance legislation in 1911 provided incomplete care to a limited number of low-income citizens. During the next three decades, dissatisfaction with the system increased despite efforts to expand the percentage of citizens covered and the range of services provided. The Beveridge Report in 1942 recommended sweeping reforms. Shortly after the end of World War II, legislation led to the creation of the NHS—which mirrored many of the Beveridge recommendations. Three decades later the Thatcher government began a series of attempts to inject competitive dynamics and financial incentives into the NHS system, culminating in the 1990 National Health Service and Community Care Act, which created the beginnings of the NHS system as we know it today. As we see in this section, the Blair government continued along the path of inserting market dynamics and patient choice into the NHS. In addition, health care was one of the public services devolved to local authorities in the late 1990s by the Blair government. Accordingly, the funding, precise organization, and nature of medical services vary somewhat among England, Northern Ireland, Scotland, and Wales.

The NHS provides a comprehensive range of services to all citizens. All patients must enroll with a GP who serves as a gatekeeper for referrals to specialists. Capitation reimbursement is the key aspect of GP compensation: it constitutes half of their income. A base salary (40 percent) and, since 2004, a quality points system for merit-based pay provide the rest. The NHS covers all physician services, hospitalization, dental and eye care, long-term care, and prescription drugs. Since 1999 a clinical committee of physicians determines each year the precise mix of services available in each service area.

Most hospitals are publicly owned and managed by one of twelve district health authorities in the NHS system. Public hospitals receive fixed global budgets from the NHS based on actuarial trends in their area. Since the 1990 reform, large hospitals with over 250 beds are able to become self-governing trusts with the freedom to raise their own capital and to set staff pay levels. Such trusts (now constituting 95 percent of all hospitals) can also keep any surplus for capital improvements. Long-term care is provided by the Community Care Sector of the NHS, which also administers public health initiatives.

Over 90 percent of the system is paid for out of general government revenues. In each of the four devolved regions, the NHS has a network of local trusts that provide primary care and purchase specialist services in their respective local districts. Although the Beveridge Report called for services to be free at the point of service, copayments have been introduced over the years that support roughly 10 percent of NHS services. Patients pay a maximum copayment of roughly $400 for dental care and are charged a $13 flat-fee copayment for prescription drugs. Low-income citizens, children, and pregnant women are exempt from dental and pharmaceutical copayments. The elderly are exempt from prescription drug copayments. Around 11 percent of British citizens have some form of private health insurance. Most have supplemental coverage for nonemergency care to avoid waiting lists in the NHS for such services.

Eliminating waiting lists was a watchword for the proposed Thatcher reforms in the 1980s and early 1990s. In contrast to most other industrialized countries, the major British health reform issue had not been cost control. Of the six countries examined in this book, the United Kingdom spent the smallest percentage of its GDP on health care—then and now. With its fixed global budgets, minimal fee-for-service reimbursement, salaried physicians, and limits on technology acquisition, the NHS has possessed from the outset many of the cost-control measures discussed in other countries. Instead, the market-oriented Thatcher government used formal program evaluations and anecdotal patient complaints to try to build support for reforms focused on improving the quality of services and the speed with which they were provided.

In passing a comprehensive reform in June 1990, the Thatcher government highlighted guaranteed maximum waiting periods for different procedures. This guarantee dovetailed with the Tories' prior strategy of building public support for change by focusing on patient-level outcomes. Guarantees aside, the principal thrust of the reform adopted was the introduction of competition for resources inside the NHS system. In addition to granting autonomy to large primary practices and hospitals, the 1990 reform enabled district health authorities (the basic administrative unit of the NHS) to purchase necessary care from an array of public and private care providers. In theory, this is the most profound aspect of the reform because the district health authorities can punish inefficient public providers by replacing them with public or private competitors. When Thatcher resigned and was replaced as prime minister by John Major in 1991, the Major government decided to increase NHS funding as an additional path toward greater responsiveness.

Contemporary Dynamics

In the 1997 election campaign, Tony Blair's Labour Party candidacy emphasized the arrival of a "third way" in health care and other policy areas that would be neither largely statist nor largely market-driven. His Conservative opponent, incumbent prime minister John Major, charged that the Labour Party would likely raise tax rates in an effort to meet its promises to reduce waiting times and improve NHS performance. Major claimed that the landmark 1990 NHS reform would continue to bear fruit if given a chance to flourish. The large Labour parliamentary majority that emerged from the 1997 elections ultimately gave the Blair government considerable leeway with which to define its vision for NHS reform.

The policy formulation stage was dominated by competing intraparty and interparty differences. Most Labour Party members argued that an injection of additional funding formed a critical element of modernizing the NHS and improving patient care. Intraparty divisions widened, however, on the role of decentralization and competition within the system. Tony Blair, a native of Scotland, was firmly committed to devolving health care administration to the four constituent nations of the United Kingdom. In addition, he supported an agenda of enhanced patient choice and a continuation of some of the competitive dynamics associated with the Conservative reform agenda. More progressive backbenchers opposed the market-oriented reforms and, in particular, argued forcefully that Thatcher's creation of independent GP clinics would lead to doctors who placed profits over the interest of their patients. Conservatives, on the other hand, wanted to see the 1990 reforms maintained. Indeed, some Tories sided with voices in the insurance industry who favored a shift toward a system of competing private insurers in a government-mandated national health insurance program more similar to the French and German models.

The initial steps of the Blair government in 1997 and 1998 pleased the more progressive elements of the Labour Party. The government reversed the Thatcher reform that gave GP clinics potential autonomy and focused on increasing funding levels for the NHS. Given the diversity of internal perspectives and the complexity of the issues, the government opted to spend three years developing a specific vision for sweeping reform. The 2000 NHS Plan outlined the path the Blair government would take in health reform. To the dismay of progressive Labour backbenchers and to the surprise of many

Conservatives, the Blair government invigorated the system of hospital trusts established under Thatcher; insisted that the primary care trusts offer a menu of provider and treatment options to every patient; continued the pursuit of shortened waiting times and the provision of more services per expenditures; and reformed the remuneration of GP clinics. Rather than the fund-holding model of autonomous GP clinics, beginning in 2004 all GP salaries would include a merit-based component based on evaluations of the quality of care provided and the efficiency of their practices. In turn, the continuation of the hospital trust system granted greater funding and operating autonomy to high-performing hospitals. In 2004 the government replaced a firm reliance on fixed, global hospital budgets with a new system in which a base budget would be supplemented with a patient-based supplement calculated on a DRG-basis (termed a "healthcare resource group" [HRG] in British jargon). Also in 2004, the NHS bureaucracy was decentralized into a network of twenty-eight Strategic Health Authorities that set performance targets, monitor performance, and reward hospitals and GP clinics that meet the stated goals.

The implementation of the sweeping reforms initiated by the Blair government in the four years preceding his 2007 resignation proved to be a complex affair, given the many dimensions of change. Administrative, clinical, financial, geographic, and managerial reforms were superimposed over a brief period. To try to ensure improved services amid the many structural changes, the Blair government increased health spending from 6.8 percent of GDP in 1997 to 8.6 percent by 2007.

In initial assessments, governmental and nongovernmental studies have demonstrated a decline in waiting times for nonemergency services as well as an increase in the treatment and health care provider options presented to patients. The Blair government trumpeted these studies as evidence of policy success, and Gordon Brown's government has thus far continued along the lines established by the NHS ten-year plan presented in 2000. The debate over policy evaluation in the broader policy network centers on a different question: were these successes generated by the changes in administrative and incentive structures, or were they driven primarily by the Blair government's considerable injection of new financial resources in the health sector? The answers that emerge from this debate will help to frame the policy debate for the next electoral cycle.

Health reform during the Blair government demonstrates the role that personal popularity and a large parliamentary majority can play in deepening party discipline. Blair's commitment to enhanced use of financial incentives in the NHS proved unpopular with many rank-and-file legislators in private conversations. However, Blair's centrality to the emergence of the large "New Labour" majority gave him considerable latitude in guiding the direction of policy reform. Now that the Labour parliamentary majority has shrunk and Blair has retired from electoral politics, the legacy of the Blair reforms to the NHS will be determined by future British voters and politicians.

Italy

Background: Policy Process and Policy History

In Italy the process for health policy making differs from the process for other policy areas. In other areas the lead role is played by the central government within a unitary state. Since passage of the 1979 National Health Service Law, however, the locus of health policy making shifted to the twenty regional governments. Those governments set global budgets and arbitrate fee schedules and other matters for the local health units (USLs) in their respective territories. The USLs administer services via contracts for a combination of public ambulatory clinics, public hospitals, and private providers. At their creation in 1979, the USLs became public enterprises governed by boards appointed to represent the partisan balance of forces in the regional government. The central government sets the basic parameters for services that must be provided, but the regions can determine whether to provide additional services. Policies are largely implemented (and reforms discussed) between the regional governments and the boards of their respective USLs.

The health sector was the first major function transferred from the central government to the regions. Health expenditures, funded by transfers from the central government and by revenues raised at the regional level, constituted a majority of regional government budgets throughout the 1980s. Some proponents of decentralization at the national level trumpeted the passage of the 1979 law as the first step toward the creation of meaningful regional governments. In contrast, as time passed, critics grumbled that regional administration of the health sector was more politicized and less professionalized than it had been at the national level. In particular, some observers questioned the professional credentials of not just the boards governing the USLs but also of the general managers charged with directing the USLs' activities. Others pointed out that the central government's pledge to cover revenue shortfalls at the regional level gave little incentive to both the regional governments and the USLs to administer their services efficiently.

Italy had developed a government-mandated system earlier on in the twentieth century. If anything, the Italian system of numerous sickness funds organized by occupational groups was more complex than its French and German counterparts. By the 1970s over 90 percent of the Italian population was covered. As the system expanded, many observers came to criticize the disparities in care across occupations, the duplication of effort and services across public and private care providers, and the continuing exclusion of the unemployed and several other categories of citizens.

In 1978 the so-called national solidarity government—a heterogeneous coalition that included the support of the traditionally excluded Communists—tackled these criticisms by adopting the national health service model. The reform, passed in January 1979, promised to provide universal coverage free to the user at the point of service. In 1992 a major organizational and financial reform created a more decentralized system.

Italians are currently guaranteed access to the National Health Service (SSN). Similar to the British NHS after the Thatcher and Blair reforms, the Italian system is a patchwork of public ambulatory clinics, public hospitals, and private providers contracted by the USLs responsible for providing care mandated by the national and regional governments. Coverage is portable across localities and regions. Some regions cover items not included in the national mandate. The system covers general and specialist physician services, hospitalization, prescription drugs, maternity, and dental care.

Most of the hospital sector is public. Since the 1992 reform, large public hospitals can separate administratively from the USL. Such hospitals must run balanced budgets and can spend surpluses on additional capital acquisitions or staff compensation incentives. About 30 percent of the population has some form of private insurance—to cover copayments, to extend coverage to additional services, and in many cases to provide comprehensive insurance as an alternative to the SSN.

Traditionally, a slim majority of funding came from payroll taxes (of which employers paid a larger share than employees). Government subsidies from general revenues filled in gaps in revenues and provided coverage for the unemployed. In 1998 the D'Alema government moved to fund the entire system out of general government revenues at the national and regional levels—thus eliminating the use of payroll taxes in health financing. In particular, a new value-added tax (VAT) collected by regional governments will bear primary responsibility for funding the health service. The reform also created a National Solidarity Fund by which the central government tries to adjust for the uneven tax bases across the regional governments. These financing changes toward the use of general revenues in pursuit of more evenly distributed funding mirrors the system already employed in the United Kingdom.

Patients pay a copayment of up to $54 for each outpatient service. They pay a copayment of up to 50 percent for most prescriptions. Several categories of persons are exempt from the copayment and deductible requirements: children (six years and under), disabled persons, and low-income patients who already qualify for welfare assistance. Out-of-pocket payments are twice as important in Italian health finance as they are in the United Kingdom: in 2008 they comprised over one-fifth of total health spending.

The Italian SSN has been the subject of reform efforts almost annually since its inception in 1979. As we noted earlier, copayments have been introduced on an increasing number of services. In some cases, governments revoked major copayment hikes, only to reinstate them (often at higher levels) later. Copayment increases and a reduction in the number and nature of exempt pharmaceuticals have reduced prescription drug use per capita. These decisions helped to control costs by controlling utilization, but they also helped to place the efficiency of the SSN on the institutional agenda. Critics of copayments did not always succeed in defeating the introduction of (or increase in) copayments on certain services, but they did force the major parties to consider reform measures.

In the early 1990s the Northern League became a strident advocate for market-oriented reform in the health care sector. Beset by the political stalemate and serious budgetary woes, elements of the Christian Democratic and Socialist parties began to consider serious reform of the SSN's internal dynamics and funding mechanisms. Advocates of limited use of market mechanisms were strengthened further at the policy formulation stage by events in the United Kingdom and the Netherlands, where governments were introducing similar reforms. This policy debate culminated in comprehensive reform legislation in 1992. In addition to further adjustments in copayments, a decision was made to adopt major changes in the administrative structure of the SSN. This "reform of the reform" empowered the national government to set more specific nationwide coverage and planning guidelines and to apportion funding to regional governments based on population and additional criteria. The regional governments now found themselves obligated to generate revenues to cover any expenses in excess of the national government contribution. Before the reform, the national government had pledged to cover all unforeseen health expenses. This reform made SSN funding similar to the Canadian health care system in that regional governments have an incentive to control costs to avoid raising taxes and imposing fees on their constituents. Furthermore, the 1992 reform made the USLs autonomous public enterprises no longer controlled by boards appointed to represent the partisan balance of forces in elected government. The USL general managers are chosen based on professional qualifications and receive five-year contracts with a possibility of renewal. Hospitals gained operating autonomy and would now be reimbursed on the basis of DRGs rather than on a uniform per diem basis.

Contemporary Dynamics

The 1992 reform reshaped the debate over the future of the SSN. It helped to reduce perceived and real problems associated with the politicized boards of the past. The move toward a more professionalized management made it easier to implement other elements of the 1992 reform. Fiscal reforms were designed to ensure that—at the implementation stage—managers and regional politicians would have an incentive to comply with the cost-control goals that helped to motivate the legislation. Not all implementation problems were overcome, however. One of the most controversial aspects of the 1992 legislation was not implemented in the years that followed. The reform called for citizens (and occupational groups) to be allowed to opt out of the SSN—thereby reducing much of their SSN payroll tax—beginning in 1995. In 1993 the Democratic Party of the Left (the PDS), lobbied hard for the abolition of this clause. With the 1996 election of the center-left Olive Tree coalition led by Romano Prodi, the possibility of opt-out provisions became remote. However, the major center-right parties campaigned on platforms calling for the ability to withdraw from the system or, in the case of the Northern League, for the abolition of the entire system.

The Prodi government began working on building a consensus to deepen the financial reforms begun in 1992. When the Prodi government narrowly lost a vote of confidence in 1998, the reform effort continued under the new center-left government led by D'Alema. Both governments pushed a hybrid agenda—analogous to the Blair government's aims in the United Kingdom. On the one hand, they wanted to reform health care financing to reduce the role that regional socioeconomic inequalities played in limiting the number and quality of medical services available in the poorer regions. On the other hand, they also sought to increase further the role of market incentives and government monitoring in ensuring greater effectiveness and efficiency in the health sector. The mixed agenda made it more difficult for center-right parties and interest groups to criticize the reform package. In turn, opposition to the increased use of market incentives from progressive groups was mitigated by the promise to reduce inequality.

The 1999 Health Reform Law markedly modified health finance in Italy. Regional governments were now guaranteed the vast majority of regional corporate taxation. In addition, the law launched a National Solidarity Fund in 2001; the fund is guaranteed one-fourth of VAT revenues, and those finances are supplemented with additional money from the national government. The goal of the fund is to distribute additional revenues to the poorer regional governments in pursuit of reduced disparity in the quality and availability of health care. The reform also called for a review of the list of comprehensive services that would be provided and the establishment of clinical standards for each service. In an effort to cultivate greater complementarity between the public and private sector health systems, the 1999 reform permitted private-sector providers more access to practice within the SSN and also encouraged private insurance companies to offer more supplemental insurance policies (as opposed to the frequent sale of duplicative, substitute private insurance).

The immediate implementation of the 1999 reform law took place largely under the center-right government led by Silvio Berlusconi from 2001 through 2006. The lower profile of the Northern League in this second Berlusconi-led government reduced the visibility of previous demands to permit Italian taxpayers to opt out of funding and participating in the SSN. Furthermore, the efforts of the 1999 reform to extend the use of market mechanisms and private-sector activity was largely congruent with major themes of the Berlusconi electoral campaign. As a result of these factors, the Berlusconi government implemented the core aspects of the 1999 reform law without proposing major changes. Indeed, perhaps the most noticeable health reform of the second Berlusconi government was the enactment of a ban on smoking in public areas.

In the 2006 and 2008 election campaigns, critics on the center-left argued that the Berlusconi government was not sufficiently committed to the creation of a robust National Solidarity Fund that could achieve the goal of reducing health care inequality. However, neither election campaign saw health reform rise to a prominent level on the systemic agenda. With the reelection of a third Berlusconi-led government in 2008, the immediate future seemed unlikely to generate major health policy reforms.

The reform of the SSN over time in Italy illustrates the impact of a changed vision for health policy among many European progressives. At the launching of the SSN in the late 1970s, most analysts predicted that—if and when leftist parties displaced the Christian Democrats—Italy would witness the creation of a much more centralized SSN. In stark contrast to those predictions, the Italian experience with center-left governments in the 1990s and in the early twenty-first century saw a shift toward a more decentralized health system in which market dynamics played a greater role.

European Union

Background: Policy Process and Policy History

Formally speaking, there is no health policy making process in the EU. The Maastricht Treaty mentions public health initiatives but also expressly prohibits any EU effort to harmonize "the laws and regulations of the member states" in health policy. Article 152 of the 1997 Amsterdam Treaty represents the boldest formal assertion of EU authority in health policy to date in that it calls for public health concerns to inform EU activities. However, the strongest formal power available to the EU in public health is the creation of recommendations to the member states. Article III-178 of the 2003 draft text of the (as yet unratified) European Constitution would have clarified further than any previous accord the role of the EU in public health. Nonetheless, the closing, seventh paragraph of the draft article makes it clear: "Union action in the field of public health shall fully respect the responsibilities of the Member States for the organisation and delivery of health services and medical care."

Because the shared belief of the member state governments holds that curative care policy is the exclusive competency of national governments, only informal health policy mechanisms are in place in the EU, and they focus on public health concerns. The member states' health ministers meet periodically to share information and to develop, as needed, coordinated approaches to meet public health challenges. This episodic form of public health coordination expanded in response to the outbreaks of mad cow disease and hoof-and-mouth disease in the early twenty-first century. The European Commission formed a set of recommendations in 2003 that culminated in the creation of the European Centre for Disease Prevention and Control.

Amid the absence of a health policy mandate in the curative care realm, the locus of EU intervention in this sector stems not from health-centric organizations, but rather from the ongoing regulatory activities of the EU and from the judicial decisions handed down by the Court of Justice of the European Communities. The diffuse call for EU activity to be informed by public health concerns has motivated a majority of the Commission's twenty-four directorates-general to invoke public health rationales for some of its directives. Thus the Directorate-General for Health and Consumers is not the only arm of the Commission potentially engaged in health policy. The Commission has no express authority in health policy, but it does have authority to influence the regulation of working conditions, purchasing arrangements, and equality of treatment of consumers—all in the pursuit and defense of a European single market. In turn, the EU judicial system arbitrates disputes regarding whether EU community-wide standards can be imposed over national practices and standards in a variety of activities.

Contemporary Dynamics

During the 1990s and the 2000s, the EU's Council of Ministers and the Court of Justice made several binding decisions that have affected the course of health policy and of medical services more broadly. During the 1990s, many of these policy decisions took place in a policy network in which health policy and medical professionals were largely absent. The health community had (wrongly) assumed that the formal recognition of member state competence in health policy would keep their sector free of EU decisions. The events of the ensuing years would eventually change that perception of so-called benign neglect. As a result, in the early twenty-first century, health policy interest groups have shown more interest in lobbying EU officials.

As discussed in Chapter 10, the EU has taken a growing interest in higher education policy since the 1970s. Part of that activity focused on creating common standards for various degree paths. In 1993 an EU directive created common standards for recognizing medical and nursing degrees issued within the community. Although historically each country (and its respective professional associations) retained sovereignty over when and how to recognize degrees earned in other countries, the EU's pursuit of common professional standards and equal national treatment created an end-run around the long-standing autonomy of national medical and nursing professions. Although this directive was challenged in the courts, the Court of Justice upheld the principle that nondiscrimination among member states requires that medical and nursing degrees earned in one member state be recognized by all other member states—provided that they meet the minimum standards established by the EU directive. This decision was opposed by many professional associations. However, despite this innovative ruling, the mobility of doctors and nurses has remained relatively limited.

The evolution of a different 1993 EU action, Directive 93/104/EEC, came to have a more profound impact on curative care in the early twenty-first century. This 1993 labor policy, often referred to as the Working Time Directive, established a series of common, EU-wide labor standards in pursuit of harmonized work conditions across the single market. Among the standards involved are a maximum weekly total of 48 hours and a minimum daily rest period of 11 hours. A 2000 amendment to this directive expressly included physicians as being subject to this labor policy. Medical interns and residents traditionally are on call for very long hours in the United States and elsewhere around the world. Advocates of this form of extended medical training argue that it exposes young doctors to the widest possible array of diagnostic and treatment scenarios. Critics, including advocates of extending this particular EU labor standard to include physicians, argue that it constitutes an unfair and potentially dangerous labor practice.

The implementation of this extension of the Working Time Directive into the medical community quickly brought about a legal challenge. In the 2000 *SiMAP* case (Case C-303/98, ECR 1-7963), the Court of Justice rejected the argument that physicians were resting when they were sleeping in the clinic or hospital during their on-call hours. The Court ruled that all on-call hours constituted hours worked and, thus, must be counted toward the legal weekly maximum of 48 hours. In the 2003 *Jaeger* case (C-151/02, ECR 2003 I-08389), the Court ruled that physicians, upon waking up from an on-call nap that took them past their daily work limit, were entitled immediately to the legally prescribed compensatory rest. Many national health ministries fought these decisions because the full implementation of these uniform labor standards has forced a sea-change both in physician training and in how emergency clinics are staffed. Rather than serving on-call for extended hours, interns and residents must now be scheduled for shorter periods of time to ensure compliance with EU law. This requires more staffing. In addition, some initial studies have sided with the traditional pedagogical defense of lengthy on-call training: they argue that physicians are now exposed to fewer "teaching moments" over the course of their clinical training.

The two preceding examples of EU activity in health policy illustrate a role via the regulation of professional credentials and labor practices. Perhaps the next frontier of EU activity in health policy may stem from a desire to have EU consumers treated equally when they cross national borders between member states. A host of EU laws attempt to prevent citizens from being discriminated against when they travel within the EU. When patients find themselves living in a different member state from their country of citizenship, two Court of Justice decisions require national health insurance systems to fund insurees' medical treatments even when the provider is in another member state. Some observers have asked whether the evolution of policy and case law will lead to an expansion of "medical tourism" in which affluent citizens try to identify the best country in which to receive various medical treatments.

The dynamics of EU activity in health policy illustrate the logic of "spillover" in the expansion of EU competencies. To date, the EU still has no formal role in curative care policy. Instead, competency over health services is reserved for member state governments. Nonetheless, the actions of EU institutions in pursuit of their identified competencies in labor practices, professional credentialing, and nondiscrimination of EU citizens have led to laws, regulations, and court cases that shape the contours of health policy.

Cross-national Trends

In the 1990s and the early twenty-first century we can observe considerable convergence in the content of health policies. All six countries have enacted reforms designed to control costs. Most countries have pursued the creation of electronic medical record-keeping systems. In addition, there has been some convergence toward a mixed approach to health policy as a whole. The most market-oriented country, the United States, has increased government involvement, whereas the two countries employing the national health service model (the United Kingdom and Italy) pursued reforms designed to inject some market mechanisms into their health care systems. In terms of health policy outcomes, the United States is exceptional in that it has the worst outcomes on several major indicators, despite spending more money than any other industrialized country. Consideration of the contemporary dynamics of reform on this policy issue highlights cultural and economic factors as central to agenda setting, whereas political and institutional influences are important in the decision-making process.

Policy Outputs

Most industrialized countries pursue one of two options: a national health service or mandated national health insurance via a mix of public and private providers. The latter option is by far the most common. Among the six countries examined in this book (and compared to other countries as well), the United States has opted for minimal government activity in the health sector. Italy and the United Kingdom have adopted the national health service model, and France, Germany, and Japan have adopted the prevailing model in the industrialized world: mandatory national health insurance.

During the 1990s and the early twenty-first century, these countries instituted reforms aimed at curtailing costs in one or more sectors of their respective health care systems. Copayments have been adopted in new areas and increased in existing areas in all six countries. Copayments represent an attempt to reduce costs in two senses. First, they transfer a portion of the cost from the government-funded or government-mandated plan to the patient. Second, they can influence patients' choices about utilization—provided that patients do not have a supplemental insurance policy to cover the copayments.

These countries' governments have taken a harder stance, to varying degrees, in negotiating fee schedules for physician services. This is particularly true in France and Germany, where the climate for negotiations has been more publicly bitter than in years past. This same dynamic of increased tension has occurred in the predominantly private U.S. system as physicians complain about tighter fee schedules and utilization reviews conducted by private insurers.

Policy Outcomes

Although the reform concerns are fairly similar in some senses, significant differences remain in the health policy models and in the levels of health care expenditures in the six countries. Are these policy differences associated with any differences in policy outcomes? Here we examine briefly outcomes in the three main policy problems discussed at the beginning of this chapter: health outcomes, access to curative care, and cost control.

It is difficult to assess the role of government policy in promoting good health outcomes across individuals or across countries. One might think that average life expectancy is a good health indicator because it measures the basic threshold of health: continued life. However, life expectancy is problematic as a measure of how well the health care system is performing because life span is affected by a variety of factors including diet, exercise, surroundings, genetics, stress, and health care. For this reason, studies of comparative health policy often rely on infant mortality statistics (the number of infants who die prior to age one) as an indicator of health system performance. Although factors other than access to care and its quality influence infant mortality rates, this measure has fewer additional intervening factors than does life expectancy. Table 8-1 provides infant mortality and life expectancy statistics for the six countries examined here.

In 2006 the United States had the highest infant mortality rate and the lowest life expectancy at birth among the six countries. The United States also experienced the least improvement in its infant mortality rate from 1996 to 2006. These outcomes have often been used in the policy debate to criticize the effectiveness of the market-maximized model. The lowest infant mortality rates (albeit by a small margin in some cases) are found in the countries with mandatory health insurance (France, Germany, and Japan) and in Italy. The United Kingdom is in the middle of the pack.

On the access issue, the United States also does not compare favorably to the other six countries. In the United States, 45 to 50 million people lack health insurance at any given time. A few other countries allow citizens above a high income threshold to opt out of health insurance, but most choose not to do so. Thus about 15 percent of the U.S. population has no health insurance, whereas in the other five (and most other) industrialized countries less than 1 percent of citizens lack access to a comprehensive health care program, and those who do tend to be wealthy.

One might assume, then, that the United States' relatively poor performance in health indicators and in access to health care is simply the result of a societal choice to spend fewer resources on health care. Such a scenario

Table 8-1 Infant Mortality and Life Expectancy in Six Countries, 1996 and 2006

Country	Infant Mortality in 1996 (% of live births)	Infant Mortality in 2006 (% of live births)	% Change in Infant Mortality (1996–2006)	Life Expectancy at Birth in 1996 (years)	Life Expectancy at Birth in 2006 (years)	% Change in Life Expectancy (1996–2006)
France	0.49%	0.38%	–22%	78.1	80.7	3.3%
Germany	0.50	0.38	–24	76.9	79.8	3.8
Italy	0.62	0.37	–40	78.7	81.2	3.2
Japan	0.38	0.26	–32	80.3	82.4	2.6
United Kingdom[a]	0.61	0.50	–18	76.9	79.1	2.9
United States	0.73	0.67	–8	76.1	78.1	2.6
Average	*0.56*	*0.43*	*–24*	*77.8*	*80.2*	*3.1*

SOURCE: Organisation for Economic Co-operation and Development (2009b).

[a]The life expectancy data are for 1996 and 2005.

Table 8-2 Health Care Spending in Six Countries, 1996 and 2006

Country	Total Health Spending in 1996 (% of GDP)	Total Health Spending in 2006 (% of GDP)	Change in Spending (1996–2006)	Government Health Spending in 1996 (% of GDP)	Government Health Spending in 2006 (% of GDP)	Change in Spending (1996–2006)
France	10.4%	11.0%	6%	8.3%	8.7%	7%
Germany	10.4	10.5	1	8.5	8.1	–5
Italy	7.4	9.0	22	5.2	6.9	33
Japan	7.0	8.1	16	5.8	6.6	14
United Kingdom	6.8	8.5	25	5.6	7.0	25
United States	13.5	15.8	17	6.1	7.1	16
Average	*9.3%*	*10.5%*	*14%*	*6.6%*	*7.4%*	*15%*

SOURCE: Organisation for Economic Co-operation and Development (2009b)

would certainly be congruent with the view that a private sector approach (1) enables people to choose precisely how much health care they want and (2) provides for greater efficiency via the operation of the free market. Nevertheless, precisely the opposite pattern of events has occurred. The United States spends significantly more than these other countries on health care (as a look at Table 8-2 indicates), yet it performs poorly relative to those thriftier countries.

In 2006 the United States spent nearly 16 percent of its GDP on health care. In the other five countries healthcare spending averaged 9.4 percent. Despite the largely market-oriented nature of the U.S. system, government health expenditures as a percentage of GDP remain very close to the average for all six countries. Another way to look at these trends is in terms of spending per person. In 2006 the United States spent $6,933 per person on health care. Norway ($4,507), Switzerland ($4,165), and Luxembourg ($4,162) were the only other industrialized countries in the world spending over

$4,000 per person. Among the other five countries examined in this book, average annual spending per person was $3,005—less than half what the United States spends. The average across all industrialized economies was just over $2,900 per person. Furthermore, among the six countries examined in this book, the United States spent a higher percentage of GDP on government-funded health care programs than all but France and Germany, despite covering a smaller percentage of the population in public programs. Efforts to explain higher health care spending in the United States point to several factors including:

- Higher administrative costs due to the variety of insurance plans (estimated by some analysts to constitute as much as 20 percent of costs)
- Fee-for-service reimbursement of both outpatient and hospital physicians
- The absence of firm global budgets for hospitals
- Defensive medicine (that is, multiple and expensive tests to protect against potential malpractice lawsuits)
- Cost-shifting from the uninsured and underinsured to the insured

Understanding Policy Reform

Thinking back to the case studies, you can see how popular discontent (or its absence) has shaped the reform agenda. In France and Germany, reform proposals have focused on maintaining the current system while restraining costs in various ways. In the other four countries, major reform proposals have been debated.

However, discontent with the system alone does not imply that sweeping reform is on the way. As we have seen in other policy areas, decision making and implementation are subject to a variety of influences beyond general public opinion and political trends. For example, with its solid, one-party legislative majority, the Thatcher government was able to pass reforms similar to proposals that failed in Sweden, where they were advocated by many leaders of a shakier, four-party coalition government. The structural decentralization of decision making in the United States made it easier for opponents of reform to block new proposals that had considerable public support in some sectors. In the realm of implementation, professional patterns and loyalties limited the adoption of some market-oriented behaviors in the British reform, whereas cultural obstacles slowed the Japanese provision and utilization of long-term care called for in 1992 legislation and, later, in the 2000 Gold Plan and the 2006 Health Reform Law.

Although widespread concern over health care as a priority does not guarantee that government action will be taken (much less predetermine its nature), it does guarantee that health care will remain on the agenda. This is especially true given that the percentage of elderly citizens is on the rise in all six countries. Senior citizens incur the largest health care expenditures per capita of any age group. They also are the one category of citizens that receives government health care in some fashion in all six countries. Health policy will continue to find a place on systemic and institutional agendas in the 2010s as the baby-boom generation reaches retirement age.

SUGGESTED READINGS

Behan, Pamela. 2006. *Solving the Health Care Problem: How Other Nations Succeeded and Why the United States Has Not.* Albany: State University of New York.

Blank, Robert H., and Viola Burau. 2004. *Comparative Health Policy.* New York: Palgrave Macmillan.

Colby, Mark A. 2004. *The Japan Healthcare Debate: Diverse Perspectives.* Folkestone: Global Oriental.

Dutton, Paul V. 2007. *Differential Diagnoses: A Comparative History of Health Care Problems and Solutions in the United States and France.* Ithaca, N.Y.: ILR Press.

Freeman, Richard. 2000. *The Politics of Health in Europe.* Manchester: Manchester University Press.

Funigiello, Philip J. 2005. *Chronic Politics: Health Care Security from FDR to George W. Bush.* Lawrence: University Press of Kansas.

Giaimo, Susan. 2002. *Markets and Medicine: The Politics of Health Care Reform in Britain, Germany, and the United States.* Lansing: Michigan State University Press.

Graig, Laurene. 1999. *Health of Nations: An International Perspective on U.S. Health Care Reform,* 3rd ed. Washington, D.C.: CQ Press.

Johnson, James A., and Carleen H. Stoskopf. 2010. *Comparative Health Systems: Global Perspectives.* Sudsbury, Mass.: Jones & Bartlett Publishers.

Klein, Rudolf. 2006. *The New Politics of the NHS: From Creation to Reinvention,* 5th ed. Oxford: Radcliffe.

Mechanic, David. 2006. *The Truth About Health Care: Why Reform Is Not Working in America.* New Brunswick, N.J.: Rutgers University Press.

Moon, Marilyn. 2006. *Medicare: A Policy Primer.* Washington, D.C.: Urban Institute.

Moran, Michael. 1999. *Governing the Health Care State: A Comparative Study of the United Kingdom, the United States, and Germany.* Manchester: Manchester University Press.

Patel, Kant, and Mark E. Rushefsky. 2006. *Health Care Politics and Policy in America,* 3rd ed. Armonk: M. E. Sharpe.

Rovner, Julie. 2009. *Health Care Politics and Policy A to Z,* 3rd ed. Washington, D.C.: CQ Press.

Smith, David G., and Judith D. Moore. 2008. *Medicaid Politics and Policy, 1965–2007.* New Brunswick, N.J.: Transaction Publishers.

Thai, Khi V., Edward T. Wimberley, and Sharon M. McManus. 2002. *Handbook of International Health Care Systems.* New York: Marcel Dekker.

Chapter 9 Social Policy

In many countries the largest portion of the government budget is spent on social policy, the dizzying variety of government efforts to boost citizens' standards of living. Social policy initiatives include pension programs, unemployment and disability benefits, subsidies to support families with dependent children, and assistance to families and individuals with low incomes. Because of the diverse nature of social policies, these initiatives are referred to collectively in many ways. Policy experts also use the terms *income maintenance policy* or *family policy*, yet not all such policies maintain incomes or deal explicitly with families. In the United States, one often hears the term *welfare policy*, although social security and many other social programs are frequently excluded from the welfare debate. In this book, we use the term *social policy* because it captures the many ways in which government tries to protect and directly improve people's standards of living.

Common Policy Problems

Prior to the late nineteenth century, government social policies were a patchwork of emergency initiatives and a few standing programs whose implementation was dominated by favoritism. As increasing numbers of citizens gained the right to vote and to organize freely, many began to pressure the government to provide a social safety net in the economic sphere for people who suffered visible misfortunes and to try to alleviate poverty more generally. These dynamics in democratic governments often led nondemocratic governments to create programs to avoid disappointing their citizens. As governments devoted more and more resources to these efforts, other citizens became concerned about the rising cost of social policy. In the late twentieth and early twenty-first centuries, governments sought to fine-tune social policies in response to the increasing globalization of domestic economies.

Four major groups of citizens—children, the elderly, the infirm, and the recently unemployed—have been at the center of social policies in industrialized countries for a century now. These groups include people who for one reason or another can make a claim that they cannot support themselves at the moment. Children are too young to work, senior citizens might be too old, the infirm are too ill, and the recently unemployed were working but happened to lose their jobs. Because these are situations that most citizens can visualize facing, public pressure for government programs to deal with these **situationally poor** citizens has been considerable. Social policies began in earnest in this area as governments responded to demands to alleviate these common problems.

Over time, governments moved to respond to another challenge: alleviating poverty among the **chronically poor**, that is, people who are of working age but are having a hard time escaping poverty. Obviously, alleviating poverty among the economically active can be attacked through many sorts of policies. In Chapter 6, we saw how macroeconomic policies try to create an economic environment propitious for economic growth and job creation. Later, in Chapter 10, we see how government tries to promote economic opportunity for individuals via education policy. In this chapter we deal with government efforts to alleviate poverty by providing economic benefits directly to individuals.

Dealing with poverty is a difficult problem for all governments, although policymakers confront fewer impoverished citizens in industrialized countries than in poorer countries. In industrialized countries, 5 to 20 percent of the population lives in poverty. In late-industrializing countries, the percentage of people living in poverty ranges from about 15 percent to more than 50 percent. There are more poor people in these countries, and governments typically dedicate far fewer resources to social policy. This resource gap has three major dimensions. First, the total economic resource base is smaller—as measured by gross domestic product (GDP) per person—in late-industrializing countries. Second, governments in late-industrializing societies are smaller: taxes as a percentage of GDP are around half as high as taxes in industrialized countries. In other words, the government has a smaller share of what was already a smaller economic pie. Third, social policy represents a much smaller portion of government expenditure in late-industrializing countries.

As social policies have expanded in industrialized countries, another policy issue has emerged: concern about the present and future costs of those government initiatives. These cost-control concerns spring from a variety of sources. First, political support for dealing with poverty has been uneven—particularly for programs dealing with chronic poverty. In some industrialized countries in northern Europe, particularly during the economic boom of the 1950s and 1960s, programs dealing with the chronically poor faced limited opposition. Since the 1980s (amid slower economic growth), opposition has grown. In other countries, particularly the United States, a significant number of citizens have opposed these efforts from the outset. Second, the largest set of social policies in most countries relates to old-age pensions; however, as societies age the proportion of active workers to retirees continues to fall. For example, in the United States in the year 2000 just 12.3 percent of the population was over age sixty-four. By the year 2050 it is projected to be 20.3 percent. If current pension benefits are to be defended, then ever smaller numbers of workers will be called on to pay more into social security. The United States is not an exception; the percentage of the population that is elderly is rising in all of the industrialized countries. In the oldest of these societies, Japan, the share of senior citizens in the national population is projected to rise from 17.2 to 35.9 percent over the same fifty-year period (Adema 2006: 12). This demographic pressure has placed cost control even higher on the policy agenda. Assistance programs in the social policy sphere comprise the largest component of government spending in the industrialized countries. These governments face a true political dilemma: should they decrease benefits to control costs, or should they protect those benefits by either cutting other programs or raising taxes?

This difficult decision is made more complicated by the impact of economic globalization. Globalization presents two major sets of challenges for social policy. First, as global economic competition expands to include firms from more and more areas of the world, many unskilled and semiskilled workers in industrialized countries face the prospect of losing their jobs to similar employees in late-industrializing countries who are working for lower wages. This situation forces domestic governments into a bind regarding social policy. On the one hand, the dislocation associated with greater competition increases demands on existing social policies to pay out benefits to unemployed workers. On the other hand, because some of that unemployment is blamed on high compensation levels in the industrialized world, the dislocation creates political pressure to reduce social policy benefit levels in an effort to avoid losing these jobs to foreign competitors. Critics of this approach often call for renewed emphasis on education and on-the-job training so that vulnerable citizens can obtain the skills needed to produce more competitive products and in turn to merit higher wages.

The second impact of globalization on social policy stems from economic integration efforts. As nation-states enter binding agreements to remove barriers to economic exchange, they not only reduce tariffs but also often call for an end to restrictions on the movement of investment capital and labor. The free flow of products, labor, and capital creates the possibility that workers will strive to move to countries with better social policy benefits while investors will attempt to move production to low-benefit countries. Domestic governments in high-benefit countries fear that this puts them in a lose-lose situation, often referred to as **social dumping**, in which workers with low skills will move to high-benefit countries to enjoy greater social policy benefits while employers will move abroad to avoid the higher tax burden associated with those programs. As a result, economic integration can lead to calls for international coordination on social policy in an effort to create a more level playing field within the association. From Ross Perot's charge that a "great sucking sound" would pull U.S. and Canadian firms to Mexico within the North American Free Trade Agreement (NAFTA) to calls for a greater social policy coordination in the European Union (EU), economic integration is placing international social policy coordination on the agendas of many industrialized countries. Box 9-1 illustrates the visible differences in social security taxation in the six countries examined in this book.

Box 9-1 **In Depth: Social Security Contributions, Social Dumping, and Unemployment**

In media discussions, social dumping usually refers to the possibility that workers might move to countries that have higher benefit levels embedded in social policies while employers might move their firms to countries with lower levels of government-mandated social security contributions. Some analysts have challenged this presentation of the issues because it implies that workers and firms each have high mobility. Several studies have demonstrated that individual employees are less likely to move than firms. In addition, because most firms are small and medium-sized businesses, they are also unlikely to move.

Working from this perspective, some analysts have argued that high social security contributions may not result in a visible influx of foreign workers nor in a highly visible flight of businesses. Instead, social security contributions may serve as a factor that decreases both people's willingness to form new businesses and existing firms' willingness to take on new workers. These sorts of studies try to highlight the relationship between high social security contributions and national unemployment rates. Although many factors influence unemployment, the ability of social policy reformers to construct tables similar to the one shown below forms an important part of the contemporary debate over social policy:

Country	Average Employee Social Security Payroll Tax Rate (2008)	Average Employer Social Security Payroll Tax Rate (2008)	Unemployment Rate (2008)
France	20%	41%	7.8%
Germany	20	20	7.3
Italy	10	32	6.8
Japan	12	13	4.0
United Kingdom	11	13	5.6
United States	8	9	5.8

SOURCE: Tax rate data are from *OECD Tax Database*, www.oecd.org/ctp/taxdatabase; standardized unemployment data are from *OECD Economic Outlook*, no. 85 (2009a).

Major Policy Options

Once the government decides to provide economic assistance directly to individuals, how might this goal be accomplished? Social policy design involves three basic choices: (1) How does one determine who qualifies for this assistance, (2) how redistributive is the program, and (3) how will the assistance be provided?

Two major approaches can be taken to determining who qualifies for social policy benefits: the **public assistance** model and the **social insurance** model. In the public assistance approach, sometimes called social assistance, eligibility for benefits is **means-tested**. Recipients must demonstrate economic need to qualify for benefits. Advocates of this approach argue that means-testing enables governments to target resources to the truly needy—thereby alleviating extreme poverty without spending government resources on self-supporting individuals. This logic has proven powerful in countries with an individualist heritage such as Australia and the United States; both countries' social policies are predominantly means-tested. Critics of public assistance charge that this approach poses logistical and political problems. On the logistical side, critics note that the truly needy often struggle to prove their eligibility while others cheat the system by using fraudulent documents to qualify for benefits they should not receive. On the political side, critics assert that reliance on means-tested programs makes it difficult to build public support for social policy because few people want to envision themselves as poverty-stricken individuals. This attitude can stigmatize recipients of public assistance and can make such programs more vulnerable to political attacks.

Critics of public assistance favor a social insurance approach to social policy. In this model, all citizens in a given circumstance are eligible for assistance regardless of their degree of economic need. For example, all families with minor-aged children might receive benefits, all senior citizens might receive pensions, or all unemployed persons might receive income supplements. Because of the absence of means-testing, this approach creates **entitlements**. Citizens pay taxes to support these programs with the knowledge that they cannot be denied benefits. Because many citizens can imagine themselves having children, growing old, or temporarily losing a job, the social insurance approach helps to build support for social policy by ensuring taxpayers that they will get back some of their taxes in government benefits. Critics of social insurance charge that this political appeal creates new problems not faced by public assistance programs. Because citizens are sold on these programs through the promise of future benefits, they do not want to see benefit levels cut. However, as the number of active workers per dependent citizen (the young and the aged) decreases, it becomes harder and harder to protect benefits without increasing the taxes paid by working citizens.

A second policy choice involves determining how redistributive each social policy should be. That is, how much money should be taken from some taxpayers to pay for others' benefits? The public assistance approach is explicitly redistributive: everyone pays taxes to support the program, but many people may never meet the relevant poverty test to qualify for benefits. In contrast, the social insurance approach leaves open the possibility that all citizens may benefit. As a result, governments can choose to limit the redistributive element in social insurance programs. This means that programs can be based on either the principle of **individual equity** or the principle of **basic needs**. According to the individual equity principle, citizens can expect to receive benefits in accordance with their level of contributions: you get back what you paid in. According to the basic needs principle, the government sets benefit levels at a certain standard and then pays each citizen a common benefit. The basic needs approach combines an entitlement with some redistribution: everyone benefits, but wealthy contributors help to subsidize the benefits paid out to the needy. Social insurance pensions are also redistributive over time. The contributions of younger citizens fund pensions for current senior citizens; however, the younger citizens contribute to the pension system with the knowledge that their retirements will be funded by future generations. Distrust over the feasibility of maintaining current benefit levels in countries with aging populations is a major political problem in contemporary public pension policy in industrialized countries.

A third choice faced by government is determining how to provide economic assistance. That is, what policy instruments should be used? Often benefits are provided via government **transfers** to the individual. These transfers could be cash payments or they could involve in-kind benefits—for example, food or government services. Another instrument of social policy involves government **subsidies** for certain basic needs. For example, government could spend money to make food, public transportation, or housing available at abnormally low prices. A third option consists of the use of **tax expenditures**, which, as discussed in Chapter 6, reduce citizens' tax obligations when they spend their money for certain purposes. Lower sales taxes on food and income tax deductions for dependents and for owning a home are examples of the tax expenditure approach to social policy.

Explaining Policy Dynamics

What contextual factors influence policymakers as they try to meet the varied challenges of social policy? Similar to research on health policy, most studies of social policy making have been national case studies complemented by several comparative case studies. Cultural forces are particularly visible in this research, but economic, political, and institutional factors can also influence the path of social policy.

Cultural Explanations

Cultural traditions form one of the most widely discussed influences on social policy making. Much of the policy analysis in this area takes the family of nations approach introduced in Chapter 2. Anglo-American countries have had a greater tendency to emphasize the role of the individual than have societies from different cultural traditions. As a result, some scholars (Castles and Mitchell 1993) assert that Anglo-American traditions serve as a brake on social policy (or as a force for contraction). Conversely, the Scandinavian family of nations is seen as more collectivist in its cultural norms, which helps to fuel more support for government expansion in social policy.

Studies of the emergence and development of the welfare state in advanced industrial societies note that the liberal tradition of individualism had deeper roots and more political impact in the Anglo-American countries than in other industrialized countries. This cultural obstacle of a strongly liberal tradition is said to have slowed the initiation of major welfare policies (Flora and Alber 1981), lowered transfer spending levels (Castles 1982b), and created distinctive welfare policies (Esping-Andersen 1990; Oorschot, Opielka, and Pfau-Effinger 2008) in those countries.[1] The logic of this deeper cultural explanation is that individualism simultaneously reinforces both a reluctance to provide government programs for able-bodied working citizens and a distrust of government solutions to societal problems. The United States is often said to be the most individualistic of the Anglo-American countries in terms of its approach to social policy issues (King 1973; Skocpol 1992).

Economic Explanations

As noted in Chapter 2, the convergence thesis (Wilensky 1975) argues that as countries become industrialized countries (usually measured by GDP per capita), they are likely to experience similar social and political pressures that culminate in the adoption of a wide range of similar welfare policies—in part because those greater economic resources provide greater breathing room for the expansion of government spending and activity. The convergence thesis can be used to explain the timing of welfare policy initiation and the level of welfare spending in countries around the world (Flora and Alber 1981). It has been less useful, however, for explaining differences among industrialized countries.

Some studies of public opinion support for social spending in industrialized countries show a negative relationship between public support for increased welfare spending and national economic fortunes in the 1980s. First, the greater the national wealth (measured again by GDP per capita), the lower the support for social spending tends to be. Second, the greater the income equality across a society, the lower the support for social spending (Roller 1995). This alternative vision—specific to the study of industrialized countries alone—turns Wilensky's convergence thesis on its head. As industrialized countries become more affluent, it may be harder for most citizens to support reaching out to less fortunate citizens via social policies because they may feel that such policies are no longer necessary.

Short-term economic conditions also shape decision making. As noted in Chapter 6, rising unemployment tends to put more demand on a variety of social policy services—unemployment insurance, poverty relief programs, and the like. This increased demand for social spending due to higher unemployment usually occurs with no compensating rise in economic growth that

---

[1] For an effort to draw finer distinctions among the welfare practices in the Anglo-American countries, see Castles and Mitchell (1993).

would generate more revenues to pay for those higher expenditures. Writing on European social policy developments, Vic George asserted in the mid-1990s that the "most obvious and most powerful economic pressure for increased welfare spending today is unemployment" (1996: 184). In addition to the direct impact that rising unemployment rates can have on demand for social spending, chronic unemployment can indirectly increase demand for social spending over the medium run. Long-term unemployment has been associated with higher rates of mental and physical illness and with the dissolution of families (Sinfield 1984), thereby increasing demands for other social policies.

Another economic influence on social policy stems from the impact of the international economic environment. Scholars focusing on contemporary economic globalization assert that increased economic competition is a factor that motivates a reconsideration of social policies (Giddens 2007; Gould 1993). This competition occurs both among industrialized countries (Preece, 2009) and between industrialized countries and newly industrialized countries (characterized by lower wages and less expensive social policies). Some analysts have argued that the pressures of globalization have motivated a move away from universalist social insurance policies in search of an "affordable welfare state" (George and Miller 1994: 17). In this context, the path toward a more affordable welfare state involves reducing the role of entitlement programs or replacing such programs with programs based on fixed annual budgets as a means of capping social expenditures.

Political Explanations

From a cross-national perspective in the welfare state literature, political parties are frequently cited as an influence on social policy. Leftist political parties played an important role in stimulating the emergence and evolution of the welfare state in most industrialized countries, whereas rightist parties worked to slow its development (Castles 1982b). Schmidt (1982) demonstrated that leftist prime ministers were strongly associated with the expansion of public revenues from 1950 to 1975. In contrast, the few countries without powerful leftist parties—Canada, Switzerland, and the United States—manifested the slowest growth in government and in welfare spending. Analyses of the evolution of welfare states during the 1990s and 2000s, however, have identified ways in which Christian democratic and social democratic parties have been moving toward more similar stances on several social policy issues (Seeleib-Kaiser, van Dyk, and Roggenkamp 2008).

Another political factor that influences social policy decision makers is the nature of interest group competition. In most policy areas, several groups of economically comfortable citizens or firms are organized participants in the policy network, with a vested interest in protecting and enhancing the scope of government activity. Consider, for example, the role of economic sectors that employ immigrant laborers in immigration policy making, the teacher and parent associations active in education policy, the conservationist and environmental watchdog groups working on various ecological issues, the physician associations and retiree organizations active in health policy formulation, and so on. In contrast, the primary constituencies of social policy are among the least affluent and least organized portions of any country. This situation has given rise to what former U.S. budget director David Stockman dubbed the weak clients thesis. Stockman observed that amid a search to reduce government spending, well-organized interest groups were better able to defend their portions of the budget (even for expenditures that public opinion generally opposed) than were scattered voices calling for the preservation of social spending (Greider 1981).

Institutional Explanations

A broad cross-national literature explores the relevance of institutional distinctions for welfare state policies and for government decision making more generally. Several cross-national studies of the evolution of the welfare state note that federal states have tended to have lower levels of welfare spending than unitary states (Cameron 1978; Wilensky 1975). Federalism's mix of responsibilities can provide more opportunities for opponents of welfare spending to intervene in the political process and slow the growth of the welfare state. This pattern holds for both large and small federal countries and when one controls for population size. While acknowledging that federalism can pose an obstacle for social policy advocates, revisionist research in the early twenty-first century has added some qualifiers to the conventional wisdom portraying federalism as an obstacle for social policy (Obinger, Leibfried, and Castles 2005). First, although federalism can be an obstacle, its impact is contingent on other cultural, economic, and political conditions. Second, just as federalism can block or slow the adoption of new social policy programs it can also protect existing policies from retrenchment or elimination.

Another often-discussed institutional obstacle to sweeping policy change is the use of presidential executive-legislative relations. Weaver and Rockman (1993a) provide a useful summary of the advantages for major policy enactment said to be provided by parliamentary executives "with parliamentary systems featuring stronger party discipline, greater recruitment of ministers from the legislature, greater centralization of legislative authority in the cabinet, and greater centralization of accountability" (p. 11). This excerpt from Weaver and Rockman is taken from the framing introductory chapter to their edited volume on the relevance of executive-legislative distinctions for a variety of domestic and foreign policy issues in industrialized countries. Near the end of that same volume, Weaver and Rockman (1993b) conclude that the relationship between parliamentary and presidential systems and policy making has proven more contingent on factors other than its straightforward presentation would imply. As noted in other policy chapters, institutional factors help to frame opportunities and obstacles for policymakers, but they do not always determine which policy outputs are chosen.

International Policy Making

Although the case studies that follow focus on domestic policy efforts, economic integration involving five of these countries has placed international coordination on the political agenda. The NAFTA debate in the United States highlighted concerns that the freer movement of products and of investment among Canada, Mexico, and the United States might lead employers to move firms to Mexico to avoid taxes associated with more generous social policies. Although this debate has not led to a binding NAFTA-wide social policy, it did lead to a side agreement on labor policy in which the Mexican government pledged to increase the enforcement of existing protections for unionized and nonunionized workers. In turn, Canada and the United States pledged to provide financing to assist in those efforts.

Given the longer history of the EU, it should not be surprising that social policy coordination has been on the agenda in Europe longer than it has in the United States. Although the Treaty of Rome called for the creation of a common social fund when the European Economic Community was launched, it took nearly two decades for the fund to be established. The pursuit of more in-depth economic integration associated with the single-market initiative of the late 1980s reinvigorated discussions of social policy coordination. The initial social charter of the late 1980s evolved into the social chapter of the 1990s in the Maastricht Treaty and later into the so-called social community of the EU in the early twenty-first century. We explore EU social policy in greater detail later in this chapter.

Because social policy is such a diverse area, it would be impossible to cover all aspects of this policy area in the case studies. For that reason, we have chosen to focus on family policy, that is, government social programs designed specifically for children and their parents.

United States

Background: Policy Process and Policy History

The political process for family policy is more complex in most countries than it is for most of the other policy areas treated in this book. By complex we mean that policy formulation and decision making occur in many arenas and that a multitude of interest groups tend to participate actively. The only other policy area that perhaps approaches this level of complexity is spending policy. However, even in spending policy, in most countries the broad outlines of policy formulation and decision making are usually shaped through the leadership of one or two government agencies.

Why is the family policy network more complex in the United States and elsewhere? First, the diversity of individuals whose pocketbooks are affected by family policies is greater than in most policy areas. Second, the variety of conceivable policy instruments opens the path to meaningful contributions from many agencies, legislative committees, and interest groups. Finally, the multitude of policies in place gives many government agencies and legislative oversight committees jurisdiction over different elements of family policy. The result is a diffuse process such that the nature of family policy making tends to resemble fairly closely the major dynamics of policy making in the country as a whole.

In the decentralized world of policy making in the United States, family policy exhibits the most complex policy network of all. Many programs are managed by the Department of Health and Human Services. Some aspects fall under the Department of Labor, others are implemented by the Department of the Treasury, and a few fall under the Department of Agriculture. Furthermore, the nature of the federal policies in the United States is such that many crucial decisions are made by state governments. Major reforms need to gain not only executive approval but also the approval of both houses of Congress. A host of subcommittees within various committees in both chambers play an active role in policy formulation and decision making. In the House the Ways and Means, Education and Labor and Appropriations Committees have been central. In the Senate the Agriculture, Nutrition and Forestry (because of the Food Stamp program); Finance; Appropriations; and Health, Education, Labor, and Pensions committees have been crucial. Interest group involvement is varied. By some estimates, nearly one-sixth of registered interest groups are active in health and social policy formation.

The United States relies more than any other industrialized country on a means-tested approach to family policy. Nothing on the political horizon indicates that a shift will occur toward greater use of a social insurance approach. In fact, the United States tightened eligibility requirements in the 1990s and 2000s—embarking on what has constituted the most substantial welfare reform in a generation. The 1996 Personal Responsibility and Work Opportunity Reconciliation Act (PRWORA) and its subsequent evolution reshaped U.S. social policy into the form it takes today—particularly in its insistence of firm maximum time limits for most public assistance programs, tougher means-testing, and expanded insistence on employment.

The United States, like Japan, has never had a universal child allowance. Instead, the United States has used means-tested transfers, means-tested tax credits, and universal tax deductions to supplement incomes for families with children. The main means-tested transfer program during most of the twentieth century, Aid to Families with Dependent Children (AFDC), had its origins in the 1935 Social Security Act—a major element of the Roosevelt administration's New Deal initiatives in response to the Great Depression. Although the program originally provided cash benefits only for children with deceased or incapacitated fathers, since the 1950s it also provided support to single parents (usually mothers). To be eligible for AFDC, families had to meet both a means test and also an assets test. The 1996 welfare reform led to the conversion of AFDC into the current Temporary Assistance for Needy Families (TANF) program. The federal guarantee of AFDC funds shifted to block grants to the states that are contingent on state policies meeting reform guidelines. These block grants for TANF cover not only the former AFDC expenses but also initiatives previously funded as the JOBS and Emergency Assistance programs. TANF benefits are limited to a maximum of five years (although states could conceivably exempt 20 percent of families for hardship), and recipients must be working or preparing to work as soon as possible, but no later than two years after entering the TANF program. In this federal system, standards vary considerably from state to state as do benefit levels, but the 1996 reform set a firm set of targets that tied future federal funding to adherence to the federal guidelines. In particular, states had to ensure by 2004 that 90 percent of participants from two-parent households and at least half of all adult participants were meeting the workfare guidelines. The federal government pays, on average, for about half of the TANF program, and the state government pays the rest. In addition, many states receive federal matching funds for forming an Emergency Assistance program within TANF for specific purposes (for example, burial costs, first and last month rental housing payments, and utility payments).

In addition to these means-tested transfers for families with children, the United States provides various tax concessions for children. For generations, the U.S. tax code has permitted tax deductions for adult and minor dependents. In 1976 the Earned-Income Tax Credit (EITC) program was initiated for families with children under age nineteen. This refundable, means-tested credit was created in response to criticism that the dependent tax deduction transfers more money to middle- and upper-income families than to poor families. Families with annual incomes of no more than $37,000 are conceivably eligible for some tax credit. The size of the credit rises with the number of dependent children and shrinks as income nears the threshold; the maximum annual tax credit is less than $5,000. The crucial aspect of the EITC program is that many participants get a tax refund as a result of their earned-income tax credit. Beyond the EITC program, since 1998 there has also been a child tax credit program with a broader eligibility threshold for its means test that enables all but upper-income households to claim the credit.

Child care policies provide another example of the emphasis on means-testing and tax expenditures in U.S. family policy. The United States provides a tax deduction for parents who put their children in licensed child care facilities. About half of all state governments provide additional tax deductions and tax credits for child care expenses. In addition to these universal tax expenditures, a variety of federal programs try to subsidize child care for low-income families that meet relevant eligibility criteria (for example, the Child Care and Development Fund, Head Start, and the Social Services Block Grant program). Despite these subsidies targeted at low-income families, such families spend a disproportionate amount of their income on child care. The average U.S. family purchasing day care for two children in 2004 spent 19 percent of its income for that service; low-income families spent over 27 percent, and high-income families spent 13 percent (Organization for Economic Co-operation and Development [OECD] 2009c).

Just as in the area of child allowances, the United States is a policy outlier in its maternity and parental leave policies. Among the six countries examined in this book, the United States is the only one that does not require employers to provide paid maternity leave. In fact, only with the 1993 Family and Medical Leave Act did the government require employers to provide twelve weeks of unpaid leave for childbirth, adoption, or care for dependent family members. This unpaid leave (which many workers cannot afford to use) is mandatory only for employees in firms with fifty or more workers. Less than half of all women are employed in such firms. A handful of state governments provide some form of limited pay during maternity leave.

Other forms of social policy are available. Poor families with gross incomes less than 130 percent of the official poverty line standard and less than $2,000 in disposable assets can receive vouchers to purchase foodstuffs via the Food Stamp program that was created in 1939. During the 1990s and 2000s, the paper vouchers were replaced with electronic debit cards that in some states are also used for other public assistance programs. As a result of the move away from stamps, since October 2008 this program has been called officially the Supplemental Nutritional Assistance Program (SNAP). Finally, families that receive TANF benefits are also eligible for medical benefits under the Medicaid program. Medical benefits are a crucial issue in family policy in the United States because—unlike all other industrialized countries—the United States has no universal health insurance program (see Chapter 8). Between 45 and 50 million U.S. citizens lack health insurance.

The context of family policy making in the United States is different from that found in other countries in several respects—perhaps principally in the area of public attitudes. Many people in the United States believe that transfer programs breed sloth and should be limited. In public opinion polls from 1975 through the late 1980s, less than half of the respondents supported government intervention on behalf of the poor (Schlesinger and Lee 1994).

From 1980 into the 1990s, the United States engaged in a prolonged period of policy formulation and debate. The major reforms advocated were the addition of work requirements (dubbed workfare) and the creation of a sunset period for the provision of benefits. From January 1981 through January 1993, this debate took place in the context of a divided government in which Republican presidents called for welfare reform while Democratically controlled legislatures zigzagged between expansion of benefits in some programs and contraction of benefits in others. The majority of the few program expansions in this conflictive atmosphere were unfunded mandates in which the federal government could agree to pass an initiative—but only if state governments were responsible for funding.

The Republican Party in January 1995 gained control of the legislature for the first time in well over a generation. The reduction over time in the proportion of the Republican caucus protective of the status quo, and the presence in the White House of a Democratic president who was committed to some forms of social policy change, opened the door to a new decision-making stage under a changed balance of forces at the federal level. The result was the passage of PRWORA, the biggest change in federal social policy since the 1960s. The legislation tightened means-test standards, limited the maximum benefit period, and inserted new back-to-work incentives and requirements into several programs. The formula for food stamps was changed to reduce benefit levels almost 20 percent by the year 2002. This reform formed the backdrop of the debate over social policy in the 2000 presidential campaign.

Contemporary Dynamics

In the 2000 election campaign, family policy was not a high-profile issue. Both presidential candidates—Al Gore and George W. Bush—tended to claim that PRWORA had been a success. Furthermore, each candidate took credit for the successes. Al Gore served as vice president when Bill Clinton signed the bill into law and then presided over its implementation. In turn, George W. Bush noted that the reform lined up well with the Republican Party's agenda for welfare reform. During the campaign, the agenda-setting process had more to do with other elements of their respective platforms. Gore criticized Bush for being too interested in providing sweeping tax cuts for wealthy Americans, and Bush charged that Gore would mismanage the surplus and end up raising taxes.

Once Bush emerged as the winner of the 2000 election, his administration's high-profile domestic priorities were tax reform and education reform. Social policy formulation—a hot-button political issue during the 1980s and 1990s—attained a lower profile. A variety of incremental changes and reforms were discussed, but the main contours of the 1996 reform did not face a serious challenge in Congress nor in most public opinion polls. President Bush expanded the executive branch's use of the "charitable choice" element of the 1996 reform, which enabled faith-based groups to receive federal funding for implementing social welfare initiatives. Some Republicans, including many in the Bush administration, wanted to use the pending reauthorization of the welfare system to tighten further the work requirements. Most Republicans favored limiting federal financial obligations to the program over time.

Conversely, some Democrats wanted to create more discretion in the eligibility rules for state governments, and most Democrats wanted to expand or maintain funding in real terms over time.

Against this political backdrop, Congress debated an extended reauthorization of the TANF program and other elements of the welfare system in 2005. President Bush's reelection and Republican majorities in both chambers gave his party the upper hand. However, the lack of a filibuster-proof majority in the Senate (and the slim numerical majority more broadly) meant that the House bill was likely to be more conservative than the Senate version. To move toward passage in the Senate, ultimately the Republican legislative leadership and the Bush administration agreed to remove language that would have increased the workfare requirements beyond the level of the 1996 law to 70 percent of all adult recipients. In addition, there was a slight upswing in funding for the federal child care program from 4.8 to 5 billion dollars. However, on balance the content of the welfare provisions of the 2005 Deficit Reduction Act lined up with the Republican Party's desire to maintain the core elements of the TANF program and to cut federal spending slowly over time by reauthorizing $16.6 billion each year through 2010. Once inflation is taken into account, federal spending for the TANF program on balance will decline.

Implementation of most aspects of this program reauthorization went smoothly because there were no major changes in eligibility rules, benefit levels, or other key dimensions of the TANF program. The major new detail was that states had been able to get credit toward the workfare participation rule by getting beneficiaries not just employed but also off of the welfare roll. The 2005 reauthorization, at the insistence of the Republican Party, created a new blank slate in which state governments lost previous credit for getting people off of welfare but could begin claiming credit again in 2006 and beyond. The TANF program had seen its number of participants fall by half between 1996 and 2000; participation declined an additional 30 percent by 2005. Accordingly, although many states had maintained their eligibility for block grants by meeting prior targets for reducing the number of welfare recipients, the new rules forced all states to begin new reductions in the number of recipients.

The intent of PRWORA was and is clear: the federal government wants to limit further both the number of people receiving welfare transfers and the time period of benefits. The legislation proposed to meet these goals through a variety of means, and it succeeded, as demonstrated by the program enrollment trends cited previously. Nevertheless, even though PRWORA's proponents champion the decreased number of welfare recipients as an indicator of program success, the policy evaluation debate over time has been more complicated. Supporters also pointed to a decline in the population below the poverty line from 10 percent in 1997 to less than 9 percent in 2000. Critics of the workfare approach note that the poverty rate increased to 10 percent by 2003, remained at that level through 2007, and then nudged higher in 2008. Furthermore, opponents of workfare observe that half of the TANF recipients who leave the program have jobs that leave them below the poverty line. They argue that—rather than rushing to get as many recipients out of the TANF system as quickly as possible—the government should be providing a more effective set of job training and education programs that will require a higher level of TANF benefits over a longer time period. The election of Democratic presidential candidate Barack Obama, despite his endorsement of workfare as a guiding principle, may reopen this policy debate in the years of his presidency.

The saga of contemporary social policy reform in the United States is a microcosm of several fundamental features of U.S. politics since the 1980s—frequent periods of divided government, weaker party discipline (especially in the Senate), an important role for state governments, and a wide open field for interest group politics. These factors make it difficult for the federal government to make sweeping policy changes. That said, major reform is not impossible in this political system. The passage of the 1996 legislation bears witness to the fact that change is possible—albeit time-consuming.

Japan

Background: Policy Process and Policy History

The central ministry for social policy in Japan is the Ministry of Health and Welfare. The lead agency for family policy is the Children and Family Bureau, which is responsible for family allowances, child care, and public assistance policies. Family leave and unemployment insurance are supervised by the Ministry of Labor. The Ministry of Finance has played a crucial role as well in determining the fiscal parameters for family policy. Major reforms have tended to involve prolonged negotiations between the relevant ministries, the leaders of coalition partners or party factions, and heads of major employer organizations and labor unions.

Although a few social policy measures were initiated during the Depression and World War II (including the establishment of the first Ministry of Welfare), the bulk of contemporary family policy has its origins in legislation passed after the war. The 1947 Child Welfare Law was followed by a variety of other measures designed to provide a minimum standard of living for children; the 1947 law calls on all Japanese citizens "to ensure that all children have basic economic security" (Ozawa 1991: 2). Despite the universal standard that this implies, the policy instruments chosen to meet that goal have tended to be means-tested. As Japan begins a new century, the challenge of devoting sufficient resources to meet that goal has increased amid a wave of economic and political crises from which Japan seemed immune just a few years earlier.

Compared with other industrialized countries, Japan was late to adopt child allowances as part of the country's social policy. The 1971 Children's

Allowance Law initially provided allowances only for third and subsequent children. The law currently provides means-tested allowances for all children, and higher benefits (double the initial amount) are paid for third and subsequent children. Recipients must have a family income below a ceiling that varies according to the number of dependents. All parents receive a lump-sum childbirth allowance. In addition to this program, single mothers not receiving benefits from the Old-Age, Survivors, and Disability Insurance program are also eligible for a child support allowance that has a less stringent means test and pays benefits until children reach age eighteen (age twenty if the children are disabled). Parents with mentally or physically disabled children are also eligible for a means-tested special child dependent's allowance. The tax code provides a deduction for children and other dependents.

Since 1947 child care for preschoolers has been provided for all children whose parents or relatives cannot provide care (due to work responsibilities or disability). Fees in both public and private child care centers are based on a single, universal sliding scale tied to income. The government subsidizes the difference between the fee charged and a universal per-child fee collected by the centers; the local and central governments share the funding burden equally.

Maternity leave is provided for a maximum of fourteen weeks under the 1947 Labor Standards Law. Compensation is at two-thirds of the relevant reference wage. The issue of parental leave for child (and elder) care has entered the Japanese legislative agenda only recently. In 1992 the government passed the Child Care Leave Law, which requires most firms to provide either parent (not simultaneously) with unpaid leave during a child's first year. Since 1992 leave policy has been a topic of repeated legislative debate regarding whether to shift to paid leave. Currently, the parental leave policy provides a maximum benefit of roughly 40 percent of salary.

The impoverished are potentially eligible for public assistance under the 1950 Livelihood Protection Act. All other income supplements (including child allowances) are counted as income in the means-test standard. There is also an assets test. For those who qualify for assistance, the program pays a benefit designed to bring people up to roughly three-fifths of the median family income in their region. Because of social stigma and ignorance, far fewer than half of those eligible for public assistance have applied for benefits during the entire history of the program. As a result of smaller benefits and lower participation, Japan has historically spent the smallest percentage of GDP on public assistance of the six countries examined in this book.

Japan was arguably the only one of the six countries in which an expansion of family policy was under serious discussion at the start of the 1990s. Japan engaged in electoral system reform in the 1990s to deal with discontent about one-party domination and corruption scandals. In Japan's newly more fluid political environment, the major postreform political parties all publicly contemplated some expansion of the family welfare system. The most visible example of this expansionist tendency was found in family leave policy. Some of the newly formed political parties helped to put this issue on the public agenda by pointing out how Japan—despite its rapid ascent to economic heights at or beyond European standards—had yet to enact this basic element of European family policy. In 1992 Japan passed its first parental leave legislation—calling for unpaid parental leave during a child's first year of life. As nearly half of all mothers moved to accept this leave, pressure increased to provide some form of paid leave. Rather than dulling attention on the issue, implementation of this initial reform raised the profile of the issue once the Liberal Democratic Party (LDP) lost its control of the executive in 1993. The Japan New Party (at the helm of the first post-LDP coalition government) called for some form of paid leave, as did the Social Democratic Party. The LDP, in its effort to regain the political initiative, upped the ante by calling for a comprehensive review of the entire social policy framework. In 1994 the Unemployment Insurance Act was amended to provide a leave benefit at 25 percent of previous earnings. The Hashimoto government, a coalition led by Liberal Democrats and Social Democrats, passed in 1995 a compromise expansion of the leave system, which called on all firms to provide at least three months of child or elder care leave per family.

Contemporary Dynamics

As noted above, the more competitive political atmosphere of the 1990s was associated with an upswing in proposals to expand social policy on the family to provide categories of assistance that had previously been denied. The two central policy areas under debate were the family allowance program and recently created parental leave program. On the one hand, the insertion of new spending initiatives onto the institutional agenda might seem odd in the early twenty-first century when the Japanese government was trying to control costs associated with the elderly in health care and pensions policy.

On the other hand, examined within that broader context of the industrialized country with the oldest population, one can see the logic that helped propel family policy into the reform agenda: many political parties and bureaucrats wanted to increase the Japanese birth rate as part of an integrated strategy to deal with the aging demographic trends in Japan. For two generations, LDP politicians and bureaucrats had been generally reluctant to expand welfare policies. Mounting demographic pressures helped to reduce that traditional reluctance—as did the LDP's parliamentary coalition with the Buddhist-informed New Komeito Party following its creation in 1998. Once the LDP and New Komeito formed a parliamentary alliance in pursuit of broader family policies, the only serious question became, how large an expansion of public activity in this sphere would be pursued? Because labor unions and center-left political parties had long supported initiatives in this area, they were not opponents of policy expansion. In turn, potential business opposition to these proposals was minimized by the demographic arguments noted earlier.

Following his rise to the post of prime minister in 2001, Junichiro Koizumi pursued an expansion of family allowances and parental leave. The Diet passed legislation that increased the maximum age for participating children from six to twelve years of age; this basically doubled the potential number of recipients of family allowances by 2006 when Koizumi left office. In turn, a 2004 reform to the parental leave system expanded the compensation for child-care-based parental leave from 25 to 40 percent of one's base salary.

The implementation of these policies within the government went fairly smoothly. No new bureaucratic structures needed to be created because the central reforms were to the eligibility rules and benefit levels. Existing cultural patterns proved a greater obstacle. Despite increasing the benefit level, it remained difficult to convince fathers to claim parental leave during their children's first year of life. Only a tiny minority—less than 1 percent in some studies—of Japanese fathers claimed child care leave benefits in the first year of the expanded benefit.

Given that much emphasis was placed on the desire to stimulate higher birth rates, policy evaluation debates have paid considerable attention to fertility indicators. The Japanese fertility rate (the average number of children born to a woman during her lifetime) had fallen below the replacement level of 2.1 births in the early 1970s and continued to decline over the next three decades to 1.26 in 2005. In this context, many policymakers celebrated the slight uptick in fertility rates to 1.32 in 2006 (OECD 2009e). As of this writing, however, it remains to be seen whether this observed rise is the beginning of a sustained trend in Japan or simply an aberration.

The debate over family policy in Japan in the 1990s and 2000s demonstrates that in a fluid political environment, examples from abroad may be used more powerfully. New and changing political movements attempt to stake out positions to attract (what they hope are) uncommitted voters by calling for policy innovations previously ignored on the public agenda. The presence of family leave policies in so many other industrialized countries made it a safer issue on which to call for expansion of government activity. The use of such policies in other countries gave the issue credibility that might otherwise have been lacking. Further, the reform of both family leave and family allowances demonstrates the usefulness of a crisis in generating broad support for policy reform. Advocates of change argued successfully that the graying of Japanese society constituted a crisis that demanded policy change.

Germany

Background: Policy Process and Policy History

The central elements of family policy in Germany are currently managed by two major ministries. The Ministry of Labor and Social Affairs is in charge of the social security system, family allowances, and means-tested poverty assistance. The Ministry of Family Affairs, Senior Citizens, Women, and Youth supervises child care programs and other family social services. These ministries work with the Economics Ministry, Finance Ministry, and the chancellor in formulating new family policy initiatives. As in other policy areas, the interest group structure is less freewheeling and more centralized in Germany than in France. The two major employers' associations—the Federation of German Industry and the Confederation of German Employers' Associations—and the German Federation of Trade Unions have been of particular historical relevance in family policy making.

The German pattern of caring for families has been a combination of means-tested programs and universal benefits that provide cradle-to-grave protection. The German constitution requires the government to establish and maintain basic social welfare rights, and family policy has fallen under this umbrella. Several contemporary family policies (maternity benefits and unemployment insurance, for example) trace their roots to the late nineteenth and early twentieth centuries. However, most legislation designed to protect families has been adopted since 1949. The German political parties' attempts to outbid each other for moderate votes have resulted in the steady expansion of these programs by conservatives as well as socialists. The partisan debate has concerned the precise nature of government activity—a debate that in recent years has gained significance in a changing German economic environment.

Germany has traditionally adopted **pronatalist family policies** that reward parents for having additional children and encourage increasing family size. The first German pronatalist policies date back to the Weimar Republic and were continued with racist rather than pro-family intentions in the Nazi era. Since 1949 the German government has continued in the pronatalist tradition. The family allowance has varied with the political climate in the country; Social Democratic governments have created more universal benefits, and Christian Democratic leaders have based these allowances more often on means-testing. Presently all German parents receive the same annual benefit (roughly $2,700) for each of their first three children, but larger allowances are paid for fourth and subsequent children. Poorer families that meet means-test requirements are eligible for a supplemental benefit.

Taxation in Germany is designed to encourage women to focus on their role as mothers. The tax system rewards married couples by taxing them at a much lower rate than unmarried individuals, and German couples with a financially dependent spouse also receive generous tax credits. In combination, these policies create a powerful incentive for married women to remain at home with their children. Among all industrialized countries, Germany trails only the United States in its use of tax expenditures for these and other social policy purposes.

Although Germany currently offers a wide array of child care options, this was not always the case. The German government traditionally viewed child care as the responsibility of parents, relatives, and neighbors. However, since the 1970s, day care has been heavily subsidized by government. Limited government funds are also available for parents who arrange for child care in their homes. The 1991 Child Care Act states that all children, but especially preschoolers, have a right to develop fully through private and public organizations.

Maternity leave is provided through a social insurance program that dates back to 1883. This program is funded through employer, employee, and government contributions. Employed women enrolled in a sickness fund who have worked for a designated period of time are entitled to fourteen weeks of maternity leave at 100 percent of previous earnings up to a cap of $18 per day that was instituted in the mid-1990s; employers can provide additional benefits. Parents may also take up to five days of leave each year for each sick child under age eight. Since 1986 a parental leave program has operated in Germany. The program currently allows one parent (at a time) to take job-protected leave for child rearing at two-thirds of the parent's normal salary. This leave could extend to a maximum of thirty-six months. The relatively long leave period reflects, in part, a desire to decrease the unemployment rate by creating job openings.

Relatively few direct benefits are targeted toward the poor in Germany. This dearth of benefits has traditionally reflected the small number of Germans living in poverty; in addition, many of the poor have been foreign guest workers with few guaranteed rights. For poverty-stricken Germans, direct payments for food, housing, clothing, and other necessities are available, but these expenditures are a small proportion of the national budget. To receive public assistance, individuals must have no income or assets and cannot receive assistance from relatives. They are required to seek employment unless it would endanger the raising of children. Parents of children under age three who receive public assistance are not required to work, and those with children ages three to six must work only part time. A child-rearing benefit was introduced in Germany in 1986 for parents who are unable to work full time because they are taking care of their children. The child-rearing benefit is available to parents in the labor force and homemakers and cannot be received simultaneously with unemployment benefits. In addition to central government programs, some state governments also provide assistance to families. Finally, parents may claim family assistance under a young family program for children under age two. This is a one-time payment upon the birth or adoption of a child. These special family allowances are all means-tested.

The support and expansion of social policies in Germany was not a problem in times of economic growth. In the 1980s and 1990s, however, an economic downturn and the challenges of reunification focused attention on controlling the cost of social programs. This was especially true as rising unemployment and an economic slowdown reduced payments into social insurance funds at the same time that demands for unemployment benefits and worker retraining programs increased. In the 1990s the prospect of budget deficits for the first time in the postwar era, resulting from the underestimated costs of reunification, further focused attention on cost reduction.

The decisions adopted by Helmut Kohl's government in the 1990s called for modest cost reduction and not for a wholesale attack on the welfare state. Maternity leave benefits were capped, and many other benefits (such as child allowances) were not increased in real terms. This understated approach to social policy reform proved easier to adopt and to implement than was the case in France. Reductions in benefits were easier to implement by the Kohl government's ability to play the inflation card. The long-standing aversion to inflation in Germany faced its most serious challenge in over a generation because of the expenses associated with reunification. In the context of a once-in-a-lifetime event—reunification—it was difficult for labor unions or the Social Democrats to mount vigorous public opposition to slight spending reductions.

Contemporary Dynamics

The triumph of the "red-green" coalition of Social Democrats and Greens in the 1998 elections marked the end of Kohl's sixteen-year chancellorship and his center-right coalition government. The center-left government led by Gerhard Schröder faced considerable pressure—from party activists and organized labor—to reverse the trend of stagnant and falling benefit levels. Part of the 1998 election campaign had centered on the theme that the Kohl government had been indifferent to the plight of the poor and disadvantaged; Schröder at times called Kohl the "unemployment chancellor," in reference to high and rising joblessness during the second half of Kohl's lengthy government. Welfare reform was clearly a major agenda item at the start of the new center-left government.

At the same time, the policy formulation process revealed differences not just between the two major parties but also within the Social Democratic Party (SPD) itself. Schröder presented himself as a reformist figure within his own party who, like Tony Blair in the British Labour Party, would pursue a "third way" that would improve social welfare while avoiding an increase in taxation. Conversely, Oskar Lafontaine led a more traditionally progressive wing of the SPD that advocated an expansion in social spending as a central element of the Social Democratic agenda. Labor unions and many other social movements tended to side with the Lafontaine wing while business groups supported Schröder's call for welfare reform and labor law changes as a path toward reducing business tax rates (see Chapter 7) and stimulating job growth.

Early in Schröder's first government, emphasis was placed on expanded benefits to promote birth rates. As in Japan at the time, the government defended pronatalist policies as one of several steps toward dealing with an aging society. In 2000 the basic family allowance benefit rose by nearly 10 percent. Then, in 2001, the government adjusted by 10 to 12 percent the brackets within the sliding-income-based scale that determines benefit levels of eligible families; this marked the first time since 1986 that the German government had adjusted this aspect of the payment scale. While these pronatalist spending reforms moved through the legislature, Schröder spent time building a broader coalition in support of his vision for major welfare reform. In February 2002 he established a welfare reform commission—chaired by Peter Hartz, the head of Volkswagen. The commission's report in August endorsed a sweeping set of "workfare" reforms analogous to the 1996 PRWORA reforms in the United States and the Blair government's reforms in the United Kingdom in the late 1990s. After narrowly winning reelection in the September 2002 elections in a campaign that emphasized welfare reform as part the SPD's Agenda 2010, the Schröder government enacted the so-called Hartz reforms between 2003 and 2004. The 2003 reforms shortened the maximum period of normal unemployment benefits to twelve months and made it easier for firms to hire and fire workers in several job categories. The even more controversial 2004 reform law added a series of new work requirements and means tests that made it more difficult to qualify for public assistance; this second law also completely transformed the policy toward workers who remain unemployed for long periods of time. Under previous policy, workers with many years of service could receive over half of their prior salary in long-term unemployment insurance. Under the new law that entered into effect in 2005, those unemployed for more than one year could receive a flat-rate maximum benefit of a little over $6,500 per year. The reduction in benefit levels was used to help pay for a series of tax cuts (see Chapter 7).

Implementation of the Hartz reforms generated a firestorm of controversy. The labor movement held many rallies in protest. Business groups, in contrast, supported the workfare concept but claimed that the Schröder government had not gone far enough. The biggest initial impact occurred within the SPD itself. Lafontaine helped lead the formation of a splinter movement that created a new political party to the left of the SPD and the Greens. When the red-green coalition lost a subnational election in May 2005, Schröder called for new nationwide elections to be held one year early, in September 2005.

Given the controversy over these welfare reforms, policy evaluation took place in the midst of an election campaign held less than a year after their full implementation. Supporters of the Hartz reforms claimed that too little time had elapsed to observe the effect of these reforms on unemployment rates. Critics charged that the die had been cast as Germany had betrayed its obligations to working families. The 2005 elections produced a stalemate in which neither Schröder's red-green coalition nor the center-right bloc led by Angela Merkel gained a majority. This culminated in the creation of the "grand coalition" government headed by Merkel but staffed with many SPD leaders.

The German experience demonstrates the impact of policy learning as the Schröder team and the Hartz Commission emphasized the utility of labor flexibility and workfare policies in the United States and the United Kingdom as a driving force behind lower unemployment rates. At the same time, the aftermath of the Hartz reforms illustrates how traumatic major policy shifts can be for long-running political parties. The bloc led by Lafontaine saw the shift in social policy as a betrayal of Social Democratic principles and resolved to form a new political party as a vehicle to make their case to the voters in the years to come.

France

Background: Policy Process and Policy History

As noted in Chapter 3, the precise number and nature of cabinet ministries is not fixed in France. Each cabinet minister has the ability to form ministries over existing permanent agencies and bureaus as a reflection of his or her priorities. For example, the family allowance program in France is administered by the National Fund of Family Allocations (CNAF). This means that CNAF could be placed under the bailiwick of the economic or finance ministry; however, in most situations it falls to an employment or labor ministry or to a welfare ministry. For example, in the center-left cabinet established by Lionel Jospin in 1997, the CNAF came under the supervision of the Ministry of Employment and Solidarity; in the center-right government established by François Fillon in 2007, the CNAF came under the supervision of the Ministry of Labor, Social Relations, Family, Solidarity, and Cities. The CNAF has a permanent bureaucracy and a permanent advisory council. Although the notion of an advisory council is a potentially corporatist one, the pluralist nature of French interest groups creates a variety of representatives for each set of interests. Representatives of the same basic interest often have decidedly different ideological perspectives. This diversity of interests at the table has given French governments some political space to maneuver as governments of different political stripes can appeal to different groups to gain support for pet initiatives.

Besides the CNAF, other agencies and ministries are influential in family policy decisions. Often the pressure for changes in spending levels emerges out of the budget, economic, and/or finance ministries, which then consult with the supervisory ministry or ministries to set parameters for family policy that the relevant agencies need to meet. Support of these executive decisions in the legislature tends to depend on perceptions of public reaction to the proposed changes.

France provides to its citizens an extensive array of universal and means-tested family subsidies. Government assistance to families began in the early twentieth century with policies such as an unemployment insurance program (1905), maternity leave (1913), and a child allowance program (1932). Family programs were improved and expanded after World War II.

Building on this tradition, the 1958 constitution of the Fifth Republic declares a national responsibility for families. The prominence of left-wing movements, the activities of labor unions, the influence of Catholic social teachings, and concern over a declining birth rate have been important factors promoting a generous system of family supports in France.

As in Germany, France has a pronatalist child allowance policy. This policy is a clear response to concerns about low birth rates and population decline. France introduced a child allowance program in 1932 to provide assistance to employees with dependent children. This program was modified in 1939 to eliminate support for first children and increase payments for subsequent children, to a maximum of three children. Currently, all parents with two children under age seventeen (age twenty if the children are students) receive an annual allowance of at least $2,101. As an incentive to have a large family, the allowance increases by another $2,500 for a third child and continues to grow by roughly $2,500 for each additional child after that. The family allowance is not considered taxable income and is financed through payroll taxes. Low-income families are also eligible for several means-tested supplements to the child allowance.

Taxation policy in France also reflects a pronatalist orientation because parents significantly reduce their income tax burden when they have more children. In contrast to most other countries, taxation in France is based on the family rather than the individual. Tax concessions to parents for third and subsequent children are twice the amount allowed for the first and second children. Further, French parents do not pay income tax until their income reaches nearly 1.8 times the income of the average production worker. As a result, only half of French households pay income taxes (see Chapter 7).

France has one of the most comprehensive child care systems in the industrialized countries. The government provides a system of tuition-free preschools for all children aged three to six through the public education system. These preschools are funded through employer and employee contributions. Publicly financed and operated day care centers are also widely available, as are before- and after-school care facilities. These facilities are funded largely at the local level and involve some form of direct contribution from parents. In addition to the universal availability of child care, parents are also given tax concessions for children in public day care and for the cost of private day care in their homes. The child care system, despite its breadth, is criticized because demand for public day care outpaces supply and because of apparent inequities from region to region.

Government-sponsored maternity leave has been available in France since 1913. The program has some restrictions based on family size and length of employment, but generally speaking the French have universal access to paid maternity leave. Female employees now enjoy leave from work at full pay for at least sixteen weeks for each of their first two children. As with other family benefits, the length of the maternity leave and level of benefits increases with the number of children in the family. Fathers may take from three to fourteen days of leave at full pay when their children are born. French parents are also entitled to cash maternity benefits for birth and adoption. These benefits are financed through a social insurance fund based on payroll taxes and government contributions. Parental leave is available during the first three years of a child's life for up to one-year intervals for either parent. The paid leave varies between $400 and $1,000 per month depending on one's income level and how many hours one works (if any) during the leave.

Public assistance is available in the form of means-tested relief for both single and married parents. For low-income families with children, this benefit consists of housing, medical care, and help in finding employment. This assistance is intended to provide the minimum level of income necessary to help people get back on their feet. The extent of this benefit depends on income and household size. Another income-based program provides a basic income level to single parents who have a child under age three or for one year after the individual becomes a single parent.

When Jacques Chirac captured the French presidency in 1995, he inherited a sizable center-right majority in the legislature. His election ended a period of cohabitation between opposing political forces in the executive. Chirac and premier Alain Juppe tried to use Chirac's triumph as further evidence of an agenda-setting mandate for a reduction of the government's role in social policy. This initiative also could be presented as part of the general effort to cut costs and to reduce the budget deficit (particularly in response to pressures to meet EU budgetary standards). They argued that social reform could reduce the size of the public workforce and the flow of transfer payments to individual citizens—thereby improving the macroeconomic climate.

These reform efforts were widely opposed by organized labor and by French citizens more generally. Unions participating in the general strike launched in December 1995 were quick to refer to these twin efforts at privatization and social reform as evidence that the Juppe government was callously indifferent to the needs of the common person. The initial announcements of cuts in social spending prior to the strike were attacked repeatedly in the press and in person-on-the-street media interviews that demonstrated popular support for many of the strikers. The Juppe government appeared to be caught off guard by the adherence to the strike across different sectors of the economy. The wave of protests and criticism led the Juppe cabinet to withdraw most of its social policy reforms at the decision-making stage because the Gaullists and the Republicans feared the possibility of an electoral backlash that could threaten to reduce their large majority in the legislature.

Contemporary Dynamics

As it turned out, this retreat on social policy reform came too late to meet this electoral concern. The early attacks on social policy by the Juppe cabinet helped to fuel the electoral defeat of Juppe's center-right coalition in 1997. The victory of Jospin's center-left coalition kept welfare reform high on the systemic and institutional agendas. Jospin had promised to increase assistance to the disadvantaged but faced considerable budget constraints generated by the process of European monetary unification.

The debate over policy formulation produced a wide range of proposed reforms to all elements of the social policy system. The Communist Party and other leftist parties pressed for higher benefit levels and greater coverage of the French population. Business groups continued to press for a reduction in payroll taxes as a path toward reducing unemployment in France. The center-right bloc criticized the leftist proposals as a recipe for disaster.

The Jospin government decided ultimately to steer a middle course in which elements of both the pro-labor and the pro-business proposals would be adopted. In particular, the Jospin government argued that greater targeting of benefits was needed to raise the level of assistance to the neediest segments of the population without raising tax levels. The first reform in late 1997 aimed at the heart of France's long-standing pronatalist policies: the government eliminated the universal family allowance program and replaced it with a system completely reliant on means-testing that raised benefits to those who qualified. Like the Juppe government that had preceded it, the Jospin government faced widespread protests upon the implementation of this measure in 1998. Leftist movements led these protests, but many upper- and middle-income people also opposed the change because they were the ones losing their family allowance benefits. By mid-1998 the Jospin government restored the universal component of the family allowance in an effort to salvage the rest of its reform agenda. In 1999, with much fanfare, the Jospin government guaranteed full access to health care to poor residents. In turn, in 2000 (after over two years of negotiations) a major reform of the unemployment insurance system increased benefit levels and job training but also tightened eligibility requirements by increasing the work requirements.

The implementation of the welfare-to-work reforms shared similarities with the subsequent experience in Germany in the mid-2000s. The technical implementation of the reforms went relatively smoothly, but the political implications of the reforms were diverse and divisive. Leftist political parties and social movements criticized these reforms as a betrayal of workers' interests. They argued that there were now few or no differences between the social policy platforms of the Socialists and the Gaullists. The center-right bloc countered that the Jospin reforms were insufficient to save the system and improve economic conditions. From the far right, the National Front maintained that French social policy measures were too generous for non-French residents. The decibel level of policy evaluation reached a fever pitch in the first-round presidential election campaign in early 2002. Jospin's campaign argued that these reforms had protected the disadvantaged while stimulating a considerable reduction in the unemployment rate from 11.5 percent in 1997 to 8.4 percent in 2002. Ultimately, the center-left vote in the first round fragmented amid a handful of challengers who each claimed that they would be more progressive than Jospin. This dispersion lowered Jospin's vote total to 16.2 percent, leaving him in third place and out of the decisive runoff election.

Once Gaullist Jacques Chirac defeated National Front leader Jean-Marie Le Pen in the May 2002 runoff, the center-right bloc garnered a large majority in the June 2002 legislative elections. The center-right bloc pursued an extension of the Jospin-era reforms by increasing still further the use of work requirements via a 2003 reform on the major public assistance program (*revenu minimum garanti*, or guaranteed minimum income) while also expanding benefits to families during the first year of a child's life. The reelection of a center-right legislative majority in 2007—combined with the election of the new Gaullist leader, Nicolas Sarkozy, to the presidency—seemed to indicate that the welfare-to-work approach would remain at the center of the social policy debate for the foreseeable future.

The dynamics of social policy in France in the 1990s demonstrate just how effective interest groups can be when they can mobilize vocal public support for their stated position. Although we often consider interest groups as agents of backroom politics and quiet lobbying, they are perhaps most powerful when they win the war for public opinion to put pressure on cabinets and legislators. In a democracy, the threat of an electoral backlash against an unpopular policy decision is a powerful political tool. In France during the mid-1990s Juppe government, the weak clients thesis did not hold because advocates of social spending succeeded in mobilizing public opposition to the proposed cuts. In turn, the initial mobilization against the Jospin government's elimination of the universal family allowance was swift and effective perhaps precisely because it affected negatively affluent families (who had lost their benefits as a result of the shift toward means testing). The difficulty of shifting partisan preferences also became apparent as time passed. Similar to the experience of Gerhard Schröder in Germany in 2005, the pursuit of "third way" reforms by the Jospin government generated a split in the unity of the center-left bloc as the more leftist components of Jospin's coalition campaigned vigorously against him in the 2002 elections.

United Kingdom

Background: Policy Process and Policy History

Although the dynamics of family policy have always been more centralized in the United Kingdom than in the other countries examined in this book, a greater decentralization of the policy network existed in the family policy area than in other British policies prior to this century. Tony Blair's government in 2001 placed social policy into a single unit, the new Department of Work and Pensions, by merging the Department of Social Security with the labor components of the Department of Education and Employment. The various components of this department work closely with the prime minister and the finance minister (the chancellor of the exchequer) in formulating potential policy reforms. Although formal and informal consultation with interest groups is ongoing, most major reforms have tended to take the shape of the electoral campaign platforms that led to a new party forming the government.

By the early 1900s the British had introduced policies to provide old-age pensions, unemployment insurance, and public housing. A widely read plan for postwar reconstruction, the 1942 Beveridge Report, resulted in policies that now provide a series of government-sponsored services. Nevertheless, apart from the National Health Service (see Chapter 8), the United Kingdom has few comprehensive, universal social programs. With the exception of the initial level of family allowances, the majority of family policies are means-tested. During the 1980s and 1990s, Conservative governments emphasized the importance of market mechanisms. In family policy, this ideological thrust was associated with a significant reduction in the level of benefits in most areas.

Family allowances have been distributed in various forms in the United Kingdom since the end of World War II. Whatever their form, these allowances have always been intended to equalize the incomes of parents and individuals without children, as well as to acknowledge the additional costs of child rearing. As such, the child allowance program is a universal benefit financed through general government revenue. Since 1976 the child benefit has been a weekly nontaxable payment to mothers and legal guardians. It is universal for children under age sixteen (age nineteen if the children are students), but the highest benefit is paid for the first child. The annual value of the child benefit is roughly $1,570 per child. An additional child tax credit is available to all but high-income families. Finally, a means-tested family tax credit is also available to low-income parents; this program was created under the Blair government to replace a previous means-tested transfer program.

Taxation in Britain has been based on the individual since 1989, with each taxpayer entitled to one exemption. When the universal child benefit was introduced in 1976, existing tax deductions for families with dependent children, which had been in place since 1909, were eliminated. Child care expenses are not tax deductible, but the Blair government expanded child tax credits for working families with the express purpose of subsidizing day care.

The United Kingdom clearly has a shortage of child care options, especially publicly funded care. In a departure from the European model, the standard for day care in the United Kingdom is private provision. In part this reflects a traditional reluctance by both the public and the government to encourage mothers to participate in the workforce. The vast majority of children under age three are cared for by parents or other relatives, with class being an important determinant of the type of child care arrangement used.

Middle- and upper-class parents tend to employ nannies. Although employment for lower- and middle-class women has become more of a financial necessity, a corresponding movement toward direct public provision of day care services has not followed. Government day care centers have tended to be for children who are considered disadvantaged. Public day care is typically provided by local authorities, but these services vary widely and are generally not of high quality. The Blair government extended considerably the provision of tax credits to working families to assist them in obtaining child care.

Maternity leave has been provided for British women since 1911. Currently, the first six weeks are compensated at 90 percent of earnings. Up to an additional thirty-three weeks of leave are subsidized by a flat-rate weekly benefit (valued at a little under $1,000 per month). After meeting certain conditions relating to wages and length of service, women can opt for up to an additional thirteen weeks of unpaid maternity leave with a guarantee of reinstatement. Under the Thatcher government (1979–1990), the requirements for maternity leave were tightened for employees and relaxed for employers. Many women do not take the full leave because only the first six weeks provide substantial compensation. Fathers can take one or two weeks of paternity leave at the same flat-rate benefit provided for the bulk of the maternity leave. There was historically no official provision for parental leave. Via a 1999 reform, parents gained up to a maximum of thirteen weeks of unpaid leave.

The British approach to poverty relief has historically lacked generosity in comparison with most European countries. Prior to 1948 the British government assisted the poor under the provisions of the 1834 Poor Law, which created poorhouses for so-called paupers, who were forced to relinquish their basic citizenship rights upon entry. Most assistance to the poor came from religious and charitable organizations. In 1948 national public assistance programs were initiated that were expanded in the 1960s and 1970s. The 1992 Social Security Act and the 1995 Jobseekers Act provide the frameworks that currently apply in the area of poverty relief; the 1995 reform shifted most assistance from the more open-ended Social Security System toward the "workfare" approach of the Jobseekers Allowance program, which provides means-tested benefits to able-bodied residents. The new standards were intended by the Conservative Party to reduce the available level of benefits; keep spending down; and encourage the voluntary, informal, and private sectors to cover the difference. Under the Blair government, as we will see shortly, the welfare-to-work approach continued, but the level of benefits and government job training assistance rose markedly for those who meet the means test.

Under Margaret Thatcher's leadership, the Conservative Party sought to move government out of the social welfare business by placing increasing emphasis on personal responsibility and the market. Winning the executive in the stagflationary 1970s—amid a period of prolonged British economic decline—Thatcher chose to place welfare reform (and the reduction of government activity more generally) in the context of making the United

Kingdom economically competitive again. When Thatcher's parliamentary majority was expanded comfortably by the 1983 elections (held after the victory in the Falklands War with Argentina), the Conservative government moved more vigorously to restructure the welfare system over the rest of the decade. Most of the major institutions charged with providing family assistance saw their powers curtailed and functions changed. Although public opinion polls showed that support for universal family assistance did not decline significantly, Thatcher built support for her reform program by convincing many voters that the old benefits and services could be maintained only by increasing taxes. A willingness to pay more in taxes to maintain or increase social services was not apparent among the majority of British citizens during the Thatcher era.

Contemporary Dynamics

This trend in public opinion would not be lost on Thatcher's immediate successor as prime minister, John Major, nor on Labour Party leader Tony Blair. In the 1997 election campaign, both the Tories and Labour called for stable or increased social spending but promised to provide it without raising taxes significantly. Blair's New Labour program—the centerpiece of his huge victory in the May 1997 elections—even trumpeted a large dose of Thatcher's emphasis on personal responsibility. In office, the Blair government promised to develop a series of New Deal initiatives that would transform British social policy.

The policy formulation process was part of a sweeping reconsideration of government activity in family policy, education, job training, unemployment insurance, pensions, and health care. The more traditional elements of the Labour Party emphasized the importance of improving benefit levels that had declined over the prior two decades of Conservative governments; they were supported by organized labor and progressive social movements. Business groups emphasized a desire to retain and enhance labor flexibility and to keep taxes under control. The Conservative Party promised that it would be the best vehicle for extending the welfare-to-work reforms that had been launched under the Thatcher and Major governments.

After more than one year of debate and study, the Blair government enacted a series of major social policy reforms in 1999 that combined elements of both approaches—the provision of higher benefit levels and the insistence on work requirements and strenuous means-testing. A preexisting means-tested cash benefit program was transformed into the Working Families Tax Credit. Reforms to the maternity leave system extended benefits to some poor mothers who did not meet the previous eligibility requirements and created a new system of unpaid parental leave. The largest reform package redesigned the Jobseekers Allowance program by increasing the benefit levels, tightening eligibility requirements further, and increasing government services to job seekers.

This last component of the Blair reforms presented the greatest implementation challenges. A new integrated system of employment assistance was created in which each unemployed person was assigned a personal adviser to serve as a point of contact with the national system of job bureaus, job training centers, and many other social services. To ease the burden of this transition, the so-called ONE program was implemented in stages with a series of pilot centers followed by the creation of the envisioned nationwide network. During the first years of the new program, the Blair government determined that the most disadvantaged participants needed additional job training and higher benefit levels (to enable them to go through that process of extended assistance).

When Blair stepped down from the prime minister's post in 2007, he emphasized considerable progress in social policy. The government had increased family policy spending (as a percentage of GDP) by 25 percent from 1997 to 2003. In turn, child poverty rates also fell by one-fourth by 2005. The Blair government's rebuttal to critics of the welfare-to-work approach argued that improved targeting of social spending enabled a substantial rise in benefit levels with an additional investment of less than 1 percent of GDP.

The United Kingdom's experience with family policy making in the 1990s and 2000s demonstrates two central features of British political dynamics. First, the combination of strong party discipline, a unitary state, and plurality elections paves the way for governments to pursue bold reform initiatives. Second, this increased reform capability is not limitless. Governments that steer too far away from the voters do so at their own risk. The Major government moved to the center to avoid furthering the perception that the Conservative Party had become overly callous under Thatcher. At the same time, Tony Blair finished a fifteen-year-long effort to demonstrate that the Labour Party would not simply rush to restore every social program that was modified or eliminated during the Thatcher era. Instead, the Blair government worked within the welfare-to-work approach inherited from the Conservative Party but claimed to have improved it via better provision of services and greater public spending.

Italy

Background: Policy Process and Policy History

Most family policy issues in Italy come under the jurisdiction of the Ministry of Labor, Health and Social Policies. The core agency is the General Directorate for Welfare, which supervises family allowances and other public assistance programs. Many of these other programs are designed and implemented at the local government level. The finance minister has always been a part of the family policy process, but this role grew during the 1990s as Italy struggled to bring down its budget deficit, and the finance minister has remained more engaged in this century. As in other areas, compromises worked out among different party leaders represented in and across the relevant ministries have not always translated smoothly into new legislation.

Italian family policy has undergone an evolution similar to social policy in Germany. First, a variety of unemployment, disability, and pension programs were initiated at the turn of the century. Then, between the world wars, new family programs responded to both the Great Depression and the fascist rhetorical emphasis on solidarity. After World War II, Italy experienced the greatest economic growth in its modern history, and some of the resulting resources were devoted to an expansion of family policy funding and programming—often via universal social insurance policies.

Child allowances were introduced for all workers under Benito Mussolini. In the postwar era, allowances initially varied by region and by occupation, but by the 1970s Italy had moved to a universal flat-rate monthly benefit per child. Over the next decade, amid burgeoning government deficits, successive governments inserted means-tested restrictions: families earning more than twice the national average receive no child allowances, whereas those earning between 150 and 200 percent of the average receive partial benefits. The maximum benefit per household varies in accordance with the income level of the family, the number of children, and whether it is a single- or a two-parent household. Additional means-tested transfer programs exist for low- and middle-income families with three or more children. The tax code provides additional support for families. Tax deductions exist for children and other dependent family members. In addition, a tax credit for children pays out an equal benefit per child. Several public assistance programs exist at the local government level with funding from the central government.

Since the 1970s, universal child care for preschoolers has been provided via child care centers and kindergartens. The centers are run by local governments with funding support from the central government. Since 1950, female employees have been entitled to five months of paid maternity leave (beginning two months prior to delivery). The maternity leave program provides benefits at 80 percent of previous earnings. Either parent can also opt for an additional six months of leave, at 30 percent of earnings, during the child's first eight years. Another five months of unpaid parental leave can be obtained beyond the maximum limit for paid parental leave. Female employees are also entitled to paid parental leave to care for sick children under age three.

During the 1990s, efforts to reform Italian social policy were shaped not just by fiscal pressures visible in several other countries but also by widespread disaffection with the national government. The political dynamic of two generations of Italians—coalition governments dominated by the Christian Democrats—collapsed during the 1980s in the midst of corruption scandals that damaged the traditional governing parties. In this volatile climate, social policy reform emerged on the systemic agenda in the 1990s amid a climbing budget deficit and increasing attacks on the exchange rate. In 1994 the newly elected Berlusconi government proposed a substantial reform of the pension system as well as reductions in family policy benefits in several areas. Berlusconi, beset by problems within his own coalition, lost a no-confidence vote after less than a year in office. His nonpartisan successor, Lamberto Dini, presented himself as a technocrat concerned about the ability of Italy to meet its obligations under the Maastricht agreement on fiscal policy (see Chapter 6). Dini shepherded through a budget that reduced the rate of increase for family spending but made no major family policy reforms. He did broker a pension reform that reduced medium-run fiscal pressures on the retirement system by reducing future benefits and introducing a new supplemental, investment-based pension.

The 1996 election produced a center-left victory led by the PDS, the major faction of the once-communist party. The new government under Romano Prodi pledged fiscal and social responsibility. Prodi's governing platform called for a welfare state compatible with fiscal responsibility, which he deemed essential given Italy's need for sharp deficit reduction to meet Maastricht Treaty criteria for European monetary unification. The Prodi government increased benefits for family allowances and—especially—for child care but left the basic policy frameworks intact. The Refounded Communists (the other faction of the old communist party) pulled their support away from the Prodi government in October 1998 on the grounds that Prodi had not done enough to protect social spending. The subsequent center-left coalition government under Massimo D'Alema expanded the parental leave benefit in 2000 by extending the maximum age of the attended child from three to eight years. In general, however, the major policies of the Prodi government were left in place.

Contemporary Dynamics

The 2001 elections restored social policy reform as a significant component of the systemic agenda. Berlusconi called for a contradictory mix of tax cuts, public works spending, further pension reform to reduce costs, higher benefits for current retirees, and a reworking of the welfare and labor market systems that would increase the role of work requirements. The center-left Olive Tree coalition tried to characterize their opponents as indifferent toward the fate of the impoverished. Berlusconi's coalition received a large enough majority to govern this time (unlike in 1994) without the support of the Northern League—the coalition partner that spoke the most insistently in favor of substantial cuts in social policy spending.

While the Northern League called for major spending cuts and a dramatic reduction in payroll taxes, Berlusconi's own Forza Italia and its other coalition partners argued on behalf of a slower reduction in social spending coupled with an increase in eligibility requirements for many means-tested programs. Center-left political parties and labor unions argued for the protection of benefit levels along the lines of the policies pursued under the previous two Olive

Tree governments. Business confederations argued for lower payroll taxes and improved labor flexibility to make it easier to hire and fire workers. As this debate continued during 2002, a violent event shifted some of the tone of the debate: the leftist terrorist group the Red Brigades assassinated Marco Biagi. Biagi had been the Berlusconi advisor most associated with the development of "workfare" reforms. Most groups and individuals across the political spectrum repudiated the assassination; in its aftermath, it helped to lower the decibel level of the policy formulation debate. By July 2002 three dozen employer and labor associations signed an accord calling for a negotiated consensus on social policy reform that embraced many elements of Biagi's past proposals.

In 2003 the so-called Biagi Law mandated a dramatic restructuring of Italian social policy toward labor. New work requirements were introduced for welfare beneficiaries and for the long-term unemployed. In turn, the law called for the creation of a national network of local employment agencies that can be public, for-profit, or nonprofit in nature; these are to be linked in a national jobs database accessible to employers and job-seeking individuals. Other labor law reforms made it much easier to hire and fire workers in a series of different short-term job categories. During this second Berlusconi government, family allowance benefits were left untouched—slowly reducing the value of those benefits over his five-year term. In one area, however, the Berlusconi government supported the upswing in benefits endorsed by the prior Olive Tree governments: child care spending commitments were maintained and continued to grow in the 2000s as they had in the late 1990s.

The Berlusconi government, like the Koizumi government in Japan, defended the child care spending increases as part of a pronatalist policy that would make labor markets work more efficiently. The Biagi Law presented even greater implementation challenges than the analogous changes pursued by the Blair government. In the United Kingdom, the ONE program mandated the transformation of many existing government-run social services into an integrated network. In contrast, the Biagi Law called for the creation of a unified employment system out of a loose network of employment agencies, many of which were formed after the law took effect. Furthermore, the evolution of the reform also called for more job training than the system was able to provide initially.

In the 2006 election campaign, the Berlusconi government took credit for the decline in unemployment rates from 9.1 percent in 2001 to 7.7 percent in 2005. Berlusconi's opponents on the center-left countered that the reduction in unemployment had been sharper under the previous center-left governments, during which the jobless rate fell from 11.2 to 9.1 percent. Prodi's center-left coalition won a narrow majority in 2006, but the defeat of his government in a January 2008 vote of confidence culminated in new elections, which Berlusconi's coalition won. As of this writing, there is no reason to assume that Berlusconi's third government will abandon the social policy approach that his government took earlier in the decade.

The Italian experience demonstrates some of the special difficulties faced by multiparty coalition governments. When the executive needs the support of several parties with different ideologies and different core constituencies of voters, policy reform of any magnitude can be decidedly difficult to conduct. The first Berlusconi government and the first Prodi government were toppled because of disagreements among coalition partners with different regional and ideological constituencies. During the first several months of Berlusconi's second government, it was not at all clear that a firm coalition could be mobilized in support of a "workfare" reform bill. The killing of welfare-to-work advocate Biagi mobilized a willingness to accept many of his suggestions that might not have existed otherwise. This is an important reminder that politics is a decidedly human activity in which relationships among the participants in public debate frame their willingness to compromise (and their willingness to criticize).

European Union

Background: Policy Process and Policy History

Social policy coordination has been on the agenda in Europe for a long time. Article 123 of the 1957 Treaty of Rome called for the creation of a European Social Fund (ESF). Member states initially put this action on the back burner as they focused instead on reducing tariff and nontariff barriers to trade. However, after northern European countries began to experience increased social problems with foreign guest workers in the 1970s (see Chapter 5), the ESF was created in 1974. During the 1970s and 1980s, as the European Community expanded to include several relatively poorer countries, ESF spending rose to provide job training and unemployment benefits to workers in Greece, Ireland, Portugal, and Spain who were harmed by the initial transition to freer competition with the major European economies. When the 1987 Single European Act called for steps to realize the Treaty of Rome's call for free movement of labor, pressure for a coordinated social policy rose to minimize the possibility of widespread social dumping.

These concerns led to the adoption of a European Charter of the Fundamental Social Rights of Workers (or Social Charter) in 1989 by eleven of the then-twelve member states; the United Kingdom, under the vocal opposition of the Thatcher government, refused to sign the agreement. The Social Charter is a proclamation of principles that did not lead to many concrete initiatives because of the need for unanimity under traditional EC voting rules. Even the eleven countries in the Social Charter found it difficult to agree on specific community-wide social policies. The Maastricht Treaty included a social chapter of similar goals that the United Kingdom again refused to sign. The other EU members agreed to form a Social Community that could make some labor market policy decisions via a qualified majority voting system. Maastricht's emphasis on labor policy harmonization would eventually produce perhaps the first major EU directive on social policy—the 1996 parental leave directive that established minimum standards for parental leave throughout the EU.

Contemporary Dynamics

Later in the 1990s the negotiation of a new framework treaty for the EU created a new opportunity for agenda setting in EU social policy. Article 137 of the Amsterdam Treaty called on the Council of Ministers to develop measures to increase cooperation among member state governments to fight social exclusion. Although the treaty left family policy as an exclusive competency of the member states, Article 137 sounded a clarion call for the EU to induce greater coordination of social policy efforts in the name of reducing exclusion. Subsequent to the Amsterdam Treaty, a special summit in Lisbon created an initial policy process for the EU in an area in which it was now charged with combating exclusion while it was still instructed not to make direct policies. At Lisbon in 2000, the Council of Ministers endorsed the so-called "open method of coordination" (OMC) as a mechanism for policy coordination in the EU. To avoid violating member states' sovereignty in family policy, the European Commission is charged with facilitating consultations among member governments that will produce common objectives and indicators. In turn, the pursuit of those shared objectives shall involve information sharing and strategic reports among the Commission and the member states. A new era of EU social policy was born.

In the initial policy formulation debate, the Commission tended to tread lightly in deference to member states' exclusive competency in family policy and in social policy more broadly. Commission members supported the suggestions of member state governments that the OMC approach should emphasize fact-finding and research. Indeed, it proved difficult to build support for a specific set of social exclusion priorities. To maintain momentum, support grew in the Commission for a loose mandate for research as a path to initiate cooperation and dialogue in this policy area.

In December 2001 the member states and the Commission endorsed a five-year research agenda called the Community Action Program to Combat Social Exclusion. The three major goals established involved (1) improving the understanding of social exclusion and poverty, (2) organizing the exchange of information regarding national action plans to fight poverty and exclusion, and (3) capacity building with an eye toward improving future policies. Toward these loose shared ends, the EU dedicated over $100 million over the years 2002–2006. The Community Action Program sponsored studies of the causes and characteristics of exclusion, meetings and conferences in pursuit of developing best practices to combat poverty, and broadened pan-European networking to raise the profile of these issues in national and regional settings.

Given the very diffuse research mandate, it is perhaps not surprising the program's official report detailed a series of ways in which greater shared purpose could produce more satisfying and useful research findings. Although the report acknowledged the crucial role of many local factors in determining both the dynamics of social exclusion and the utility of various social policy instruments, it argued that future OMC efforts should aspire to develop a more shared understanding of which social policy goals merited community-wide attention.

In the policy evaluation process, this initial OMC effort culminated in policy change: the EU decided to blend its existing competencies in labor market policies with this newer initiative to combat social exclusion. Specifically, the next community action plan for the years 2007–2013, called PROGRESS, will combine the pursuit of the European Employment Program with another round of research and consultative roundtables regarding the fight against social exclusion and poverty. As of this writing, it remains to be seen whether this innovation will mark an eventual increase in EU social policy activity (via potential linkages to labor market dynamics) or if the PROGRESS program will instead constitute a point of inflection in which the EU resolves to limit its social policy making to labor issues more narrowly defined.

As with health policy, EU social policy dynamics speak to the importance with which member states guard the independence of their welfare policies. At the same time, the evolution of the EU has seen a gradual build-up during the 1990s and 2000s of rhetorical emphasis on the importance of social policy coordination. We may be observing the beginning stages of a much longer process. If it took nearly half a century for the European Community to shift from a call for a single market toward a host of single-market policies, the period from the late 1980s through the late 2000s constituted the first half of a similarly capacity-building process in the realm of social policy.

Cross-national Trends

As with tax policy, the general social policy approach of the three continental European countries (France, Germany, and Italy) differs from that found in the other three countries. The continental countries tend to have more universalist policies, whereas the other three pursue means-testing measures more frequently. In general, universalist policies tend to be associated with lower rates of relative poverty. Despite the superior performance of universalist policies (and of higher social spending) in reducing relative poverty, in the 1990s and 2000s all six countries enacted reforms that relied more frequently on means tests (or tightening existing means standards). Furthermore, all six countries have, at times, frozen or reduced welfare benefit levels. Although the use of means-testing as a prevalent feature of social policy efforts was familiar outside of continental Europe, it represents a new development in France, Germany, and Italy. Efforts to explain this change have tended to focus on the impact of globalization and, in particular, the push toward deficit reduction implied by monetary unification. Amid the restructuring efforts, we also consider reasons why the level of social spending on family policy proved more resilient than the prevailing political debate might imply.

Policy Outputs

A clear division appears to exist between countries that have tended to rely more on means-tested policies (Japan, the United Kingdom, and the United States) and those that have opted more often for universalist social insurance policies (France, Germany, and Italy). In making such a generalization, however, we are referring to differences of degree in the mix of instrument choices.

The mix of public and private responsibility and of means-tested and universal policies is summarized in Table 9-1. No country relies exclusively on means-tested policies. For example, all countries employ a social insurance approach to unemployment benefits (and to public pensions). At the same time, even the three countries with the predominantly universalist approach (France, Germany, and Italy) employ several means-tested programs for poverty relief.

Universalist social insurance policies tend to be more politically viable because they guarantee benefits to all. This approach makes it easier to build political coalitions that will protect and raise the benefit packages associated with the programs. In contrast, means-tested packages are more vulnerable to political attack because the beneficiaries—the impoverished—are often not well organized politically. This supposition that social insurance policies lead to higher benefit levels generally holds true for child allowances in these six countries in 2008. The three countries with the longest universalist child allowance traditions (France, Germany, and the United Kingdom) provided an average annual benefit for a two-child family of over $3,500, whereas the average child allowance in Italy, Japan, and the United States was $500 (U.S. Social Security Administration, 2009). As Table 9-2 demonstrates, these child allowance trends follow the pattern for overall spending on family policy. France, Germany, and the United Kingdom spent an average of 2.6 percent of GDP while the other three countries spent half as much on family policy. The data for the United Kingdom represent a particularly compelling example of how social insurance programs can generate support for funding even in a comparatively hostile political environment.

Beyond direct spending levels, countries also engage in social policy via tax expenditures. As noted in this chapter, the United States has the most active program of social tax expenditures—providing benefits toward the sorts of activities discussed in this chapter valued at well over 1.5 percent of net national income in 2005. Germany's tax expenditures in social policy also exceeded 1 percent of net national income; each of the other four countries' tax expenditures constituted less than 1 percent (OECD 2009c).

Table 9-1 Social Policy Models, 1980–2008

Country	Child Allowances	Child Care Funding	Paid Family Leave Policy	Unemployment Insurance
France	SI (1980–1995) Mixed (1995–1997) MT (1997–1998) Mixed (1998–2008)	Public>Private	Maternity and parental (1984–2008)	SI
Germany	SI (1980–1982) Mixed (1982–2008)	Public>Private	Maternity and parental (1986–2008)	SI
Italy	Mixed	Public>Private	Maternity and parental	SI
Japan	MT	Private>Public	Maternity and parental (1994–2008)	SI
United Kingdom	SI (1980–1985) Mixed (1985–2008)	Private>Public	Maternity (1984–2008)	SI (1980–1994) Mixed (1995–2008)
United States	MT	Private>Public	None	SI

SI = social insurance; MT = means-tested; Mixed = mix of SI and MT.

Table 9-2 Public Spending on Family Policy per Gross Domestic Product (1985–2003)[a]

Country	Family Policy Spending per GDP (1985)	Family Policy Spending per GDP (1995)	Family Policy Spending per GDP (2003)
France	2.7%	2.7%	3.0%
Germany	1.8	1.8	1.9
Italy	0.9	0.6	1.2
Japan	0.4	0.4	0.7
United Kingdom	2.3	2.4	2.9
United States	0.6	0.6	0.7

SOURCE: Organisation for Economic Co-operation and Development (2009c).

[a]Public social spending encompasses funding of poverty relief, family allowances, maternity and parental leave, food benefits, child care, and other social services. It also includes cash rebates generated by tax credits; however, it excludes tax expenditures that do not generate cash payments.

Policy Outcomes

Given this variety of policy mixes, which countries have been most successful at limiting poverty? Poverty can be defined in a multitude of ways. The notion of **absolute poverty** implies some basic needs standard beneath which citizens are said to be poor. This threshold varies substantially from expert to expert and from government to government. This lack of agreement on a common standard makes meaningful cross-national comparison of absolute poverty statistics difficult.

Table 9-3 Relative Poverty (mid-1980s to mid-2000s)[a]

Country	Mid-1980s	Mid-1990s	Mid-2000s
France	7.6%	6.9%	6.5%
Germany	6.3	8.5	11.0
Italy	10.3	14.2	11.4
Japan	12.0	13.7	14.9
United Kingdom	6.2	9.8	8.3
United States	17.9	16.7	17.1

SOURCE: Organisation for Economic Co-operation and Development (2009e).

[a]Percentage of the population earning less than 50 percent of the median income.

Poverty can also be defined in a relative sense. Perhaps the most common definition of **relative poverty** in industrialized countries has been used by the Luxembourg Income Study and by the Organisation for Economic Co-operation and Development countries. They define the relative poverty rate as the percentage of households that earn less than 50 percent of the median household income (adjusted for family size).

Table 9-3 presents data on relative poverty for the six countries examined in this book. Two of the three countries that have the highest spending commitments in family policy have noticeably lower poverty rates (France and the United Kingdom). The partial exception is Germany. Germany had a below-average poverty rate in the 1980s and early 1990s until the pressures of reunification raised poverty significantly over the ensuing decade (particularly with the incorporation of eastern Germany, with its higher level of poverty). It remains to be seen if Germany can lessen the relative poverty inherited from reunification. The two countries with the greatest reliance on means-tested programs (Japan and the United States) have higher poverty rates. The poverty rate is considerably higher in the United States than in the other countries.

Why do the countries with more universalist policies tend to have lower relative poverty rates? At least two interrelated explanations are possible. First, social insurance policy advocates would argue that the universalist approach helps to prevent many potentially poor citizens from experiencing prolonged poverty by allowing families at the lower end of the middle-income range to save during good years. In contrast, means-tested policies (especially those involving assets tests) often require citizens to become desperately poor before receiving government assistance. As a result, by the time government help arrives, citizens are in a deeper hole that is harder to escape. Second, as noted earlier, universalist policies are easier to defend politically, which ensures greater policy continuity over time—thereby allowing the policies a better opportunity to succeed.

Understanding Reform Dynamics

One might assume that all countries—because they certainly share a desire to reduce poverty—would move over time toward increasingly greater use of social insurance policies. However, in reviewing the six case studies, one sees the trend line in the 1980s and 1990s moving toward a redefinition rather than an expansion of government activity in social policy. This restructuring is taking place on two different levels: policy instruments and funding levels. First and foremost, there is a visible trend toward greater means-testing in the area of child allowances (see Table 9-1). In 1980 only Japan and the United States had means-tested child allowances. By the mid-1990s the other four countries had stepped up the role of means-testing in pursuing a mixed approach to child allowances. Further, shifts to means-testing and tightening of existing needs standards are on the systemic and institutional agendas of all of these countries. In particular, the shift toward greater work requirements as an eligibility requirement for poverty relief and for unemployment insurance was a well established trend by the early twenty-first century. Second, in all six countries, the policy debate focused heavily on constraining the growth of social policy expenditures. In pensions policy, several of these countries engaged in dramatic reforms. However, in family policy, not all benefits were viewed as costs that hurt the business climate. Quite the contrary, several of these countries—especially Italy, Japan, and the United Kingdom—expanded public spending on child care as an infrastructural investment that was heralded as good for families and good for business. It is no surprise that these three countries experienced the biggest increases in family policy spending per GDP in the early twenty-first century.

As discussed throughout this chapter, reforms aimed at limiting government responsibilities in social policy have taken place amid more generalized debates regarding deficit reduction, tax relief, and labor market reform. This is not mere coincidence. Social policy broadly defined is the largest single category of government spending in industrialized countries. As long as deficit reduction and tax relief remains high on the political agenda, we can expect social policy to be a spending category under the microscope.

How long should one expect the welfare-to-work reform movement to last? The Anglo-American countries have long been skeptical about universalist social policies. For those countries, the contemporary contraction in government intervention in this area is part of an ongoing debate in society and among the major political parties. In the continental European countries, with citizens and major parties historically more supportive of welfare initiatives, this shift represents a novelty. The 1990s marked the first decade since the end of World War II in which government intervention in social policy decreased. In the case studies, French, German, and Italian politicians placed a heavy rhetorical emphasis on the budgetary demands of monetary unification as a rationale for a contraction of the welfare state. In turn, in the 2000s more emphasis was placed on a flexible work environment as a potential tool in the fight against unemployment. Time will tell whether governments will continue to rely heavily on means-testing and employment requirements over the next decade.

SUGGESTED READINGS

Alcock, Peter, and Gary Craig, eds. 2001. *International Social Policy: Welfare Regimes in the Developed World*. Basingstoke, United Kingdom: Palgrave.

Buchs, Milena. 2007. *New Governance in European Social Policy: The Open Method of Coordination*. Basingstoke, England: Palgrave Macmillan.

Clasen, Jochen, ed. 1999. *Comparative Social Policy: Concepts, Theories and Methods*. London: Blackwell.

Clasen, Jochen. 2005. *Reforming European Welfare States: Germany and the United Kingdom Compared*. Oxford: Oxford University Press.

Currie, Janet M. 2006. *The Invisible Safety Net: Protecting the Nation's Poor Children and Families*. Princeton: Princeton University Press.

Esping-Andersen, Gøsta. 1990. *The Three Worlds of Welfare Capitalism*. Cambridge: Polity.

Ferrera, Maurizio, and Elisabetta Gualmini. 2004. *Rescued by Europe?: Social and Labour Market Reforms in Italy from Maastricht to Berlusconi*. Amsterdam: Amsterdam University Press.

Goldberg, Gertrude S., and Marguerite G. Rosenthal, eds. 2002. *Diminishing Welfare: A Cross-national Study of Social Provision*. Westport, Conn: Auburn House.

Haas, Linda, and Steven K. Wisensale, eds. 2006. *Families and Social Policy: National and International Perspectives*. Binghamton, N.Y.: Haworth Press.

Haskins, Ron. 2006. *Work over Welfare: The Inside Story of the 1996 Welfare Reform Law*. Washington, D.C.: Brookings Institution Press.

James, Allison, and Adrian L. James, eds. 2008. *European Childhoods: Cultures, Politics and Childhoods in Europe*. Basingstoke, United Kingdom: Palgrave Macmillan.

Karger, Howard J., and David Stoesz. 2010. *American Social Welfare Policy: A Pluralist Approach*, 6th ed. New York: Allyn & Bacon.

Kasza, Gregory J. 2006. *One World of Welfare: Japan in Comparative Perspective*. Ithaca, N.Y.: Cornell University Press.

Kvist, Jon, and Juho Saari, eds. 2007. *The Europeanisation of Social Protection*. Bristol, U.K.: Policy Press.

Schoppa, Leonard J. 2006. *Race for the Exits: The Unraveling of Japan's System of Social Protection*. Ithaca, N.Y.: Cornell University Press.

Seeleib-Kaiser, Martin, ed. 2008. *Welfare State Transformations: Comparative Perspectives*. Basingstoke, United Kingdom: Palgrave Macmillan.

Smith, Timothy B. 2004. *France in Crisis: Welfare, Inequality, and Globalization Since 1980*. Cambridge: Cambridge University Press.

Taylor-Gooby, Peter, ed. 2004. *New Risks, New Welfare: The Transformation of the European Welfare State*. Oxford: Oxford University Press.

Chapter 10 Education Policy

Since the end of World War II, education expenditures have represented the fastest growing area of public spending. Across all countries in the Organisation for Economic Co-operation and Development (OECD), total funding for educational institutions at all levels rose over the past decade and rose on average by 19 percent between 2000 and 2005 alone (OECD 2008a). By 2005 education spending absorbed on average 6.1 percent of the gross domestic product (GDP) and 13.2 percent of total public expenditures. Education is prominent on national political agendas not only because of its budgetary prominence but also because of its integral role in society. The most basic interests and values of a society are represented in education policy. Often the definition of what constitutes such basic interests and values is a matter of great controversy.

Common Policy Problems

The most striking feature of the education debate today is the nearly universal and perpetual call for national education reform. Better education has become the prescription for creating individual success, social harmony, and international competitiveness. Political leaders often argue that the solutions to their nations' most pressing problems are to be found in the schools or, more specifically, in reformed schools. When citizens feel that their country is faltering in some fundamental respect, they, too, often blame the schools. Dissatisfaction with economic development and progress is increasingly likely to take the form of a backlash against schools and educators.

An important education policy problem concerns the question of **access to schooling**, or whom education is for. A nation's position on this issue is generally considered to be an important indicator of the **equality of opportunity** in a society. The equality of opportunity perspective assumes that school systems can compensate for existing social and economic inequalities in a society. The assumption is that universal access to schooling will serve as a leveler, as opposed to less open education systems that perpetuate existing social or economic divisions. Opponents of this view of education access believe that individuals differ innately in their capabilities and are not equally capable of benefiting from an education. Thus efforts to equalize education access squander resources. Supporters of the latter perspective advocate access to education systems based on achievement, especially in secondary schools and universities. Concerns about whether all students are receiving the same type of education and about the substance of education also involve a debate over **liberal versus vocational education**. This is a debate between an orientation in which education is aimed at reducing social and economic inequalities and a market orientation that emphasizes education to promote global competitiveness.

The definition of education policy objectives has evolved over time and remains an unsettled issue: what should students learn? The list of potential objectives raised in the political debate is almost endless. Possible objectives include basic literacy, critical thinking skills, a well-rounded grounding in many fields of study, building of a shared national history and values, and technical training for a particular career—to name just a few. This problem area frequently raises questions about courses of study, national standards, and national testing or assessment programs.

The issue of who controls the education system is another education policy problem. Different countries create more or less centralized administrative structures. For example, federal political systems such as the United States tend to be more decentralized, delegating responsibility for education to the local level. In contrast, unitary political systems such as France and Japan are traditionally characterized by centralization of education decision-making authority at the national level. In most industrialized countries, the trend in recent years has been toward greater decentralization. Another dimension of the control over education is the issue of **public versus private schooling**. This dimension often involves the question of whether to permit religious schools to exist and of the appropriate allocation of public funds to these schools, where they exist. Nonreligious private schooling also raises concerns over control, in particular through pressures for more parental control and choice relative to local schools.

In considering the most pressing public policy choices encountered in the education arena, we focus on three areas of concern: (1) who will be educated, (2) what will that education entail, and (3) who will control the education system? All three issues are typically controversial, and in most countries a widely accepted view of schooling continues to be elusive.

Major Policy Options

Policies that emphasize equality of opportunity are not the norm in most education systems. Many countries determine access to secondary and post-secondary education by means of competitive exams or other evaluations of an individual's **merit**. Because such mechanisms tend to reward those who were better off prior to entering the system, these policy choices tend to reinforce rather than reduce existing inequalities. For example, European systems, which rely on competitive exams, have traditionally reinforced rather than overcome class distinctions, with only a small percentage of university students coming from the middle and working classes. In systems that have adopted equality of opportunity policies, such as in the United States, the emphasis on promoting equality has declined. In short, although the implication of a universal right to education is access for all, education policies in most countries stress merit over egalitarianism, thereby reinforcing existing inequalities.

The debate over liberal versus vocational education also results in policy controversy. Proponents of liberal, or general, education advocate traditional training of students in the classics as well as reading, writing, and arithmetic to provide for the full development of the individual. Supporters of vocational, or technical, training emphasize the development of useful skills that translate directly into specific occupational opportunities. This latter policy orientation raises questions about which skills are most needed to produce a well-trained, competitive global labor force and who should receive which skills. For example, who will be trained as workers, who as executives? Who will make these decisions? And what will this training entail?

Related to the question of what students should learn, a continuing matter of controversy in education policy concerns the content of the **curriculum**, or the course of study that education institutions offer. Should the curriculum be governed by **equality of provision**? That is, should the curriculum ensure that all students in an education system receive the same type of education, particularly with respect to subject matter? The content of the curriculum is not merely a question of liberal versus vocational education; rather, it involves debates over adopting Western, non-Western, multicultural, feminist, or religious perspectives. Because both economic outcomes and societal values are at stake, curricular reform is the source of considerable controversy. In recent years, pressures to adopt national curricula have increased in most industrialized countries. Adoption of such curricula entails the creation of a national standard for what students should know and be able to do in order to ensure equality of provision throughout the country.

Pressures to adopt a national curriculum often are accompanied by a move to create comprehensive standardized testing systems to assess student achievement and to measure equality of outcomes. Such tests also can be a matter of intense debate. Many critics of standardized tests argue that these exams are biased in favor of advantaged students and that they penalize students from diverse socioeconomic, ethnic, and racial backgrounds. Others question the ability of standardized tests to measure learning at all, particularly when it comes to assessing writing or the ability to reason or argue. Thus calls for curriculum reform are extremely contentious and meet with vehement opposition from educators, who often disagree with new education goals, reject restrictions on their academic freedom, and resent the reduction of education to "teaching to the test."

The locus of education decision-making power has a number of important implications for the nature of education policy. For example, where education funding is decentralized (meaning education funds rely on local revenue-raising capabilities), inequalities in expenditures per pupil are much more likely to occur among a nation's schools. In systems where education is controlled centrally, spending per pupil is likely to be equalized from locality to locality, and from student to student. As a result, increased centralization is a common response to calls for greater equality of provision. Centralization also permits the development of more common curricular goals and facilitates the pursuit of such goals by increasing the state's power over comprehensive policy implementation. Further, centralization of decision making also enables better monitoring of outcomes, particularly in regard to national education goals.

In decentralized systems, education policy is made at all levels of government—national, state, and local—resulting in a less focused policy agenda and greater access to this agenda. These systems exhibit a marked absence of national education policy. Decentralization also translates into somewhat greater potential for effective protest against controversial decisions (for example, textbook or curriculum choices), because the responsible policymakers tend to be more accessible and susceptible to pressure than are remote national politicians. Further, the initiation of policy change and participation in the decision-making process by educators tends to be less difficult in decentralized systems because educators tend to be more autonomous and to have developed their own power and financial resources. Local administration also allows for greater participation by local community members in these processes. Meaningful involvement in education decision making by both educators and citizens is far less likely in centralized systems where change is instituted by national politicians and bureaucrats. For these reasons, many observers believe that decentralized systems are more democratic.

A recent version of the decentralization approach to education reform emphasizes the need for parents to be able to choose among the schools in a system. School choice programs are intended to give parents more control over their children's education. Such programs involve financial assistance for education that is provided directly to individuals, not schools. Parents would be free to spend these funds at the school of their choice. The assumption of such an approach is that by giving parents the ability to take their "business" elsewhere, government would create a more competitive environment among schools and improve education quality overall. Under such a system, each school would presumably focus its efforts on attracting the greatest number of students (and additional funds) by improving the services it provides. The idea of school choice typically includes a variety of approaches: tuition tax credits, privately financed tuition reimbursement programs, an increased number of public charter schools, and tax-funded **vouchers** (Box 10-1).

Striking an appropriate balance between public and private education providers is a difficult and controversial task for political leaders. The desire of some parents to educate their children as they see fit creates conflict with national education policies. Countries differ in their approach to resolving

Box 10-1 **In Depth: The Voucher Movement in the United States**

A recent policy innovation in education is the voucher. This option involves the government issuing parents a voucher, or coupon, representing tax dollars they would use to pay tuition at the school of their choice, public or private (presumably only a partial payment for private schools). The assumption is that such a system increases parents' ability to evaluate and choose the educational styles and curriculum best suited to their children. Such a system, it is argued, relies on competition to improve schools as parents avoid poor quality schools, which then forces public schools to improve to compete with the presumed higher quality of private schools.

Public support for school choice in the United States has grown since the early 1990s. Public opinion polls indicate that a majority of the population favors allowing parents to send their children to the school of their choice (public, private, or religious) with government funding. Support has risen across socioeconomic groups for the general idea of school choice, but especially for vouchers, as those living in economically disadvantaged areas have come to view vouchers as their best chance for improving the educational opportunities available to their children.

Some of those who oppose the use of vouchers claim that their advocates want these vouchers to be available to all income groups, however, not just low-income families. To date, most voucher proposals and programs in the United States involve an income cap, but many opponents claim that the ultimate goal is universal vouchers. Were these to be implemented, the country's educational systems would become even more unequal, opponents claim, because private schools can accommodate only a small percentage of the country's students.

Opponents of the voucher system argue that such a system would reinforce and encourage existing social and economic divisions and would not improve most schools. Instead, dual education systems based on socioeconomic factors would emerge, with private schools improving and public schools worsening. For these reasons, they argue, the use of vouchers would serve the interests of a privileged few and remove their interest in the overall quality of public education. Those opposed to such a system further maintain that it reduces the diversity of experiences that public schools provide by serving students with different backgrounds.

this conflict. Some countries, such as the United States, allow religious schools to exist but deny government funding to these institutions. This approach usually results in a marked inequality in the provision of education in that private religious schools are less well equipped (or are better equipped but at tremendous cost to parents).

The public versus private schooling issue also encompasses nonreligious private schools. These institutions are most controversial in countries where private school students enjoy a distinct advantage over public school students, especially in university admissions or in seeking employment, thereby allowing the wealthy to maintain their privileged status. The controversy tends to surround the right of these institutions to exist and may be manifested in abolition campaigns. Such campaigns usually maintain that those who can afford to do so should not be allowed to purchase a better education at private schools. Controversy in this policy area intensifies to the degree that successful private schools highlight the deficiencies of public schools. That is, where the quality of public schools is poor, people are more likely to resent private institutions.

Explaining Policy Dynamics

The study of the education policy-making process is often described as being more descriptive than theoretical. Scholars tend to describe the processes surrounding education reform in the industrialized countries (particularly beyond the United States) rather than place their studies within some wider or explicitly theoretical framework. Although the atheoretical nature of this field has changed somewhat in recent years, our understanding of policy processes in this area is often based on descriptive case studies, primarily focusing on the United States and the other Anglo-American countries.

Cultural Explanations

Cultural factors are commonly used to explain education policy reform. Researchers note the importance of public attitudes both for setting the reform agenda and for policy outputs. More specifically, contemporary movements for reform are argued to have emerged from widespread public perceptions that education systems had lowered their standards and were failing to prepare students to function in a more competitive economic environment (Ambler 1987). These attitudes resulted in reforms that stressed a return to basic education; emphasized discipline and effort; and focused on training students to serve more internationalized, high-technology, knowledge-based economic systems.

Another cultural explanation for contemporary reform involves the prevailing ideology in a country. Researchers note a shift in values in industrialized countries relative to education. From the 1930s to 1980, education policy in many countries focused on equity and social justice, whereas since the early 1980s education policy has stressed freedom and excellence. This value shift is argued to reflect the resurgence of classic liberal ideology—favoring deregulation, decentralization, and varying degrees of privatization (Eliason 1996; Lauglo 1996). This return to a liberal ideology results in education reforms that stress economic efficiency, choice, and market mechanisms (Iannacone 1988). More specifically, this ideological shift is apparent in the move from an emphasis on equality and access to education to an emphasis on education excellence, selectivity, and choice (Boyd 1996; Boyd and Kerchner 1987). In the Anglo-American countries, resurgent liberalism in the 1980s and early 1990s led reform advocates to argue that schools should be subject to regulation by market forces rather than by the government—and thus be forced to respond to parental demands (Ambler 1987; Chubb and Moe 1990). These reform advocates argued that school choice would achieve three goals: higher average academic achievement, lower costs, and greater equality of opportunity.

Cultural perspectives also point to the importance of culturally based education traditions in defining a country's approach to reform. This literature stresses the importance of deeply imbued cultural attitudes about the most desirable kinds of knowledge, the best ways of transmitting it, and the means for deciding who will benefit from education. These values are shared across cultures and influence education policy decisions. Thus the emphasis on individualism and equality of opportunity that characterizes Anglo-American countries, as opposed to the more collectivist and social equality cultural norms found in France or Germany, have significant implications for questions about education access, content, and control (Fowler, Boyd, and Plank 1993; Fusarelli 2003; McLean 1988, 1995; Rust and Blakemore 1990). In the United States, for example, important cultural values include an emphasis on freedom, quality, efficiency, and equity, with education policy outputs reflecting, at least in part, the country's positions on these values at the time (Marshall, Mitchell, and Wirt 1989). Conversely, in Japan, the cultural importance of group identity, uniformity, hierarchy, and centralization results in very different policy outputs (Wray 1999).

Economic Explanations

Many researchers argue that education reforms can be explained by concerns about globalization and increasing international economic competition. Reform efforts are viewed as having been stimulated in part by worries about more intense global competition and the need to develop a better educated workforce to enable countries to compete effectively and enhance their global economic position (Boyd 1996; Boyd and Kerchner 1987; Wirt and Hartman 1986). As industrialized countries increasingly are defined by interdependent, postindustrial, and knowledge-based economic systems, their demands for more effective schooling escalate. In this context, existing approaches to education are viewed as slow, outdated, and incapable of producing necessary improvements in student preparation. These perceptions result in pressures on the government to design and implement centrally controlled standards and accountability schemes for their school systems (Boyd and Kerchner 1987; Cibulka 1996; Coombs 1985; Eliason 1996; Ginsburg et. al. 1990; McLean 1995; Wirt and Hartman 1986).

Political Explanations

The partisanship thesis introduced in Chapter 2 can be important for understanding education reform, particularly when examining cross-national differences in education spending. As expected, left-wing governing parties are more likely to favor and achieve increased government spending on education. However, as Ambler (1987) notes, although changes in partisan control may affect education spending levels, the inherent complexity and relative autonomy of education institutions create particularly strong resistance to other types of education reforms. He argues that sometimes, even when a party that comes to power is intent on major reform (such as the Conservatives under Thatcher in the United Kingdom or the Socialists under Mitterrand in France), the nature of the education system itself (its size, complexity, and tendency toward bureaucratic inertia) may interfere with that party's capacity to achieve its goals.

A multitude of scholars, examining the full range of industrialized countries, point to the influence of highly mobilized, powerful, and entrenched interests in affecting education reforms. In all countries, interest groups (especially teachers' unions but also parents associations, education administrators, business groups, and religious groups) place limits on the ability of governments to initiate and implement widespread education reforms. In pluralist systems, interest group activities are seen as a prime driver of education decision making, but such movements also are argued to play a strong role under more corporatist arrangements. In the education policy area, interest groups are frequently argued to be strong enough to override the distinction between unitary and federal political systems regarding the access they provide such groups. Even in unitary political systems, groups representing the various sectors of the education establishment have been highly successful in shaping reforms (Ambler 1987; Cibulka 2001; Elmore 1997; Fusarelli 2003; Kogan 1971; McLean 1988; Rust and Blakemore 1990; Spring 1998).

Institutional Explanations

Institutional approaches to understanding education policy reform focus on the degree of centralization of political authority. In most policy areas, centralization of decision-making authority is regarded as being advantageous for reform. In examining education reforms, however, researchers take issue with the centralization thesis. They note that centralization is most effective in policy areas in which power is centralized in the hands of relatively few individuals. In education policy, this is usually not the case, even in more centralized political systems. The size and complexity of education systems—as well as their relative autonomy—is the problem here (Ambler 1987). Education systems may create a powerful set of vested interests. For example, in France (a highly centralized country), successful education reforms require broad support in public opinion as a means of getting the system moving because of the strength and inertia of the education establishment. Such public support is necessary to put pressure on teachers and their unions to accept change. In the absence of such public support, the education establishment often is able to block or delay new policies proposed by government, with centralization giving government no great advantage (Duclaud-Williams 1988). Along these same lines, however, decentralized systems are argued to fare no better in enacting education reforms because of the multiple points at which these same opponents of reform can block change.

International Policy Making

When it comes to education policy, little in the way of international policy making exists. Education policy is a domain in which countries are very protective of their national sovereignty and in which a high degree of policy flexibility and independence is maintained. There are no major international agreements that establish norms or practices for education. Beyond national sovereignty issues, the lack of international cooperation on these matters may also reflect the fact that in many countries education policy making is highly decentralized. Lower levels of government often are reluctant enough to surrender authority over education policy to their own central governments. As a result, it is even more difficult to envision them transferring their decision-making powers to some still further removed external body.

Education is a policy area in which the European Union (EU) has exercised considerable restraint. This is true regarding its present policy position and its plans for the future. Under the Maastricht Treaty, the EU's education mandate is to play a supporting role to the member states. The treaty does not authorize the union to issue directives or regulations pertaining to education that are legally binding on members. Instead, the EU's role is to encourage cooperation by member states on education issues and to supplement and support their education efforts. Beyond these activities, we currently find no other major international education policies at work.

United States

Background: Policy Process and Policy History

The United States, with its multiple centers of decision-making power, has no comprehensive national education policy. Specific education goals and spending levels vary across both states and localities. Because the financing of education at the local level usually is based on property taxes, funding differs markedly across school districts. Typically students who live in more affluent districts attend better quality schools than do children living in poorer areas. To address this inequality, states and the federal government have created policies aimed at equalizing education provision across districts. The most recent policy innovations in this regard require states and localities to comply with federal education mandates to receive federal education funds. In this sense, U.S. policies are becoming somewhat more similar to the centralized approach common in other industrialized countries.

Constitutionally, education is a state responsibility, although most states have delegated authority to operate and finance schools to local education authorities, or school districts. The federal government plays a limited role in the governance of education but provides funding to states and school districts, mostly to support programs for students with special educational needs. The government also provides financial aid to students in the form of scholarships and loans to support their participation in postsecondary education. State and local school districts provide the vast majority of funds for public elementary and secondary education. Because no state has taken responsibility for financing public schools, nor do any seem likely to do so, the tradition of local autonomy is likely to live on.

This diffusion of jurisdiction has fostered a profusion of uncoordinated policies. The United States has over 15,000 school districts (governed through school boards by more than 95,000 citizens), and in recent years a shift to greater federal and state regulation of local districts has been made in order to create greater equality and effectiveness. The United States is unique with respect to the number of issues and responsibilities that these local school boards confront: everything from budgets to maintenance to the curriculum. These boards are burdened with many responsibilities that in other countries are dispersed among many levels of government and bureaucrats. Local school boards also tend to be highly politicized.

The issue of school choice has been on the political agenda in the United States since the 1980s, first in the form of an unsuccessful effort to create a national system of vouchers (although some states and localities have introduced the use of vouchers) and then with charter school plans that many states have adopted. Charter school laws create independent public schools that are largely free from government control but are held accountable for education results agreed upon in each school's charter.

The United States has traditionally endorsed the view that all citizens have a right to an education. This belief reflects the notion that a key element of effective democracy is an educated citizenry. Thus education is regarded as important not only for the improvement and success of the individual but also for molding democratic citizens. Reflecting this emphasis, the U.S. education system expanded during the twentieth century, and the average level of education attainment rose.

Compulsory education begins at age six or seven in the majority of states, but most children enter kindergarten in a public elementary school at age five. Compulsory schooling ends at age sixteen in over half the states, but a large majority of young adults (73 percent in 1990–1996) continue their education and receive regular high school diplomas at age seventeen or eighteen. Full-time primary schooling begins at age six and ends at age twelve or thirteen. Students then enter middle school (grades 6–8) or junior high school (grades 7–9) and then proceed to secondary school for grades 9–12 (or 10–12). This pathway results in a single-track system. Secondary schools in the United States provide a choice between general, college preparatory, or vocational tracks (the latter do not provide comprehensive vocational training of the sort found in Germany, however). About two-thirds of students enroll in the college preparatory and general tracks, and just under one-third enroll in the vocational track.

The United States does not have a national curriculum or curriculum framework, although since 2001 states have developed curriculum frameworks and performance standards to meet the requirements of the federal No Child Left Behind Act (2002). Specification of the curriculum and selection of textbooks are usually delegated by the states to local school districts. Also in line with No Child Left Behind, since 2001 states have mandated statewide testing programs to assess individual student performance against state-established performance standards (these standards must be approved by the U.S. Department of Education). Across the country, students are tested annually in grades three to eight in reading and math, and all students are tested at least once per level (elementary, middle, and high school) in science.

Recent efforts at education reform have placed increasing emphasis on the provision of vocational alternatives at the secondary level. One area of controversy with respect to vocational education has concerned the type of training that should be provided. For example, should students be trained for one specific job, should they be provided with more general skills that can later be refined through on-the-job training, or should they receive a comprehensive education combined with specific job skills? Because this question generally remains unanswered, the United States has advanced in the provision of vocational education far less than have the other industrialized countries.

Contemporary Dynamics

Education policies in the United States have been undergoing continuous reform since the early 1980s. Two reform trends have influenced U.S. education systems: the imposition of uniform standards and a push for greater accountability. Reforms in the United States are based on an assumption that academic achievement will be improved by establishing rigorous education standards, uniform curricula, and assessment tests. The goal of such reforms is better quality, not greater equity. Early criticisms of the U.S. education system emerged from within the business community; these criticisms in turn tapped into growing public concerns about the deteriorating quality of public schools.

Concerns about education related to international competitiveness date back to 1983 with the publication of a federal commission's report, *A Nation at Risk*. The report claimed that the United States was losing its ability to compete in an increasingly competitive global marketplace. This was blamed on an education system that had failed to do its job, as evidenced by almost two decades of decline in student achievement levels. *A Nation at Risk* launched what is commonly referred to as the excellence movement, which argued that the United States had to intensify its education approach to increase rigor, raise graduation standards for students and teachers, and reemphasize the importance of education overall. The business community and public opinion quickly galvanized around the report's findings, and education reform became situated firmly on the country's institutional agenda, where it has remained to the present day. In a clear example of the outside initiation agenda-setting model, reaction to this report almost single-handedly placed education reform on the institutional agenda for nearly three decades.

Despite the prominent position of education reform on the institutional agenda in the 1980s and 1990s, comprehensive reform proved difficult to achieve. The Reagan administration initially responded to this agenda by devolving a great deal of education decision-making authority to states and reducing the federal government's role overall. Beyond this, the administration did not develop any comprehensive response to calls for change. After a protracted and highly partisan debate, President George H. W. Bush's America 2000 plan failed to win congressional approval—in a classic example of the effects of divided government and the policy gridlock it can produce. President Clinton's Goals 2000 plan was enacted by Congress in 1994, again after intense debate, but failed to achieve all of its intended results in the implementation stage, where powerful education interest groups failed to support the reforms and actively worked to obstruct these new policies.

By the time President George W. Bush arrived in office in 2001, education issues still figured prominently on the institutional agenda. Comprehensive reform had not yet been fully achieved, despite the continuing national uproar surrounding the poor state of American education, which was seen as both expensive and ineffective. In response, and following through on a campaign pledge, President Bush introduced his education reform plans three days after his inauguration in 2001. The centerpiece of his standards, teaching, and accountability plan is known as No Child Left Behind (NCLB). The primary goal of NCLB was for all students to be "proficient" in reading, mathematics, and science by the 2013–2014 academic year. Under the legislation, federal financial support to schools would be tied to students' progress on annual standardized tests. Since 2005 NCLB requires testing for students in grades 3 through 8 every year in reading and math. Since 2008, science testing also is mandatory at least once per level of schooling (elementary, middle, and high school). In addition, each year, a sample of fourth- and eighth-grade students from each state must participate in the National Assessment of Educational Progress program in reading and math. The law also requires states and school systems to develop standards for what students should know and be able to do. Finally, NCLB mandates that teachers be "highly qualified" for their positions. Based on their testing results, schools face penalties if they fail to meet the established standards (or, at a minimum, make "adequate yearly progress" [AYP] toward these standards). If schools fail to improve after four years, their principals can be fired. Under NCLB, schools must provide parents with annual reports. The policy also intends for parents to be given the chance to move their children from poor quality schools or to receive funds to pay for tutors.

The No Child Left Behind Act was signed into law in 2002 after a year of debate and compromise. When it was approved, the law was considered to be the most sweeping federal legislation in the country's history. Remarkably, given that political conflict is inevitable in large-scale education reform in the United States, the NCLB bill was embraced on both sides of the aisle and by key education policy stakeholders. This legislation constitutes one of the rare instances of collaboration between Democratic congressional leaders and the Bush White House. There was general bipartisan agreement about the overall aim of the legislation—ensuring the education of every child. In addition, consensus was encouraged by the president, who quickly dropped private school vouchers from the reform in the face of Democratic objections, rather than digging in on the issue, which was important to many Republicans. National standards and increasing accountability, the bill's core values, were embraced not just by Republicans but also by many Democrats. During debate on the bill, teachers, administrators, and the public also endorsed the principles on which NCLB was based, especially the idea that it was designed to help correct the imbalance between wealthier and poorer school districts.

The widespread embrace of NCLB did not last for long, however. Since its implementation in 2002, NCLB has been the source of tremendous controversy. As implementation of the plan proceeded, state resistance mounted and politicians from both parties have become increasingly unhappy with the law. Many states were dissatisfied with insufficient levels of federal funding and the law's strict timetables for raising student achievement. By 2004, bills challenging the law had been introduced in thirty-one state legislatures. These bills primarily reflected states' unhappiness over being forced to implement the law "on the cheap." The states were not off-base with this perception; Congress appropriated $27 billion less than it authorized for the bill's implementation, leaving states with unaffordable, unfunded NCLB mandates. The National Education Association, the country's largest teachers' union, and eight school districts in three states sued the Department of Education on the grounds that forcing states to fund the law's implementation themselves violates a provision of NCLB. The state of Connecticut also threatened to sue on this basis.

As implementation proceeded, the law also came under fire from local school officials, who viewed the law's implementation as too focused on standardized testing, resulting in too much classroom time being devoted to "teaching to the test." The law was due for reauthorization in 2007, but the highly charged controversy that its implementation generated made lawmakers skittish in the approach to an election year and the review was postponed. Most lawmakers and educators agree that NCLB has big problems that need to be fixed, although some evidence, such as higher test scores, indicates a shrinking performance gap between rich and poor students and improved urban schools, which suggests that some aspects of the law have worked. The law's reauthorization will be the first education reform project for the Obama administration.

Comprehensive education reform in the United States, both the decision to engage in reform and the nature of the reform itself, resulted from a set of interrelated factors. For twenty years, fears about the country losing its ability to compete in the global marketplace drove public attitudes on education reform. These concerns were echoed by the business community, which sought to shape education systems to meet its employment needs. The perception that U.S. students did not measure up to their peers in other industrialized countries—and that this shortcoming was detrimental to the country's future economic strength—was sufficient to drive large-scale reform. In addition, the ease with which this legislation passed was a remarkable exception to the typical pattern of executive-legislative relations in the United States. In this instance, we observed the effects of a rare consensus between Democratic leaders in Congress and a Republican president in the White House. This consensus reflected, at least in part, the legacy of failed education reform efforts over the previous two decades. By 2001 there was widespread agreement that the time had come to make comprehensive education reform a reality. At the implementation stage, this bipartisan consensus broke down, however, and the president's signature domestic policy achievement ran into a host of difficulties that have set the stage for yet another overhaul of U.S. education policies in the near future.

Japan

Background: Policy Process and Policy History

The national government administers education in Japan through the Ministry of Education, Culture, Sports, Science and Technology (known as the Ministry of Education or MEXT). The Ministry of Education creates guidelines for the curriculum and courses, and approves textbooks. National government education expenditures include direct expenditures for national education activities (for example, operating national universities and schools); specific subsidies for the education activities of other institutions (that is, prefectures, municipalities, private schools, and research organizations); and local allocation of a tax grant, part of which is for education. Boards of education exist at the prefectural and municipal levels. Prefectural boards administer schools (upper secondary and special education) established by the prefectures, whereas municipal boards administer mainly elementary and lower secondary schools established by the local authorities.

A commitment to the widespread provision of education in Japan can be traced to the nineteenth century. A Fundamental Code of Education was promulgated in 1872 that established literacy as a national goal. After World War II, the Japanese education system was reorganized in line with the U.S. model. Until 1987 the plan for Japan's education system was laid out in the 1947 Fundamental Law on Education. This system experienced reform for the first time in the late 1980s and early 1990s. Subsequent reforms were enacted in 2004.

The primary education policy objective in Japan is declared to be the provision of equal access to a high quality of education to all students in the country, regardless of where they live. Compulsory education is from ages six to fifteen, with upper secondary schools serving those aged fifteen to eighteen. Nearly 97 percent of students graduating from lower secondary schools go on to upper secondary schools (which are not compulsory). Japan has a single-track school system comparable to that found in the United States.

Upper secondary schools admit entrants based on a selection process that considers student credentials, scholastic test records, and other factors. This selection process determines the distribution of students among upper secondary schools, not access to education, which is universal. For university admissions, however, students take a standard commercially developed test as well as tests administered by each university. University admissions are based almost exclusively on performance on these entrance exams; this system has produced what is widely viewed as an excessively competitive examination process.

About 25 percent of students go on to universities and 30 percent to other forms of postsecondary education. In principle a student may apply to any university from any upper secondary school, but in practice a strong link exists between the status of the upper secondary school attended and university admissions. In seeking admission to a particular university, Japanese students are more likely to have based their choice on the placement and status of an institution's graduates than on the quality of its education program. Reflecting these conditions, efforts have been developed to reduce the single criterion of a standard exam score in career guidance, and schools have been encouraged to diversify their selection criteria.

The national government sets curriculum standards for elementary, lower secondary, and upper secondary schools. The Ministry of Education has issued a document called the Course of Study, which defines Japan's general education standards for curricula, textbooks, and entrance exams. These standards provide the basic framework for curricula including the aims of each subject and school activity, the content of teaching at each grade level, and the basis for teacher training. Curriculum revisions were enacted from 1992 to 1994 that emphasized independent learning activities and students thinking for themselves rather than the traditional one-dimensional transmission of knowledge and skills from teacher to student. More recent (and controversial) reforms, in 2007, list "public spirit" and an "attitude of loving the nation" as important education goals. The reforms are designed to imbue students with a better sense of the nation's history and culture. Each school is left to organize its curriculum as it sees fit to reflect these guidelines and to take into account the conditions of the community and the school as well as the characteristics and development levels of its pupils.

Student performance in meeting the objectives of the national curriculum is assessed by individual teachers on a case-by-case basis rather than through national examinations. At the secondary level, studies have traditionally been focused on academic subjects; an extensive vocational education program does not exist. In postsecondary education, technical and junior colleges provide technical and vocational education.

Contemporary Dynamics

As in the United States, Japan is concerned about international competitiveness and education reform. Since the mid-1980s many Japanese have been critical of the country's education system for failing to create the sort of workers that employers need in an increasingly competitive global marketplace. More specifically, the public became concerned that the system was failing to encourage creativity and individualism and that this had serious ramifications for the abilities of Japan's future workforce. Unlike most of the countries examined in this book, however, Japan was unsuccessful in moving its education system in dramatically new directions in the 1980s and 1990s. In particular, little movement had been made away from a highly centralized system of control. Rather, small-scale reforms ushered in during the 1990s focused on changing the internal aspects of education, such as reducing the stress of the competitive exams or changing the manner in which teachers were trained. By the late 1990s, public dissatisfaction with the education system was such that substantial reform seemingly became inevitable. Higher education was the first sector to be tackled, reflecting strong public sentiment that universities were failing to adequately prepare students in multiple ways.

In 1999 then–prime minister Junichiro Koizumi initiated higher education reform in earnest, requesting that the MEXT present him with a reform plan. In a marked break from the traditional hallmarks of Japan's educational system, the prime minister's request made clear his interest in the possibility of privatizing the country's public university system. The policy development process was distinguished by a protracted period of bureaucratic infighting between MEXT and METI (the Ministry for Economy, Trade and Industry) and their supporting interest groups. METI was a powerful advocate for economic liberalization in the country overall and strongly encouraged higher education reforms that were oriented toward the demands of industry and greater institutional autonomy. MEXT was reluctant initially to move in METI's preferred direction lest it undermine its own substantial power over the education system. In addition, a move toward privatization constituted a dramatic cultural shift in the Japanese approach to education. In the past, reform efforts that stressed individualism, competition, or autonomy were rejected by the ministry because they contradicted accepted cultural norms. However, MEXT eventually conceded to the prime minister and METI's preferences, recognizing that the momentum for a liberalizing reform of the system—both within the government and among the general public—was too powerful to overcome or resist. Determined to gain the upper hand in the reform process, the ministry presented an even more market-oriented reform proposal than had been advocated by METI or the prime minister. Although its proposal made dramatic concessions in the area of university autonomy, the plan also was constructed to ensure that MEXT retained considerable power over the university system by maintaining indirect control via bureaucratic guidance.

Thus a series of cabinet-level decisions from April 1999 to November 2002 culminated in the 2003 National University Corporation Law and five related laws, all of which easily received parliamentary approval. In April 2004 all public universities were converted to National University Corporations (NUCs), in the most dramatic reform to the Japanese education system since the late nineteenth century. Under the law, universities were granted administrative independence to foster competition and to allow them to develop partnerships with industry. The reforms made major changes to universities' missions, budgetary systems, patterns of governance, and their relationship with the central government, while maintaining a role for MEXT in planning and decision making.

Education reform in Japan is a policy area in which change comes as a result of bureaucratic consultation and decision making rather than through legislative debate or law making. Thus the policy formulation and decision-making stages of education reform occurred not in the Diet but in a bureaucratic and cabinet-level consultation process. Based on a mandate from the prime minister, the Ministry of Education pursued reform through administrative guidance, which eliminates opportunities for debate, opposition, or the exertion of external influence. This is a process of incremental change within existing frameworks that leaves little space for opposition. Because policy change occurred and continues to occur through administrative rather than legislative action, few implementation concerns surround education reforms.

The drive for education reform in Japan can be explained largely by economic factors. Although the Japanese economy was strong in the 1980s, the Japanese became increasingly concerned that their education system was not training students adequately to be creative and innovative—two qualities recognized as essential to future economic success. The 2004 reform of Japan's universities, in particular the acceptance of movement toward greater privatization and liberalization, is a notable change from earlier attempts at reform. Traditionally, the Japanese education system does not emphasize individuality, competition, and freedom, reflecting the traditional Japanese value system. Consequently, previous reform efforts that have stressed individualism, choice, and school autonomy were rejected because they contradicted accepted cultural norms. By early in the twenty-first century, however, ongoing and intensifying concerns about the country's global economic competitiveness proved more influential than traditional values, and a major reform of the higher education system was accomplished.

Germany

Background: Policy Process and Policy History

The control of education in Germany reflects the country's federal structure. According to Article 7 of the Basic Law, the entire school system is under the control of the state governments, but this responsibility in practice is shared by federal and state governments. In each state, schools are usually maintained by either municipalities or the state, whereas higher education institutions are state-level institutions. Education legislation and its administration is developed and adopted largely by the states. States and municipalities carry over 90 percent of education expenditures. Each of the sixteen state governments enjoys full control over the organization and structure of its education system. Since 1971 the states have been legally bound to maintain comparable basic structures in their school systems, and a Standing Conference of the Ministers of Education and Cultural Affairs meets regularly to provide for greater harmonization of policies across school systems.

The German education system traditionally was seen by many as the envy of the world. It was distinguished by the high quality of its graduates and the considerable attention paid to vocational education at the secondary and post-secondary levels. As a result, citizen dissatisfaction and subsequent calls for education reform historically have not been as strong in Germany as in many of the other countries we are considering. However, German policymakers have addressed questions of reform in recent years, particularly with respect to higher education, although not on the scale observed in some other countries.

German education structures involve a multi-track system offering general, technical, and vocational options. Full-time education is compulsory between the ages of six and fifteen or sixteen (depending on the state). Part-time education is compulsory until the age of eighteen for students who do not choose to pursue upper secondary education full time. Part-time education takes place in vocational schools in a dual system that combines practical on-the-job training with in-school theoretical instruction. Secondary school students receive one of three qualifications: a lower secondary school qualification after eight or nine years of schooling (with or without vocational training), an intermediate school qualification after ten years (vocational or nonvocational), or an upper secondary qualification after twelve or thirteen years. Students who leave school with lower or intermediate secondary qualifications are likely to enter vocational training in the dual system or serve a two- to three-year apprenticeship.

Higher education in Germany consists of either professional colleges or universities, entrance to which requires an upper secondary school qualification. A reform process is under way in this sector in an effort to improve institutional efficiency and address problems of insufficient space. An identified problem in higher education is the length of time it takes students to complete their education, which averages around seven years. Insufficient space has forced the government to introduce admissions restrictions in some subject areas. Until recently, tuition was free at public institutions; some states now impose tuition fees in their higher education institutions.

State ministries of education develop their curricula to reflect guidelines developed at the national level. To ensure some degree of uniformity in curricula and standards across states, a standardization process has been developed. The Standing Conference of the Ministers of Education and Cultural Affairs oversees state education systems to ensure a baseline of provision across the states while respecting state autonomy. The process of incorporating the five new eastern states has raised some concern over whether such a balance will be sustained in the future or whether the federal government will have to intervene to ensure the maintenance of such standards.

Reflecting a decentralized education system, Germany does not use national testing or large-scale assessments of students. In particular, state governments are resistant to any movement toward cross-state comparisons. The German government monitors the performance of the education system by paying strict attention to teacher training, establishing compulsory curricula for all sixteen states for all subjects and areas of study in all types of schools, and ensuring that textbooks comply fully with the curriculum.

Among the industrialized countries, Germany has one of the most well-developed and extensive systems of vocational schools. A clear goal of the government is that no young person should begin his or her working life without some form of vocational training. Currently, about 1.6 million students are receiving some form of vocational training, and vocational schools are required for all young people under age eighteen who attend no other type of school. This training is a joint effort between private business and industry and the public sector. In addition, at the postsecondary level, two- to three-and-a-half-year internships are available that provide a paid training allowance that increases for each year of service. More than 500,000 German firms participate in the apprenticeship program.

Contemporary Dynamics

Until recently, the generally strong state of the German education system meant that education reform was not a perennial political battle in this country. Overall, quality and efficiency were not education concerns. However, like the other countries examined here, concerns about globalization, the workforce, and especially mounting financial pressures placed notions of competition, autonomy, and efficiency on the education reform agenda. This was particularly true in the higher education sector. Unlike other aspects of the education system, higher education has been subject to reform attempts over the past several decades. By the late 1980s, common complaints about the higher education system included too-long periods of study (some lasting as long as ten years), overflowing lecture halls, too little contact between teachers and students and between researchers and industry, and a lack of comparability between German and international qualifications. In June 1995 Foreign Minister Klaus Kinkel called for reform of higher education based on his feeling that such reforms were needed to make Germany more competitive in foreign trade. The result was the 1998 Framework Law on Higher Education (which amended the 1976 Framework Act). This law aimed at improving performance, giving universities greater autonomy, and making them more competitive at the international level. Following this law, states were required to reform their higher education policies. The reforms led to many changes, but the financial pressures on higher education continued to be significant. Thus, despite the recent reforms, demands continued for further government action, particularly from students, but also from within the German business community and among some conservative politicians. Perhaps more important, there now were calls from university heads, as well as conservative-controlled state governments, for the government to introduce student fees to increase university revenues.

The question of tuition fees was a controversial one: opponents feared them as a first step in releasing the state from its obligation to fund higher education (or, at a minimum, increasing the likelihood of significant reductions in state support) and as unfairly limiting access to higher education only to those who could afford it. More generally, opponents did not believe that the government should be in the business of "selling" education to students. Advocates for tuition fees believed such fees would make universities more competitive and encourage students to complete their degrees more quickly. They also argued that fees represented the only feasible way to finance an ever-expanding higher education system in the future. University rectors favored tuition fees as a last resort to solve the ongoing and worsening fiscal crisis in higher education. On the right wing of the political spectrum, both the Christian Democratic Union (CDU) and the Free Democratic Party were fee supporters. On the left, the Social Democratic Party (SPD) and the Green Party were committed to the principle of government-supported higher education and opposed tuition fees, arguing in particular that they would be prohibitive for many students and, as such, economically discriminatory. Not surprisingly, students of all political stripes were generally opposed to the introduction of fees, as were most academics.

In a reflection of partisan differences on the issue (and in the lead-up to a general election), the Social Democratic–Green Party governing coalition in 2002 passed a law in the Bundestag guaranteeing students' rights to complete their first university degree program free of charge. The introduction and passage of this education reform was somewhat unusual for Germany, where education policies are not usually introduced at the federal level because states are constitutionally individually responsible for their own education systems. The 2002 law (the sixth amendment to the 1976 Framework Act) prohibited all German states from charging fees to students who were taking more than the usual length of time to complete their degrees. The law was directed toward states like Baden-Württemberg, which had begun charging undergraduates who had been pursuing their degree for more than six years $550 a semester in 1998. All the states that charged fees before the 2002 ban were controlled by Christian Democratic or conservative-dominated governments. In introducing the ban, Gerhard Schröder's government argued that these fees violated the principle of equal opportunity for all Germans, regardless of their socioeconomic status. But, in the lead-up to a general election, this also was a tactical move by the SPD, since their CDU rivals were staunch fee supporters. The Social Democrats believed the fee ban would be a vote-winner, since most Germans viewed free education as a fundamental right.

The government's majority control of the Bundestag made the law's passage easily achieved. Its enactment, however, created considerable unrest at the state level. Although the law acknowledged that exceptions could be made to the jurisdiction of individual states, six states (all controlled by the opposition parties) immediately challenged the measure in the Federal Constitutional Court, arguing that it violated states' self-rule in educational and cultural matters and that it was an unconstitutional interference into the states' higher education budgetary autonomy. The Federal Court ruled, in January 2005, that the law was unconstitutional on the grounds that it violated the constitutional rights of German states to regulate higher education. The Court's decision dismissed all legal obstacles to the introduction of fees at universities across Germany. Further, although before 2005 states could charge fees only to students who significantly exceeded their regular study time, after the Court decision this principle no longer applied. Immediately following the ruling, several states announced the introduction of tuition fees (notably, states governed by the SPD continued to shun fees). In most states, the introductory fees were capped at 500 euros per semester, although the amount varied across states.

The implementation of fees across the country (now for all students, not just those taking an unusually long time to complete their studies) was met by widespread and angry student protests. Those opposed to the reforms embraced the mantra "Education is no commodity." To students, the tuition fees constituted an assault on their fundamental rights. They occupied Berlin's city hall, staged tuition boycotts, and sued in court to have the tuition requirement removed. Professors (who are not permitted to strike) staged lectures in busy public spaces to draw attention to the issue. Although students' dissatisfaction with the fees remains apparent, the policy has since 2005 safely enjoyed the protection of Angela Merkel's CDU-controlled government.

The 2002 reform attempt illustrates the difficulty the German government faces in introducing education legislation at the central level. Even when the governing coalition controls a strong majority at the center, the constitutional authority accorded to the states in the education realm makes nationwide educational policy making nearly impossible. Intensive debate continues perennially between the federal government and the states about the nature of reform. What little is decided upon by the central government is often diluted by the states, which are protective of their powers in educational matters. In this instance, federalism, as well as the disparate educational perspectives of the main political parties, made it impossible for the central government to impose reform on the education system as whole. Reform ultimately occurred by 2005, but in the exact opposite direction from what the SPD-controlled government intended. The states' powers to check the federal government's plans—either through voting in the Bundesrat or, in this case, via the Constitutional Court—give them the upper hand in determining the direction of policy.

The German government's decision to place higher education reform on the institutional agenda reflected the influence of economic factors. Problems in higher education had been pointed out by German students and others for many years; however, the government did not respond until concerns became based on arguments about the country's loss of international economic competitiveness. Once the German economy faltered in the early 1990s, concerns that the country was losing its competitive edge became widespread; at the same time, universities came under increasing budgetary pressure. The government's response was not comprehensive; instead, it constituted a political power-play, and the federal nature of the German political system determined the eventual path of this reform effort. Finally, partisan differences played an important role—the federal government was controlled by the SPD, which opposed fees, whereas the states that challenged the law were controlled by Christian Democrats. In the end, reform happened, but not the reform the SPD-controlled federal government had in mind when it initiated the policy reform process in 2002.

France

Background: Policy Process and Policy History

In 1985 the French government began the process of transferring some education decision-making powers to regional administrations and decentralizing education responsibilities to elected local authorities. Each level of government was made responsible for a tier of education: communes for nursery and primary school management, departments for maintenance and construction of lower secondary schools, and regions for upper secondary schools and for education planning. Secondary schools and universities were made more independent, although postsecondary education continues to be largely centrally controlled.

Despite such changes, however, a good deal in the French education system remains under the domain of the national government, including teacher recruitment and pay, the framing and implementation of general education policy, the national curriculum and the national exam, and the right to confer university diplomas. National government also continues to fund two-thirds of total expenditures on education. By the late 1980s education expenditures made up the largest part of the national budget.

The French education system has been public, uniform, compulsory, and centralized since the late nineteenth century. Education in France continues to be widely considered the foremost national priority, both to impart knowledge and to transmit a sense of national identity. Education also is seen as a democratic right and is viewed as an important mechanism for creating equality of opportunity.

Among the industrialized countries, France has one of the highest levels of education activity: French students spend longer in school (an average of 18.9 years) and are more likely to go on to higher education. Education in France is compulsory for ages six to sixteen and is divided into primary, secondary, and upper secondary levels. General, vocational, and technological education is provided at the secondary level. Higher education is open to all holders of secondary degrees (the *baccalaureat*).

The 1989 Education Act makes a clear commitment to creating equality of education opportunities, with an emphasis on equal access and outcomes. The French education system was expanded substantially in the 1980s in an endeavor to ensure that 80 percent of eligible students would complete upper secondary level education and obtain the *baccalaureat*. As a result of this expansion, in the 1990s approximately 70 percent of eligible students entered upper secondary education, twice as many as in 1980. This increase has also resulted in a significant increase in higher education enrollments—2.1 million enrolled in universities in 1996, compared with just over 1 million in 1980.

Under the 1989 Education Act, new standards for the country's common curriculum were adopted. This curriculum, set at the national level, defines both subject matter and the number of hours to be devoted to each subject; it may not be modified at the regional level. At the secondary level, students are offered some optional courses, such as a foreign language, but must also complete the national curriculum.

France has a national assessment procedure. The Ministry of Education examines students on a regular basis to note their level of achievement. National assessment tests are given at the third year of elementary education, the end of lower secondary education, and the beginning of upper secondary education. Assessment is also achieved through monitoring of students' progress through the education system and their learning skills and social behavior in school.

The French education system has increasingly moved to some form of secondary level vocational education (from a system traditionally focused exclusively on academics). Recent education reforms resulted in the extension of the *baccalaureat* to cover a wide range of vocational options in addition to the traditional general and technical subjects. France also offers an apprenticeship program for students over age sixteen, in which they learn a trade partly in employment under an apprenticeship trainer and partly in education institutions. Nearly all students who do not go on to university enter some form of vocational training.

Contemporary Dynamics

During the 2007 presidential campaign, the right-wing Union for a Popular Movement (UPM) candidate Nicolas Sarkozy regularly emphasized an urgent need to reform France's higher education system. Early in that campaign, Sarkozy argued that it was time for France to address such controversial issues as university admissions criteria, tuition fees, and institutional autonomy. Failure to do so, he argued, would prevent French universities from competing on the global stage, and universities would continue to fall short of meeting France's economic needs and, in particular, its workforce demands. As the election neared, Sarkozy maintained his focus on higher education reform but pulled back from some of his earlier, more controversial positions (for example, support for tuition fees) and concentrated on what he thought would be less divisive issues, such as university governance and autonomy. At the time, France's centralized, state-centered, bureaucratic model was mirrored in its university system: all universities were public, all professors were civil servants, admissions were completely open, and the system was entirely publicly funded. In 2007 these institutions also were generally regarded as failures—no French university was found in the world's top forty, more than half of students dropped out after their first year, large numbers of those who continued after one year failed to earn a degree, and many of those who did graduate found themselves unprepared for the workforce. Hence, Sarkozy's claim that university reform was urgently needed seemed valid.

Upon taking office, and following through on his election pledges, Sarkozy declared higher education reform to be an "absolute priority" for his government's first year. The first major piece of legislation the prime minister, François Fillon, introduced to the parliament was on higher education. The proposed reform was designed to grant universities autonomy in spending, staffing decisions, and facilities management. As introduced, the proposal was bold and far reaching for a policy sector infamously opposed to change and very effective at obstructing reform.

The difficulties associated with enacting education reforms in France became apparent immediately after the reform's unveiling. The government was well aware of the typical response to the sort of reforms it was proposing: vociferous student and teachers' union resistance, usually leading to reform failure. The proposed legislation quickly drew intense criticism from student groups, teachers' unions, and the opposition parties. Soon after the bill's introduction, the main student organization in the country threatened to unleash large-scale protests. As those opposed to the reforms were mustering their forces, President Sarkozy took an unusual approach to the reform process: he personally conducted negotiations with student unions, and as a result, several provisions of the draft law were amended or deleted entirely. The government clearly intended to avoid the pitfalls of past education reforms by trying to garner the support of key stakeholders through compromise and concessions before the law was approved.

Opposition to the bill focused on three issues. First, students were concerned that a proposal to allow universities to choose whether to operate more autonomously would create a two-tier higher education system. After extended parliamentary debate, the plan to introduce an autonomy option was delayed for five years. Second, the government planned to reduce the size of university governing boards from between thirty and sixty members to twenty. This reduction would have dramatically altered existing decision-making arrangements among students, academics, staff, and unions. In addition, outside groups, such as regional authorities and businesses, were to be included on the boards and given more influence, reflecting the president's intention to forge closer links among universities, the economy, and business. In talks with the president, a compromise of thirty members was reached (with increased student representation) that largely maintained the proportional influence of the various stakeholder groups. Third, students strongly objected to a provision to introduce admissions criteria for entry to master's-level programs. The first draft of the bill proposed to allow universities to select their master's students at the entry to the degree program, rather than between the first and second years of schooling, which was the standing practice. This provision was dropped from the bill entirely after the student unions met with the president.

The Law on the Autonomy and Responsibilities of Universities was enacted in August 2007, in part because even the most ardent opponents of the new law recognized that the country's higher education system was in dire need of reform. The law passed with solid majority support in the National Assembly on a vote of 165 to 46, with only the opposition Socialist, Green, and Communist parties voting against it. The final law achieved far more than earlier reform attempts, although its final version was noticeably less comprehensive than the government had intended. Not only did the Sarkozy government succeed in passing reform in a notoriously difficult policy sector, but it did so based on consensus among educators and students regarding the urgent need for the sort of reform the bill proposed. In this instance, the policy-making process proceeded quite differently than in the past. The government actively sought to negotiate and then make concessions before the law was voted on. The more traditional practice would have involved ignoring opposition during the parliamentary stage and then making concessions, or backing down entirely, at the implementation stage.

Even so, implementation of the 2007 law was not trouble-free. Reflecting the government's earlier concessions—and unusual for France in the aftermath of passage of a major education reform—large public demonstrations were *not* held following the bill's adoption. This was a notable achievement for the Sarkozy government. However, by April 2009 regular, albeit small, protests against the reform were commonplace. University professors objected to a range of new rules, such as requirements for regular performance reviews and the transfer of new powers to university presidents to hire, promote, and manage staff. Although the reforms did not involve tuition fees or admissions standards, students remain suspicious of any hint of competition or privatization of the universities, such as their new capacity to engage in private fund-raising. Despite the concessions they received from the government when the law was being debated, these student groups remain wary of change. A number of trade unions and parent-teacher organizations, led by the university lecturers union, view the law as an attack on the basic right to education. The Socialist Party shared this view of the law when it was introduced and remains opposed to it. Nonetheless, implementation of the law has proceeded despite this general sense of uneasiness among key stakeholders.

The policy reform process in this instance clearly reveals the important role a unified governing party can play in enacting widespread reform. Strong leadership at the top, combined with a unified and disciplined parliamentary party at the time of this decision, enabled the government to successfully pursue a major reform in one of the country's most intractable policy areas. In the past, significant divisions within the governing coalitions meant that reform could not succeed. In addition, the president clearly learned from past experience: previous reforms failed because interest groups were able to block reforms they opposed, often first within the legislature and then on the streets. He attempted to forestall both stages of interest group activity by meeting and negotiating with key stakeholders—a strategy that was by and large successful. Finally, the success of this reform effort demonstrates the importance of political support within the parliamentary majority, key stakeholders, and the electorate at large. In the end, all were convinced that the time had come to engage in reform.

United Kingdom

Background: Policy Process and Policy History

The principle of decentralization is an important dimension of British education policy. More specifically, power has been decentralized in that individual local schools have been given more authority, and it has been centralized in that this reform has taken place within a framework of national evaluation and curriculum control. Both Margaret Thatcher's and John Major's governments supported a process of moving education authority from producers (that is, teachers and administrators) to consumers (parents and students).

Power in certain areas of education policy also is centralized through a mandatory national curriculum for core subjects and a set of nationally administered and determined tests. The national Department for Children, Schools and Families and the Department for Innovation, Universities and Skills establish and administer the statutory framework of the education system and establish national education policy, working with other central and local government bodies. The public sector predominates in British education (with attendance by over 90 percent of children), although the diversity of providers is growing. About 7 percent of children attend a variety of tuition-charging independent schools (or public schools). Independent schools are funded privately and are permitted to opt out of the national curriculum, although many conform to at least some of its guidelines. Since 1998 there have been four types of maintained schools: community schools (local authority controls the school), voluntary aided schools (almost always church schools with local authority control), voluntary controlled schools (fully in the hands of charitable organizations), and foundation schools. Foundation schools have been the focus of the Labour government: these are controlled by a governing body that employs the staff and makes admission decisions. The school land and buildings are owned by the governing body or by a charitable foundation. The foundation appoints a minority of governors. In 2005 the Labour government proposed allowing all schools to become foundation schools if they wished. The bulk of resources for education is generated at the central level, but expenditures generally take place at the local government level through local education authorities.

Education in the United Kingdom is compulsory from age five to age sixteen. The leaving age for compulsory education was raised to eighteen by the Education and Skills Act of 2008. The change will take effect in 2013 for seventeen-year-olds and in 2015 for eighteen-year-olds. In most localities, a two-tier system of primary and secondary schools operates, but some areas have a three-tier system of first, middle, and upper or high schools. Although the majority of schools are comprehensive, some areas also have grammar and secondary modern schools that cater specifically to children in the higher and lower ability ranges, respectively. Secondary schools specializing in particular subjects areas, such as technology or languages, have developed as well.

At the end of compulsory schooling, students may either enter a one- to two-year course of study in what is known as the sixth form of a school, or study at one of more than 450 further education colleges. These institutions offer three types of certificates: in education (A levels), broad-based vocational qualifications, or job-specific vocational qualifications in one- to two-year programs. Nearly one-third of students then go on to higher education.

All compulsory-age students in government-run (maintained) schools follow a national curriculum that is at the heart of a drive to improve standards and to provide a minimum entitlement for students. The curriculum involves twelve subjects, the core of which are mathematics, science, and English. The curriculum was established under the 1988 Education Reform Act and was revised and scaled back in January 1995 in response to complaints that it was far too comprehensive and consequently unmanageable. The curriculum began changing again after 2000. The biggest modification—requiring citizenship as a foundation subject in secondary schools—was enacted in September 2002.

Formal assessment of students with national testing begins at age seven and is followed up at ages eleven and fourteen. These assessment points correspond to the end of key stages in the national curriculum. At ages sixteen and eighteen, several public examinations (the General Certificate of Secondary Education and the A levels) are the main assessment instruments. The government also planned to introduce nationwide baseline assessment and testing for five-year-olds in 1997. The introduction of such tests has been highly contentious, with the tests criticized for a lack of integrity and their hurried introduction. The government has since reviewed and modified the testing process, although the policy of nationwide tests has not been abandoned.

Vocational education has yet to be addressed in a comprehensive manner in the United Kingdom. The country offers no vocational alternative to the academic course at the secondary level. Government education policy also plans for all sixteen- and seventeen-year-olds not in full-time education to be in training or in a job, preferably with training. A system of youth credits gives all sixteen- and seventeen-year-old dropouts access to a Modern Apprenticeships and Youth Training program. Limited attention has been paid to making vocational courses available to students who choose not to pursue academic courses after age sixteen, but this is not yet a systematic effort.

Contemporary Dynamics

As elsewhere, the drive for education reform in the United Kingdom in the 1980s and early 1990s began with a sense that the education system was failing to prepare students for new economic challenges. Education policy reform arrived on the institutional agenda in the United Kingdom as a result of pressures similar to those observed in the other industrialized countries. In particular, the move to reform reflected a belief that the education system was not up to challenges presented by increasing international economic competition. Such competition from abroad generated a belief that increased education system effectiveness needed to be achieved through an emphasis on standards and performance. Efficiency, competition, performance, and quality became important reform keywords.

In 1997 the Labour Party campaigned under the leadership of Tony Blair on an education platform—"education, education, education" was the party's central campaign motto. The education theme continued to play a prominent role in the party's 2001 and 2005 general election campaigns. From the outset, the Blair government pursued an aggressive education policy reform agenda that emphasized choice, competition, autonomy, and efficiency. The earliest

Blair education reforms were targeted at primary level schooling, with far less activity at the secondary and tertiary levels. The Blair government inherited a higher education system confronted by a number of serious challenges—decreasing public funding, increasing student numbers, rising costs, and growing pressure to respond to the demands of a competitive global economy. Although higher education reform had been on the institutional agenda in the United Kingdom since the mid-1990s, the Blair government did not turn its full attention to higher education reform until its second term, in 2001.

The number of students enrolled in British universities began to increase in the late 1980s—doubling between 1987 and 1997—without a commensurate increase in the level of funding. This situation contributed to a growing sense that the country was faced with a higher education crisis. In response, in 1996 the Conservative-controlled government formed a Commission of Inquiry charged with making recommendations about higher education's role, organization, and funding into the twenty-first century. To address the funding crisis, the commission recommended that university students be responsible for a portion of the cost of their education, when they could afford to do so. The prospect of changing the system of cost-free education generated considerable debate within the Labour Party, traditionally the party most strongly in favor of free public education at all levels. Reflecting the divisions within the party over this issue, and despite serious objections in some quarters, the Blair government in 1997 opted to move only a small portion of the costs of university education to students via an up-front tuition fee (of around 1,100 pounds).

Amidst great controversy, the Blair government's position on fees began to change during its second term. The small up-front fees introduced in 1997 had proven insufficient to address the crisis presented by rising higher education costs and insufficient funding, and, as a result, the government moved further in the direction of full-blown tuition fees. In 2004 the government introduced to parliament a higher education bill. Consistent with a 2003 white paper on higher education, but in direct contradiction to the party's 2001 election manifesto and then–education minister David Blunkett's 2001 pledge that there would be no levying of university fees in the next parliament, the bill's main provision was the introduction of variable tuition fees of up to 3,000 pounds beginning in 2006. To generate additional revenues, the new fees would provide each university with some freedom to price their own courses as they saw fit, based on what they thought the market would bear. At the time, the cost of higher education was the same at all British universities, regardless of quality. Under provisions of the new bill, some universities would charge more than others, but no more than the 3,000 pound cap. Reflecting his belief that market policies could and should be applied to the higher education sector in the interest of promoting greater efficiency, competition, and autonomy, Blair argued that the price of degrees should vary across universities according to their cost and their value to the student. The introduction of fees was to be accompanied by a system of deferred student loans (no student would be required to pay fees up front) and means-tested grants.

The parliamentary approval process for the bill involved the greatest controversy the Blair government had faced thus far and constituted a real challenge to the government's authority. There was intense opposition to the bill within the parliamentary Labour Party. Upon the bill's introduction, nearly 160 Labour members of Parliament signed a Commons motion opposing the bill. The motion was partly a reflection of these members' strong opposition to tuition fees in principle, but it also was a reaction to the prime minister's position on the Iraq war, which made the fees vote potentially a referendum on Blair's leadership. Labour members of Parliament were unhappy with fees for a variety of reasons. Some members fundamentally opposed any sort of fee and favored increasing taxes to fund education; others argued that having to accrue debt to attend university would scare off poor students; others accepted the idea of fees but did not like the variability aspect, fearing the eventual creation of an education marketplace. Across these groups, many Labour members of Parliament resented being asked to vote for a policy that had been ruled out explicitly in the party manifesto, and members sitting in marginal seats feared electoral retribution from Labour voters most affected by the fees. Overall, for many Labour members of Parliament, the idea of tuition fees deeply contradicted fundamental party principles.

In the face of this dissension in the party, the prime minister described the legislation as "a very major flagship reform" from which "there will be absolutely no retreat." He added, "of course my authority is on the line." He did not, however, back down from his commitment to the bill, confident, as ever, in his ability to persuade his party to stand by him at the bill's final vote. Public opinion polls showed that large majorities of the population were opposed to the fees. The Conservative and Liberal Democratic parties also were opposed. The Tories thought the funding crisis could be resolved by simply cutting student numbers, whereas the Liberal Democrats advocated levying higher taxes on the rich.

The bill passed through its second reading in the Commons by just five votes (the overall Labour majority was 161 seats). Opponents continued to work against the measure through its final reading in March 2004. After intensive lobbying of Labour members of Parliament by the education minister, Charles Clarke, and Labour whips, the bill passed with only a slight margin—just twenty-eight votes. In the end, the vote was not a referendum on Blair's leadership. Some members realized that voting against Blair would make the party appear incapable of governing, and others decided they did not want to remove him from office. Thus the prime minister survived the biggest backbench rebellion of his government, and his funding reform bill became law as the Higher Education Act of 2004. Despite high levels of dissatisfaction among students about the new charges, implementation of the law proceeded without any impediments.

The Blair government's achievement in enacting variable tuition fees was significant. Although passage of the law was more difficult than one would typically anticipate in this majority-party system, in the face of considerable parliamentary party opposition, the government ultimately was able to secure enough votes to enact a major change in higher education policy. The nature of the reform itself is significant because (1) it was a first step away from a fully publicly funded higher education system, and (2) for the first time it introduced the possibility of competition between institutions. As such, it created the possibility that future governments will give universities even more autonomy and move the higher education sector closer to market mechanisms. As we have observed elsewhere, the principles of autonomy, efficiency, and competition played a significant role in shaping the content of higher education reform in the United Kingdom.

Italy

Background: Policy Process and Policy History

The Italian government's central Ministry of Education, University and Research supervises and coordinates all education activities carried out in the country by public and private institutions. The ministry governs curriculum and syllabus changes and administers budgetary activities and school staffing decisions. Regional governments oversee school building and maintenance, the management of vocational education, the provision of training, specialization and teacher requalification, and counseling and guidance services. Provinces provide equipment, services, and nonteaching staff to schools; and local councils manage services necessary for running schools in their own areas. Education is funded primarily at the central level (90.5 percent of education expenditures). The remainder is covered by regions, provinces, and municipalities.

This pattern reflects the traditional Italian view that education should be controlled and financed by national government. Since the early 1990s, however, the issue of control has been debated. There has been a strong movement for local autonomy and increased input in running schools by those most involved in education—parents, students, and teachers. Although most Italians still want education to be funded at the central level, a more clearly defined and rigorous curriculum is desired, and many Italians believe that this goal can be achieved only through more local control. This perceived need for a more open and participatory structure has been the subject of tremendous debate, yet nothing has been resolved. Italy may eventually move to a greater, but not complete, level of autonomy in which the central government funds education and sets standards for and monitors outcomes, while local schools adapt national mandates to local needs and take advantage of local resources.

Education in Italy is compulsory for all children aged six to sixteen. Compulsory education is divided into primary and lower secondary schools, with

98 percent of the relevant age groups enrolled. More than 80 percent of students continue their education for four to five additional years in a variety of secondary school types: general education, elementary teachers' training schools, technical education with different specializations, vocational education for various working activities fields, or fine arts institutes and schools. Nearly three-fourths of secondary school graduates go on to some form of postsecondary education, either in vocational programs or some form of university. Graduates of general education and five-year vocational schools are qualified for university entrance.

Italian students are given the option of enrolling in any Italian school, even in a district in which they do not live or pay property taxes. To inform students' and parents' choices, individual schools are asked to make available information about their education programs. The issue of vouchers recently made it onto the education policy agenda in Italy, with some supporters advocating their use for Catholic and private schools. Not surprisingly, the Catholic schools and other private schools have been especially strong advocates of vouchers, rather than Italian parents more generally, given that Italian students already have the option of choosing to attend any public school.

The Italian government supports a common national curriculum in the interests of promoting Italian culture and providing education equity for all students. The national minister of education enacts national curricular programs approved by the parliament and gives approval for experimental curricula in selected schools. An elementary school curriculum implemented in 1990 emphasized new teaching methods, more disciplinary-based teaching, and the teaching of a foreign language from grade 3 onward. The middle school curriculum has been in place since 1979.

National examinations are administered in Italy at the lower secondary level, where students are tested in all subjects. Students passing the examinations receive a certificate that is required for admission to the upper secondary level. There also are national periodical assessments for lower secondary programs, but schools are not required to administer these tests. These assessments are of limited utility, however, because performance feedback to schools is minimal, although the results of examinations are made public.

Important reforms were made in technical and vocational education in Italy in the 1990s. Significant reform has been made in the technical institutes to prepare young people adequately for future employment. Post-diploma courses were introduced for higher professional qualifications, and vocational institutes also underwent curriculum reform. In the last two years of the five-year vocational course, some teaching hours are now devoted to job-training activities under the responsibility of the regions. This reform is intended to result in a broader basic education that is followed by vocational training. In addition, a diploma in all languages of the EU was created for students who successfully complete a three-year course after compulsory schooling, to increase their job mobility.

Contemporary Dynamics

Among the six countries examined in this book, Italy has spent the least amount of time engaged in education reform in the contemporary era. By the late 1990s, only two landmark education reforms had been enacted in Italy, the 1859 Casati law, which created the existing education system, and a major reform undertaken in 1923, the Gentile reform. Other important but smaller reforms have been undertaken since then, such as the introduction of a single middle school curriculum in 1962 and the opening of higher education to universal access in 1969. Although calls for more substantial reforms were issued regularly, consensus about how to approach such reforms was lacking to such a large degree that most Italians talked about the impossibility of reform when it came to education matters. Thus the basic shape of the education system in Italy remained largely unchanged throughout most of the twentieth century. This lack of change should not be taken as an indication of widespread satisfaction, however. On the contrary, Italians have increasingly recognized that their students perform at lower levels than students in other industrialized countries. As a result, since the 1980s pressure has continued to mount for the government to initiate reforms to raise the skill levels of students about to enter the workforce. These concerns were strongly related to concerns about Italy's ability to increase its economic competitiveness both within the EU and internationally.

By the end of the last century, the absence of comprehensive education reform had become especially problematic in higher education. Over a thirty-year period (1965–1995), Italian universities experienced a fourfold increase in the size of their student populations. This tremendous growth was not accompanied by any meaningful change in the structure of the university system, nor by funding increases. Although multiple higher education reform laws had been proposed since 1960s, none made it to a final vote in the parliament. These reform failures were partly a byproduct of persistent government instability but also reflected the presence of a mobilized and effective academic community that wields considerable political clout and is perennially opposed to change. By the late 1990s, the Italian higher education system was perceived to be in desperate need of reform. Among the long-standing problems confronting Italian universities were rigid ministerial control over curricula, financing, and degrees and the common view that institutions were inefficient and ineffective. These perceptions were supported by many objective indicators: at the end of the last century, Italy ranked near the top of industrialized countries in dropout rates and near the bottom in employment rates for graduates.

In 1999 Romano Prodi's center-left government formed an ad hoc group of academics (known as Gruppo Martinotti, after the director, Guido Martinotti) to discuss guidelines for higher education reform. University rectors and other academics were asked to directly inform the drafting of higher education reform legislation. The reform process was given added momentum and definition by the Bologna Process initiatives that recently had been drafted at the European level. The government seized on the Bologna Process as one impetus for higher education reform and also as a source for guidance in framing the content of the reform. This collaborative and inclusive approach at the policy development stage, combined with a widely shared view that the higher education system was in urgent need of reform, allowed the Prodi government to quickly propose and pass comprehensive education reform in the legislature without extensive debate. This was a marked break from patterns of education policy making in Italy. The approved laws were intended to reduce dropout rates, to reduce the average duration of university study, to improve the employability conditions for university degree holders, and to make graduates competitive in both domestic and global labor markets. The laws were implemented through a series of ministerial decrees that went into effect in the 2000–2001 academic year.

The speed and ease with which the law was passed, as well as the absence of a full public vetting of the proposed law, may explain, at least in part, the controversy that emerged during the implementation phase of the reform decrees. Supporters (namely, business and academic leaders who had been involved in the early phase of the reform process) argued that the new policies would lead the Italian system toward European standards, in particular with respect to efficiency. They also were keenly aware of the need for modernization and fully supported the reform's implementation. However, the majority of Italian academics below the administrative level (who had not been included in the reform process) strongly resisted the new reforms. In the main, they objected to moving toward what they viewed as the Anglo-Saxon model for organizing teaching and curriculum that was suggested by the Bologna Process. In their view, such a model would reduce the overall quality of Italian degrees. In addition, for many, a degree program designed largely to improve students' employability signaled the cultural decline of the Italian university system. Despite their strong objections, Italian academics were not powerful enough as a group to stop the reform in the implementation stage. In the end, implementation of the reform was accomplished because of the government's early consultation with university rectors on the content of the reform. The leadership of the academic community was persuaded that the university system had to change, and they were comfortable with the reform and especially with the education minister, who was a former rector himself. In this instance, all the conditions were in place for this reform to be accepted widely and implemented quickly.

In Italy the movement for education policy reform was driven by concerns about global competition and demands for a more flexible and highly skilled workforce and by a belief that students were less well educated than in the past. Additional pressures came from European-level imperatives. By including members of the education establishment in the policy formulation process, and by incorporating their criticisms and concerns into the policy proposal, the Italian government hoped to avoid much of the opposition from strong education interest groups that traditionally hindered the adoption and implementation of reforms. In the past, needed reforms failed to advance in Italy because consensus about how to approach reform was consistently lacking. In this instance, the government established a consensus among educational leaders about reform in the early phase of the policy process. This proved to be an effective strategy not only for passing the reform legislation but also for implementing it.

European Union

Background: Policy Process and Policy History

EU member states have traditionally viewed education policy as an area reserved for national decision makers. This orientation continues into the contemporary period. Primary responsibility for education policy remains with the members states in both the Treaty on European Union and in the draft Constitutional Treaty. As such, the European Commission's Directorate-General for Education and Culture has a limited legal basis and few financial resources. The Commission has sought greater harmonization in this policy area, but its efforts have been resisted.

This resistance notwithstanding, the Commission has steadily extended its reach in education policy over the past fifty years. Although education policy is not a clearly defined EU competency, a set of emerging political objectives can be identified that guide the EU's activities with respect to higher education in particular that constitute a genuine EU policy framework in this sector. Although this framework complements rather than competes with national policies, in recent years the EU has had a substantial impact on national higher education policy making. No similar initiatives have been undertaken with respect to other educational levels.

Early on, the EU focused its educational activities on vocational training and defining professional qualifications. Its initiatives in this area were accepted because they were deemed necessary to facilitate the free movement of workers for the common internal market. In 1987 the EU introduced the ERASMUS student mobility initiative, which expanded the EU's influence over higher education with respect to university networking and credit transfers. The ERASMUS scholarship program has supported well over a million European students studying outside their European home countries. More recently, two European-level policy developments, the Lisbon Strategy and the Bologna Process, have had a more noticeable influence on higher education policy reform within the member states. Although neither policy initiative provides a mandate for EU action in higher education, both have allowed the Commission to assert itself in national higher education policy arenas with considerable success. Today, in most member states, national higher education policies increasingly conform to the standards laid out in these plans. The

Bologna Process in particular has initiated profound changes in higher education systems across Europe and beyond, with the net result being marked uniformity across systems, as if an EU mandate had existed. These reforms have been initiated by national governments, but most of the policies proposed clearly reflect the Bologna standards. In effect, an EU education policy framework does exist.

Since 2000 the European Commission has developed its higher education policy portfolio beyond Bologna and Lisbon and has noticeably increased its European higher education profile. This is particularly true in the area of research, where the Commission has pushed for a European Research Council, advocated strongly for greater emphasis on research on a European scale, and sought to provide financial support for research endeavors. All told, we observe an increasingly central role for the European Commission's policy statements on education in shaping the higher education discourse across member states. In many countries, political leaders have found the EU's objectives for higher education to be a useful impetus and framework for reforms.

Contemporary Dynamics

In 1999 nothing resembling a European common market in education existed. Across European countries, degree programs were incompatible, credits did not transfer easily, and student mobility in both education and labor markets was constrained. In addition, dropout rates were high, and many students took longer than average time to complete their studies. Further, across European countries there were serious concerns about the declining quality of higher education relative to the rest of the world.

The 1999 Bologna Process is a Europe-wide commitment to restructuring European higher education systems that emerged in response to these concerns. The Bologna Process is officially nothing more than a declaration of shared higher education goals. It is not EU law, and it does not involve formally binding obligations. The name derives from the June 1999 meeting in Bologna, Italy, at which the higher education ministers of thirty-nine European countries met to declare their intention to construct a "European Higher Education Area" by 2010 that would resemble a common market. This area would be characterized by "greater compatibility and comparability of the systems of higher education." The ministers hoped to see the implementation of a common higher education structure across the agreement's signatory countries. The primary objective of the Bologna Process is to increase the effectiveness and efficiency of undergraduate and postgraduate university teaching. To this end, Bologna calls for curricular harmonization, as well as convergence in the structure and length of study for university degrees. These changes, it was believed, would result in more efficient higher education institutions, lowered dropout rates, and increased mobility for students and researchers.

Policy making at the Bologna meetings was intergovernmental, but this agreement did not result in a treaty or binding EU law. Bologna is notable as a European initiative because it extends beyond EU countries; as such, the agreement was clearly outside formal EU policy-making processes, although the European Commission played an important role at the Bologna meetings. Although the Bologna Process is not official EU policy and did not evolve via normal EU policy-making channels, it is considered here as EU policy because its impact on higher educational systems across the EU has been notable.

Although European political leaders welcomed the Bologna Process as an impetus for higher education reforms that had been stalled for decades, students across Europe have been unhappy with the changes it has encouraged in their countries' higher education systems. In France and Italy, for example, student protesters decried the adoption of an Anglo-Saxon educational model. In these countries and others, many students and professors also objected to, in their view, Bologna's emphasis on education for employability, rather than learning for learning's sake.

Although often the source of great controversy in European countries, implementation of the Bologna Process turned out to be more successful than would probably have been anticipated in 1999. The Process's reform agenda has been implemented in a decentralized manner, with each signatory country proceeding as it sees fit at the national level. However, its implementation has been closely monitored and advanced since 1999 by European-level reports, conferences, and communications, which were formally structured around biennial meetings of ministers financed by the European Commission. These meetings function as a system of monitored cooperation, involving regular reporting, troubleshooting, and developing follow-up mechanisms. This regular, formal interaction between the signatory states has produced a sense of obligation among them and maintained their commitment to the process. Despite fierce resistance in some quarters, by 2007 nearly three-quarters of Bologna Process participants had over 60 percent of students enrolled in courses of study compatible with the new degree structure recommended at Bologna.

As of 2009, forty-six European countries had committed to the Bologna Process—twenty-seven from the EU and nineteen other countries, including Russia and Turkey. Representatives of these countries met in Leuven in April 2009 to declare the Bologna Process a success. With few exceptions, higher education systems do constitute a "European Higher Education Area," and universities across Europe now adhere to a European credit transfer system, standardized diploma supplements that detail what students have learned, and a common degree structure. One of the major achievements of Bologna is the structure of curriculum. Most European higher education systems have abandoned their traditional degree structures, where students earned a degree in four or five years, to a three-year bachelor's and two-year master's degree curriculum. In short, despite the nonharmonizing, nonregulating, intergovernmental nature of the Bologna Process, it became the most powerful force for change in higher education public policy across Europe. Today, nearly all European countries are playing the Bologna Process game.

Cross-national Trends

In reviewing the broader cross-national trends in these six countries, we consider here the choices these countries have made with respect to education provision and how well their education systems have performed in terms of access to education and student achievement. All six countries have engaged to varying degrees in education policy reforms in recent years, with a pattern of mixed results regarding students' access to education and their education achievements.

Policy Outputs

Among the industrialized countries examined in this book, most have been engaged in an ongoing process of education reform since the 1990s or earlier. Cross-national variation exists in the degree of interest in changing the control, administration, financing, and evaluation of education systems, but generally all countries have addressed at least some, if not all, of these issues. These countries have made a variety of choices, ranging from creating more centralized control systems to ones that are highly decentralized to a mixture of the two, and from systems based on loose education standard frameworks to rigid systems of national curriculum control. In most countries, the reform process also has included a focus on evaluating and creating education standards and improving assessment tools to respond to the public's demand for greater education accountability and productivity.

In these countries, education reforms have been directed toward some or all of the following: improving quality and efficiency, monitoring students' progress more comprehensively and systematically, closing the gap between standards and actual learning, and, for some countries, improving vocational training and managing the transition from work to school. Included in their reforms in the 1990s have been curriculum revisions, standardized and centralized testing, and new approaches to school governance, with an increased emphasis on market-based mechanisms. The most comprehensive reforms have been undertaken in the United Kingdom and the United States (through the introduction of new policy instruments in nearly all these areas). The other four countries have tinkered with various aspects of education provision but avoided dramatic, wholesale change.

Another area of policy outputs involves education spending in these six countries. In all areas of education, the United States spends more than

Table 10-1 Expenditures per Student in Public and Private Institutions, 2005

Country	Annual Expenditure per Student (in equivalent U.S. dollars)		
	Primary Education	*Secondary Education*	*Tertiary Education*
France	$5,365	$8,927	$10,995
Germany	5,014	7,636	12,446
Italy	6,835	7,648	8,026
Japan	6,744	7,908	12,326
United Kingdom	6,361	7,167	13,506
United States	9,156	10,390	24,370

SOURCE: Center for Educational Research and Innovation (2008).

Table 10-2 Educational Expenditures as a Percentage of Gross Domestic Product (GDP)

Country	Direct Public Expenditure for Educational Institutions (percentage of GDP)		
	1995	2000	2005
France	6.6%	6.4%	6.0%
Germany	5.4	5.1	5.1
Italy	4.8	4.8	4.7
Japan	5.0	5.1	4.9
United Kingdom	5.2	5.0	6.2
United States	6.6	7.0	7.1

SOURCE: Center for Educational Research and Innovation (2008).

most other industrialized countries. At the primary and secondary levels, U.S. expenditures per pupil are among the highest of the OECD countries. As Table 10-1 indicates, the United States outspent the other five countries at both public and private primary and secondary levels per pupil in 2005, especially for primary education. At all levels, the United States spent more than the other five countries. If we consider government education expenditures as a percentage of GDP (Table 10-2), the United States also spends more than all the other countries. By 2005, OECD countries were spending 6.1 percent of their collective GDP on education at all levels (Center for Educational Research and Innovation 2008: 2). Overall, the United States spent a higher percentage of GDP on education than the other five countries (National Center for Education Statistics 2009: vi). From 2000 to 2005, public spending on education rose in the United States and the United Kingdom, decreased in France, and remained stable in Germany, Italy, and Japan (Center for Educational Research and Innovation 2008: 13). Notably, though, from 1995 to 2005, public expenditure on education as a proportion of all public spending grew in all countries except France. In these countries, spending on education rose at least as fast as public spending in other sectors.

Policy Outcomes

How do countries compare with respect to education outcomes? If one were to assume that higher spending translates automatically into better quality education, then one would expect the quality of U.S. education to be especially high. On the issue of access to education, the United States is performing fairly well. Enrollment in primary education in the United States in 2006 was at the median level for high-income economies; enrollment in the United States is basically universal, as it is in most industrialized countries. Enrollment in upper secondary education is now the norm in the industrialized countries examined in this book. In Japan and Germany, over 90 percent of students were enrolled in and graduated from upper secondary education in 2006. The figures for the United States in 2006 were slightly below the OECD average due to higher dropout rates.

In higher education, the United States' emphasis on access has shown the most tangible results: enrollment rates in the United States were about twice the median level found in other industrialized countries (Center for Educational Research and Innovation 2008: 217). Although higher education is also accessible to increasing numbers of people in all industrialized countries, considerable variations in participation rates are observed from country to country. The greater use of postsecondary education in the United States stems from an emphasis on general education at the secondary level. The one-track system used in the United States leads to higher enrollments in postsecondary education in two ways. First, more U.S. students meet the entrance requirements to go to universities and colleges. Second, because high schools have fewer vocational programs, students who want a vocational degree or certificate often pursue that training at the postsecondary level. Italy again performs poorly relative to the other countries in higher education participation.

Although the United States has done well in providing access to education, the performance of the system (as measured by student scores on achievement tests) has been decidedly mixed. The 2006 Progress in International Reading Literacy Study, which measures reading levels in students' fourth year of formal study, found reading literacy in the United States unchanged from 2001 but above the international average. The United States ranked fourteenth among the forty countries studied, behind Italy and Germany, but ahead of Italy and France (Japan does not participate in this study). In science and mathematics, students from the United States have not fared well in cross-national studies. In a variety of studies from the 1970s through the early 2000s, the average U.S. student performed at or, more often, considerably below the median for other industrialized countries. Also, in most studies, the top U.S. students did not perform in math and science as well as the best students in other countries. The 2007 Trends in International Math and Science Study (TIMSS) showed some improvement for U.S. students since 1995 for math scores (to above the TIMSS average) but no movement in science (still below the average). Of the countries considered in this book, Japanese students placed highest in both math and science. Significantly, students with the best exam performances were from countries that tended to have education systems based on mandatory national curricula and testing.

Cross-national comparisons suggest that increased spending on education is not a foolproof solution to improving education outcomes. Money can help, but it is not a cure-all. The United States, like other countries, finds itself pressed to engage in education reform in an environment characterized by declining resources, rising expectations, and limited consensus. In all countries, such factors are simultaneously incentives for and barriers to meaningful reform.

Understanding Policy Reform

Reflecting on the case studies, we see that these industrialized countries have come to recognize that they no longer can maintain their global economic status through mass production because low labor costs in late-industrializing countries allow them to engage in mass production for a fraction of the cost in industrialized countries. Thus, for these richer industrialized countries, the primary remaining economic niche is found in employment sectors that require highly skilled, well-educated workers. In large part, recognition of this economic situation initially pushed the movement for education reform in these countries. This recognition especially fueled the return to the basics, and the increased emphasis on curriculum content and accountability. These reform efforts reflect a widespread interest in producing a more highly skilled and technologically competent workforce. Because these driving forces for reform remain, policymakers likely will continue to be confronted with pressure for significant education change, regardless of the results of their ongoing reforms.

Citizens in industrialized countries have increasingly come to view education systems, correctly or incorrectly, as being ineffective. A widely held opinion in many settings is that education standards either have fallen or have not been set sufficiently high. As a result, the focus of education reform has switched from inputs (such as financing) to outcome control (especially through greater emphasis on curriculum and testing). Popular concern and dissatisfaction with the education system have been high in all countries. Noticeable levels of citizen concern are partly the result of cross-national comparisons of student performance (usually based on standardized exam results). For example, although German and Japanese students tended to score much higher than students from other industrialized countries on such exams, falling test scores in recent years have resulted in the population's having a stronger sense of education failure. As a result, the pressure for comprehensive education reform has increased in these countries. Strong pressure for reforms also is related to economic conditions: countries facing economic difficulties are more likely to pursue significant education restructuring than are those in relatively good economic shape. This relationship was evident in all of the countries examined here, as economic downturns produced significant impetus for intensive education reform.

Education reforms also are related to a return to market-based mechanisms and individualistic orientations in many industrialized countries. As governments began to emphasize the virtues of privatization, decentralization, deregulation, and market forces, these principles began to be applied outside the sphere of economic systems. As dissatisfaction with education performance emerged in these countries, these more liberal political values provided ready solutions to many areas of concern. In the United Kingdom, Japan, and France, we see a clear example of this pattern of influence, as school autonomy and non-public-funding policies were ardently pursued.

Education policy implementation was no easy task in any of the countries examined in this book, but it proved especially difficult in the less centralized political systems. In all six countries, implementation was impeded by the broad number of participants involved and the power of entrenched education bureaucracies. Education systems offer multiple points at which opponents of prior policy decisions can attempt to change the course of those policies. This is especially true in political systems where the control of education remains firmly in the hands of lower levels of government, as in the United States and Germany. In these countries, the passage of reforms was not enough to effect widespread change because powerful interests at the implementation stage were able to exercise their clout. In contrast, in Japan, where the entire education system is controlled tightly by the education bureaucracy, implementation was of far less concern. The experience of these six countries implies that dramatic policy changes are more difficult to achieve in this policy area because an extensive array of interests (many of whom control the systems that are the targets of reform) have a stake in preventing innovation from occurring and had the means to do so. This is not to say that change is impossible, however. The experiences of Italy and France, in which the policy-making process emphasized consensus among the major actors early on, may yet teach the industrialized countries a valuable lesson.

Our focus in this chapter has been on ongoing efforts to reform education systems. Given where most countries are in the reform process, the next step for these countries is to evaluate the effects of these reforms and proceed from there. The industrialized countries will continue to face pressures for further reform because of ongoing concern about being competitive in the global economic system. Many parents, students, politicians, and business people continue to feel that their countries' education systems are not capable of addressing new economic challenges, in particular the demand for better educated and more highly skilled workers.

SUGGESTED READINGS

Anderson, Lee. 2007. *Congress and the Classroom: From the Cold War to "No Child Left Behind."* University Park: Pennsylvania State University Press.

Chakrabarti, Rajashiro, and Paul E. Peterson. 2009. *School Choice International: Exploring Public-Private Partnerships.* Cambridge: MIT Press.

Cummings, William. 2003. *The Institutions of Education: A Comparative Study of Educational Development in Six Core Nations.* Oxford: Symposium Books.

Debray, Elizabeth. 2006. *Politics, Ideology, and Education: Federal Policy during the Clinton and Bush Administrations.* New York: Teachers College Press.

Eades, J. S., Roger Goodman, and Yumiko Hada. 2005. *The 'Big Bang' in Japanese Higher Education: The 2004 Reforms and the Dynamics of Change.* Melbourne, Australia: Trans Pacific Press

Horner, Wolfgang. 2007. *The Education Systems of Europe.* Dordrecht: Springer.

Maassen, Peter. 2007. *University Dynamics and European Integration.* Dordrecht: Springer.

Meyer, Heinz-Dieter, and William Boyd. 2001. *Education between State, Markets and Civil Society.* Mahwah, N.J.: L. Erlbaum Associates.

Tsuchiya, Okano. 1999. *Education in Contemporary Japan.* Cambridge: Cambridge University Press.

Wray, Harry. 1999. *Japanese and American Education: Attitudes and Practices.* Westport, Conn.: Bergin and Garvey.

Chapter 11 Environmental Policy

Since the early 1980s environmental issues have become increasingly prominent on policy agendas in all the industrialized countries, including the six examined in this book. These issues are important for policymakers in political terms (as reflected in the effort of political parties and political leaders to appear "green"); in terms of the dimensions of the problems, which include global warming, global destruction of the ozone layer, global deforestation, and global overpopulation; and in terms of the sheer number of issues—for example, air, water, ground, and noise pollution; radioactivity; toxic waste; pesticides; and endangered species—and the possible solutions. Although substantial environmental gains have been achieved in most industrialized countries, the process of environmental protection has been more difficult, costly, and frustrating than policymakers initially foresaw, and much remains to be done.

Common Policy Problems

Industrialized countries make choices regarding environmental policies in a number of important areas. A relatively clearly defined and shared set of environmental issues confronts policymakers in each of the industrialized countries examined in this book. In this section and in the case studies we focus on problems related to air pollution, one of the first environmental issues that industrialized countries recognized and addressed. The process of postwar industrialization and a general reliance on fossil fuels for energy meant that by the late 1960s most industrialized countries began to experience significant air pollution problems and by the early 1970s the first air pollution control policies began to be implemented. As a result, each of the six countries has a substantial environmental protection record.[1]

The term *ambient air quality*, which refers to air in our immediate surroundings, is common in discussions about the air we breathe. Deterioration in ambient air quality generally results from an increase in the number of contaminants present in the atmosphere—largely the result of the burning of

[1] For more detailed discussions of environmental issues in these countries, see the series *Environmental Performance Reviews,* published since the 1990s by the Organisation for Economic Co-operation and Development (2001, 2002a, 2002b, 2002c, 2005a, 2005b). Included in this series are in-depth treatments of environmental problems and policies for each of the countries examined in this book.

fossil fuels in industrial and transport activities. These contaminants are produced at far greater levels than can be processed naturally and are absorbed into the air relatively easily.

Air-polluting contaminants include both particles and gases. The term *particulate matter* refers to solids—including ash, soot, and lead—that are released into the atmosphere in industrial emissions and exhaust gases. The most important polluting gases include carbon monoxide (CO), which is emitted primarily from gasoline engines. Sulfur oxides (SO_x), such as sulfur dioxide (SO_2), are produced by burning sulfur-containing fuels (when combined with water vapor, SO_2 forms sulfuric acid and falls as acid rain). Volatile organic compounds (VOCs), which include many compounds that are known carcinogens or that have climate-changing properties, contribute to the large-scale formation of ozone and smog. Nitrogen oxides (NO_x), especially nitrous oxide, are byproducts of fossil fuel burning at high temperatures; these oxides combine with VOCs to produce smog. Finally, chlorofluorocarbons (CFCs) are compounds with a chemical composition such that part of the molecule, when released in the atmosphere, is highly destructive to ozone molecules.

Scientific studies demonstrate that both short- and long-term exposure to emissions containing these gases or particulates cause serious health problems in humans. Air pollution also endangers people indirectly by causing significant harm to plant and animal life. The threat from these emissions is compounded by the interaction effects of these pollutants, which can be more hazardous than exposure to each of the compounds separately.

The existence of such air pollutants in recent years also has created growing concern about ozone layer depletion. Increasingly, scientific evidence has supported the argument that the earth's ozone layer has gradually become depleted or developed holes as a result of polluting human activities. Such damage is thought to be an environmental danger because of the ozone layer's role in shielding the earth from dangerous wavelengths of ultraviolet rays. When this layer is depleted, the level of ultraviolet radiation that reaches the earth increases significantly. Increases in levels of ultraviolet radiation are linked to increases in skin cancer rates, possible weakening of the human immune system, crop loss, and forest damage. The most significant factor in ozone layer depletion is believed to be the production of CFCs in commercial activities.

Air pollution also creates another area of government concern with respect to the problem of global warming. This problem is caused by substances known as trace gases (so named because they make up less than 1 percent of atmospheric gases). They are also known as **greenhouse gases**, because they allow heat from the sun to enter the earth's atmosphere and then trap it, creating a greenhouse effect. These greenhouse gases are usually vital to the earth's ecology: they ensure that average temperatures are suitable to sustain life. However, human activities cause a harmful buildup of these gases, and the excess cannot be processed through the earth's natural capacity to recycle these gases. As these gases (such as carbon dioxide, or CO_2) build up, the atmosphere's capacity to capture heat radiated from the earth's surface increases, which raises the average temperature of the earth's surface. Should global warming increase, it is generally held that higher temperatures would likely produce a range of harmful effects—including rising sea levels, changes in agricultural production patterns, and warmer weather patterns.

Major Policy Options

In all industrialized countries, environmental protection policies usually are designed with one of two goals in mind. Policies such as those regulating automobile emission standards may be intended to prevent additional environmental contamination from occurring. Alternatively, policies may be aimed at eliminating existing contamination, for example, through a policy of planting forests to absorb excess gases already in the atmosphere. Public policies designed to achieve either, or both, of these objectives may take several forms.

The most widely used environmental protection policy instruments are **direct regulations** (or **command-and-control policies**) imposed by governments. Regulatory policies tend to look very similar from country to country. They typically are either framework policies, which allow latitude in their interpretation and implementation, or detailed laws, which permit little discretion in their application. Environmental regulations usually define permissible levels of pollutants and place limits on their discharge in the interest of reaching established target levels.

Although the content of these policies tends to be similar from country to country, a significant degree of difference in direct regulation policies is observed in the sanctions for noncompliance. Penalties for noncompliance may include criminal liabilities with fines as a penalty and the possibility of personal liability for responsible individuals. Alternatively, sanctions may include modifying, suspending, or revoking a license to operate. Governments may also be given the power to clean up after a pollution incident, with the costs paid by the polluter. Polluters also may be required to pay significant damages for civil liability. The enforcement of such penalties may generate costly adverse publicity for the polluter. In most industrialized countries, these noncompliance penalties have become stricter and are enforced more vigorously than in the past.

In the 1990s governments in many industrialized countries moved away from a command-and-control approach to environmental problems toward new policy instruments. As environmental problems persisted, the regulations of the 1970s and 1980s came to be seen as economically inefficient, difficult to implement and enforce, and unsuited to new forms of pollution, especially "nonpoint" sources of pollution. As a result, policymakers began to search for mechanisms that were more flexible, incentive based, and noncoercive. Among the new policy instruments adopted are green product labeling, eco-taxation, emission trading (or cap-and-trade) schemes, and voluntary agreements.

Industrialized countries may also develop **voluntary agreements** between the government and producers to reduce pollution levels. These agreements are usually used in conjunction with other policy instruments. They typically are negotiated directly between government and industry or are developed independently by industry (reflecting a genuine environmental concern, a concern about positive public relations, or both). These agreements are not legally binding but instead involve mutually agreed upon goals and target dates. Across industrialized countries, the use of voluntary agreements has risen dramatically since the early 1990s.

In some industrialized countries, policymakers have begun to address environmental problems by stressing the importance of market mechanisms through the use of **economic incentives**. These incentives include tax breaks for corporations that implement pollution controls, pollution charges or taxes, deposit-refund systems, and tradable discharge permits. These policies involve what are known as **polluter pays principles**, in which individuals are charged for their environmentally harmful activities, or **user pays principles**, which involve additional costs for consumers of environmentally hazardous products. Since the late 1990s, environmentally related taxes have become widespread across most industrialized countries.

Although such policy instruments are increasingly being discussed by policymakers, some industrialized countries continue to be reluctant to use such incentives to control environmental pollution. This reluctance probably reflects a natural bureaucratic preference for regulatory policies. In addition, opponents of incentives argue that these policies are too complex to be administered and that they offer less certainty that specific pollution reduction goals will be achieved. Others argue that economic instruments can be effective only when polluters, both producers and consumers, accept a notion of shared responsibility and have accurate information about the effects of their activities, conditions that are difficult to achieve.

An important environmental policy instrument for industrialized countries, particularly in the face of the globalization of many environmental problems, is the use of international environmental agreements. Since the late 1980s a number of international agreements have been developed that set pollution reduction targets for individual participant countries. One of the earliest of these agreements was the 1987 Montreal Protocol on Substances That Deplete the Ozone Layer, which forty-nine countries ratified. Other international agreements include the 1992 United Nations Framework Convention on Climate Change (FCCC) and the Convention on Biological Diversity, also drafted in 1992. One of the more controversial international agreements is the 1997 Kyoto Protocol on global warming. Box 11-1 provides a more in-depth look at these agreements regarding climate change.

Box 11-1 **In Depth: Climate Change Agreements**

The first international agreement to address the climate change problem was developed at the 1992 Earth Summit in Rio de Janeiro, Brazil. This document, the United Nations Framework Convention on Climate Change (FCCC), was intended to stabilize, not eliminate, greenhouse gas concentrations in the atmosphere. Under the FCCC, the industrialized countries made voluntary commitments to reduce their levels of greenhouse gas emissions to 1990 levels by 2000. Overall, 154 countries signed the FCCC, and it went into effect in March 1994. The United States was one of the first countries to ratify this agreement. It was estimated in 1999 that roughly half of the participating countries would meet the FCCC targets by 2000.

In the face of rising concerns about continued increases in carbon dioxide (CO_2) and other greenhouse gas emissions, a consensus emerged that further international action was needed. As a result, the Kyoto Protocol to the FCCC was adopted in December 1997. The protocol set more ambitious goals for reducing greenhouse gas emissions and involved binding commitments (though it lacked effective enforcement mechanisms). The Kyoto Protocol committed the industrialized countries to specific, binding emission targets for six key greenhouse gases, especially CO_2, methane, and nitrous oxide.

By 2008 the Kyoto Protocol had been signed by 174 countries, including the European Union, Canada, Japan, and China, and entered into force in February 2005. The United States is the only Group of 8 country that failed to ratify the protocol, which would have committed the United States to a target of reducing three greenhouse gases by 7 percent below 1990 levels between 2008 and 2012—instead, its greenhouse gas emissions rose more than 16 percent between 1990 and 2005. Bill Clinton's administration indicated that it would not submit the protocol for ratification in the Senate until developing countries also acted to reduce their greenhouse gas emissions. This position in part reflected a 1997 Senate resolution that the United States should not become a party to the agreement until developing countries also submit to binding targets. In March 2001 George W. Bush's administration announced that it was "unequivocally" opposed to the Kyoto Protocol. The president declared that the protocol was "fatally flawed" and antithetical to U.S. economic interests and withdrew all U.S. support for it.

In late 2007 the first global discussions on a new framework to replace the Kyoto Protocol, which expires in 2012, were held in Bali, Indonesia. At Bali, negotiators agreed to begin two years of negotiations to be concluded in Copenhagen in December 2009, but they made no firm commitments to new goals for greenhouse gas reductions, reflecting intense debate between European states and the United States over new obligations to limit emissions. Although European states argued strongly in favor of deeper international commitments, the United States opposed them. American arguments against binding targets were criticized heavily—at one point the U.S. ambassador was booed by conference delegates—and the U.S. delegation backed down, agreeing to work on a new, post-2012 agreement that would obligate countries to take on new commitments to limit greenhouse gas emissions and aid developing countries with sustainable development. The resulting Bali Action Plan established an Ad Hoc Working Group on Long-Term Cooperative Action, which met for the first time in April 2008. This group was scheduled to present its findings to the fifteenth meeting of the parties to the FCCC in Copenhagen in December 2009.

Explaining Policy Dynamics

The existing research on environmental policy reform rests largely on a case study approach; thus large-scale theorizing about these issues is generally lacking, and most work in the area is highly descriptive. Existing analytical work points primarily to the importance of institutional factors in explaining both policy reform and outcomes.

Cultural Explanations

A cultural factor that may influence environmental policy reform involves citizens' definition of their rights and freedoms with respect to the environment. Widely held social values, such as the right to own and drive an automobile, the importance of the open road, the freedom to drive at high speeds, or the freedom to fish and use waterways, are argued to influence a government's ability to impose more restrictive environmental policies. Where such things are viewed as right and proper, they are rarely challenged when it comes to making decisions about environmental policies (O'Riordan and Jordan 1996).

Not surprisingly, environmental policy reforms often reflect public opinion and priorities. In countries where environmental policy has yet to arouse public concern, governments face greater difficulty in enacting reforms. Conversely, in countries where populations are more mobilized on certain environmental issues, reform may be easier to pursue (depending on whether a match exists between public opinion and the government of the day). This pattern is especially relevant for understanding the policy reform process when the policy agenda has been determined by external rather than internal pressures (Collier and Lofstedt 1997; Crepaz 1995; Jansen, Osland, and Hanf 1998; McBeath and Rosenberg 2006; Vernon 1993). Further, in countries where postmaterialism is a relevant cultural attribute, public concern about the environment may account for the increasing prominence of environmental issues on political agendas (Inglehart and Baker 2000).

Economic Explanations

Environmental policy reform may also be affected by economic pressures arising from globalization and increased international competitiveness. For example, reforms involving environmental taxes have been difficult to adopt in industrialized countries. These reforms are often rejected on the grounds that they impede international competitiveness. In such cases, policy reform is affected by a perception that the policies will reduce the chances of making national industry profitable in a globally competitive environment (Jansen, Osland, and Hanf 1998).

Cost considerations also influence the environmental policy reform process. For example, the economic costs of achieving CO_2 emission targets are viewed as either the most critical factor for national decision making or one of the most influential factors. Where estimated costs of a particular policy are low, support for the policy will be more readily forthcoming; where the policy involves tremendous expense, cost becomes a decisive factor in mustering opposition to reform. Thus cost is a critically influential factor when great expense is required to achieve the target but is less influential when the cost is small or uncertain or when environmental improvements may be economically beneficial (Kawashima 1997).

In most industrialized countries, the values and norms of business and industry also may influence environmental policy reform. Business and industrial interests often place primary emphasis on maximizing economic growth and the value of material wealth in a society. These interests often play an important role in defining the way environmental problems are defined, as well as in developing the various solutions that are given serious consideration (Ophuls and Boyan 1992; Schnaiberg and Gould 1994; Schnaiberg, Watts, and Zimmerman 1986).

Political Explanations

As we noted in earlier chapters, the ideology of the governing party in a country often determines the nature of policy reform. This relationship often holds true with respect to environmental policy. In particular, because organized environmental interests are usually allied with the political center or the left, we expect centrist or leftist governments to be more likely to pursue substantial environmental policy reform (Scruggs 1999).

Researchers also observe that the extent to which citizens participate in environmentalist movements or parties varies greatly from country to country. Not surprisingly, wider and more frequent reform efforts occur in countries where such movements are active than in those where they are conspicuously absent. Some countries have highly active interest organizations that continually demand more environmentally oriented policies and more effective environmental administration. In other countries, the government is subject to no significant political pressure concerning environmental policy, from either specific groups or the population at large.

Institutional Explanations

Many scholars argue for the importance of institutional arrangements in accounting for environmental policy reform (Hanf and Jansen 1998; Jager and O'Riordan 1996; Jansen, Osland, and Hanf 1998; Scruggs 1999; Weale 1992). Some scholars emphasize a lack of coordination and cooperation between different levels of government as an important influence. They note that although environmental problems offer substantial scope for action at lower levels of government and most countries have taken a good deal of initiative at these levels, central governments often pay little attention to such efforts when drawing up national environmental programs. This lack of cooperation frequently results in duplications of effort, squandering of resources, and, overall, ineffective policy reforms (Jansen, Osland, and Hanf 1998).

Another important institutional factor may be the nature of a country's electoral system. Proportional representation electoral systems are argued to create the possibility for greater success in environmental protection, because they encourage the representation of smaller and more particularized interests. Under such a system, green parties are more likely to gain policy influence either by gaining access to elected office themselves or by compelling the more mainstream parties to accommodate those interests (Schreurs 2002; Scruggs 1999).

Researchers also have pointed to the importance of interest representation systems for explaining policy reform. Corporatist political systems are widely held to be more amenable to broader environmental policy reforms because they are more consensual and amenable to compromise. Pluralist systems are argued to allow for the blockage of such reforms because of their adversarial and competitive nature. Because environmental policies involve collective goods and action, they are argued to be more difficult to achieve in pluralist systems, which allow various interests to intervene in the policy process to defend their own interests. In particular, environmental policies impose costs on private economic interests, which are highly motivated to prevent the adoption of such policies. Although these policies are generally of aggregate benefit, particular sectors and individuals may lose out, resulting in considerable opposition to some measures—opposition to which pluralist systems are more likely to respond (Crepaz 1995; Enloe 1975; Lundqvist 1980; Steel, Clinton, and Lovrich 2003; Scruggs 1999; Vogel 1986).

O'Riordan and Jordan (1996) point to policy networks as important institutional factors that influence the direction and development of environmental policies. They argue that policy networks provide both an enabling and a constraining filter to policy development. Stable policy communities become an effective constraint to radical policy change because they tend to change slowly, if at all. Where policy networks exist, governments faced with new policy problems are forced to negotiate with and gain the support of relevant and important communities if they want their policies implemented. In such settings, these networks can place significant constraints on large-scale reform.

Lundqvist (1974) argues that the highly technical and standards-based nature of environmental policy makes policy development and implementation more difficult in a federal system. A federal structure may interfere with the technical connection between the national government, which sets standards, and those agencies responsible for monitoring and implementation at lower levels of government. As a result, effective policy making in federal political systems takes more time (because policies need to be articulated more fully) and requires consensus building (because multiple actors are involved). In unitary political systems, the existence of more immediate connections between various governmental actors concerned with standards typically reduces the need for consensus building or policy elucidation. Lundqvist further argues that federal systems may also result in the development of more lenient standards than policymakers prefer, as well as a greater ability to delay actions because policy making in federal systems involves multiple decision-making points. At the same time, he notes that unitary political systems often result in reforms that deprive lower levels of government of the flexibility needed to cope with local problems when implementing reforms. Desai (2002) notes that countries with highly fragmented and decentralized policy and administrative systems are more likely to have national environmental policy reform that moves in fits and starts—advancing in some areas and retreating in others—and that, as a result, appears piecemeal and disconnected. Conversely, environmental policy is likely to have a clearer and more comprehensive focus, though not necessarily in a pro-environment direction, in more centralized political systems.

Scruggs (1999) argues that the relationship between the executive and the legislature is important to the degree that these two government branches are divided. In a unified legislative-administrative structure, policy continuity, consensus, and accountability will be enhanced. Where significant divides exist between the executive and the legislature, government will be less capable of providing consensual decisions about public goods and thus will be even less successful in achieving substantial reform.

International Policy Making

Policymakers in industrialized countries increasingly acknowledge that the environment in one country is not distinct from the environment in another and that environmental problems do not respect national territorial boundaries. Instead, most environmental issues have an international dimension or at least a regional or transborder component. This phenomenon is commonly known as the **globalization of the environment**. In policy terms, this globalization has meant that although effective environmental policies can be developed at the national level, identifying and addressing the regional and global dimensions of these problems also is necessary. This awareness has resulted in the development of a substantial number of international environmental agreements. A system of global environmental governance—consisting of intergovernmental and nongovernmental organizations, framework environmental laws, financing institutions, and mechanisms for implementing treaty mechanisms—now exists and continues to expand.

Environmental protection policies in the United States, Canada, and Mexico may be affected by some provisions of the North American Free Trade Agreement (NAFTA), which has a clear environmental component. NAFTA's environmental provisions are intended to ensure that environmental conditions in the agreement's three signatory countries do not hamper trade or give one country a comparative advantage over the others. Under the agreement, none of the three countries may lower its environmental regulatory standards to attract investment. In addition, the agreement encourages the integration of environmental policies and a raising of environmental standards in these countries while protecting each country's right to set its own level of environmental protection.

NAFTA was also accompanied by a supplemental agreement on environmental cooperation that was drafted in 1993 at the encouragement of the Clinton administration. The supplemental agreement came in response to unprecedented pressures from many U.S. environmental groups with respect to trade issues. The agreement was intended to foster environmental cooperation and to improve enforcement of national environmental laws; however, it does not require the signatory countries to adopt any new environmental laws. It established a North American Commission on Environmental Cooperation, which has some powers to impose fines or trade sanctions for the failure to enforce existing environmental laws. Thus far, NAFTA's strongest impact on environmental policies has been seen in Mexico.

Environmental protection is one of the best developed policy areas within the European Union (EU). Approximately 300 environmental laws have been adopted since 1957, and roughly 200 are currently being implemented by member states. It is now possible to talk of a comprehensive EU environmental policy regime. The majority of these laws are directives to be adopted by individual member states and transposed into national laws. Today, responsibility for environmental policy making in Europe has shifted to the EU level to a remarkable degree, although national politics still produce noticeable policy differences across countries. The EU has developed some of the most comprehensive and innovative environmental policies found among the industrialized countries, reflecting a strong commitment to environmental protection that is supported by the EU member states and the majority of European citizens.

In the case studies that follow, we focus our consideration of contemporary policy dynamics on these countries' most recent attempts to meet their international commitments in preventing climate change under the Kyoto Protocol. These attempts typically involve efforts to reduce CO_2 concentrations in the atmosphere by reducing consumption of fossil fuels in both the energy and transport sectors. In all six countries, these efforts have been a primary focus of attempts at environmental policy reform since 1990, with the systemic agenda having been set largely through external influences.

United States

Background: Policy Process and Policy History

The development and administration of environmental policy in the United States can be very complex because it occurs at multiple points in the government system. Responsibility for the development of environmental policies lies with a variety of executive branch offices, departments, and agencies, including the Environmental Protection Agency (EPA), the principal environmental bureaucratic agency. Congress, under its constitutional jurisdiction to regulate interstate commerce and control activities on federal lands, also passes specific, detailed (rather than framework) environmental policies. These laws may be implemented by either the executive branch or the states, depending on their specific provisions. Further, both criminal and civil actions may be used in the U.S. judicial system for implementing and enforcing environmental legislation, and many environmental cases are heard in federal courts. Strong compliance and enforcement are notable features of federal environmental management in the United States.

Although primary responsibility for environmental protection traditionally is placed in the federal government's hands (to harmonize regulations nationwide and to equalize the protection burden), individual states also may develop their own environmental policies that extend, or possibly supersede, federal mandates (albeit under strict federal oversight). Other states have laws that prevent them from toughening federal standards. Many states also have created their own bureaucratic structures to develop and implement environmental policies. States have become particularly active in developing environmental policies since the mid-2000s, when federal inaction on climate change issues compelled them to act on their own initiative.

A general policy of shared authority and cooperative arrangements exists between federal and state governments to implement and enforce national environmental laws. The federal government may authorize states to issue permits and take enforcement actions that are consistent with national-level policies. Local governments also have the authority to address environmental problems in their areas. Increasingly, states and localities have sought more independence in their environmental protection efforts and have objected to federal programs that require action without supplying the necessary funds.

The United States has pursued air quality improvements since the early 1970s. Environmental policy on air quality in the United States primarily takes the form of direct regulations that set strict standards. More than in other industrialized countries, air quality standards in the United States are enforced through stiff penalties and noncompliance fees. The United States also uses economic instruments and voluntary agreements to control air pollution, although historically to a lesser degree than direct regulations. The focus of air quality management policies is primarily on removing existing contaminants rather than on pollution prevention.

Air pollution control in the United States falls under the 1970 Clean Air Act (amended in 1977 and 1990), which calls for the creation of a set of national ambient air quality standards. Under the 1970 act, technology-based emission levels were set for eight compounds classified as hazardous air pollutants. This list of air contaminants was extended to 189 compounds in

1990, with a requirement for technology-based control standards to be developed for each (these standards replaced the quantitative, health-based risk assessments introduced in 1977). Ambient air quality is not monitored on a national basis but is checked at various points throughout the country.

George W. Bush's administration attempted to further amend the Clean Air Act with the introduction of the 2002 Clean Skies Bill. Among other things, the bill called for cuts in SO_x, NO_x, and mercury emissions from power plants through a cap-and-trade system. After three years of highly partisan deliberation, Congress failed to pass the bill. The administration then proceeded to implement many of the Clean Skies proposals via executive orders. Many of these orders were highly controversial, as they rescinded previous environmental policies. For example, an executive order was issued to repeal the new source review section of the 1977 Clean Air Act. This provision required older coal-fired plants, oil refineries, and other industrial facilities to install state-of-the-art pollution control equipment if they were to be modified to increase production or extend facility life. The repeal of this provision constituted a significant environmental policy development that occurred despite Congress's having failed to agree to it.

Emission controls for mobile sources of air contaminants have been in use in the United States since the 1960s. Stringent exhaust limits for passenger cars were instituted in 1981, following fuel-efficiency standards in 1978 that were strengthened progressively until 1985. Unleaded gasoline was introduced in the United States in 1975, and the complete phase-out of vehicles running on leaded gasoline was concluded in 1996. To reduce CO emissions, the use of oxygenated gasoline, particularly in winter, is required in thirty-one U.S. cities, and the use of reformulated gasoline with lower hazardous emissions is being introduced in select areas. The 1990 Clean Air Act amendments further tightened and introduced new controls. These controls included standards for cleaner fuels, new vehicle emission limits, inspection programs (many of which already existed at the state level), and changes in transportation policy to encourage van pooling and carpool lanes.

The United States makes use of voluntary agreements in air quality management, mostly to promote energy-efficiency improvements but also to reduce emissions. The Climate Challenge, a recent voluntary agreement between the Department of Energy and major utilities, involves a pledge to limit or reduce greenhouse gas emissions in the most cost-effective way possible under strict performance measures. More than 80 percent of U.S. electric utilities are party to the agreement. Voluntary agreements were particularly popular during the Clinton and George W. Bush administrations, because a voluntary approach also allowed for the formulation of policy without seeking congressional authorization.

Economic instruments, especially those based on user pays principles, are not an important air pollution control mechanism in the United States. The one strict use of tax incentives involves a significant tax on CFCs to facilitate their phase-out. Some market-based mechanisms, such as the use of emission trading systems, particularly for SO_2 allowances and CFC emission permits, are used to help reduce air pollution at minimum cost. Under such systems, a company that reduces emissions below a required level can receive credits usable against higher emissions elsewhere; companies may also trade emission credits. Under the SO_2 program, allowances for SO_2 emissions may be bought, sold, or traded among utilities or industrial plants with the intention of reducing compliance costs to industry. The goal of these trading systems is to balance combined emissions within an aggregate limit. The United States also makes limited use of environment-specific subsidies and has created some tax programs aimed at funding damage compensation or clean-up activities performed by government.

The United States is party to both regional and international agreements to reduce air contaminant emission levels. In the 1991 Air Quality Agreement with Canada, the United States committed to reducing SO_x emission levels between 2000 and 2010 with a 40 percent decrease from 1980 levels. The United States also has agreements with Mexico, such as the 1992 Integrated Border Environmental Plan and the 1996 Border XXI Program, and participates in agreements on long-range transport of air pollutants, such as the acid rain program and the NO_x and VOC protocol. The United States was the first industrialized country to ratify the FCCC. Like most industrialized countries, the United States signed the Kyoto Protocol but withdrew its support for the agreement in 2001. Since 2001 the United States has played a less significant role in the development, implementation, and encouragement of global environmental agreements with respect to air quality than was true in the past. The Obama administration has committed itself to returning the country to the leading edge in this regard.

Contemporary Dynamics

The election of George W. Bush in 2000 dramatically altered the U.S. environmental policy agenda. As a conservative Republican, President Bush placed far more emphasis on economic development than on environmental protection. The president's natural inclination away from environmental issues was exacerbated first by September 11, 2001, and then by the war in Iraq. In the aftermath of these events, the prominent environmental challenges facing the country—especially climate change—virtually disappeared from the national political agenda.

Environmental policy did not merely experience benign neglect from 2001 to 2008. On the administration's first day in office in 2001, it issued a moratorium on all of the Clinton administration's environmental policies. The administration used its powers of appointment to staff the Environmental Protection Agency and the Departments of Energy, Agriculture, and the Interior with individuals who were more sympathetic to industry than to the environment and then used these institutions to advance an industry-friendly, antiregulatory environmental agenda. For most of its time in office, the Bush administration expended the bulk of its environmental policy energy on weakening, undermining, or ignoring existing domestic environmental laws, while global agreements were rejected completely. The few environmental policies enacted in this period were more likely to be voluntary than regulatory. The government actively sought to roll back the impressive environmental policy gains the country had realized since the 1970s.

The United States ratified and sought to comply with the FCCC and signed but withdrew from the Kyoto Protocol. After this withdrawal, for most of the Bush administration's tenure, the United States distanced itself from climate change policy, in particular, making a full-scale retreat from binding targets and timetables. The Bush administration did not necessarily have a mandate to tackle climate change issues from 2001 to 2008, since these issues received little attention during either the 2000 or the 2004 elections. Nevertheless, these issues were already on the systemic agenda because the United States was presented with a serious greenhouse gas emissions problem, public support for fighting climate change was high and growing over this period, and the emissions picture was continuing to worsen. In this policy area there was an outside initiation model of agenda setting, in which interests and actors outside the government attempted to raise the profile of an issue already on the systemic agenda with the government. Their efforts ultimately proved fruitless, however, since the Bush administration did not enact national policies to address climate change. Among the industrialized countries, the United States is the world's largest emitter of greenhouse gases. Only China has higher emission levels. With less than one-twentieth of the world's population, the United States produces nearly one-fourth of its greenhouse gas emissions, and U.S. CO_2 emission levels were 16 percent higher in 2005 than in 1990. As in other industrialized countries, in the United States CO_2 emission levels continue to rise because of the continuing increase in motor vehicle use, despite the implementation of strict emission controls. A tradition of low gasoline prices and easy access to fossil fuels has increased people's reliance on individual transportation and discouraged fuel efficiency and alternative energy generation.

Even before 2001, the U.S. government did not go as far as formulating policies that involve specific CO_2 emission targets because of the perceived negative influence such targets would have on the domestic economy. Here we are referring to the cost factor—namely, that increasing energy efficiency in the country overall will have real economic costs in both the short and long terms. Although citizens demonstrated interest in climate change issues, prior to 2001 they were not overly alarmed and were especially persuaded by arguments that emission reductions would clash with their right to move about freely and cheaply and that such reductions would involve greater expense to them individually (in terms of both energy and transport costs). Without pressure from the public and with intense opposition from industry, political leaders had only weak incentives to place on the institutional agenda CO_2 emission targets or other economic instruments for controlling emissions.

Significant opposition to setting specific targets for CO_2 emissions (and other greenhouse gases) comes in particular from industrialists, who argue that they are hurt by more stringent emission standards and increased costs of transport and that such costs affect their international competitiveness and result in lost jobs. Industry has encouraged the use of voluntary standards, which most supporters of environmental control argue will achieve little. Businesses also fear that emission targets will result in higher energy prices. Echoing the concerns of industry, many Republicans charge that the Kyoto Protocol imposes costly environmental controls on U.S. businesses while giving developing countries an unfair competitive advantage by easing restrictions facing them—all in an effort to address an environmental problem they believe does not exist.

Supporters of more stringent efforts to control CO_2 emissions in the United States include, not surprisingly, environmentalists and scientists. Environmental organizations were highly critical of the Bush administration for not pursuing more aggressively the reduction of CO_2 emissions. Given the pattern of partisan control of Congress from 2001 to 2007 and the fact that none of these groups enjoys the support of (or access to) the Republican Party, they had little influence on environmental policy making.

In this political context, the Bush administration made no significant attempt to control CO_2 emissions and, in particular, was uninterested in making any carbon reduction commitments. Its major greenhouse gas emission reduction effort was the 2003 Climate Change Initiative, which called for slowing the growth of greenhouse gas emissions to cut "greenhouse gas intensity" (the ratio of greenhouse gases to economic output) by 18 percent by 2012. This slower growth was to be accomplished through voluntary reporting of emissions by companies and voluntary reductions, as well as through an expanded climate research program and incentives to develop new technologies. Observers had no real expectations that these policies would reduce emissions.

Democrats in Congress made some attempts to initiate climate change legislation after seizing control of the House in the 2006 congressional elections, but these reform efforts amounted to nothing, illustrating the difficulty of resolving environmental policy conflicts in an era of intense partisan divide. Decisions on environmental policy require Congress to reconcile the conflicting views of multiple interests and constituencies, a task made all the more difficult in the face of partisan polarization. For over a decade, Congress was unable to pass either sweeping Republican environmental changes or moderate Democratic reforms. Democratic legislative efforts in the 110th Congress did move climate change issues to the front burner; however, these initiatives laid a foundation for sweeping climate change legislation to be considered early in the Obama administration, through the 2009 American Clean Energy and Security Act.

The U.S. government's failure to set emission reduction targets or introduce economic instruments to reduce CO_2 emissions, especially from the transport sector, reflects the presence of several formidable obstacles to reform. First, during the Bush years, the combination of Republican control of the legislature (at least until the 2006 elections), strong business opposition, and the close relationship between the Republican Party and industry meant that efforts to set CO_2 reduction targets and new emission standards were not pursued. Second, cultural influences play a role in the lack of resistance to this approach, in that Americans are strongly attached to their right to own and operate vehicles. The culture of the open road is an important part of the national psyche, and policies that increase the cost of motor vehicle use are politically risky. Third, public opinion in the United States in the past was only weakly mobilized about global warming, creating little pressure for immediate action. Fourth, industry and consumer advocacy groups have been effective in lobbying against the adoption of economic instruments to reduce emissions, claiming that the costs are too high and that the country's economic competitiveness will be threatened. Several political factors also play an important role. The lack of an environmental party in the United States (in part reflecting the country's single-member district plurality electoral system) reduces pressure to address environmental issues in Congress. In the 2007–2009 congressional sessions, the existence of divided government, as well as intense partisan polarization, presented formidable obstacles to reform. In particular, the Republican Party's opposition to any discussion of global warming issues meant that little action was taken.

Japan

Background: Policy Process and Policy History

In Japan, primary responsibility for the development of environmental policy lies with the national Diet. Japan's forty-seven prefectures and the municipalities organized below them also are permitted to draft policies that are in line with national laws. Such policies typically are aimed at toughening national standards or responding to specific prefectural problems. Thus all prefectures, as well as many municipalities, have their own pollution control policies. Further, where air pollution levels are particularly high, prefectural governments are required by the national government to develop integrated pollution prevention plans.

The relationship among national, prefectural, and municipal governments generally is well coordinated through the ministries of the Japanese bureaucracy. Since a government reorganization in 2001, environmental issues are coordinated by the Ministry of the Environment at the central level. Implementation and enforcement of environmental laws is passed on to the prefectures and sometimes municipalities, with close supervision from the national government, resulting in a high degree of policy effectiveness.

The Japanese government has vigorously pursued air quality management since the late 1960s and has made considerable progress in reducing air pollution levels. This reduction was accomplished through a combination of strong direct regulation and widespread use of voluntary agreements with industry, with only limited use of economic instruments. An important environmental policy emphasis in Japan is on air pollution prevention, especially through improved pollution control technology and strict standards. Since the 1990s Japan has been a strong advocate for and participant in global environmental agreements.

Environmental quality standards and emission standards in Japan are strictly controlled through direct regulations. The 1968 Air Pollution Control Law put in place limits on both stationary emissions (that is, from industrial and combustion facilities) and motor vehicle exhaust. Subsequent restrictions on emissions have made Japan's requirements among the strictest in the world. Emission targets were established for the major air contaminants in the early 1970s and are revised as new scientific data are gathered. For areas with more serious air pollution, the Area-wide Total Pollutant Load Control System was introduced in 1974 through amendments to the 1968 law. This policy determined the maximum tolerable emission levels for SO_x in these areas to conform to environmental quality standards. The policy was extended to NO_x in 1981. Accompanying these emission controls in Japan is one of the most extensive and effective air pollution monitoring systems found among the industrialized countries.

Japan also has introduced some of the world's strictest measures to control motor vehicle emissions. Passenger car and heavy vehicle emission standards and NO_x standards have been strengthened gradually, emphasizing the use of best-available technology. From early on, the Japanese government emphasized the development of technological improvements for new vehicles, favoring the use of catalytic converters. Vehicles are subject to emission inspections at one- to three-year intervals. Fuel quality improvements accompanied new vehicle technology. All gasoline was lead free by 1987, and sulfur levels in diesel fuel were reduced. Vehicle emissions are further controlled through a 1992 NO_x law to accompany more restrictive vehicle emission standards with special measures in designated areas to reduce NO_x emissions, and still stricter standards went into effect in 2000–2004.

Voluntary agreements are an important component of environmental policy making in Japan, probably to a greater extent than is found in the other industrialized countries. Local governments and citizens' groups have signed a number of voluntary agreements with industry to control both emissions and fuel use; these agreements encourage the use of best-available pollution control technology and energy-efficiency measures. By the early 2000s, over 40,000 agreements between government and industry were in effect. Japanese industries are strong advocates for the use of voluntary agreements, and industry associations have been influential in striking such agreements.

The use of economic instruments in Japan is limited primarily to incentives (in the form of tax relief or low-interest loans) for investment in air pollution prevention and control equipment, mostly for industry, but also to encourage the replacement of older vehicles with newer, less polluting ones. For example, companies that install or improve their air pollution control equipment receive tax exemptions and may depreciate this equipment at special rates. Other economic incentives, such as emission charges, tradable permits, or eco-taxes have not been adopted in Japan in response to strong business opposition to such measures.

Since the 1980s the Japanese government has placed increasing emphasis on international environmental issues and has become a strong advocate of international cooperation in this area. Japan is an active partner in international attempts to control air quality as supporter of the Montreal Protocol, the FCCC, and the Kyoto Protocol. Japan also has increased its financial support and technology transfers to less developed countries to assist in their efforts to improve their environmental conditions. Further, Japan was one of the first countries to create a national government structure (the Global Warming Prevention Headquarters) specifically to address global environmental issues.

Contemporary Dynamics

Japan ratified the FCCC in 1993 and committed itself to stabilizing CO_2 emissions at 1990 levels by 2000. The country also ratified the Kyoto Protocol in 2002, and it went into effect in 2005. Despite strong mitigation efforts since the early 1990s, Japan has not been wholly successful in reducing greenhouse gas emissions. In 2006 Japan's CO_2 emissions were 6.3 percent above 1990 levels, meaning that its emissions remain above its Kyoto Protocol target. Current estimates indicate that Japan needs to cut emissions by 13.8 percent from 1990 levels to meet its assigned Kyoto Protocol target by 2012. In Japan, as in the other industrialized countries, CO_2 emissions from the transport sector continue to present an important obstacle to meeting these goals, despite substantial gains in the 1980s and 1990s. Transport-related emissions have continued to rise since 1990 as the number of vehicles in use has risen sharply. Further, consumer preference for larger, more powerful vehicles has resulted recently in a decline in the fuel efficiency of passenger cars in use. Emissions of CO_2 from the road transport sector will continue to present a difficult environmental problem for Japanese policymakers, particularly as they attempt to meet the stringent binding targets of the Kyoto Protocol. In this context, the government has placed further CO_2 emission reductions on the country's institutional agenda.

Early on, the Japanese government formulated policies under its 1990 Action Program to Arrest Global Warming, which laid out a strategy to stabilize greenhouse gas emissions between 1990 and 2000. The 1990 program was replaced by the 1997 Guidelines on Measures to Prevent Global Warming; these guidelines were revised in 2002 after Japan ratified the Kyoto Protocol and again in 2005 (when their name was changed to the Kyoto Protocol Target Achievement Plan). These plans all emphasize voluntary action rather than strict obligations; hence, measures to achieve emission reduction targets include developing new technologies, strengthening forest management to enhance the absorption of CO_2, and promoting scientific research and public education, energy conservation measures, and international cooperation.

The most notable policy reform relating to CO_2 emission reductions surrounded the adoption of the 1998 Law Concerning the Promotion of Measures to Cope with Global Warming. Like its predecessor, the 1993 Basic Law for the Environment, the 1998 law was notable not so much for what it accomplished but for what it failed to achieve. The 1998 law and its amendments in 2002, 2005, and 2008 serve as a basic law for Japan's climate change policy. Although the law specifies clear roles for national and local government, business and industry, and citizens in mitigating climate change, the law imposes no legal obligations on any of these groups and involves only voluntary action to reduce greenhouse gas emissions. As is the norm in Japan, the law was the product of a consensus-building process between government and polluting industries, with limited chance for public input. Business preferences were translated directly into policies via tight and close networks with government ministries.

The policy formulation stage of this legislation took place through close consultations between industry and the bureaucracy. The Environment Agency (replaced by the Ministry of the Environment in 2001) advocated the introduction of strict regulatory measures as well as a carbon tax as a means of reducing CO_2 emissions. This proposal brought strong opposition from several other government ministries, especially the Ministry of Economy, Trade and Industry (METI) and the Ministry of International Trade and Industry (MITI), both of which are connected closely to business leaders. In addition, the country's most powerful business organization, the *Keidranen*, strongly opposed the introduction of stricter environmental regulations that would impose costly obligations on industry, or the implementation of a carbon tax, which they also perceived as economically detrimental. Industry, METI, and MITI all argued that economic growth should take precedence over environmental concerns. Because the Ministry of the Environment is much less influential than these other two powerful ministries, the proposed legislation was weakened considerably during the negotiation process, and the tax was omitted entirely. The final policy strongly emphasizes technological solutions because business preferred them over reducing overall production and consumption. As is often the case in Japan, industry's close connection to the bureaucracy was highly effective in influencing policy development.

Although environmental groups were unhappy with the climate law, they had no say in its formulation, nor were they able to influence the decision-making process. Environmental groups exist in Japan, but a strong national-level movement does not exist and a green party has not emerged. The strong industrial-bureaucratic linkage in Japan, combined with relatively few access points to the highly centralized decision-making process, meant that interest groups were weak and ineffective overall. In addition, because policymakers are unreceptive to citizen involvement on environmental issues (indeed, on most issues) at the national level, public opinion made no difference.

At present there are no significant implementation concerns for policies in this area. The implementation of all environmental policies remains under strict bureaucratic control. Environmental policies receive ample bureaucratic attention and are implemented efficiently. As Japan's government continues to develop policies to meet its existing commitments, it likely will be forced to create new sorts of policy instruments in this area, many of which may be more controversial among the general public and industry. For example, the government has yet to develop a taxation system for vehicle ownership and fuel use that would provide incentives for the use of more fuel-efficient passenger cars, commercial vehicles, and ships that emit less CO_2. The use of economic instruments such as taxes and charges may be the next policy approach to be adopted.

The reform process in Japan is explained by two key factors: economic concerns and the existence of a closed policy network in this policy area. The Japanese government's CO_2 emission control policies have thus far failed to include economic instruments (most notably, taxes) that could make significant inroads toward the country's emission reduction goals. This situation reflects the ability of industry to prevent the adoption of measures that involve significant costs, based on arguments that such measures will reduce international competitiveness. Because environmental policy formulation and decision making occur through a pattern of close consultation between business and industry, with no room for environmental groups or public opinion in the policy formulation or decision-making process, policy outputs reflect the wishes of industry and the bureaucracy. The absence of a strong environmental interest group at the national level in Japan, coupled with little public interest in the problem of global warming, results in little pressure being placed on the government to open up this policy network for more debate and discussion.

Germany

Background: Policy Process and Policy History

The German constitution does not allocate legislative responsibility for the environment to different levels of government. As a result, the distribution of environmental responsibility has differed among environmental areas. In most cases, federal environmental law supersedes state law. Air quality management has fallen predominantly under the domain of the federal government. Federal environmental policy is managed by the Federal Ministry for the Environment, Nature Conservation, and Nuclear Safety, created in 1986.

The German constitution makes state governments responsible for implementation of environmental protection laws. Once environmental standards are set, the federal government's authority ends and the states are responsible for enforcement. State governments are usually free to establish specific institutional arrangements for carrying out these laws, thereby creating the possibility for notable differences at the implementation stage. With respect to air quality management, state governments may grant permits; set penalties, fines, or sanctions; monitor ambient air pollution; and identify so-called investigation and smog areas. They are also responsible for developing emission inventories and air pollution abatement plans for these areas. Finally, the states are permitted to develop their own policies for locally specific air pollution problems, such as traffic control in smog-prone areas.

Successful environmental policy implementation in Germany requires a significant degree of cooperation between the federal government and the states. To facilitate this process, a number of highly effective committees and working groups exist, comprising both federal and state representatives, that facilitate coordination and cooperation. For example, the Conference of Environment Ministers includes ministers from both levels of government. These bodies are generally successful in harmonizing environmental policy enforcement in the states.

Concern over air quality has been a central focus of German environmental policy making since the early 1970s, and climate change appeared as an important political issue in the mid-1980s. Since the 1990s, Germany has been one of the leading industrialized countries in terms of its climate change policies, from reductions in overall greenhouse gas emissions to the development of a strong institutional capacity and comprehensive knowledge base. German policy especially focused on pollution prevention, emphasizing the development of technology-oriented standards and new methods for eliminating air pollution. Germany has transposed the EU's environmental directives into national law and is party to all international agreements on air quality. Even further, the German government has actively sought to set the global climate policy agenda at international negotiations since the late 1980s.

The primary mechanism for controlling air pollution in Germany is direct regulation adopted at the federal level. Such regulations involve emission standards, the use of best-available technology, fuel quality standards, and product standards. The foundation of air management policy in Germany is the 1974 Federal Immission Control Act.[2] The 1974 act provides an overarching framework for licensing of industrial facilities, air pollution

---

[2] The term *immission* refers in this context to the concentration of a substance in an environmental medium.

monitoring, and enforcement. More than twenty ordinances are involved in the implementation of the act. In addition, three administrative regulations, the most important of which is the Technical Instruction on Air Quality Control (TI Air), are implemented uniformly throughout the country and have addressed numerous pollutants from a variety of sources. Overall, the German air quality management program is one of the strictest and most successful in the industrialized countries.

Many of the air quality regulations that Germany has implemented are targeted to control production facilities. In particular, the government has focused on limiting emissions from large combustion installations. The Ordinance on Large Combustion Plants set stringent emission standards based on best-available technology for dealing with SO_x and NO_x emissions. Industrial sources of air pollutants are regulated under the TI Air that calls for the adoption of continuously evolving state-of-the art controls. The TI Air is invoked on the premise that the higher the potential risk of a pollutant, the more stringent the controls or emission limits should be. This regulation thus involves best-available control technology requirements and emission limits specific to individual industries. Emission limits are set for all industrial pollutants.

This emission control approach is accompanied in Germany by the setting of ambient air quality standards (or, as the Germans call them, *immissions values*) under TI Air. These standards are linked directly to the process of licensing polluting facilities. To obtain a license, industries must demonstrate that they will keep their immission values within acceptable levels or implement additional controls to meet these standards. Although ambient air quality is not monitored at the national level, state governments are required to maintain monitoring systems in more polluted areas.

Federal regulations and economic instruments aimed at transport-related pollution focus on controlling automobile emissions and fuel quality. These regulations involve the use of state-of-the-art technology, emission standards for heavy vehicles, periodic inspection of older vehicles, and bans on leaded gasoline and certain fuel additives. Economic incentives in regulating emissions include reduced taxes on cars with three-way catalytic converters and on vehicles that use unleaded gasoline or that have diesel engines with lower particulate emissions. An eco-tax was introduced in 1999 that imposed a levy on electricity consumption and raised all existing fuel taxes.

Germany also has implemented a fairly elaborate system of smog control in which the states designate areas with high concentrations of air pollutants that lead to smog incidents. At the federal level, three grades of smog intensity are defined: when the second level is exceeded, traffic restrictions are issued; when the third level is exceeded, industrial activity is halted. Smog areas are defined in both western and eastern Germany, and in recent years, smog levels in the west rarely have triggered a second-level warning.

Although German environmental policy remains highly regulatory in nature, several new policy instruments have been developed recently. Within the EU, Germany is now one of the highest users of voluntary agreements. Germany is a full participant in the EU Emission Trading System and has effectively implemented EU environmental directives. Germany also is a leader in the global movement to protect the environment. The country is party to many international agreements setting overall emission reduction goals and standards for transborder air pollution control as well as global measures. Germany also is a strong supporter of global efforts to prevent climate change and to protect the ozone layer. For example, Germany was the first country to have completed CFC reductions called for under the Montreal Protocol.

Contemporary Dynamics

Like the United States and Japan, Germany has committed to reducing its greenhouse gas emissions under the FCCC and the Kyoto Protocol and has achieved substantial reductions in these emissions since the late 1990s. Although a portion of these reductions accrued because of the rapid collapse of the eastern states' economies in the early 1990s, they also reflect increasing energy efficiency across all economic sectors over the past decade. Unlike in most other industrialized countries, in Germany, CO_2 emissions from the transport sector have declined since 2000. Germany's greatest progress was achieved in greenhouse gas emissions reductions (especially CO_2) through the 1990s, with some slowing of this trend by the mid-2000s. In this context, successive governments have placed further CO_2 emission reductions on the country's institutional agenda. Germany continues to pursue further, ambitious greenhouse gas emission reduction targets, recently committing to a 40 percent reduction in CO_2 emissions by 2020. This ambitious target goes well beyond Germany's international commitments as well as those made by any other industrialized country to date.

Notably, changes in the political composition of governing coalitions have not led to climate policy reversals. Instead, political leaders of all stripes have endorsed increasingly stringent national environmental goals. In 2007, at the German Energy Summit, current center-right chancellor Angela Merkel declared climate protection to be the biggest challenge of the twenty-first century. Her government continued to push for extensive climate policy that was consistent with the agenda pursued by her predecessor Gerhard Schröder's center-left government.

The continued ability of the German government to set such stringent emission reduction targets emerged from an unusual and early agenda-setting experience. In 1987 the government set up a nonpartisan inquiry commission (the Enquete Commission) to study climate change. In 1990 this commission issued three reports that created the basis for a common definition of the problem, climate change, while recommending the adoption of strict emission reduction targets. Because the commission, rather than political parties, the

Bundestag, interest groups, or ministries, reached this conclusion, it was possible to establish a broad national consensus around which to act. The commission's reports raised the public's awareness of climate change issues and set the institutional agenda for reform via a mobilization model that endures.

Because Germany emphasizes informal consultations in the policy-making process, particularly with industry but also with environmental groups, most climate change policy measures tend not to be strongly opposed by industry or the general public. The German population tends to be relatively more environmentally aware and environmentally demanding than the public in other industrialized countries and traditionally is less likely to oppose significant environmental reforms. These policies also are associated with no unusual implementation concerns.

Despite public consensus on global warming problems, initial attempts to extend Germany's frequent use of economic instruments to a CO_2 tax were unsuccessful. Environmental interest groups, the Green Party, scientists, and the center-left Social Democratic Party favored developing such a tax, and in 1996 the Social Democratic Party and the Free Democratic Party together proposed a CO_2 tax in the Bundestag. The decision-making stage for this policy proposal was marked by a great deal of controversy. The proposal was denounced by the Christian Democratic Union/Christian Social Union (CDU-CSU) as unfeasible and expensive. Fearing a loss of international competitiveness, German industrial associations also opposed the proposal and instead pushed for voluntary agreements. The government was not prepared to force the adoption of a tax despite it's being a necessary means to reach the country's ambitious emission reduction target. Instead, industry's opposition ruled the day, and the government conceded to industry's calls for voluntary agreements.

The idea of an eco-tax did not die, however. In the lead-up to the 1998 elections, environmental groups staged a major public campaign in favor of eco-taxation. The campaign was stridently opposed by industry groups. When the election produced a coalition government (between the Social Democratic Party and its junior partner, the Green Party), the eco-tax window of opportunity was reopened. In the coalition agreement, the two parties committed to pursuing eco-tax reform. Naturally, the Greens favored environmental taxation (with strong support from environmental nongovernmental organizations). The Social Democrats supported the idea because tax revenues would be used to benefit workers and employers. The tax plan introduced to the parliament in 1999 envisioned a five-step reform to be phased in through 2003. This timing was intended to allow companies to adjust to the tax increase while maintaining their economic competitiveness. Although the proposal generated considerable debate, with vocal opposition from the business sector and a high degree of skepticism from German citizens, the unified governing coalition was able to ensure the bill's passage in the parliament, and the new tax went into effect in 1999.

The eco-tax policy encountered some difficulty in the implementation phase as the annual increases in the tax rate generated intense political opposition. Rising fuel prices generated mass popular protests in 2000. These protests prompted the main opposition parties (the CDU-CSU and the Free Democratic Party) to demand that the government rescind the tax. The CDU-CSU tabled a parliamentary initiative to this effect, which was rejected by the coalition majority. The government did, however, adopt measures to compensate those most affected by fuel price increases, namely, commuters and lower-income households. Although the tax remains in place, the rate has not increased, diluting the tax policy's guiding principle—imposing price increases to discourage the continued use of nonrenewable energy sources—and reducing its environmental impact.

Despite the German government's commitment to environmental policy reform and a relatively high degree of public mobilization on environmental issues, the move to more stringent economic instruments to control CO_2 was not easily achieved. The initial failure to adopt an environmental tax to meet the country's stringent emission targets can be explained by both economic and political factors. Concerns about the competitive position of the German economy mean that policy choices must be justified to both the public and industry in terms of their cost neutrality. Thus arguments that environmental policies destroy jobs and reduce industrial competitiveness carry significant weight in policy debates. Measures seen as threatening to economic growth or the country's global competitiveness may be destined to fail, especially given the corporatist arrangements that exist between government and industry. The pattern of close consultation in policy making between these players means that any measures perceived as harmful to industry are less likely to succeed. This dynamic changed considerably, however, with the movement of the Green Party into the governing coalition. In 1999 their presence in government was enough to counter substantial industrial opposition to tax reform and reverse the earlier policy outcome.

France

Background: Policy Process and Policy History

Environmental policy in France has been managed by the Ministry of the Environment since 1971. A new super-ministry, the Ministry of Ecology and Sustainable Development, was created by President Jacques Chirac in 2002. The ministry is a large bureaucratic organization with wide-ranging responsibilities, covering most areas of environmental protection, including energy and transport, and overseeing a large number of environmental agencies. For example, the ministry oversees twenty-four regional directorates of industry, research, and environment (DRIREs), along with twenty-six regional departments of the environment. The DRIREs include among their responsibilities air quality management and local implementation of national policies. The minister of the environment also leads an interministerial committee for environmental affairs that includes representatives from all government ministries and is charged with ensuring the integration of policies across ministries and reviewing the actions of ministries to ensure that they reflect environmental requirements. In general, the environmental policy process in France has involved central-level actors playing a key role in both policy making and implementation.

Most environmental policies in France are adopted at the national level (although some regions also have their own administrative structures) and are then implemented at the lower levels of government, particularly at the department level through the local branches of different ministries. Many useful policy coordination mechanisms are at work in this system. In general, the environmental policy process in France is relatively well managed and effective.

Although France came later to the process of environmental protection than many of its European neighbors, its record on air quality management, which came into full force in the 1980s, is still viewed as being comprehensive, well coordinated, and effective. The government made a clear commitment to environmental protection in 2005 by incorporating an Environmental Charter into the French constitution. The government uses a variety of policy options for environmental protection, traditionally relying most heavily on direct regulations but moving increasingly toward economic instruments. France has transposed most of the EU's environmental directives into national law, has made a serious attempt to implement these laws, and is a strong supporter of further EU action on the environment.

The majority of environmental policies directed toward air pollution in France are direct regulations. The French government first set air quality objectives with the 1961 Law on the Control of Atmospheric Pollution and Odors; these objectives were further defined in a 1977 law on classified facilities, which set standards for emissions from stationary sources based on best-available technology. A national air quality monitoring system introduced in 1974 is run by associations throughout the country. To improve energy efficiency and mitigate climate change—with a goal of stabilizing greenhouse gas emissions at 1990 levels by 2010—France adopted its first National Climate Plan in 2000. This was followed in 2004 by a more ambitious plan, which included a carbon tax, biofuels, energy labeling, and fuel price increases. These plans include about 100 measures intended to address seven greenhouse gas emission sectors. The measures envisioned in the plans are developed by an interministerial agency led by the prime minister in consultation and negotiation with a range of environmental stakeholders (sectoral ministry representatives, scientific experts, nongovernmental organizations, lobbies, and unions). This extensive consultation process often results in noticeable differences between policy proposals and the final measures adopted, reflecting the influence of powerful interests in the process.

Most French policies to control emissions are economic instruments (including government subsidies for public transport and cleaner technology development, road taxes and pricing, and fiscal measures to promote sales of fuel-efficient vehicles). Recognizing that fuel consumption and CO_2 emissions are directly proportional, the French government uses fuel taxes effectively to control transport emissions. Taxes on petroleum products, in the form of gasoline and diesel taxes, are high compared to those found in other industrialized countries. Regulatory policy in this area is limited to greater speed limit enforcement and vehicle inspections, and voluntary agreements have been signed with car manufacturers to limit CO_2 emissions by 2005. Government and industry also set up a working group on reducing these emissions and entered into a voluntary agreement for the development of alternatively powered vehicles. The government presented a biofuel plan in 2006.

The French government supports and participates actively in international cooperative efforts on the environment. France is a full participant in the EU Emission Trading System and has effectively implemented EU environmental directives. France is a signatory to all the major international agreements with regard to the major air pollutants and on more global issues such as ozone-depleting substances. Under President Sarkozy, France has begun to take on a global environmental leadership role, particularly within the EU.

Contemporary Dynamics

France ratified the FCCC and the Kyoto Protocol, and since 1990 France has made progress in reducing emissions. In general, France has a less severe problem with CO_2 emissions than other industrialized countries. France has already reduced CO_2 emissions more per capita than any other EU country, and only Sweden has done better among the Organisation for Economic Cooperation and Development (OECD) countries. These low levels reflect the structure of the economy, the country's energy resources, and the effects of government action. In particular, hydroelectric and nuclear power account for about 90 percent of the country's power generation, resulting in lower CO_2 emission levels. France is on its way to meeting its Kyoto target, although continued increases in emissions from the transport sector keep climate change issues on the institutional agenda.

Despite some success in reducing emissions, France has yet to put in place the sort of strict, binding measures for greenhouse gas emissions required to meet its targets in the face of continued increases in emissions. Owing to the influence of business interests and other lobbies, the national government has not yet imposed the needed regulations or standards, favoring instead incentives (tax credits or subsidies) and information (energy labeling, public awareness campaign), especially in the transport sector. Despite recent improvements in fuel efficiency and motor vehicle emissions, the country's expanding transport sector places increasing pressure on air quality through the increased volume of emissions of many pollutants.

Lionel Jospin's center-left coalition government, with a green partner (the Verts—the largest French Green party), in 1999 introduced the first National Climate Plan. This plan included three categories of preventive measures: emission trading and voluntary agreements, economic instruments in the form of a carbon tax, and measures to promote energy efficiency and the use of renewable energy sources such as wind power. The second measure, the carbon tax (or TGAP-Energie), was brought before the parliament in 1999. Under the plan, companies using the equivalent of over 100 tonnes of oil per year (some 40,000 companies in all) were to pay a tax of 260 francs per tonne of carbon equivalent.

The proposed reform encountered resistance in several quarters but in particular from industrial and agricultural groups. After intense interministerial negotiation, strong pressure from industry groups, and robust debate in the parliament, the government made several concessions on its original proposal. In particular, to maintain their economic competitiveness, the most energy-intensive firms were exempted from the tax, provided that they attained emission reduction targets set out in voluntary agreements to be signed with the government. Firms failing to meet their agreements would need to pay a tax on excess emissions. Farmers and food producers also were exempted, as well as primary energy producers and chemicals companies. In the end, the higher energy taxes on industry that were envisioned in the plan were weakened substantially, lessening the potential environmental impact of the policy.

Despite these significant concessions, a case against the tax was brought before the Constitutional Council by opposition party members in December 2000. The court struck down the TGAP-Energie as unconstitutional, arguing that it failed to respect the principle of equality in taxation. The court ruled that the tax in its proposed form discriminated among categories of energy consumers, and this aspect of the National Climate Plan was abandoned. In this instance, strong resistance from market actors obstructed the implementation of a significant eco-tax reform and left the government with a significantly weakened climate change policy.

The court's decision led to a continued sidelining of eco-tax proposals. By 2002 there was a strong sentiment in the country against eco-taxation on industry and other economic instruments. Successive governments, included the Sarkozy government, have remained receptive to arguments from industry against carbon taxes on the grounds that they are ineffective in environmental terms and disabling in economic terms. The conventional wisdom has been that companies need to be persuaded rather than forced to reduce their emissions to protect their economic competitiveness. To date, a clear lack of political will to revive a carbon tax or to introduce other economic instruments has persisted.

Support for moving from regulatory policies to market-oriented measures (especially increasing taxes) is weaker in France than in Germany or the United Kingdom. Although strict emission targets and carbon taxes are supported by environmental groups, they have no support among industrialists or the public. Even when in a governing position, the Verts, with the support of environmental groups and center-left parties, lacked the political resources to bring the carbon tax to fruition. The French public had become more interested in climate change issues over the 1990s, but popular mobilization for policy reform is still lacking, especially compared to some other industrialized countries, and environmentalists remained in a relatively marginalized position. Taken together, these attitudes resulted in little political will to act on these issues.

France has no technical implementation concerns related to existing air quality policies—although to the extent that some of these policies involve real economic costs for users, they are easier to implement in times of economic growth than in an economic downturn. The real challenge in meeting environmental policy targets is government inaction in implementing national objectives—plans are laid out, but the political will to follow through has been lacking. Objectives often are not translated into actionable measures that are then monitored and enforced.

The absence of credible reforms to meet the more stringent targets the country faces under the Kyoto Protocol is the result of a lack of mobilization on these issues among the French public. Public indifference is partly the result of concerns about economic growth and competitiveness, and neither the public nor the government has any interest in new policy measures that will increase the costs of transport and production. Further, substantial reductions in the past have significantly reduced the public's and the government's sense of urgency, putting little pressure on the government to act. Under President Sarkozy, this policy environment is expected to remain stable.

United Kingdom

Background: Policy Process and Policy History

Environmental policy in the United Kingdom is controlled at the central level. Until 1997 such policy was managed by the Department of the Environment. The new Labour government in 1997 merged the environment department with transport and regional planning, to form the Department of the Environment, Transport and the Regions (DETR) to improve policy formulation and integration. After the 2001 election, another reorganization created the Department for Environment, Food and Rural Affairs (DEFRA), which combined the environment section of DETR with the old Ministry of Agriculture, Fisheries, and Food. This is now the main environmental policy making department. The transport sector was redesignated as the Department for Transport.

The United Kingdom has a long history of environmental policy making that has emphasized pollution control rather than pollution prevention. Environmental policies in the United Kingdom involve the use of direct regulations, economic instruments, and international agreements. The United Kingdom has made an effort to adopt and implement all EU environmental directives and is a strong supporter of an integrated European environmental program.

British environmental policy has stressed the use of direct regulation. Air quality was controlled primarily under the provisions of the 1956 Clean Air Act (revised in 1968 and consolidated in 1993), which regulated emissions of particulates. In the area of air quality, the United Kingdom traditionally resisted pressure to set quantitative targets for air pollution emission reductions or ambient air quality standards. When such targets were set, it was generally in response to requirements imposed by EU directives or international agreements. Under the provisions of the 1995 Environment Act, however, the secretary of state for the environment was charged with producing a national air quality strategy that involved targets and standards to serve as a general framework for air quality management efforts.

The 1997 National Air Quality Strategy set quantitative, dated targets for eight common air pollutants, based primarily on their effects on human health but also with attention paid to their broader environmental effects (seven of these objectives were later incorporated into the 1997 Air Quality Regulation Act). This strategy requires local authorities (under a system known as local air pollution control created by the 1990 Environmental Protection Act) to monitor air quality in their localities and, where these standards are not likely to be met by 2005, to create air quality management areas and develop plans for meeting these goals in these areas. The Labour government completed a review of this strategy in 1998 and introduced new standards based on this review in early 2000. The most recent air quality strategy was introduced in 2007. The 1999 Pollution Prevention and Control Act introduced a new integrated pollution prevention and control system that was phased in between 2000 and 2007.

The United Kingdom has a regular system for testing and inspecting motor vehicles for exhaust emissions and introduced a plan for roadside vehicle emission testing. Motor vehicle emissions are controlled under the 1972 and 1974 Road Traffic Acts. Since 1991 the United Kingdom has tested hydrocarbon and CO_2 emissions, and smoke emissions from light diesel vehicles have been tested since 1993. In addition, since 1992 all new vehicles must be fitted with catalytic converters. Regulatory policies also govern fuel quality, although the sulfur content of fuel is regulated only in London.

The British government has encouraged the use of unleaded fuel througl tax differentials for leaded and unleaded gasoline since 1986. The sal of leaded gasoline was banned in 2000. The use of economic instrumen traditionally was otherwise limited, but the Labour government in 1998 indicated its intention to provide further economic incentives for environmental protection. A climate change levy was introduced in 2001, and the U.K. Emissions Trading Scheme (a precursor to the EU Emission Trading System) was launched in 2002. The United Kingdom was the first industrialized country to introduce a market-based emission trading scheme.

Voluntary agreements have begun to be used more extensively in the United Kingdom. In 2001, as part of the U.K. Climate Change Program, more than forty industry associations, representing some 6,000 companies, negotiated climate change agreements with DEFRA. Under these agreements, the companies signed on to quantitative targets for improvements in energy efficiency or carbon emissions in return for an 80 percent discount on the climate change levy.

The United Kingdom has a strong record on developing, ratifying, and fully implementing international environmental agreements. The United Kingdom also supports European efforts to reduce transborder air pollution (a large portion of which the United Kingdom produces) and is a strong supporter of the major global agreements on ozone depletion, acid rain, and prevention of climate change. The country also is a full participant in the EU Emission Trading System and has effectively implemented EU environmental directives. The British government advocates developing measures that allow for the effective implementation and enforcement of these agreements and supports future environmental cooperation among countries. By the mid-1990s, around 80 percent of the United Kingdom's environmental legislation had its origins in EU directives.

Contemporary Dynamics

The United Kingdom is one of the few EU countries on track to meet and surpass its Kyoto target. This has been achieved through the development of a comprehensive set of policies and measures. Even though industrial emissions have fallen, however, residential and transport-sector greenhouse gas emissions have increased. In fact, transport is expected to account for all of the country's projected increases in CO_2 emissions between 1970 and 2020. Under the EU burden sharing agreement (and the Kyoto Protocol), the United Kingdom committed to reducing its emissions by 12.5 percent based on 1990 levels by 2010. The government set a domestic goal that went even urther, with plans to cut CO_2 emissions by 20 percent below 1990 levels by 010.

The 2000 U.K. Climate Change program set out policies and measures to ove toward this domestic goal. In response to a recommendation by the yal Commission on Environmental Pollution, the Labour government de a further commitment in its 2003 energy white paper to putting the ntry on the path toward a reduction in CO_2 emissions of some 60 percent from current levels by about 2050, with real progress to be made by 2020. The white paper did not set specific targets, however. In a 2006 review of the country's progress toward meeting its targets, DEFRA reported that although the United Kingdom was on track to meet and exceed its Kyoto Protocol target, further effort was needed to attain a domestic goal of 20 percent by 2010 (this goal was set in the Labour Party's 2001 general election manifesto). Based on the 2006 report, this commitment was reduced to an aspiration (with perhaps a 15 to 18 percent goal more likely to be accomplished). In this context, the government has placed further CO_2 emission reductions on the country's institutional agenda.

Environmental policy formulation continues the government's tradition of close consultation between regulatory agencies and industry. Because core policy networks in the United Kingdom remain strong, meaning that at best environmental groups are consulted only intermittently in the policy process, these closed policy communities have been successful at preventing stricter emission controls and defending producer interests. The Labour government, through the creation of several discussion forums, has worked to encourage a broader consultative process. But a closed and bureaucratic culture remains, with strong involvement by industry groups in environmental policy design. These groups continue to enjoy a privileged position as providers of technical knowledge and as consultants on the practicality of environmental policy proposals. There is a small green party movement in the United Kingdom, and a strong and well-organized lobby for the environment exists. However, environmental groups often find it difficult to gain access to this formulation process.

Environmental issues over the past decade have maintained a low profile in British politics. They did not figure prominently in the 1997, 2001, or 2005 election campaigns. The major political parties correctly perceived environmental issues as not being significant vote winners. Nonetheless, since 2005 increasing evidence indicates that climate change has emerged as a more politically relevant issue. In recent public opinion polls, the environment has consistently been one of the top issues the public believes require government attention.

Since coming to power in 1997, the Labour government has regularly changed its approach to environmental issues, to environmental governance, and to environmental policy content. The Labour government's commitment to reducing CO_2 emissions to 20 percent of their 1990 levels by 2010 (higher than the Kyoto target) required dramatic policy changes. The government initially favored annual increases in fuel taxes of at least 6 percent on average above inflation (1 percent higher than the previous government's commitment). In 1999, however, the government announced its decision to eliminate these annual increases (the so-called fuel tax escalator) in response to industrial pressures. The Labour government also entered into voluntary agreements with auto manufacturers to meet vehicle fuel-efficiency targets.

The government introduced a controversial climate change levy in April 2001 that applied to business use of electricity, gas, and solid fuels (but not fuel oil and energy from renewable sources) consumed by the public and business sectors. To ward off business opposition, the revenue from this tax is recycled to businesses, primarily through reductions in employer national insurance contributions and is used to support new plans to promote energy efficiency and renewable energy. Despite these concessions, industrial groups remained opposed to the levy. Because the levy was aimed at the downstream use of energy rather than at reducing the carbon intensity of energy use, it was viewed as unlikely to be sufficient to meet the country's climate targets. As such, the expectation in 2001 was that further costly measures (at least in the view of industry) were likely.

In an effort to deflect future increases in the climate change levy, industry mobilized to present its own environmental policy solutions. In particular, industry groups were determined to prevent the adoption of a carbon energy tax. These efforts resulted in a plan for an emission trading scheme, which was first mentioned in a government report in 1998 but not fully developed. The first proposals for such a scheme were generated by industry, in documents circulated in 2000 by the U.K. Emissions Trading Group (formed by the Federation of British Industry and the Advisory Committee on Business and the Environment to produce a blueprint for a scheme). The group's proposals were well received, and DEFRA began consultations with industry, academics, environmental groups, and traders on rules for a trading scheme. With strong industry support, the United Kingdom was the first country to introduce a market-based emission trading scheme. Introduced in 2002, it predated the EU Emission Trading System. The U.K. scheme operated from 2002 to 2005, when the country began to participate in the EU plan.

The nature of adopted policy reforms in the United Kingdom reflects the influence of those concerned about economic costs and international competitiveness. Despite its commitment to significant reductions in CO_2 emissions, the government has not been entirely successful in pursuing the policies necessary to achieve these goals. Industrial concerns have a strong capacity to influence the content of environmental policy because the policy formulation process is based on consultative arrangements between industry and government that usually exclude advocates for more stringent environmental policies. At the decision-making stage, single-party government ensures that policy decisions made in this consultation process survive in the resulting legislation and are implemented effectively.

Italy

Background: Policy Process and Policy History

Government policies for environmental protection in Italy begin with the 1947 Italian constitution, which guarantees individuals' right to health and safeguards the natural, historic, and cultural heritage of the nation. Environmental legislation may be drafted by the Italian parliament, by the government, or by regional authorities. Protection of the environment also is pursued through decrees issued by the president of the republic, the president of the Council of Ministers, or by an individual minister with delegation from the parliament.

Most environmental policies in Italy are drafted at the level of central government and implemented by lower levels of government, which can result in varying levels of implementation across regions. The 20 regions and 103 provinces have varying abilities to carry out these responsibilities owing to differences in size, resources, and administrative structures. The effectiveness of Italian environmental policies is generally viewed as being limited by the weaknesses of regional and provincial institutions and by a lack of coordination and linkage between central and regional levels, particularly in terms of defining responsibilities and providing adequate financial support for implementation costs. In addition, the Italian government's rigid regulatory framework provides local authorities with little to no discretion in the policy implementation process.

Italy established a national-level Ministry of the Environment in 1986 that coordinates and integrates environmental activities in the country and creates new policy instruments. This is now called the Ministry of the Environment and Land Protection (MATT). This and other central-level environmental institutions are relatively short on human and financial resources. The ministry is charged with developing and administrating Italy's three-year environmental management programs, which lay out plans for allocating central revenues to the regions and provinces for environmental expenditures. These plans are the primary source of environmental money for subnational levels of government.

Italy faces real challenges regarding environmental policy coordination among central, regional, and other levels of government. National-level institutions lack both the resources and organizational strength to manage the policy process effectively. In addition to their own weaknesses, central government agencies thus far have had great difficulty in guaranteeing uniform implementation of regulations across regions, reflecting a high degree of subnational government autonomy. To improve this coordination, additional monetary resources, stronger enforcement mechanisms, and improved monitoring capabilities are needed at the central and regional levels. Such improvements will be possible only to the degree that the regional and local administrative units are strengthened (institutionally and financially) so that they can effectively fulfill their responsibilities.

The Italian government has been developing policies to improve air quality since the 1960s. Laws governing air quality are extremely complex and inconsistently implemented. Policies focus primarily on eliminating pollution rather than on preventing it and include a combination of direct regulations, economic incentives, and voluntary and international agreements. Italian environmental laws reflect the content of nearly all EU environmental directives. Italy's environmental legislation is highly reactive, usually prompted primarily by EU directives or environmental emergencies, although often with significant delay. The country's main air quality targets derive from EU and international efforts.

The main thrust of the Italian government's air quality management effort is through direct regulation. Italy's first comprehensive air quality legislation, the Clean Air Law, was adopted in 1966. Before this legislation, Italian air quality policies were piecemeal efforts that addressed specific, localized problems. Air pollution is now regulated under the 1988 Industrial Air Pollution Law, which allocates a wide range of responsibilities to the regions for both improving and monitoring air quality. Regions are charged with developing plans for protecting, conserving, and cleaning up their territories while complying with national air quality limits; setting emission limits based on best-available technology within national guidelines; establishing air pollution monitoring; and reporting annually on air quality. Provinces are also required to monitor air emissions to meet national criteria.

Italy controls industrial emissions by issuing licensing permits for new and existing installations. Regional authorities issue permits to facilities that can demonstrate that emissions will fall within existing limits and that measures will be taken to prevent air pollution with current technology. In some regions, these responsibilities are passed on to the provinces. These requirements resulted in a large number of industrial plants requiring inspection and monitoring (estimated at between 300,000 and 600,000 premises) in an environment of limited resources and fragmented administration. Given these problems, a system of self-certification has been adopted.

The Italian government has introduced motor vehicle emission controls, including requiring all newly registered cars to be low-emission vehicles (equipped with three-way catalytic converters), in line with EU directives. Italy currently requires periodic emission inspections for all vehicles. The government also has proposed economic incentives to eliminate older vehicles and has adopted policies regarding fuel quality. Since 1978 taxes on all motor vehicle fuels have increased to such a degree that Italy's fuel prices and taxes are some of the highest among the OECD countries. Voluntary agreements among the government, trade unions, and auto manufacturers encourage the development of electric cars and the development of low-emission public transport. Agreements with oil industries also are used to improve fuel quality through lead and benzene content restrictions for gasoline and sulfur limits for diesel fuel. To control air pollution, Italy uses several mechanisms designed to control traffic in regions where severe pollution is a problem, particularly where air pollution has damaged historical buildings and artifacts. These measures typically include restricting access to the regions to public transport and low-emission vehicles or instituting odd-even plate access on alternate days.

Italy is a participant in international cooperative efforts, both within the EU and on regional and global levels. The country has ratified most international air quality agreements and has integrated EU air quality directives into national law. Italy ratified the Kyoto Protocol in 2002 and began to pursue its targets in 2005. A lack of financial and personnel resources at the national, regional, and local levels, however, has resulted in an incomplete record with respect to the implementation and monitoring of these agreements. Italy is a full participant in the EU Emission Trading System, although until recently Italy had the dubious distinction of being the EU member state most frequently brought before the Court of Justice of the European Communities for failing to comply adequately with EU environmental directives.

Contemporary Dynamics

A rise in CO_2 emission levels from the transport sector presents a continuing challenge to Italian policymakers. Although Italy had one of the lowest levels of CO_2 emissions per capita among the OECD countries in the 1990s, the country's total emissions increased 4.4 percent in 1990–1999 and by 2005 had increased 12.3 percent since 1990. Despite a decrease in CO_2 emissions from manufacturing industries, as in other industrialized countries, the gains achieved by existing emission policies are being offset by transport and energy production emissions, and stricter and more comprehensive policies are needed, particularly because current target levels of CO_2 are unlikely to be achieved at current rates of expansion in the transport sector. The government has placed further CO_2 emission reductions on the country's institutional agenda.

Italy's official climate change strategy appears to be thin in content, especially regarding the transport sector. In 1994 the Ministry of the Environment formulated the National Program for Limiting CO_2 Emissions, which approaches CO_2 emission control largely through the use of economic instruments such as government subsidies for public transport, traffic management systems, alternatively powered vehicle development, and new technologies; fiscal measures to support sales of fuel-efficient vehicles; and vehicle fleet renewal. Italy has yet to use voluntary agreements to address CO_2 concerns, and specific regulations have been developed that relate only to speed limits outside of cities.

The 1994 program was updated and published as the Guidelines for National Policies and Measures for Reduction of Greenhouse Gas Emissions in 1997 and adopted by the government in 1998. The update was carried out by the Interministerial Committee for Economic Planning (CIPE), which takes all key decisions on Italy's climate policy and approves all associated initiatives. The program is the current basis for Italy's climate change policy. Implementation of the program is mainly through voluntary reduction targets and is accompanied by economic incentives, rather than regulations, and as such has not provided a clear legal framework. In 1999 and 2000, new policies using instruments such as regulatory measures, market-oriented actions, and fiscal incentives in the form of a carbon tax were introduced but then reversed by the Berlusconi government in 2001, which preferred a flexible rather than command-and-control approach. In 2002 CIPE presented a new government strategy to achieve emission targets in a National Action Plan for 2003–2010 for the Reduction of Greenhouse Gas Emissions, as well as Revised Guidelines for National Policies Regarding the Reduction of Greenhouse Gas Emissions. However, little was accomplished in implementing these plans between 2002 and 2006. The short-lived and politically tenuous Prodi government (2006–2008) was unsuccessful in addressing environmental problems. In 2008 the second Berlusconi government initiated a review of the 2002 national plans, with the intention of updating national emission projections and identifying new measures to be implemented.

Since 2000 climate change policy has appeared intermittently on the systemic agenda but with little real effect. The general political upheaval that Italy has experienced since the first half of the 1990s hindered consistent environmental policy development, especially as the office of environment minister changed hands several times, and none of the office's occupants took environmental issues that seriously. As a result, although an extensive body of environmental policy exists, it is unsystematic and disjointed and implementation has been problematic.

Internal pressures have not played much of a role in environmental policy making in Italy. Although in the 1980s Italy had an active green party movement, by the 1990s the party had become fragmented and factionalized. Environmental issues have not been a high priority for mainstream partisan organizations. For example, attempts by the Ministry of the Environment to introduce environmentally conscious taxation and economic incentives in the Italian Financial Law did not succeed because partisan consensus about the problem is lacking. Although environmental interest groups have some ability to affect the policy process, they have not had a significant impact in this issue area of late, in particular because of a lack of citizen mobilization. Among Italian citizens, concern about environmental issues has been increasing and there is a general desire to see things improve, although this has not translated into strong political mobilization.

As in other areas of environmental policy, any air pollution policy measures face implementation difficulties in Italy because of a lack of coordination at the national, regional, and local levels and because of a lack of resources to monitor fully the process. Much remains for the Italian government to do when it comes to controlling CO_2 emissions. In particular, concrete measures concerning the transport sector are needed. For example, Italy has not gone as far as other industrialized countries with respect to vehicle inspections, exhaust emission controls, or the promotion of alternatives to road transport. In addition, Italy has yet to eliminate many of the country's transport-related tax deductions.

The lack of any substantial efforts to meet Italy's international commitments may be explained by economic, political, and institutional factors. Italian industrial and business interests have blocked the introduction of strong economic instruments for CO_2 emission controls on the grounds that such instruments will reduce the country's economic competitiveness and hinder economic growth. Given a general sense of economic uncertainty, the Italian government has been receptive to these claims. Politically, the Italian green parties are ineffective environmental policy advocates, the mainstream political parties are uninterested in the environment, and the environmental interest groups are not important actors. As a result, the government faces little effective political pressure to act. Institutionally, the political disarray in Italy since the 1990s resulted in environmental issues dropping on and off the systemic and institutional agendas, and a policy approach that is too often incoherent and ineffective. This pattern appears likely to persist under Prime Minister Berlusconi.

European Union

Background: Policy Process and Policy History

The European Community (EC) did not include among its original objectives environmental protection. The 1957 Treaty of Rome did not address environmental issues, and the EC did not address multinational environmental concerns until the 1970s. A series of environmental action programs was introduced in 1973, with the sixth program introduced in 2002. These programs had no legal basis and were intended primarily to eliminate barriers to a common market rather than to focus on environmental issues. Environmental protection was not recognized as a formal obligation of member states until the Single European Act in 1987, certain provisions of which defined the EC's environmental policy goals and established a legal foundation for its actions. Beyond simply defining environmental protection as a priority, the environmental sections of the 1986 act called for the EC to consider environmental protection to be an integral part of all EC laws, whatever their primary focus. These commitments were reinforced and extended in the 1991 Maastricht Treaty. The majority of environmental policies are now adopted through qualified majority voting in the Council of Ministers and approval by the European Parliament. The Treaty of Amsterdam did not extend the EU's environmental goals but committed the EU to further consolidate the progress that has already been made by stating that environmental concerns be integrated into all EU policy making. The Nice Treaty reaffirmed the EU's environmental commitments. At the treaty conference in 2000, a declaration was adopted affirming member states' intention "to see the European Union play a leading role in promoting environmental protection in the Union and in international efforts promoting the same objective at the global level."

By the early 2000s, the EU had over 300 environmental policies in place. The bulk of this legislation, mainly in the form of regulations and directives, was adopted in the 1970s and 1980s. Application of the principle of subsidiarity as outlined in the Maastricht Treaty slowed the pace of policy making in the 1990s. The regulatory slowdown also reflected a push from industry and some governments for more flexible EU policies. Since the 1990s the EU has developed broader framework directives focused on long-term goals; these efforts emphasize new policy instruments and give member states more room to maneuver at the implementation stage. By the late 1990s the EU also began to be more active in policy development on the global stage. Since the 1970s the EU has established a strong policy record on air quality, covering a wide range of issues, from road vehicle and industrial plan emissions to acid rain reduction and limits on specific pollutants.

The EU member states generally have transposed EU environmental directives into national legislation. As in other policy areas, however, subsequent implementation and enforcement of these policies has not been uniform across the member states. In particular, the lack of EU enforcement mechanisms and resources, as well as cross-national differences in administrative structures (and differences within countries), has produced uneven policy effectiveness. States with well-established environmental protection records, a strong philosophical commitment to the environment, and existing environmental policy administrative infrastructures are more likely to have implemented EU directives effectively (although implementation in these countries also is less than perfect).

In 1994 the European Environment Agency was established at the supranational level. The agency primarily has an information-providing, integrationist role rather than being responsible for environmental regulation or monitoring enforcement of EU laws. As such, many analysts view as limited the prospects for more successful enforcement of EC environmental directives. These difficulties with implementation and enforcement notwithstanding, EU environmental policy making is viewed widely as having encouraged environmental improvements that would not otherwise have occurred and as one of the best examples of cross-national policy integration.

Decision making for most EU environmental policies is made via qualified majority voting and the co-decision procedure, making the European Parliament an equal partner with the Council of Environmental Ministers. Of the three main policy-making institutions, the European Parliament has traditionally been the most committed to environmental protection. A separate directorate-general XI for the environment (DG-XI) was established by the European Commission in 1981, although a commissioner was not appointed until 1989. The DG-XI has primary responsibility for environmental policy in the early stages of policy formulation. It formally consults and negotiates with other commissioners and other directorate-generals before policy proposals are passed to the Council of Ministers and the European Parliament. Conflicts of interest between member states often complicate decision making in the Council of Ministers. In particular, differences between "greener" countries (like Denmark, Germany, and the Netherlands) and poorer countries that have been more reluctant to implement stringent environmental standards over concern about impeding economic growth can be difficult to reconcile. Another challenge for EU policymakers has been balancing lofty environmental goals with different levels of environmental commitment and regulatory capability across member states. The decisions of the Court of Justice of the European Communities have had a significant impact on the development of environmental policy in the EU. The Court has consistently supported the view that the EU should have a broad legislative competence in this domain, even though this competence originally did not appear in the Treaty of Rome.

The EU has emerged as a global policy leader. It played a key role in the formulation and adoption of the FCCC and the Kyoto Protocol. The internal EU Emission Trading System, implemented in 2005, is the world's first international carbon trading system. The EU's 2007 Energy Policy for Europe (EPE) clearly indicated that addressing global climate change is a top EU policy priority. The EPE commits the EU to independently reducing its greenhouse gas emissions by 20 percent by 2020 (based on 1990 levels), and if other industrialized countries commit to this same target, the EU will raise its target to 30 percent. Many observers view the EPE as setting the bar for the new round of global climate negotiations to be concluded in late 2009.

Contemporary Dynamics

In the late 1990s, climate change issues arrived on the EU's institutional agenda via external pressures, namely, its participation in the Kyoto Protocol. The EU's main policy response for meeting its Kyoto target is the EU Emission Trading System, adopted in 2003 and introduced in 2005. The decision to implement an emission trading scheme was a somewhat remarkable policy development. In the mid to late 1990s, most EU member states, EU institutions, environmental groups, and industries were not interested in an international emission trading program, preferring instead domestic-based emission reduction programs. However, in 1997, when the EU found itself weighing its options for implementation of the Kyoto Protocol across member states, it was clear that new policy instruments had to be developed to achieve the stringent Kyoto targets. At the time, a proposed EU directive on a carbon tax had proved too controversial in the Council of Ministers and was poised to fail because of the absence of unanimity on it. Without the tax scheme as a policy option, the search was on for other potentially high-impact measures.

The Commission first floated the idea of an emission trading scheme in 1998 via a series of in-house communications. In March 2000 it issued a "green paper" calling for the creation of a centralized and harmonized emission trading system to respond to the Kyoto Protocol. To secure the support of key stakeholders, the Commission formed a European Climate Change Program Working Group focused on such a system. This handpicked group consisted of industry, environmental group, and Commission representatives. Review and negotiations within this group and with their larger constituencies resulted in policy change, with the Commission making several concessions to industry and member states' concerns. The group's final report on the core plan for the system endorsed the scheme unanimously.

Interest groups clearly played a role in the EU Emission Trading System decision-making process. In all environmental policy areas in the EU, interest group lobbying is significant and effective. The Commission consulted industry groups directly, and consumer and other public interest groups also had representation on the Commission working group. Public opinion usually does not play a direct role in EU decision making, although the position of the European Parliament (in this instance, in support of the policy) usually reflects public sentiment. In the case of the Emissions Trading System, the public wanted to see something done to comply with the Kyoto Protocol and mitigate climate change.

Emission trading was ultimately easier to sell to industry than taxes since the former was seen as being cost-effective. To environmental groups (and the European Parliament), the system was seen as environmentally effective. For member states' governments, the scheme presented a workable model for implementing the Kyoto targets, and because both environmental groups and industry supported the approach, it was politically palatable. The Commission framed the scheme for its key stakeholders and built support within the member states, the Commission, Parliament, industry, and environmental groups. The Commission itself was responsive to demands from states for a more decentralized system in the negotiation process.

The Commission's work might not have been enough, though, given some substantial differences of opinion among member states. As late as 2001, most member states remained opposed or indifferent to the emission trading scheme. This state of opinion changed dramatically, however, when the United States withdrew its support of the Kyoto Protocol. U.S. rejection put the global climate change regime in jeopardy. EU leaders felt considerable pressure to sustain the protocol and to demonstrate EU unity in the face of U.S. resistance. The need to show EU leadership was enough to convince many opponents to support the scheme. In short, the emission trading scheme became a mechanism not only for implementing the Kyoto Protocol across Europe but also for saving the agreement.

The Commission formally proposed the emission trading scheme directive in October 2001. It required adoption by qualified majority voting among the member states in the Council of Environment Ministers and a co-decision with the Parliament. The final emission trading scheme directive, proposing the first international (and largest) emission trading system to date, was adopted by the Council in July 2003. The main shape and content of the directive remained intact through the decision-making process. The EU Emission Trading System was launched formally in January 2005, covering some 11,500 installations across the EU. The program ran in a pilot phase from 2005 to 2007. The Kyoto commitment period of 2008–2012 is the system's second, and more substantial, phase. Following a review of the first phase, the Commission in January 2008 proposed a revised emission trading scheme directive for the 2013–2020 period.

The scheme's decentralized approach to setting national emission caps has created some difficulties in the implementation stage. A key instrument in implementing the system is the development of national allocation plans. Set individually by each state (with the approval of the Commission), each plan involved varying levels of ambition and commitment across member states. In practice, the decentralized nature of the scheme produced a "race to the bottom" in which member states had strong incentives to allocate carbon credits generously and to set targets for major emitters that were far too high, to protect their own industries. As a result, many large polluters were not required to reduce emissions, nor did they purchase credits because many already had a surplus. As such, the reforms suggested for 2012 involve greater centralization of allocation authority.

The adoption and design of the EU Emission Trading System came about mainly as a result of the broad consultative process the Commission used during the policy development phase. The member states' and others' ability to directly influence the Commission to make changes to the scheme's original design, as well as the decision of the Commission to establish a knowledge base using external expertise, resulted in broad consensus about the policy's content. In addition, the United States' exit from the Kyoto Protocol unified the member states' positions, and anticipation of Kyoto ratification proved important for keeping the EU Emission Trading System decision-making process on track, given that it was to be the primary mechanism (in the absence of a carbon tax) for complying with the protocol.

Cross-national Trends

We are now able to consider the overall approach to greenhouse gas emission reductions in the six countries discussed in this book, as well as how effective their policies have been in improving air quality. As we review these broader cross-national trends, we observe a striking similarity with respect to policy choices and outcomes. These patterns of environmental policy reform may be attributed to the interaction of cultural, political, economic, and institutional factors.

Policy Choices

Direct regulations were by far the most common policy instrument used to address air quality management. For the most part, air quality management policies involve varying degrees of emission controls and limits, usually by controlling pollution at its source through a national set of targeted emission levels. The exceptions to this pattern are Germany and Japan, where such measures also are accompanied by regulations that strongly encourage the development of new technologies and the use of best-available technologies.

The use of economic incentives for pollution control has become more common, but it is not widespread in all of the countries examined here. In countries where economic incentives are a part of air quality policy frameworks, they most commonly involve fuel taxes. Such incentives include direct taxes on gasoline sales, differential tax rates for leaded and unleaded gasoline, and reduced taxes on fuel-efficient vehicles or on vehicles that use unleaded gasoline. The Italian and French governments traditionally have led the way with such policies, imposing the highest fuel tax rates among our six countries. Germany and the United Kingdom also have enacted fuel taxation policies. The United States is a clear outlier when it comes to fuel taxation. Policymakers in the United States are not inclined to attempt to reduce fuel consumption by using taxes to increase fuel prices, especially as oil prices have gone up. In the 2000s Germany and the United Kingdom both successfully introduced eco-taxes.

Several countries, including the United States, have experimented with other economic incentive policies, such as emission trading or deposit-refund systems, tax rebates for technology development, or fees for emissions, but the use of such policies is still not widespread (although all the EU countries participate in the EU Emission Trading System). This cross-national pattern of low usage has begun to change, however. Policymakers have been more likely to consider alternative policy mechanisms, such as product charges and tradable permit systems, because regulatory devices are viewed as having reached their effective limits and pressures are increasing to improve the cost-effectiveness of solutions to environmental problems. Along these lines, the United Kingdom developed the first national emission trading system. Even so, regulatory mechanisms are likely to remain the primary environmental policy instrument for most industrialized countries.

A pattern of cross-national variation also is observed with respect to the use of voluntary agreements. Such agreements have become more common in all industrialized countries and are now used in all the countries examined here. Even in countries that use such agreements to a limited degree, such as France and Italy, they are only a small part of the nation's overall air pollution policy framework. The extreme exception to this pattern is Japan, where some 40,000 voluntary agreements between government and industry have been signed and effectively implemented. Since the early 1990s, however, the use of such agreements appears to be on the rise in all countries.

Finally, five of our six countries have been willing participants in transborder and international air quality management agreements. Most of these countries are leaders in the movement to address environmental issues on a global scale. Five countries have implemented the major international agreements on air pollution control, albeit with varying degrees of compliance and effectiveness. These international agreements play an important role in agenda setting in these countries. Between 2001 and 2008, the United States was the clear outlier in this regard, as it reneged on its commitment to the Kyoto Protocol and withdrew from all global negotiations in the period examined in this book.

Policy Outcomes

Several trends can be observed in the effects of air quality policy during the 1990s and 2000s. First, the policies implemented by these six countries have generally been effective in reducing air emission levels and improving ambient air quality. Second, although substantial gains have been made, some of this progress has been eroded by continuing hazardous emissions in some sectors, particularly from the transport sector. Third, cross-national differences in policy implementation and coordination have resulted in a pattern of differential policy outcomes.

How well have these countries done in reducing their levels of the most common air pollutants—that is, of SO_x, NO_x, and CO_2? As Table 11-1 indicates, their records are mixed, with a significant degree of cross-national variation. All six countries reduced their levels of air pollutants and improved ambient air quality during the 1990s and early 2000s. However, some countries have made far more progress in this effort than others. The European countries' early commitments to reduce SO_x emissions have been achieved via a combination of effective policy mixes and structural changes to their economies. The United States was less successful in this area. Although reductions in NO_x were less dramatic across all countries, the European countries have also accomplished a good deal with respect to this pollutant, whereas the United States was less successful.

Although several countries have reduced air emission levels significantly for some pollutants, emission levels for other pollutants have been reduced only marginally, or even increased, in some of these countries. Emission levels for most air pollutants remain above OECD averages, and the levels of many pollutants continue to rise. In the United States, this trend implies that air quality and economic growth continue to be strongly related and also reflects an energy-intensive consumption pattern. The best record on air quality management is found in Germany, where the major air pollutant emission levels are the most strictly controlled and effectively reduced.

Although these six countries have made good progress since the 1970s in improving air quality, reducing emission levels, and removing health risks, they are all in danger of sacrificing these gains to increased emission levels, especially from the transport sector. Since 1990, industrialized countries have experienced a remarkable increase in the size of their motor vehicle stocks, an

Table 11-1 Trends in Atmospheric Emissions

	Emissions of SO_x (thousands of metric tons)			Emissions of NO_x (thousands of metric tons)			CO_2 Emissions from Energy Use (millions of metric tons)		
Country	*1990*	*2005*	*Percent Change*	*1990*	*2005*	*Percent Change*	*1980*	*2005*	*Percent Change*
France	1333	465	–65	1840	1206	–34	355	388	9.3
Germany	5350	560	–90	2861	1443	–50	968	813	–16.0
Italy	1794	417	–77	1941	1114	–43	398	454	14.0
Japan	991	751	–24	2032	1920	–6	1058	1214	14.7
United Kingdom	3687	706	–81	2966	1627	–45	558	530	–5.0
United States	20,925	13,272	–37	22,830	16,982	–26	4850	5817	19.9

SOURCE: Organisation for Economic Co-operation and Development (2007).

Table 11-2 Trends in the Transport Sector

	Road Network Length (thousands of kilometers)			Total Number of Motor Vehicles (thousands)			Road Traffic Volume (billions of kilometers traveled)		
Country	*1990*	*2005*	*Percent Change*	*1990*	*2005*	*Percent Change*	*1990*	*2004*	*Percent Change*
France	806	1006	24.8%	28,460	36,169	27.1%	407	523	28.5%
Germany	501	645	28.7	32,222	48,034	49.1	489	585	19.6
Italy	807	871	7.9	29,910	38,941	30.2	352	515	46.3
Japan	1115	1193	7.0	56,491	74,037	31.0	629	826	31.3
United Kingdom	382	413	8.1	23,831	32,173	35.0	405	493	21.7
United States	6154	6429	4.5	188,799	241,195	27.8	3440	4763	38.5

SOURCE: Organisation for Economic Co-operation and Development (2007).

accompanying increase in motor vehicle usage, and an increase in the size of their transport infrastructures (Table 11-2).

Paradoxically, although individual motor vehicle emission levels have decreased in these countries, the tremendous increases in motor vehicle volume and usage have rapidly eroded these gains. In all six countries, the transport sector's relative contribution to air pollution, especially CO_2 emissions, has increased dramatically since 1980 (Table 11-3). The increased emission levels generated by these enlarged transport sectors might well eliminate the air quality gains of the past twenty years—and reduce these countries' chances of meeting their targets for CO_2 emission reductions.

The challenge for governments, as they seek to further reduce greenhouse gas emissions, is to continue to devise strategies for reducing motor vehicle use, both by private individuals and by business and industry. This goal may be achieved through policies that encourage the development of alternative

Table 11-3 CO_2 Emissions from Transport, 1980–2005

Country	CO_2 Emissions (millions of metric tons)		
	1980	*2005*	*Percent Change*
France	89.7	134.5	49.9%
Germany	130.2	158.5	21.7
Italy	71.8	119.1	65.8
Japan	156.7	249.2	59.0
United Kingdom	90.5	129.1	42.7
United States	1,237.6	1813.3	46.5

SOURCE: Organisation for Economic Co-operation and Development (2007)

forms of transportation (in particular, public mass transportation systems) and that provide better incentives to citizens to use these systems (for example, through increased use of economic policy instruments, such as higher taxes on vehicles and fuel). Other alternatives include increased emphasis on research and development on new technologies (for example, for the development of vehicles fueled by cleaner alternatives to gasoline) or the provision of information and education to change public behavior, in particular with the goal of increasing public transport usage and stabilizing private vehicle use.

Countries with more coordinated environmental policy structures have had a greater degree of success in implementing and monitoring environmental control systems. For example, the German environmental bureaucracy involves a substantial degree of coordination between federal and state authorities. In addressing air pollution problems, this system has allowed for comprehensive management programs that are implemented uniformly across the country and are effective in achieving their objectives. Similarly, Japan has well-coordinated and integrated environmental policy making and implementation processes, which has resulted in generally more favorable policy outcomes in that country.

The complexity of the relationships between different levels of government in the United States is a complicating factor in establishing effective air pollution control, although controls are managed somewhat through stricter national-level enforcement of regulations. These differences were not related solely to the policy coordination difficulties often found between levels of government in federal systems. The United Kingdom, despite its unitary system of government, traditionally had an environmental policy process that was also hampered by coordination and implementation difficulties and that reduced policy effectiveness. These shortcomings have been addressed recently through the creation of an integrated pollution control system. Thus, despite a general cross-national pattern of air pollution policy convergence, marked differences in management of the policy implementation process have produced variation in policy outcomes.

Understanding Policy Reform

The case studies indicate that the interaction of cultural, economic, political, and institutional variables is key to understanding environmental policy reform. In particular, these variables are important for understanding why none of the six countries adopted the more stringent economic measures (for example, some form of an environmental tax on CO_2 emissions) believed to be necessary to reach the ambitious CO_2 emission reduction targets of the Kyoto Protocol.

Citizens' expectations about their rights and freedom with respect to the environment were a strong influence in the reform process only in the United States. There, the fact that citizens are strongly attached to their right to own and operate a vehicle, as well as the culture of the open road, limits the possibility that the government will adopt tax measures that increase the cost of motor vehicle use. The other industrialized countries have, in fact, increased the costs of motor vehicle use in order to reduce CO_2 emission levels to a far greater degree than is observed in the United States. In particular, the other countries have higher gasoline taxes.

The difficulty the six countries experienced in introducing strict economic measures was related partly to a lack of citizen mobilization around climate change issues. Although most of these countries have active environmental movements, such movements tend not to be highly effective in mobilizing the general public around climate change issues, in part because of the long-term nature of the problem. Citizens tend to be more aroused about environmental issues whose effects they already observe. In countries where climate change has yet to produce active political mobilization, such as the United States, Italy, and France, governments faced greater difficulty in enacting reforms. The U.S. government, for example, failed to even place such measures on the country's institutional agenda. Even in countries where the population was more involved, however, the political influence of those opposed to the introduction of more stringent measures was often sufficient to override popular opinion.

Economic factors greatly influenced the six countries' policy responses to emission reduction goals. The introduction of environmental taxes to achieve CO_2 emission reductions was opposed (or not even considered) in four countries for reasons of international economic competitiveness. Environmental taxes were ruled out because they were seen to reduce industrial profitability. Because these proposed reforms impose costs on private economic interests, such interests are highly motivated to prevent their adoption. Thus, in an environment in which high priority is given to economic growth and industrial competitiveness, environmental reforms that increase the costs to industry or consumers fail to be enacted. As a result, less effective voluntary agreements are introduced as alternatives to environmental taxes.

In all six countries, a variety of institutional frameworks benefit the interest groups opposed to economic instruments. More specifically, this reform situation reflects the power of industrial interests. Whether through the operation of closed policy networks, corporatist arrangements, or intensive lobbying efforts, industrial lobbies were successful in all six countries in opposing the introduction of economic measures. Thus a close connection exists between industry and government in this policy area in a variety of institutional settings, and industry has the ability to influence both policy formulation and policy decision making.

SUGGESTED READINGS

Axelod, Regina S., David Leonard Downie, and Norman J. Vig. 2005. *The Global Environment: Institutions, Law and Policy.* Washington, D.C.: CQ Press.

Desai, Uday. 2002. *Environmental Politics and Policy in Industrialized Countries.* Cambridge: MIT Press.

Dryzek, John S., and David Schlosberg, eds. 2006. *Debating the Earth: An Environmental Politics Reader.* Oxford: Oxford University Press.

Knill, Christoph, and Duncan Liefferink. 2007. *Environmental Politics in the European Union.* Manchester, U.K.: Manchester University Press.

McCormick, John. 2001. *Environmental Policy in the European Union.* New York: Palgrave.

Morgenstern, Richard D., and William A. Pizer, eds. 2007. *Reality Check: The Nature and Performance of Voluntary Environmental Programs in the United States, Europe and Japan.* Washington, D.C.: Resources for the Future.

Rosenbaum, Walter A. 2008. *Environmental Politics and Policy,* 7th ed. Washington, D.C.: CQ Press.

Schreurs, Miranda A. 2003. *Environmental Politics in Japan, Germany and the United States.* Cambridge: Cambridge University Press.

Vig, Norman J., and Michael Faure, eds. 2004. *Green Giants? Environmental Policies of the United States and the European Union.* Cambridge: MIT Press.

Vig, Norman J., and Michael E. Kraft, eds. 2006. *Environmental Policy: New Directions for the Twenty-first Century,* 6th ed. Washington, D.C.: CQ Press.

Chapter 12 Conclusion

Diverse policy-making contexts shaped different reform dynamics in the six countries examined in this book. The differences in the countries' cultural norms, public opinion trends, economic conditions, political party systems, interest group politics, and governing institutions clearly are meaningful. Amid this diversity, however, two major trends stand out. First, many issues formerly considered to be domestic concerns are becoming increasingly internationalized. Second, in virtually all seven of the policy areas examined in this book, cost-control concerns are a more visible influence on policy making than they were in past decades.

Contemporary Trends

Given the diversity of policy concerns addressed in this book, some people might expect that no clear trends could be identified across seven policy areas in six countries. Even though all six countries are industrialized and wealthy, with relatively large economies compared to most of the world, they are quite different from one another in many respects. Some countries have centralized government systems (France, Japan, and the United Kingdom), and others are much more decentralized (Germany and the United States). The British and Italian governments embarked on substantial administrative reforms that decentralized the management of several public policies, whereas the other four countries retained considerable administrative stability. Some countries have been world economic powers for centuries (France and the United Kingdom), whereas the economies of others took off only after World War II (Italy and Japan). From the 1980s and through the early twenty-first century, some countries embarked on sweeping political reform (Italy and Japan). Other polities have been marked by partisan conflicts and voter swings (France, Italy, and the United States). In the same time period, two countries (Germany and the United Kingdom) had remarkably durable governments with one set of political forces controlling the prime ministry for lengthy periods. In Germany, Helmut Kohl's coalition of Christian Democrats and Free Democrats governed for over sixteen years without interruption. In turn, in the United Kingdom, each of the two major parties exercised control of executive-legislative relations for well over a decade—the Conservatives from 1979 to 1997 and the Labour Party from 1997 to 2009 (and still counting as of July 2009).

Through the case studies in the preceding chapters we have seen different situations in which cultural, economic, political, and institutional distinctions among these countries have shaped policy making. For example, we have seen multiple illustrations of how the Westminster system of government is best suited to the party government model of policy making. British chief executives faced the smallest number of defeats in the legislature. At the same time, however, we observed in the poll tax affair under Margaret Thatcher (and in the Blair government's foreign policy decision to aid the U.S. military in invading and occupying Iraq) that the Westminster model makes it possible for governments to pursue measures that are visibly out of line with public opinion. When that occurs, the clear line of accountability can disrupt the government in charge. Thatcher lost popularity and resigned amid a leadership challenge, whereas Blair lost popularity and resigned in 2007 (perhaps doing so to avoid facing a leadership challenge later in the decade).

Conversely, we saw several situations in which coalition governments in France, Italy, and Japan were supported by unstable voting majorities and public opinion trends. In many instances this volatility increased tensions or resulted in reversals of past policies—perhaps most obviously in the December 1995 general strike in France against the Juppe government's proposed spending cuts. Japanese governments, for the first time in decades, also faced some of these same pressures from unstable voting trends and weak ties among political parties in several of the governing coalitions in the 1990s and the early twenty-first century.

Coalition government need not, however, be synonymous with policy volatility and failed reform efforts. If the coalition parties can agree on a platform and the voters demonstrate stable support for those parties, the prospects for more coherent policy making over time are considerable. We observed this situation in many policy areas in Germany during the enduring Kohl government of the 1980s and 1990s. Perhaps the most visible tension in the coalition of Christian Democrats and Free Democrats occurred in disputes over tax policy; on most other issues (including, eventually, asylum law reform) the two coalition partners were able to agree on how to proceed. The subsequent center-left coalition government led by Gerhard Schröder in Germany and the reform-seeking coalition of the LDP and *Komeito* led by Junichiro Koizumi in Japan also enjoyed considerable success in adopting the policies they pursued.

The United States case studies demonstrated why Charles Lindblom developed the incrementalist decision-making model through the study of U.S. policy making. The many decision points in the U.S. system, resulting from its mix of federalism and presidentialism, combine with undisciplined political parties to make major reforms more difficult to push through the system. In most policy areas in the 1990s and 2000s, a series of incremental reforms were made to existing policies. The major exception to that trend is in social policy. After many years of criticism of existing policies, through public opinion, in the media, and within the Republican Party, President Bill Clinton signed into law a series of major social policy changes in 1996. Major reform is not impossible in the U.S. institutional framework, but it tends to be time consuming.

The Increasing Internationalization of Public Policy

International agreements and international economic forces have in various ways worked to shape the policy agenda and to frame viable policy options in the policy formulation and decision-making stages. In several of these policy areas, industrialized countries' commitments to various external directives, accords, or binding agreements influenced their policy agendas. In particular, in this book, we have detailed the ways in which the European Union's formal and informal institutions have increasingly framed public policy decisions in the union's member countries. In immigration policy, for example, the European countries were faced with questions of what to do about population inflows that arose as a result of the elimination of border controls between EU member states. For Italy, in particular, this meant substantial external pressures from other member states to strengthen the country's border controls, resulting in the adoption of many new policies. Contemporary environmental policy agendas reflected all six countries' participation in international accords to reduce greenhouse gas emissions. Further, the Maastricht budget deficit targets provided the impetus for considerable deficit reduction in France, Germany, and Italy during the second half of the 1990s. The Stability and Growth Pact subsequently maintained pressure on EU member states to keep present and future budget deficits under control. As we saw in Chapters 8 and 10, even in the two policy areas in which the formal competencies of the EU are the weakest—health care and education—the influence of the EU has had an impact on policy making.

Internationalization had an effect on policy decisions in all six countries beyond the efforts these countries made to fulfill their obligations under international agreements. We also observed the effects of increasing international economic competition on policy reform decisions. In education, for example, the reform pressures that all six countries experienced in the 1980s and 1990s were a direct result of citizens' and industry's perceptions that educational systems had to be improved to increase these countries' international economic competitiveness. Similar arguments were used to oppose the use of costly economic instruments to reduce carbon dioxide emissions. Industrial interests in these six countries consistently and effectively argued that increased taxation or environmental charges would hurt these countries' global economic positions. Fiscal policies in these countries also were visibly influenced by global economic factors—specifically, by the requirements of European integration, by the increased interdependence among countries, or in some cases by both factors. These factors affected both fiscal policy agenda setting and the policy decision-making stage. The quest to reduce budget deficits that resulted from international financial market pressures and economic integration motivated these governments to increase revenues through tax policy reform.

Concern for Spending Restraint

Another major trend evident in these six countries was a desire to constrain the growth of overall public expenditures. Calls for fiscal restraint have been so common since the 1980s that they are now part of the normal state of affairs. The contemporary period marks the end of a long upswing in government spending. From the end of World War II through 1995, government expenditures as a percentage of gross domestic product (GDP) rose steadily in these and other industrialized countries. As Table 12-1 indicates, by 1995 spending met or approached 40 percent of GDP in all but Australia, Japan, and the United States.

In the late 1990s and the early twenty-first century, however, the pace of spending expansion slowed everywhere. In nearly all industrialized countries, government spending as a percentage of GDP declined or remained stable from 1995 to 2007. Government spending per GDP fell in the late 1990s in the United States but then rose steadily in the early twenty-first century amid the twin decisions to cut taxes while engaging in extended military operations in Afghanistan and Iraq. The only industrialized country that increased public spending significantly between 1995 and 2007 was Portugal.

Why are most industrialized countries so concerned with restraining expenditures? As noted earlier, part of this fiscal pressure comes from international currency and financial markets. The speed with which today's financial markets react to events makes countries risk averse in their fiscal policies. National governments would rather be seen as fiscally sound than risk a run against their currency or a loss of demand for government bonds. Within the euro zone of the EU, as we saw in Chapter 6, the fiscal targets for participation in European monetary integration provided an additional international rationale for restraining public expenditure.

Today's fiscal conservatism also stems from a growing realization that current government commitments in pension and health policy are headed for financial trouble because of demographic changes. Specifically, as the populations of these countries age, the ratio of workers paying into the system per pensioner is on the decline and will fall significantly in the early decades of the twenty-first century. To compensate for this decline, governments may decide to decrease the amount of benefits paid out, increase the tax rate, or both. This decision presents a major difficulty for governments because publicly managed pensions have come to be seen as guarantees provided to the citizenry.

Table 12-1 Government Spending as a Percentage of GDP, 1960–2007

Country	1960	1970	1980	1990	1995	2000	2005	2007
France	34.6%	38.9%	46.2%	49.6%	54.4%	53.4%	52.3%	52.3%
Germany	32.0	37.6	46.9	43.8	54.8	45.1	46.9	44.1
Italy	30.1	34.2	45.6	53.1	52.5	46.1	48.1	47.9
Japan	20.7	19.3	32.7	31.3	36.5	39.0	38.4	36.0
United Kingdom	32.6	39.3	44.6	41.8	44.1	36.6	44.2	44.1
United States	27.8	32.2	33.2	33.6	37.0	34.2	36.6	37.4
Average	*29.6*	*33.6*	*41.5*	*42.2*	*44.4*	*42.1*	*44.6*	*43.6*
Australia	22.1	25.5	34.1	33.5	38.2	32.3	34.8	34.2
Austria	32.1	39.2	48.5	48.5	56.5	50.7	50.0	48.7
Belgium	30.3	36.5	51.7	50.7	52.0	47.9	52.1	48.3
Canada	28.9	35.7	40.7	46.7	48.5	40.2	39.3	39.1
Finland	26.7	31.3	38.2	44.4	61.5	47.1	50.3	47.3
Greece	17.4	22.4	30.3	47.8	45.8	43.5	43.3	44.0
Ireland	28.0	39.6	N.A.	37.8	41.2	31.5	33.7	35.7
Netherlands	33.7	45.5	62.5	49.4	56.4	43.2	44.8	45.3
Norway	29.9	41.0	49.4	49.7	50.9	46.1	42.3	41.0
Portugal	17.0	21.6	N.A.	40.6	43.4	44.7	47.6	45.8
Spain	13.7	22.2	32.4	39.7	44.4	38.6	38.4	38.8
Sweden	31.1	43.7	65.7	56.2	65.3	55.9	54.0	51.3
Average	*25.9*	*33.7*	*45.4*	*45.4*	*50.3*	*43.5*	*44.2*	*43.3*
Average for all	*27.2%*	*33.7%*	*43.9%*	*44.3%*	*49.1%*	*43.1%*	*44.3%*	*43.4%*

SOURCE: For the years 1960–1980, data are from OECD (1982). For the years 1985–1990, data are from OECD (2000). For the years 1995–2007, data are from *OECD Economic Outlook*, no. 85 (Paris: OECD, 2009a).

N.A. = not available.

This sense of entitlement derives from two sources. First, in all six countries, pensions are funded on a social insurance basis: all citizens who have made certain contributions are eligible at retirement age for a pension, regardless of income. Second, today's workers have spent their lives paying into the system in anticipation of receiving a pension that provides for a certain standard of living.

The politics of pensions put governments in a real bind. Almost all voting-age citizens have a stake in the defense of current pension benefits because either they are already retirees or they have begun to pay into the pension system. However, governments fear that raising tax levels to maintain benefit levels will also generate political opposition. Governments face a true dilemma in which raising payroll taxes and reducing benefits are both bound to generate discontent. As a result, many governments have made only minor reforms thus far to their pension systems. Italy, where the pension system was running the largest deficit, is the only one of these countries that visibly reshaped its pension system in the 1990s and 2000s.

In the absence of major pension reform, knowledge of the coming deficits has been used as a political argument in favor of fiscal restraint in other policy areas. We saw that argument emerge in regard to health care and social policy, in particular. Calls for fiscal responsibility drew on three major sources: a need to prepare for the retirement of the baby-boom generation, a need to improve governments' positions in international financial markets, and, in France, Germany, and Italy, a desire to meet the fiscal targets placed in the monetary unification effort.

Learning Lessons by Comparing Policies

We have offered in this book many examples that suggest the limitations of the extent to which countries may learn from one another. The cultural, economic, political, and institutional context of policy making as well as the decisions made by individual human beings can block the adoption of policies deemed desirable by some or perhaps even many policy analysts and sectors of society. For example, the United States' history as a country of immigrants colors the debate over the adoption of restrictive immigration legislation. Italy's political, economic, and geographic divisions made it difficult to reduce the deficit in a series of governments pledged to do so. France increased only slightly the use of direct taxes over the years because of a long suspicion that tax avoidance and tax evasion are widespread responses to such tax instruments. Japanese cultural norms slowed the adoption of long-term health care policies and have made implementation of those reforms more difficult for a series of governments. The liberal tradition of individualism in the United Kingdom led that country to adopt mainly means-tested social policies, whereas most European countries chose a more universalistic approach. A variety of forces in Germany supported expanding the adoption of user-pays instruments in environmental protection; however, a host of economic problems (and tax hikes) associated with reunification blocked the successful creation of such measures in the 1990s and 2000s.

In short, the construction of public policies involves a variety of considerations that may constrain the usefulness of comparisons with other countries. Countries may face slightly different problems. They may confront similar problems but in different political, economic, or sociocultural contexts. In particular, the dynamics of the policy subsector in each country often play a crucial role in determining the precise policy mix chosen.

Nevertheless, cross-national comparisons can and do help in the effort to meet citizens' needs via the design, passage, and implementation of public policies. We have seen many examples of a broad consensus in policy choice—a consensus built on an examination of national and cross-national experiences. Countries desiring to limit the flow of immigration have learned that restrictive immigration laws require enhanced enforcement measures for effective implementation. Countries with different political parties in charge have attempted to control their deficits to avoid the currency instability found in countries with higher deficits. Throughout the twentieth century, governments moved to an increasing use of direct taxes because such instruments permit a more nuanced use of tax expenditures as well as the pursuit of tax progressivity goals. Industrialized countries have learned that an effective set of public health initiatives is a crucial first step toward the achievement of better health outcomes. In the curative care sector in the early twenty-first century, countries have learned that the creation of an electronic medical record can aid in the pursuit of better medical treatment and of more cost-efficient patient billing. Governments know that social insurance policies are useful for guaranteeing political (and financial) support for national pension systems. Compulsory public education at the primary and secondary levels is a response to the achievements of the first countries to adopt this policy. In environmental policy, countries are realizing that regulation is of limited effectiveness and are beginning to supplement regulation with the use of economic incentives.

In many situations, comparisons among countries can be useful. Even when comparisons do not lead to the virtually wholesale adoption of another country's policy, comparisons can often shift the national debate in a new, useful direction. We hope, therefore, that this book has helped readers to brainstorm more constructively about building solutions to public problems at home and abroad.

Glossary

absolute poverty A poverty measure that establishes a basic needs threshold beneath which citizens are said to be poor.

access to schooling The issue of who receives schooling.

actuarial fairness An approach to medical insurance that groups people according to their risk factors. Healthy individuals in low-risk occupations are grouped with similar individuals and pay lower insurance rates, whereas high-risk patients are forced to pay higher insurance rates in recognition of the greater likelihood that they will require care.

administrative evaluation One of the three major arenas of policy evaluation, in which the government itself evaluates public policies.

agenda setting The stage of the policy-making process at which problems come to the attention of policymakers.

asylum seekers Individuals who are already present in a country where refuge is sought or who are at the border requesting entry.

back door immigration Illegal entry into a country.

ballotage system A two-round variation of the single-member district plurality electoral system that requires a majority to win in the first round. If no candidate wins, the top vote-getters compete again under plurality rules.

basic needs An approach to social insurance programs in which the government sets benefit levels based on a certain standard below which no individual should fall.

behavioralism The school of thought in political science that focuses on the political behavior of individuals and groups throughout society.

bottom-up implementation A view of implementation that focuses on how informal customs and considerations, faced by those who implement policies, block the fulfillment of what policy decision makers originally intended.

capitation A system for reimbursing physicians based on how many patients they treat, not how many services they provide.

catch-all parties Coalitions of voters with weaker organizational structures, memberships drawn from disparate backgrounds, and programs based on less clearly defined goals or visions than are found in more traditional parties.

chronically poor Individuals who are of working age but who have a hard time escaping poverty.

command and control policies Environmental policies that involve direct regulation and monitoring by government.

consolidation A model of agenda setting in which the government places on the institutional agenda an issue already visible on the systemic agenda. The government does not need to mobilize support for maintaining the issue on the institutional agenda; instead, it relies on existing public interest in the issue.

convergence thesis The theory that as countries industrialize, they develop similar policy concerns.

copayment A partial payment for medical services that patients are required to pay at the time that care is delivered.

corporatism A pattern of interest group activity in which fewer, larger groups participate actively in the policy-making process and government tries more often to include these major groups in systematic discussions of policy-making issues relevant to the policy network.

cost-benefit analysis Under the rational decision-making model, this type of analysis is used to identify all benefits (positive impacts) and costs (negative impacts) of a policy proposal and to select the option most likely to reach policymakers' goals at an acceptable cost.

countercyclical fiscal policies The practice of running deficits to escape recession and running surpluses in times of economic growth.

curriculum The course of study that educational institutions follow.

dealignment The weakening of voters' ties to existing political parties and a resulting shift in voter behavior.

debt service The interest and principal payments made on a country's national debt.

decision making The stage of the policy-making process at which the relevant public authority decides to create a new policy, to modify an existing policy, or to take no new action.

deficit The situation that occurs when governments spend more money than they take in.

depolarization The tendency for political parties to move toward the moderate center of the political spectrum.

direct government instruments Public policies that include direct regulations, the direct provision of services, the operation of state-owned enterprises, and the like.

direct regulations Environmental policies that involve the setting of restrictions and requirements by government.

direct taxes Tax instruments that are levied as a percentage of income earned by a person or a firm.

divided government A situation in which the executive and the legislature are controlled by different political parties.

economic incentives Environmental policy instruments that use market mechanisms, such as tax breaks, pollution charges, or deposit systems, to reduce pollution.

employer-mandate An approach to health care in which premiums are tied to wages.

entitlements Social insurance programs under which citizens cannot be denied benefits.

equality of opportunity The assumption that school systems can compensate for existing social and economic inequalities in a society. Universal access to schooling is believed to serve as a leveler, as opposed to less open educational systems that perpetuate existing social or economic divisions.

equality of provision The attempt to ensure that all students in an educational system are receiving the same type of education, particularly with respect to subject matter.

excise tax A tax charged on a particular good, such as tobacco or liquor.

external controls Illegal-immigration control measures designed to prevent foreigners from entering the country without permission, such as more effective policing of borders and airports.

family of nations A group of countries whose cultural similarities help to produce similar policy-making dynamics and in some cases comparable policy decisions.

family reunification Legal immigration that involves entry into a country by the spouses and children of legal residents and citizens.

federal political system A political system in which one or two meaningful levels of government exist above the local level; each level has its own constitutionally defined policy-making responsibilities.

fee-for-service A system for reimbursing physicians in which doctors are paid a fee for each service performed.

flat tax Income-neutral direct taxes that charge all citizens a uniform rate.

front door immigration Legal entry into a country, usually for family reunification or through employment-based immigration.

fusion of powers The constitutional division of authority in which the executive derives from and is responsible to the legislature.

garbage can decision making A policy decision-making model that rejects the idea that governments systematically weigh policy alternatives. Decisions are instead the result of multiple factors interacting in the policy environment, or garbage can.

gatekeeper system A health care organization cost-cutting mechanism that requires patients to see a general practitioner to receive a referral before seeing a specialist.

globalization The idea that a country's national political, economic, and social life is increasingly affected by what occurs beyond the country's borders.

globalization of the environment The fact that the environment in one country is not distinct from the environment in another and that environmental problems do not respect national territorial boundaries.

government bonds Instruments created by governments to make up for a budget deficit. Investors purchase the bonds, and the government agrees to pay back the value of the bond plus interest over a certain period of time.

greenhouse gases Atmospheric gases that allow heat from the sun to enter the earth's atmosphere and then trap it, creating a greenhouse effect.

gridlock A situation that occurs when political, ideological, or other differences between the executive and the legislature make it more difficult for the government to develop policies.

guest worker programs Foreign labor recruitment programs in which foreign workers are given temporary work residence permits.

health maintenance organizations A form of health insurance in the United States in which premiums are used to hire a group of physicians who provide a comprehensive range of services to the plan's members.

humanitarian immigration Immigration of asylum seekers and refugees, who seek entry into a country as protection from political or other forms of persecution in their home countries.

illegal immigration The unauthorized entry of immigrants into a country, typically through clandestine means or visa overstaying.

income-neutral A tax system that has no impact on the distribution of income in a country.

incremental decision making A descriptive model of decision making according to which political factors constrain decision makers from the pursuit of all possible alternatives; the result is that only marginal changes are made to existing policies.

indirect taxes Tax instruments that are not based on taxpayers' incomes. These instruments include sales taxes or the value-added tax.

individual equity An approach to social insurance programs in which citizens receive benefits in accordance with their level of contributions.

inside initiation A model of agenda setting in which interest groups attempt to influence the institutional agenda almost entirely in private. Where this model exists, no attempt is made to expand the visibility of the policy debate on the systemic agenda.

institutional agenda Issues that have attracted the attention of government officials and have become the focus of public policy making.

interest aggregation The process of taking a wide range of citizen viewpoints and demands and translating them into a more manageable and more specific number of policy alternatives.

interest groups Private organizations that set out to influence public policy in specific areas of concern to their members.

internal controls Illegal-immigration control measures that allow for the legal supervision of immigrants in order to guarantee that they leave when their visas expire and that they do not work without authorization.

iron triangle A political subsystem controlled by the relevant bureaucratic agencies, the relevant legislative subcommittees, and the major interest groups dedicated to a given policy area. Together these three groups exert influence in the policy area, and policy decisions in that area are closed to outside influence.

issue network A political subsystem in which a loose mix of government and non-government actors is actively involved in policy formulation. Membership in the network is flexible over time.

issue voting The tendency of voters to base their votes on the policy programs of competing parties on issues that matter to them, rather than on their strong sense of identification with a particular party.

judicial evaluation Policy evaluation conducted by the courts in response to a specific legal complaint against a public policy.

Kaldor criterion Standards for evaluating cost-benefit analyses, according to which policy decisions must provide more benefits than costs to society as a whole (even if some people suffer net losses). When applied, the preferred policy option is the one that provides the highest net benefits.

Keynesianism The school of thought in economics that argues for deficit spending as a government policy tool to help the economy grow out of tough times.

legal immigration Immigration for the purposes of family reunification or for employment sanctioned by government.

legislative judicial review The power of courts to declare legislation and executive actions unconstitutional and, thereby, to nullify laws.

liberal versus vocational education The debate over whether education should be aimed at reducing social and economic inequalities or at promoting global competitiveness. Proponents of liberal, or general, education advocate traditional training of students in the classics, reading, writing, and arithmetic in order to provide for the full development of the individual. Vocational, or technical, training supporters emphasize the development of useful skills that translate directly into specific occupational opportunities.

limits on technology acquisition A health care cost-control measure that places limits on the acquisition of medical technology by hospitals and private physicians.

mandatory national health insurance An approach to health care in which the government guarantees all citizens access to care, with multiple payers and multiple providers.

manifestly unfounded claims Asylum seekers' petitions for entry into a country that fail to demonstrate absolute proof of political persecution.

market economies Economic systems based on private ownership and the market, not the government, as the central economic coordinating mechanism.

market instruments Public policies that attempt to motivate certain behaviors within a largely free market.

market-maximized An approach to health care in which the government provides no guarantee of access through either public hospitals or mandatory health insurance.

mass party A well-organized political party that has a large number of active members drawn from a particular social cleavage and that is committed to pursuing a particular political ideology or a distinctive set of policy goals.

means-tested A method for determining eligibility for social assistance that is based on recipients' economic need.

median voter model The explanation of partisan trends that argues that political parties try to develop policies that will appeal to the widest range of voters, regardless of whether those policy positions contradict their traditional perspective on the issue at hand. This process results in the emergence of catch-all parties.

merit The belief that access to education should reflect the fact that individuals differ innately in their capabilities and are not equally capable of benefiting from an education. Those who emphasize merit oppose equal access to education for all.

mixed economies Economic systems that combine capitalist free-market principles, including private ownership, with some level of state ownership, some central economic planning, and a higher level of government regulation.

mixed instruments Public policies that rely on some combination of direct government intervention, market incentives, and voluntary persuasion.

mobilization A model of agenda setting in which the government is the group interested in setting the institutional agenda.

moderate pluralism A description of political systems in which political parties tend toward the center of the political spectrum.

multiparty system A political system in which multiple parties enter elections and achieve elected office. Parties represent a narrow range of interests and do very little interest aggregation.

national debt The sum total of the future financial obligations that the government owes to others.

national health service An approach to health care in which citizens are guaranteed access to most services through a system paid for and administered directly by the government.

new institutionalism An approach to the study of the policy-making process that focuses on institutional influences on policy making. This approach emphasizes formal rules and informal norms and patterns in governmental institutions, as well as the role of institutional considerations in framing nongovernmental organizations' participation in policy making.

non-refoulement principle The principle in international law that imposes legal and moral obligations on countries not to reject foreign asylum applicants if such rejection entails their being returned to a place where they are in danger of being persecuted.

optimizing adjustment A model of policy decision making in which decision makers do not consider widely divergent options but are willing to consider fairly significant changes from the status quo.

outside initiation An agenda-setting model in which organized interest groups attempt to raise the profile of an issue on the systemic agenda. By forming allegiances with other groups, raising citizen awareness, and lobbying the government these groups attempt to move their concerns onto the institutional agenda.

overloaded government A situation in which the sum total of the demands placed on government grows faster than both public spending and public revenues.

Pareto optimality The criterion that states that when evaluating the results of a cost-benefit analysis, policy decisions must make at least one person better off while making no one worse off.

parliamentary systems Governmental systems in which the chief executive is elected by the legislature and can be removed for any reason by the legislature as it sees fit.

partisanship thesis A theory of policy making that holds that parties are central to the policy process. In particular, political parties tied to the organized labor movement are argued to support an expansion in the scope of government activity in policy areas supported by labor unions, and the range of government activity is more likely to expand when such parties are in power.

party discipline The likelihood of legislators voting with their own party in the legislature.

party government A governing situation in which one party controls the executive branch and holds a majority in the legislative branch.

party system The number of parties that are viewed as having a serious chance of winning elections in a country, as well as the extent of competition between these parties.

pluralism A pattern of group activity in which many interest groups or other actors compete openly for the government's attention and in which political power is dispersed.

plurality In electoral systems, the requirement that the winning candidate must receive the most votes cast in an election.

pocketbook voting A pattern of voting behavior in which election results reflect the state of the national economy and, at times, individual economic fortunes. For example, if the country's economy is seen as reasonably strong, the incumbent party tends to do well with many voters—regardless of their traditional party ties or ideology.

point of service plan A hybrid form of managed care health insurance in the United States in which patients can choose to see a specialist who does not participate in the plan if they are willing to pay a higher copayment.

polarization In party systems, the degree of emotional or political distance between political parties.

polarized pluralism A description of political systems in which political parties tend to be more ideologically distant from one another. In such systems, parties tend to move away from the center of the political system toward the left and right poles.

policy evaluation The stage of the policy-making process at which judgments are made about the effects of public policies.

policy formulation The stage of the policy-making process at which proposed policy alternatives are weighed, the nature of the problem itself is debated, and policy proposals are developed.

policy implementation The stage of the policy-making process at which public policies are put into effect.

policy instruments The specific actions taken by government to put public policies into effect.

policy network All of the different actors who usually participate actively in a given policy area. A policy network is defined by the nature of the relationship between government and nongovernment participants.

policy outcomes The consequences of government activity, or what public policies produce.

policy outputs The government's actions to carry out and enforce its policies.

policy science A field of study focusing on what governments do rather than how institutions are organized.

political evaluation An arena of policy evaluation that takes place within existing policy networks, with interest groups providing feedback to government and influencing public opinion.

polluter pays principles Economic incentive policies in which individuals are charged for their environmentally harmful activities.

postentry controls Immigration policies that attempt to control immigrants', especially asylum seekers', activities and experiences once they are within a country's borders.

postindustrial A description of the changed employment structure of industrialized countries, with greater employment opportunities in the service sector than in manufacturing or agriculture.

postmaterialism A description of the changed attitudinal structure of industrialized countries, with citizens placing greater emphasis on freedom of expression, quality of life, greater political participation, the environment, or gender and sexual equality concerns than on physical or material well-being.

preentry controls External immigration-control mechanisms designed to prevent immigrants from making it across a country's borders.

preference system An immigration policy instrument that allocates a certain number of visas per year for particular categories of immigrants.

preferred provider organizations The gatekeeper system used in the United States, which not only requires patients to be referred to a specialist by a general practitioner but also usually limits patients to the selection of doctors who agree to the insurer's fee schedule.

presidential systems Governmental systems in which the chief executive is elected separately from the legislature to a fixed term and can be removed by the legislature only upon charges of dereliction of duty.

principal-agent model A model of bureaucratic activity in which the bureaucratic agents' control of information and expertise limits the authority of the principal political officials.

progressive A tax system in which the wealthy pay a higher percentage of their income in taxes than the poor. Such a system redistributes income from the rich to the poor.

pronatalist family policies Social policies that reward parents for having additional children and that encourage increasing family size.

proportional representation The allocation of legislative seats in an electoral district roughly according to the proportion of the vote that a party's slate received.

public assistance A social policy benefit model in which eligibility for benefits is means-tested.

public goods Services generally deemed necessary for a basic quality of life that are unlikely to be provided by the marketplace because it is not in any individual's self-interest to produce them.

public policies Intentional courses of action designed by government bodies and officials to accomplish specific goals or objectives.

public versus private schooling An education debate involving the question of permitting religious schools to exist and, where they exist, of the appropriate allocation of public funds.

pull factors A country's characteristics that make it attractive to immigrants.

push factors A country's characteristics that affect individuals' decisions to emigrate, including overpopulation, poverty, unemployment, natural disaster, or war.

rational decision making A prescriptive model of decision making that emphasizes the even-handed consideration of all alternatives and the consequences of those alternatives.

realignment The process whereby individuals form attachments to new political parties corresponding to new forms of social identification.

referendum An election in which voters choose among specific policy options, typically involving a yes-no vote on one issue.

refugees Individuals found outside their home country (typically in refugee camps) who are seeking entry into another country for protection from persecution.

regressive A tax system that forces the poor to pay a higher percentage of their income in taxes than the rich. Such a system redistributes income from the poor to the wealthy.

regularization programs Immigration programs that provide legal amnesty (and usually naturalized citizenship) for illegal immigrants who satisfy certain conditions such as entry into the country before a certain date, good health, regular employment, or a valid passport.

relative poverty A poverty measure that creates a relative standard to assess comparable levels of poverty across a society or across countries.

risk-pooling An approach to medical insurance that groups people based on the principle that everyone is at risk of needing care due to chronic illness or accidents. This risk is pooled across a large number of currently healthy and unhealthy individuals to provide maximal coverage at lowest cost.

satisficing decision making A descriptive model of decision making in which the bounded rationality of decision makers limits their ability to give full consideration to all alternatives and their consequences.

separation of mandate In presidential systems, the fact that the chief executive derives strength from his or her direct election independently from the legislature. The executive has a personal mandate to govern, whereas the legislature also has its own independent electoral mandate.

separation of powers The constitutional division of authority among the executive, legislative, and judicial branches of government.

side door immigration Entry to a country through temporary immigration programs.

single-member district plurality The allocation of legislative seats based on the division of the country into a relatively large number of legislative districts; each district is assigned one seat in the legislature. Once an election is held and the results are tallied, the candidate who receives the most votes is the elected representative from that district.

single-payer An approach to health care that guarantees all citizens access via a single program in which almost all funds come from the government but care is provided privately.

situationally poor Individuals who for one reason or another (unemployment, illness, or old age) cannot support themselves.

social cleavages Social criteria by which people are grouped in a society.

social dumping The movement of low-skill individuals from countries that provide fewer social benefits to countries with more generous social benefits systems. Employers move to countries that provide fewer social benefits because of the lighter tax burdens associated with lower levels of benefits.

social insurance A model for determining access to social policy benefits in which all citizens in a given circumstance are eligible for assistance regardless of their degree of economic need.

social insurance programs Government programs that provide for health care, old age benefits, unemployment, and the like.

social market economy An economic system in which the government combines support for the private sector and the free market (with nearly all enterprises under private control). A high level of government intervention is designed to create a framework for economic growth.

subsidies A social policy instrument that involves the government spending money to make services available to the needy at abnormally low prices.

supply-side school The school of economists who believe that decreasing taxes and increasing government spending will stimulate investment and economic growth.

surplus The situation that occurs when governments take in more money than they spend.

swing voters Voters who demonstrate no strong loyalty to any political party from one election to another but instead base their voting choices on candidates' personalities, perceptions of candidates' competence and leadership abilities, more specific policy promises of one party or another, and the like.

systemic agenda The set of citizens' concerns and issues that may be placed on a country's institutional agenda.

tax avoidance The practice of managing money in such a way as to minimize the tax liability.

tax brackets In tax systems, the increments used to determine taxation rates for specific levels of income.

tax credits A feature of some tax systems in which the cost of a particular activity is counted as a credit toward the taxes owed.

tax deductions A feature of some tax systems in which the government allows citizens to reduce their amount of taxable income by taking into account charitable contributions and the like.

tax evasion The illegal refusal to pay taxes owed under the law.

tax expenditures Public policies in which the government reduces citizens' tax obligations when they spend their money for certain purposes, such as through lower sales taxes on food or tax deductions for home ownership.

tax protest Citizens' opposition to taxes that is generated by perceived injustice.

tax revolt Citizens' opposition to taxes that results from a perception that taxation is unjust in its execution and unfair in principle.

top-down implementation A view of implementation that focuses on how policy design at the leadership level frames how policies will be implemented.

traditionalism Political science analyses that focus on formal government institutions and that make normative judgments about preferred institutional forms.

transfers Government economic assistance provided to citizens via direct cash payments to individuals or in-kind benefits.

two-party system A political system in which two major political parties present broad policy alternatives to the electorate in an effort to appeal to the broadest possible segment of the electorate.

unitary political system A political system in which only one meaningful level of government exists above the local level. In such systems, only the central government has constitutionally derived policy-making authority (for all stages of the policy-making process).

user pays principles Economic incentive policies that involve additional costs for consumers of environmentally hazardous products.

volatility A tendency for patterns of partisan support to shift dramatically from election to election as both the issues of the day and parties' and the electorate's positions change.

voluntary agreements Nonbinding agreements between government and producers to reduce pollution levels.

voluntary instruments Public policies in which speeches by public officials and publicly authorized commercials encourage people to adopt certain behaviors.

vouchers Coupons, representing tax dollars, that parents use to pay tuition at the school of their choice, public or private.

welfare states States that provide extensive social insurance benefits to their citizens.

Westminster model A model of government in which a parliamentary system is combined with a plurality electoral system.

References

Abel-Smith, Brian. 1994. *The Reform of Health Care Systems: A Review of Seventeen OECD Countries.* Paris: Organisation for Economic Co-operation and Development.

Adam, Antonis and Pantellis Kammas. 2007. "Tax policies in a globalized world: Is it politics after all?" *Public Choice* 133: 321–341.

Adema, Willem. 2006. "Social Assistance Policy Development and the Provision of a Decent Level of Income in Selected OECD Countries." *OECD Social, Employment and Migration Working Papers,* No. 38.

Alesina, Alberto, and Nouriel Roubini with Gerald Cohen. 1997. *Political Cycles and the Macroeconomy.* Cambridge: MIT Press.

Ambler, John. 1987. "Constraints on Policy Innovation in Education: Thatcher's Britain and Mitterrand's France." *Comparative Politics* 20:85–105.

Anderson, Odin. 1972. *Health Care: Can There Be Equity?* New York: Wiley.

Apap, Joanna. 2004. *Justice and Home Affairs in the EU: Liberty and Security Issues After Enlargement.* Northampton, Mass.: Edward Elgar.

Baldwin-Edwards, Martin, and Martin Schain. 1994. "The Politics of Immigration: Introduction," in *The Politics of Immigration in Western Europe,* edited by Martin Baldwin-Edwards and Martin Schain. London: Frank Cass.

Barro, Robert. 1989. "The Neoclassical Approach to Fiscal Policy," in *Modern Business Cycle Theory,* edited by Robert Barro. Cambridge: Harvard University Press.

Basinger, Scott and Mark Hallerberg. 2004. "Remodeling the Competition for Capital: How Domestic Politics Erases the Race to the Bottom." *American Political Science Review* 98: 261–276.

Beck, Howard, and Steven Camarota. 2002. *Elite vs. Public Opinion: An Examination of Divergent Views on Immigration.* Washington, D.C.: Center for Immigration Studies.

Beramendi, Pablo and David Rueda. 2007. "Social Democracy Constrained: Indirect Taxation in Industrialized Democracies." *British Journal of Political Science* 37: 619–641.

Betz, Hans-George. 1991. *Post-modern Politics in Germany: The Politics of Resentment.* London: Macmillan.

Betz, Hans-George. 1994. *Radical Right-wing Populism in Western Europe.* Basingstoke, U.K.: Macmillan.

Blake, Charles H., and Jessica R. Adolino. 2001. "The Enactment of National Health Insurance: A Boolean Analysis of Twenty Advanced Industrial Countries." *Journal of Health Politics, Policy and Law* 26:679–708.

Blank, Robert H., and Viola Burau. 2004. *Comparative Health Policy.* New York: Palgrave Macmillan.

Borelli, Stephen, and Terry Royed. 1995. "Government Strength and Budget Deficits in Advanced Democracies." *European Journal of Political Research* 28:225–260.

Boyd, William. 1996. "The Politics of Choice and Market-Oriented School Reform in Britain and the United States," in *The Reconstruction of Education,* edited by Judith Chapman, William Boyd, Rolf Lander, and David Reynolds. London: Cassell.

Boyd, William, and Charles Kerchner. 1987. "Introduction," in *The Politics of Excellence and Choice in Education,* edited by William Boyd and Charles Kerchner. Philadelphia: Falmer Press.

Brochman, Grete, and Tomas Hammar, eds. 1999. *Mechanisms of Immigration Control: A Comparative Analysis of European Regulation Policies.* Oxford: Berg Publishers.

Cameron, David. 1978. "The Expansion of the Public Economy: A Comparative Analysis." *American Political Science Review* 72:1243–1261.

Castles, Francis, ed. 1982a. *The Impact of Parties: Politics and Policies in Democratic Capitalist States.* London: Sage.

Castles, Francis. 1982b. "The Impact of Parties on Public Expenditure," in *The Impact of Parties: Politics and Policies in Democratic Capitalist States,* edited by Francis Castles. London: Sage.

Castles, Francis, ed. 1993. *Families of Nations: Patterns of Public Policy in Western Democracies.* Aldershot, U.K.: Dartmouth Publishing.

Castles, Francis, and Deborah Mitchell. 1993. "Worlds of Welfare and Families of Nations," in *Families of Nations: Patterns of Public Policy in Western Democracies,* edited by Francis Castles. Aldershot, U.K.: Dartmouth Publishing.

Castles, Francis, and Rudolf Wildenmann, eds. 1986. *The Future of Party Government,* vol. 1: *Visions and Realities of Party Government.* New York: DeGruyter.

Center for Educational Research and Innovation. 2008. *Education at a Glance: OECD Indicators, 2008.* Paris: Organisation for Economic Co-operation and Development.

Chubb, John, and Terry Moe. 1990. *Politics, Markets and America's Schools.* Washington, D.C.: Brookings Institution Press.

Cibulka, James. 1996. "The Evolution of Education Reform in Great Britain and the United States: Implementation Convergence of Two Macro-policy Approaches," in *The Reconstruction of Education,* edited by Judith Chapman, William Boyd, Rolf Lander, and David Reynolds. London: Cassell.

Cibulka, James. 2001. "The Changing Role of Interest Groups in Education: Nationalization and the New Politics of Education Productivity." *Educational Policy* 15:12–40.

Cigler, Allan J., and Burdett A. Loomis, eds. 2007. *Interest Group Politics,* 7th ed. Washington, D.C.: CQ Press.

Clingermayer, James, and B. Dan Wood. 1995. "Disentangling Patterns of State Debt Financing." *American Political Science Review* 89:108–120.

Cobb, Roger, Jennie-Keith Ross, and Marc Howard Ross. 1976. "Agenda Building as a Comparative Political Process." *American Political Science Review* 70:126–138.

Cohen, Wesley, and Daniel Levinthal. 1990. "Absorptive Capacity: A New Perspective on Learning and Innovation." *Administrative Science Quarterly* 35:128–152.

Collier, Ute, and Ragnar Lofstedt. 1997. "Comparative Analysis and Conclusions," in *Cases in Climate Change Policy,* edited by Ute Collier and Ragnar E. Lofstedt. London: Earthscan Publications.

Confalonieri, Maria, and Kenneth Newton. 1995. "Taxing and Spending: Tax Revolt or Tax Protest?" in *The Scope of Government,* edited by Ole Borre and Elinor Scarbrough. Oxford: Oxford University Press.

Congleton, Roger, and Birgitta Swedenborg, eds. 2006. *Democratic Constitutional Design and Public Policy: Analysis and Evidence.* Cambridge: MIT University Press.

Coombs, Philip. 1985. *The World Crisis in Education: The View from the Eighties.* New York: Oxford University Press.

Cornelius, Wayne, Philip Martin, and James Hollifield. 1994. "Introduction: The Ambivalent Quest for Immigration Control," in *Controlling Immigration: A Global Perspective,* edited by Wayne Cornelius, Philip Martin, and James Hollifield. Stanford: Stanford University Press.

Cowart, A. T. 1978. "The Economic Policies of European Governments, Part II: Fiscal Policy." *British Journal of Political Science* 8:425–439.

Crepaz, Markus. 1995. "Explaining National Variations of Air Pollution Levels: Political Institutions and Their Impact on Environmental Policy-making." *Environmental Politics* 4:391–414.

Crepaz, Markus. 2001. "Veto Players, Globalization and the Redistributive Capacity of the State: A Panel Study of 15 OECD Countries." *Journal of Public Policy* 21: 1–22.

De Haan, Jakob, and Jan-Egbert Sturm. 1994. "Political and Institutional Determinants of Fiscal Policy in the European Community." *Public Choice* 80:157–172.

Desai, Uday. 2002. *Environmental Politics and Policy in Industrialized Countries.* Cambridge: MIT Press.

Duclaud-Williams, Roger. 1988. "Policy Implementation in the French Public Bureaucracy: The Case of Education." *West European Politics* 11:81–101.

Eckstein, Harry. 1960. *Pressure Group Politics: The Case of the British Medical Association.* London: Allen and Unwin.

Eliason, Leslie. 1996. "Educational Decentralization as a Policy Strategy in an Era of Fiscal Stress," in *The Reconstruction of Education,* edited by Judith Chapman, William Boyd, Rolf Lander, and David Reynolds. London: Cassell.

Elmore, Richard. 1997. "The Politics of Education Reform." *Issues in Science and Technology* 14:41–50.

Enloe, Cynthia. 1975. *The Politics of Pollution in Comparative Perspective: Ecology and Power in Four Nations.* New York: David McKay.

Esping-Andersen, Gøsta. 1990. *The Three Worlds of Welfare Capitalism.* Princeton: Princeton University Press.

Fetzer, Joel. 2000. *Public Attitudes Toward Immigration in the United States, France, and Germany.* Cambridge: Cambridge University Press.

Flora, Peter, and Jens Alber. 1981. "Modernization, Democratization and the Development of Welfare States in Western Europe," in *The Development of Welfare States in Europe and America,* edited by Peter Flora and Arnold Heidenheimer. New Brunswick, N.J.: Transaction.

Fowler, Frances, William Boyd, and David Plank. 1993. "International School Reform: Political Considerations," in *Reforming Education: The Emerging Systemic Approach,* edited by Stephen Jacobson and Robert Berne. Thousand Oaks, Calif.: Corwin Press.

Franzese, Robert. 2000. "Electoral and Partisan Manipulation of Public Debt in Developed Democracies, 1956–1990," in *Institutions, Politics, and Fiscal Policy,* edited by Rolf Strauch and Jürgen von Hagen. Boston: Kluwer Academic Press.

Freeman, Gary. 1995. "Modes of Immigration Politics in Liberal Democratic Societies." *International Migration Review* 29:881–903.

Freeman, Gary. 1998. "The Decline of Sovereignty? Politics and Immigration Restriction in Liberal States," in *Challenge to the Nation-state,* edited by Christian Joppke. Oxford: Oxford University Press.

Freeman, Gary. 2001. *Controlling a New Migration World.* London: Routledge.

Freeman, Gary. 2006. "National Models, Policy Types, and the Politics of Immigration in Liberal Democracies." *West European Politics* 29:227–247.

Freitag, Markus, and Pascal Sciarini. 2001. "The Political Economy of Budget Deficits in the European Union: The Role of International Constraints and Domestic Structure." *European Union Politics* 2:163–189.

Fusarelli, Lance D. 2003. *The Political Dynamics of School Choice: Negotiating Contested Terrain.* New York: Palgrave Macmillan.

George, Vic. 1996. "The Demand for Welfare," in *European Welfare Policy: Squaring the Welfare Circle,* edited by Vic George and Peter Taylor-Gooby. London: Macmillan.

George, Vic, and S. Miller, eds. 1994. *Social Policy Towards 2000: Squaring the Welfare Circle.* London: Routledge.

Giaimo, Susan. 2002. *Markets and Medicine: The Politics of Health Care Reform in Britain, Germany, and the United States.* Lansing: Michigan State University Press.

Giddens, Anthony. 2007. *Europe in the Global Age.* Cambridge, U.K.: Polity.

Gimpel, James, and James Edwards. 1998. *The Congressional Politics of Immigration Control.* Boston: Allyn and Bacon.

Ginsburg, M., et al. 1990. "National and World System Explanations of Education Reform." *Comparative Education Review* 34:474–499.

Glaser, William. 1978. *Health Insurance Bargaining: Foreign Lessons for Americans.* New York: Gardener.

Gould, Arthur. 1993. *Capitalist Welfare Systems: A Comparison of Japan, Britain, and Sweden.* London: Longman.

Grant, J. Tobin, and Stephen T. Mockabee. 2002. "Tax Policy Attitudes and the 1996 Presidential Election." *American Politics Research* 30: 459–475.

Greider, William. 1981. "The Education of David Stockman." *Atlantic Monthly,* December, pp. 27–54.

Grilli, V., D. Masciandaro, and G. Tabellini. 1991. "Political and Monetary Institutions and Public Financial Policies in the Industrial Countries." *Economic Policy* 10:341–392.

Grindle, Merilee, and John Thomas. 1991. *Public Choices and Policy Change: The Political Economy of Reform in Developing Countries.* Baltimore: Johns Hopkins University Press.

Guiraudon, Virginie. 1997. "Policy Change Behind Gilded Doors: Explaining the Evolution of Aliens' Rights in Contemporary Western Europe, 1974–1994." Ph.D. dissertation, Harvard University.

Guiraudon, Virginie. 2000. "European Integration and Migration Policy: Vertical Policy-making as Venue Shopping." *Journal of Common Market Studies* 38:251–271.

Guiraudon, Virginie. 2001. *Controlling a New Migration World.* London: Routledge.

Guiraudon, Virginie, and Gallya Lahav. 2000. "A Reappraisal of the State Sovereignty Debate: The Case of Migration Control." *Comparative Political Studies* 33:163–195.

Gurowitz, Amy. 1999. "Mobilizing International Norms: Domestic Actors, Immigrants, and the Japanese State." *World Politics* 51:413–445.

Hacker, Jacob S. 2004. "Dismantling the Health Care State? Political Institutions, Public Policies and the Comparative Politics of Health Reform." *British Journal of Political Science* 34:693–724.

Hadenius, Axel. 1985. "Citizens Strike a Balance: Discontent with Taxes, Content with Spending." *Journal of Public Policy* 5:349–363.

Hagemann, R., B. Jones, and R. Montador. 1988. "Tax Reform in OECD Countries: Motives, Constraints, and Practice." *OECD Economic Studies* 10:185–226.

Hahm, Sung Deuk, Mark Kamlet, and David Mowery. 1996. "The Political Economy of Deficit Spending in Nine Industrialized Parliamentary Democracies." *Comparative Political Studies* 29:52–77.

Hall, Peter. 1986. *Governing the Economy: The Politics of State Intervention in Britain and France.* New York: Oxford University Press.

Hall, Peter. 1990. "Policy Paradigms, Experts, and the State: The Case of Economic Policy-making in Britain," in *Social Scientists, Policy, and the State,* edited by Stephen Brooks and Alain Gagnon. New York: Praeger.

Hallerberg, Mark, and Jürgen von Hagen. 1999. "Electoral Institutions, Cabinet Negotiations, and Budget Deficits Within the European Union," in *Fiscal Institutions and Fiscal Performance,* edited by James Poterba and Jürgen von Hagen. Chicago: University of Chicago Press.

Hanf, Kenneth, and Alf-Inge Jansen. 1998. "Environmental Policy: The Outcome of Strategic Action and Institutional Characteristics," in *Governance and Environment in Western Europe: Politics, Policy and Administration,* edited by Kenneth Hanf and Alf-Inge Jansen. New York: Longman.

Hansen, John Mark. 1998. "Individuals, Institutions, and Public Preferences over Public Finance." *American Political Science Review* 92:513–532.

Hansen, Randall. 2000. *Citizenship and Immigration in Post-War Britain.* Oxford: Oxford University Press.

Haycraft, John. 1987. *Italian Labyrinth.* London: Penguin.

Heclo, Hugh. 1978. "Issue Networks and the Executive Establishment," in *The New American Political System,* edited by Anthony King. Washington, D.C.: American Enterprise Institute.

Heisler, Martin. 1986. "Transnational Migration as a Small Window on the Diminished Autonomy of the State." *The Annals* 485:153–166.

Hicks, Alexander, and Duane Swank. 1992. "Politics, Institutions, and Welfare Spending in Industrialized Democracies, 1960–1982." *American Political Science Review* 86:658–674.

Hollifield, James. 1992. *Immigrants, Markets and States.* Cambridge: Cambridge University Press.

Hollifield, James. 2004. "The Emerging Migration State." *International Migration Review* 38:885–911.

Howlett, Michael and M. Ramesh. 1995. *Studying Public Policy: Policy Cycles and Policy Subsystems.* New York: Oxford University Press.

Huseby, Beate. 1995. "Attitudes Toward the Size of Government," in *The Scope of Government,* edited by Ole Borre and Elinor Scarbrough. Oxford: Oxford University Press.

Iannacone, Lawrence. 1988. "From Equity to Excellence," in *The Politics of Excellence and Choice in Education,* edited by William Boyd and Charles Kerchner. Philadelphia: Falmer Press.

Immergut, Ellen. 1992. *Health Politics: Interests and Institutions in Western Europe.* Cambridge: Cambridge University Press.

Inglehart, Ronald, and Wayne Baker. 2000. "Modernization, Cultural Change and the Persistence of Traditional Values." *American Sociological Review* 65:19–51.

International Social Science Programme. 1996. *Role of Government III Survey.* Cologne: Zentralarchiv fuer Empirische Sozialforschung, University of Cologne.

International Social Science Programme. 2006. *Role of Government IV Survey,* retrieved from http://zacat.gesis.org/webview/index.jsp?object=http://zacat.gesis.org/obj/fStudy/ZA4700.

Jacobs, Lawrence. 1993. *The Health of Nations: Public Opinion and the Making of American and British Health Policy.* Ithaca: Cornell University Press.

Jacobson, David. 1996. *Rights Across Borders.* Baltimore: Johns Hopkins University Press.

Jager, Jill, and Tim O'Riordan. 1996. "The History of Climate Change Science and Politics," in *Politics of Climate Change: A European Perspective,* edited by Tim O'Riordan and Jill Jager. New York: Routledge.

Jansen, Alf-Inge, Oddgeir Osland, and Kenneth Hanf. 1998. "Environmental Challenges and Institutional Changes," in *Governance and Environment in Western Europe: Politics, Policy and Administration,* edited by Kenneth Hanf and Alf-Inge Jansen. New York: Longman.

Jenson, Jane. 1989. "Paradigms and Political Discourse: Protective Legislation in France and the United States Before 1914." *Canadian Journal of Political Science* 22:235–258.

Joppke, Christian. 1998. "Immigration Challenges the Nation-state," in *Challenge to the Nation-state,* edited by Christian Joppke. Oxford: Oxford University Press.

Joppke, Christian. 1999. *Immigration and the Nation-state.* Oxford: Oxford University Press.

Katzenstein, Peter. 1985. *Small States in World Markets: Industrial Policy in Europe.* Ithaca: Cornell University Press.

Kawashima, Yasuko. 1997. "A Comparative Analysis of the Decision-making Processes of Developed Countries Toward CO_2 Emissions Reduction Targets." *International Environmental Affairs* 9:95–126.

Kindleberger, Charles. 1967. *Europe's Postwar Growth: The Role of the Labor Supply.* Cambridge: Harvard University Press.

King, Anthony. 1973. "Ideas, Institutions and the Policies of Governments: A Comparative Analysis—Part III." *British Journal of Political Science* 3:409–423.

King, Anthony. 1975. "Overload: Problems of Governing in the 1970s." *Political Studies* 23:284–296.

Klein, Rudolf. 2006. *The New Politics of the NHS: From Creation to Reinvention,* 5th ed. Oxford: Radcliffe.

Kogan, Maurice. 1971. *The Politics of Education.* New York: Penguin.

Lahav, Gallya. 2004. *Immigration and Politics in the New Europe: Reinventing Borders.* Cambridge: Cambridge University Press.

Lasswell, Harold. 1951. "The Policy Orientation," in *The Policy Sciences: Recent Developments in Scope and Method,* edited by Daniel Lerner and Harold Lasswell. Stanford: Stanford University Press.

Lauglo, Jon. 1996. "Forms of Decentralization and Their Implication for Education," in *The Reconstruction of Education,* edited by Judith Chapman, William Boyd, Rolf Lander, and David Reynolds. London: Cassell.

Layard, Richard, and Stephen Glaister, eds. 1994. *Cost-Benefit Analysis*. Cambridge: Cambridge University Press.

Layton-Henry, Zig. 1992. *The Politics of Immigration Control*. Oxford: Blackwell.

Lindblom, Charles. 1959. "The Science of Muddling Through." *Public Administration Review* 39:79–88.

Lindblom, Charles. 1968. *The Policy-making Process*. Englewood Cliffs, N.J.: Prentice-Hall.

Linder, Stephen, and B. Guy Peters. 1989. "Instruments of Government: Perceptions and Contexts." *Journal of Public Policy* 9:35–58.

Lindert, Peter. 2004. *Growing Public: Social Spending and Economic Growth Since the Eighteenth Century*, vols. 1–2. Cambridge: Cambridge University Press.

Lundqvist, Lennart. 1974. *Environmental Policies in Canada, Sweden and the United States: A Comparative Overview*. Beverly Hills, Calif.: Sage.

Lundqvist, Lennart. 1980. *The Hare and the Tortoise: Clean Air Policies in the United States and Sweden*. Ann Arbor: University of Michigan Press.

Maioni, Antonia. 1997. "Parting at the Crossroads. The Development of Health Insurance in Canada and the United States, 1940–1965," *Comparative Politics* 29:411–431.

March, James, and Johan Olsen. 1976. "Organization Choice Under Ambiguity," in *Ambiguity and Choice in Organizations*, edited by James March and Johan Olsen. Bergen, Norway: Universitetsforlaget.

March, James, and Johan Olsen. 1984. "The New Institutionalism: Organizational Factors in Political Life." *American Political Science Review* 78:734–749.

Marmor, Theodore. 1997. "Global Health Policy Reform: Misleading Mythology or Learning Opportunity," in *Health Policy Reform, National Variations and Globalization*, edited by Christa Altenstetter and James Björkman. New York: St. Martin's Press (for the International Political Science Association).

Marmor, Theodore, and David Thomas. 1972. "Doctors, Politics and Pay Disputes: 'Pressure Group Politics' Revisited." *British Journal of Political Science* 2:421–442.

Marshall, Catherine, Douglas Mitchell, and Frederick Wirt. 1989. *Culture and Education Policy in the American States*. New York: Falmer Press.

May, Peter. 1991. "Reconsidering Policy Design: Policies and Publics." *Journal of Public Policy* 11:187–206.

McBeath, Jerry, and Jonathan Rosenberg. 2006. *Comparative Environmental Politics*. Dordrecht, Netherlands: Springer.

McLaren, Lauren. 2001. "Immigration and the New Politics of Inclusion and Exclusion in the European Union: The Effect of Elites and the EU on Individual-Level Opinions Regarding European and Non-European Immigrants." *European Journal of Political Research* 39:81–108.

McLean, Martin. 1988. "The Conservative Education Policy in Comparative Perspective." *British Journal of Educational Studies* 36:200–217.

McLean, Martin. 1995. *Educational Traditions Compared*. London: David Fulton Publishers.

Messere, Ken, ed. 1998. *The Tax System in Industrialized Countries*. Oxford: Oxford University Press.

Messina, Anthony. 1989. *Race and Party Competition in Europe*. Oxford: Clarendon Press.

Messina, Anthony. 1990. "Political Impediments to the Resumption of Labour Migration in Western Europe." *West European Politics* 3:31–46.

Messina, Anthony. 1995. "Immigration as a Political Dilemma in Britain: Implications for Western Europe." *Policy Studies Journal* 23:686–699.

Money, Jeannette. 1999. *Fences and Neighbors: The Political Geography of Immigration Control.* Ithaca: Cornell University Press.

Morone, James. 1995. "Nativism, Hollow Corporations, and Managed Competition: Why the Clinton Health Care Reform Failed." *Journal of Health Politics, Policy and Law* 20:391–398.

Morrissey, Oliver, and Sven Steinmo. 1987. "The Influence of Party Competition on Post-war UK Tax Rates." *Politics and Policy* 15:195–206.

Mulas-Granados, Carlos. 2004. "Voting Against Spending Cuts: The Electoral Costs of Fiscal Adjustments in Europe." *European Union Politics* 5:467–493.

National Center for Education Statistics. 2009. *Comparative Indicators of Education in the United States and Other G-8 Countries.* Washington, D.C.: U.S. Department of Education.

Navarro, Vicente. 1995. "Why Congress Did Not Enact Health Care Reform." *Journal of Health Politics, Policy and Law* 20:455–462.

Norton, Philip, ed. 1999. *Parliaments and Pressure Groups in Western Europe.* London: Frank Cass.

Obinger, Herbert, Stephan Leibfried, and Francis Geoffrey Castles, eds. 2005. *Federalism and the Welfare State: New World and European Experiences.* Cambridge: Cambridge University Press.

Ophuls, William, and A. S. Boyan. 1992. *Ecology and the Politics of Scarcity Revisited: The Unraveling of the American Dream.* New York: Freeman.

Organisation for Economic Co-operation and Development. 1982. *OECD Economic Outlook: Historical Statistics 1960–1980.* Paris: Organisation for Economic Co-operation and Development.

Organisation for Economic Co-operation and Development. 1999. *OECD in Figures.* Paris: Organisation for Economic Co-operation and Development.

Organisation for Economic Co-operation and Development. 2000. *OECD Economic Outlook,* No. 67. Paris: Organisation for Economic Co-operation and Development.

Organisation for Economic Co-operation and Development. 2001. *Environmental Performance Reviews: Germany.* Paris: Organisation for Economic Co-operation and Development.

Organisation for Economic Co-operation and Development. 2002a. *Environmental Performance Reviews: Italy.* Paris: Organisation for Economic Co-operation and Development.

Organisation for Economic Co-operation and Development. 2002b.*Environmental Performance Reviews: Japan.* Paris: Organisation for Economic Co-operation and Development.

Organisation for Economic Co-operation and Development. 2002c. *Environmental Performance Reviews: United Kingdom.* Paris: Organisation for Economic Co-operation and Development.

Organisation for Economic Co-operation and Development. 2005a. *Environmental Performance Reviews: France.* Paris: Organisation for Economic Co-operation and Development.

Organisation for Economic Co-operation and Development. 2005b. *Environmental Performance Reviews: United States.* Paris: Organisation for Economic Co-operation and Development.

Organisation for Economic Co-operation and Development. 2006. *OECD Factbook.* Paris: Organisation for Economic Co-operation and Development.

Organisation for Economic Co-operation and Development. 2007. *OECD Environmental Data, Compendium 2006/2007.* Paris: Organisation for Economic Co-operation and Development.

Organisation for Economic Co-operation and Development. 2008a. *Education at a Glance: OECD Indicators 2008.* Paris: Organisation for Economic Co-operation and Development.

Organisation for Economic Co-operation and Development. 2008b. *International Migration Outlook: Annual Report.* Paris: Organisation for Economic Co-operation and Development.

Organisation for Economic Co-operation and Development. 2008c. *OECD Economic Outlook,* No. 84. Paris: Organisation for Economic Co-operation and Development.

Organisation for Economic Co-operation and Development. 2008d. *OECD in Figures.* Paris: Organisation for Economic Co-operation and Development.

Organisation for Economic Co-operation and Development. 2009a. *OECD Economic Outlook,* No. 85. Paris: Organisation for Economic Co-operation and Development.

Organisation for Economic Co-operation and Development. 2009b. *OECD Health Data 2009.* Paris: Organisation for Economic Co-operation and Development.

Organisation for Economic Co-operation and Development. 2009c. *OECD Social Expenditure Database,* retrieved from www.oecd.org/els/social/expenditure.

Organisation for Economic Co-operation and Development. 2009d. *OECD Tax Database,* retrieved from www.oecd.org/ctp/taxdatabase.

Organisation for Economic Co-operation and Development. 2009e. *Society at a Glance 2009: OECD Social Indicators.* Paris: Organisation for Economic Co-operation and Development.

Oorschot, Wim van, Michael Opielka, and Birgit Pfau-Effinger. 2008. *Culture and Welfare State: Values and Social Policy in Comparative Perspective.* Cheltenham, U.K.: Edward Elgar.

O'Riordan, Tim, and Andrew Jordan. 1996. "Social Institutions and Climate Change," in *Politics of Climate Change: A European Perspective,* edited by Tim O'Riordan and Jill Jager. New York: Routledge.

Ozawa, Martha. 1991. "Child Welfare Programs in Japan." *Social Service Review* 65:2.

Patel, Kant, and Mark Rushefsky. 1998. *Politics, Power and Policy Making: The Case of Health Care Reform in the 1990s.* New York: M. E. Sharpe.

Pempel, T. J., ed. 1990. *Uncommon Democracies: The One-party Dominant Regimes.* Ithaca: Cornell University Press.

Pempel, T. J. 1992. "Bureaucracy in Japan." *PS: Political Science and Politics* 25:19–24.

Perlmutter, Ted. 1996. "Bringing Parties Back In: Comments on 'Modes of Immigration Politics in Liberal Democratic Societies.'" *International Migration Review* 30:375–389.

Peters, B. Guy. 1991. *The Politics of Taxation: A Comparative Perspective.* Cambridge: Basil Blackwell.

Peters, B. Guy. 1995. *The Politics of Bureaucracy,* 4th ed. New York: Longman.

Preece, Daniel V. 2009. *Dismantling Social Europe: The Political Economy of Social Policy in the European Union.* Boulder: First Forum Press.

Pressman, Jeffrey, and Aaron Wildavsky. 1973. *Implementation: How Great Expectations in Washington Are Dashed in Oakland.* Berkeley: University of California Press.

Quadagno, Jill. 2004. "Why the United States Has No National Health Insurance: Stakeholder Mobilization Against the Welfare State, 1945–1996." *Journal of Health and Social Behavior* 45:25–44.

Raffel, Marshall. 1997. "Dominant Issues: Convergence, Decentralization, Competition, Health Services," in *Health Care and Reform in Industrialized Countries,* edited by Marshall Raffel. University Park: Pennsylvania State University Press.

Rich, Paul. 1990. *Race and Empire in British Politics.* Cambridge: Cambridge University Press.

Rodrik, Dani. 1998. "Why Do More Open Economies Have Bigger Governments?" *Journal of Political Economy* 106: 997–1032.

Roemer, Milton. 1977. *Comparative National Policies on Health Care.* New York: Marcel Dekker.

Roller, Edeltraud. 1995. "The Welfare State: The Equality Dimension," in *The Scope of Government,* edited by Ole Borre and Elinor Scarbrough. Oxford: Oxford University Press.

Rose, Richard, and Terrance Karran. 1986. *Taxation by Political Inertia.* London: Macmillan.

Roubini, Nouriel, and Jeffrey Sachs. 1989. "Political and Economic Determinants of Budget Deficits in the Industrial Democracies." *European Economic Review* 33:903–938.

Rust, Val, and Kenneth Blakemore. 1990. "Educational Reform in England and the United States." *Comparative Education Review* 17:160–179.

Sassen, Saskia. 1998. "The De Facto Transnationalizing of Immigration Policy," in *Challenge to the Nation-state,* edited by Christian Joppke. Oxford: Oxford University Press.

Sassen, Saskia. 1999. *Guests and Aliens.* New York: The New Press.

Schain, Martin. 1987. "The National Front in France and the Construction of Political Legitimacy." *West European Politics* 10:229–252.

Schain, Martin. 1988. "Immigration and Changes in the French Party System." *European Journal of Political Research* 16:597–621.

Schain, Martin. 2006. "The Extreme Right and Immigration Policy-making: Measuring Direct and Indirect Effects." *West European Politics* 29:270–289.

Scharpf, Fritz. 1997. *Games Real Actors Play: Actor-Centered Institutionalism in Policy Research.* Boulder: Westview.

Schlesinger, Mark, and Taeku Lee. 1994. "Is Health Care Different? Popular Support of Federal Health and Social Policies," in *The Politics of Health Care Reform,* edited by James Morone and Gary Belkin. Durham: Duke University Press.

Schmidt, Manfred. 1982. "The Role of Parties in Shaping Macroeconomic Policy," in *The Impact of Parties: Politics and Policies in Democratic Capitalist States,* edited by Francis Castles. London: Sage.

Schnaiberg, Allan, and Kenneth Gould. 1994. *Environment and Society: The Enduring Conflict.* New York: St. Martin's Press.

Schnaiberg, Allan, Nicholas Watts, and Klaus Zimmerman. 1986. *Distributional Conflicts in Environmental Resource Policy.* Aldershot, U.K.: Gower.

Schnapper, Dominique. 1994. "The Debate on Immigration and the Crisis of National Identity," in *The Politics of Immigration in Western Europe,* edited by Martin Baldwin-Edwards and Martin Schain. London: Frank Cass.

Schreurs, Miranda. 2002. *Environmental Politics in Japan, Germany and the United States.* New York: Cambridge University Press.

Scruggs, Lyle. 1999. "Institutions and Environmental Performance in Seventeen Western Democracies." *British Journal of Political Science* 29:1–32.

Sears, David, and Jack Citrin. 1985. *Tax Revolt: Something for Nothing in California.* Cambridge: Harvard University Press.

Seeleib-Kaiser, Martin, Silke van Dyk, and Martin Roggenkamp. 2008. *Party Politics and Social Welfare: Comparing Christian and Social Democracy in Austria, Germany and the Netherlands.* Cheltenham, U.K.: Edward Elgar.

Shapiro, Martin, and Alec Stone. 1994. "The New Constitutional Politics of Europe." *Comparative Political Studies* 26:397–420.

Simon, Herbert. 1957. *Models of Man: Social and Rational.* New York: Wiley.

Sinfield, A. 1984. "The Wider Impact of Unemployment," in *High Unemployment,* edited by OECD. Paris: Organisation for Economic Co-operation and Development.

Skocpol, Theda. 1992. *Protecting Soldiers and Mothers: The Political Origins of Social Policy in the United States.* Cambridge: Belknap Press of Harvard University Press.

Smith, Martin. 1994. "Policy Networks and State Autonomy," in *The Political Influence of Ideas: Policy Communities and the Social Sciences,* edited by Stephen Brooks and Alain Gagnon. New York: Praeger.

Soysal, Yasemin. 1994. *The Limits of Citizenship.* Chicago: University of Chicago Press.

Spring, Joel. 1998. *Conflict of Interests: The Politics of American Education.* New York: Longman.

Starr, Paul. 1982. *The Social Transformation of American Medicine.* New York: Basic Books.

Statham, Paul, and Andrew Geddes. 2006. "Elites and the 'Organized Public': Who Drives British Immigration Politics and in Which Direction?" *West European Politics* 29:248–269.

Steel, Brent, Richard Clinton, and Nicholas Lovrich. 2003. *Environmental Politics and Policy: A Comparative Approach.* Boston: McGraw-Hill.

Steinmo, Sven. 1993. *Taxation and Democracy: Swedish, British, and American Approaches to Financing the Modern State.* New Haven: Yale University Press.

Steinmo, Sven, and Jon Watts. 1995. "It's the Institutions, Stupid! Why Comprehensive National Health Insurance Always Fails in America." *Journal of Health Politics, Policy and Law* 20:329–372.

Stone, Deborah. 1980. *The Limits of Professional Power.* Chicago: University of Chicago Press.

Swank, Duane and Sven Steinmo. 2002. "The New Political Economy of Taxation in Advanced Capitalist Democracies," *American Journal of Political Science* 46: 642–655.

Tsebelis, George. 2002. *Veto Players: How Political Institutions Work.* Princeton: Princeton University Press.

Tuohy, Carolyn. 1999. *Accidental Logics: The Dynamics of Change in the Health Care Arena in the United States, Britain, and Canada*. New York: Oxford University Press.

United Nations High Commissioner for Refugees. 2006. *Refugees by the Numbers, 2006*. Geneva: United Nations High Commissioner for Refugees.

United Nations High Commissioner for Refugees. 2007. *Protecting the Refugees and the Role of the UNHCR 2007-08*. Geneva: United Nations High Commissioner for Refugees.

U.S. Social Security Administration. 2009. *Social Security Programs Throughout the World* series, retrieved from www.ssa.gov/policy/docs/progdesc/ssptw/.

van Waarden, Frans. 1992. "Dimensions and Types of Policy Networks." *European Journal of Political Research* 21:29–52.

Vernon, Raymond. 1993. "Behind the Scenes: How Policymaking in the European Community, Japan and the United States Affects Global Negotiations," *Environment* 35:12–29.

Vogel, David. 1986. *National Styles of Regulation: Environmental Policy in Great Britain and the United States*. Ithaca: Cornell University Press.

Weale, Albert. 1992. *The New Politics of Pollution*. Manchester, U.K.: Manchester University Press.

Weaver, R. Kent, and Bert Rockman. 1993a. "Assessing the Effects of Institutions," in *Do Institutions Matter? Government Capabilities in the United States and Abroad*, edited by R. Kent Weaver and Bert Rockman. Washington, D.C.: Brookings Institution Press.

Weaver, R. Kent, and Bert Rockman. 1993b. "When and How Do Institutions Matter?" in *Do Institutions Matter? Government Capabilities in the United States and Abroad*, edited by R. Kent Weaver and Bert Rockman. Washington, D.C.: Brookings Institution Press.

Weissberg, Robert. 2002. "The Problem with Polling." *The Public Interest* 148: 37–48.

Welch, Susan. 1985. "The 'More for Less' Paradox: Public Attitudes on Taxing and Spending." *Public Opinion Quarterly* 49:310–316.

Wildavsky, Aaron. 1975. *Budgeting: A Comparative Theory of Budgeting Processes*. Boston: Little, Brown.

Wilensky, Harold. 1975. *The Welfare State and Equality*. Berkeley: University of California Press.

Wilsford, David. 1991. *Doctors and the State: The Politics of Health Care in France and the United States*. Durham: Duke University Press.

Wilson, James. 1989. *Bureaucracy: What Government Agencies Do and Why They Do It*. New York: Basic Books.

Winner, Hannes. 2005. "Has Tax Competition Emerged in OECD Countries? Evidence from Panel Data." *International Tax and Public Finance* 12: 667–687.

Wirt, Frederick, and Grant Hartman. 1986. *Education, Recession and the World Village: A Comparative Political Economy of Education*. Philadelphia: Falmer Press.

Wray, Harry. 1999. *Japanese and American Education: Attitudes and Practices*. Westport, Conn.: Bergin and Garvey.

Yergin, Daniel, and Joseph Stanislaw. 1998. *The Commanding Heights: The Battle Between Government and the Marketplace That Is Remaking the Modern World*. New York: Simon and Schuster.

Index

Boxes, figures, notes, and tables are indicated with b, f, n, and t following the page number.